MINNESOTA
ILLUSTRATED
GOLF COURSE DIRECTORY

MINNESOTA
ILLUSTRATED
GOLF COURSE DIRECTORY

CHRISTOPHER SULLIVAN · TIMOTHY SULLIVAN
EVERGREEN PUBLICATIONS

COPYRIGHT © 1996 EVERGREEN PUBLICATIONS
CHRISTOPHER SULLIVAN, TIMOTHY SULLIVAN
THIRD EDITION, FIRST PRINTING

All rights reserved. No part of this book may be reproduced or transmitted in any form without the permission of Evergreen Publications except for review purposes.

ISBN 0-9633480-3-5

Evergreen Publications
3824 Willow Way
Eagan, Minnesota 55122

Printed and bound in U.S.A.

Please write to the address above for additional copies of this book. Quantity pricing is available. The information in this book is also available in computer format.

DISCLAIMER
All information contained herein was provided exclusively to Evergreen Publications. Data was gathered through written correspondence and telephone surveying. Due to uncontrollable circumstances, information may change without notice. Evergreen Publications reserves the right to revise this publication and to make changes whenever necessary without obligation of notifying any person of such revisions or changes. Evergreen Publications welcomes any new or updated information.

A NOTE FROM THE PUBLISHER
It is best to call ahead to the golf course you plan to visit to get the most up-to-date information. The publishing process is complicated and requires a great deal of time. It makes it necessary to collect data well in advance. Data was collected for this issue from February through December, 1995. Because of these constraints, changes made during the winter months for the forthcoming season will not be reflected.

DEDICATION

This directory is dedicated to all Minnesota golfers.

We know that each of you will utilize this Directory in discovering Minnesota golf courses. Whatever the reason, we hope that it is beneficial to you and your golfing party.

We wish to extend sincere and heartfelt thanks to our wives

...Sue and Nichole...

for their dedication, patience, support, and useful suggestions throughout the entire project. We also want to thank our families and friends for their enthusiasm and encouragement, which helped to make it all possible.

Have a good round, Minnesota!

Christopher Sullivan

Chris has been golfing in Minnesota for eight years. He has a BA degree in Journalism from the University of Minnesota.

Timothy Sullivan

Tim has been a Minnesota golfer for ten years. He has an Electronics diploma and an associate degree in Computer Science.

TABLE OF CONTENTS

FORWARD
Introduction I
Key/Explanation .... III-VI

DIRECTORY
Public/Semi-Private/Private Courses 1-418

Courses are listed alphabetically (A-Z) by course name. All listings are identified by region using the following key:

Northwest Region

Northeast Region

Southwest Region

Southeast Region

INDEXES
Course Index 419
City Index 423

INTRODUCTION

An Illustrated Golf Course Directory...

As golf continues to be a favorite pastime for many, the resources available for golfing information are relatively scarce. Who has the right greens fee to fit your budget? Which course will offer a challenge as you polish up your swing?

Every golf course varies in difficulty, price and availability. That's why we've put together one source of information that puts it all at your fingertips!

In our first edition, we set out in the fall of 1991 to gather information on all golf courses in the state of Minnesota. We went from all corners compiling a list of over 400 golf courses. We surveyed courses directly with correspondence and phone calling. With determination, we released *The 1993 Minnesota Statewide Golf Course Directory* in November 1992.

Our second edition, entitled *The Minnesota Illustrated Golf Course Directory,* was released in March 1994. We renamed it slightly to emphasize its graphic approach to available information. It became a popular and valuable resource for thousands of Minnesota golfers.

We now present you with our third edition of *The Minnesota Illustrated Golf Course Directory* with much enthusiasm. We have updated the information for you and added nearly 100 more listings to this collection. We have also invested in higher quality printing for you, including better graphics and durable perfect binding.

Whether you are headed out for your first tee-off, or you've been playing for years, *The Minnesota Illustrated Golf Course Directory* will help you get where you want to go. We wish you all an enjoyable and successful season.

I

KEY/EXPLANATION

1 **COURSE NAME**   18 Regulation Public

100 Minnesota Drive
Minnesota City, Minnesota 55555
000/000-0000 Clubhouse/Proshop

3 HOURS   6 am to 10 pm
SEASON   Apr 1 to Nov 15

4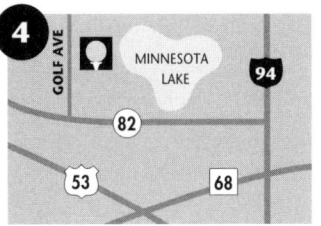

2	RESERVATIONS	000/000-0000 0 days
		Weekends only $0 fee
		Walk-on: good/fair

GREEN FEES	M-F	S-S
Adult	$00/0	$00/0
Senior	$00/0	$00/0
Junior	$00/0	$00/0
Twilight	$0 (5 pm)	$0 (5 pm)
	Memberships available	

PAYMENT	Credit: Visa® MasterCard®
	Non–local checks accepted

LEAGUES	Men:	M (4-10 pm)
	Women:	T (9-10 am)
	Other:	F (6-9 pm)

MEMBERSHIPS	USGA, PGA, MGA, MPGA
PROFESSIONAL	John Doe

FEATURES		
Putting green	Y	
Driving range	Y	$0-0
Practice area	N	
Golf carts		
Power (gas)	Y	$0/0
Pull carts	Y	$0/0
Club rental	Y	$0/0
Club storage	Y	$0/yr
Caddies	Y	$0
Proshop		
Regular	Y	
Refreshments		
Restaurant	Y	
Lounge	Y	
Snacks	Y	
Clubhouse		
Showers	Y	$0
Lockers	Y	$0
Lodging	Y	$0

Located 3 miles west of I-94. Exit west on Cty Rd 82, then north on Golf Ave. Course 1 mile on right.

6

	MEN					WOMEN		
	BACK	FRONT	PAR	HDCP	FRONT	PAR	HDCP
1	345	337	4	9	320	4	9
2	325	300	4	15	270	4	13
3	345	330	4	13	288	4	7
4	310	304	4	17	300	4	11
5	335	330	4	7	325	4	5
6	166	158	3	11	129	3	17
7	425	410	4	1	335	4	1
8	515	489	5	3	435	5	3
9	300	285	4	5	240	4	15
Out	3066	2943	36		2642	36	
10	370	360	4	6	350	4	8
11	287	277	4	16	257	4	14
12	364	344	4	10	295	4	12
13	145	135	3	18	130	3	18
14	364	348	4	8	333	4	10
15	338	314	4	4	276	4	6
16	240	228	4	16	210	4	16
17	355	350	4	2	345	4	2
18	492	482	5	12	439	5	4
In	2955	2838	36		2635	36	
Total	6021	5781	72		5277	72	
Rating	68.6	67.5			69.4		
Slope	113	111			111		

5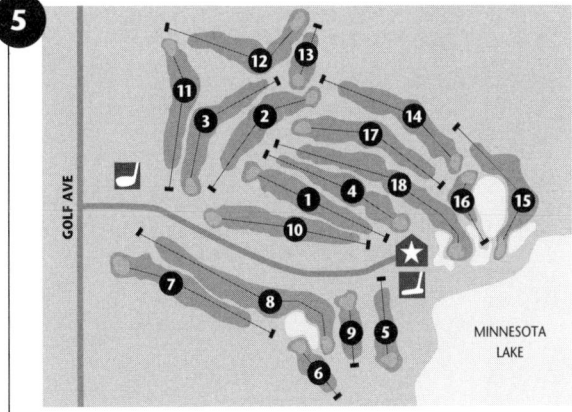

GOLF COURSE DIRECTORY

KEY/EXPLANATION

①

COURSE NAME   **18 Regulation Public**

　　　　　　　　　　　　　　　　　　　　　　　Total number │ Course type:
　　　　　　　　　　　　　　　　　　　　　　　of holes　　│ Public, Semi-private
　　　　　　　　　　　　　　　　　　　　　　　　　　　　 　or Private

Region (counties are outlined):
Southeast, Southwest, Northwest, Northeast   Course category: Regulation, Executive or Par-3

②

RESERVATIONS	000/000-0000	0 days
	Weekends only	$0 fee
	Walk-on: good/fair	
GREEN FEES	M-F	S-S
Adult	$00/0	$00/0
Senior	$00/0	$00/0
Junior	$00/0	$00/0
Twilight	$0 (5 pm)	$0 (5 pm)
	Memberships available	
PAYMENT	Credit: Visa® MasterCard®	
	Non–local checks accepted	
LEAGUES	Men:	M (4-10 pm)
	Women:	T (9-10 am)
	Other:	F (6-9 pm)
MEMBERSHIPS	USGA, PGA, MGA, MPGA	
PROFESSIONAL	John Doe	

— Reservation phone number
— Advance time for reservation
— Reservation information and fee, if applicable
— Walk-on chances for weekday/weekend (good, fair or poor)

— Range of days to define weekday and weekend rates

— Green fees for 18 holes/9 holes for age group: Adult, Senior or Junior (Sr/Jr together on one line when prices are same)
— Twilight discount rate (time begins when provided)
— Misc. pricing information: memberships, group discounts, etc.

— Course terms of payment other than cash and restrictions if provided; proper i.d. always required
(Note: "non-local" includes local check acceptance)

— League type, day, time if provided
(Note: on many courses, public play may continue during league times. Call for specific restrictions)

— Membership associations as provided:
　USGA　United States Golf Association
　NGF　National Golf Foundation
　PGA　Professional Golf Association
　LPGA　Ladies Professional Golf Association
　GCSAA　Golf Course Superintendents Assn. of America
　CMAA　Club Managers Association of America
　MGA　Minnesota Golf Association

Course personnel and/or professional

IV   THE MINNESOTA ILLUSTRATED

KEY/EXPLANATION

3

HOURS	6 am to 10 pm
SEASON	Apr 1 to Nov 15

├── Course hours (Note: hours may vary for weekend/weekday)
├── Course season guidelines as provided (Note: may change due to weather)

FEATURES		
Putting green	Y	
Driving range	Y	$0-0
Practice area	N	
Golf carts		
Power (gas)	Y	$0/0
Pull carts	Y	$0/0
Club rental	Y	$0/0
Club storage	Y	$0/yr
Caddies	Y	$0
Proshop		
Regular	Y	
Refreshments		
Restaurant	Y	
Lounge	Y	
Snacks	Y	
Clubhouse		
Showers	Y	$0
Lockers	Y	$0
Lodging	Y	$0

├── Availability: Y = Yes, N = No

├── Range fees (quantities vary)

├── Type of cart (gas, electric) for 18 holes/9 holes
├── (Note: both types available if left blank)
├── Pull cart fee for 18 holes/9 holes
├── Club rental fee for 18 holes/9 holes (Note: club sets may vary)
├── Club storage fee (Note: may be for members only)
├── Caddy fee

├── Proshop rating based on available merchandise categories:
    1) tees & balls, 2) clubs & bags, 3) shoes & clothing
    Basic = only one category; Regular = any two categories;
    Extended = all three categories; N = no categories available

├── Clubhouse fees (Shower fee generally refers to towel rental)

├── Fee for lodging on course premises (generally base price per person)

4

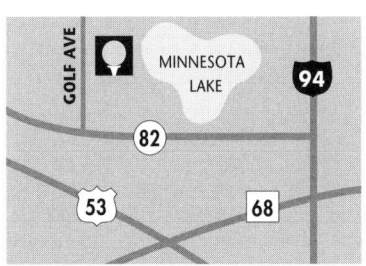

Located in Minnesota City. Course is west of I-94 on County Road 82, then north on Golf Avenue.

Vicinity map may include the following symbols:

    Course location
    94 Interstate highways
    53 US Highways
    68 Minnesota highways
    82 County roads

├── Directions from nearest town, city or highway

GOLF COURSE DIRECTORY   V

KEY/EXPLANATION

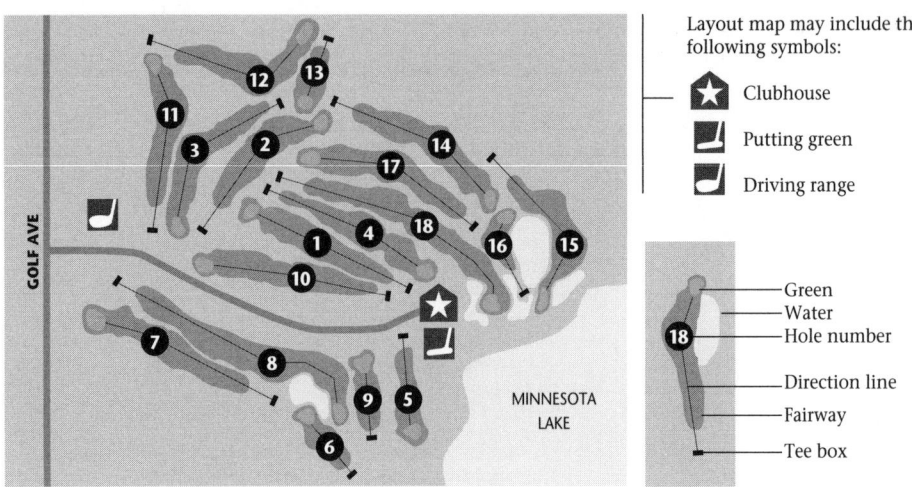

5 — Layout map may include the following symbols:
- ★ Clubhouse
- Putting green
- Driving range

- Green
- Water
- Hole number
- Direction line
- Fairway
- Tee box

6

	MEN				WOMEN		
	BACK	FRONT	PAR	HDCP	FRONT	PAR	HDCP
1	345	337	4	9	320	4	9
2	325	300	4	15	270	4	13
3	345	330	4	13	288	4	7
4	310	304	4	17	300	4	11
5	335	330	4	7	325	4	5
6	166	158	3	11	129	3	17
7	425	410	4	1	335	4	1
8	515	489	5	3	435	5	3
9	300	285	4	5	240	4	15
Out	3066	2943	36		2642	36	
Total	6021	5781	72		5277	72	
Rating	68.6	67.5			69.4		
Slope	113	111			111		

— Tee box location, par, handicap (if available) for hole

— Hole number, yardage, par and handicap (Note: Men par/hdcp listed for front tees)

— Total yardages and par for nine holes (In and Out for 9- and 18-hole course; "Name" for multiple nine-hole or 27-hole courses)

— Total yardages and par for 18 holes; Ratings and slope measured for 18 holes

VI   **THE MINNESOTA ILLUSTRATED**

DIRECTORY

PUBLIC COURSES

SEMI-PRIVATE COURSES

PRIVATE COURSES

AFTON ALPS GOLF COURSE
18 Regulation Public

6600 Peller Avenue South
Hastings, Minnesota 55033
612/436-1320 Clubhouse/Proshop

HOURS	7 am to Dusk
SEASON	April to October

RESERVATIONS	612/436-1320	
	Walk-on: good/poor	
GREEN FEES	M-F	S-S
Adult	$14/10	$17/10
Senior	$13/8	$17/10
Junior	$14/10	$17/10
Twilight	NA	NA
PAYMENT	Credit: Visa® MasterCard®	
	Non-local checks accepted	
LEAGUES	Men: T (pm)	
	Women: T (pm)	
	Business: Th (pm)	
	Couples: F (pm)	
MEMBERSHIPS	MGA	
OWNER	Paul Augustine	
MANAGER	Penny Brown	

FEATURES	
Putting green	Y
Driving range	N
Practice area	N
Golf carts	
Power (gas)	Y $16/10
Pull carts	Y $2.50
Club rental	Y $7
Club storage	N
Caddies	N
Proshop	
Regular	Y
Refreshments	
Restaurant	Y
Lounge	Y
Snacks	Y
Clubhouse	
Showers	N
Lockers	N
Lodging	N

Located in Hastings. Course is about 3 miles east of MN Highway 95 on County Road 20, then north on Peller Avenue.

	MEN FRONT	PAR	HDCP	WOMEN FRONT	PAR	HDCP
1	308	4	7	283	4	7
2	147	3	17	128	3	17
3	308	4	15	267	4	15
4	460	5	1	395	5	1
5	332	4	13	289	4	13
6	463	5	3	395	5	3
7	493	5	5	439	5	5
8	295	4	9	288	4	9
9	189	3	11	160	3	11
Out	2995	37		2644	37	
10	348	4	14	297	4	14
11	282	4	12	263	4	12
12	159	3	16	146	3	16
13	260	4	10	216	4	10
14	328	4	4	276	4	4
15	128	3	18	115	3	18
16	448	5	2	377	5	2
17	304	4	8	272	4	8
18	276	4	6	260	4	6
In	2533	35		2222	35	
Total	5528	72		4866	72	
Rating	67.2			68.8		
Slope	110			118		

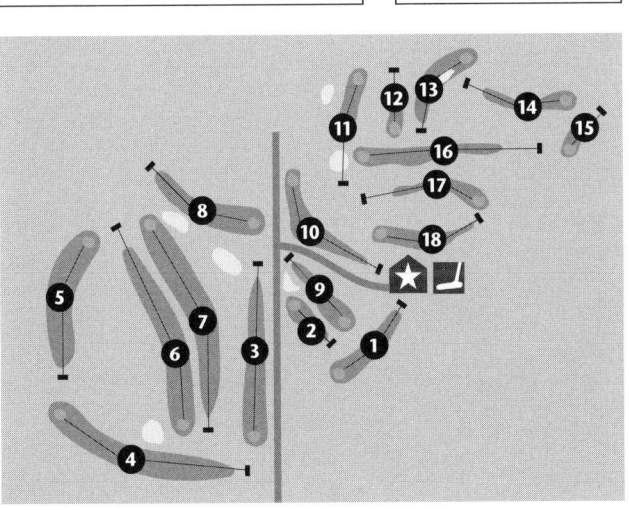

GOLF COURSE DIRECTORY

ALBANY GOLF CLUB

18 Regulation Public

500 Church Avenue, P.O. Box 338
Albany, Minnesota 56307
612/845-2505 Clubhouse/Proshop

RESERVATIONS	612/845-2505 3 Days
	Walk-on: good/good

GREEN FEES	M-F	S-S
Adult	$15/10.25	$16.75/12
Senior	$10	$16.75/12
Junior	$7	$16.75/12
Twilight	NA	NA

PAYMENT	Credit: Visa® MasterCard®
	Non-local checks accepted

LEAGUES	Men:	T
	Women:	W
	Senior:	M

MEMBERSHIPS	USGA, PGA, GCSAA, MGA

MANAGER	Paul Wellenstein
SUPERINTENDENT	Tom Kasner
PROFESSIONAL	Paul Wellenstein

HOURS	7:30 am to Dusk
SEASON	April to October

FEATURES		
Putting green	Y	
Driving range	Y	$2.75
Practice area	Y	
Golf carts		
Power (gas)	Y	$18/10
Pull carts	Y	$1.75
Club rental	Y	$5
Club storage	Y	$25/yr
Caddies	N	
Proshop		
Extended	Y	
Refreshments		
Restaurant	N	
Lounge	Y	
Snacks	Y	
Clubhouse		
Showers	Y	
Lockers	Y	
Lodging	N	

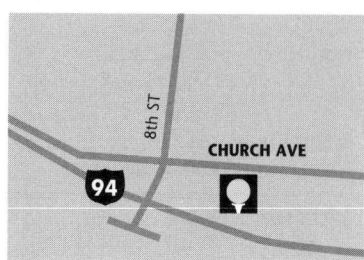

Located in Albany. Course entrance is just north of I-94 on 8th street, then east on Church Avenue.

	MEN				WOMEN		
	BACK	FRONT	PAR	HDCP	FRONT	PAR	HDCP
1	315	310	4	11	290	4	11
2	395	376	4	7	340	4	7
3	166	149	3	13	125	3	13
4	402	319	4	5	214	4	5
5	424	382	4	3	372	5	3
6	357	347	4	9	337	4	9
7	532	517	5	1	404	5	1
8	366	349	4	15	319	4	15
9	251	249	4	17	241	4	17
Out	3208	2998	36		2642	37	
10	553	503	5	10	426	5	10
11	169	157	3	16	114	3	16
12	339	324	4	14	309	4	14
13	414	402	4	2	400	5	2
14	382	330	4	4	290	4	4
15	135	129	3	18	115	3	18
16	350	339	4	12	321	4	12
17	343	333	4	8	263	4	8
18	515	476	5	6	388	5	6
In	3207	2993	36		2626	37	
Total	6415	5991	72		5268	74	
Rating	69.8	68.0			69.9		
Slope	115	111			116		

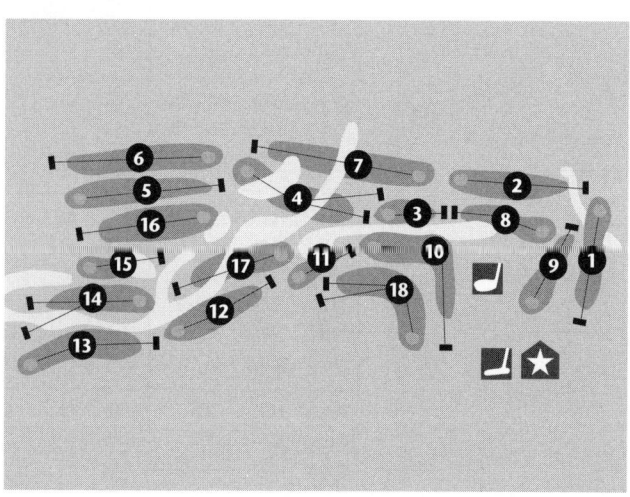

THE MINNESOTA ILLUSTRATED

ALBERT LEA GOLF CLUB

18 Regulation Semi-Private

1701 Country Club Road
Albert Lea, Minnesota 56007
507/377-1683 Clubhouse/Proshop

HOURS	7:30 am–Dusk
SEASON	April to October

RESERVATIONS	507/377-1683 3 days
	Walk-on: fair/poor

GREEN FEES	M-F	S-S
Adult	$16/10	$20/13
Senior	$16/10	$20/13
Junior	$16/10	$20/13
Twilight	NA	NA

PAYMENT	No credit cards accepted
	Non-local checks accepted

LEAGUES	Men: W
	Women: T

MEMBERSHIPS	USGA, NGF, GCSAA,
	CMAA, MGA

OWNER	Continental Golf Corp.
MANAGER	Michael Edling
SUPERINTENDENT	Damon Morgan
PROFESSIONAL	Michael Edling

FEATURES	
Putting green	Y
Driving range	Y
Practice area	Y
Golf carts	
Power (gas)	Y
Pull carts	N
Club rental	N
Club storage	Y
Caddies	N
Proshop	
Extended	Y
Refreshments	
Restaurant	Y
Lounge	Y
Snacks	Y
Clubhouse	
Showers	Y
Lockers	Y
Lodging	N

Located in Albert Lea. Course is south of I-90 on Bridge Avenue, then west on Richway Drive to Country Club Road.

	MEN			WOMEN		
	FRONT	PAR	HDCP	FRONT	PAR	HDCP
1	255	4	17	245	4	17
2	460	5	11	400	5	11
3	485	5	9	460	5	9
4	225	3	7	145	3	7
5	155	3	15	155	3	15
6	390	4	1	326	4	1
7	312	4	8	253	4	8
8	336	4	10	291	4	10
9	282	4	18	276	4	18
Out	2900	36		2551	36	
10	380	4	3	313	4	3
11	185	3	13	135	3	13
12	355	4	5	310	4	5
13	116	3	14	98	3	14
14	467	5	6	415	5	6
15	339	4	16	284	4	16
16	338	4	12	323	4	12
17	345	4	2	301	4	2
18	476	5	4	416	5	4
In	3001	36		2595	36	
Total	5901	72		5146	72	
Rating	69.4			70.0		
Slope	121			123		

Course layout map not provided.

GOLF COURSE DIRECTORY

ALBION RIDGES GOLF COURSE
18 Regulation Public

7771 20th Street NW
Annandale, Minnesota 55302
612/963-5500 Clubhouse/Proshop

RESERVATIONS	612/963-5500 1 week
	Walk-on: fair/poor

GREEN FEES	M-F	S-S
Adult	$14.40/9.30	$18/12
Senior	$12.60/8.40*	$18/12
Junior	$12.60/8.40*	$18/12
Twilight	NA	NA
	*M-F am only	

PAYMENT	Credit cards not accepted
	Non-local checks accepted

LEAGUES	None

MEMBERSHIPS	USGA, GCSAA, MGA

OWNER	Dennis & JoAnn Olson
MANAGER	JoAnn Olson
SUPERINTENDENTS	Brooks Ellingson

HOURS	Dawn to Dusk
SEASON	April-November

FEATURES	
Putting green	Y
Driving range	Y
Practice area	N
Golf carts	
Power (gas)	Y
Pull carts	Y
Club rental	Y
Club storage	N
Caddies	N
Proshop	
Extended	Y
Refreshments	
Restaurant	N
Lounge	N
Snacks	Y
Clubhouse	
Showers	Y
Lockers	Y
Lodging	N

Located east of Albion Center on Wright Cty 105. Cty Rd 105 is 5 miles south of MN 55 and 9 miles north of US 12.

	MEN				WOMEN		
	BACK	FRONT	PAR	HDCP	FRONT	PAR	HDCP
1	376	346	4	13	336	4	9
2	512	500	5	3	428	5	5
3	356	344	4	11	332	4	11
4	178	169	3	15	129	3	17
5	352	334	4	7	237	4	3
6	396	366	4	5	340	4	7
7	363	340	4	9	317	4	13
8	181	161	3	17	144	3	15
9	523	505	5	1	487	5	1
Out	3237	3065	36		2750	36	
10	375	343	4	14	311	4	14
11	376	351	4	8	296	4	4
12	175	151	3	16	104	3	18
13	521	497	5	2	388	5	2
14	376	351	4	12	326	4	12
15	149	139	3	10	120	3	16
16	419	395	4	6	335	4	6
17	522	488	5	4	352	5	8
18	376	369	4	10	344	4	10
In	3289	3084	36		2584	36	
Total	6526	6149	72		5334	72	
Rating	71.1	69.5			70.8		
Slope	124	120			122		

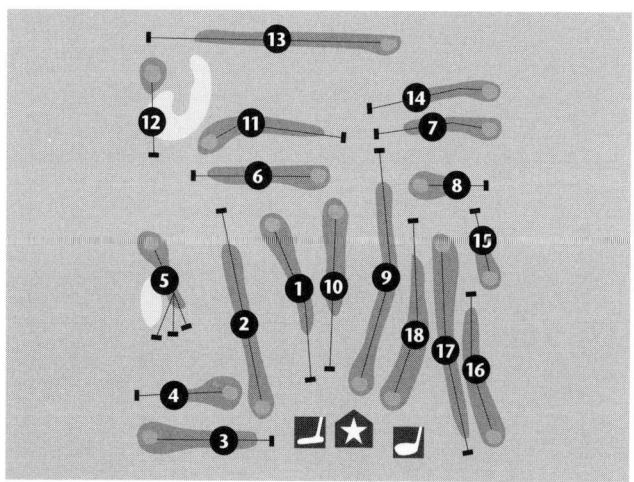

ALEXANDRIA GOLF CLUB

18 Regulation Semi-Private

2300 North Nokomis, P.O. Box 206
Alexandria, Minnesota 56308
612/762-3604 Clubhouse
612/763-3605 Proshop

HOURS	Dawn to Dusk
SEASON	April to October

FEATURES	
Putting green	Y
Driving range	N
Practice area	N
Golf carts	
Power (gas)	Y
Pull carts	Y
Club rental	Y
Club storage	N
Caddies	N
Proshop	
Regular	Y
Refreshments	
Restaurant	Y
Lounge	Y
Snacks	Y
Clubhouse	
Showers	N
Lockers	N
Lodging	N

RESERVATIONS	612/763-3605
	Walk-on: good/fair

GREEN FEES	M-F	S-S
Adult	Call	Call
Senior	Call	Call
Junior	Call	Call
Twilight	NA	NA

PAYMENT	Credit: Visa® MC® Discover®
	Non-local checks accepted

LEAGUES	Men:	Various
	Women:	Various

MEMBERSHIPS	USGA, PGA, GCSAA, MGA

PROFESSIONAL	John Basten

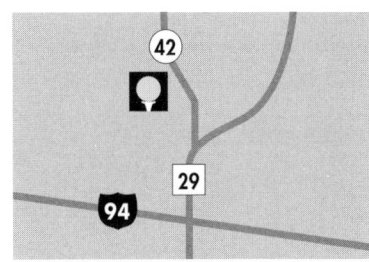

Located north of Alexandria. Course is north of I-94 on MN Highway 29, then north on County Road 42.

	MEN			WOMEN		
	FRONT	PAR	HDCP	FRONT	PAR	HDCP
1	315	4	15	298	4	13
2	321	4	11	306	4	11
3	406	4	1	389	4	5
4	404	4	7	389	5	3
5	409	4	5	399	4	9
6	500	5	17	492	5	1
7	130	3	13	77	3	17
8	363	4	9	275	4	15
9	403	4	3	394	5	7
Out	3241	36		3029	38	
10	329	4	10	320	4	14
11	320	4	16	312	4	10
12	471	5	18	440	5	4
13	184	3	6	110	3	18
14	530	5	2	456	5	2
15	390	4	4	383	4	6
16	375	4	8	367	4	8
17	154	3	14	147	3	16
18	340	4	12	331	4	12
In	3093	36		2866	36	
Total	6310	72		5895	74	
Rating	69.7			72.5		
Slope	117			120		

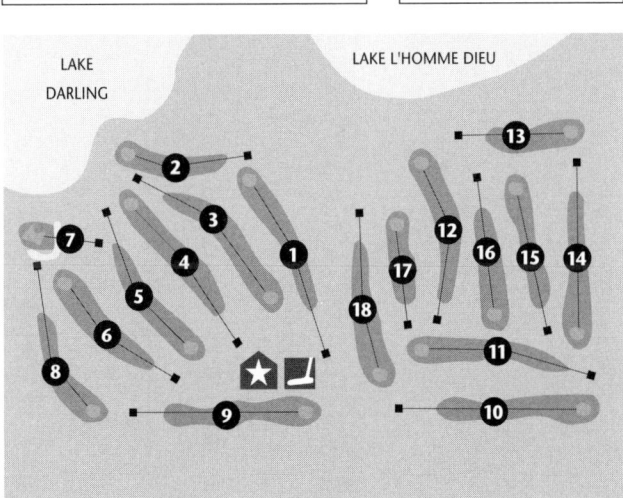

GOLF COURSE DIRECTORY

ALL SEASONS GOLF COURSE   9 Par-3 Public

7552 West Point Douglas Road
Cottage Grove, Minnesota 55016
612/459-2135 Clubhouse/Proshop

HOURS	8 am to Dusk
SEASON	April-November

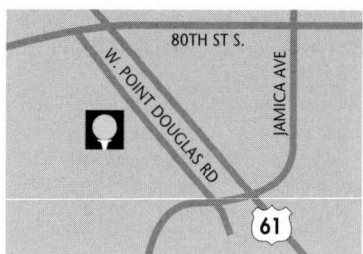

RESERVATIONS	612/459-2135	
	Walk-on: good/good	

GREEN FEES	M-F	S-S
Adult	$10/6	$10.50/6.50
Senior	$9/5	$9/5
Junior	$9/5	$9/5
Twilight	NA	NA

PAYMENT	Credit: Visa® MasterCard®
	Non-local checks accepted

LEAGUES	Women: T (pm)
	Junior: W (am)

MEMBERSHIPS	USGA, PGA, GCSAA, MGA

MANAGER	Jeff Rayburn

FEATURES	
Putting green	Y
Driving range	Y
Practice area	N
Golf carts	
Power	N
Pull carts	Y
Club rental	Y
Club storage	N
Caddies	N
Proshop	
Regular	Y
Refreshments	
Restaurant	N
Lounge	N
Snacks	Y
Clubhouse	
Showers	N
Lockers	N
Lodging	N

Located in Cottage Grove. Exit US Hwy 61 onto west 80th St S. Then south on West Point Douglas Rd. Course on right.

	MEN			WOMEN		
	FRONT	PAR	HDCP	FRONT	PAR	HDCP
1	130	3	4	130	3	4
2	72	3	9	72	3	9
3	154	3	1	154	3	1
4	83	3	7	83	3	7
5	122	3	5	122	3	5
6	130	3	3	130	3	3
7	157	3	2	157	3	2
8	71	3	8	71	3	8
9	87	3	6	87	3	6
Out	1006	27		1006	27	
1	130	3	4	130	3	4
2	72	3	9	72	3	9
3	154	3	1	154	3	1
4	83	3	7	83	3	7
5	122	3	5	122	3	5
6	130	3	3	130	3	3
7	157	3	2	157	3	2
8	71	3	8	71	3	8
9	87	3	6	87	3	6
In	1006	27		1006	27	
Total	2012	54		2012	54	
Rating	48.4			50.0		
Slope	62			71		

Course layout map
not provided.

ANGUSHIRE GOLF COURSES

9 Regulation/9 Par-3 Public

224 Waite Avenue
St. Cloud, Minnesota 56301
612/251-9619 Clubhouse/Proshop

RESERVATIONS	612/251-9619 2 days	
	Walk-on: good/fair	
GREEN FEES	M-F	S-S
Adult	$13.50/8.50	$14.75/9.75
Senior	$11/7.25	$14.75/9.75
Junior	$13.50/8.50	$14.75/9.75
Twilight	NA	NA
PAYMENT	No credit cards accepted	
	Non-local checks accepted	
LEAGUES	Men: W (pm)	
	Women: M (pm), T (am)	
	Seniors: Th (8:30-10 am)	
MEMBERSHIPS	USGA, NGF, PGA, GCSAA, CMAA	
OWNER	Mary Weyrens Tasto	
SUPERINTENDENT	Lynn Richert	
PROFESSIONAL	Tom Ramler	

HOURS	8 am to Dusk
SEASON	April to October
FEATURES	
Putting green	Y
Driving range	N
Practice area	N
Golf carts	
Power (gas)	Y
Pull carts	Y
Club rental	Y
Club storage	N
Caddies	N
Proshop	
Regular	Y
Refreshments	
Restaurant	N
Lounge	N
Snacks	Y
Clubhouse	
Showers	N
Lockers	N
Lodging	N

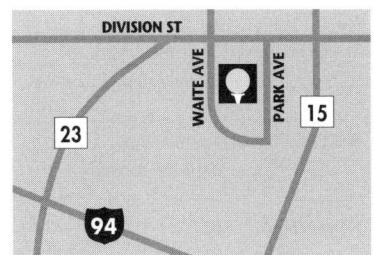

Located in St. Cloud. Course is just three blocks south of Division Street (Highway 23) on Waite Avenue South.

	MEN			WOMEN		
	FRONT	PAR	HDCP	FRONT	PAR	HDCP
1	318	4		318	4	
2	180	3		180	3	
3	314	4		314	4	
4	273	4		273	4	
5	403	4		403	4	
6	512	5		512	5	
7	275	4		275	4	
8	170	3		170	3	
9	263	4		263	4	
Reg	2708	35		2708	35	
1	128	3		128	3	
2	110	3		110	3	
3	132	3		132	3	
4	192	3		192	3	
5	153	3		153	3	
6	98	3		98	3	
7	191	3		191	3	
8	106	3		106	3	
9	172	3		172	3	
Par-3	1282	27		1282	27	
Total	3990	62		3990	62	
Rating	65.6			68.0		
Slope	109			113		

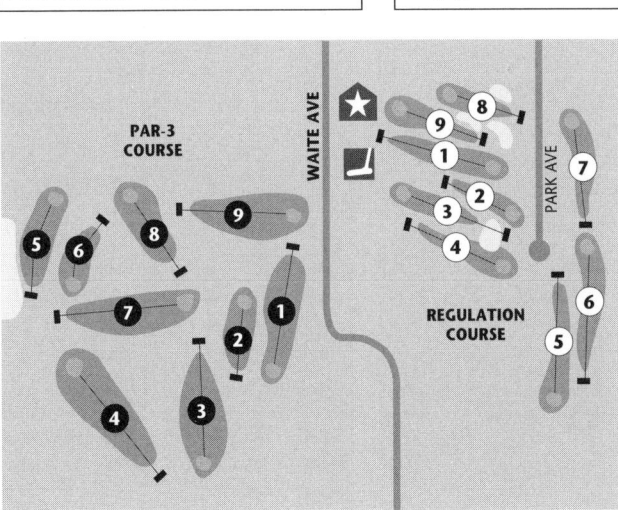

GOLF COURSE DIRECTORY

APPLE VALLEY GOLF COURSE

9 Executive Public

8661 West 140th Street
Apple Valley, Minnesota 55124
612/432-4647 Clubhouse/Proshop

HOURS	Dawn to Dusk
SEASON	April–November

RESERVATIONS	612/432-4647 1 week
	Walk-on: good/fair

GREEN FEES	M-F	S-S
Adult	$12.75/8	$13.75/9
Senior	$11/7*	$13.75/9
Junior	$11/7*	$13.75/9
Twilight	NA	NA
	* Before 1 pm	

PAYMENT	No credit cards accepted
	Local checks only

LEAGUES	Men: T (evening)
	Women: M,T (morning)

MEMBERSHIPS	None

OWNER	Joel & Julie Watrud

FEATURES	
Putting green	Y
Driving range	N
Practice area	Y
Golf carts	
Power	N
Pull carts	Y $1.50
Club rental	Y $3
Club storage	Y
Caddies	N
Proshop	
Regular	Y
Refreshments	
Restaurant	N
Lounge	Y
Snacks	Y
Clubhouse	
Showers	N
Lockers	N
Lodging	N

Located in Apple Valley. Course is about one mile south of I-35E on County Road 11/140th Street.

	MEN			**WOMEN**		
	FRONT	PAR	HDCP	FRONT	PAR	HDLP
1	244	4		244	4	
2	115	3		115	3	
3	251	4		251	4	
4	149	3		149	3	
5	117	3		117	3	
6	243	4		243	4	
7	266	4		266	4	
8	242	4		242	4	
9	143	3		143	3	
Out	1770	32		1770	32	
1	244	4		244	4	
2	115	3		115	3	
3	251	4		251	4	
4	149	3		149	3	
5	117	3		117	3	
6	243	4		243	4	
7	266	4		266	4	
8	242	4		242	4	
9	143	3		143	3	
In	1770	32		1770	32	
Total	3540	64		3540	64	
Rating	NA			NA		
Slope	NA			NA		

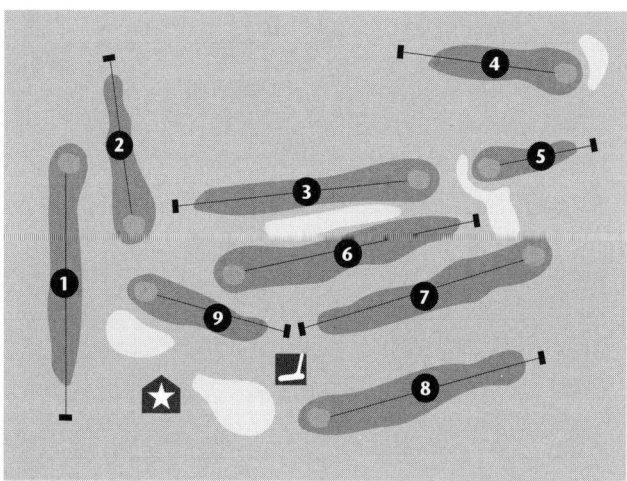

APPLETON GOLF CLUB

9 Regulation Semi-Private

331 East Wyman Avenue
Appleton, Minnesota 56208
612/289-2511 Clubhouse/Proshop

RESERVATIONS	Reservations not accepted
	Walk-on: good/good

GREEN FEES	M-F	S-S
Adult	$13/7	$15/9
Senior	$13/7	$15/9
Junior	$13/7	$15/9
Twilight	NA	NA

PAYMENT	No credit cards accepted
	Non-local checks accepted

LEAGUES	Men: T (pm)
	Women: W (pm)

MEMBERSHIPS	MGA

MANAGER	Dana D. Spry
GREENSKEEPER	Craig Johnson

HOURS	7:30 am to Dusk
SEASON	April–November

FEATURES	
Putting green	Y
Driving range	N
Practice area	N
Golf carts	
Power (gas)	Y $15/10
Pull carts	N
Club rental	Y
Club storage	Y
Caddies	N
Proshop	
Basic	Y
Refreshments	
Restaurant	Y
Lounge	N
Snacks	Y
Clubhouse	
Showers	N
Lockers	N
Lodging	N

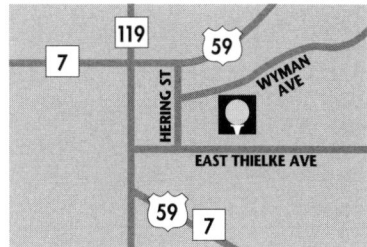

Located in Appleton. Course is just south of Highway 59 on North Hering Street, then east on Wyman Avenue.

	MEN				WOMEN		
	BACK	FRONT	PAR	HDCP	FRONT	PAR	HDCP
1	320	310	4	17	280	4	17
2	485	479	5	11	406	5	11
3	378	376	4	1	311	4	1
4	502	492	5	7	435	5	7
5	569	564	5	3	479	5	3
6	300	295	4	9	225	4	9
7	205	195	3	5	165	3	5
8	131	121	3	15	121	3	15
9	163	153	3	13	142	3	13
Out	3053	2985	36		2564	36	
1	320	310	4	18	280	4	18
2	485	479	5	12	406	5	12
3	378	376	4	2	311	4	2
4	502	492	5	8	435	5	8
5	569	564	5	4	479	5	4
6	300	295	4	10	225	4	10
7	205	195	3	6	165	3	6
8	131	121	3	16	121	3	16
9	163	153	3	14	142	3	14
In	3053	2985	36		2564	36	
Total	6106	5970	72		5128	72	
Rating	69.0	68.4			69.0		
Slope	113	111			113		

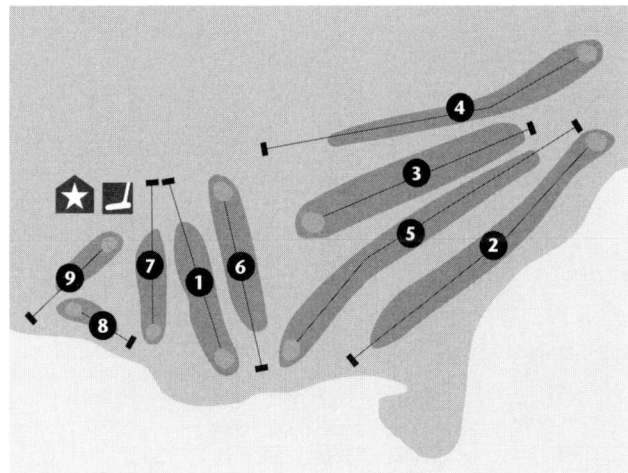

GOLF COURSE DIRECTORY

APPLEWOOD HILLS GOLF COURSE

18 Regulation Public

11840 60th Street North
Stillwater, Minnesota 55082
612/439-6544 Clubhouse
612/439-7276 Proshop

HOURS	6:30 am - Dusk
SEASON	April to October

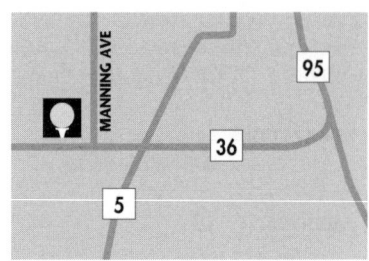

FEATURES	
Putting green	Y
Driving range	Y $2.50/5
Practice area	Y
Golf carts	
Power (gas)	Y
Pull carts	Y
Club rental	Y
Club storage	N
Caddies	N
Proshop	
Extended	Y
Refreshments	
Restaurant	Y
Lounge	Y
Snacks	Y
Clubhouse	
Showers	N
Lockers	Y
Lodging	N

Located in Stillwater. Course is just north of Highway 36 on County Road 15 (North Manning Avenue).

RESERVATIONS	612/439-7276 3 Days
	Walk-on: fair/poor

GREEN FEES	M-F	S-S
Adult	$17/9	$19/10
Senior	$14/7	$19/10
Junior	$14/7	$19/10
Twilight	$6	NA

PAYMENT	Credit: Visa® MasterCard®
	Non-local checks accepted

LEAGUES	Men: Various
	Women: Various

MEMBERSHIPS	USGA, PGA, GCSAA, MGA

MANAGER	Neil Wilson
SUPERINTENDENT	Scott Melby
PROFESSIONAL	Neil Wilson & Fred Habbermil

	MEN					**WOMEN**		
	BACK	FRONT	PAR	HDCP		FRONT	PAR	HDCP
1	129	118	3	17		107	3	17
2	152	145	3	13		128	3	13
3	161	148	3	7		137	3	7
4	155	139	3	15		121	3	15
5	145	134	3	9		123	3	9
6	229	211	3	11		200	4	11
7	220	209	3	3		156	3	3
8	256	247	4	5		224	4	5
9	327	318	4	1		216	4	1
Out	1774	1659	29			1412	30	
10	326	318	4	2		298	4	2
11	381	360	4	6		315	4	6
12	138	128	3	12		118	3	12
13	159	146	3	8		133	3	8
14	339	323	4	14		313	4	14
15	342	330	4	4		302	4	4
16	153	140	3	16		130	3	16
17	254	244	4	10		234	4	10
18	159	146	3	18		132	3	18
In	2241	2135	32			1975	32	
Total	4025	3794	61			3387	62	
Rating	58.7	57.9				58.8		
Slope	88	86				92		

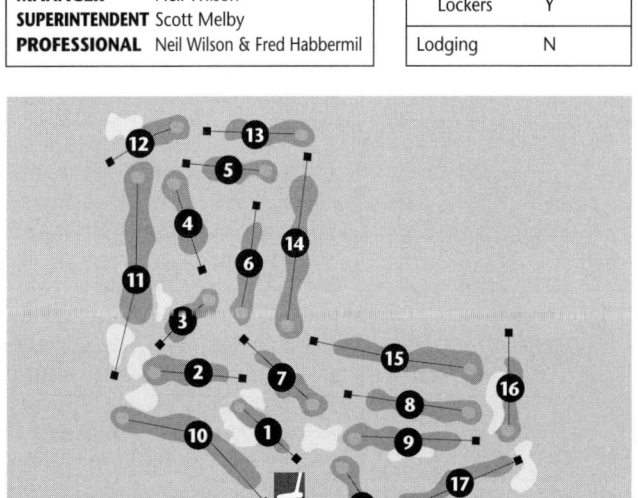

ARROWWOOD GOLF CLUB   18 Executive Semi-Private

2100 Arrowwood Dr., P.O. Box 639
Alexandria, Minnesota 56308
612/762-8337 Clubhouse/Proshop

HOURS	7 am to Dusk
SEASON	April-November

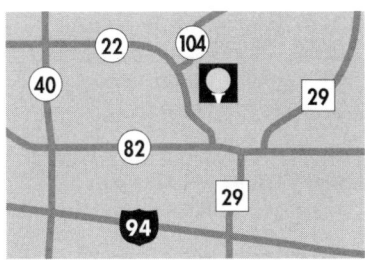

| RESERVATIONS | 612/762-8337 1 week |
| | Walk-on: fair/fair |

GREEN FEES	M-F	S-S
Adult	$22/17	$24/19
Senior	$22/17	$24/19
Junior	$22/17	$24/19
Twilight	NA	NA

| PAYMENT | Credit: Visa® MC® AmEx® |
| | Non-local checks accepted |

LEAGUES	Men: W (pm)
	Women: T (pm)
	Mixed: Th (pm)

| MEMBERSHIPS | USGA, LPGA, GCSAA, MGA |

OWNER	Dave Hartvigsen
MANAGER	D. Ziesmer, P. Hertwig
PROFESSIONAL	Dave Kluver

FEATURES	
Putting green	Y
Driving range	N
Practice area	N
Golf carts	
Power (gas)	Y
Pull carts	Y
Club rental	Y
Club storage	N
Caddies	N
Proshop	
Extended	Y
Refreshments	
Restaurant	Y
Lounge	Y
Snacks	Y
Clubhouse	
Showers	N
Lockers	N
Lodging/Resort	Y

Located in Alexandria. Course is north of I-94 on Hwy 29, Cty Rd 82 east, Cty Rd 22 north, then Cty Rd 104 east.

	MEN			WOMEN		
	FRONT	PAR	HDCP	FRONT	PAR	HDCP
1	500	5	8	490	5	1
2	324	4	9	314	4	8
3	126	3	15	117	3	16
4	367	4	3	362	4	5
5	496	5	6	433	5	13
6	400	4	2	385	4	4
7	402	4	1	328	4	7
8	147	3	16	131	3	15
9	366	4	4	354	4	6
Out	3128	36		2914	36	
10	269	4	14	233	4	17
11	273	4	10	263	4	3
12	184	3	5	174	3	2
13	128	3	17	123	3	14
14	292	4	13	284	4	10
15	297	4	12	292	4	9
16	98	3	18	88	3	18
17	272	4	7	264	4	12
18	288	4	11	288	4	11
In	2101	33		1999	33	
Total	5229	69		4913	69	
Rating	65.8			69.0		
Slope	116			119		

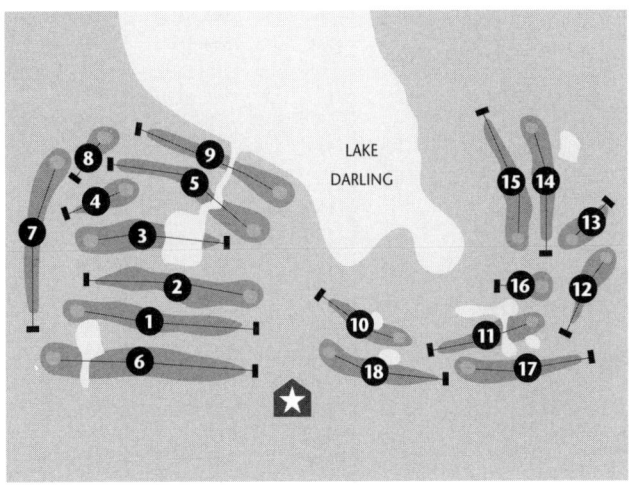

AUSTIN COUNTRY CLUB 18 Regulation Private

474 28th Street NE, P.O. Box 474
Austin, Minnesota 55912
507/437-7631 Clubhouse
507/433-7736 Proshop

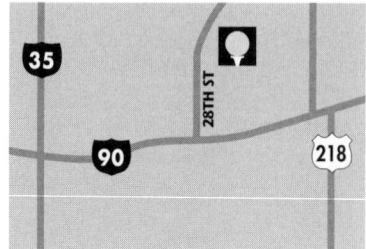

| **HOURS** | 7 am to Dusk |
| **SEASON** | April to October |

FEATURES

Putting green	Y
Driving range	Y
Practice area	N

| **RESERVATIONS** | 507/433-7736 |
| | Members only |

GREEN FEES	M-F	S-S
Adult	$19.50/12	$19.50/12
Senior	$19.50/12	$19.50/12
Junior	$19.50/12	$19.50/12
Twilight	NA	NA
	Members and guests only	

Golf carts	
Power (elec)	Y
Pull carts	Y
Club rental	N
Club storage	Y
Caddies	N

| **PAYMENT** | Credit: Visa® MasterCard® |
| | Non-local checks accepted |

Proshop	
Extended	Y
Refreshments	
Restaurant	Y
Lounge	Y
Snacks	N
Clubhouse	
Showers	Y
Lockers	Y

LEAGUES	None
MEMBERSHIPS	USGA, PGA, GCSAA, MGA
MANAGER	Mike Nelson
PROFESSIONAL	Mike Hasley

| Lodging | N |

Located in Austin. Course entrance is about 1/4 mile north of I-90 on 28th Street NE.

	MEN					**WOMEN**		
	BACK	FRONT	PAR	HDCP		FRONT	PAR	HDCP
1	435	422	4	3		377	4	3
2	500	485	5	13		475	5	5
3	337	337	4	11		328	4	9
4	430	410	4	5		383	5	15
5	420	406	4	1		388	5	13
6	397	397	4	9		372	4	1
7	138	125	3	17		108	3	17
8	513	505	5	7		415	5	7
9	163	145	3	15		125	3	11
Out	3035	2894	35			2663	35	
10	337	327	4	6		295	4	2
11	335	326	4	18		258	4	16
12	475	462	5	10		327	4	8
13	160	152	3	16		132	3	18
14	426	416	4	2		346	4	6
15	180	169	3	12		150	3	14
16	537	528	5	4		419	5	12
17	380	369	4	8		356	4	4
18	357	345	4	14		340	4	10
In	3187	3094	36			2623	35	
Total	6520	6326	72			5594	73	
Rating	71.2	70.6				71.7		
Slope	128	127				127		

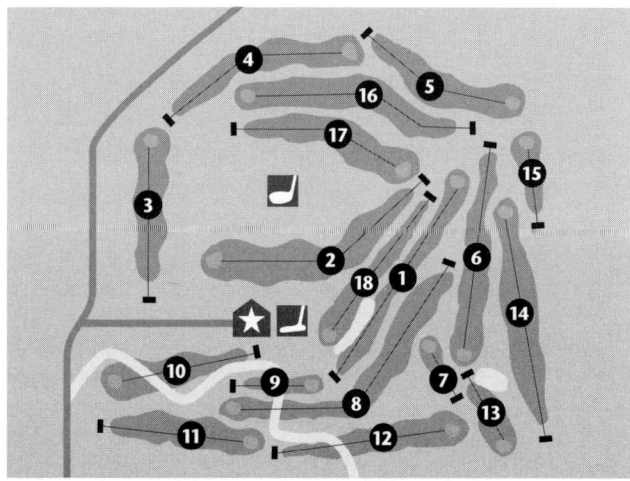

THE MINNESOTA ILLUSTRATED

BABBITT GOLF COURSE

9 Regulation Public

2806 Highway 21
Babbitt, Minnesota 55706
218/827-2603 Clubhouse/Proshop

HOURS	8 am to 9 pm
SEASON	May to October

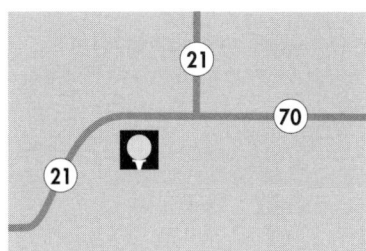

RESERVATIONS	218/827-2603
	Walk-on: fair/good

GREEN FEES	M-F	S-S
Adult	$16/10	$16/10
Senior	$16/10	$16/10
Junior	$16/10	$16/10
Twilight	NA	NA

PAYMENT	Credit cards not accepted
	Non-local checks accepted

LEAGUES	Men: W (pm)
	Women: T (4-7 pm)

MEMBERSHIPS	USGA, MGA
OWNER	Babbitt Golf Association
MANAGER	Pat MacDowell

FEATURES	
Putting green	Y
Driving range	N
Practice area	Y
Golf carts	
Power (gas)	Y
Pull carts	Y
Club rental	Y
Club storage	Y
Caddies	N
Proshop	
Extended	Y
Refreshments	
Restaurant	N
Lounge	N
Snacks	Y
Clubhouse	
Showers	N
Lockers	N
Lodging	N

Located west of Babbitt. Course is about 1/2 mile west of the Cty Rd 70/Hwy 21 junction on the south side of Hwy 21.

		MEN			WOMEN		
	BACK	FRONT	PAR	HDCP	FRONT	PAR	HDCP
1	342	331	4	13	331	4	11
2	382	370	4	9	365	4	7
3	178	150	3	17	150	3	17
4	437	425	4	1	401	5	3
5	381	370	4	7	370	4	5
6	510	500	5	5	445	5	1
7	189	182	3	15	182	3	15
8	372	361	4	11	300	4	9
9	392	333	4	3	280	4	13
Out	3183	3022	35		2824	36	
1	342	331	4	14	331	4	12
2	382	370	4	10	365	4	8
3	178	150	3	18	150	3	18
4	437	425	4	2	401	5	4
5	381	370	4	8	370	4	6
6	510	500	5	6	445	5	2
7	189	182	3	16	182	3	16
8	372	361	4	12	300	4	10
9	392	333	4	4	280	4	14
In	3183	3022	35		2824	36	
Total	6366	6044	70		5648	72	
Rating	69.4	68.0			71.4		
Slope	117	114			116		

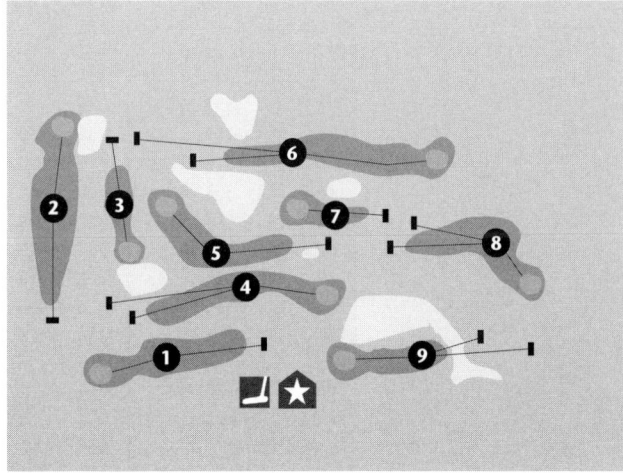

GOLF COURSE DIRECTORY

13

BAKER NATIONAL GOLF COURSE

LEA-LAKE COURSE/18 Reg Public

2935 Parkview Drive
Medina, Minnesota 55340
612/473-0800 Clubhouse/Proshop

HOURS	7 am to Dusk
SEASON	April-November

RESERVATIONS	612/473-0800 3 days
	Walk-on: good/fair

GREEN FEES	M-F	S-S
Adult	$22/13	$22/13
Senior	$19/11.50	$19/11.50
Junior	$10/5.50	$10/5.50
Twilight	NA	NA
	Patron cards available	

PAYMENT	Credit: Visa® MasterCard®
	Non-local checks accepted

LEAGUES	Men: Various
	Women: Various

MEMBERSHIPS	USGA, NGF, PGA, GCSAA, MGA

MANAGER	Michael Turnbull
PROFESSIONAL	Ken Little, Seth Zimmerman

FEATURES	
Putting green	Y
Driving range	Y $3.5-10
Practice area	Y
Golf carts	
Power (gas)	Y $20/11
Pull carts	Y $2.50
Club rental	Y $7
Club storage	N
Caddies	N
Proshop	
Extended	Y
Refreshments	
Restaurant	N
Lounge	N
Snacks	Y
Clubhouse	
Showers	Y
Lockers	Y
Lodging	N

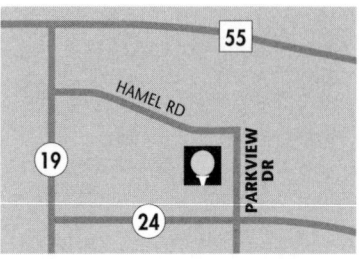

Located south of Hwy 55 in Medina. Take Cty Rd 19 south to Cty Rd 24 east. Take Parkview Dr (Rd 201) north 1 mile.

		MEN				**WOMEN**		
	BACK	FRONT	PAR	HDCP		FRONT	PAR	HDCP
1	466	440	4	3		417	5	1
2	159	146	3	17		130	3	17
3	446	425	4	1		378	5	7
4	530	473	5	5		399	5	3
5	348	324	4	13		280	4	13
6	468	447	5	7		382	5	5
7	162	139	3	15		109	3	15
8	396	379	4	9		289	4	11
9	409	384	4	11		355	4	9
Out	3384	3157	36			2739	38	
10	512	491	5	10		431	5	2
11	410	379	4	8		330	4	8
12	181	150	3	18		130	3	18
13	538	528	5	6		410	5	4
14	422	359	4	4		300	4	10
15	182	180	3	14		157	3	16
16	348	328	4	12		274	4	12
17	360	327	4	16		270	4	14
18	425	395	4	2		354	5	6
In	3378	3137	36			2656	37	
Total	6762	6294	72			5395	75	
Rating	74.2	71.8				72.7		
Slope	133	128				129		

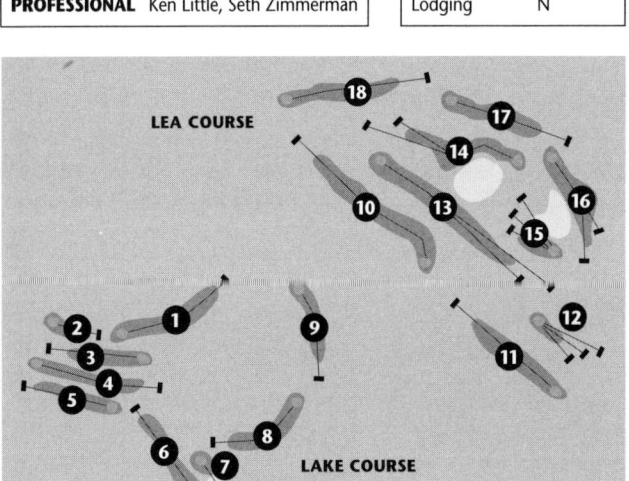

THE MINNESOTA ILLUSTRATED

BAKER NATIONAL GOLF COURSE

EVERGREEN COURSE/9 Exec Public

2935 Parkview Drive
Medina, Minnesota 55340
612/473-0800 Clubhouse/Proshop

HOURS	7 am to Dusk
SEASON	April-November

| RESERVATIONS | 612/473-0800 3 days |
| | Walk-on: good/fair |

GREEN FEES	M-F	S-S
Adult	$8	$8
Senior	$6	$6
Junior	$4	$4
Twilight	NA	NA
	Patron cards available	

| PAYMENT | Credit: Visa® MasterCard® |
| | Non-local checks accepted |

| LEAGUES | Men: Various |
| | Women: Various |

| MEMBERSHIPS | USGA, NGF, PGA, GCSAA, MGA |

MANAGER	Michael Turnbull
SUPERINTENDENTS	Keith Greeninger
PROFESSIONAL	Ken Little, Seth Zimmerman

FEATURES	
Putting green	Y
Driving range	Y $3.5-10
Practice area	Y
Golf carts	
Power (gas)	Y $20/11
Pull carts	Y $2.50
Club rental	Y $7
Club storage	N
Caddies	N
Proshop	
Extended	Y
Refreshments	
Restaurant	N
Lounge	N
Snacks	Y
Clubhouse	
Showers	Y
Lockers	Y
Lodging	N

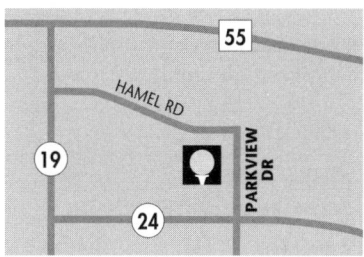

Located south of Hwy 55 in Medina. Take Cty Rd 19 south to Cty Rd 24 east. Take Parkview Dr (Rd 201) north 1 mile.

		MEN			WOMEN	
	FRONT	PAR	HDCP	FRONT	PAR	HDCP
1	169	3	5	137	3	5
2	186	3	4	186	3	4
3	322	4	1	322	4	1
4	227	4	6	227	4	6
5	244	4	2	244	4	2
6	118	3	8	118	3	8
7	134	3	7	134	3	7
8	85	3	9	85	3	9
9	165	3	3	165	3	3
Out	1650	30		1618	30	
1	169	3	5	137	3	5
2	186	3	4	186	3	4
3	322	4	1	322	4	1
4	227	4	6	227	4	6
5	244	4	2	244	4	2
6	118	3	8	118	3	8
7	134	3	7	134	3	7
8	85	3	9	85	3	9
9	165	3	3	165	3	3
In	1650	30		1618	30	
Total	3300	60		3236	60	
Rating	56.8			59.8		
Slope	83			89		

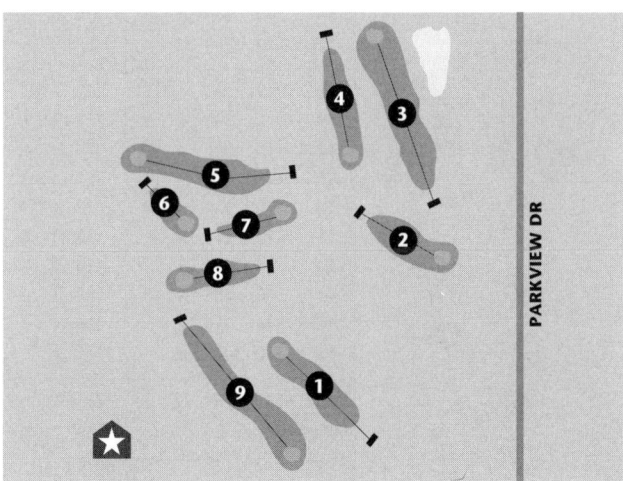

GOLF COURSE DIRECTORY

BALMORAL GOLF COURSE

18 Regulation Public

Route 3, Box 119
Battle Lake, Minnesota 56515
218/367-2055 Clubhouse
218/864-5414 Proshop

RESERVATIONS	218/367-2055 1 week	
	Walk-on: good/fair	
GREEN FEES	M-F	S-S
Adult	$20/13	$20/13
Senior	$20/13	$20/13
Junior	$20/13	$20/13
Twilight	$15/10	NA
	Multi-round cards available	
PAYMENT	Credit: Visa® MasterCard®	
	Non-local checks accepted	
LEAGUES	Men: Th (pm)	
	Women: W (am)	
MEMBERSHIPS	NGF, GCSAA, MGA	
OWNER/MGR	Michael Helmquist	
PROFESSIONAL	Jay Christenson	

HOURS	Dawn to Dusk	
SEASON	April to October	
FEATURES		
Putting green	Y	
Driving range	Y	
Practice area	Y	
Golf carts		
Power (gas)	Y	$20/12
Pull carts	Y	$2
Club rental	Y	$6/4
Club storage	Y	
Caddies	N	
Proshop		
Extended	Y	
Refreshments		
Restaurant	N	
Lounge	N	
Snacks	Y	
Clubhouse		
Showers	N	
Lockers	N	
Lodging	N	

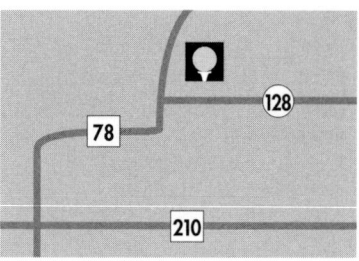

Located north of Battle Lake. Course is about 9 miles north of Battle Lake or 16 miles south of Perham on Highway 78.

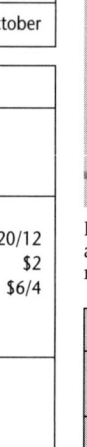

	MEN				WOMEN		
	BACK	FRONT	PAR	HDCP	FRONT	PAR	HDCP
1	410	400	4	2	353	4	2
2	150	140	3	18	130	3	18
3	469	464	5	8	457	5	8
4	361	356	4	6	346	4	6
5	444	439	5	16	419	5	16
6	312	305	4	12	234	4	12
7	178	170	3	14	160	3	14
8	322	320	4	10	313	4	10
9	376	370	4	4	358	4	4
Out	3022	2964	36		2770	36	
10	289	282	4	17	272	4	17
11	374	366	4	3	351	4	3
12	390	386	4	5	376	4	5
13	462	458	5	15	397	5	15
14	340	330	4	13	310	4	13
15	219	217	3	9	152	3	9
16	507	500	5	1	410	5	1
17	193	185	3	11	165	3	11
18	336	316	4	7	296	4	7
In	3110	3040	36		2729	36	
Total	6132	6004	72		5499	72	
Rating	69.1	68.5			71.0		
Slope	115	114			116		

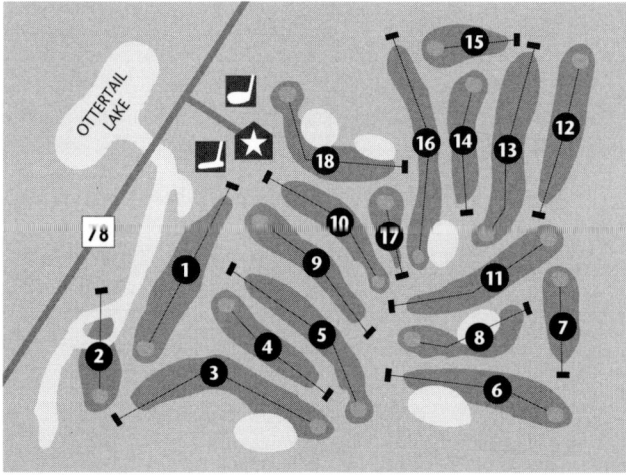

BEARPATH GOLF CLUB

18 Regulation Private

17600 Pioneer Trail
Eden Prairie, Minnesota 55347
612/975-0000 Development Corp.

HOURS	Dawn to Dusk
SEASON	April-November

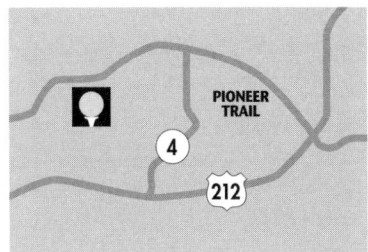

RESERVATIONS	No reservations accepted
	Members only

GREEN FEES	M-F	S-S
Adult	Call	Call
Senior	Call	Call
Junior	Call	Call
Twilight	NA	NA
	Members and guests only	

PAYMENT	Credit: Visa® MasterCard®
	Non-local checks accepted

LEAGUES	None

MEMBERSHIPS	USGA, PGA, GCSAA, MGA

PROFESSIONAL	Call

FEATURES	
Putting green	Y
Driving range	Y
Practice area	Y
Golf carts	
Power (elec)	Y
Pull carts	Y
Club rental	Y
Club storage	Y
Caddies	N
Proshop	
Extended	Y
Refreshments	
Restaurant	Y
Lounge	Y
Snacks	Y
Clubhouse	
Showers	Y
Lockers	Y
Lodging	N

Located in Eden Prairie. Course entrance is about 3 miles west of U.S. Highway 169/212 on Pioneer Trail.

		MEN			WOMEN		
	BACK	FRONT	PAR	HDCP	FRONT	PAR	HDCP
1	390	350	4		275	4	
2	520	500	5		415	5	
3	400	360	4		280	4	
4	410	370	4		290	4	
5	455	410	4		320	4	
6	190	170	3		135	3	
7	375	340	4		260	4	
8	175	155	3		100	3	
9	540	510	5		425	5	
Out	3455	3165	36		2500	36	
10	465	420	4		325	4	
11	195	175	3		135	3	
12	535	505	5		420	5	
13	185	165	3		130	3	
14	385	350	4		270	4	
15	545	515	5		430	5	
16	345	310	4		240	4	
17	410	370	4		290	4	
18	430	400	4		300	4	
In	3495	3210	36		2540	36	
Total	6950	6375	72		5040	72	
Rating	NA	NA			NA		
Slope	NA	NA			NA		

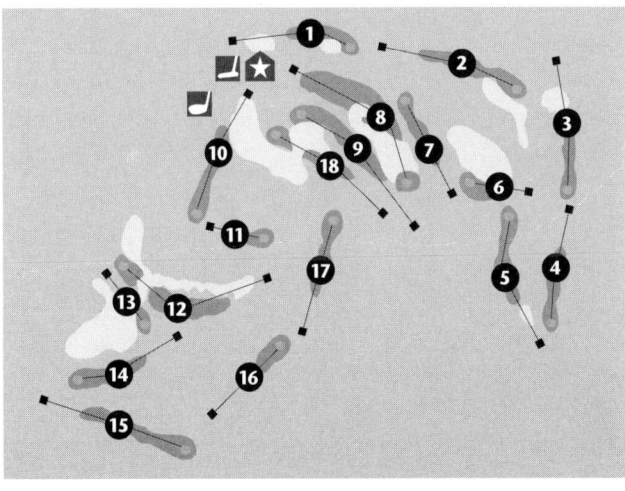

 **BELLWOOD OAKS GOLF COURSE** 18 Regulation Public

13239 210th Street East
Hastings, Minnesota 55033
612/437-4141 Clubhouse/Proshop

HOURS	6 am to Dusk
SEASON	April-November

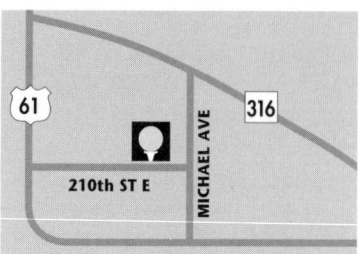

Located south of Hastings. Course is about 1/2 mile east of U.S. Highway 61 on 210th Street East.

RESERVATIONS	612/437-4141 5 days
	Walk-on: fair/poor

GREEN FEES	M-F	S-S
Adult	$15/9.50	$15/9.50
Senior	$13/8.50	$15/9.50
Junior	$15/9.50	$15/9.50
Twilight	NA	NA

PAYMENT	No credit cards accepted
	Non-local checks accepted

LEAGUES	Men: Various
	Couples: Various

MEMBERSHIPS	GCSAA, MGA

OWNER	Don Raskob
MANAGER	Don Raskob

FEATURES		
Putting green	Y	
Driving range	N	
Practice area	Y	
Golf carts		
Power (gas)	Y	$20/12
Pull carts	Y	$2
Club rental	Y	$7
Club storage	N	
Caddies	N	
Proshop		
Basic	Y	
Refreshments		
Restaurant	N	
Lounge	N	
Snacks	Y	
Clubhouse		
Showers	Y	
Lockers	Y	
Lodging	N	

	MEN				WOMEN		
	BACK	FRONT	PAR	HDCP	FRONT	PAR	HDCP
1	387	369	4	8	353	4	8
2	503	482	5	16	462	5	15
3	387	379	4	4	362	4	5
4	160	146	3	10	135	3	17
5	380	372	4	6	242	4	6
6	182	171	3	12	150	3	9
7	301	290	4	18	245	4	18
8	434	409	4	2	312	4	7
9	500	480	5	14	460	5	10
Out	3234	3098	36		2721	36	
10	494	478	5	11	460	5	12
11	393	380	4	5	364	4	4
12	360	352	4	13	291	4	16
13	372	363	4	7	294	4	13
14	481	461	5	17	433	5	11
15	405	387	4	15	306	4	14
16	424	410	4	1	385	5	2
17	226	204	3	3	156	3	1
18	386	374	4	9	297	4	3
In	3541	3409	37		2986	38	
Total	6775	6507	73		5707	74	
Rating	71.3	70.2			71.2		
Slope	115	112			115		

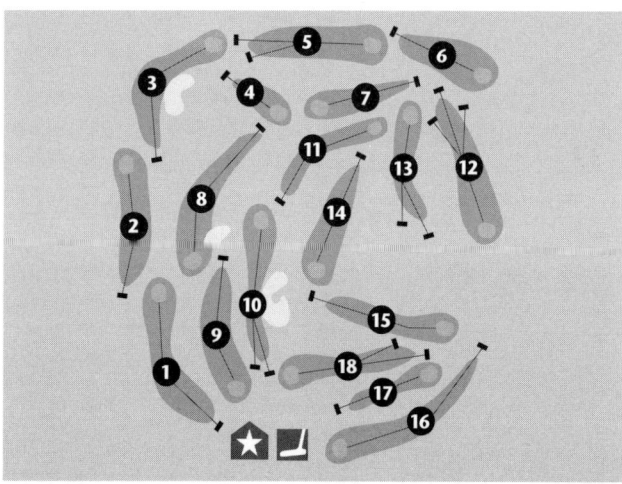

BEMIDJI TOWN & COUNTRY CLUB

18 Regulation Semi-Private

P.O. Box 622
Bemidji, Minnesota 56601
218/751-4535 Clubhouse
218/751-9215 Proshop

RESERVATIONS	218/751-9215	
	Walk-on: fair/fair	
GREEN FEES	M-F	S-S
Adult	$28/15	$28/15
Senior	$28/15	$28/15
Junior	$28/15	$28/15
Twilight	NA	NA
PAYMENT	Credit: Visa® MasterCard®	
	Non-local checks accepted	
LEAGUES	Men: Th	
	Women: W	
MEMBERSHIPS	USGA, NGF, PGA, GCSAA, MGA	
MANAGER	Tom Johans	
PROFESSIONAL	Paul Grovum	

FEATURES		
HOURS Dawn to Dusk		
SEASON April-November		
Putting green	Y	
Driving range	Y	
Practice area	N	
Golf carts		
Power (gas)	Y	$22/11
Pull carts	Y	$2
Club rental	Y	
Club storage	Y	
Caddies	N	
Proshop		
Extended	Y	
Refreshments		
Restaurant	Y	
Lounge	Y	
Snacks	Y	
Clubhouse		
Showers	Y	
Lockers	Y	
Lodging	N	

Located in Bemidji. Course entrance is east of County Road 21 on Birchmont Beach Road.

	MEN				WOMEN		
	BACK	FRONT	PAR	HDCP	FRONT	PAR	HDCP
1	350	345	4	9	286	4	11
2	295	290	4	17	257	4	15
3	305	298	4	13	293	4	9
4	490	485	5	5	360	4	3
5	389	369	4	7	301	4	5
6	400	392	4	3	297	4	7
7	186	163	3	11	154	3	13
8	387	377	4	1	375	5	1
9	171	161	3	15	152	3	17
Out	2973	2880	35		2475	35	
10	275	267	4	16	262	4	16
11	498	489	5	6	405	5	2
12	413	403	4	2	400	5	6
13	405	390	4	8	353	4	8
14	350	330	4	12	273	4	14
15	359	350	4	14	347	4	10
16	313	306	4	18	300	4	12
17	353	347	4	10	257	4	18
18	424	417	4	4	409	5	4
In	3390	3299	37		3006	39	
Total	6363	6179	72		5481	74	
Rating	70.3	69.2			69.3		
Slope	124	122			121		

Course layout map not provided.

GOLF COURSE DIRECTORY

BENSON GOLF CLUB

18 Regulation Public

2222 Atlantic Avenue
Benson, Minnesota 56215
612/842-7901 Clubhouse/Proshop

HOURS	8 am to Dusk
SEASON	April-November

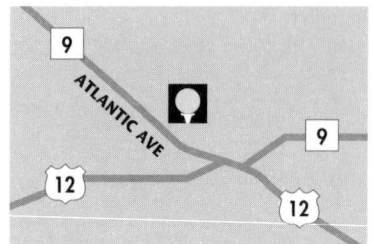

RESERVATIONS	612/842-7901 1 week
	Walk-on: good/good

GREEN FEES	M-F	S-S
Adult	$15/10	$17/12
Senior	$15/10	$17/12
Junior	$15/10	$17/12
Twilight	NA	NA
	Friday/weekend specials	

FEATURES	
Putting green	Y
Driving range	Y $2.5-3.5
Practice area	N
Golf carts	
Power (gas)	Y $18/12
Pull carts	Y $2
Club rental	Y $5
Club storage	Y $25/yr
Caddies	N
Proshop	
Extended	Y
Refreshments	
Restaurant	Y
Lounge	Y
Snacks	Y
Clubhouse	
Showers	N
Lockers	Y
Lodging	N

Located north of Benson. Course is about 1 mile north of U.S. Highway 12 on Highway 9 (Atlantic Avenue).

PAYMENT	No credit cards accepted
	Non-local checks accepted

LEAGUES	Men: T (pm)
	Women: W (am & pm)

MEMBERSHIPS	USGA, NGF, PGA, GCSAA, MGA

MANAGER	Sandy Moesenthin
SUPERINTENDENT	Dave Sime
PROFESSIONAL	Jim Carlson

	MEN				WOMEN		
	BACK	FRONT	PAR	HDCP	FRONT	PAR	HDCP
1	395	390	4	11	350	4	9
2	170	164	3	15	116	3	17
3	344	332	4	17	263	4	15
4	342	328	4	5	288	4	1
5	419	388	4	1	274	4	3
6	315	305	4	9	213	4	11
7	513	507	5	7	416	5	7
8	196	188	3	13	170	3	13
9	531	525	5	3	465	5	5
Out	3225	3127	36		2555	36	
10	520	514	5	6	385	5	5
11	307	294	4	14	282	4	11
12	398	352	4	4	322	4	3
13	171	159	3	10	127	3	9
14	273	254	4	18	232	4	15
15	393	380	4	2	294	4	1
16	554	497	5	8	445	5	7
17	161	134	3	16	124	3	13
18	355	348	4	12	222	4	17
In	3132	2932	36		2433	36	
Total	6357	6059	72		4988	72	
Rating	70.2	68.8			68.6		
Slope	122	120			118		

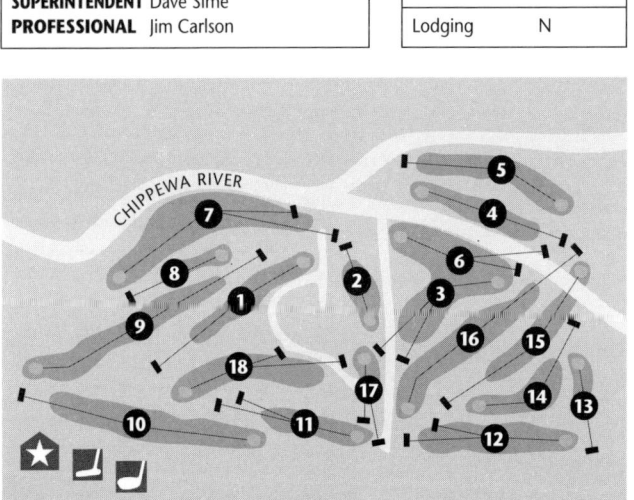

THE MINNESOTA ILLUSTRATED

BENT CREEK GOLF CLUB

18 Regulation Private

14490 Valley View Road
Eden Prairie, Minnesota 55344
612/937-0789 Clubhouse
612/937-9347 Proshop

RESERVATIONS	612/937-9347 7 days	
	Members only	
GREEN FEES	M-F	S-S
Adult	$35/20	$40/20
Senior	$35/20	$40/20
Junior	$20	$20
Twilight	NA	NA
	Members and guests only	
PAYMENT	Credit: Visa® MasterCard®	
	Non-local checks accepted	
LEAGUES	Women: T (pm), Th (am)	
MEMBERSHIPS	USGA, PGA, GCSAA, MGA	
MANAGER	R. Larson	
SUPERINTENDENT	Kevin Benson	
PROFESSIONAL	Chet Cashman	

HOURS 7 am to 9 pm
SEASON April–November

FEATURES
Putting green	Y	
Driving range	Y	$2.50-5
Practice area	N	
Golf carts		
Power (elec)	Y	$24/12
Pull carts	Y	$2.50
Club rental	Y	$10
Club storage	Y	
Caddies	Y	$10
Proshop		
Extended	Y	
Refreshments		
Restaurant	Y	
Lounge	Y	
Snacks	Y	
Clubhouse		
Showers	Y	
Lockers	Y	
Lodging	N	

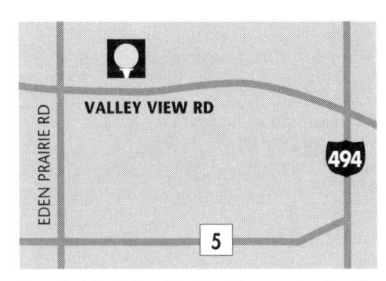

Located in Eden Prairie. Course is about one mile west of Interstate-494 on Valley View Road.

	\multicolumn{4}{c}{MEN}	\multicolumn{3}{c}{WOMEN}
	BACK	FRONT	PAR	HDCP	FRONT	PAR	HDCP
1	510	493	5	7	460	5	3
2	135	116	3	17	80	3	17
3	340	323	4	11	300	4	11
4	415	400	4	1	368	4	1
5	310	300	4	13	295	4	13
6	380	360	4	5	325	4	5
7	405	385	4	3	340	4	7
8	180	170	3	15	160	3	15
9	360	347	4	9	335	4	9
Out	3035	2894	35		2663	35	
10	500	482	5	12	413	5	12
11	330	314	4	16	293	4	14
12	410	374	4	10	360	4	8
13	400	380	4	4	281	4	6
14	185	157	3	14	145	3	10
15	425	400	4	2	332	4	4
16	504	482	5	8	434	5	2
17	160	137	3	18	125	3	16
18	420	410	4	6	410	5	18
In	3334	3136	36		2793	37	
Total	6369	6030	71		5456	72	
Rating	70.9	69.4			72.7		
Slope	123	120			130		

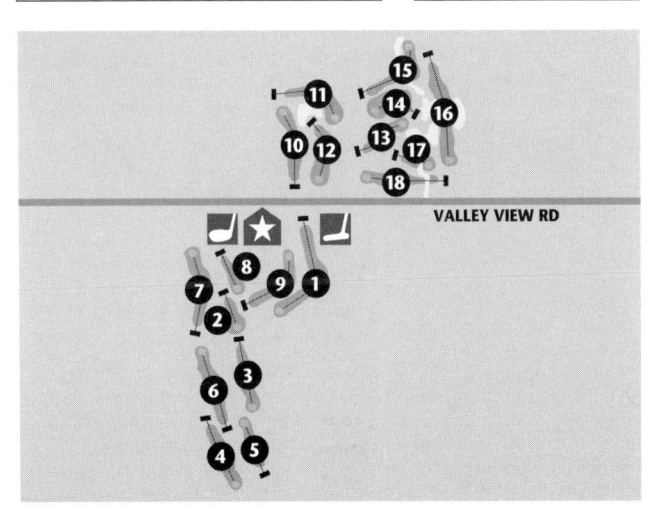

GOLF COURSE DIRECTORY

BENTWOOD CLIMAX MUNICIPAL GOLF CLUB

9 Regulation Public

Highway 75 North, P.O. Box 118
Climax, Minnesota 56523
218/857-3545 Clubhouse/Proshop

HOURS	Dawn to Dusk
SEASON	April to October

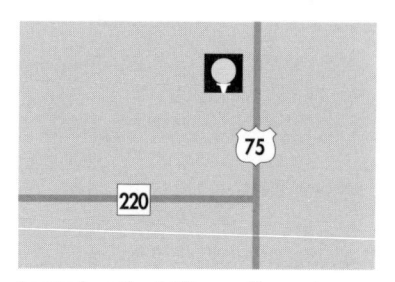

RESERVATIONS	218/857-3545	
	Walk-on: good/fair	

GREEN FEES	M-F	S-S
Adult	Call	Call
Senior	Call	Call
Junior	Call	Call
Twilight	NA	NA

PAYMENT	No credit cards accepted
	Non-local checks accepted

LEAGUES	Men: Various
	Women: Various

MEMBERSHIPS	MGA

PROFESSIONAL	Call

FEATURES	
Putting green	Y
Driving range	N
Practice area	N
Golf carts	
Power (gas)	Y
Pull carts	Y
Club rental	Y
Club storage	N
Caddies	N
Proshop	
Regular	Y
Refreshments	
Restaurant	N
Lounge	Y
Snacks	Y
Clubhouse	
Showers	N
Lockers	N
Lodging	N

Located north of Climax. Course is one mile north of MN Highway 220 on U.S. Highway 75.

	MEN			WOMEN		
	FRONT	PAR	HDCP	FRONT	PAR	HDCP
1	313	4	4	280	4	4
2	151	3	8	140	3	8
3	437	5	1	385	5	1
4	108	3	9	104	3	9
5	434	5	3	363	5	2
6	327	4	6	302	4	6
7	389	4	2	379	4	3
8	300	4	5	280	4	5
9	293	4	7	267	4	7
Out	2752	36		2500	36	
1	313	4	4	280	4	4
2	151	3	8	140	3	8
3	437	5	1	385	5	1
4	108	3	9	104	3	9
5	434	5	3	363	5	2
6	327	4	6	302	4	6
7	389	4	2	379	4	3
8	300	4	5	280	4	5
9	293	4	7	267	4	7
In	2752	36		2500	36	
Total	5504	72		5000	72	
Rating	66.2			68.8		
Slope	101			117		

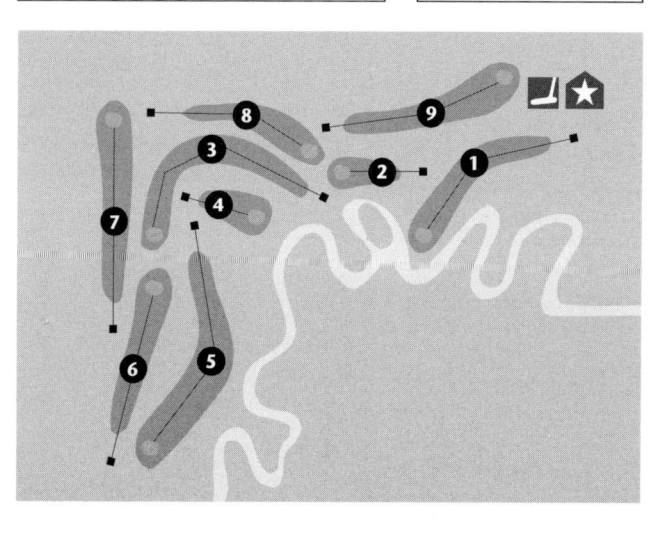

THE MINNESOTA ILLUSTRATED

BIG LAKE GOLF CLUB

9 Par-3 Public

18 Cary Road
Cloquet, Minnesota 55720
218/879-4221 Clubhouse
218/879-1197 Proshop

HOURS	8 am to Dusk
SEASON	Apr-November

FEATURES		
Putting green	Y	
Driving range	N	
Practice area	Y	
Golf carts		
Power (gas)	Y	$12/6
Pull carts	Y	$2
Club rental	Y	$3
Club storage	Y	
Caddies	N	
Proshop		
Extended	Y	
Refreshments		
Restaurant	Y	
Lounge	Y	
Snacks	Y	
Clubhouse		
Showers	N	
Lockers	N	
Lodging (camp)	Y	

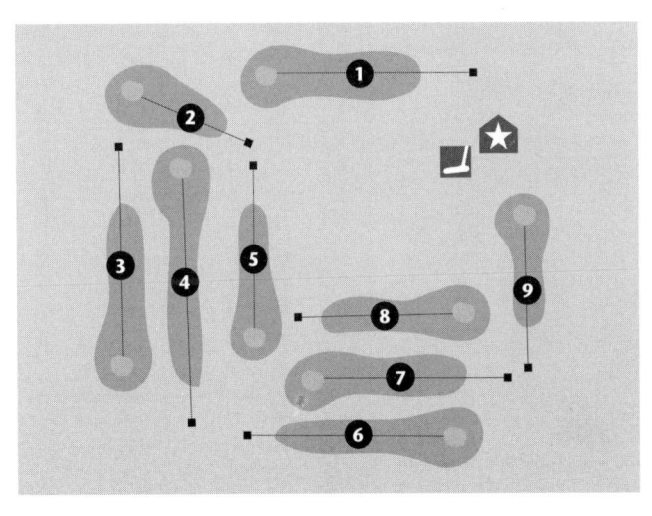

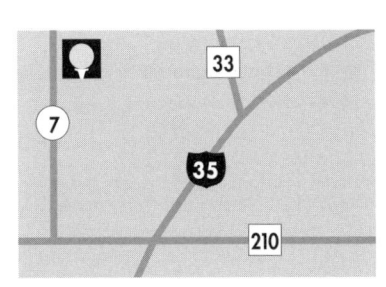

Located south of Cloquet. Course is west of I-35 on Highway 210, then north on County Road 7.

RESERVATIONS	218/879-1197	
	Walk-on: good/fair	
GREEN FEES	M-F	S-S
Adult	$10/8	$10/8
Senior	$10/8	$10/8
Junior	$10/8	$10/8
Twilight	NA	NA
PAYMENT	No credit cards accepted	
	Non-local checks accepted	
LEAGUES	Men: T (3-7 pm)	
	Women: W (9-12 am)	
	Couples: W (5-8 pm)	
MEMBERSHIPS	NGF	
OWNER	Jalmer & Joyce Angell	

	\multicolumn{3}{c}{MEN}	\multicolumn{3}{c}{WOMEN}
	FRONT	PAR	HDCP	FRONT	PAR	HDCP
1	170	3	5	170	3	5
2	129	3	8	129	3	8
3	210	3	3	210	3	3
4	220	3	2	220	3	2
5	145	3	6	145	3	6
6	210	3	1	210	3	1
7	189	3	4	189	3	4
8	150	3	7	150	3	7
9	142	3	9	142	3	9
Out	1565	27		1565	27	
1	170	3	5	170	3	5
2	129	3	8	129	3	8
3	210	3	3	210	3	3
4	220	3	2	220	3	2
5	145	3	6	145	3	6
6	210	3	1	210	3	1
7	189	3	4	189	3	4
8	150	3	7	150	3	7
9	142	3	9	142	3	9
In	1565	27		1565	27	
Total	3130	54		3130	54	
Rating	NA			NA		
Slope	NA			NA		

GOLF COURSE DIRECTORY

BIRCH BAY GOLF COURSE

9 Regulation Semi-Private

1771 Birch Drive West
Nisswa, Minnesota 56468
218/963-4488 Clubhouse
800/450-4481 Proshop

HOURS	7 am to Dusk
SEASON	April to October

FEATURES	
Putting green	Y
Driving range	N
Practice area	Y

RESERVATIONS	800/450-4481 1 week
	Walk-on: good/good

GREEN FEES	M-F	S-S
Adult	$20/13	$20/13
Junior	$20/13	$20/13
Senior	$20/13	$20/13
Twilight	$8.50 (4pm)	$9.50 (5pm)

Golf carts		
Power (gas)	Y	$20/13
Pull carts	Y	$2.75
Club rental	Y	$4
Club storage	Y	$25/yr
Caddies	N	

PAYMENT	Credit: Visa® MasterCard®
	Non-local checks accepted

Proshop	
Extended	Y
Refreshments	
Restaurant	N
Lounge	N
Snacks	Y
Clubhouse	
Showers	Y
Lockers	Y

LEAGUES	Women: M (4:30 pm)

MEMBERSHIPS	GCSAA, MGA

Lodging	Y $44 up

OWNER/MGR	Butch & Kathy Brown

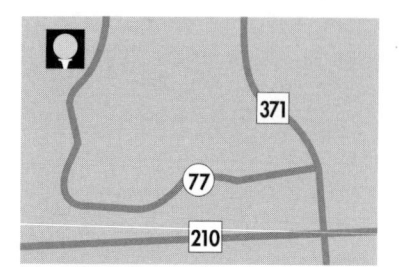

Located north of Brainerd. Course entrance is west of Highway 371 on County Road 77.

	MEN			**WOMEN**		
	FRONT	PAR	HDCP	FRONT	PAR	HDCP
1	330	4	5	270	4	5
2	310	4	7	270	4	7
3	337	4	4	304	4	4
4	460	5	6	400	5	6
5	230	4	9	230	4	9
6	255	4	2	205	4	2
7	354	4	3	324	4	3
8	439	4	1	380	5	1
9	190	3	8	175	3	8
Out	2900	36		2558	37	
1	330	4	5	270	4	5
2	310	4	7	270	4	7
3	337	4	4	304	4	4
4	460	5	6	400	5	6
5	230	4	9	230	4	9
6	255	4	2	205	4	2
7	354	4	3	324	4	3
8	439	4	1	380	5	1
9	190	3	8	175	3	8
In	2900	36		2558	37	
Total	5800	72		5116	74	
Rating	69.4			70.6		
Slope	122			121		

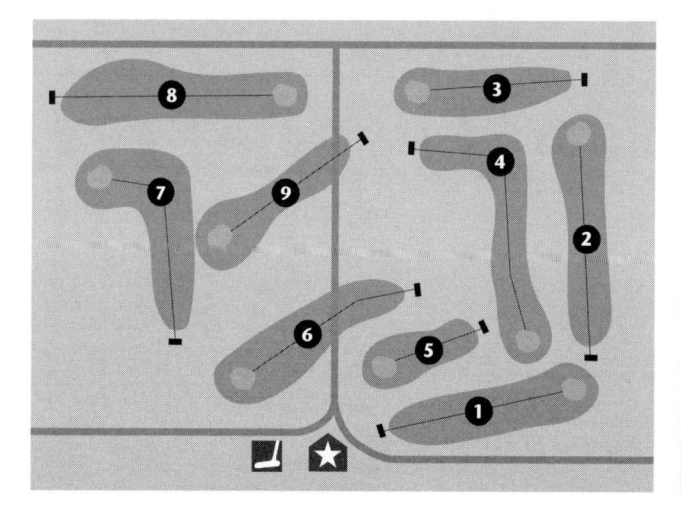

THE MINNESOTA ILLUSTRATED

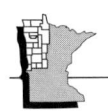

BIRCHWOOD GOLF COURSE

9 Regulation Public

Golf Course Road, P.O. Box 432
Pelican Rapids, Minnesota 56572
218/863-6486 Clubhouse/Proshop

HOURS	7 am to Dusk
SEASON	April to October

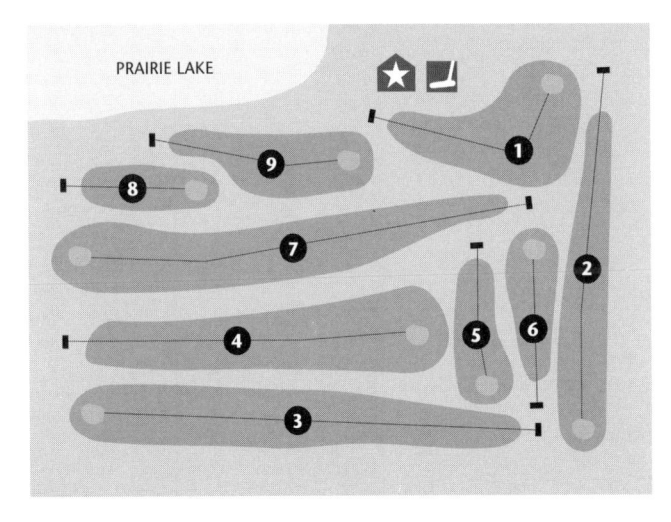

RESERVATIONS	218/863-6486
	Walk-on: good/poor

GREEN FEES	M-F	S-S
Adult	$12.50/8.50	$12.50/8.50
Senior	$12.50/8.50	$12.50/8.50
Junior*	$4/4	$4/4
Twilight	NA	NA

*Rate for age 12 and under
10 punch card available

PAYMENT	No credit cards accepted
	Non-local checks accepted

LEAGUES	Men: W (3 pm-dusk)
	Women: Th (7 am-11am)

MEMBERSHIPS	MGA

OWNER	Brian & Connie Evenson

FEATURES		
Putting green	Y	
Driving range	Y	$2-3
Practice area	N	
Golf carts		
Power (gas)	Y	$14.50
Pull carts	Y	$1.50
Club rental	Y	$2
Club storage	Y	
Caddies	N	
Proshop		
Extended	Y	
Refreshments		
Restaurant	N	
Lounge	N	
Snacks	Y	
Clubhouse		
Showers	Y	
Lockers	Y	
Lodging	N	

Located 1 mile north of Pelican Rapids. Course entrance is west of Highway 59 on Golf Course Road.

		MEN			WOMEN	
	FRONT	PAR	HDCP	FRONT	PAR	HDCP
1	204	4	9	204	4	7
2	326	4	3	312	4	4
3	388	4	1	378	5	3
4	343	4	2	333	4	2
5	134	3	7	134	3	8
6	188	3	5	175	3	6
7	435	5	4	425	5	1
8	130	3	8	130	3	9
9	300	4	6	276	4	5
Out	2448	34		2367	35	
1	204	4	9	204	4	7
2	326	4	3	312	4	4
3	388	4	1	378	5	3
4	343	4	2	333	4	2
5	134	3	7	134	3	8
6	188	3	5	175	3	6
7	435	5	4	425	5	1
8	130	3	8	130	3	9
9	300	4	6	276	4	5
In	2448	34		2367	35	
Total	4896	68		4734	70	
Rating	64.2			67.8		
Slope	112			115		

GOLF COURSE DIRECTORY

BIRNAMWOOD PUBLIC GOLF COURSE   9 Par-3 Public

12424 Parkwood Drive
Burnsville, Minnesota 55337
612/890-7964 Clubhouse/Proshop

HOURS	Dawn to Dusk
SEASON	April-November

RESERVATIONS	612/890-7964 1 week
	Walk-on: poor/poor

GREEN FEES	M-F	S-S
Adult	$6.75	$7.25
Senior	$5.25	$7.25
Junior	$4.25	$7.25
Twilight	NA	NA

PAYMENT	No credit cards accepted
	Non-local checks accepted

LEAGUES	Men: Various
	Women: Various
	Juniors: Various

MEMBERSHIPS	USGA, NGF, MGA

OWNER	City of Burnsville
MANAGER	Jeff Curlo

FEATURES		
Putting green	Y	
Driving range	N	
Practice area	N	
Golf carts		
Power (gas)	Y	$8
Pull carts	Y	$1.50
Club rental	Y	$2.50
Club storage	Y	$20/yr
Caddies	N	
Pro shop		
Basic	Y	
Refreshments		
Restaurant	N	
Lounge	N	
Snacks	Y	
Clubhouse		
Showers	N	
Lockers	Y	
Lodging	N	

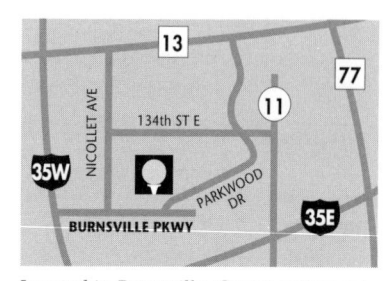

Located in Burnsville. Course entrance is east of I-35W on Burnsville Parkway, then northeast on Parkwood Drive.

	MEN			**WOMEN**		
	FRONT	PAR	HDCP	FRONT	PAR	HDCP
1	122	3	8	122	3	8
2	123	3	7	123	3	7
3	171	3	1	171	3	1
4	139	3	2	139	3	2
5	109	3	9	109	3	9
6	139	3	5	139	3	5
7	165	3	3	165	3	3
8	142	3	6	142	3	6
9	157	3	4	157	3	4
Out	1258	27		1258	27	
1	122	3	8	122	3	8
2	123	3	7	123	3	7
3	171	3	1	171	3	1
4	139	3	2	139	3	2
5	109	3	9	109	3	9
6	139	3	5	139	3	5
7	165	3	3	165	3	3
8	142	3	6	142	3	6
9	157	3	4	157	3	4
In	1258	27		1258	27	
Total	2516	54		2516	54	
Rating	51.6			53.4		
Slope	71			74		

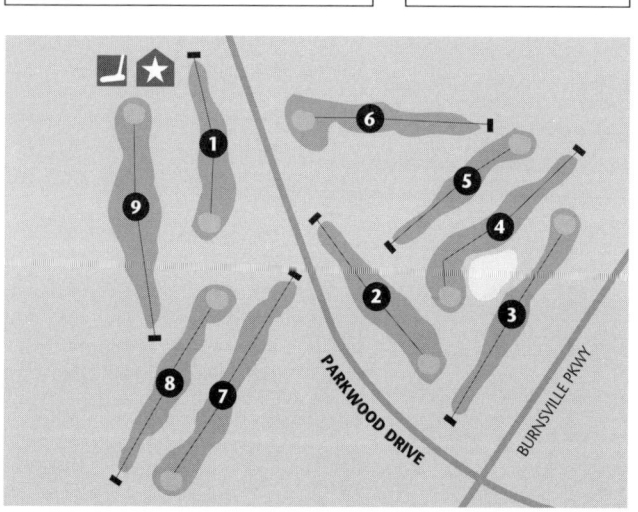

BLACKDUCK GOLF CLUB

9 Regulation Public

P.O. Box 380
Blackduck, Minnesota 56630
218/835-7757 Clubhouse/Proshop

HOURS	8 am to Dusk
SEASON	April to October

RESERVATIONS	218/835-7757
	Walk-on: good/good

GREEN FEES	M-F	S-S
Adult	$12/10	$15/12
Senior	$12/10	$15/12
Junior	$8/6	$8/8
Twilight	NA	NA

PAYMENT	Credit: Visa® MC® Discover®
	Non-local checks accepted

LEAGUES	None

MEMBERSHIPS	USGA, LPGA, MGA

OWNER	City of Blackduck
MANAGER	Duane T. Dueffert

FEATURES		
Putting green	Y	
Driving range	N	
Practice area	N	
Golf carts		
Power (gas)	Y	$7
Pull carts	Y	$1
Club rental	Y	$3
Club storage	N	
Caddies	N	
Proshop		
Extended	Y	
Refreshments		
Restaurant	N	
Lounge	N	
Snacks	Y	
Clubhouse		
Showers	N	
Lockers	Y	
Lodging	N	

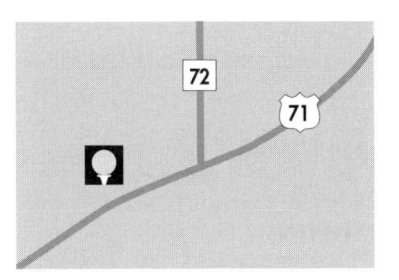

Located west of Blackduck. Course is about 1/2 mile west of MN Highway 72 on the north side of US Highway 71.

	MEN			WOMEN		
	FRONT	PAR	HDCP	FRONT	PAR	HDCP
1	475	5	4	395	5	1
2	345	4	7	345	4	3
3	322	4	5	276	4	8
4	198	3	2	198	4	9
5	471	5	8	381	5	6
6	393	4	1	278	4	4
7	153	3	6	153	3	7
8	292	4	9	292	4	5
9	380	4	3	360	5	2
Out	3029	36		2678	38	
1	475	5	4	395	5	1
2	345	4	7	345	4	3
3	322	4	5	276	4	8
4	198	3	2	198	4	9
5	471	5	8	381	5	6
6	393	4	1	278	4	4
7	153	3	6	153	3	7
8	292	4	9	292	4	5
9	380	4	3	360	5	2
In	3029	36		2678	38	
Total	6058	72		5356	76	
Rating	69.4			72.0		
Slope	120			119		

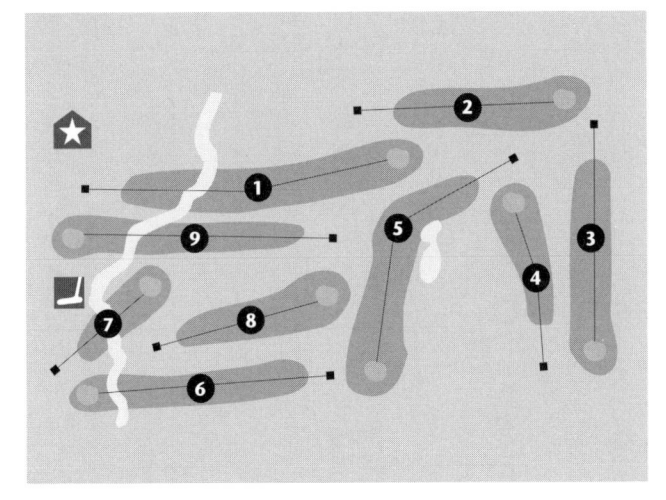

GOLF COURSE DIRECTORY

BLOOMING PRAIRIE COUNTRY CLUB

9 Regulation Public

North Highway 218, P.O. Box 788
Blooming Prairie, Minnesota 55917
507/583-2887 Clubhouse/Proshop

HOURS	7 am to Dusk
SEASON	April to October

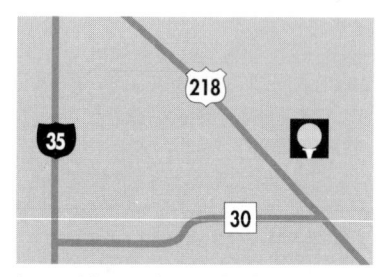

Located four miles north of Blooming Prairie. Course entrance is north of MN Highway 30 on U.S. Highway 218.

RESERVATIONS	No reservations accepted	
	Walk-on: good/fair	
GREEN FEES	M-F	S-S
Adult	$10/8	$16/10
Senior	$10/8	$16/10
Junior	$10/8	$16/10
Twilight	NA	NA
PAYMENT	No credit cards accepted	
	Non-local checks accepted	
LEAGUES	Men: M (pm)	
	Women: T (pm)	
	Couples: F (pm)	
MEMBERSHIPS	MGA	
MANAGER	Paul Smith	
SUPERINTENDENT	Mike Lea	

FEATURES		
Putting green	Y	
Driving range	N	
Practice area	N	
Golf carts		
Power (gas)	Y	$16/10
Pull carts	Y	$2
Club rental	Y	$3
Club storage	Y	$12/yr
Caddies	N	
Proshop		
Regular	Y	
Refreshments		
Restaurant	N	
Lounge	N	
Snacks	Y	
Clubhouse		
Showers	Y	
Lockers	Y	$12/yr
Lodging	N	

	MEN			WOMEN		
	FRONT	PAR	HDCP	FRONT	PAR	HDCP
1	456	5	5	368	5	1
2	170	3	15	160	3	15
3	361	4	3	275	4	11
4	363	4	9	317	4	9
5	147	3	17	127	3	17
6	476	5	1	367	5	3
7	347	4	7	340	4	7
8	358	4	11	358	5	5
9	302	4	13	291	4	13
Out	2980	36		2603	37	
1	456	5	6	368	5	2
2	170	3	16	160	3	16
3	361	4	4	275	4	12
4	363	4	10	317	4	10
5	147	3	18	127	3	18
6	476	5	2	367	5	4
7	347	4	8	340	4	8
8	358	4	12	358	5	6
9	302	4	14	291	4	14
In	2980	36		2603	37	
Total	5960	72		5206	74	
Rating	67.2			69.0		
Slope	109			111		

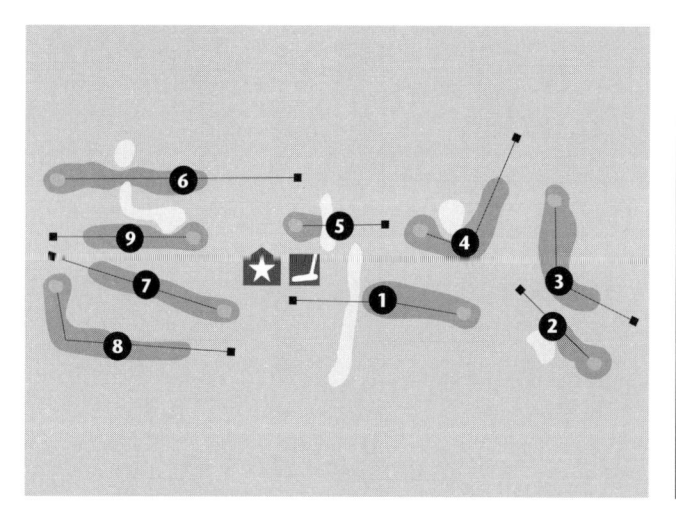

THE MINNESOTA ILLUSTRATED

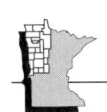

BLUEBERRY PINES GOLF CLUB

18 Regulation Public

Route 2, P.O. Box 76
Menahga, Minnesota 56464
218/564-4657 Clubhouse
218/564-4653 Proshop

HOURS	6 am to Dusk
SEASON	April to October

FEATURES	
Putting green	Y
Driving range	Y
Practice area	N
Golf carts	
Power (gas)	Y
Pull carts	N
Club rental	Y
Club storage	Y
Caddies	Y
Proshop	
Extended	Y
Refreshments	
Restaurant	Y
Lounge	Y
Snacks	Y
Clubhouse	
Showers	N
Lockers	N
Lodging	N

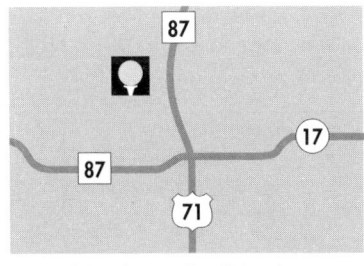

Located 3 miles north of Menahga on US Hwy 71/MN Hwy 87. Course is on the west side of US Hwy 71/MN Hwy 87.

| **RESERVATIONS** | 218/564-4653 1 week |
| | Walk-on: fair/fair |

GREEN FEES	M-F	S-S
Adult	$21/13	$23/15
Senior	$16/10*	$19/12*
Senior	$16/10*	$19/12*
Twilight	$8 (5 pm)	$10 (5 pm)
	*Rate after 2 pm	

| **PAYMENT** | Credit: Visa® MC® AmEx® |
| | Non-local checks accepted |

| **LEAGUES** | Men: W (5:30 pm) |
| | Women: Th (5:30 pm) |

| **MEMBERSHIPS** | USGA, PGA, GCSAA, MGA |

| **SUPERINTENDENT** | Lee Kirtchgatter |
| **PROFESSIONAL** | Scott Roth |

	MEN				WOMEN		
	BACK	FRONT	PAR	HDCP	FRONT	PAR	HDCP
1	469	447	5	15	385	5	7
2	447	406	4	1	349	4	3
3	531	500	5	5	427	5	1
4	162	150	3	17	113	3	17
5	376	349	4	9	248	4	11
6	339	305	4	13	233	4	15
7	415	365	4	3	316	4	5
8	200	185	3	11	144	3	13
9	395	379	4	7	302	4	9
Out	3334	3086	36		2547	36	
10	401	367	4	8	308	4	12
11	512	486	5	4	409	5	2
12	408	395	4	6	307	4	10
13	360	305	4	16	267	4	14
14	192	155	3	14	115	3	18
15	379	344	4	12	252	4	6
16	406	377	4	2	294	4	4
17	157	124	3	18	103	3	16
18	514	482	5	10	422	5	8
In	3329	3035	36		2477	36	
Total	6663	6121	72		5024	72	
Rating	72.6	70.2			69.3		
Slope	128	123			123		

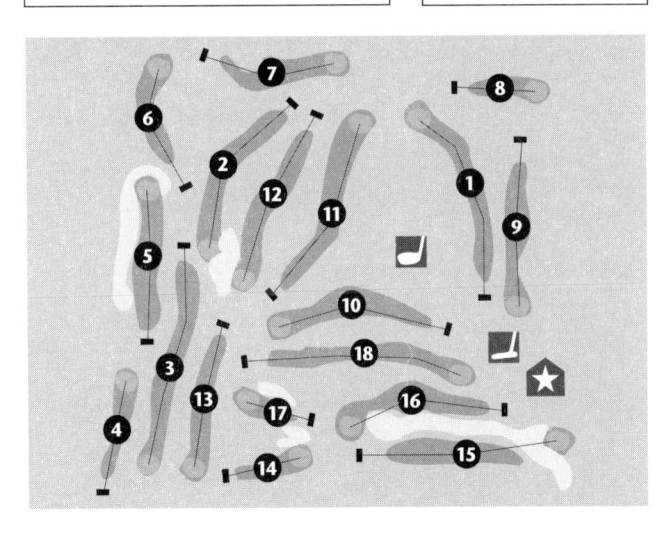

GOLF COURSE DIRECTORY

BLUFF CREEK GOLF COURSE

18 Regulation Public

1025 Creekwood
Chaska, Minnesota 55318
612/445-5685 Clubhouse/Proshop

HOURS	Dawn to Dusk
SEASON	April–November

RESERVATIONS	612/445-5685 1 week
	Reservations required
	Walk-on: good/poor

GREEN FEES	M-Th	F-S
Adult	$17/12.50	$20/12.50
Senior	$12/8.50	$20/12.50
Junior	$17/12.50	$20/12.50
Twilight	NA	NA

| **PAYMENT** | No credit cards accepted |
| | Non-local checks accepted |

| **LEAGUES** | Men: None |
| | Women: None |

| **MEMBERSHIPS** | USGA, NGF, MGA |

| **OWNER** | Norman Berglund, Art Johnson |
| **MANAGER** | Scott E. Fiedler |

FEATURES		
Putting green	Y	
Driving range	Y	$3.75
Practice area	N	
Golf carts		
Power (gas)	Y	$20/11.5
Pull carts	Y	$2.65
Club rental	Y	$11/6.5
Club storage	N	
Caddies	N	
Proshop		
Basic	Y	
Refreshments		
Restaurant	Y	
Lounge	Y	
Snacks	Y	
Clubhouse		
Showers	Y	
Lockers	N	
Lodging	N	

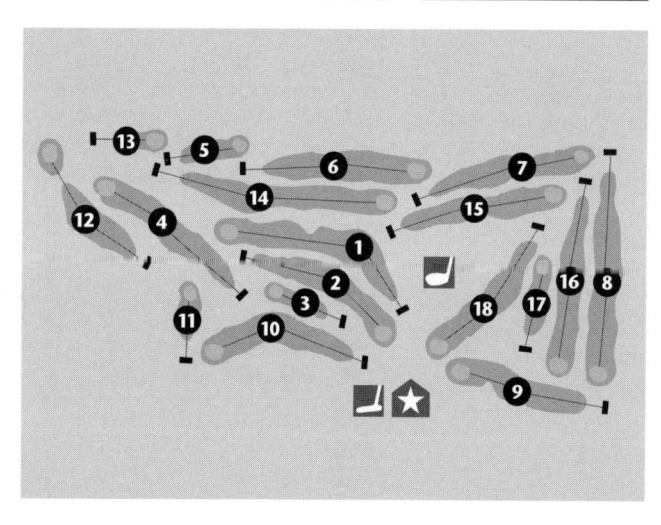

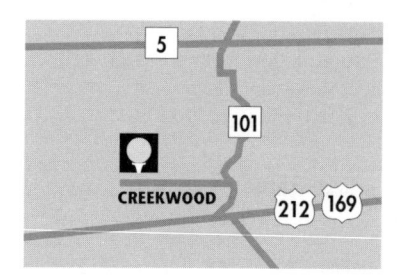

Located in Chaska. Course is south of Hwy 5 or north of U.S. Hwy 169/212 on Hwy 101, then west on Creekwood.

		MEN			**WOMEN**		
	BACK	FRONT	PAR	HDCP	FRONT	PAR	HDCP
1	535	528	5	10	377	5	6
2	388	382	4	8	273	4	14
3	186	182	3	12	165	3	16
4	413	400	4	2	302	4	4
5	171	164	3	14	146	3	18
6	413	407	4	5	387	5	12
7	415	408	4	4	276	5	10
8	481	475	5	15	375	5	8
9	376	368	4	11	254	4	2
Out	3378	3314	36		2555	38	
10	394	386	4	6	366	5	11
11	143	135	3	18	120	3	15
12	364	358	4	1	339	5	1
13	149	140	3	17	121	3	17
14	511	467	5	16	447	5	5
15	404	398	4	9	378	5	9
16	433	427	4	3	289	5	7
17	206	200	3	13	179	3	13
18	377	371	4	7	299	4	3
In	2981	2882	34		2538	38	
Total	6359	6196	70		5093	76	
Rating	69.9	69.1			68.3		
Slope	115	114			109		

BRACKETT'S CROSSING COUNTRY CLUB

18 Regulation Private

17976 Judicial Road
Lakeville, Minnesota 55044
612/435-7600 Clubhouse
612/435-7700 Proshop

HOURS	7 am to Dusk
SEASON	April-November

FEATURES		
Putting green	Y	
Driving range	Y	$2.75
Practice area	N	
Golf carts		
Power (gas)	Y	$24
Pull carts	Y	$3
Club rental	Y	$10
Club storage	Y	$75/yr
Caddies	N	
Proshop		
Extended	Y	
Refreshments		
Restaurant	Y	
Lounge	Y	
Snacks	Y	
Clubhouse		
Showers	Y	
Lockers	Y	
Lodging	N	

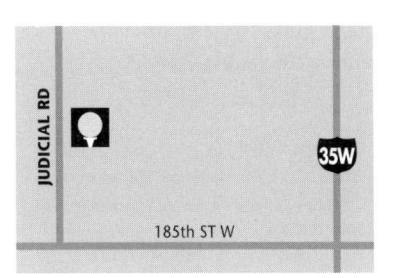

RESERVATIONS	612/435-7700 5 days
	Members only

GREEN FEES	M-F	S-S
Adult	$30/15	$35/17.50
Senior	$30/15	$35/17.50
Junior	$30/15	$35/17.50
Twilight	NA	NA
	Members and guests only	

PAYMENT	No credit cards accepted Local checks only
LEAGUES	Various
MEMBERSHIPS	USGA, NGF, PGA, GCSAA, CMAA, MGA
SUPERINTENDENT	Tom Proshek
PROFESSIONAL	Steve Jensen

Located in Lakeville. Course entrance is one mile west of I-35W on 185th Street, then 1/2 mile north on Judicial Road.

	MEN				WOMEN		
	BACK	FRONT	PAR	HDCP	FRONT	PAR	HDCP
1	425	420	4	4	411	5	2
2	199	176	3	12	142	3	12
3	500	490	5	10	315	4	10
4	435	419	4	2	305	4	16
5	194	182	3	18	156	3	18
6	377	345	4	16	311	4	14
7	437	390	4	6	384	5	4
8	445	408	4	8	380	4	6
9	427	360	4	14	344	4	8
Out	3439	3190	35		2748	36	
10	436	423	4	1	418	5	1
11	429	405	4	3	394	5	3
12	133	131	3	17	113	3	17
13	377	359	4	13	353	4	7
14	525	474	5	11	331	4	9
15	408	383	4	7	235	4	13
16	186	173	3	15	130	3	15
17	409	400	4	5	292	4	11
18	532	528	5	9	371	5	5
In	3435	3275	36		2637	37	
Total	6874	6465	71		5385	73	
Rating	73.4	71.6			72.3		
Slope	128	124			126		

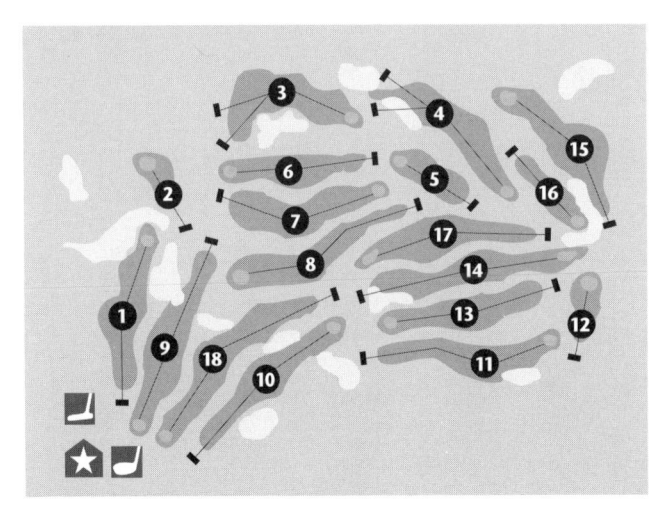

GOLF COURSE DIRECTORY

BRAEMAR GOLF CLUB

27 Regulation Public

6364 Dewey Hill Road
Edina, Minnesota 55439
612/941-2072 Clubhouse/Proshop

RESERVATIONS	612/941-2072 1 day	
	Walk-on: fair/poor	
GREEN FEES	M-F	S-S
Adult	$21/11.50	$21/11.50
Senior	$21/11.50	$21/11.50
Junior	$21/11.50	$21/11.50
Twilight	$11.50	$11.50
PAYMENT	Credit: Visa® MasterCard®	
	Non-local checks accepted	
LEAGUES	Men: Various	
	Women: Various	
MEMBERSHIPS	USGA, NGF, PGA, GCSAA, MGA	
MANAGER	John Valliere	
SUPERINTENDENT	John Nylund	
PROFESSIONAL	Joe Greupner	

HOURS	6:30 am to Dusk	
SEASON	April-November	
FEATURES		
Putting green	Y	
Driving range	Y	$5
Practice area	N	
Golf carts		
Power	Y	$20
Pull carts	Y	$2.25
Club rental	Y	$6
Club storage	Y	$35
Caddies	Y	$10-12
Proshop		
Extended	Y	
Refreshments		
Restaurant	Y	
Lounge	Y	
Snacks	Y	
Clubhouse		
Showers	Y	
Lockers	Y	
Lodging	N	

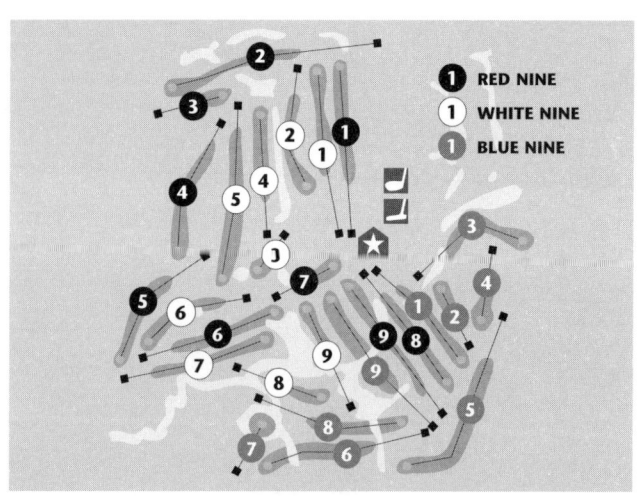

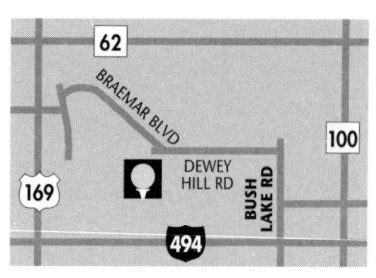

Located in Edina. Course is west of Bush Lake Road on Dewey Hill Road.

	MEN				**WOMEN**		
	BACK	FRONT	PAR	HDCP	FRONT	PAR	HDCP
1	485	445	4	5	372	4	13
2	546	530	5	1	415	5	3
3	179	160	3	15	140	3	17
4	432	426	4	3	406	5	5
5	414	406	4	7	376	4	9
6	411	402	4	13	395	4	11
7	177	165	3	17	160	3	15
8	395	380	4	9	330	4	7
9	488	471	5	11	415	5	1
RED	3527	3385	36		3009	37	
1	493	381	4	3	359	4	11
2	343	337	4	15	332	4	9
3	141	120	3	17	115	3	17
4	358	351	4	13	335	4	7
5	485	476	5	7	444	5	1
6	411	396	4	1	388	5	3
7	420	413	4	5	384	4	5
8	245	227	3	9	152	3	15
9	316	300	4	11	221	4	13
WHITE	3212	3001	35		2730	36	
1	372	361	4	11	322	4	9
2	181	169	3	15	140	3	15
3	377	351	4	7	322	4	11
4	195	185	3	13	164	3	13
5	511	497	5	5	443	5	7
6	504	484	5	3	444	5	1
7	146	129	3	17	101	3	17
8	388	377	4	1	280	4	7
9	491	472	5	9	454	5	3
BLUE	3165	3025	36		2670	36	
R/W	6739	6386	71		5739	73	
Rating	71.8	70.6			73.4		
Slope	124	121			129		
W/B	6377	6026	71		5400	72	
Rating	71.6	70.1			72.0		
Slope	129	126			126		
B/R	6692	6410	72		5679	73	
Rating	73.0	71.9			73.8		
Slope	134	131			131		

- RED NINE
- WHITE NINE
- BLUE NINE

BRAEMAR GOLF CLUB

9 Executive Public

6364 Dewey Hill Road
Edina, Minnesota 55439
612/941-2072 Clubhouse/Proshop

RESERVATIONS	612/941-2072 1 day
	Walk-on: fair/poor

GREEN FEES	M-F	S-S
Adult	$7	$7
Senior	$7	$7
Junior	$6	$6
Twilight	NA	NA

PAYMENT	Credit: Visa® MasterCard®
	Non-local checks accepted
LEAGUES	Men: Various
	Women: Various
MEMBERSHIPS	USGA, NGF, PGA, GCSAA, MGA
MANAGER	John Valliere
SUPERINTENDENT	John Nylund
PROFESSIONAL	Joe Greupner

HOURS	6:30 am to Dusk
SEASON	April-November

FEATURES	
Putting green	Y
Driving range	Y $5
Practice area	N
Golf carts	
Power	Y
Pull carts	Y
Club rental	Y
Club storage	N
Caddies	N
Proshop	
Extended	Y
Refreshments	
Restaurant	Y
Lounge	Y
Snacks	Y
Clubhouse	
Showers	Y
Lockers	Y
Lodging	N

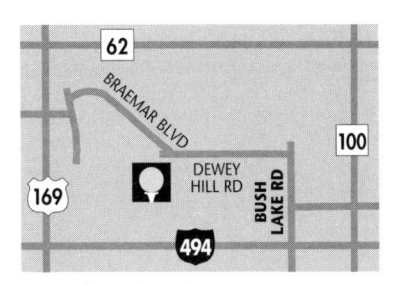

Located in Edina. Course entrance is north of I-494 on Bush Lake Road, then west on Dewey Hill Road.

	MEN			**WOMEN**		
	FRONT	PAR	HDCP	FRONT	PAR	HDCP
1	190	3		185	4	
2	110	3		100	3	
3	142	3		132	3	
4	152	3		140	3	
5	326	4		299	4	
6	113	3		96	3	
7	295	4		288	4	
8	144	3		114	3	
9	157	3		140	3	
Out	1629	29		1494	30	
1	190	3		185	4	
2	110	3		100	3	
3	142	3		132	3	
4	152	3		140	3	
5	326	4		299	4	
6	113	3		96	3	
7	295	4		288	4	
8	144	3		114	3	
9	157	3		140	3	
Out	1629	29		1494	30	
Total	3258	58		2988	60	
Rating	56.2			57.4		
Slope	83			85		

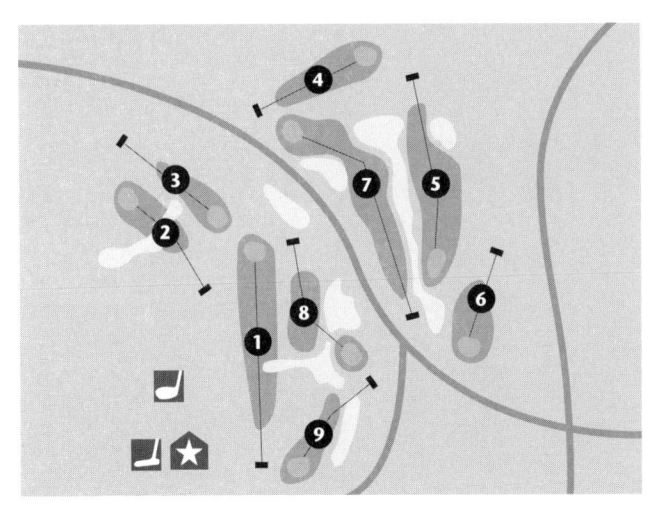

GOLF COURSE DIRECTORY

BREEZY POINT RESORT

CHAMPIONSHIP COURSE/18 Regulation Public

HCR 2, P.O. Box 70
Breezy Point, Minnesota 56472
218/562-7177 Clubhouse
218/562-7166 Proshop

RESERVATIONS	800/950-4960 2 days	
	Walk-on: good/fair	

GREEN FEES	M-F	S-S
Adult	$30/19	$35/21
Senior	$30/19	$35/21
Junior	$30/19	$35/21
Twilight	$15/9.50	$17.50/10.50

PAYMENT	Credit: Visa® MasterCard® AmEx® Discover® Non-local checks accepted

LEAGUES	None

MEMBERSHIPS	USGA, MGA

MANAGER	Jerry Hoffman
PROFESSIONAL	Jim Harmon

HOURS 7 am to Dusk

SEASON April to October

FEATURES

Putting green	Y	
Driving range	Y	$3-4.50
Practice area	N	

Golf carts		
Power (gas)	Y	$23.50
Pull carts	Y	$2.75
Club rental	Y	$15
Club storage	N	
Caddies	N	

Proshop	
Extended	Y
Refreshments	
Restaurant	Y
Lounge	Y
Snacks	Y
Clubhouse	
Showers	N
Lockers	N

| Lodging | Y | Call |

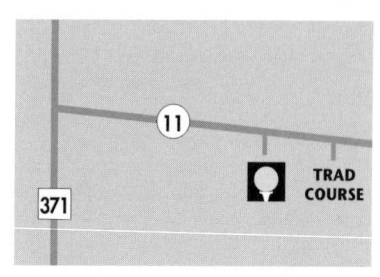

Located in Breezy Point. Course entrance is 5 miles east of Highway 371 on County Road 11.

	MEN				WOMEN		
	BACK	FRONT	PAR	HDCP	FRONT	PAR	HDCP
1	341	309	4	8	290	4	8
2	300	269	4	18	249	4	16
3	442	428	4	4	405	5	6
4	520	510	5	6	490	5	4
5	178	168	3	12	148	3	14
6	379	349	4	16	329	4	12
7	500	483	5	2	458	5	2
8	313	308	4	14	298	4	10
9	215	207	3	10	200	4	18
Out	3188	3031	36		2867	38	
10	436	421	4	3	406	5	7
11	479	438	4	7	402	5	9
12	185	149	3	17	125	3	17
13	363	353	4	13	343	4	11
14	353	347	4	11	328	4	15
15	497	452	5	1	366	5	1
16	354	323	4	9	288	4	3
17	193	181	3	15	144	3	13
18	553	507	5	5	449	5	5
In	3413	3171	36		2851	38	
Total	6601	6202	72		5718	76	
Rating	70.6	68.8			72.1		
Slope	115	112			122		

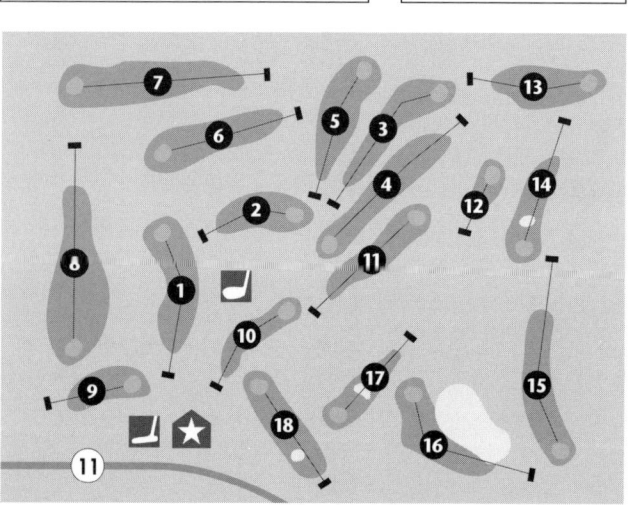

BREEZY POINT RESORT

TRADITIONAL COURSE/18 Regulation Public

HCR 2, P.O. Box 70
Breezy Point, Minnesota 56472
218/562-7177 Clubhouse
218/562-7166 Proshop

HOURS	7 am to Dusk
SEASON	April to October

RESERVATIONS	800/950-4960 2 days
	Walk-on: good/fair

GREEN FEES	M-F	S-S
Adult	$30/19	$35/21
Senior	$30/19	$35/21
Junior	$30/19	$35/21
Twilight	$15/19.50	$17.50/10.50

PAYMENT	Credit: Visa® MasterCard® AmEx® Discover®
	Non-local checks accepted

LEAGUES	None

MEMBERSHIPS	USGA, MGA

MANAGER	Jerry Hoffman
PROFESSIONAL	Jim Harmon

FEATURES

Putting green	Y	
Driving range	Y	$3-4.50
Practice area	N	
Golf carts		
Power (gas)	Y	$23.50
Pull carts	Y	$2.75
Club rental	Y	$15
Club storage	N	
Caddies	N	
Proshop		
Extended	Y	
Refreshments		
Restaurant	Y	
Lounge	Y	
Snacks	Y	
Clubhouse		
Showers	N	
Lockers	N	
Lodging	Y	Call

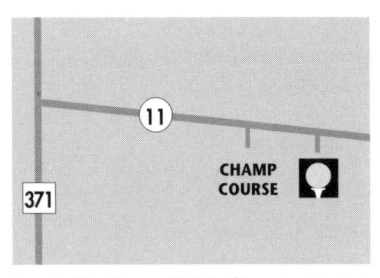

Located in Breezy Point. Course entrance is 5 miles east of Highway 371 on County Road 11.

	MEN			**WOMEN**		
	FRONT	PAR	HDCP	FRONT	PAR	HDCP
1	307	4	9	307	4	3
2	145	3	15	145	3	15
3	241	4	17	241	4	17
4	275	4	13	275	4	9
5	367	4	1	367	5	1
6	156	3	11	156	3	13
7	354	4	3	354	5	7
8	318	4	7	318	4	11
9	370	4	5	370	5	5
Out	2533	34		2533	37	
10	346	4	12	346	4	4
11	182	3	18	182	3	14
12	305	4	10	305	4	12
13	171	3	16	171	3	18
14	292	4	14	292	4	10
15	330	4	4	330	5	16
16	318	4	2	318	4	6
17	350	4	8	350	4	2
18	365	4	6	300	4	8
In	2659	34		2594	35	
Total	5192	68		5127	72	
Rating	64.3			69.0		
Slope	105			109		

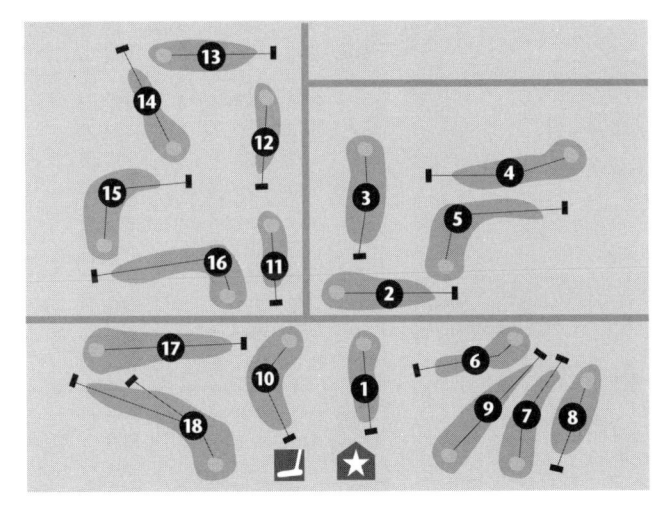

GOLF COURSE DIRECTORY

THE BRIDGES OF MOUNDS VIEW

9 Executive Public

8290 Coral Sea Street
Mounds View, Minnesota 55112
612/785-9063 Clubhouse/Proshop

HOURS	Dawn to Dusk
SEASON	April to October

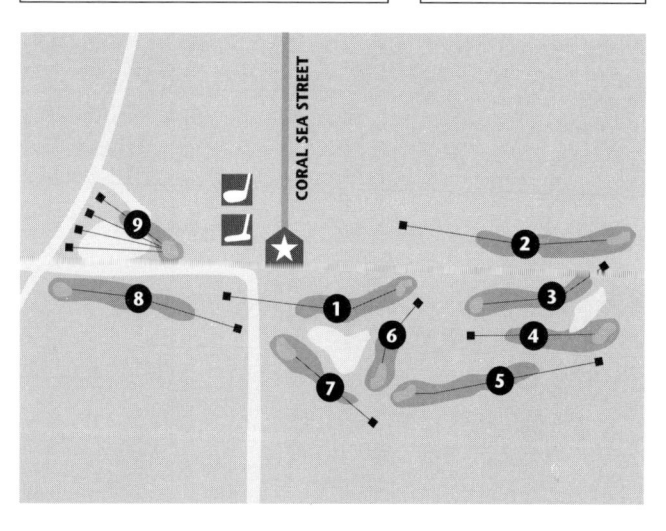

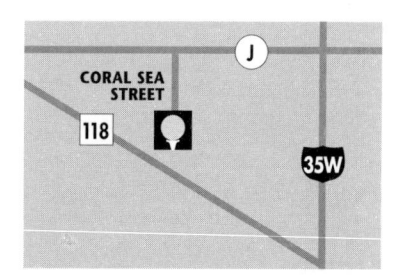

Located in Mounds View. Course is west of I-35W on County Road J, then 1/4 mile south on Corel Sea Street.

RESERVATIONS	612/785-9063 3 days
	Walk-on: fair/fair

GREEN FEES	M-F	S-S
Adult	$13/8	$13/8
Senior	$13/7	$13/8
Junior	$13/7	$13/8
Twilight	NA	NA

PAYMENT	Credit: Visa® MasterCard®
	Non-local checks accepted

LEAGUES	Men: Various
	Women: Various

MEMBERSHIPS	USGA, PGA, GCSAA, MGA

SUPERINTENDENT	Mike Mueller
PROFESSIONAL	Brus von Ende

FEATURES		
Putting green	Y	
Driving range	Y	
Practice area	Y	
Golf carts		
Power (gas)	Y	$9
Pull carts	Y	$1.50
Club rental	Y	
Club storage	N	
Caddies	N	
Proshop		
Regular	Y	
Refreshments		
Restaurant	N	
Lounge	N	
Snacks	Y	
Clubhouse		
Showers	N	
Lockers	N	
Lodging	N	

	MEN				WOMEN		
	BACK	FRONT	PAR	HDCP	FRONT	PAR	HDCP
1	356	329	4	2	249	4	3
2	476	455	5	1	380	5	1
3	177	155	3	8	133	3	5
4	142	121	3	9	100	3	9
5	290	266	4	4	242	4	2
6	122	98	3	6	74	3	7
7	146	123	3	7	100	3	8
8	351	333	4	3	308	4	6
9	182	156	3	5	115	3	4
Out	2242	2038	32		1723	32	
1	356	329	4	2	249	4	3
2	476	455	5	1	380	5	1
3	177	155	3	8	133	3	5
4	142	121	3	9	100	3	9
5	290	266	4	4	242	4	2
6	122	98	3	6	74	3	7
7	146	123	3	7	100	3	8
8	351	333	4	3	308	4	6
9	182	156	3	5	115	3	4
In	2242	2038	32		1723	32	
Total	4484	4076	64		3446	64	
Rating	61.2	59.4			58.6		
Slope	95	91			93		

BRIGHTWOOD HILLS GOLF COURSE

9 Executive Public

1975 Silver Lake Road
New Brighton, Minnesota 55112
612/638-2150 Clubhouse/Proshop

HOURS	Dawn to Dusk
SEASON	April to October

RESERVATIONS	612/633-2150 5 days	
	Walk-on: fair/poor	

GREEN FEES	M-F	S-S
Adult	$7	$8
Senior	$6	$8
Junior	$7	$8
Twilight	NA	NA

PAYMENT	Credit: Visa® MasterCard®
	Non-local checks accepted

LEAGUES	Men: Various
	Women: Various

MEMBERSHIPS	GCSAA, MGA

MANAGER	Mary Burg
SUPERINTENDENT	Chris Wolla

FEATURES		
Putting green	Y	
Driving range	N	
Practice area	Y	
Golf carts		
Power (gas)	N	
Pull carts	Y	$1.50
Club rental	Y	$3
Club storage	N	
Caddies	N	
Proshop		
Regular	Y	
Refreshments		
Restaurant	N	
Lounge	N	
Snacks	Y	
Clubhouse		
Showers	Y	
Lockers	N	
Lodging	N	

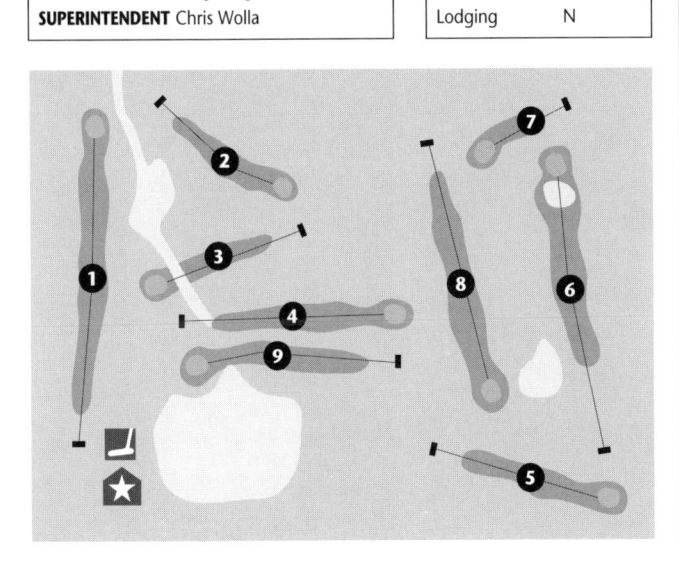

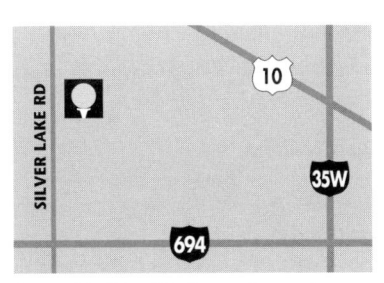

Located in New Brighton. Course is about 1 1/2 miles north of I-694 on Silver Lake Road.

	MEN			**WOMEN**		
	FRONT	PAR	HDCP	FRONT	PAR	HDCP
1	281	4		252	4	
2	135	3		124	3	
3	119	3		114	3	
4	175	3		144	3	
5	134	3		120	3	
6	235	4		195	4	
7	90	3		74	3	
8	240	4		211	4	
9	164	3		150	3	
Out	1573	30		1384	30	
1	281	4		252	4	
2	135	3		124	3	
3	119	3		114	3	
4	175	3		144	3	
5	134	3		120	3	
6	235	4		195	4	
7	90	3		74	3	
8	240	4		211	4	
9	164	3		150	3	
In	1573	30		1384	30	
Total	3146	60		2768	60	
Rating	55.0			55.6		
Slope	83			88		

GOLF COURSE DIRECTORY

BROCKWAY GOLF CLUB

9 Regulation Semi-Private

13500 South Robert Trail
Rosemount, Minnesota 55068
612/423-5222 Clubhouse/Proshop

HOURS	6:30 am to Dusk
SEASON	April to October

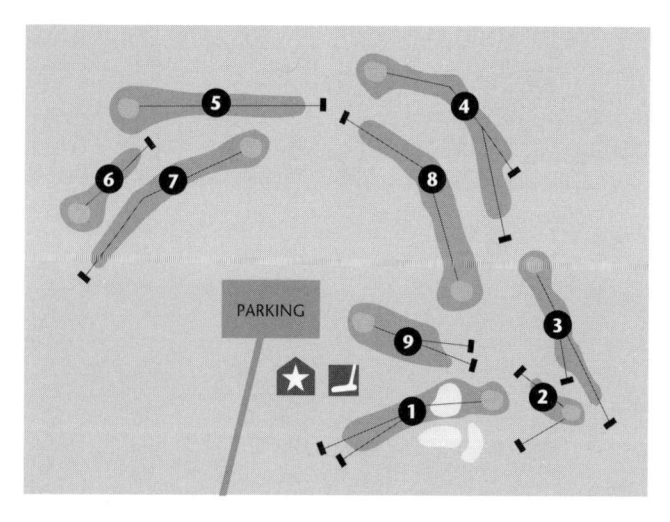

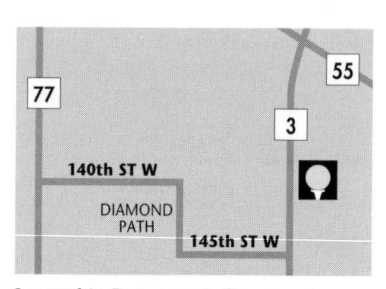

Located in Rosemount. Course entrance is about 6 miles south of Highway 55 on Highway 3.

RESERVATIONS	612/423-5222 1 week
	Walk-on: good/fair

GREEN FEES	M-F	S-S
Adult	$17/12	$17/12
Senior	$10*	$17/12
Junior	$10*	$17/12
Twilight	$10.95	$10.95
	* Rate before 11 am	
	10 play & F ($8.50) specials	

PAYMENT	No credit cards accepted
	Non-local checks accepted

LEAGUES	Various

MEMBERSHIPS	USGA, MGA

OWNER	Wintz Companies
MANAGER	Curt Walker

FEATURES	
Putting green	Y
Driving range	N
Practice area	Y
Golf carts	
Power (gas)	Y $16/9.5
Pull carts	Y $1.75
Club rental	Y $8
Club storage	N
Caddies	N
Pro shop	
Regular	Y
Refreshments	
Restaurant	N
Lounge	N
Snacks	Y
Clubhouse	
Showers	N
Lockers	N
Lodging	N

	MEN					**WOMEN**		
	BACK	FRONT	PAR	HDCP	FRONT	PAR	HDCP
1	328	313	4	5	263	4	5
2	195	180	3	3	103	3	9
3	330	325	4	6	309	4	3
4	382	373	4	4	269	4	7
5	272	263	4	9	253	4	8
6	209	200	3	2	185	3	1
7	482	477	5	1	383	5	4
8	555	530	5	7	479	5	2
9	186	179	3	8	174	3	6
Out	2939	2840	35		2418	35	
1	328	313	4	5	263	4	5
2	195	180	3	3	103	3	9
3	330	325	4	6	309	4	3
4	382	373	4	4	269	4	7
5	272	263	4	9	253	4	8
6	209	200	3	2	185	3	1
7	482	477	5	1	383	5	4
8	555	530	5	7	479	5	2
9	186	179	3	8	174	3	6
In	2939	2840	35		2418	35	
Total	5878	5680	70		4836	70	
Rating	68.0	66.0			68.0		
Slope	119	117			116		

THE MINNESOTA ILLUSTRATED

BROOKLAND EXECUTIVE NINE GOLF COURSE
9 Executive Public

8232 Regent Avenue North
Brooklyn Park, Minnesota 55443
612/561-3850 Clubhouse/Proshop

HOURS	6 am to Dusk
SEASON	April-November

| **RESERVATIONS** | 612/561-3850 2 days |
| | Walk-on: good/fair |

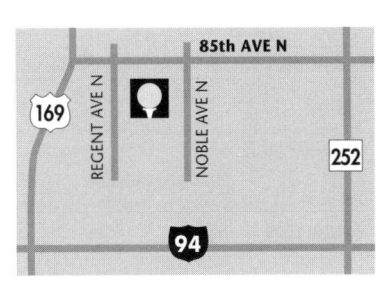

GREEN FEES	M-F	S-S
Adult	$7.50	$7.50
Senior	$6.50	$6.50
Junior	$6.50	$6.50
Twilight	NA	NA

| **PAYMENT** | No credit cards accepted |
| | Non-local checks accepted |

| **LEAGUES** | Women: Various |

| **MEMBERSHIPS** | USGA, NGF, MGA |

OWNER	City of Brooklyn Park
MANAGER	Bob Slind
SUPERINTENDENT	Bob Slind

FEATURES	
Putting green	Y
Driving range	N
Practice area	N
Golf carts	
Power (gas)	Y $10
Pull carts	Y $1.50
Club rental	Y $3.50
Club storage	N
Caddies	N
Proshop	
Extended	Y
Refreshments	
Restaurant	N
Lounge	N
Snacks	Y
Clubhouse	
Showers	N
Lockers	N
Lodging	N

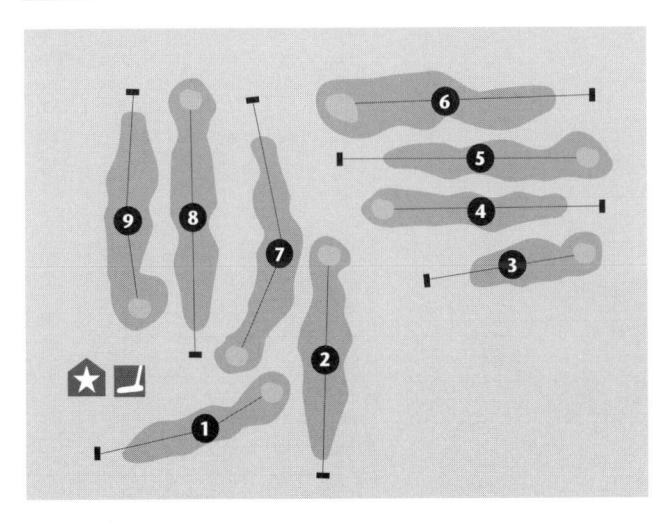

Located in Brooklyn Park. Course entrance is two blocks south of 85th Avenue on Regent Avenue.

	MEN			**WOMEN**		
	FRONT	PAR	HDCP	FRONT	PAR	HDCP
1	144	3	9	144	3	9
2	178	3	7	178	3	7
3	118	3	8	118	3	8
4	169	3	6	169	3	6
5	210	3	5	210	3	5
6	214	3	2	214	3	2
7	298	4	3	261	4	3
8	266	4	4	221	3	4
9	252	4	1	186	3	1
Out	1849	30		1701	28	
1	144	3	9	144	3	9
2	178	3	7	178	3	7
3	118	3	8	118	3	8
4	169	3	6	169	3	6
5	210	3	5	210	3	5
6	214	3	2	214	3	2
7	298	4	3	261	4	3
8	266	4	4	221	3	4
9	252	4	1	186	3	1
In	1849	30		1701	28	
Total	3698	60		3402	56	
Rating	57.2			59.0		
Slope	88			85		

GOLF COURSE DIRECTORY

BROOKLYN PARK GOLF COURSE

9 Executive Public

7720 Lakeland Avenue North
Brooklyn Park, Minnesota 55445
612/425-9978 Clubhouse/Proshop

RESERVATIONS	612/425-9978	3 days
	Walk-on: good/good	
GREEN FEES	M-F	S-S
Adult	$14.50/8.25	$14.50/8.25
Senior	$14.50/8.25	$14.50/8.25
Junior	$14.50/8.25	$14.50/8.25
Twilight	NA	NA
	Senior, Junior rate incentives available at special times	
PAYMENT	No credit cards accepted	
	Non-local checks accepted	
LEAGUES	Men: None	
	Women: None	
MEMBERSHIPS	None	
MANAGER	Lyn Joyner	

HOURS 6:30am to Dusk
SEASON March–November

FEATURES	
Putting green	Y
Driving range	N
Practice area	N
Golf carts	
Power (gas)	Y
Pull carts	Y $1
Club rental	Y $4
Club storage	N
Caddies	N
Proshop	
Basic	Y
Refreshments	
Restaurant	N
Lounge	N
Snacks	Y
Clubhouse	
Showers	N
Lockers	N
Lodging	N

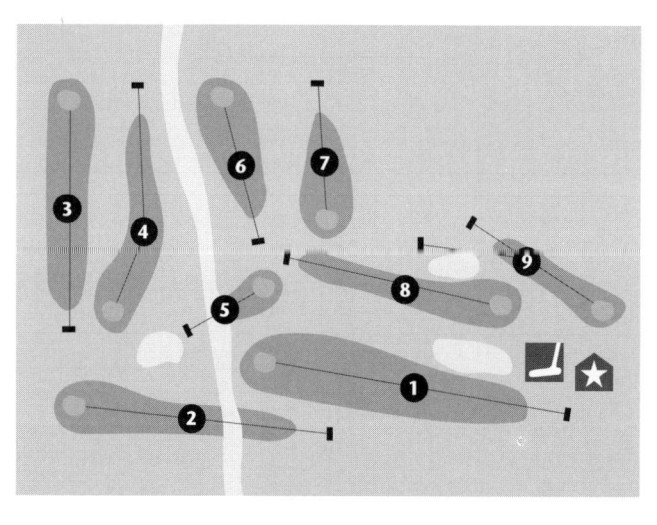

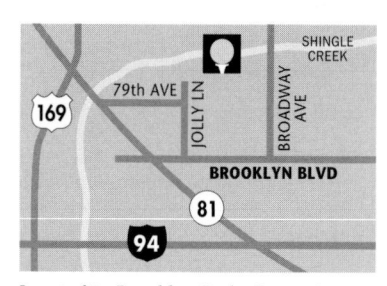

Located in Brooklyn Park. Course is east of County Road 81 on Brooklyn Blvd, then north on Jolly Lane.

	MEN			WOMEN		
	FRONT	PAR	HDCP	FRONT	PAR	HDCP
1	300	4	2	300	4	2
2	260	4	9	230	4	9
3	325	4	6	325	4	6
4	325	4	7	325	4	7
5	175	3	8	110	3	8
6	230	3	1	230	3	1
7	205	3	5	205	3	5
8	225	3	3	225	3	3
9	190	3	4	190	3	4
Out	2235	31		2140	31	
1	300	4	2	300	4	2
2	260	4	9	230	4	9
3	325	4	6	325	4	6
4	325	4	7	325	4	7
5	175	3	8	110	3	8
6	230	3	1	230	3	1
7	205	3	5	205	3	5
8	225	3	3	225	3	3
9	190	3	4	190	3	4
In	2235	31		2140	31	
Total	4470	62		4280	62	
Rating	NA			NA		
Slope	NA			NA		

BROOKTREE MUNICIPAL GOLF COURSE

18 Regulation Public

1369 Cherry Street
Owatonna, Minnesota 55060
507/451-0730 Clubhouse/Proshop

RESERVATIONS	507/451-0730 3 days
	Walk-on: good/fair

GREEN FEES	M-F	S-S
Adult	$13/9	$15/10
Senior	$13/9	$15/10
Junior	$13/9	$15/10
Twilight	NA	NA

PAYMENT	Credit: Visa® MasterCard®
	Non-local checks accepted

LEAGUES	Men: Various
	Women: Various

MEMBERSHIPS	USGA, PGA, CGSAA, MGA

MANAGER	Chuck Kriska
SUPERINTENDENT	Rick Smith

HOURS	7 am to Dusk
SEASON	April to October

FEATURES	
Putting green	Y
Driving range	N
Practice area	Y
Golf carts	
Power (gas)	Y $16/10
Pull carts	Y $2
Club rental	Y $6
Club storage	Y
Caddies	N
Proshop	
Extended	Y
Refreshments	
Restaurant	N
Lounge	Y
Snacks	Y
Clubhouse	
Showers	Y
Lockers	Y
Lodging	N

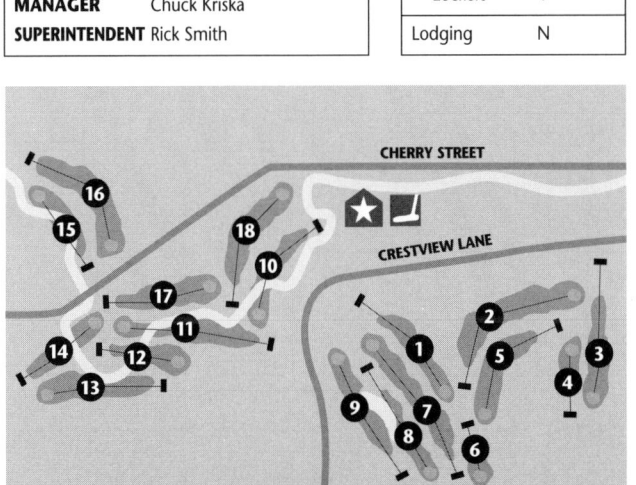

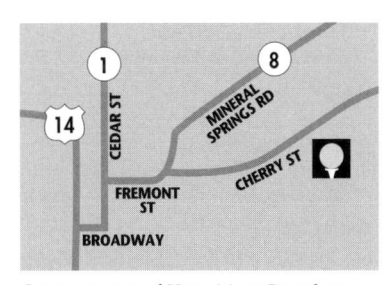

Course is east of Hwy 14 on Broadway, north on Cedar, east on Fremont, north on Mineral Springs, then east on Cherry.

	MEN				**WOMEN**		
	BACK	FRONT	PAR	HDCP	FRONT	PAR	HDCP
1	408	390	4	11	343	4	7
2	532	515	5	3	410	5	5
3	424	404	4	7	331	4	9
4	230	211	3	17	160	3	17
5	409	391	4	13	333	4	13
6	194	174	3	15	157	3	15
7	521	509	5	5	430	5	3
8	404	382	4	9	283	4	11
9	440	422	4	1	403	5	1
Out	3562	3399	36		2850	37	
10	360	356	4	8	328	4	8
11	522	513	5	6	459	5	2
12	195	148	3	18	145	3	18
13	385	385	4	2	336	4	4
14	355	345	4	12	329	4	12
15	171	166	3	14	126	3	14
16	284	275	4	16	265	4	16
17	427	422	4	4	355	4	6
18	387	381	4	10	341	4	10
In	3086	2991	35		2684	35	
Total	6648	6390	71		5534	72	
Rating	71.9	70.8			71.3		
Slope	121	118			121		

GOLF COURSE DIRECTORY

BROOKVIEW GOLF COURSE

18 Regulation/9 Par-3 Public

200 Brookview Parkway
Golden Valley, Minnesota 55426
612/544-8446 Clubhouse/Proshop

HOURS	6 am to Dusk
SEASON	April-November

RESERVATIONS	612/544-8446 2 days
	Walk-on: fair/fair

GREEN FEES	M-F	S-S
Adult	$20/12	$20/12
Senior	$20/12	$20/12
Junior	$20/12	$20/12
Twilight	NA	NA
	Patron cards/rates available	

PAYMENT	Credit: Visa® MasterCard®
	Non-local checks accepted

LEAGUES	Men: Various
	Women: Various

MEMBERSHIPS	USGA, PGA, MGA

MANAGER	Kris Tovson
PROFESSIONAL	Scott Leer

FEATURES		
Putting green	Y	
Driving range	Y	$4.25
Practice area	N	
Golf carts		
Power (gas)	Y	$20/12
Pull carts	Y	$2
Club rental	Y	
Club storage	N	
Caddies	N	
Proshop		
Regular	Y	
Refreshments		
Restaurant	Y	
Lounge	Y	
Snacks	Y	
Clubhouse		
Showers	Y	
Lockers	Y	
Lodging	N	

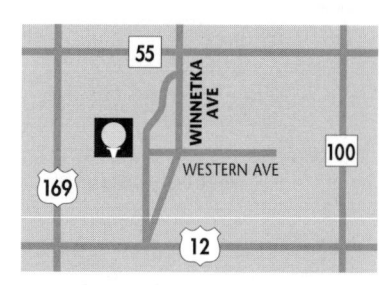

Located in Golden Valley. Course is south of MN Highway 55 on Winnetka Avenue, then west on Western Avenue.

		MEN				WOMEN		
	BACK	FRONT	PAR	HDCP		FRONT	PAR	HDCP
1	360	354	4	11		330	4	9
2	465	460	5	9		444	5	1
3	544	520	5	3		412	5	3
4	173	166	3	13		120	3	15
5	318	310	4	17		240	4	13
6	375	331	4	5		323	4	11
7	399	394	4	1		363	4	5
8	203	193	3	7		164	3	17
9	308	304	4	15		301	4	7
Out	3145	3032	36			2697	36	
10	380	372	4	2		345	4	6
11	358	351	4	12		301	4	12
12	159	155	3	16		145	3	18
13	346	336	4	8		326	4	8
14	337	324	4	14		303	4	16
15	561	547	5	6		426	5	4
16	534	509	5	4		475	5	2
17	135	126	3	18		111	3	14
18	414	357	4	10		334	4	10
In	3224	3077	36			2766	36	
Total	6369	6109	72			5463	72	
Rating	70.2	69.0				71.2		
Slope	122	120				121		

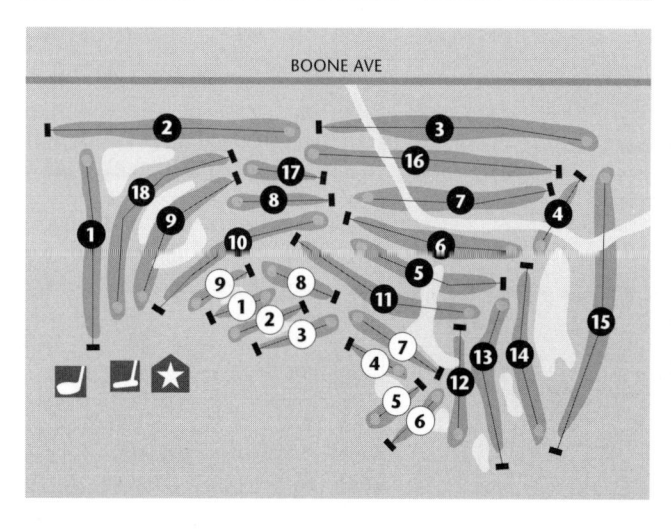

BUFFALO HEIGHTS GOLF COURSE

9 Regulation Public

905 S. Highway 25, P.O. Box 318
Buffalo, Minnesota 55313
612/682-2854 Clubhouse/Proshop

HOURS	7 am to Dusk
SEASON	April–November

FEATURES	
Putting green	Y
Driving range	N
Practice area	N
Golf carts	
Power	Y $19/12
Pull carts	Y $2
Club rental	Y $6
Club storage	N
Caddies	N
Proshop	
Extended	Y
Refreshments	
Restaurant	Y
Lounge	Y
Snacks	Y
Clubhouse	
Showers	N
Lockers	N
Lodging	N

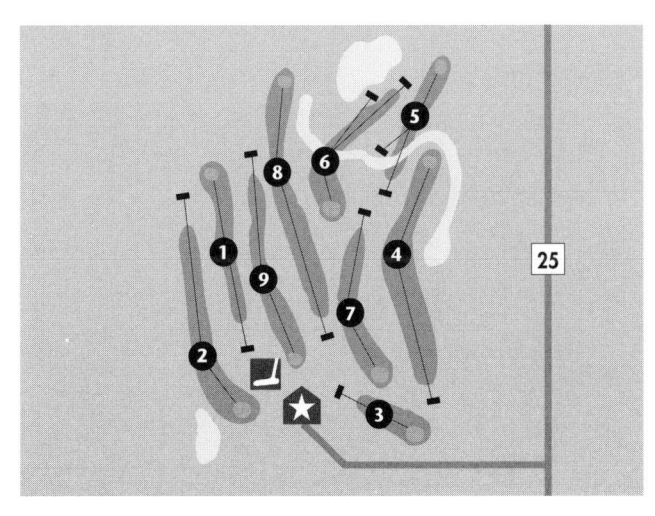

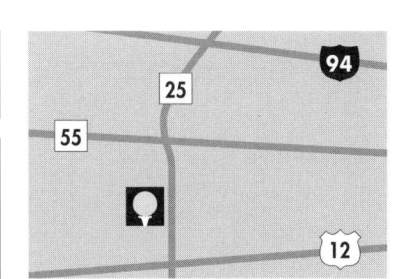

Located in Buffalo. Course entrance is about three miles south of MN Highway 55 on MN Highway 25.

RESERVATIONS	612/682-2854 2 days
	Walk-on: good/fair

GREEN FEES	M-F	S-S
Adult	$15.50/10.50	$17.50/12.50
Senior	$15.50/10.50	$17.50/12.50
Junior	$15.50/10.50	$17.50/12.50
Twilight	NA	NA

PAYMENT	Credit: Visa® MC® AmEx®
	Non-local checks accepted

LEAGUES	Men: Various
	Women: Various

MEMBERSHIPS	USGA, PGA, GCSAA, MGA

PROFESSIONAL	Steve Suerth

	MEN			**WOMEN**		
	FRONT	PAR	HDCP	FRONT	PAR	HDCP
1	343	4	13	329	4	9
2	365	4	9	350	4	1
3	158	3	17	148	3	15
4	441	4	1	431	5	7
5	314	4	15	201	4	17
6	339	4	7	318	4	5
7	325	4	11	316	4	11
8	517	5	5	442	5	3
9	390	4	3	302	4	13
Out	3192	36		2837	37	
1	343	4	16	343	4	12
2	365	4	8	365	4	10
3	162	3	18	158	3	18
4	475	5	12	441	5	4
5	175	3	10	314	4	6
6	349	4	6	339	4	8
7	325	4	14	325	4	14
8	442	4	2	517	5	2
9	399	4	4	390	5	16
In	3035	35		3192	38	
Total	6227	71		6029	75	
Rating	70.0			75.0		
Slope	120			128		

GOLF COURSE DIRECTORY

BUFFALO RUN GOLF CLUB

18 Regulation Public

1710 Montrose Blvd
Buffalo, Minnesota 55313
612/682-4476 Clubhouse/Proshop

RESERVATIONS	612/682-4476	
	Walk-on: fair/fair	
GREEN FEES	M-F	S-S
Adult	$18/12	$20/12
Senior	$18/12	$20/12
Junior	$18/12	$20/12
Twilight	NA	NA
PAYMENT	No credit cards accepted	
	Non-local checks accepted	
LEAGUES	Men: Various	
	Women: Various	
MEMBERSHIPS	MGA	
MANAGER	David Lamm	

HOURS	Dawn to Dusk
SEASON	April-November

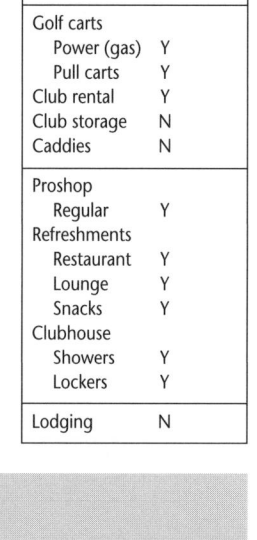

FEATURES	
Putting green	Y
Driving range	Y
Practice area	Y
Golf carts	
Power (gas)	Y
Pull carts	Y
Club rental	Y
Club storage	N
Caddies	N
Proshop	
Regular	Y
Refreshments	
Restaurant	Y
Lounge	Y
Snacks	Y
Clubhouse	
Showers	Y
Lockers	Y
Lodging	N

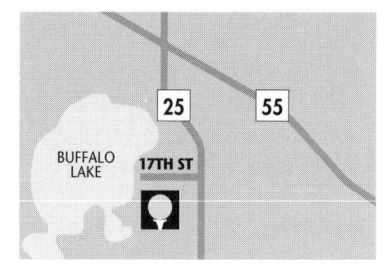

Located in Buffalo. Course entrance is about 1/4 mile west of MN Highway 25 on 17th Street.

	MEN				**WOMEN**		
	BACK	FRONT	PAR	HDCP	FRONT	PAR	HDCP
1	411	396	4	3	381	4	1
2	391	362	4	5	275	4	7
3	335	270	4	7	215	4	13
4	418	413	4	1	344	3	1
5	385	352	4	11	333	4	11
6	382	376	4	9	290	4	5
7	153	148	3	15	143	3	17
8	533	500	5	13	437	5	9
9	385	341	4	17	326	4	15
Out	3393	3158	36		2744	36	
10	369	364	4	14	312	4	10
11	346	338	4	12	212	4	18
12	428	355	4	6	315	4	8
13	151	148	3	16	145	3	12
14	453	356	4	4	331	4	6
15	330	325	4	8	117	3	16
16	662	617	5	2	572	5	2
17	147	142	3	18	137	3	14
18	413	409	4	10	387	4	4
In	3299	3054	35		2528	35	
Total	6369	6109	71		5463	71	
Rating	71.8	69.9			71.4		
Slope	128	124			121		

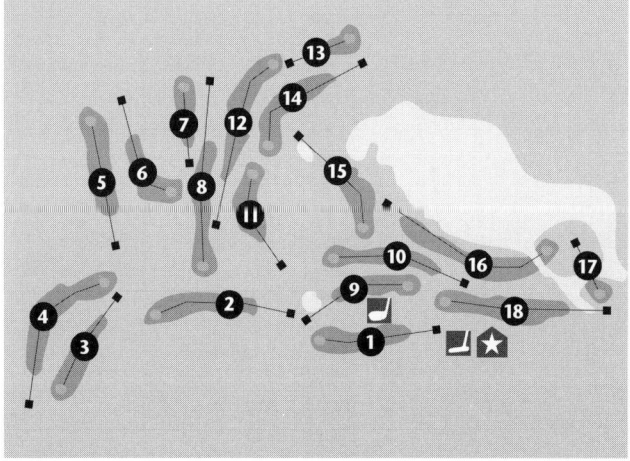

44

THE MINNESOTA ILLUSTRATED

BUNKER HILLS GOLF COURSE

27 Regulation Public

Highway 242 & Bunker Hill Drive
Coon Rapids, Minnesota 55448
612/755-4141 Clubhouse/Proshop
612/755-4444 Seasons Restaurant

HOURS	6 am to Dusk
SEASON	April-November

FEATURES		
Putting green	Y	
Driving range	Y	$2
Practice area	Y	
Golf carts		
Power (gas)	Y	$24
Pull carts	Y	$2
Club rental	Y	$10/5
Club storage	N	
Caddies	N	
Proshop		
Extended	Y	
Refreshments		
Restaurant	Y	
Lounge	Y	
Snacks	Y	
Clubhouse		
Showers	Y	
Lockers	Y	
Lodging	N	

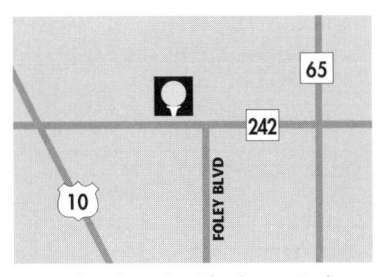

RESERVATIONS	612/755-4141 3 days
	Walk-on: good/poor

GREEN FEES	M-F	S-S
Adult	$25/12	$27/12
Senior	$25/12	$27/12
Junior	$25/12	$27/12
Twilight	NA	NA

PAYMENT	No credit cards accepted
	Non-local checks accepted

LEAGUES	Men: Various
	Women: Various

MEMBERSHIPS	USGA, NGF, PGA, GCSAA, MGA

PROFESSIONAL	Dick Tollette, Jr.

Located in Coon Rapids. Course is three miles west of Hwy 65 on Hwy 242.

		MEN			WOMEN		
	BACK	FRONT	PAR	HDCP	FRONT	PAR	HDCP
1	410	390	4	5	370	4	2
2	413	386	4	2	332	4	3
3	372	358	4	6	293	4	9
4	501	479	5	4	429	5	4
5	437	414	4	1	358	4	1
6	180	160	3	8	141	3	8
7	380	361	4	7	301	4	5
8	180	160	3	9	140	3	7
9	545	525	5	3	430	5	6
NORTH	3418	3233	36		2794	36	
1	430	410	4	3	390	4	1
2	368	347	4	4	278	4	2
3	164	142	3	9	96	3	9
4	474	451	5	5	405	5	5
5	370	350	4	7	330	4	7
6	515	495	5	6	475	5	4
7	220	200	3	8	180	3	8
8	450	430	4	1	320	4	6
9	390	370	4	3	350	4	3
EAST	3381	3195	36		2824	36	
1	425	405	4	3	385	4	1
2	530	510	5	6	430	5	7
3	195	175	3	8	140	3	4
4	360	340	4	9	320	4	9
5	550	530	5	2	430	5	6
6	440	420	4	1	400	5	8
7	400	380	4	4	360	4	2
8	240	220	3	5	180	3	5
9	380	360	4	7	340	4	3
WEST	3520	3340	36		2985	37	
N/E	6799	6428	72		5618	72	
Rating	72.7	71.0			72.6		
Slope	130	126			126		
E/W	6901	6535	72		5509	73	
Rating	73.4	71.7			74.2		
Slope	133	129			128		
W/N	6938	6573	72		5779	73	
Rating	73.1	71.5			73.4		
Slope	135	131			130		

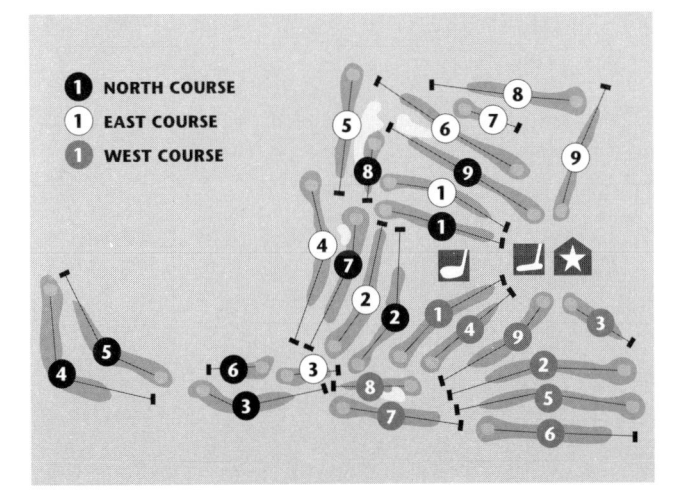

- NORTH COURSE
- EAST COURSE
- WEST COURSE

GOLF COURSE DIRECTORY

BUNKER HILLS GOLF COURSE

9 Executive Public

Highway 242 & Bunker Hill Drive
Coon Rapids, Minnesota 55448
612/755-4141 Clubhouse/Proshop
612/755-4444 Seasons Restaurant

RESERVATIONS	612/755-4141 3 days	
	Walk-on: poor/poor	
GREEN FEES	M-F	S-S
Adult	$7	$7
Senior	$7	$7
Junior	$7	$7
Twilight	NA	NA
PAYMENT	No credit cards accepted	
	Non-local checks accepted	
LEAGUES	Men: Various	
	Women: Various	
MEMBERSHIPS	USGA, NGF, PGA, GCSAA, MGA	
PROFESSIONAL	Dick Tollette, Jr.	

HOURS	Dawn to Dusk
SEASON	April-November

FEATURES	
Putting green	Y
Driving range	Y
Practice area	Y
Golf carts	
Power (gas)	Y
Pull carts	Y
Club rental	Y
Club storage	N
Caddies	N
Proshop	
Extended	Y
Refreshments	
Restaurant	Y
Lounge	Y
Snacks	Y
Clubhouse	
Showers	Y
Lockers	Y
Lodging	N

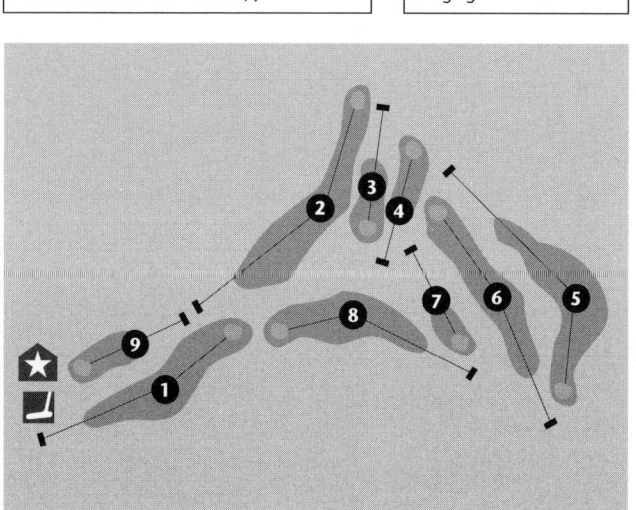

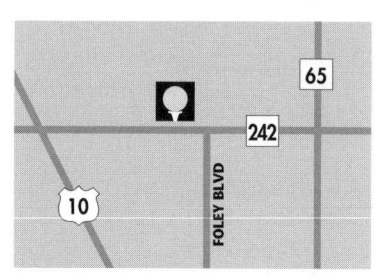

Located in Coon Rapids. Course is three miles west of MN Highway 65 on MN Highway 242.

	MEN			**WOMEN**		
	FRONT	PAR	HDCP	FRONT	PAR	HDCP
1	330	4	1	295	4	1
2	350	4	3	305	4	3
3	170	3	7	135	3	7
4	160	3	6	140	3	6
5	375	4	4	290	4	4
6	325	4	5	275	4	5
7	130	3	8	105	3	8
8	325	4	2	255	4	2
9	135	3	9	108	3	9
Out	2300	32		1908	32	
1	330	4	1	295	4	1
2	350	4	3	305	4	3
3	170	3	7	135	3	7
4	160	3	6	140	3	6
5	375	4	4	290	4	4
6	325	4	5	275	4	5
7	130	3	8	105	3	8
8	325	4	2	255	4	2
9	135	3	9	108	3	9
In	2300	32		1908	32	
Total	4600	64		3816	64	
Rating	60.6			60.0		
Slope	87			87		

BURL OAKS GOLF CLUB

18 Regulation Private

5400 North Arm Drive
Mound, Minnesota 55364
612/472-4909 Clubhouse/Proshop

HOURS	7 am to Dusk
SEASON	April to Oct 31

RESERVATIONS	612/472-4909 1 week Members only	
GREEN FEES	M-F	S-S
Adult	Call	Call
Senior	Call	Call
Junior	Call	Call
Twilight	NA	NA
	Members and guests only	
PAYMENT	Credit: Visa® MC® Discover® Non-local checks accepted	
LEAGUES	Men: W (all day) Women: T (8 am, 6:30 pm) Th (8-10:30 am)	
MEMBERSHIPS	USGA, PGA, GCSAA, MGA	
MANAGER	Mike Larson	
SUPERINTENDENT	Tom Natzel	
PROFESSIONAL	Jerry Kroc, John Syversen	

FEATURES	
Putting green	Y
Driving range	Y
Practice area	Y
Golf carts	
Power (gas)	Y
Pull carts	Y
Club rental	Y
Club storage	Y
Caddies	N
Proshop	
Extended Refreshments	Y
Restaurant	Y
Lounge	N
Snacks	Y
Clubhouse	
Showers	Y
Lockers	Y
Lodging	N

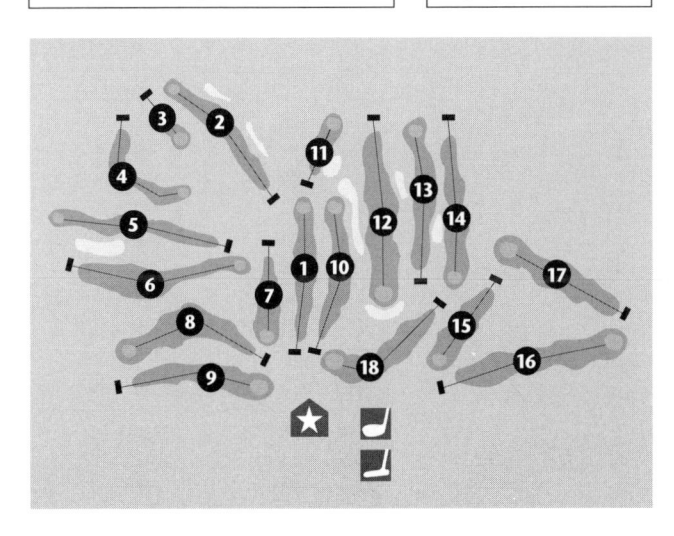

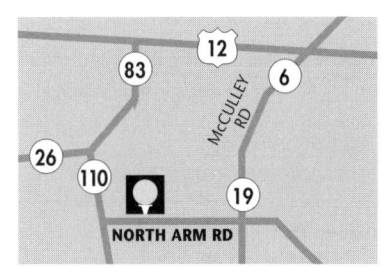

Located in Mound. Course is south of Highway 12 on Cty Road 6/Cty Road 19, then 1 mile west on North Arm Drive.

		MEN			WOMEN		
	BACK	FRONT	PAR	HDCP	FRONT	PAR	HDCP
1	389	363	4	15	308	4	7
2	494	480	5	5	403	5	13
3	144	134	3	17	104	3	15
4	400	394	4	7	317	4	9
5	501	489	5	13	378	5	11
6	403	350	4	11	287	4	5
7	202	192	3	9	92	3	17
8	405	390	4	1	354	4	1
9	387	374	4	3	338	4	3
Out	3325	3166	36		2581	36	
10	398	385	4	2	312	4	10
11	180	155	3	18	132	3	18
12	474	454	5	14	432	5	6
13	414	390	4	8	371	4	8
14	395	369	4	6	362	4	2
15	221	163	3	16	138	3	16
16	450	430	4	4	400	5	14
17	388	368	4	12	345	4	4
18	352	332	4	10	282	4	12
In	3272	3046	35		2774	36	
Total	6597	6212	71		5355	72	
Rating	72.8	71.1			71.9		
Slope	131	127			123		

GOLF COURSE DIRECTORY

CANBY GOLF CLUB
9 Regulation Private

P.O. Box 85
Canby, Minnesota 56220
507/223-5607 Clubhouse/Proshop

RESERVATIONS	507/223-5607	
	Members only	

GREEN FEES	M-F	S-S
Adult	Call	Call
Senior	Call	Call
Junior	Call	Call
Twilight	NA	NA
	Members and guests only	

PAYMENT	No credit cards accepted
	Non-local checks accepted

LEAGUES	Men: Call
	Women: Call

MEMBERSHIPS	MGA

PROFESSIONAL	Call

HOURS	Dawn to Dusk
SEASON	April to October

FEATURES	
Putting green	Y
Driving range	N
Practice area	N
Golf carts	
Power (gas)	Y
Pull carts	Y
Club rental	Y
Club storage	N
Caddies	N
Proshop	
Regular	Y
Refreshments	
Restaurant	N
Lounge	Y
Snacks	Y
Clubhouse	
Showers	Y
Lockers	Y
Lodging	N

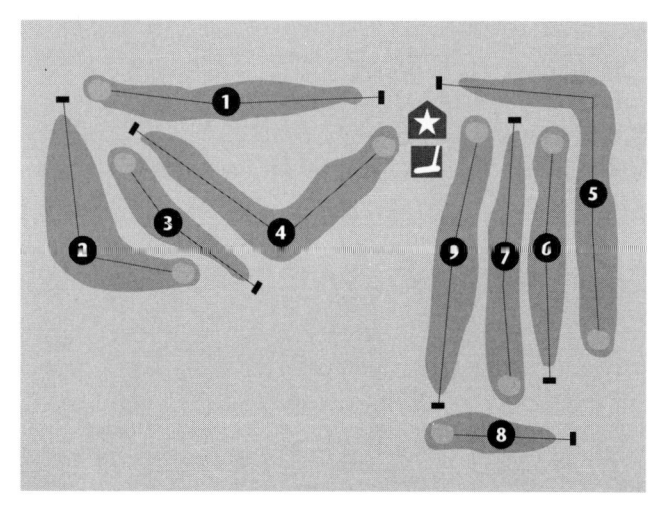

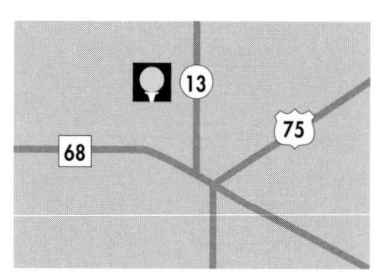

Located north of Canby. Course is about three miles north of MN Highway 68 on County Road 13.

	MEN			WOMEN		
	FRONT	PAR	HDCP	FRONT	PAR	HDCP
1	428	4	1	326	5	1
2	347	4	8	347	4	8
3	219	3	2	199	3	2
4	472	5	4	391	5	4
5	531	5	3	333	4	3
6	352	4	7	292	4	7
7	395	4	5	320	4	5
8	135	3	9	124	3	9
9	396	4	6	396	5	6
Out	3275	36		2728	36	
1	428	4	1	326	5	1
2	347	4	8	347	4	8
3	219	3	2	199	3	2
4	472	5	4	391	5	4
5	531	5	3	333	4	3
6	352	4	7	292	4	7
7	395	4	5	320	4	5
8	135	3	9	124	3	9
9	396	4	6	396	5	6
In	3275	36		2728	36	
Total	6550	72		5456	72	
Rating	71.6			71.4		
Slope	117			114		

CANNON GOLF CLUB

18 Regulation Public

8606 295th Street East
Cannon Falls, Minnesota 55009
507/263-3126 Clubhouse/Proshop

HOURS	6 am to Dusk
SEASON	April to October

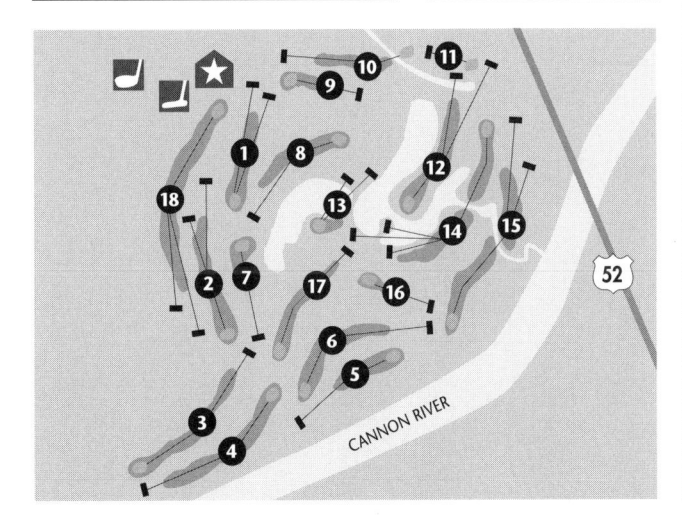

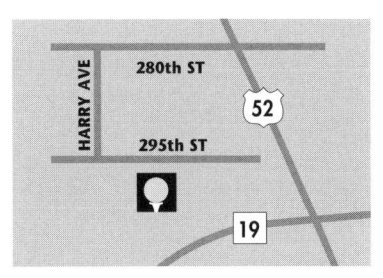

Located in Cannon Falls. Course is west of U.S. Highway 52 on 280th St, south on Harry Avenue, then east on 295th St.

RESERVATIONS	507/263-3126
	Walk-on: good/fair

GREEN FEES	M-Th	F-S
Adult	$18/12	$22/15
Senior	$12/9	$22/15
Junior	$18/12	$22/15
Twilight	$10	$10

PAYMENT	Credit: Visa® MasterCard®
	Non-local checks accepted

LEAGUES	Men: Various
	Women: Various

MEMBERSHIPS	USGA, NGF, PGA, GCSAA, MGA

MANAGER	Sarah Richards, Bob Carnel
SUPERINTENDENT	Jeff Backstrom
PROFESSIONAL	Sarah Richards

FEATURES		
Putting green	Y	
Driving range	Y	$3
Practice area	N	
Golf carts		
Power (gas)	Y	$22/11
Pull carts	Y	$1.50
Club rental	Y	$4
Club storage	N	
Caddies	N	
Proshop		
Extended	Y	
Refreshments		
Restaurant	N	
Lounge	Y	
Snacks	Y	
Clubhouse		
Showers	Y	
Lockers	Y	
Lodging	N	

	MEN				WOMEN		
	BACK	FRONT	PAR	HDCP	FRONT	PAR	HDCP
1	351	345	4	11	309	4	11
2	361	337	4	5	279	4	5
3	414	406	4	1	325	4	1
4	456	444	5	9	413	5	9
5	308	285	4	13	262	4	13
6	413	366	4	3	358	4	3
7	221	202	3	7	148	3	7
8	333	326	4	15	318	4	15
9	163	161	3	17	119	3	17
Out	3020	2872	35		2512	35	
10	297	295	4	14	244	4	14
11	122	103	3	12	73	3	12
12	387	339	4	2	269	4	2
13	178	155	3	18	129	3	18
14	523	518	5	6	425	5	6
15	537	525	5	8	453	5	8
16	169	154	3	16	139	3	16
17	325	317	4	10	309	4	10
18	543	530	5	4	458	5	4
In	3079	2936	36		2499	36	
Total	6099	5808	71		5011	71	
Rating	69.2	67.9			68.9		
Slope	123	120			121		

GOLF COURSE DIRECTORY

CARRIAGE HILLS COUNTRY CLUB

18 Regulation Public

3535 Wescott Hills Drive
Eagan, Minnesota 55123
612/686-7008 Clubhouse
612/452-7211 Proshop

RESERVATIONS	612/452-7211 3 days	
	Walk-on: good/poor	
GREEN FEES	M-Th	F-S
Adult	$17/12	$19/13
Senior	$11/7*	$19/13
Junior	$11/7*	$19/13
Twilight	NA	NA
	*Before 3 pm	
PAYMENT	No credit cards accepted	
	No checks accepted	
LEAGUES	Men: Various	
	Women: Various	
MEMBERSHIPS	MGA	
MANAGER	Tom Westbrook	

HOURS	6 am to 9 pm	
SEASON	April to October	
FEATURES		
Putting green	Y	
Driving range	N	
Practice area	N	
Golf carts		
Power (gas)	Y	$21/12
Pull carts	Y	$2
Club rental	Y	$5
Club storage	N	
Caddies	N	
Proshop		
Basic	Y	
Refreshments		
Restaurant	N	
Lounge	N	
Snacks	Y	
Clubhouse		
Showers	N	
Lockers	N	
Lodging	N	

Located in Eagan. Course is one mile east of I-35E on Yankee Doodle Road, then south on Wescott Hills Drive.

	MEN			**WOMEN**		
	FRONT	PAR	HDCP	FRONT	PAR	HDCP
1	400	4	4	387	5	4
2	434	5	14	351	4	6
3	148	3	16	138	3	18
4	295	4	18	206	4	16
5	324	4	10	222	4	12
6	508	5	2	399	5	2
7	369	4	8	357	4	8
8	310	4	12	287	4	10
9	183	3	6	158	3	14
Out	2971	36		2505	36	
10	330	4	15	311	4	11
11	370	4	5	357	4	3
12	395	4	3	337	5	5
13	533	5	1	397	5	1
14	146	3	7	134	3	7
15	346	4	13	284	4	15
16	158	3	11	129	3	9
17	349	4	9	274	4	17
18	316	4	17	306	4	13
In	2943	35		2529	36	
Total	5914	71		5034	72	
Rating	67.2			68.2		
Slope	108			109		

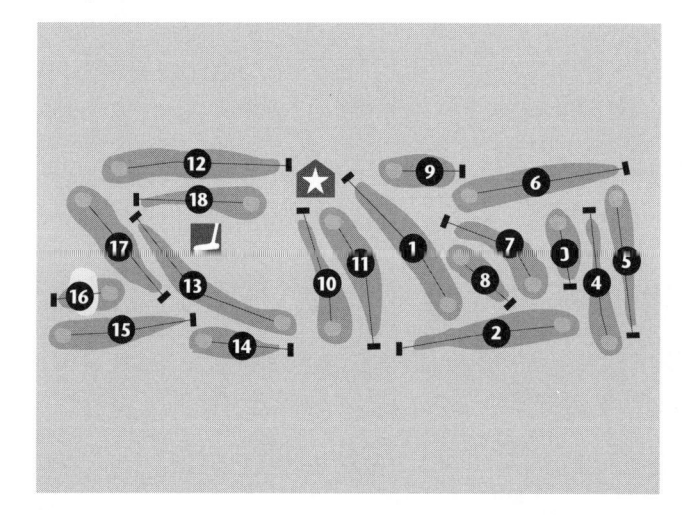

THE MINNESOTA ILLUSTRATED

CASTLE HIGHLANDS GOLF COURSE

18 Regulation Semi-Private

Route 5, P.O. Box 328
Bemidji, Minnesota 56601
218/586-2681 Clubhouse/Proshop

RESERVATIONS	218/586-2681	
	Walk-on: good/good	
GREEN FEES	M-F	S-S
Adult	$18/13	$18/13
Senior	$18/13	$18/13
Junior	$18/13	$18/13
Twilight	NA	NA
PAYMENT	Credit: Visa® MasterCard®	
	Non-local checks accepted	
LEAGUES	None	
MEMBERSHIPS	USGA, NGF, GCSAA, MGA	
OWNER	Robert & Cynthia Dolan	
MANAGER	Cynthia Dolan	
SUPERINTENDENT	Robert Dolan II	
PROFESSIONAL	Robert Dolan	

HOURS	Dawn to Dusk		
SEASON	April-November		
FEATURES			
Putting green	Y		
Driving range	Y	$2-4	
Practice area	Y		
Golf carts			
Power (gas)	Y	$20	
Pull carts	Y	$3	
Club rental	Y	$3	
Club storage	N		
Caddies	N		
Proshop			
Extended	Y		
Refreshments			
Restaurant	N		
Lounge	Y		
Snacks	Y		
Clubhouse			
Showers	N		
Lockers	N		
Lodging	N		

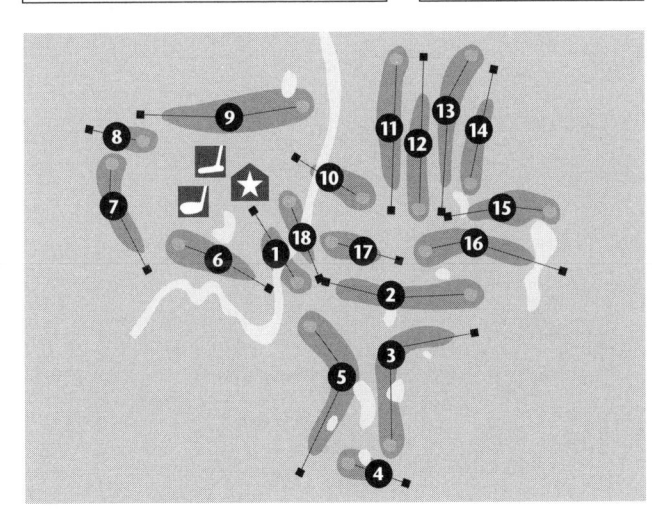

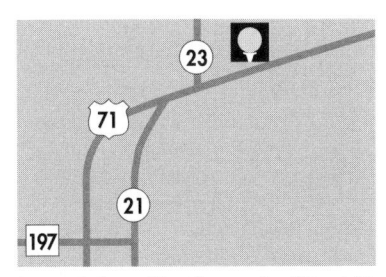

Located about 10 miles north of Bemidji. Course is north of US Highway 71 on the east side of County Road 23.

	\multicolumn{4}{c}{**MEN**}	\multicolumn{3}{c}{**WOMEN**}
	BACK	FRONT	PAR	HDCP	FRONT	PAR	HDCP
1	180	166	3	9	136	3	4
2	465	461	5	4	360	5	3
3	470	465	5	3	405	5	11
4	130	127	3	16	127	3	15
5	435	432	5	13	308	5	17
6	405	403	4	1	359	4	1
7	257	250	4	17	210	4	18
8	164	161	3	10	161	3	9
9	453	450	5	3	440	5	2
Out	2959	2915	37		2506	37	
10	208	200	3	6	125	3	10
11	290	285	4	12	285	4	8
12	262	254	4	18	254	4	14
13	255	250	4	14	250	4	6
14	136	130	3	15	130	3	12
15	263	259	4	8	259	4	7
16	371	365	4	5	307	4	5
17	337	307	4	11	212	4	16
18	165	159	3	7	120	3	13
In	2287	2209	33		1942	33	
Total	5246	5124	70		4448	70	
Rating	65.8	65.2			65.5		
Slope	111	110			112		

GOLF COURSE DIRECTORY

CASTLEWOOD GOLF COURSE

9 Regulation Public

7050 Scandia Trail North
Forest Lake, Minnesota 55025
612/464-6233 Clubhouse/Proshop

HOURS	7 am to Dusk
SEASON	April–November

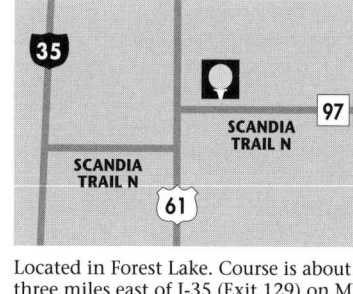

Located in Forest Lake. Course is about three miles east of I-35 (Exit 129) on MN Highway 97.

RESERVATIONS	612/464-6233	
	Walk-on: good/fair	
GREEN FEES	M-F	S-S
Adult	$15.50/9.25	$16.50/10.25
Senior	$14.50/7.25	$13.50/8.25
Junior	$14.50/7.25	$13.50/8.25
Twilight	NA	NA
PAYMENT	No credit cards accepted	
	Non-local checks accepted	
LEAGUES	Men: Various	
	Women: Various	
MEMBERSHIPS	USGA, PGA, GCSAA, MGA	
MANAGER	Ron Vannelli	
PROFESSIONAL	Curt Erickson	

FEATURES		
Putting green	Y	
Driving range	N	
Practice area	N	
Golf carts		
Power (gas)	Y	$20/12
Pull carts	Y	$2.75
Club rental	Y	
Club storage	N	
Caddies	N	
Proshop		
Extended	Y	
Refreshments		
Restaurant	Y	
Lounge	Y	
Snacks	Y	
Clubhouse		
Showers	N	
Lockers	N	
Lodging	N	

	MEN				WOMEN		
	BACK	FRONT	PAR	HDCP	FRONT	PAR	HDCP
1	531	501	5	3	387	5	3
2	149	139	3	17	126	3	17
3	356	341	4	9	315	4	9
4	260	250	4	13	245	4	13
5	217	212	3	15	200	4	15
6	558	528	5	1	415	5	1
7	363	353	4	5	343	4	5
8	383	375	4	7	365	4	7
9	349	344	4	11	340	4	11
Out	3166	3043	36		2736	37	
1	531	501	5	4	387	5	4
2	149	139	3	18	126	3	18
3	356	341	4	10	315	4	10
4	260	250	4	14	245	4	14
5	217	212	3	16	200	4	16
6	558	528	5	2	415	5	2
7	363	353	4	6	343	4	6
8	383	375	4	8	365	4	8
9	349	344	4	12	340	4	12
In	3166	3043	36		2736	37	
Total	6332	6086	72		5572	74	
Rating	70.4	69.2			71.6		
Slope	120	117			123		

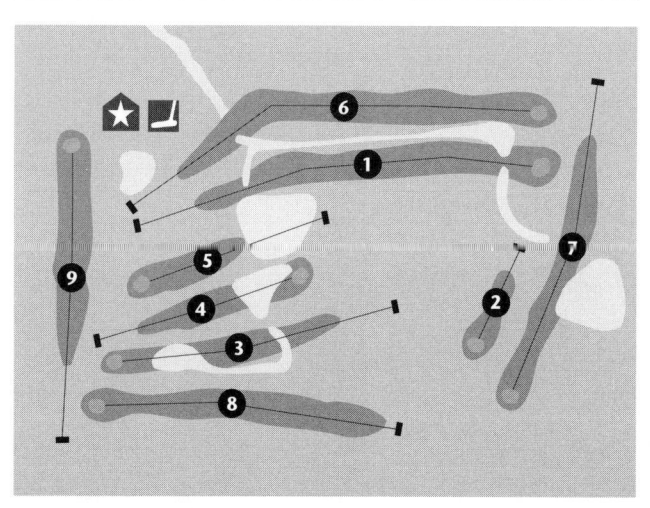

THE MINNESOTA ILLUSTRATED

CEDAR HILLS GOLF COURSE

9 Executive Public

9735 Eden Prairie Road
Eden Prairie, Minnesota 55347
612/934-1977 Clubhouse/Proshop

HOURS	Dawn to Dusk
SEASON	April–November

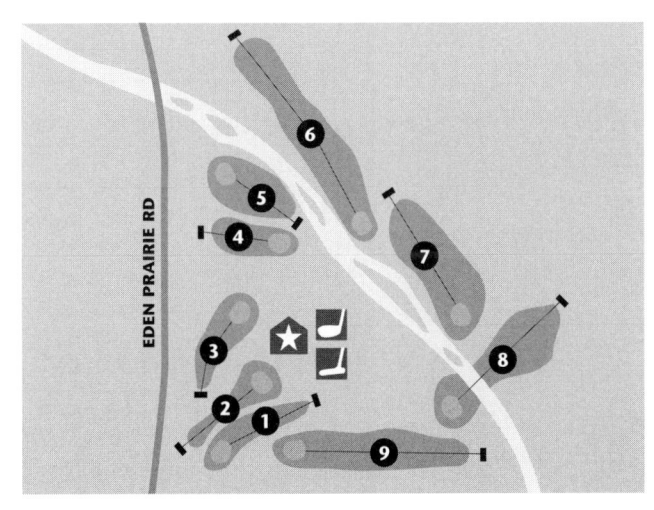

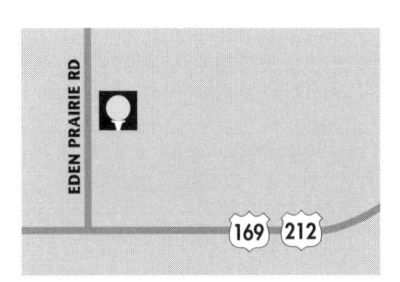

Located in Eden Prairie. Course entrance is about 1/2 mile north of Highway 212 on Eden Prairie Road.

RESERVATIONS	612/934-1977 4 days
	Walk-on: fair/poor

GREEN FEES	M-F	S-S
Adult	$15.50/9	$17.50/10
Senior	$10.50/6.50	$12.50/7.50
Junior	$15.50/9	$17.50/10
Twilight	NA	NA

PAYMENT	No credit cards accepted
	Non-local checks only

LEAGUES	Various

MEMBERSHIPS	NGF

OWNER	Brett & Tracy Hope
MANAGER	Brett & Tracy Hope

FEATURES	
Putting green	Y
Driving range	Y
Practice area	N
Golf carts	
Power (gas)	Y
Pull carts	Y
Club rental	Y
Club storage	N
Caddies	N
Proshop	
Regular	Y
Refreshments	
Restaurant	N
Lounge	Y
Snacks	Y
Clubhouse	
Showers	N
Lockers	N
Lodging	N

	MEN			**WOMEN**		
	FRONT	PAR	HDCP	FRONT	PAR	HDCP
1	123	3	7	123	3	7
2	130	3	4	130	3	4
3	89	3	6	89	3	6
4	97	3	9	97	3	9
5	109	3	8	109	3	8
6	210	3	1	210	4	1
7	175	3	3	175	3	3
8	163	3	2	163	4	2
9	230	4	5	230	4	5
Out	1326	28		1326	30	
1	123	3	7	123	3	7
2	130	3	4	130	3	4
3	89	3	6	89	3	6
4	97	3	9	97	3	9
5	109	3	8	109	3	8
6	210	3	1	210	4	1
7	175	3	3	175	3	3
8	163	3	2	163	4	2
9	230	4	5	230	4	5
In	1326	28		1326	30	
Total	2652	56		2652	60	
Rating	NA			NA		
Slope	NA			NA		

GOLF COURSE DIRECTORY

CEDAR RIVER COUNTRY CLUB

18 Regulation Semi-Private

Highway 56 West, P.O. Box 311
Adams, Minnesota 55909
507/582-3595 Clubhouse/Proshop

HOURS	7 am to Dusk
SEASON	April-November

| **RESERVATIONS** | 507/582-3595 1 week |
| | Walk-on: good/good |

GREEN FEES	M-F	S-S
Adult	$16/11	$16/11
Senior	$16/11	$16/11
Junior	$16/11	$16/11
Twilight	NA	NA

| **PAYMENT** | No credit cards accepted |
| | Non-local checks accepted |

| **LEAGUES** | Various |

| **MEMBERSHIPS** | GCSAA, MGA |

| **MANAGER** | Geneva Hamilton |
| **SUPERINTENDENT** | John Queenslend |

FEATURES		
Putting green	Y	
Driving range	Y	$2-2.50
Practice area	Y	
Golf carts		
Power	Y	$18/11
Pull carts	Y	$2
Club rental	Y	$5
Club storage	Y	$12/yr
Caddies	N	
Proshop		
Extended	Y	
Refreshments		
Restaurant	Y	
Lounge	Y	
Snacks	Y	
Clubhouse		
Showers	Y	
Lockers	Y	$16/yr
Lodging	N	

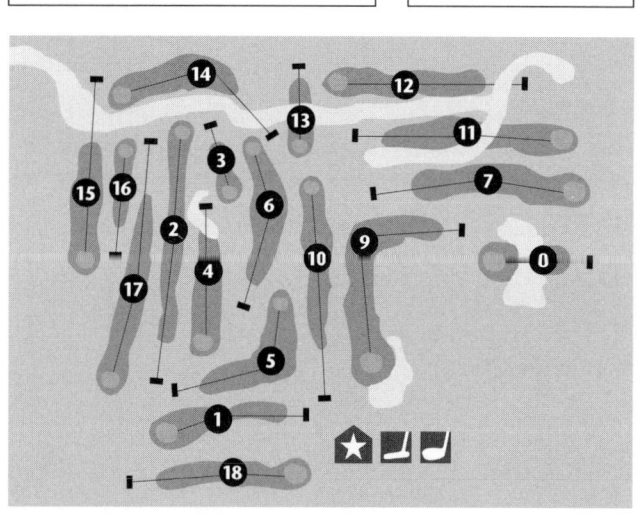

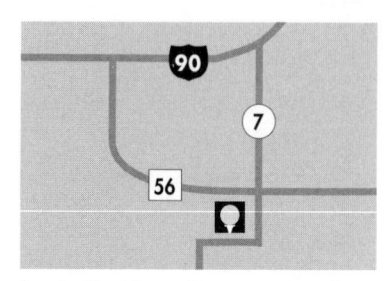

Located in Adams. Course entrance is about 12 miles south of I-90 or 1 mile west of County Road 7 on Highway 56.

	MEN				**WOMEN**		
	BACK	FRONT	PAR	HDCP	FRONT	PAR	HDCP
1	343	334	4	14	319	4	14
2	485	478	5	10	464	5	10
3	114	104	3	18	94	3	18
4	376	366	4	6	359	4	6
5	346	339	4	11	329	4	11
6	319	310	4	13	300	4	13
7	450	434	4	1	414	5	1
8	155	155	3	16	101	3	16
9	569	550	5	2	460	5	2
Out	3157	3070	36		2840	37	
10	410	393	4	7	377	5	7
11	485	471	5	3	448	5	3
12	337	319	4	9	230	4	9
13	120	110	3	15	93	3	15
14	341	329	4	5	314	4	5
15	329	323	4	12	300	4	12
16	176	168	3	17	158	3	17
17	493	488	5	4	413	5	4
18	363	354	4	8	344	4	8
In	3054	2957	36		2677	37	
Total	6211	6027	72		5517	74	
Rating	70.3	69.3			72.0		
Slope	124	122			124		

CEDAR VALLEY GOLF COURSE

18 Regulation Semi-Private

P.O. Box 1448
Winona, Minnesota 55987
507/457-3241 Clubhouse/Proshop

HOURS	Dawn to Dusk
SEASON	April to October

RESERVATIONS	507/457-3241
	Walk-on: fair/fair

GREEN FEES	M-F	S-S
Adult	Call	Call
Senior	Call	Call
Junior	Call	Call
Twilight	NA	NA

PAYMENT	No credit cards accepted
	Non-local checks accepted

LEAGUES	Men: Various
	Women: Various

MEMBERSHIPS	MGA

DIRECTOR	Rodney Sines
MANAGER	Jeni Arnold
SUPERINTENDENT	Frank Ciszak

FEATURES	
Putting green	Y
Driving range	Y
Practice area	N
Golf carts	
Power (gas)	Y
Pull carts	Y
Club rental	Y
Club storage	N
Caddies	N
Proshop	
Regular	Y
Refreshments	
Restaurant	N
Lounge	Y
Snacks	Y
Clubhouse	
Showers	N
Lockers	N
Lodging	N

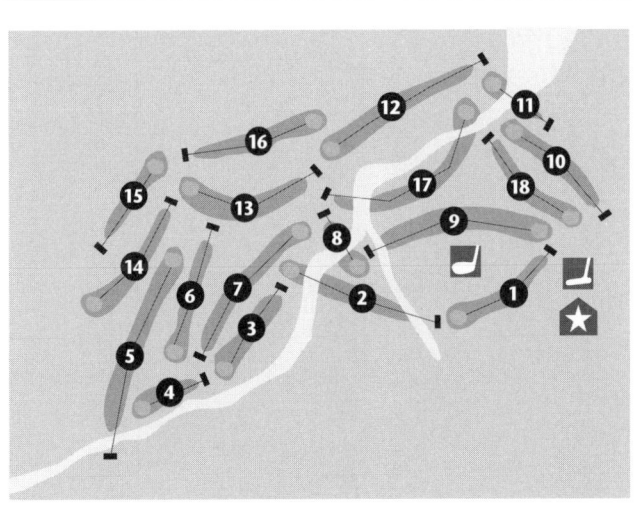

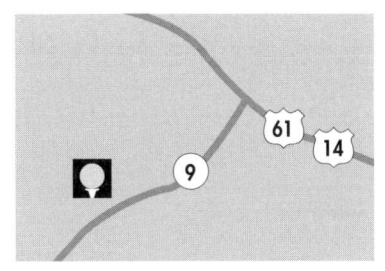

Located about 9 miles southeast of Winona. Course entrance is southwest of U.S. Highway 61 on County Road 9.

	MEN				**WOMEN**		
	BACK	FRONT	PAR	HDCP	FRONT	PAR	HDCP
1	330	320	4	15	310	4	15
2	390	370	4	7	355	4	7
3	360	350	4	13	335	4	13
4	170	160	3	11	150	3	11
5	545	535	5	3	460	5	3
6	390	380	4	9	365	4	9
7	535	529	5	5	470	5	5
8	115	115	3	17	115	3	17
9	425	380	4	1	340	4	1
Out	3260	3139	36		2900	36	
10	350	340	4	12	330	4	12
11	185	145	3	8	120	3	8
12	520	490	5	6	470	5	6
13	400	385	4	4	375	4	4
14	310	300	4	14	280	4	14
15	160	150	3	16	130	3	16
16	260	250	4	18	240	4	18
17	550	500	5	2	480	5	2
18	330	310	4	10	290	4	10
In	3065	2870	36		2715	36	
Total	6325	6009	72		5615	72	
Rating	69.5	68.0			71.7		
Slope	119	116			122		

GOLF COURSE DIRECTORY

CENTERBROOK GOLF COURSE

9 Par-3 Public

5500 North Lilac Drive
Brooklyn Center, Minnesota 55430
612/561-3239 Clubhouse/Proshop

HOURS	Dawn to Dusk
SEASON	April-November

RESERVATIONS	612/561-3239
	Walk-on: good/good

GREEN FEES	M-F	S-S
Adult	$8.50	$9
Senior	$7.50	$9
Junior	$7.50	$9
Twilight	NA	NA
	$5 Mondays till 10 am	
	$5 Saturdays till 9 am	

PAYMENT	No credit cards accepted
	Non-local checks accepted

LEAGUES	Men: Th (pm)
	Women: M,W,Th (Various)

MEMBERSHIPS	MGA

MANAGER	Arnie Mavis
SUPERINTENDENT	George Vennrich
PROFESSIONAL	Dianne Von Ende

FEATURES	
Putting green	Y
Driving range	N
Practice area	N
Golf carts	
Power (gas)	Y
Pull carts	Y
Club rental	Y
Club storage	N
Caddies	N
Proshop	
Extended	Y
Refreshments	
Restaurant	N
Lounge	N
Snacks	Y
Clubhouse	
Showers	N
Lockers	N
Lodging	N

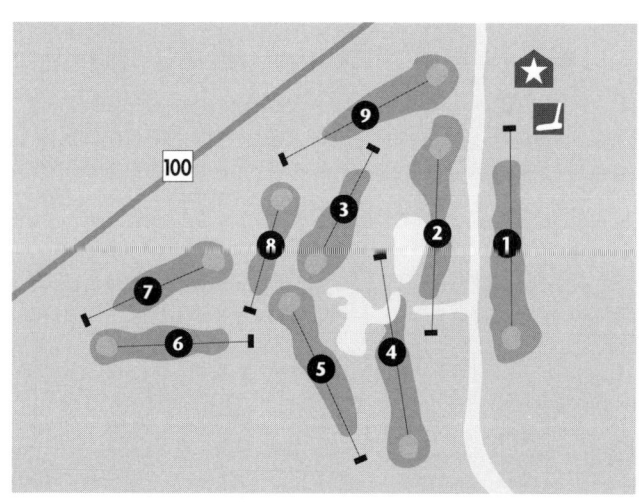

Located in Brooklyn Center. Course is east of Highway 100 on 57th Avenue, then 1/2 mile south North Lilac Drive.

	MEN				**WOMEN**		
	BACK	FRONT	PAR	HDCP	FRONT	PAR	HDCP
1	192	182	3	3	172	3	3
2	190	180	3	1	170	3	1
3	130	120	3	8	110	3	8
4	195	185	3	2	175	3	2
5	180	170	3	4	160	3	4
6	155	145	3	5	135	3	5
7	157	137	3	7	127	3	7
8	130	120	3	9	110	3	9
9	160	150	3	6	140	3	6
Out	1489	1389	27		1299	27	
1	192	182	3	3	172	3	3
2	190	180	3	1	170	3	1
3	130	120	3	8	110	3	8
4	195	185	3	2	175	3	2
5	180	170	3	4	160	3	4
6	155	145	3	5	135	3	5
7	157	137	3	7	127	3	7
8	130	120	3	9	110	3	9
9	160	150	3	6	140	3	6
In	1489	1389	27		1299	27	
Total	2958	2778	54		2598	54	
Rating	53.8	53.0			54.2		
Slope	72	70			72		

CHASKA PAR 30 GOLF COURSE

9 Executive Public

1207 Hazeltine Boulevard
Chaska, Minnesota 55318
612/448-7454 Clubhouse/Proshop

RESERVATIONS	No reservations accepted	
	Walk-on: good/fair	
GREEN FEES	M-F	S-S
Adult	$7	$8
Senior	$5	$8
Junior	$5	$8
Twilight	NA	NA
	Resident rates available	
PAYMENT	No credit cards accepted	
	Non-local checks accepted	
LEAGUES	Women: Various	
	Men: Various	
MEMBERSHIPS	MGA	
OWNER	City of Chaska	
MANAGER	Tom Redman	
SUPERINTENDENT	Mark Moeors	

HOURS	Dawn to Dusk
SEASON	April-November

FEATURES	
Putting green	Y
Driving range	N
Practice area	N
Golf carts	
Power	N
Pull carts	Y
Club rental	Y
Club storage	N
Caddies	N
Proshop	
Basic	Y
Refreshments	
Restaurant	N
Lounge	N
Snacks	Y
Clubhouse	
Showers	N
Lockers	N
Lodging	N

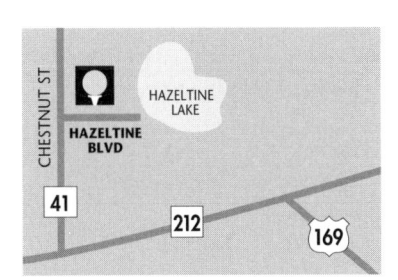

Located in Chaska. Course entrance is north of Highway 212 on Highway 41, then 2 blocks east Hazeltine Boulevard.

	MEN			**WOMEN**		
	FRONT	PAR	HDCP	FRONT	PAR	HDCP
1	129	3	8	114	3	8
2	284	4	2	262	4	2
3	136	3	6	116	3	6
4	104	3	9	95	3	9
5	140	3	5	111	3	5
6	294	4	1	264	4	1
7	156	3	4	133	3	4
8	131	3	7	101	3	7
9	271	4	3	240	4	3
Out	1648	30		1436	30	
1	129	3	8	114	3	8
2	284	4	2	262	4	2
3	136	3	6	116	3	6
4	104	3	9	95	3	9
5	140	3	5	111	3	5
6	294	4	1	264	4	1
7	156	3	4	133	3	4
8	131	3	7	101	3	7
9	271	4	3	240	4	3
In	1648	30		1436	30	
Total	3296	60		2872	60	
Rating	56.4			56.6		
Slope	89			94		

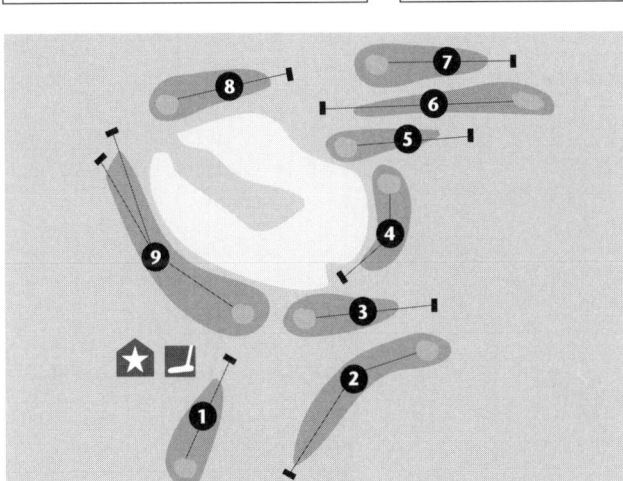

GOLF COURSE DIRECTORY

CHIPPEWA NATIONAL GOLF CLUB

9 Regulation Public

Highway 200, Southeast Shore
Leech Lake, Minnesota 56655
218/363-2552 Clubhouse/Proshop

HOURS	7 am to Dusk
SEASON	May to October

RESERVATIONS	218/363-2552
	Walk-on: good/fair

GREEN FEES	M-F	S-S
Adult	$10.50	$10.50
Senior	$10.50	$10.50
Junior	$10.50	$10.50
Twilight	NA	NA

PAYMENT	Credit: Visa® MC® Discover®
	Non-local checks accepted

LEAGUES	Men: Various
	Women: Various

MEMBERSHIPS	USGA, PGA, MGA

PROFESSIONAL	Bruce Gardner

FEATURES	
Putting green	Y
Driving range	Y
Practice area	Y
Golf carts	
Power (elec)	Y $12
Pull carts	Y $2
Club rental	Y
Club storage	N
Caddies	N
Proshop	
Basic	Y
Refreshments	
Restaurant	N
Lounge	Y
Snacks	Y
Clubhouse	
Showers	N
Lockers	N
Lodging	N

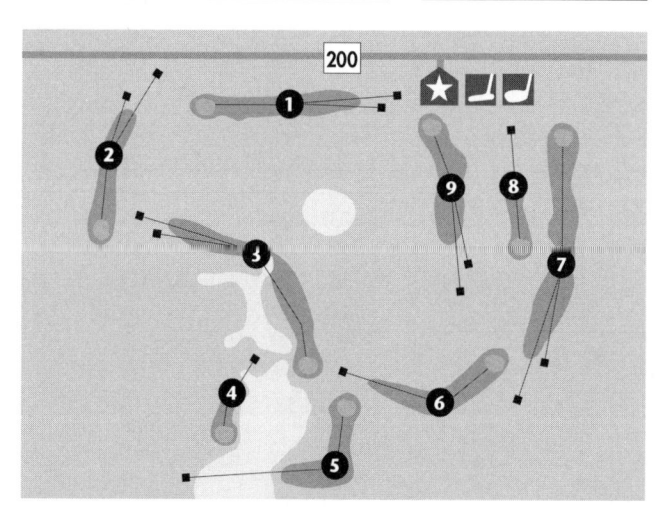

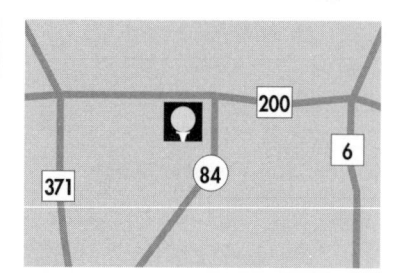

Located at SE shore of Leech Lake. Course is 15 miles east of Walker or 15 miles west of Remer on Hwy 200.

	MEN				WOMEN		
	BACK	FRONT	PAR	HDCP	FRONT	PAR	HDCP
1	380	367	4	3	342	4	3
2	356	348	4	8	284	4	8
3	437	413	5	2	397	5	2
4	155	151	3	7	151	3	7
5	328	306	4	6	291	4	6
6	377	367	4	5	359	4	5
7	530	523	5	1	403	5	1
8	196	174	3	9	160	3	9
9	361	357	4	4	312	4	4
Out	3120	3006	36		2699	36	
1	380	367	4	3	342	4	3
2	356	348	4	8	284	4	8
3	437	413	5	2	397	5	2
4	155	151	3	7	151	3	7
5	328	306	4	6	291	4	6
6	377	367	4	5	359	4	5
7	530	523	5	1	403	5	1
8	196	174	3	9	160	3	9
9	361	357	4	4	312	4	4
In	3120	3006	36		2699	36	
Total	6240	6012	72		5398	72	
Rating	70.4	69.6			75.0		
Slope	123	122			131		

CHISAGO LAKES GOLF COURSE

18 Regulation Public

P.O. Box 529
Lindstrom, Minnesota 55045
612/257-1484 Clubhouse/Proshop

HOURS	Dawn to Dusk
SEASON	April-November

RESERVATIONS	612/257-1484 2 days
	Walk-on: good/fair

GREEN FEES	M-F	S-S
Adult	$18/10	$20/12
Sr/Jr	$18/10	$20/12
Twilight	NA	NA
	Special rate: Monday's $12	

PAYMENT	Credit: Visa® MasterCard®
	Non-local checks accepted

LEAGUES	Men: M (am), W (pm)
	Women: T (am & pm)
	Couples: Th

MEMBERSHIPS	USGA, NGF, GCSAA, MGA, MPGA

MANAGER	Deb Forsman, Marge Trucheau
SUPERINTENDENT	Dave Zimmer

FEATURES		
Putting green	Y	
Driving range	Y	$2-3
Practice area	Y	
Golf carts		
Power (gas)	Y	$20/12
Pull carts	Y	$3
Club rental	Y	$7/5
Club storage	N	
Caddies	N	
Proshop		
Extended	Y	
Refreshments		
Restaurant	N	
Lounge	N	
Snacks	Y	
Clubhouse		
Showers	Y	
Lockers	Y	
Lodging	N	

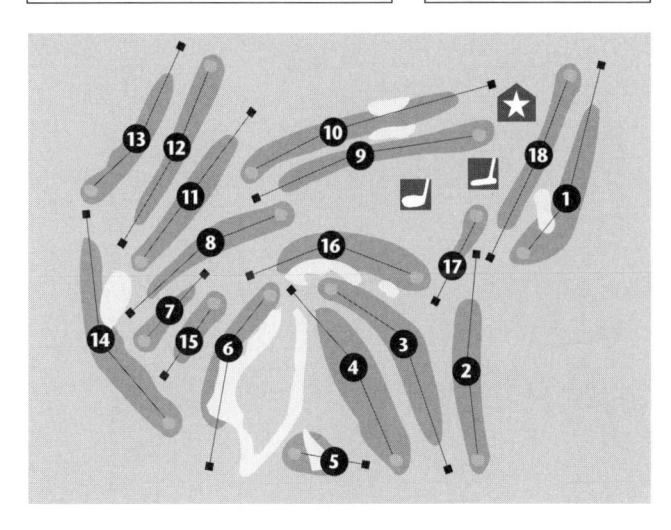

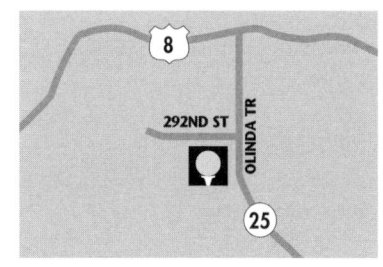

Located south of Lindstrom. Course is south of U.S. Hwy 8 on Olinda Trail (Cty Road 25), then west on 292nd Street.

	MEN				WOMEN		
	BACK	FRONT	PAR	HDCP	FRONT	PAR	HDCP
1	401	381	4	8	335	4	6
2	410	400	4	4	341	4	14
3	498	489	5	12	464	5	2
4	420	402	4	2	366	4	8
5	148	134	3	18	106	3	16
6	345	333	4	6	320	4	10
7	171	164	3	14	139	3	18
8	368	363	4	16	342	4	12
9	498	494	5	10	410	5	4
Out	3259	3160	36		2823	36	
10	526	498	5	7	433	5	3
11	362	350	4	15	336	4	13
12	360	345	4	13	333	4	7
13	364	362	4	3	328	4	5
14	468	464	5	1	446	5	1
15	186	184	3	9	174	3	15
16	416	402	4	5	346	4	9
17	192	154	3	17	142	3	17
18	396	380	4	11	353	4	11
In	3270	3139	36		2891	36	
Total	6529	6299	72		5714	72	
Rating	71.2	70.3			72.7		
Slope	119	117			124		

GOLF COURSE DIRECTORY

CHOMONIX GOLF COURSE
18 Regulation Public

646 Sandpiper Drive
Lino Lakes, Minnesota 55014
612/482-8484 Clubhouse

RESERVATIONS	612/482-8484 4 days
	Walk-on: good/good

GREEN FEES	M-F	S-S
Adult	$15/12	$17/12
Senior	$10/8	$17/12
Junior	$10/8	$17/12
Twilight	NA	NA

PAYMENT	Credit: Visa® MasterCard®
	Non-local checks accepted

LEAGUES	Men:	M (7-9:30 am)
		M-Th (4-6:30 pm)
	Women:	T (am)

MEMBERSHIPS	USGA, NGF, GCSAA, MGA

OWNER	Anoka County Parks & Rec
MANAGER	Bill Hauck
SUPERINTENDENT	Greg Iden
PROFESSIONAL	Bill Hauck

HOURS Dawn to Dusk
SEASON April–November

FEATURES		
Putting green	Y	
Driving range	Y	$3.50
Practice area	Y	
Golf carts		
Power (gas)	Y	$18
Pull carts	Y	$2.25
Club rental	Y	$8/5
Club storage	N	
Caddies	N	
Proshop		
Extended	Y	
Refreshments		
Restaurant	N	
Lounge	N	
Snacks	Y	
Clubhouse		
Showers	Y	
Lockers	Y	
Lodging	N	

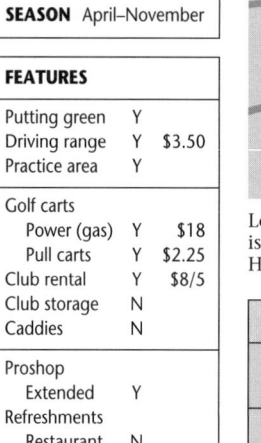

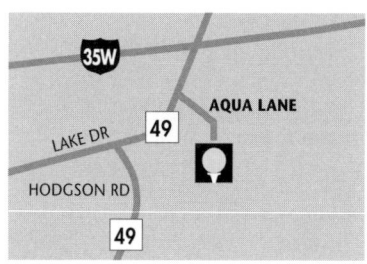

Located in Lino Lakes. Course entrance is 1 mile south of Interstate-35W on MN Highway 49, then east on Aqua Lane.

	MEN				WOMEN		
	BACK	FRONT	PAR	HDCP	FRONT	PAR	HDCP
1	525	515	5	3	497	5	3
2	215	205	3	7	174	3	7
3	399	389	4	5	354	4	5
4	476	466	5	15	426	5	15
5	167	152	3	17	142	3	17
6	424	404	4	1	390	4	1
7	387	372	4	13	362	4	13
8	355	345	4	11	328	4	11
9	372	362	4	9	347	4	9
Out	3320	3210	36		3020	36	
10	378	363	4	14	348	4	14
11	530	510	5	6	490	5	6
12	416	389	4	4	304	4	4
13	182	172	3	16	157	3	16
14	511	501	5	2	440	5	2
15	152	147	3	18	129	3	18
16	337	327	4	12	317	4	12
17	395	385	4	10	375	4	10
18	358	348	4	8	338	4	8
In	3259	3142	36		2898	36	
Total	6579	6352	72		5918	72	
Rating	71.3	70.2			73.7		
Slope	121	119			125		

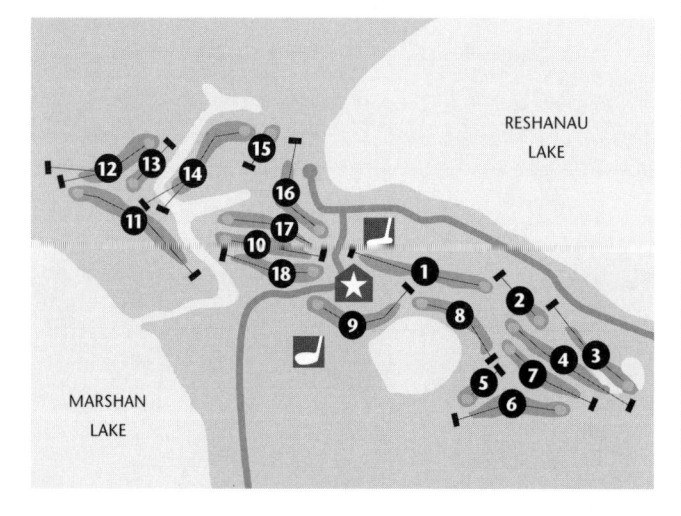

CHOSEN VALLEY GOLF CLUB

9 Regulation Semi-Private

1801 South Main Street
Chatfield, Minnesota 55923
507/867-4305 Clubhouse/Proshop

HOURS 8 am to Dusk

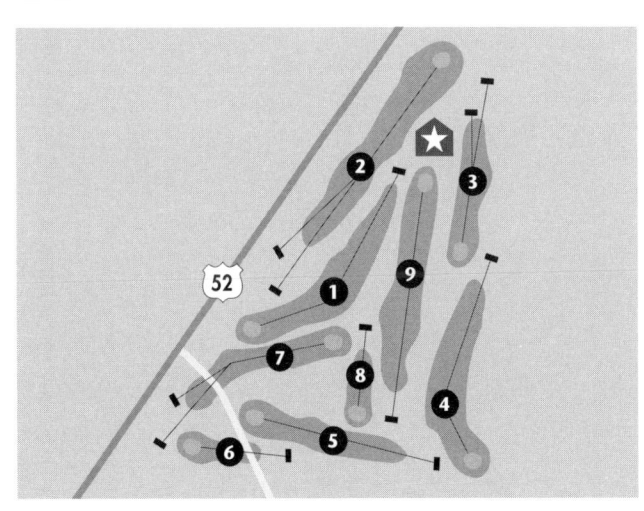

SEASON April–November

RESERVATIONS	507/867-4305 2 days	
	Weekend reservations only	
	Walk-on: good/good	
GREEN FEES	M-F	S-S
Adult	$15/10	$15/10
Senior	$15/10	$15/10
Junior	$15/10	$15/10
Twilight	NA	NA
	Special rates: M,Th $12/7	
PAYMENT	No credit cards accepted	
	Local checks only	
LEAGUES	Men: W (pm)	
MEMBERSHIPS	USGA, NGF, GCSAA, MGA	
OWNER	Chosen Valley Stockholders	
MANAGER	Bob Polikowsky	

FEATURES

Putting green	N
Driving range	N
Practice area	N
Golf carts	
Power (gas)	Y $15/10
Pull carts	Y $1.50
Club rental	Y $5
Club storage	N
Caddies	N
Proshop	
Basic	Y
Refreshments	
Restaurant	N
Lounge	N
Snacks	Y
Clubhouse	
Showers	Y
Lockers	N
Lodging	N

Located just south of Chatfield. Course entrance is south of Interstate-90 on U.S. Highway 52.

	MEN			WOMEN		
	FRONT	PAR	HDCP	FRONT	PAR	HDCP
1	371	4	3	360	4	3
2	501	5	4	457	5	4
3	265	4	8	200	3	8
4	358	4	5	340	4	5
5	334	4	6	313	4	6
6	168	3	7	98	3	7
7	385	4	1	305	4	1
8	153	3	9	138	3	9
9	398	4	2	394	5	2
Out	2933	35		2605	35	
1	371	4	4	360	4	4
2	501	5	5	457	5	5
3	200	3	3	165	3	3
4	358	4	6	340	4	6
5	334	4	7	313	4	7
6	168	3	8	98	3	8
7	385	4	1	305	4	1
8	153	3	9	138	3	9
9	398	4	2	394	5	2
In	2868	34		2570	35	
Total	5801	69		5175	70	
Rating	66.4			69.0		
Slope	108			104		

GOLF COURSE DIRECTORY

CIMARRON GOLF COURSE

9 Par-3 Public

901 Lake Elmo Avenue North
Lake Elmo, Minnesota 55042
612/436-6188 Clubhouse/Proshop

HOURS	7:30 am to Dusk
SEASON	April-November

RESERVATIONS	612/436-6188 3 days
	Walk-on: fair/good

GREEN FEES	M-F	S-S
Adult	$14/7.75	$14/7.75
Senior	$14/7.75	$14/7.75
Junior	$14/7.75	$14/7.75
Twilight	NA	NA

PAYMENT	No credit cards accepted
	Non-local checks accepted

LEAGUES	Various

MEMBERSHIPS	GCSAA, MGA

OWNER	Chateau Properties
MANAGER	Robert Lethbridge
SUPERINTENDENT	Kyle Howieson

FEATURES		
Putting green	Y	
Driving range	N	
Practice area	N	
Golf carts		
Power	N	
Pull carts	Y	$1.50
Club rental	Y	$3
Club storage	N	
Caddies	N	
Proshop		
Basic	Y	
Refreshments		
Restaurant	N	
Lounge	N	
Snacks	Y	
Clubhouse		
Showers	N	
Lockers	N	
Lodging	N	

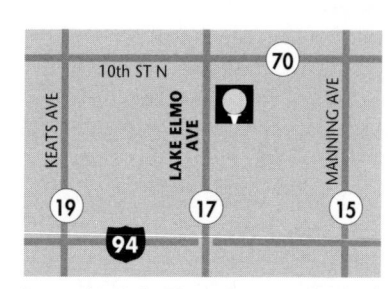

Located in Lake Elmo. Course is north of I-94 on County Road 19, east on 10th Street, then south on County Road 17.

	MEN			**WOMEN**		
	FRONT	PAR	HDCP	FRONT	PAR	HDCP
1	198	3	2	171	3	2
2	119	3	9	100	3	9
3	192	3	3	172	3	3
4	181	3	4	172	3	4
5	116	3	8	92	3	8
6	150	3	6	130	3	6
7	160	3	5	145	3	5
8	218	3	1	189	3	1
9	126	3	7	116	3	7
Out	1460	27		1287	27	
1	198	3	2	171	3	2
2	119	3	9	100	3	9
3	192	3	3	172	3	3
4	181	3	4	172	3	4
5	116	3	8	92	3	8
6	150	3	6	130	3	6
7	160	3	5	145	3	5
8	218	3	1	189	3	1
9	126	3	7	116	3	7
In	1460	27		1287	27	
Total	2920	54		2574	54	
Rating	53.8			53.6		
Slope	77			75		

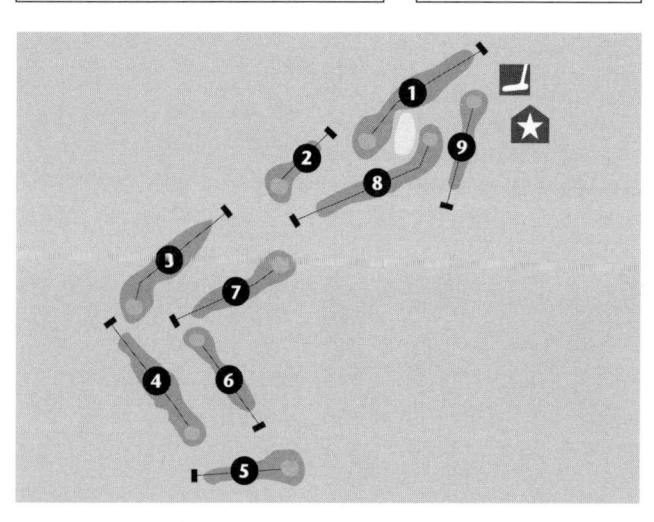

THE MINNESOTA ILLUSTRATED

CLARKS GROVE GOLF COURSE

9 Executive Public

Route 1, Box 22A
Clarks Grove, Minnesota 56016
507/256-7737 Clubhouse/Proshop

HOURS	7 am to Dusk
SEASON	April to October

RESERVATIONS	No reservations accepted
	Walk-on: good/good

GREEN FEES	M-F	S-S
Adult	$6.25	$7.75
Senior	$6.25	$7.75
Junior	$6.25	$7.75
Twilight	NA	NA

PAYMENT	No credit cards accepted
	Local checks only

LEAGUES	Men: W
	Women: T

MEMBERSHIPS	None

OWNER	Forest Peterson

FEATURES		
Putting green	Y	
Driving range	N	
Practice area	N	
Golf carts		
Power	N	
Pull carts	Y	$1
Club rental	Y	$3
Club storage	N	
Caddies	N	
Proshop		
Extended	Y	
Refreshments		
Restaurant	N	
Lounge	N	
Snacks	Y	
Clubhouse		
Showers	N	
Lockers	N	
Lodging	N	

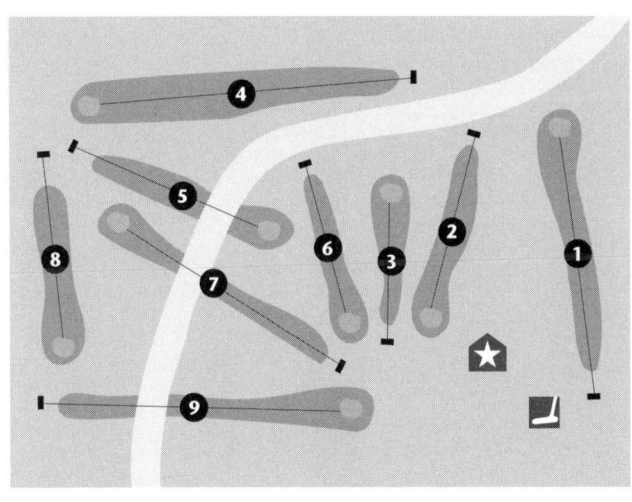

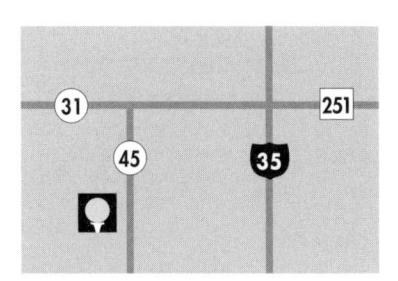

Located in Clarks Grove. Course is one mile south of MN Highway 251 on County Road 45.

	MEN			**WOMEN**		
	FRONT	PAR	HDCP	FRONT	PAR	HDCP
1	166	3	3	166	3	3
2	145	3	8	145	3	8
3	108	3	9	108	3	9
4	272	4	1	272	4	1
5	166	3	2	166	3	2
6	123	3	7	123	3	7
7	208	4	6	208	4	6
8	140	3	5	140	3	5
9	238	4	4	238	4	4
Out	1566	30		1566	30	
1	166	3	3	166	3	3
2	145	3	8	145	3	8
3	108	3	9	108	3	9
4	272	4	1	272	4	1
5	166	3	2	166	3	2
6	123	3	7	123	3	7
7	208	4	6	208	4	6
8	140	3	5	140	3	5
9	238	4	4	238	4	4
In	1566	30		1566	30	
Total	3132	60		3132	60	
Rating	NA			NA		
Slope	NA			NA		

GOLF COURSE DIRECTORY

CLEARY LAKE GOLF COURSE

9 Executive Public

18106 Texas Avenue
Prior Lake, Minnesota 55372
612/447-2171 Clubhouse/Proshop

HOURS	6 am to Dusk
SEASON	April to October

| **RESERVATIONS** | 612/447-2171 2 days |
| | Walk-on: good/fair |

GREEN FEES	M-F	S-S
Adult	$11/7.50	$11/7.50
Senior	$5*	$11/7.50
Junior	$5*	$11/7.50
Twilight	NA	NA
	*Before 4 pm	
	10 round pass available	

| **PAYMENT** | No credit cards accepted |
| | Non-local checks accepted |

| **LEAGUES** | Senior: T |

| **MEMBERSHIPS** | USGA, NGF, PGA, MGA |

| **PROFESSIONAL** | Greg Woodstrom |

FEATURES	
Putting green	Y
Driving range	Y
Practice area	N

Golf carts		
Power (gas)	Y	$9
Pull carts	Y	$2
Club rental	Y	$3
Club storage	N	
Caddies	N	

Proshop	
Regular	Y
Refreshments	
Restaurant	N
Lounge	N
Snacks	Y
Clubhouse	
Showers	N
Lockers	N

| Lodging | N |

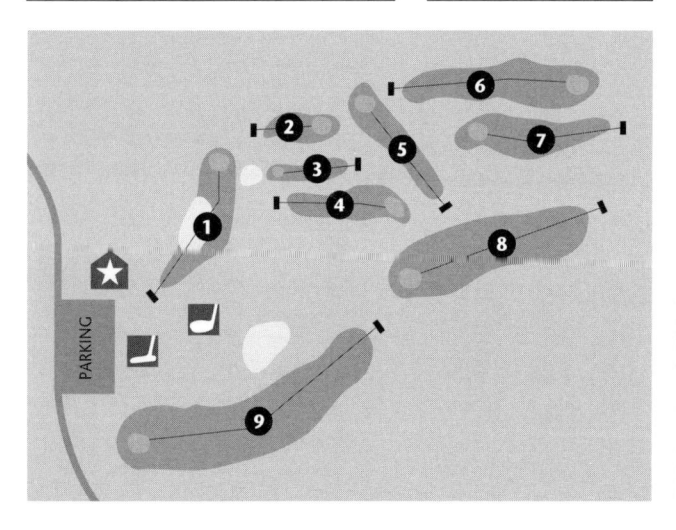

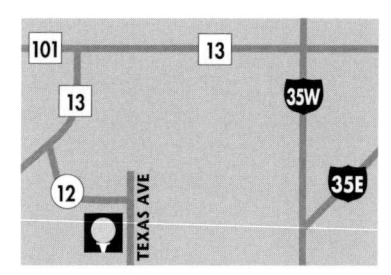

Located in Prior Lake. Course is south of MN Highway 13 on County Road 12, then south on Texas Avenue.

		MEN			WOMEN	
	FRONT	PAR	HDCP	FRONT	PAR	HDCP
1	155	3	4	155	3	4
2	118	3	8	118	3	8
3	115	3	9	115	3	9
4	145	3	7	145	3	7
5	157	3	6	157	3	6
6	237	3	2	237	4	2
7	207	3	3	207	3	3
8	209	3	5	209	3	5
9	332	4	1	332	4	1
Out	1675	28		1675	29	
1	155	3	4	155	3	4
2	118	3	8	118	3	8
3	115	3	9	115	3	9
4	145	3	7	145	3	7
5	157	3	6	157	3	6
6	237	3	2	237	4	2
7	207	3	3	207	3	3
8	209	3	5	209	3	5
9	332	4	1	332	4	1
In	1675	28		1675	29	
Total	3350	56		3350	58	
Rating	55.2			58.2		
Slope	80			88		

CLOQUET COUNTRY CLUB

9 Regulation Private

400 Country Club Dr, P.O. Box 331
Cloquet, Minnesota 55720
218/879-8858 Clubhouse
218/879-7997 Proshop

HOURS	Dawn to Dusk
SEASON	April to October

FEATURES	
Putting green	Y
Driving range	N
Practice area	Y
Golf carts	
Power (gas)	Y
Pull carts	Y
Club rental	Y
Club storage	Y
Caddies	N
Proshop	
Extended	Y
Refreshments	
Restaurant	Y
Lounge	Y
Snacks	Y
Clubhouse	
Showers	Y
Lockers	Y
Lodging	N

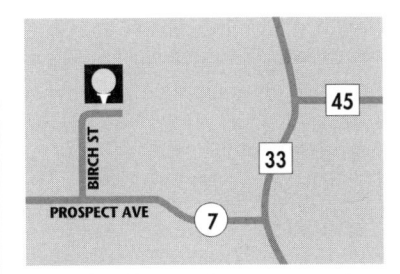

Located in Cloquet. Course is west of MN Highway 33 on Prospect Avenue / County Road 7, then north on Birch St.

RESERVATIONS	218/879-7997	
	Members only	
GREEN FEES	M-F	S-S
Adult	Call	Call
Senior	Call	Call
Junior	Call	Call
Twilight	NA	NA
	Members and guests only	
PAYMENT	Credit: Visa® MC® Discover®	
	Non-local checks accepted	
LEAGUES	Men: None	
	Women: None	
MEMBERSHIPS	USGA, PGA, GCSAA, MGA	
PROFESSIONAL	Call	

	MEN			WOMEN		
	FRONT	PAR	HDCP	FRONT	PAR	HDCP
1	310	4	14	305	4	16
2	435	4	2	425	5	10
3	200	3	12	170	3	8
4	125	3	18	115	3	14
5	530	5	6	470	5	2
6	523	5	8	403	5	6
7	363	4	10	265	4	12
8	560	5	4	500	5	4
9	145	3	16	116	3	18
Out	3191	36		2769	37	
1	330	4	15	308	4	15
2	445	4	1	428	5	9
3	233	3	5	175	3	7
4	140	3	17	120	3	13
5	501	5	11	501	5	1
6	420	4	3	420	5	5
7	393	4	9	305	4	11
8	503	5	7	503	5	3
9	185	3	13	135	3	17
In	3150	35		2895	37	
Total	6341	71		5664	74	
Rating	70.7			72.3		
Slope	129			126		

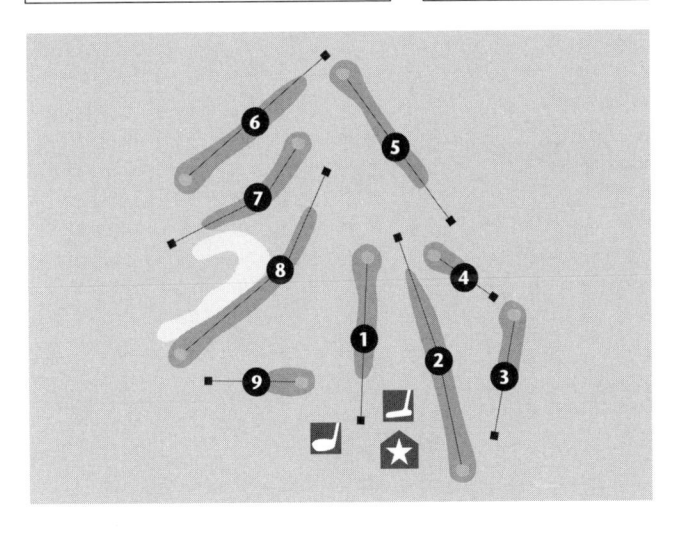

GOLF COURSE DIRECTORY

COFFEE MILL GOLF & COUNTRY CLUB

9 Regulation Semi-Private

Skyline Drive, P.O. Box 6
Wabasha, Minnesota 55981
612/565-4332 Clubhouse/Proshop

HOURS	7 am to Dusk
SEASON	April-November

RESERVATIONS	612/565-4332 4 days	
	Walk-on: good/good	
GREEN FEES	M-F	S-S
Adult	$15/9.25	$17/10.50
Senior	$15/9.25	$17/10.50
Junior	$15/9.25	$17/10.50
Twilight	NA	NA
	All day Mon-Thurs rate: $18	
PAYMENT	Credit cards not accepted	
	Non-local checks accepted	
LEAGUES	Various	
MEMBERSHIPS	USGA, GCSAA, MGA	
MANAGER	Robert Sill	
SUPERINTENDENT	Mike Pierce	

FEATURES		
Putting green	Y	
Driving range	N	
Practice area	Y	
Golf carts		
Power (gas)	Y	$18/9
Pull carts	Y	$2
Club rental	Y	$5
Club storage	N	
Caddies	N	
Proshop		
Extended	Y	
Refreshments		
Restaurant	N	
Lounge	Y	
Snacks	Y	
Clubhouse		
Showers	Y	
Lockers	N	
Lodging	N	

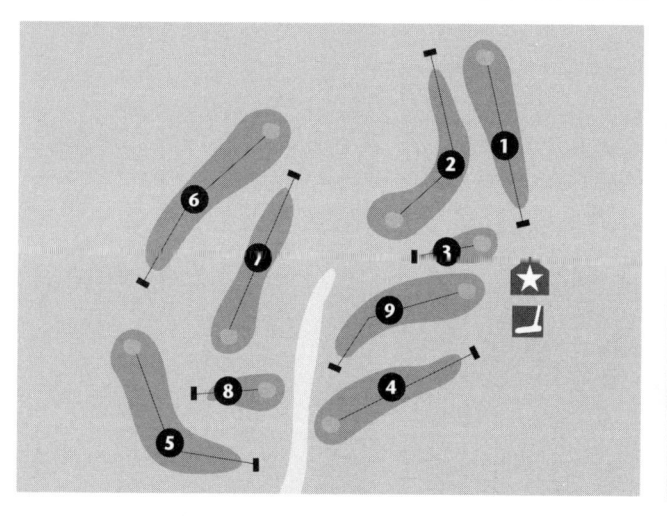

Located in Wabasha. Course entrance is about 2 miles west of U.S. Hwy 61 on Hwy 60, then north on Skyline Drive.

	MEN				**WOMEN**		
	BACK	FRONT	PAR	HDCP	FRONT	PAR	HDCP
1	397	390	4	2	379	5	7
2	498	491	5	5	432	5	6
3	195	158	3	8	126	3	8
4	362	352	4	6	328	4	1
5	546	518	5	7	460	5	5
6	405	364	4	4	329	4	2
7	375	367	4	3	294	4	4
8	187	174	3	9	160	3	9
9	409	401	4	1	330	4	3
Out	3374	3215	36		2829	37	
1	397	390	4	2	379	5	7
2	498	491	5	5	432	5	6
3	195	158	3	8	126	3	8
4	362	352	4	6	328	4	1
5	546	518	5	7	460	5	5
6	405	364	4	4	329	4	2
7	375	367	4	3	294	4	4
8	187	174	3	9	160	3	9
9	409	401	4	1	330	4	3
In	3374	3215	36		2829	37	
Total	6748	6430	72		5658	74	
Rating	70.8	69.6			71.6		
Slope	123	121			120		

THE MINNESOTA ILLUSTRATED

COKATO TOWN AND COUNTRY CLUB

9 Regulation Semi-Private

West Highway 12, P.O. Box 506
Cokato, Minnesota 55321
612/286-2007 Clubhouse/Proshop

HOURS	7 am to Dusk
SEASON	April to October

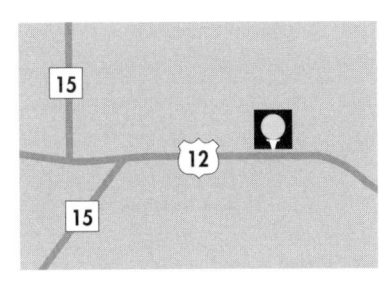

Located southwest of Cokato. Course is about 6 miles east of MN Highway 15 on U.S. Highway 12.

RESERVATIONS	612/286-2007 5 days
	Walk-on: good/fair

GREEN FEES	M-F	S-S
Adult	$15/10	$18/12
Senior	$14/9	$17/11
Junior	$15/10	$18/12
Twilight	NA	NA

PAYMENT	Credit: Visa® MasterCard®
	Non-local checks accepted

LEAGUES	Men: W (pm)
	Women: W (am)

MEMBERSHIPS	MGA

MANAGER	Sol Bernhardt

FEATURES		
Putting green	Y	
Driving range	Y	
Practice area	N	
Golf carts		
Power (gas)	Y	$10
Pull carts	Y	$1.75
Club rental	Y	$10
Club storage	Y	
Caddies	N	
Proshop		
Extended	Y	
Refreshments		
Restaurant	N	
Lounge	Y	
Snacks	Y	
Clubhouse		
Showers	Y	
Lockers	Y	$25/yr
Lodging	N	

	MEN				WOMEN		
	BACK	FRONT	PAR	HDCP	FRONT	PAR	HDCP
1	372	362	4	13	352	4	13
2	151	129	3	17	114	3	17
3	418	408	4	1	400	5	1
4	222	207	3	9	176	3	9
5	283	276	4	15	221	4	15
6	350	336	4	11	321	4	11
7	551	520	5	3	492	5	3
8	503	483	5	5	453	5	5
9	361	341	4	7	242	4	7
Out	3211	3062	36		2771	37	
10	372	362	4	14	352	4	14
11	151	129	3	18	114	3	18
12	418	408	4	2	400	5	2
13	222	207	3	10	176	3	10
14	283	276	4	16	221	4	16
15	350	336	4	12	321	4	12
16	551	520	5	4	492	5	4
17	503	483	5	6	453	5	6
18	361	341	4	8	242	4	8
In	3211	3062	36		2771	37	
Total	6422	6124	72		5542	74	
Rating	70.2	68.8			72.0		
Slope	119	117			124		

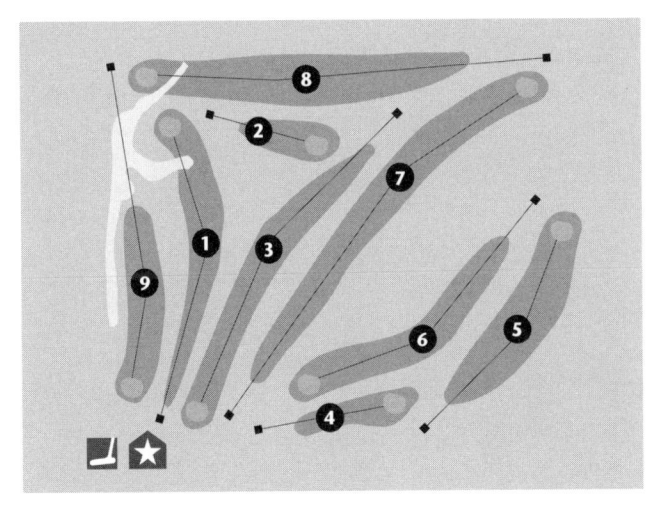

GOLF COURSE DIRECTORY

COLUMBIA GOLF COURSE

18 Regulation Public

3300 Central Avenue N.E.
Minneapolis, Minnesota 55418
612/789-2627 Clubhouse/Proshop

HOURS 6 am to 9 pm
SEASON April–November

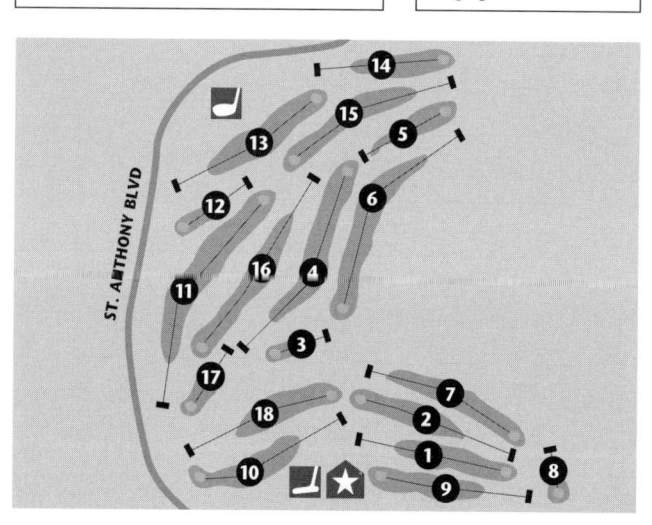

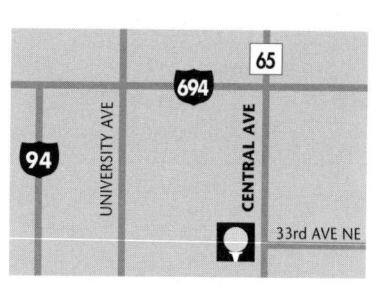

Located in northeast Minneapolis. Course entrance is about 3 miles south of I-694 on Central Avenue.

RESERVATIONS	612/789-2627 4 days	
	Weekends only $2 fee	
	Walk-on: good/good	
GREEN FEES	M-F	S-S
Adult	$18/13	$18/13
Senior	$18/13	$18/13
Junior	$18/13	$18/13
Twilight	$13 (4 pm)	$13 (4 pm)
PAYMENT	No credit cards accepted	
	Local checks only	
LEAGUES	Men: M-F (4-6 pm)	
	Women: M-F (4-6 pm)	
MEMBERSHIPS	PGA, LPGA, GCSAA, MGA	
PROFESSIONAL	William Turnquist	

FEATURES

Putting green	Y
Driving range	Y
Practice area	Y
Golf carts	
Power (gas)	Y $19/11
Pull carts	Y $2.50
Club rental	Y $4
Club storage	N
Caddies	N
Proshop	
Regular	Y
Refreshments	
Restaurant	N
Lounge	N
Snacks	Y
Clubhouse	
Showers	Y
Lockers	Y
Lodging	N

	\multicolumn{3}{c	}{MEN}	\multicolumn{3}{c	}{WOMEN}
	BACK	FRONT	PAR	HDCP	FRONT	PAR	HDCP
1	379	365	4	11	347	4	11
2	399	390	4	5	373	4	5
3	148	129	3	15	100	3	15
4	513	500	5	9	481	5	1
5	202	191	3	13	154	3	13
6	518	508	5	3	463	5	3
7	450	436	4	1	375	4	9
8	110	102	3	17	100	3	17
9	396	380	4	7	367	4	7
Out	3115	3001	35		2760	35	
10	340	330	4	10	315	4	12
11	547	532	5	4	476	5	4
12	187	170	3	16	136	3	18
13	410	400	4	6	355	4	8
14	334	321	4	14	305	4	14
15	422	407	4	2	375	4	6
16	494	480	5	12	462	5	2
17	169	154	3	18	137	3	16
18	346	336	4	8	321	4	10
In	3249	3130	36		2882	36	
Total	6364	6131	71		5642	71	
Rating	70.0	68.9			71.9		
Slope	121	119			123		

THE MINNESOTA ILLUSTRATED

COMO PARK GOLF COURSE

18 Regulation Public

1431 North Lexington Parkway
St. Paul, Minnesota 55103
612/488-9679 Clubhouse
612/488-9673 Proshop

HOURS	Dawn to Dusk
SEASON	April-November

FEATURES	
Putting green	Y
Driving range	N
Practice area	N
Golf carts	
Power (gas)	Y $20/12
Pull carts	Y $3
Club rental	Y $6
Club storage	N
Caddies	N
Proshop	
Extended	Y
Refreshments	
Restaurant	N
Lounge	N
Snacks	Y
Clubhouse	
Showers	Y
Lockers	N
Lodging	N

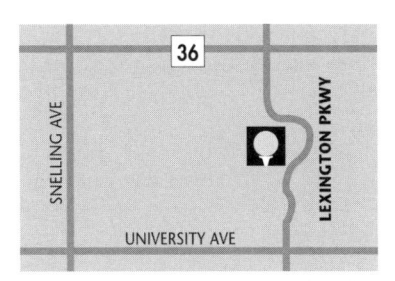

RESERVATIONS	612/488-9673
	$2 reservation fee
	Walk-on: good/fair

GREEN FEES	M-F	S-S
Adult	$18.50/13	$18.50/13
Senior	$9.25/6.50[1]	$9.25/6.50[2]
Junior	$9.25/6.50[1]	$9.25/6.50[2]
Twilight	$13 (4 pm)	$13 (4 pm)

[1] Rate before noon
[2] Rate after 4 pm

PAYMENT	Credit: Visa® MasterCard®
	Non-local checks accepted

LEAGUES	Various

MEMBERSHIPS	USGA, PGA, GCSAA, MGA

SUPERINTENDENT	Steve Dinger
PROFESSIONAL	John Shimpach

Located in St. Paul. Course is 2 1/2 miles north of University Ave or 2 miles south of Highway 36 on Lexington Parkway.

	MEN				WOMEN		
	BACK	FRONT	PAR	HDCP	FRONT	PAR	HDCP
1	345	337	4	9	320	4	9
2	325	300	4	15	270	4	13
3	345	330	4	13	288	4	7
4	310	304	4	17	300	4	11
5	335	330	4	7	325	4	5
6	166	158	3	11	129	3	17
7	425	410	4	1	335	4	1
8	515	489	5	3	435	5	3
9	200	185	3	5	140	3	15
Out	2966	2843	35		2542	35	
10	370	360	4	6	350	4	8
11	287	277	4	16	257	4	14
12	364	344	4	10	295	4	12
13	145	135	3	18	130	3	18
14	364	348	4	8	333	4	10
15	338	314	4	4	276	4	6
16	140	128	3	14	110	3	16
17	355	350	4	2	345	4	2
18	492	482	5	12	439	5	4
In	2855	2738	35		2535	35	
Total	5821	5581	70		5077	70	
Rating	68.6	67.4			70.4		
Slope	121	119			125		

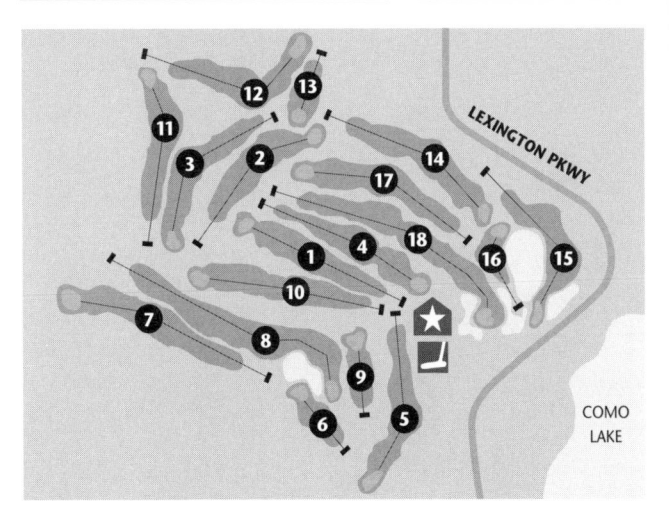

GOLF COURSE DIRECTORY

COTTONWOOD COUNTRY CLUB

9 Regulation Semi-Private

233 Shorewood Dr; Rt 1, Box 37 II
Cottonwood, Minnesota 56229
507/423-6335 Clubhouse/Proshop

HOURS 8 am to Dusk
SEASON April-November

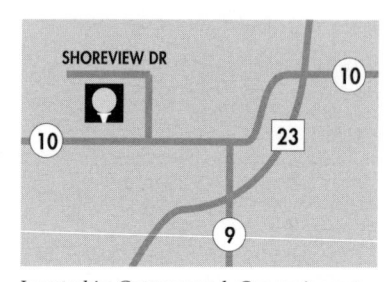

RESERVATIONS	No reservations accepted	
	Walk-on: good/good	
GREEN FEES	M-F	S-S
Adult	$12/8	$18/11
Senior	$12/8	$18/11
Junior	$12/8	$18/11
Twilight	NA	NA
PAYMENT	No credit cards accepted	
	Non-local checks accepted	
LEAGUES	Men: Th	
	Women: W	
MEMBERSHIPS	GCSAA, MGA	
MANAGER	Kathie Van Uden	
SUPERINTENDENT	Richard Rekedal	

FEATURES

Putting green	Y	
Driving range	Y	
Practice area	N	
Golf carts		
Power (gas)	Y	$12
Pull carts	Y	$1
Club rental	Y	$4
Club storage	N	
Caddies	N	
Proshop		
Regular	Y	
Refreshments		
Restaurant	Y	
Lounge	Y	
Snacks	Y	
Clubhouse		
Showers	N	
Lockers	N	
Lodging	N	

Located in Cottonwood. Course is west of MN Highway 23 on County Road 10, then north on Shoreview Drive.

	MEN				WOMEN		
	BACK	FRONT	PAR	HDCP	FRONT	PAR	HDCP
1	400	375	4	6	353	4	5
2	410	398	4	2	351	4	3
3	429	414	4	4	352	4	4
4	407	395	4	5	348	4	7
5	157	142	3	9	113	3	6
6	369	354	4	3	314	4	8
7	529	519	5	8	429	5	1
8	200	190	3	1	156	3	9
9	522	513	5	7	424	5	2
Out	3435	3325	36		2840	36	
1	400	375	4	6	353	4	5
2	410	398	4	2	351	4	3
3	429	414	4	4	352	4	4
4	407	395	4	5	348	4	7
5	157	142	3	9	113	3	6
6	369	354	4	3	314	4	8
7	529	519	5	8	429	5	1
8	200	190	3	1	156	3	9
9	522	513	5	7	424	5	2
In	3435	3325	36		2840	36	
Total	6870	6650	72		5680	72	
Rating	72.6	71.6			72.4		
Slope	122	120			120		

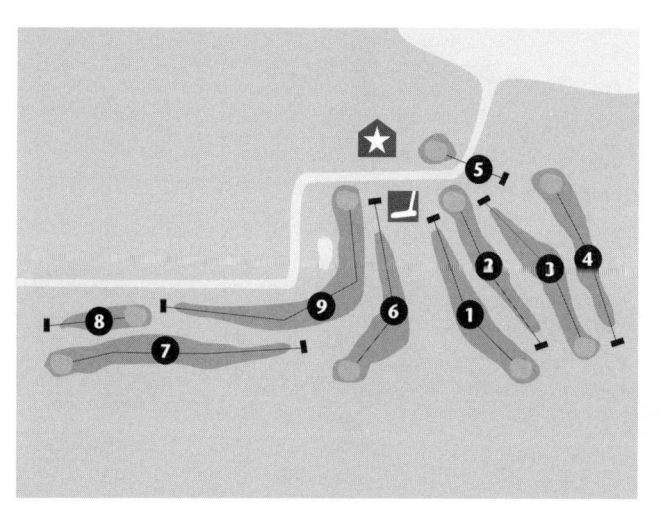

COUNTRY VIEW GOLF

18 Par-3 Public

2926 North Highway 61
Maplewood, Minnesota 55109
612/484-9809 Clubhouse/Proshop

HOURS	7 am to Dusk
SEASON	May–November

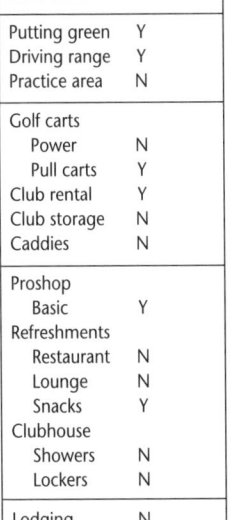

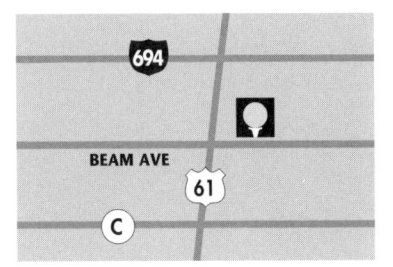

Located in Maplewood. Course entrance is about 3/4 mile south of I-694 on U.S. Highway 61.

RESERVATIONS	No reservations accepted
	Walk-on: good/fair
GREEN FEES	M-F	S-S
Adult	$10.75/6.75	$11.25/7.25
Senior	$9.25/5.25	$11.25/7.25
Junior	$10.75/6.75	$11.25/7.25
Twilight	NA	NA
	Night golfing rate: $7.25
PAYMENT	No credit cards accepted
	Local checks only
LEAGUES	Men: Various
	Women: Various
MEMBERSHIPS	None
OWNER	Mogren Brothers
PROFESSIONAL	Keith Deloia

FEATURES	
Putting green	Y
Driving range	Y
Practice area	N
Golf carts	
Power	N
Pull carts	Y
Club rental	Y
Club storage	N
Caddies	N
Proshop	
Basic	Y
Refreshments	
Restaurant	N
Lounge	N
Snacks	Y
Clubhouse	
Showers	N
Lockers	N
Lodging	N

	MEN			**WOMEN**		
	FRONT	PAR	HDCP	FRONT	PAR	HDCP
1	148	3		148	3	
2	149	3		149	3	
3	151	3		151	3	
4	110	3		110	3	
5	167	3		167	3	
6	158	3		158	3	
7	155	3		155	3	
8	172	3		172	3	
9	158	3		158	3	
FRONT	1368	27		1368	27	
1	143	3		143	3	
2	135	3		135	3	
3	155	3		155	3	
4	136	3		136	3	
5	170	3		170	3	
6	124	3		124	3	
7	167	3		167	3	
8	118	3		118	3	
9	152	3		152	3	
BACK	1300	27		1300	27	
Total	2668	54		2668	54	
Rating	NA			NA		
Slope	NA			NA		

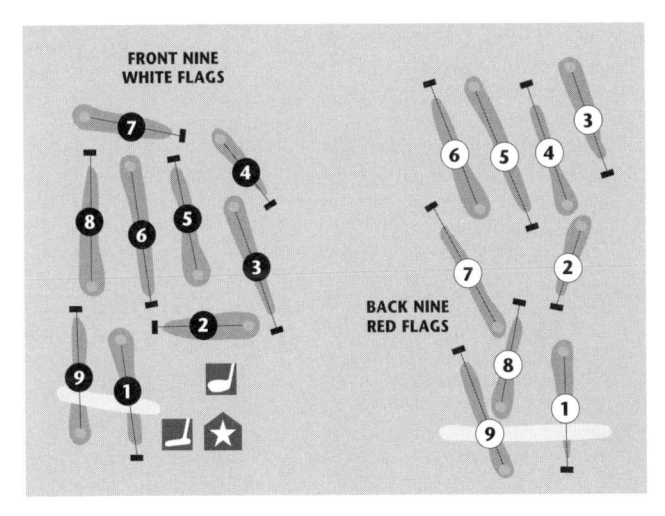

GOLF COURSE DIRECTORY

COUNTRYSIDE GOLF CLUB

9 Regulation Public

East Luon Street, P.O. Box 247
Minneota, Minnesota 56264
507/872-6335 Clubhouse/Proshop

RESERVATIONS	507/872-6335	
	Walk-on: good/fair	

GREEN FEES	M-F	S-S
Adult	Call	Call
Senior	Call	Call
Junior	Call	Call
Twilight	NA	NA

PAYMENT	No credit cards accepted
	Non-local checks accepted

LEAGUES	Men:	Various
	Women:	Various

MEMBERSHIPS	USGA, MGA

PROFESSIONAL	Call

HOURS	Dawn to Dusk
SEASON	April to October

FEATURES	
Putting green	Y
Driving range	N
Practice area	N
Golf carts	
Power (gas)	Y
Pull carts	Y
Club rental	N
Club storage	N
Caddies	N
Proshop	
Regular	Y
Refreshments	
Restaurant	N
Lounge	Y
Snacks	Y
Clubhouse	
Showers	N
Lockers	N
Lodging	N

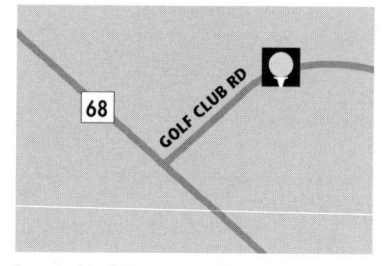

Located in Minneota. Course entrance is east of MN Highway 68 on Golf Club Road.

	\multicolumn{4}{c}{MEN}	\multicolumn{3}{c}{WOMEN}
	BACK	FRONT	PAR	HDCP	FRONT	PAR	HDCP
1	500	477	5	7	425	5	5
2	404	394	4	4	370	4	1
3	150	135	3	8	130	3	7
4	426	416	4	3	347	4	3
5	410	401	4	1	338	4	2
6	228	185	3	2	174	3	4
7	488	475	5	6	429	5	6
8	340	328	4	5	240	4	8
9	314	302	4	9	225	4	9
Out	3260	3152	36		2678	36	
1	500	477	5	7	425	5	5
2	404	394	4	4	370	4	1
3	150	135	3	8	130	3	7
4	426	416	4	3	347	4	3
5	410	401	4	1	338	4	2
6	228	185	3	2	174	3	4
7	488	475	5	6	429	5	6
8	340	328	4	5	240	4	8
9	314	302	4	9	225	4	9
In	3260	3152	36		2678	36	
Total	6520	6304	72		5356	72	
Rating	68.8	68.0			70.7		
Slope	104	102			110		

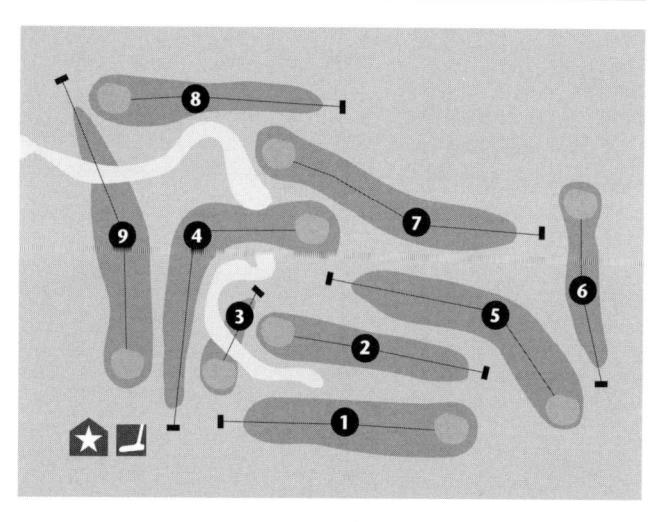

THE MINNESOTA ILLUSTRATED

CREEKS BEND GOLF COURSE

18 Regulation Public

26826 Langford Avenue
New Prague, Minnesota 56071
612/758-7200 Clubhouse/Proshop

HOURS	Dawn to Dusk
SEASON	April to October

| **RESERVATIONS** | 612/758-7200 4 days |
| | Walk-on: good/fair |

GREEN FEES	M-F	S-S
Adult	$18/10	$18/10
Senior	$15/8	$18/10
Junior	$18/10	$18/10
Twilight	NA	NA

| **PAYMENT** | No credit cards accepted |
| | Non-local checks accepted |

| **LEAGUES** | Men: Various |
| | Women: Various |

| **MEMBERSHIPS** | USGA, MGA |

OWNER	Peter & Judy Highum
	Rand & Lisa Kubes
	Dave & Jean Sticha

FEATURES	
Putting green	Y
Driving range	Y
Practice area	Y
Golf carts	
Power (gas)	Y $18/10
Pull carts	Y
Club rental	Y
Club storage	N
Caddies	N
Proshop	
Entended	Y
Refreshments	
Restaurant	N
Lounge	Y
Snacks	Y
Clubhouse	
Showers	N
Lockers	N
Lodging	N

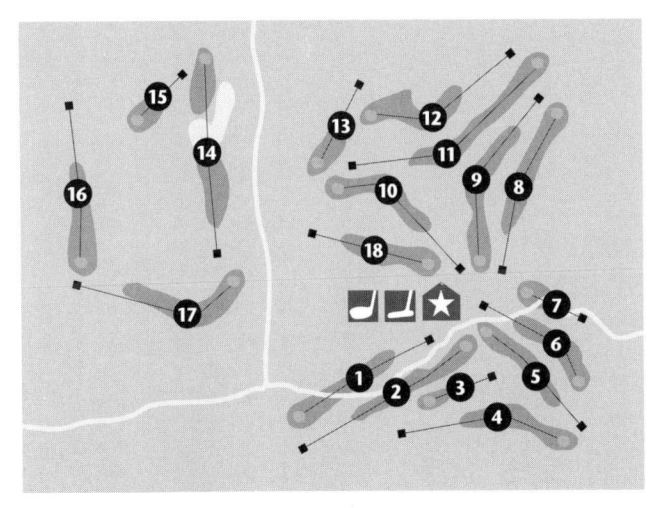

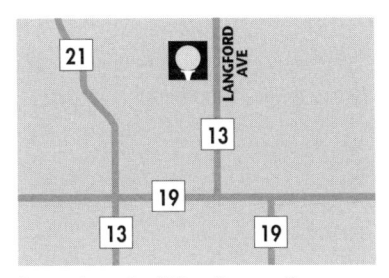

Located north of New Prague. Course entrance is about three miles north of MN Highway 19 on MN Highway 13.

	MEN			WOMEN		
	BACK	FRONT	PAR	HDCP	FRONT	PAR	HDCP
1	374	331	4		280	4	
2	450	431	5		288	5	
3	150	142	3		121	3	
4	383	361	4		297	4	
5	343	329	4		310	4	
6	293	293	4		216	4	
7	161	152	3		119	3	
8	356	346	4		294	4	
9	468	447	5		398	5	
Out	2978	2832	36		2323	36	
10	380	359	4		315	4	
11	513	488	5		475	5	
12	333	319	4		267	4	
13	204	195	3		156	3	
14	449	438	5		376	5	
15	189	176	3		106	3	
16	367	342	4		285	4	
17	396	372	4		316	4	
18	396	339	4		287	4	
In	3227	3028	36		2583	36	
Total	6205	5860	72		4906	72	
Rating	69.9	68.3			68.2		
Slope	121	117			115		

GOLF COURSE DIRECTORY

CRESTWOOD HILLS GOLF COURSE

9 Regulation Public

3340 39th Avenue Northeast
Alexandria, Minnesota 56308
612/762-8223 Clubhouse/Proshop

HOURS	7 am to Dusk
SEASON	April-November

| **RESERVATIONS** | 612/762-8223 3 days |
| | Walk-on: good/good |

GREEN FEES	M-F	S-S
Adult	$18/10.50	$19/11
Senior	$12/7	$19/11
Junior	$12/7	$19/11
Twilight	$8	NA

| **PAYMENT** | No credit cards accepted |
| | Non-local checks accepted |

LEAGUES	Men: T
	Women: W
	Couples: F (pm)

| **MEMBERSHIPS** | MGA |

| **OWNER/MGR** | Melvin & Alice Miller |

FEATURES	
Putting green	Y
Driving range	N
Practice area	N
Golf carts	
Power (gas)	Y
Pull carts	Y
Club rental	Y
Club storage	Y
Caddies	N
Proshop	
Basic	Y
Refreshments	
Restaurant	N
Lounge	Y
Snacks	Y
Clubhouse	
Showers	N
Lockers	N
Lodging	N

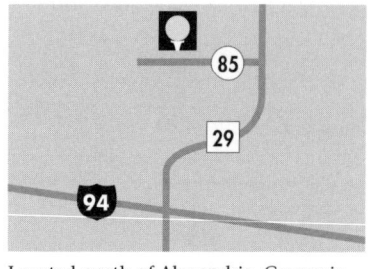

Located north of Alexandria. Course is north of I-94 on MN Highway 29, then 1/2 mile west on County Road 85.

	MEN				**WOMEN**		
	BACK	FRONT	PAR	HDCP	FRONT	PAR	HDCP
1	391	341	4	5	331	4	5
2	260	256	4	7	222	4	7
3	320	310	4	3	297	4	3
4	158	148	3	6	100	3	6
5	495	485	5	1	461	5	1
6	150	130	3	8	86	3	8
7	285	275	4	4	239	4	4
8	127	122	3	9	102	3	9
9	506	499	5	2	418	5	2
Out	2692	2566	35		2276	35	
1	391	341	4	5	331	4	5
2	260	256	4	7	222	4	7
3	320	310	4	3	297	4	3
4	158	148	3	6	100	3	6
5	495	485	5	1	461	5	1
6	150	130	3	8	86	3	8
7	285	275	4	4	239	4	4
8	127	122	3	9	102	3	9
9	506	499	5	2	418	5	2
In	2692	2566	35		2276	35	
Total	5384	5132	70		4552	70	
Rating	NA	65.4			65.8		
Slope	NA	110			112		

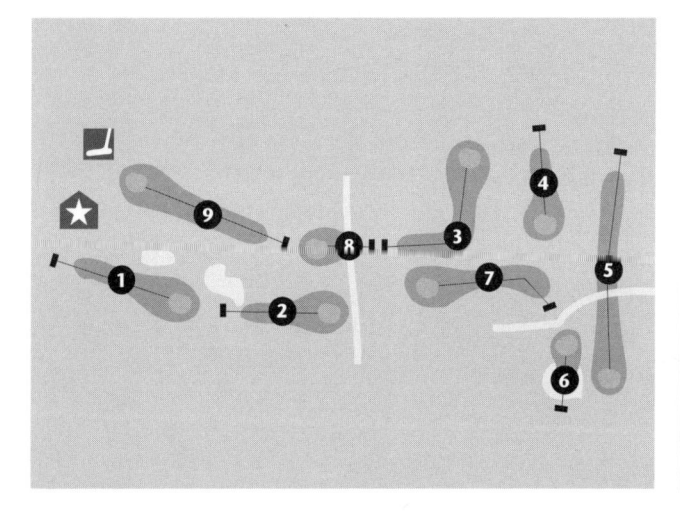

THE MINNESOTA ILLUSTRATED

CROSSLAKE GOLF COURSE

9 Executive Public

HC 83, P.O. Box 106
Crosslake, Minnesota 56442
218/692-3680 Clubhouse/Proshop

HOURS	6 am to Dusk
SEASON	May to October

RESERVATIONS	218/692-3680	
	Walk-on: good/fair	
GREEN FEES	M-F	S-S
Adult	$6	$6.50
Senior	$6	$6.50
Junior	$5	$6.50
Twilight	NA	NA
PAYMENT	No credit cards accepted	
	Non-local checks accepted	
LEAGUES	Men: Various	
	Women: Various	
MEMBERSHIPS	NGF	
OWNER	Jack & Dee Stone	
PROFESSIONAL	Jack Stone	

FEATURES		
Putting green	Y	
Driving range	Y	
Practice area	N	
Golf carts		
Power	Y	$8
Pull carts	Y	$1.25
Club rental	Y	$3
Club storage	N	
Caddies	N	
Proshop		
Regular	Y	
Refreshments		
Restaurant	N	
Lounge	N	
Snacks	Y	
Clubhouse		
Showers	N	
Lockers	N	
Lodging	N	

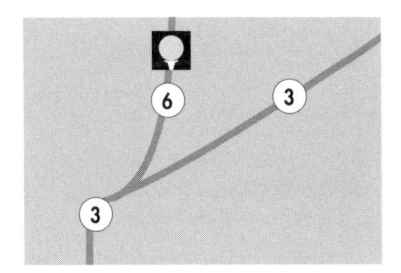

Located in Crosslake. Course entrance is about 1/2 mile north of County Road 3 on County Road 6.

	MEN			WOMEN		
	FRONT	PAR	HDCP	FRONT	PAR	HDCP
1	145	3		145	3	
2	142	3		142	3	
3	255	4		255	4	
4	145	3		145	3	
5	100	3		100	3	
6	120	3		120	3	
7	300	4		300	4	
8	175	3		175	3	
9	165	3		165	3	
Out	1547	29		1547	29	
1	145	3		145	3	
2	142	3		142	3	
3	255	4		255	4	
4	145	3		145	3	
5	100	3		100	3	
6	120	3		120	3	
7	300	4		300	4	
8	175	3		175	3	
9	165	3		165	3	
In	1547	29		1547	29	
Total	3094	58		3094	58	
Rating	NA			NA		
Slope	NA			NA		

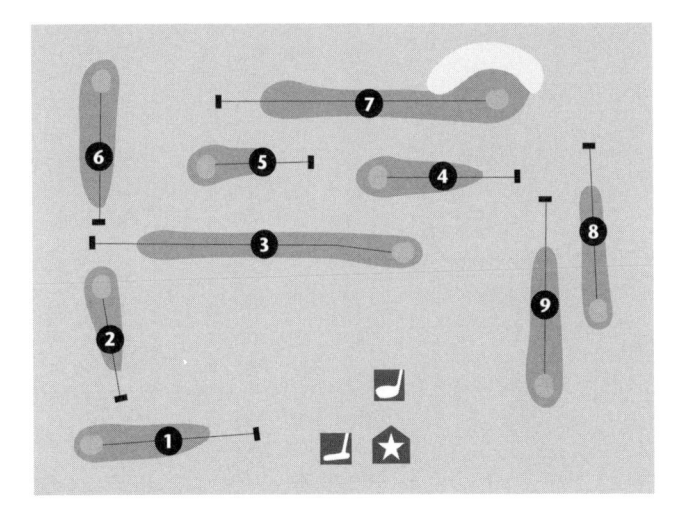

GOLF COURSE DIRECTORY

CRYSTAL LAKE GOLF COURSE

18 Regulation Public

16725 Innsbrook Drive
Lakeville, Minnesota 55044
612/432-4440 Clubhouse
612/432-6566 Proshop

HOURS	6 am to Dusk
SEASON	April-November

FEATURES	
Putting green	Y
Driving range	Y
Practice area	Y
Golf carts	
Power (gas)	Y $20/14
Pull carts	Y
Club rental	Y
Club storage	Y
Caddies	N
Proshop	
Basic	Y
Refreshments	
Restaurant	Y
Lounge	Y
Snacks	Y
Clubhouse	
Showers	Y
Lockers	Y
Lodging	N

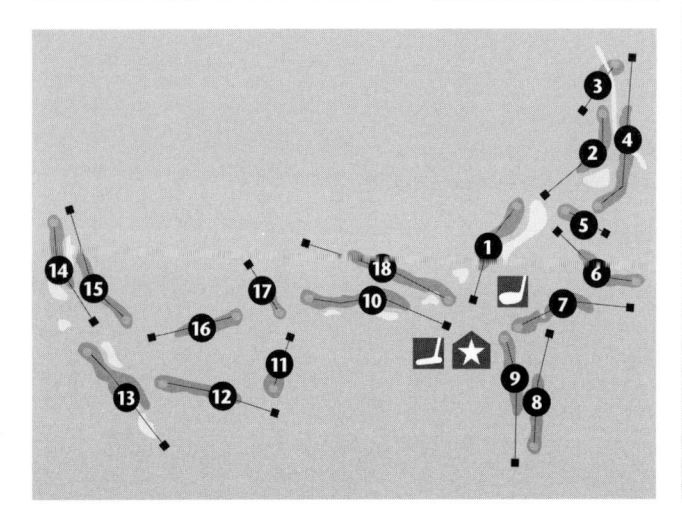

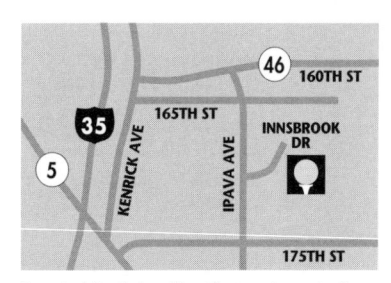

Located in Lakeville. Course is east of Kenrick Avenue on Cty Rd 46, south on Ipava Ave, then east on Innsbrook Dr.

RESERVATIONS	612/432-6566 3 days
	Walk-on: good/good

GREEN FEES	M-F	S-S
Adult	$19/12	$23
Senior	$13	$23
Junior	$19/12	$23
Twilight	NA	$ 23 (4 pm)*
*Fee includes power cart.		

PAYMENT	Credit: Visa® MasterCard®
	Non-local checks accepted

LEAGUES	Men: Th
	Women: T

MEMBERSHIPS	USGA, PGA, GCSAA, MGA

PROFESSIONAL	Joe Kreuser

	MEN					**WOMEN**		
	BACK	FRONT	PAR	HDCP	FRONT	PAR	HDCP
1	366	341	4	11	286	4	7
2	374	347	4	9	264	4	9
3	168	146	3	15	111	3	15
4	516	489	5	1	407	5	1
5	145	137	3	17	107	3	17
6	364	335	4	13	284	4	3
7	380	347	4	7	299	4	11
8	379	341	4	5	291	4	5
9	376	366	4	3	309	4	13
Out	3083	2849	35		2358	35	
10	490	464	5	2	382	5	6
11	180	160	3	16	110	3	10
12	397	369	4	4	286	4	12
13	396	373	4	14	311	4	14
14	355	329	4	10	269	4	8
15	419	389	4	12	329	4	16
16	334	304	4	6	256	4	4
17	127	109	3	18	94	3	18
18	525	492	5	8	410	5	2
In	3223	2989	36		2447	36	
Total	6306	5838	71		4805	71	
Rating	70.4	68.2			68.5		
Slope	122	118			119		

CUYUNA COUNTRY CLUB

18 Regulation Semi-Private

P.O. Box 40
Deerwood, Minnesota 56444
218/534-3489 Clubhouse/Proshop

HOURS	6 am to Dusk
SEASON	April-November

| RESERVATIONS | 218/534-3489 3 days |
| | Walk-on: good/fair |

GREEN FEES	M-F	S-S
Adult	$26/16	$28/19
Senior	$26/16	$28/19
Junior	$26/16	$28/19
Twilight	NA	NA

| PAYMENT | Credit: Visa® MasterCard® |
| | Local checks only |

| LEAGUES | Various |

| MEMBERSHIPS | USGA, GCSAA, CMAA, MGA |

| MANAGER | Keith Enstad |
| SUPERINTENDENT | Dale Lundgren |

FEATURES		
Putting green	Y	
Driving range	Y	$2
Practice area	Y	
Golf carts		
Power (gas)	Y	$22
Pull carts	N	
Club rental	Y	$5
Club storage	N	
Caddies	N	
Proshop		
Extended	Y	
Refreshments		
Restaurant	Y	
Lounge	Y	
Snacks	Y	
Clubhouse		
Showers	N	
Lockers	N	
Lodging	N	

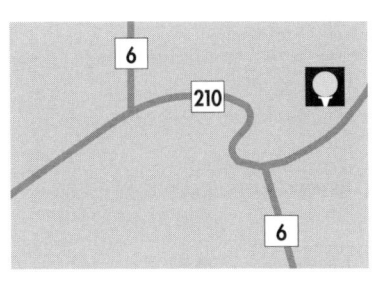

Located east of Deerwood. Course is about 1 mile east of MN Highway 6 on the north side of MN Highway 210.

		MEN				WOMEN		
	BACK	FRONT	PAR	HDCP		FRONT	PAR	HDCP
1	349	341	4	15		341	4	13
2	341	333	4	13		333	4	15
3	147	135	3	17		130	3	17
4	512	502	5	11		468	5	5
5	394	385	4	1		361	4	1
6	196	190	3	7		190	3	9
7	404	397	4	5		318	4	11
8	382	373	4	9		365	4	3
9	410	403	4	3		373	4	7
Out	3135	3059	35			2879	35	
10	355	344	4	14		308	4	12
11	414	404	4	2		359	4	2
12	152	139	3	18		124	3	18
13	483	471	5	10		406	5	6
14	351	339	4	12		295	4	14
15	328	320	4	6		296	4	10
16	508	498	5	4		462	5	4
17	167	155	3	16		145	3	16
18	380	370	4	8		353	4	8
In	3138	3040	36			2748	36	
Total	6273	6099	71			5627	71	
Rating	71.3	70.4				73.6		
Slope	129	127				135		

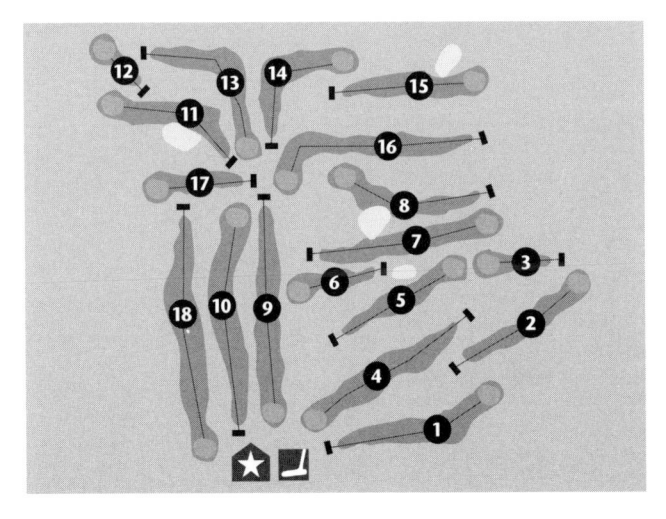

GOLF COURSE DIRECTORY

DAHLGREEN GOLF CLUB

18 Regulation Semi-Private

6940 Dahlgren Road
Chaska, Minnesota 55318
612/466-5915 Clubhouse
612/448-7463 Proshop

RESERVATIONS	612/448-7463 3 days
	Walk-on: good/fair

GREEN FEES	M-F	S-S
Adult	$18/13	$25/15
Senior	$12/8	$25/15
Junior	$17/12	$25/15
Twilight	NA	NA

PAYMENT	No credit cards accepted
	Non-local checks accepted

LEAGUES	Men: Th
	Women: T

MEMBERSHIPS	PGA, GCSAA, MGA

MANAGER	Joyce Tessman
SUPERINTENDENT	Keith Flatebo
PROFESSIONAL	Mike Malone

HOURS	6 am to Dusk
SEASON	April-November

FEATURES	
Putting green	Y
Driving range	Y
Practice area	Y
Golf carts	
Power (gas)	Y
Pull carts	Y
Club rental	Y
Club storage	Y
Caddies	N
Proshop	
Extended	Y
Refreshments	
Restaurant	Y
Lounge	Y
Snacks	Y
Clubhouse	
Showers	Y
Lockers	Y
Lodging	N

Located about 4 miles west of Chaska. Course is 1/2 mile south of Hwy 212 on Cty Rd 43, then west on Dahlgren Road.

	MEN				WOMEN		
	BACK	FRONT	PAR	HDCP	FRONT	PAR	HDCP
1	346	336	4	13	302	4	9
2	180	165	3	17	120	3	17
3	523	493	5	7	448	5	5
4	375	365	4	9	310	4	7
5	477	465	4	1	365	4	1
6	181	171	3	15	115	3	15
7	506	495	5	5	355	5	11
8	451	416	4	3	349	4	3
9	367	360	4	11	300	4	13
Out	3406	3266	36		2796	36	
10	373	362	4	14	328	4	12
11	550	525	5	6	429	5	2
12	170	158	3	16	108	3	18
13	417	411	4	2	320	4	10
14	177	170	3	18	152	3	16
15	400	392	4	12	317	4	8
16	414	400	4	4	351	4	4
17	459	379	4	10	347	4	6
18	516	503	5	8	401	5	14
In	3476	3300	36		2753	36	
Total	6882	6566	72		5417	72	
Rating	72.6	71.3			70.6		
Slope	126	123			117		

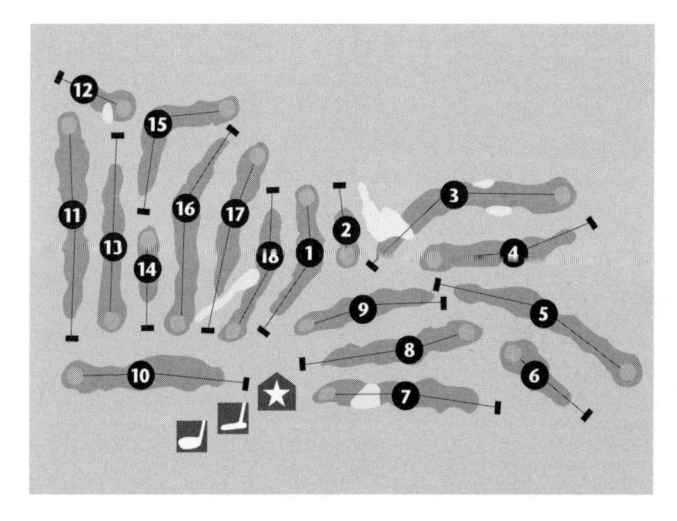

THE MINNESOTA ILLUSTRATED

DAWSON GOLF CLUB

9 Regulation Public

15th and Locust Street, P.O. Box 655
Dawson, Minnesota 56232
612/769-2212 Clubhouse/Proshop

HOURS 7 am to Dusk
SEASON April-November

RESERVATIONS	612/769-2212	
	Walk-on: good/good	

GREEN FEES	M-F	S-S
Adult	$9/7	$13/10
Senior	$9/7	$13/10
Junior	$9/7	$13/10
Twilight	NA	NA

PAYMENT No credit cards accepted
Non-local checks accepted

LEAGUES Men: Th
Women: T

MEMBERSHIPS USGA, MGA

SUPERINTENDENT LeRoy Bleyhl

FEATURES

Putting green	Y	
Driving range	N	
Practice area	Y	
Golf carts		
Power	Y	$8
Pull carts	Y	$3
Club rental	Y	$5
Club storage	N	
Caddies	N	
Proshop		
Basic	Y	
Refreshments		
Restaurant	N	
Lounge	Y	
Snacks	Y	
Clubhouse		
Showers	N	
Lockers	N	
Lodging	N	

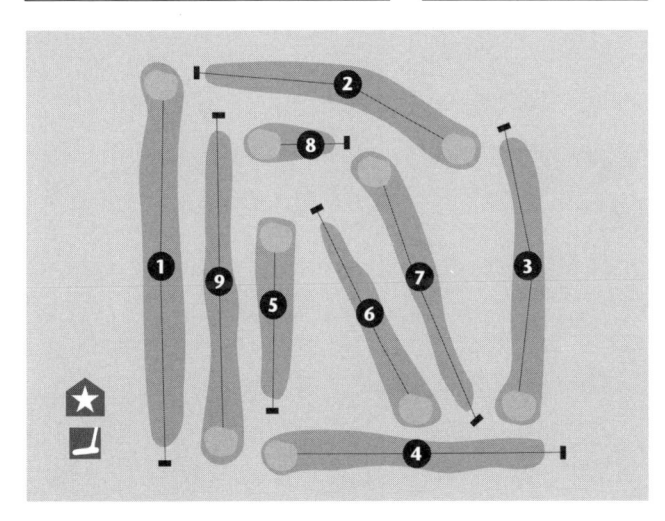

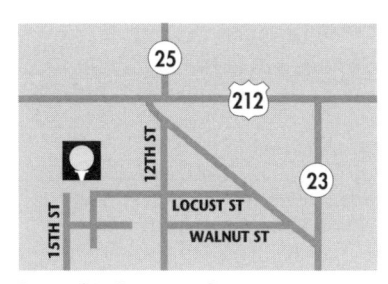

Located in Dawson. Course entrance is on the south of U.S. Highway 212 on 12th Street, then west on Locust Street.

	MEN			WOMEN		
	FRONT	PAR	HDCP	FRONT	PAR	HDCP
1	404	4	1	404	4	1
2	325	4	4	325	4	4
3	316	4	6	316	4	6
4	310	4	7	310	4	7
5	282	4	8	282	4	8
6	363	4	2	363	4	2
7	330	4	5	330	4	5
8	149	3	9	143	3	9
9	358	4	3	358	4	3
Out	2837	35		2837	35	
1	404	4	1	404	4	1
2	325	4	4	325	4	4
3	316	4	6	316	4	6
4	310	4	7	310	4	7
5	282	4	8	282	4	8
6	363	4	2	363	4	2
7	330	4	5	330	4	5
8	149	3	9	143	3	9
9	358	4	3	358	4	3
In	2837	35		2837	35	
Total	5674	70		5674	70	
Rating	67.0			73.0		
Slope	110			118		

GOLF COURSE DIRECTORY

DAYTONA COUNTRY CLUB

18 Regulation Public

14740 Lawndale Lane
Dayton, Minnesota 55327
612/427-6110 Clubhouse/Proshop

HOURS 6:30 am - Dusk
SEASON April–November

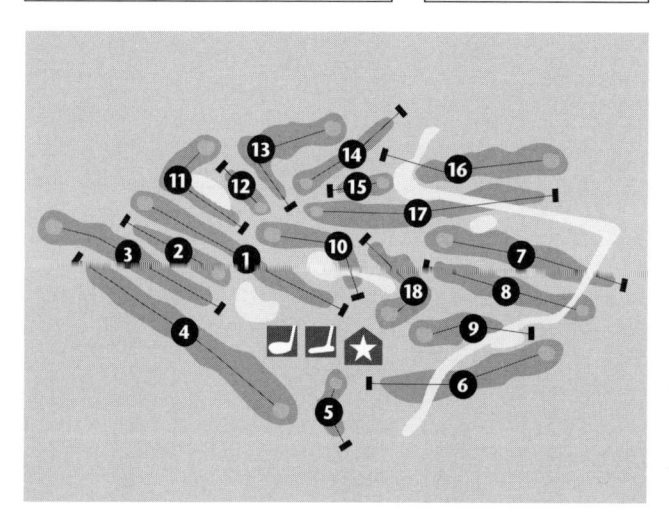

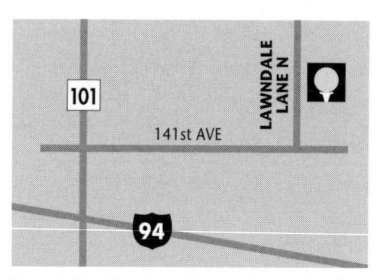

Located in Dayton. Course is north of I-94 on Highway 101, east on 141st Avenue, then north on Lawndale Lane.

RESERVATIONS	612/427-6110 1 week	
	Walk-on: good/fair	
GREEN FEES	M-F	S-S
Adult	$17/12	$20/14
Senior	$9.50/7.50	$20/14
Junior	$9.50/7.50	$20/14
Twilight	NA	NA
PAYMENT	No credit cards accepted	
	Local checks only	
LEAGUES	Men:	W, Sat (am)
		Th (4:30 pm)
	Women:	W, Sat (am)
		Th (5 pm)
MEMBERSHIPS	USGA, GCSAA, MGA	
OWNER	Gerald McCann	
SUPERINTENDENT	Chris. Hasbrouck	
PROFESSIONAL	Cyndy Meyer	

FEATURES		
Putting green	Y	
Driving range	Y	$1
Practice area	N	
Golf carts		
Power (gas)	Y	$21
Pull carts	Y	$2
Club rental	Y	$10/5
Club storage	N	
Caddies	N	
Proshop		
Regular	Y	
Refreshments		
Restaurant	Y	
Lounge	Y	
Snacks	Y	
Clubhouse		
Showers	Y	
Lockers	Y	
Lodging	N	

	MEN			WOMEN		
	FRONT	PAR	HDCP	FRONT	PAR	HDCP
1	495	5	10	424	5	8
2	172	3	16	172	3	16
3	365	4	12	306	4	12
4	502	5	8	395	5	6
5	294	4	18	288	4	14
6	381	4	2	309	4	10
7	384	4	4	326	4	4
8	358	4	6	286	4	2
9	160	3	14	140	3	18
Out	3111	36		2646	36	
10	351	4	9	320	4	1
11	401	4	1	351	5	15
12	150	3	17	150	3	17
13	544	5	7	401	5	13
14	395	4	3	304	4	7
15	176	3	15	167	3	11
16	325	4	11	320	4	5
17	542	5	5	447	5	9
18	368	4	13	362	4	3
In	3252	36		2822	37	
Total	6363	72		5468	73	
Rating	69.7			70.7		
Slope	118			112		

THE MINNESOTA ILLUSTRATED

DEER RUN GOLF CLUB

18 Regulation Public

8661 Deer Run Drive
Victoria, Minnesota 55386
612/443-2351 Clubhouse/Proshop

RESERVATIONS	612/443-2351 3 days	
	Walk-on: fair/fair	

GREEN FEES	M-F	S-S
Adult	$21/16	$25/16
Senior	$21/16	$25/16
Junior	$21/16	$25/16
Twilight	NA	NA

PAYMENT	Credit: Visa® MasterCard®
	Non-local checks accepted

LEAGUES	Various

MEMBERSHIPS	USGA, NGF, PGA, GCSAA, CMAA, MGA

SUPERINTENDENT Tim George
PROFESSIONAL Tom Abts

HOURS	Dawn to Dusk
SEASON	April–November

FEATURES		
Putting green	Y	
Driving range	Y	$3
Practice area	N	
Golf carts		
Power (gas)	Y	$21
Pull carts	Y	$3
Club rental	N	
Club storage	N	
Caddies	N	
Proshop		
Regular	Y	
Refreshments		
Restaurant	Y	
Lounge	N	
Snacks	Y	
Clubhouse		
Showers	Y	
Lockers	Y	
Lodging	N	

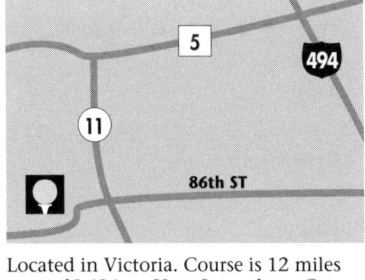

Located in Victoria. Course is 12 miles west of I-494 on Hwy 5, south on Cty Road 11, then 3/4 miles west on 6th St.

	MEN				WOMEN		
	BACK	FRONT	PAR	HDCP	FRONT	PAR	HDCP
1	381	371	4	15	361	4	15
2	156	149	3	17	129	3	17
3	416	401	4	1	361	4	5
4	498	495	5	5	438	5	3
5	383	375	4	9	365	4	9
6	196	186	3	13	166	3	13
7	361	351	4	11	341	4	11
8	478	463	5	3	423	5	1
9	369	353	4	7	343	4	7
Out	3238	3144	36		2927	36	
10	434	424	4	4	390	4	4
11	361	351	4	12	316	4	10
12	350	340	4	16	306	4	14
13	339	329	4	10	295	4	8
14	184	176	3	8	141	3	12
15	370	355	4	2	320	4	6
16	138	130	3	18	110	3	18
17	317	307	4	14	272	4	16
18	534	519	5	6	464	5	2
In	3027	2931	35		2614	35	
Total	6265	6075	71		5541	71	
Rating	70.5	69.6			72.1		
Slope	122	120			121		

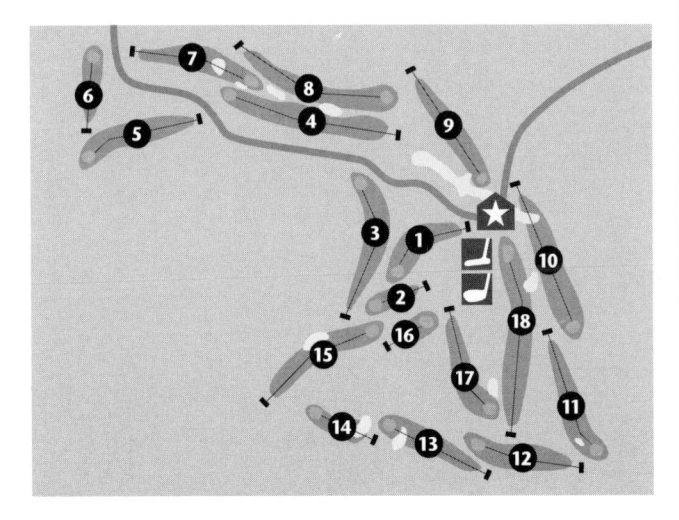

GOLF COURSE DIRECTORY

DELLWOOD HILLS GOLF CLUB

18 Regulation Private

29 East Highway 96
Dellwood, Minnesota 55110
612/426-3218 Clubhouse
612/426-4733 Proshop

RESERVATIONS	612/426-4733	
	Members only	
GREEN FEES	M-F	S-S
Adult	$35	$40
Senior	$35	$40
Junior	$35	$40
Twilight	NA	NA
PAYMENT	No credit cards accepted	
	Non-local checks accepted	
LEAGUES	Various	
MEMBERSHIPS	USGA, NGF, PGA, GCSAA,	
	CMAA, MGA	
MANAGER	Jeff Belting	
SUPERINTENDENT	John Bichner	
PROFESSIONAL	Cathy Bremer Lombritto	

HOURS	7 am to Dusk
SEASON	April-November

FEATURES	
Putting green	Y
Driving range	Y
Practice area	Y
Golf carts	
Power (gas)	Y
Pull carts	Y
Club rental	Y
Club storage	Y
Caddies	Y
Proshop	
Extended	Y
Refreshments	
Restaurant	Y
Lounge	Y
Snacks	Y
Clubhouse	
Showers	Y
Lockers	Y
Lodging	N

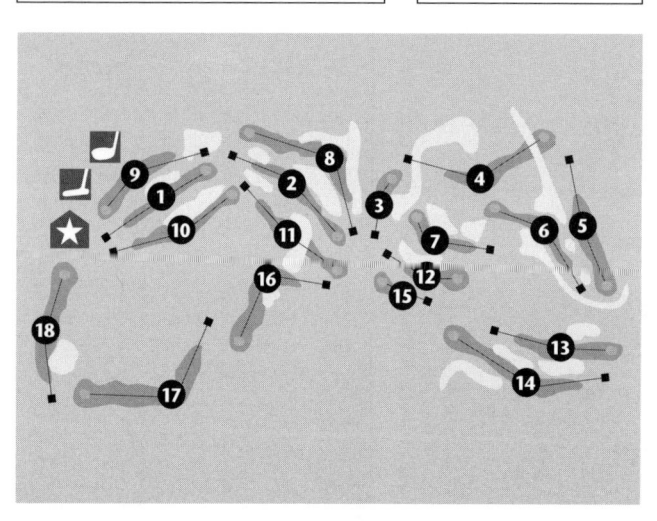

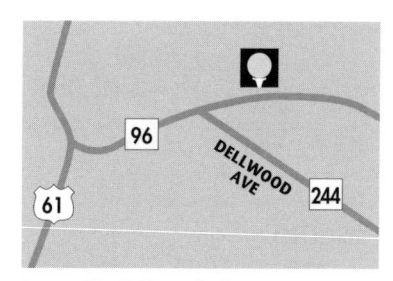

Located in Dellwood. Course entrance is about 1 3/4 miles east of US Highway 61 on the north side of MN Highway 96.

	MEN				WOMEN		
	BACK	FRONT	PAR	HDCP	FRONT	PAR	HDCP
1	386	355	4	15	320	4	13
2	436	367	4	11	279	4	15
3	175	145	3	17	120	3	17
4	483	473	5	5	404	5	1
5	435	410	4	1	326	4	11
6	413	370	4	9	340	3	3
7	240	195	3	13	188	3	7
8	516	498	5	3	416	5	5
9	401	367	4	7	322	4	9
Out	3485	3180	36		2715	36	
10	435	405	4	10	308	4	16
11	435	405	4	2	327	4	12
12	228	200	3	16	157	3	14
13	428	383	4	12	361	4	10
14	545	520	5	6	454	5	6
15	210	170	3	18	148	3	18
16	462	415	4	4	353	4	4
17	510	495	5	14	460	5	2
18	380	348	4	8	301	4	8
In	3633	3341	36		2869	36	
Total	7118	6521	72		5584	72	
Rating	74.8	72.1			73.6		
Slope	135	129			124		

THE MINNESOTA ILLUSTRATED

DETROIT COUNTRY CLUB
PINE TO PALM COURSE/18 Regulation Public

P.O. Box 1591
Detroit Lakes, Minnesota 56501
218/847-5790 Clubhouse/Proshop

HOURS	7 am to Dusk
SEASON	April-November

RESERVATIONS	218/847-5790 1 week
	Walk-on: good/poor

GREEN FEES	M-F	S-S
Adult	$22/14	$22/14
Senior	$22/14	$22/14
Junior	$22/14	$22/14
Twilight	NA	NA

PAYMENT	Credit: Visa® MasterCard®
	Non-local checks accepted

LEAGUES	Various

MEMBERSHIPS	USGA, PGA, GCSAA, MGA

SUPERINTENDENT	Brad Klein
PROFESSIONAL	Mark Holm

FEATURES	
Putting green	Y
Driving range	Y
Practice area	Y
Golf carts	
Power	Y $20
Pull carts	Y
Club rental	Y
Club storage	Y
Caddies	N
Proshop	
Extended	Y
Refreshments	
Restaurant	Y
Lounge	Y
Snacks	Y
Clubhouse	
Showers	Y
Lockers	Y
Lodging	N

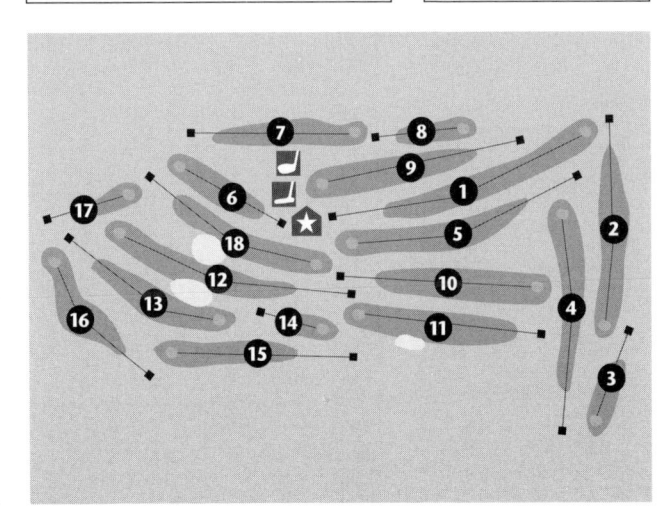

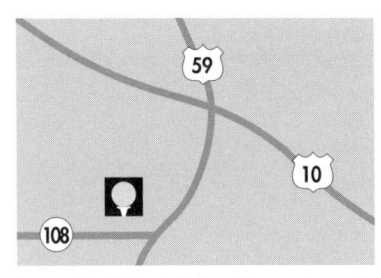

Located in Detroit Lakes. Course is south of U.S. Highway 10 on U.S. Highway 59, then west on County Road 108.

		MEN			WOMEN		
	FRONT	PAR	HDCP	FRONT	PAR	HDCP
1	512	5	3	512	5	3
2	371	4	9	360	4	5
3	213	3	15	184	3	13
4	401	4	1	368	4	1
5	459	5	5	435	5	9
6	280	4	13	258	4	17
7	286	4	11	266	4	11
8	174	3	17	161	3	15
9	396	4	7	345	4	7
Out	3092	36		2879	36	
10	384	4	2	364	4	2
11	355	4	6	312	4	10
12	450	5	4	450	5	6
13	353	4	12	353	4	4
14	151	3	16	151	3	12
15	351	4	8	284	4	16
16	289	4	14	289	4	14
17	160	3	18	160	3	18
18	356	4	10	296	4	8
In	2849	35		2659	35	
Total	5941	71		5508	71	
Rating	69.5			71.8		
Slope	124			127		

GOLF COURSE DIRECTORY

DETROIT COUNTRY CLUB
LAKEVIEW COURSE/18 Executive Public

P.O. Box 1591
Detroit Lakes, Minnesota 56501
218/847-5790 Clubhouse/Proshop

HOURS	7 am to Dusk
SEASON	April-November

RESERVATIONS	218/847-5790 1 week
	Walk-on: good/poor

GREEN FEES	M-F	S-S
Adult	$14/9	$14/9
Senior	$14/9	$14/9
Junior	$14/9	$14/9
Twilight	NA	NA

PAYMENT	Credit: Visa® MasterCard®
	Non-local checks accepted

LEAGUES	Various

MEMBERSHIPS	USGA, PGA, GCSAA, MGA

SUPERINTENDENT	Brad Klein
PROFESSIONAL	Mark Holm

FEATURES	
Putting green	Y
Driving range	Y
Practice area	Y
Golf carts	
Power	Y $20
Pull carts	Y
Club rental	Y
Club storage	Y
Caddies	N
Proshop	
Extended	Y
Refreshments	
Restaurant	Y
Lounge	Y
Snacks	Y
Clubhouse	
Showers	Y
Lockers	Y
Lodging	N

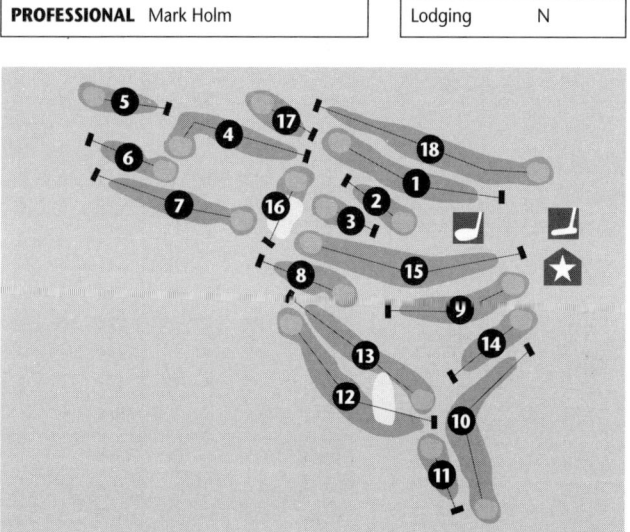

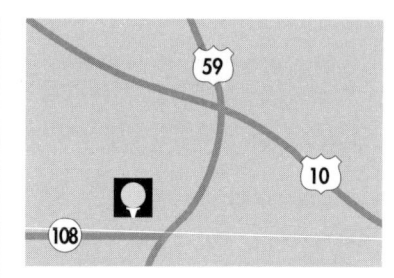

Located in Detroit Lakes. Course is south of U.S. Highway 10 on U.S. Highway 59, then west on County Road 108.

	MEN			WOMEN		
	FRONT	PAR	HDCP	FRONT	PAR	HDCP
1	300	4	3	288	4	17
2	125	3	17	120	3	5
3	133	3	15	123	3	15
4	253	4	5	225	4	1
5	180	3	11	170	3	13
6	159	3	13	145	3	11
7	328	4	1	311	4	3
8	163	3	9	150	3	9
9	300	4	7	288	4	7
Out	1941	31		1820	31	
10	341	4	10	332	4	12
11	132	3	18	115	3	18
12	345	4	6	247	4	10
13	344	4	2	333	4	2
14	125	3	16	111	3	16
15	369	4	8	358	4	6
16	134	3	14	119	3	8
17	126	3	12	116	3	14
18	450	5	4	435	5	4
In	2366	33		2166	33	
Total	4307	64		3986	64	
Rating	60.2			61.7		
Slope	96			97		

DODGE COUNTRY CLUB

9 Regulation Semi-Private

West Highway 14, P.O. Box 429
Dodge Center, Minnesota 55321
507/374-2374 Clubhouse/Proshop

HOURS	Dawn to Dusk
SEASON	April to October

RESERVATIONS	507/374-2374
	Walk-on: good/fair

GREEN FEES	M-F	S-S
Adult	$12/8	$14/10
Senior	$12/8	$14/10
Junior	$12/8	$14/10
Twilight	NA	NA

PAYMENT	No credit cards accepted
	Non-local checks accepted

LEAGUES	Men: None
	Women: None

MEMBERSHIPS	USGA, MGA

PROFESSIONAL	Call

FEATURES	
Putting green	Y
Driving range	N
Practice area	N
Golf carts	
Power (gas)	Y $14/8
Pull carts	Y $2
Club rental	Y $3
Club storage	N
Caddies	N
Proshop	
Regular	Y
Refreshments	
Restaurant	N
Lounge	N
Snacks	Y
Clubhouse	
Showers	N
Lockers	N
Lodging	N

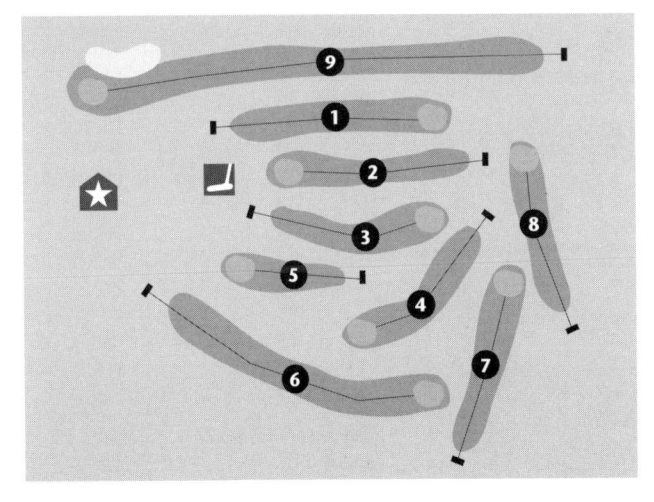

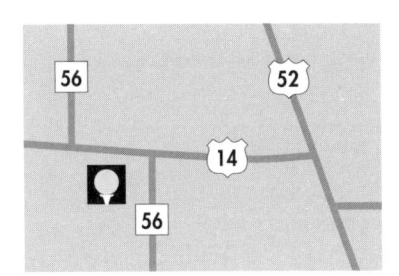

Located west of Dodge Center. Course is about one mile west of Dodge Center on U.S. Highway 14.

	MEN			**WOMEN**		
	FRONT	PAR	HDCP	FRONT	PAR	HDCP
1	353	4	4	317	4	4
2	347	4	1	317	3	1
3	321	4	7	285	3	7
4	348	4	6	310	3	6
5	134	3	8	115	3	8
6	443	5	9	393	3	9
7	368	4	5	309	3	5
8	185	3	3	174	3	3
9	501	5	2	454	3	2
Out	3000	36		2674	36	
1	353	4	4	317	4	4
2	347	4	1	317	3	1
3	321	4	7	285	3	7
4	348	4	6	310	3	6
5	134	3	8	115	3	8
6	443	5	9	393	3	9
7	368	4	5	309	3	5
8	185	3	3	174	3	3
9	501	5	2	454	3	2
In	3000	36		2674	36	
Total	6000	72		5348	72	
Rating	67.6			69.2		
Slope	107			108		

GOLF COURSE DIRECTORY

DOUBLE EAGLE GOLF CLUB

9 Regulation Public

P.O. Box 365
Eagle Bend, Minnesota 56446
218/738-5155 Clubhouse/Proshop

HOURS	7 am to Dusk
SEASON	April to October

RESERVATIONS	218/738-5155 1 week
	Walk-on: good/fair

GREEN FEES	M-F	S-S
Adult	$18/11	$18/11
Senior	$18/11	$18/11
Junior	$18/11	$18/11
Twilight	NA	NA

PAYMENT	No credit cards accepted
	Non-local checks accepted

LEAGUES	Men: W (4:30-6 pm)
	Women: Th (4:30-6 pm)
	Other: M (4:30-6 pm)

MEMBERSHIPS	None

OWNER	Ron Weibye
MANAGER	Rod Weibye
SUPERINTENDENT	Steve Weibye

FEATURES	
Putting green	Y
Driving range	Y
Practice area	N
Golf carts	
Power (gas)	Y
Pull carts	Y
Club rental	Y
Club storage	Y
Caddies	N
Proshop	
Extended	Y
Refreshments	
Restaurant	Y
Lounge	Y
Snacks	Y
Clubhouse	
Showers	N
Lockers	N
Lodging	N

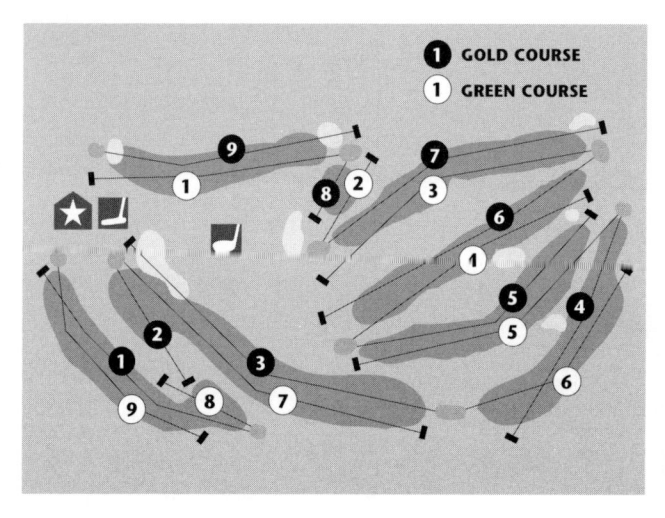

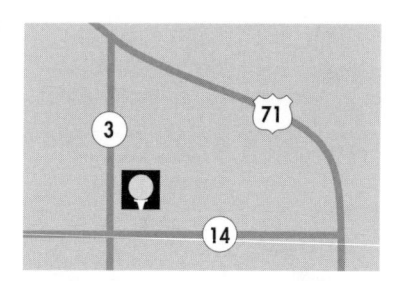

Located about 4 miles south of Eagle Bend. Course entrance is south of U.S. Highway 71 on County Road 3.

		MEN				WOMEN		
	BACK	FRONT	PAR	HDCP		FRONT	PAR	HDCP
1	431	416	4	3		396	4	2
2	200	184	3	8		136	3	9
3	572	557	5	2		433	5	1
4	368	353	4	7		343	4	6
5	460	450	4	1		427	4	4
6	500	475	5	4		429	5	3
7	485	471	5	5		359	5	5
8	144	129	3	9		114	3	8
9	376	366	4	6		283	4	7
GOLD	3536	3401	37			2920	37	
Total	7072	6802	74			5840	74	
Rating	73.3	72.1				72.8		
1	378	353	4	4		304	4	4
2	172	160	3	8		148	3	8
3	503	485	5	5		437	5	3
4	429	377	4	3		347	4	1
5	433	418	4	2		366	4	5
6	332	322	4	7		312	4	7
7	548	532	5	1		431	5	2
8	166	154	3	9		104	3	9
9	376	366	4	6		341	4	6
GREEN	3337	3167	36			2790	36	
Total	6674	6334	72			5580	72	
Rating	71.6	70.0				71.2		

- GOLD COURSE
- GREEN COURSE

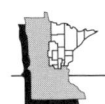

DRIFTWOOD RESORT AND GOLF COURSE

9 Executive Public

Route 1, Box 404
Pine River, Minnesota 56474
218/568-4221 Clubhouse/Proshop

HOURS	Dawn to Dusk
SEASON	April-November

RESERVATIONS	218/568-4221 1 day
	Walk-on: fair/fair

GREEN FEES	M-F	S-S
Adult	$14/8	$16/10
Senior	$14/8	$16/10
Junior	$14/8	$16/10
Twilight	NA	NA

PAYMENT	Credit: Visa® MC® AmEx®
	Non-local checks accepted

LEAGUES	None

MEMBERSHIPS	None

OWNER	The Leagjeld Family

FEATURES		
Putting green	N	
Driving range	N	
Practice area	N	
Golf carts		
Power (gas)	Y	$10/8
Pull carts	Y	
Club rental	Y	
Club storage	N	
Caddies	N	
Proshop		
Regular	Y	
Refreshments		
Restaurant	Y	
Lounge	N	
Snacks	Y	
Clubhouse		
Showers	N	
Lockers	N	
Lodging	Y	Call

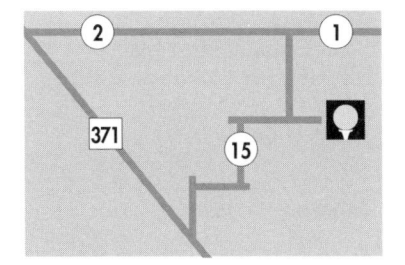

Located southeast of Pine River. Course entrance is about 6 miles northeast of MN Highway 371 on County Road 15.

	MEN			WOMEN		
	FRONT	PAR	HDCP	FRONT	PAR	HDCP
1	90	3		90	3	
2	150	3		150	3	
3	104	3		104	3	
4	110	3		110	3	
5	150	3		150	3	
6	96	3		96	3	
7	167	3		167	3	
8	220	4		220	4	
9	180	3		180	3	
Out	1237	28		1237	28	
1	90	3		90	3	
2	150	3		150	3	
3	104	3		104	3	
4	110	3		110	3	
5	150	3		150	3	
6	96	3		96	3	
7	167	3		167	3	
8	220	4		220	4	
9	180	3		180	3	
In	1237	28		1237	28	
Total	2474	56		2474	56	
Rating	NA			NA		
Slope	NA			NA		

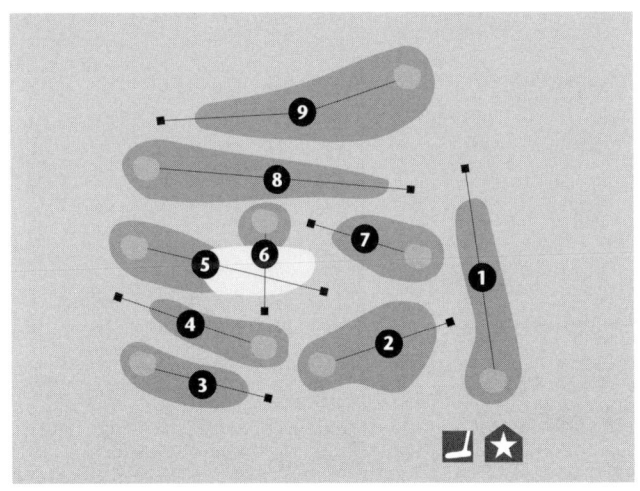

GOLF COURSE DIRECTORY

DWAN GOLF CLUB

18 Regulation Public

3301 West 110th Street
Bloomington, Minnesota 55431
612/948-8702 Clubhouse/Proshop

RESERVATIONS	612/948-8702 1 day	
	Walk-on: good/fair	
GREEN FEES	M-F	S-S
Adult	$17/11	$17/11
Senior	$17/11	$17/11
Junior	$17/11	$17/11
Twilight	NA	NA
	Patron packages available	
PAYMENT	No credit cards accepted	
	Local checks only	
LEAGUES	Various	
MEMBERSHIPS	USGA, NGF, PGA, GCSAA, MGA	
MANAGER	Rick Sitek	
SUPERINTENDENT	Arnie Bodhaine	
PROFESSIONAL	Rick Sitek	

HOURS	Dawn to Dusk
SEASON	April-November
FEATURES	
Putting green	Y
Driving range	N
Practice area	Y
Golf carts	
Power (gas)	Y
Pull carts	Y
Club rental	N
Club storage	N
Caddies	N
Proshop	
Basic	Y
Refreshments	
Restaurant	N
Lounge	Y
Snacks	Y
Clubhouse	
Showers	Y
Lockers	Y
Lodging	N

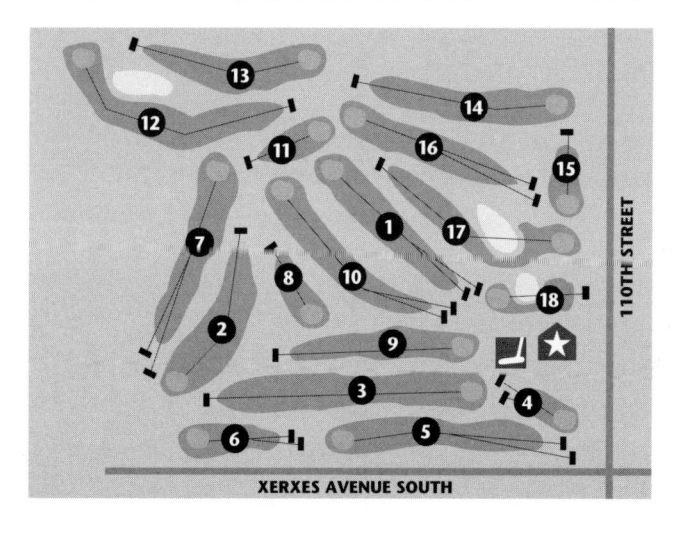

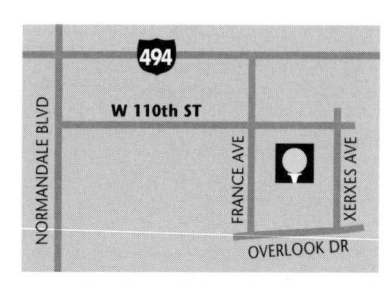

Located in Bloomington. Course is south of I-494 on France Avenue, then east on 110th Street.

	MEN				**WOMEN**		
	BACK	FRONT	PAR	HDCP	FRONT	PAR	HDCP
1	325	320	4	7	294	4	7
2	325	300	4	17	245	4	17
3	495	485	5	9	440	5	9
4	145	129	3	15	96	3	15
5	380	373	4	1	342	4	1
6	195	181	3	3	147	3	3
7	370	344	4	5	293	4	5
8	175	168	3	11	125	3	11
9	350	340	4	13	310	4	13
Out	2760	2640	34		2292	34	
10	355	347	4	4	319	4	4
11	125	120	3	18	111	3	18
12	480	450	5	8	390	5	8
13	335	327	4	10	280	4	10
14	380	373	4	6	290	4	6
15	170	160	3	12	110	3	12
16	330	321	4	14	287	4	14
17	415	409	4	2	329	4	2
18	135	128	3	16	110	3	16
In	2725	2635	34		2226	34	
Total	5485	5275	68		4518	68	
Rating	65.4	64.5			65.3		
Slope	109	107			110		

EAGLE RIDGE GOLF COURSE

18 Regulation Public

Highway 169 West, Box 197
Coleraine, Minnesota 55722
218/245-2217 Clubhouse/Proshop

HOURS	Dawn to Dusk
SEASON	April-November

FEATURES	
Putting green	Y
Driving range	Y
Practice area	N
Golf carts	
Power (gas)	Y
Pull carts	Y
Club rental	Y
Club storage	N
Caddies	N
Proshop	
Extended	Y
Refreshments	
Restaurant	N
Lounge	Y
Snacks	Y
Clubhouse	
Showers	N
Lockers	N
Lodging	N

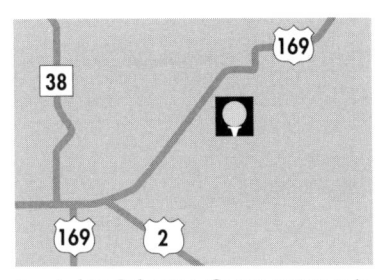

RESERVATIONS	218/245-2217 1 week
	Walk-on: good/fair

GREEN FEES	M-F	S-S
Adult	Call	Call
Senior	Call	Call
Junior	Call	Call
Twilight	NA	NA

PAYMENT	Credit: Visa® MasterCard®
	Local checks only

LEAGUES	Various

MEMBERSHIPS	GCSAA, MGA

OWNER	City of Coleraine
MANAGER	Eagle Ridge Management Corp
SUPERINTENDENT	Kurt Johnson

Located in Coleraine. Course entrance is about 5 miles north of U.S. Highway 2 on U.S. Highway 169.

	MEN				WOMEN		
	BACK	FRONT	PAR	HDCP	FRONT	PAR	HDCP
1	396	371	4	7	305	4	7
2	549	513	5	13	460	5	13
3	373	341	4	15	285	4	15
4	183	154	3	17	108	3	17
5	423	391	4	1	334	4	1
6	537	503	5	3	420	5	3
7	154	138	3	11	116	3	11
8	374	353	4	9	308	4	9
9	403	370	4	5	317	4	5
Out	3392	3134	36		2653	36	
10	414	382	4	4	320	4	4
11	374	342	4	16	287	4	16
12	204	175	3	6	113	3	6
13	432	397	4	2	335	4	2
14	559	524	5	10	441	5	10
15	349	328	4	14	263	4	14
16	506	486	5	12	396	5	12
17	148	123	3	18	103	3	18
18	394	363	4	8	309	4	8
In	3380	3120	36		2567	36	
Total	6772	6254	72		5220	72	
Rating	NA	NA			NA		
Slope	NA	NA			NA		

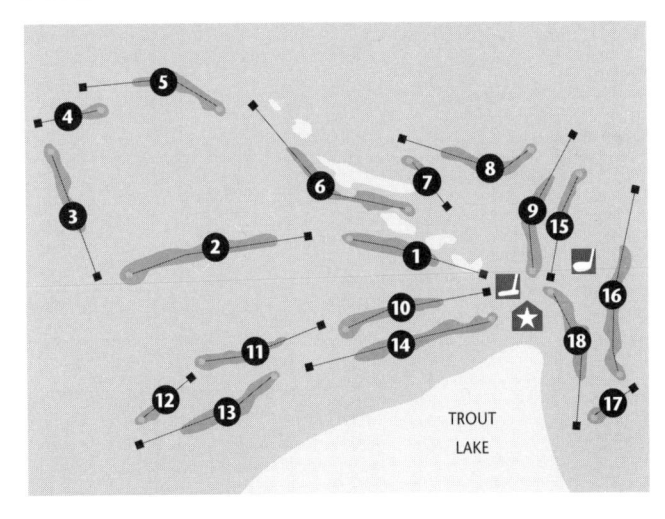

TROUT LAKE

GOLF COURSE DIRECTORY

89

EAGLE TRACE GOLFERS CLUB

18 Regulation Public

1100 Main Street
Clearwater, Minnesota 55320
320/558-6066 Clubhouse
320/558-4653 Proshop

RESERVATIONS	320/558-4653
	Walk-on: good/good

GREEN FEES	M-F	S-S
Adult	$20/12	$22/15
Senior	$18/10	$20/13
Junior	$20/12	$22/15
Twilight	NA	NA

PAYMENT	Credit: Visa® MasterCard®
	Non-local checks accepted

LEAGUES	Various

MEMBERSHIPS	MGA

OWNER	Clearwater Development

HOURS	7 am to Dusk
SEASON	April-November

FEATURES

Putting green	Y
Driving range	N
Practice area	Y
Golf carts	
Power (gas)	Y
Pull carts	Y
Club rental	Y
Club storage	N
Caddies	N
Proshop	
Extended	Y
Refreshments	
Restaurant	N
Lounge	Y
Snacks	Y
Clubhouse	
Showers	N
Lockers	N
Lodging	N

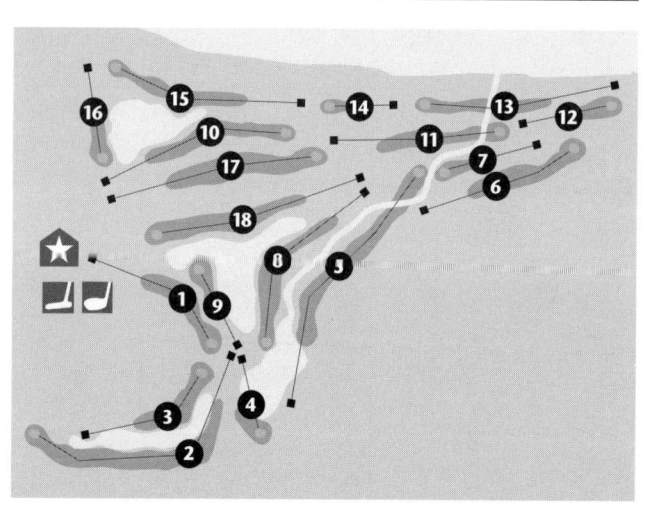

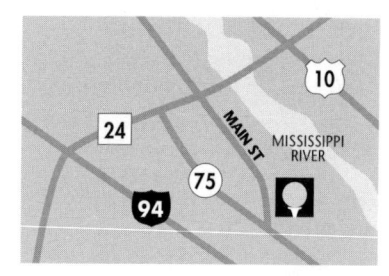

Located in Clearwater. Course is north of I-94 on MN Hwy 24, south on County Road 75, then north on Main Street.

	MEN				WOMEN		
	BACK	FRONT	PAR	HDCP	FRONT	PAR	HDCP
1	316	304	4	15	292	4	15
2	575	559	5	1	369	5	1
3	333	330	4	9	327	4	9
4	182	179	3	3	150	3	3
5	585	523	5	5	380	5	5
6	282	279	4	13	276	4	13
7	126	120	3	17	114	3	17
8	368	358	4	11	348	4	11
9	209	194	3	7	179	3	7
Out	2976	2846	35		2435	35	
10	409	385	4	6	361	4	6
11	364	353	4	2	272	4	2
12	192	178	3	16	158	3	16
13	333	330	4	8	327	4	8
14	180	157	3	12	146	3	12
15	433	418	5	14	403	5	14
16	168	153	3	18	138	3	18
17	429	414	4	10	399	4	10
18	475	427	5	4	420	5	4
In	2983	2815	35		2624	35	
Total	5959	5661	70		5059	70	
Rating	69.2	67.8			70.2		
Slope	119	117			123		

EASTWOOD GOLF CLUB

18 Regulation Public

3505 Eastwood Road Southeast
Rochester, Minnesota 55904
507/281-6173 Clubhouse/Proshop

HOURS	7 am to Dusk
SEASON	April–November

RESERVATIONS	507/281-6173 2 days
	Walk-on: good/fair

GREEN FEES	M-F	S-S
Adult	$16.50/10.50	$16.50/10.50
Senior	$16.50/10.50	$16.50/10.50
Junior	$16.50/10.50	$16.50/10.50
Twilight	NA	NA

PAYMENT	Credit: Visa® MasterCard®
	Credit for merchandise only
	Non-local checks accepted

LEAGUES	Men: None
	Women: None

MEMBERSHIPS	PGA, GCSAA, MGA

OWNER	City of Rochester
SUPERINTENDENT	Jim Bartels
PROFESSIONAL	Frank Taylor

FEATURES		
Putting green	Y	
Driving range	Y	$3
Practice area	Y	
Golf carts		
Power (gas)	Y	$16
Pull carts	Y	$2
Club rental	Y	$5.25
Club storage	N	
Caddies	N	
Proshop		
Extended	Y	
Refreshments		
Restaurant	Y	
Lounge	N	
Snacks	Y	
Clubhouse		
Showers	Y	
Lockers	Y	
Lodging	N	

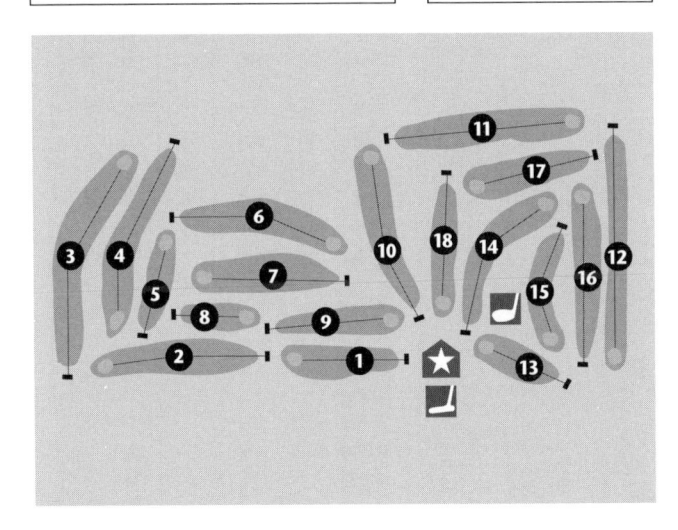

Located in Rochester. Course entrance is south of U.S. Highway 14 on Marion Road, then west on East River Road.

	MEN			**WOMEN**		
	FRONT	PAR	HDCP	FRONT	PAR	HDCP
1	348	4	13	340	4	8
2	471	5	8	401	5	2
3	462	4	2	378	4	4
4	334	4	16	274	4	13
5	162	3	18	162	3	17
6	411	4	5	292	4	9
7	411	4	4	278	4	12
8	183	3	9	183	3	16
9	360	4	12	320	4	5
Out	3142	35		2628	35	
10	329	4	14	329	4	10
11	488	5	3	411	5	1
12	428	4	1	301	4	11
13	205	3	10	154	3	15
14	356	4	11	356	4	6
15	327	4	15	314	4	7
16	395	4	6	339	4	3
17	326	4	17	275	4	14
18	182	3	7	182	3	18
In	3036	35		2661	35	
Total	6178	70		5289	70	
Rating	69.9			71.0		
Slope	119			121		

GOLF COURSE DIRECTORY

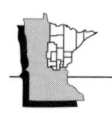

EDGE OF THE WILDERNESS GOLF COURSE

9 Regulation Public

P.O. Box 37
Big Fork, Minnesota 56628
218/743-3626 Clubhouse/Proshop

HOURS	7 am to Dusk
SEASON	April to October

RESERVATIONS	218/743-3626
	Walk-on: good/good

GREEN FEES	M-F	S-S
Adult	$15/10	$18/12
Senior	$10/7*	$18/12
Junior	$15/10	$18/12
Twilight	$5 (4 pm)	$5 (4 pm)
	*Special rate for M,W only	

PAYMENT	No credit cards accepted
	Non-local checks accepted

LEAGUES	Men: T (5:30 pm)
	Women: W (9:30 am)
	Senior: Th (9:30 am)

MEMBERSHIPS	MGA

MANAGER	Ron Bailey
SUPERINTENDENT	Gene Madsen

FEATURES		
Putting green	Y	
Driving range	Y	$2.50
Practice area	Y	
Golf carts		
Power (elec)	Y	
Pull carts	Y	
Club rental	Y	
Club storage	N	
Caddies	N	
Proshop		
Regular	Y	
Refreshments		
Restaurant	N	
Lounge	Y	
Snacks	Y	
Clubhouse		
Showers	N	
Lockers	N	
Lodging	N	

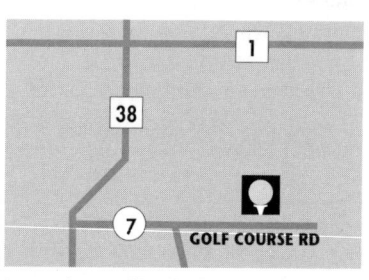

Located east of Big Fork. Course is one mile east of Highway 38 on Cty Road 7, then east on Golf Course Road.

		MEN				WOMEN		
	BACK	FRONT	PAR	HDCP		FRONT	PAR	HDCP
1	468	460	5	1		387	5	2
2	191	183	3	3		175	3	3
3	515	508	5	2		430	5	1
4	282	280	4	6		263	4	4
5	413	407	4	5		352	5	1
6	349	341	4	7		333	5	3
7	352	345	4	8		338	4	5
8	321	313	4	9		305	4	11
9	128	126	3	4		102	3	13
Out	3019	2963	36			2685	38	
1	468	460	5	1		387	5	2
2	191	183	3	3		175	3	3
3	515	508	5	2		430	5	1
4	282	280	4	6		263	4	4
5	413	407	4	5		352	5	1
6	349	341	4	7		333	5	3
7	352	345	4	8		338	4	5
8	321	313	4	9		305	4	11
9	128	126	3	4		102	3	13
In	3019	2963	36			2685	38	
Total	6038	5926	72			5370	76	
Rating	67.4	66.8				69.4		
Slope	105	104				110		

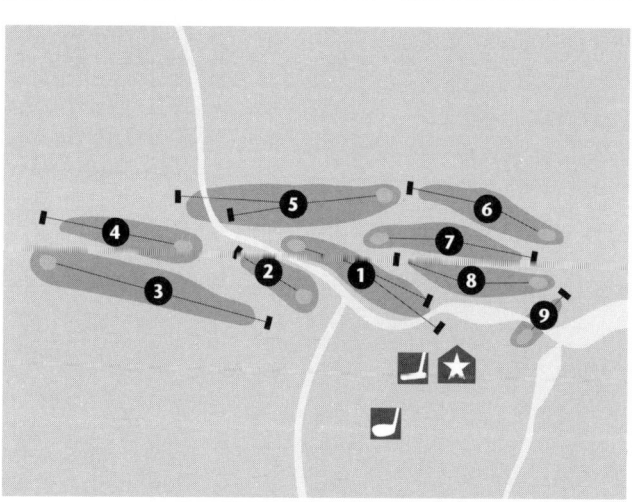

EDINA COUNTRY CLUB

18 Regulation Private

5100 Wooddale Avenue
Edina, Minnesota 55424
612/927-7151 Clubhouse
612/927-5775 Proshop

HOURS	Dawn to Dusk	
SEASON	April to October	

FEATURES		
Putting green	Y	
Driving range	Y	
Practice area	Y	
Golf carts		
Power (elec)	Y	$30
Pull carts	Y	$4
Club rental	Y	$10
Club storage	Y	
Caddies	Y	$10-14
Proshop		
Extended	Y	
Refreshments		
Restaurant	Y	
Lounge	Y	
Snacks	Y	
Clubhouse		
Showers	Y	
Lockers	Y	
Lodging	N	

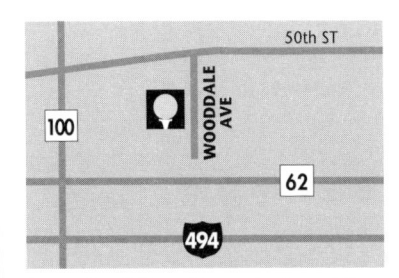

RESERVATIONS	612/927-5775 1 week Members only	
GREEN FEES	M-F	S-S
Adult	$75/37.50	$75/37.50
Senior	$75/37.50	$75/37.50
Junior	$75/37.50	$75/37.50
Twilight	NA	NA
PAYMENT	Credit: Visa® MasterCard® Local checks only	
LEAGUES	None	
MEMBERSHIPS	USGA, NGF, PGA, GCSAA, CMAA, MGA	
MANAGER	Dale Miller	
SUPERINTENDENT	Bill Johnson, Dave Simon	
PROFESSIONAL	Marty Lass, Jeff Otto	

Located in Edina. Course is about 1/2 mile east of MN Highway 100 on 50th Street, then south on Wooddale Avenue.

	MEN				WOMEN		
	BACK	FRONT	PAR	HDCP	FRONT	PAR	HDCP
1	566	414	5	5	406	5	9
2	168	150	3	17	142	3	15
3	532	478	5	3	381	5	1
4	516	423	5	9	423	5	7
5	371	314	4	11	260	4	5
6	350	326	4	13	249	4	11
7	441	313	4	1	313	4	13
8	190	143	3	15	118	3	17
9	424	307	4	7	307	4	3
Out	3558	2868	37		2599	37	
10	424	376	4	2	339	4	8
11	176	108	3	18	299	3	16
12	395	300	4	8	346	4	14
13	317	298	4	14	189	4	4
14	353	337	4	10	406	4	12
15	415	361	4	4	392	4	6
16	166	110	3	16	126	3	18
17	530	396	5	6	369	5	2
18	400	352	4	12	470	4	10
In	3176	2638	35		2936	35	
Total	6679	6353	72		5748	72	
Rating	73.3	68.0			69.5		
Slope	136	125			124		

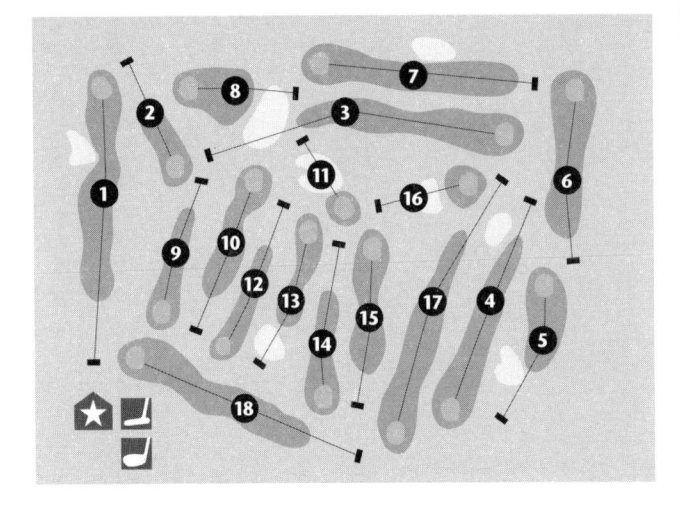

GOLF COURSE DIRECTORY

EDINBURGH USA

18 Regulation Public

8700 Edinbrook Crossing
Brooklyn Park, Minnesota 55443
612/424-9444 Clubhouse
612/424-7060 Proshop

HOURS	7 am to Dusk
SEASON	April to October

FEATURES		
Putting green	Y	
Driving range	Y	$2.50-5
Practice area	N	
Golf carts		
Power	Y	$24/12
Pull carts	Y	$2.50
Club rental	Y	$10
Club storage	Y	$30/yr
Caddies	Y	$10-12
Proshop		
Extended	Y	
Refreshments		
Restaurant	Y	
Lounge	Y	
Snacks	Y	
Clubhouse		
Showers	Y	
Lockers	Y	
Lodging	N	

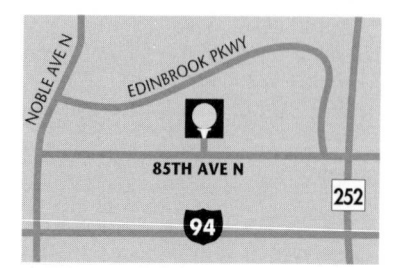

Located in Brooklyn Park. Course is two miles west of Highway 252 on 85th Ave, then north on Edinbrook Crossing.

RESERVATIONS	612/424-7060 4 days
	Reservations required
	Walk-on: fair/fair

GREEN FEES	M-F	S-S
Adult	$31	$31
Senior	$31	$31
Junior	$31	$31
Twilight	$19 (4:30pm)	$19 (4:30pm)

PAYMENT	Credit: Visa® MC® AmEx®
	Non-local checks accepted

LEAGUES	Men: Various
	Women: Various

MEMBERSHIPS	USGA, NGF, PGA, LPGA,
	GCSAA, CMAA, MGA

PROFESSIONAL	Craig Waryan

	MEN				WOMEN		
	BACK	FRONT	PAR	HDCP	FRONT	PAR	HDCP
1	510	474	5	5	440	5	5
2	193	133	3	17	93	3	17
3	408	360	4	3	304	4	3
4	514	448	5	7	425	5	7
5	335	282	4	11	258	4	11
6	195	141	3	9	124	3	9
7	424	369	4	1	341	4	1
8	165	125	3	13	101	3	13
9	520	486	5	15	449	5	15
Out	3264	2818	36		2535	36	
10	335	267	4	14	242	4	14
11	435	404	4	6	376	4	6
12	550	479	5	10	438	5	10
13	414	372	4	8	347	4	8
14	203	164	3	16	123	3	16
15	544	482	5	2	446	5	2
16	165	118	3	18	106	3	18
17	394	343	4	4	317	4	4
18	397	352	4	12	325	4	12
In	3437	2981	36		2720	36	
Total	6701	5799	72		5255	72	
Rating	73.0	68.8			71.4		
Slope	133	124			128		

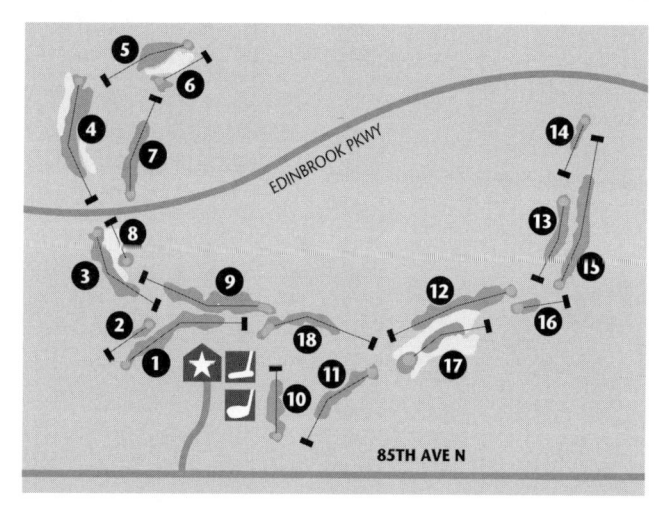

THE MINNESOTA ILLUSTRATED

ELK RIVER COUNTRY CLUB

18 Regulation Semi-Private

20015 Elk Lake Road, P.O. Box 39
Elk River, Minnesota 55330
612/441-4111 Clubhouse/Proshop

HOURS	6 am to Dusk
SEASON	April-November

| **RESERVATIONS** | 612/441-4111 1 week |
| | Walk-on: good/fair |

GREEN FEES	M-F	S-S
Adult	$18/10.50	$21/13
Senior	$10.50/7.25	$21/13
Junior	$7.25/7.25	$21/13
Twilight	NA	NA

| **PAYMENT** | Credit: Visa® MasterCard® |
| | Non-local checks accepted |

| **LEAGUES** | Men: T (pm) |
| | Women: T (am) |

| **MEMBERSHIPS** | USGA, NGF, PGA, GCSAA, MGA |

| **SUPERINTENDENT** | Jon Varty |
| **PROFESSIONAL** | Kevin Carter |

FEATURES		
Putting green	Y	
Driving range	Y	$3.75
Practice area	N	
Golf carts		
Power (gas)	Y	$20/10
Pull carts	Y	$2
Club rental	Y	$7
Club storage	N	
Caddies	N	
Proshop		
Extended	Y	
Refreshments		
Restaurant	Y	
Lounge	N	
Snacks	Y	
Clubhouse		
Showers	Y	
Lockers	Y	
Lodging	N	

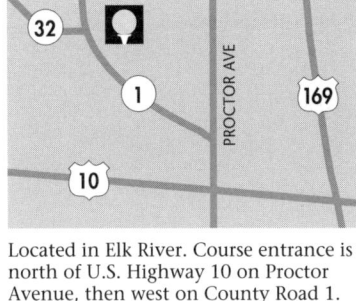

Located in Elk River. Course entrance is north of U.S. Highway 10 on Proctor Avenue, then west on County Road 1.

	MEN				**WOMEN**		
	BACK	FRONT	PAR	HDCP	FRONT	PAR	HDCP
1	425	415	4	1	405	5	5
2	170	135	3	17	135	3	17
3	335	320	4	15	275	4	13
4	180	165	3	13	160	3	15
5	470	445	5	5	425	5	1
6	375	350	4	7	325	4	9
7	370	330	4	11	310	4	11
8	510	480	5	3	385	5	3
9	415	400	4	9	395	5	7
Out	3250	3040	36		2815	38	
10	530	510	5	2	415	5	4
11	205	195	3	12	135	3	18
12	380	375	4	8	295	4	12
13	295	290	4	18	275	4	14
14	470	450	5	6	435	5	6
15	180	165	3	16	160	3	16
16	375	365	4	10	355	4	2
17	340	330	4	14	325	4	10
18	455	430	4	4	400	5	8
In	3230	3110	36		2795	37	
Total	6480	6150	72		5610	75	
Rating	71.1	69.6			72.3		
Slope	121	118			122		

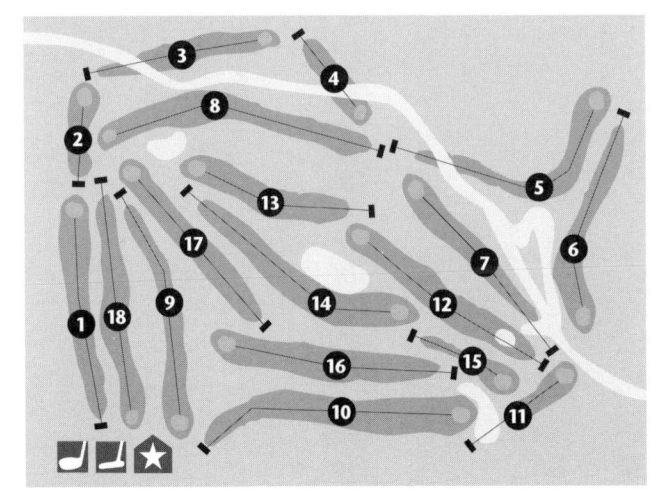

GOLF COURSE DIRECTORY

ELM CREEK GOLF LINKS

18 Regulation Public

18940 Highway 55
Plymouth, Minnesota 55446
612/478-6716 Clubhouse/Proshop

HOURS	Dawn to Dusk
SEASON	April to October

RESERVATIONS	612/478-6716 5 days
	Walk-on: good/fair

GREEN FEES	M-F	S-S
Adult	$18/12	$22/13
Senior	$8.50/6	$22/13
Junior	$8.50/6	$22/13
Twilight	NA	NA

PAYMENT	Credit: Visa® MC® AmEx®
	Non-local checks accepted

LEAGUES	Men: Various
	Women: Various

MEMBERSHIPS	NGF, PGA, GCSAA, MGA

OWNER	Mark & Mike Klatte

FEATURES	
Putting green	Y
Driving range	N
Practice area	N
Golf carts	
Power (gas)	Y $22/12
Pull carts	Y $2.50
Club rental	Y
Club storage	N
Caddies	N
Proshop	
Extended	Y
Refreshments	
Restaurant	N
Lounge	Y
Snacks	Y
Clubhouse	
Showers	N
Lockers	N
Lodging	N

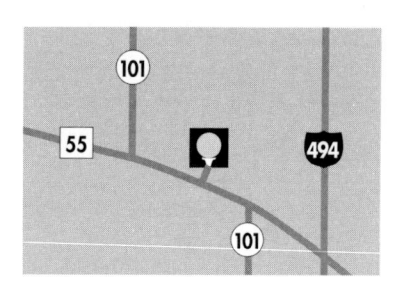

Located in Plymouth. Course entrance is about four miles west of I-494 on MN Highway 55.

	MEN BACK	FRONT	PAR	HDCP	**WOMEN** FRONT	PAR	HDCP
1	392	360	4	15	335	4	13
2	390	350	4	5	340	4	9
3	325	295	4	6	230	4	3
4	420	375	4	7	370	5	12
5	445	435	5	18	400	5	10
6	150	130	3	13	123	3	16
7	322	290	4	16	240	4	17
8	350	333	4	4	255	4	11
9	177	152	3	8	145	3	1
Out	2971	2720	35		2438	36	
10	350	346	4	14	325	4	15
11	380	330	4	9	320	4	5
12	161	140	3	10	125	3	18
13	630	500	5	1	375	5	2
14	409	345	4	11	315	4	7
15	361	332	4	12	295	4	4
16	390	370	4	3	205	1	8
17	138	113	3	17	106	3	14
18	445	315	4	2	255	4	6
In	3264	2791	35		2401	35	
Total	6235	5511	70		4839	71	
Rating	70.4	68.8			68.0		
Slope	132	128			117		

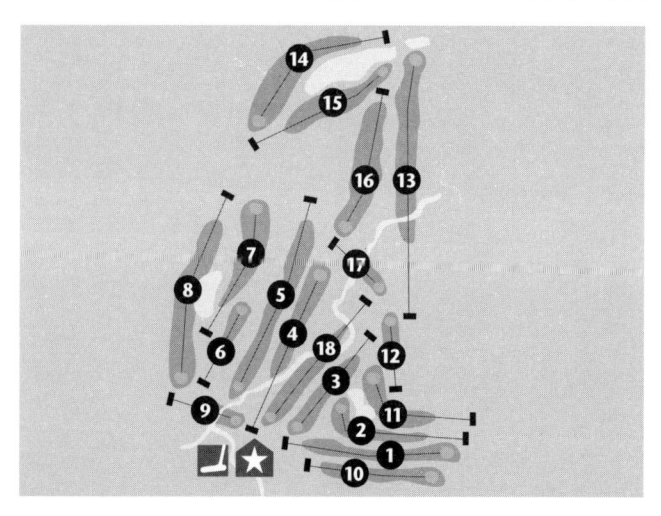

ELMDALE HILLS GOLF COURSE

9 Regulation Public

26161 Nicolai Avenue
Miesville, Minnesota 55009
507/263-2507 Clubhouse/Proshop

HOURS	6 am to Dusk
SEASON	April-November

RESERVATIONS	507/263-2507
	Walk-on: good/good

GREEN FEES	M-F	S-S
Adult	$15/9	$16/10
Senior	$15/9	$16/10
Junior	$15/9	$16/10
Twilight	NA	NA

PAYMENT	No credit cards accepted
	Non-local checks accepted

LEAGUES	None

MEMBERSHIPS	MGA

OWNER	Bruce & Diane Brage

FEATURES	
Putting green	Y
Driving range	N
Practice area	N
Golf carts	
Power (gas)	Y $16/11
Pull carts	Y
Club rental	Y
Club storage	N
Caddies	N
Proshop	
Extended	Y
Refreshments	
Restaurant	N
Lounge	Y
Snacks	Y
Clubhouse	
Showers	N
Lockers	N
Lodging	N

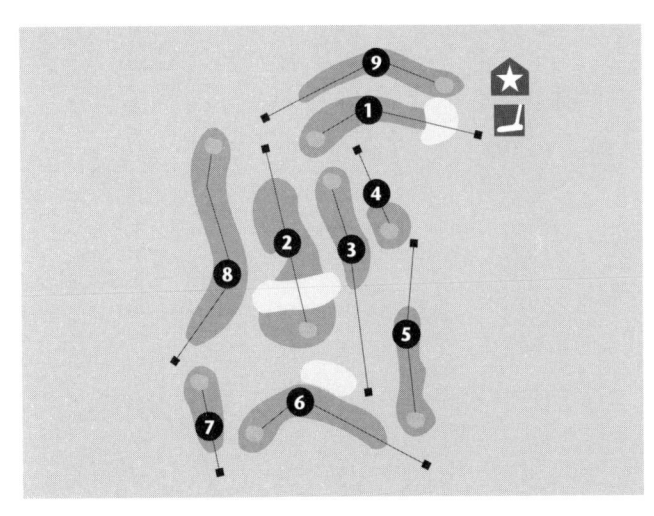

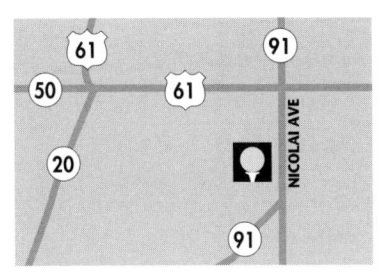

Located south of Miesville. Course is about 2 miles south of U.S. Highway 61 on County Road 91/Nicolai Avenue.

		MEN			WOMEN		
	BACK	FRONT	PAR	HDCP	FRONT	PAR	HDCP
1	297	288	4	8	253	4	6
2	505	498	5	7	396	5	2
3	405	387	4	6	300	4	5
4	147	139	3	9	103	3	9
5	380	360	4	3	290	4	3
6	328	323	4	1	246	4	4
7	192	171	3	4	100	3	7
8	470	460	5	2	390	5	1
9	395	383	4	5	311	4	8
Out	3119	3009	36		2389	36	
1	297	288	4	8	253	4	6
2	505	498	5	7	396	5	2
3	405	387	4	6	300	4	5
4	147	139	3	9	103	3	9
5	380	360	4	3	290	4	3
6	328	323	4	1	246	4	4
7	192	171	3	4	100	3	7
8	470	460	5	2	390	5	1
9	395	383	4	5	311	4	8
In	3119	3009	36		2389	36	
Total	6238	6018	72		4778	72	
Rating	70.6	69.6			68.8		
Slope	125	123			112		

GOLF COURSE DIRECTORY

ELY GOLF COURSE

9 Regulation Public

P.O. Box 507
Ely, Minnesota 55731
218/365-5932 Clubhouse/Proshop

RESERVATIONS	218/365-5932	
	Walk-on: fair/fair	
GREEN FEES	M-F	S-S
Adult	Call	Call
Senior	Call	Call
Junior	Call	Call
Twilight	NA	NA
PAYMENT	No credit cards accepted	
	Non-local checks accepted	
LEAGUES	Men: Various	
	Women: Various	
MEMBERSHIPS	USGA, MGA	
PROFESSIONAL	Call	

HOURS Dawn to Dusk
SEASON April to October

FEATURES	
Putting green	Y
Driving range	N
Practice area	N
Golf carts	
Power (gas)	Y
Pull carts	Y
Club rental	Y
Club storage	N
Caddies	N
Proshop	
Basic	Y
Refreshments	
Restaurant	N
Lounge	N
Snacks	Y
Clubhouse	
Showers	N
Lockers	N
Lodging	N

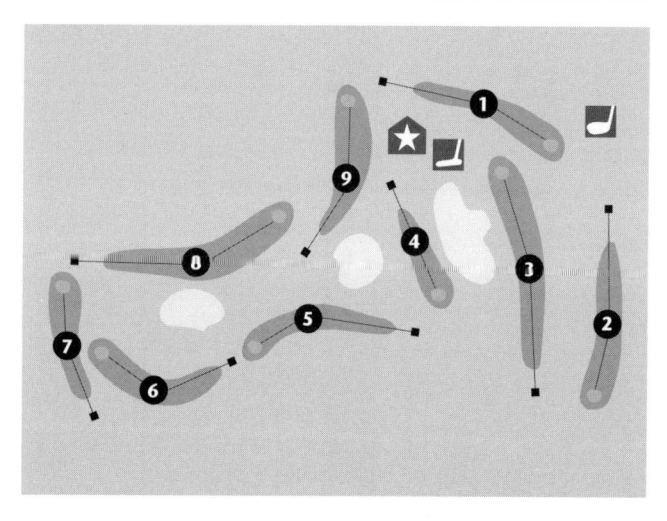

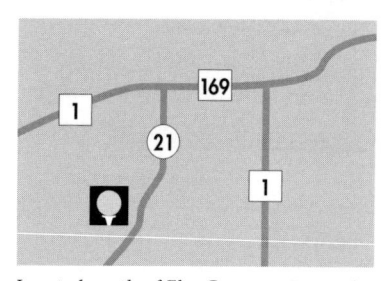

Located south of Ely. Course entrance is about one mile south of MN Highway 169 on County Road 21.

	MEN			WOMEN		
	FRONT	PAR	HDCP	FRONT	PAR	HDCP
1	366	4	9	360	4	2
2	396	4	8	387	4	8
3	539	5	6	524	5	6
4	157	3	5	150	3	5
5	343	4	2	313	4	9
6	385	4	3	373	4	1
7	117	3	1	111	3	3
8	506	5	4	443	5	7
9	419	4	7	411	5	4
Out	3228	36		3072	37	
1	366	4	9	360	4	2
2	396	4	8	387	4	8
3	539	5	6	524	5	6
4	157	3	5	150	3	5
5	343	4	2	313	4	9
6	385	4	3	373	4	1
7	117	3	1	111	3	3
8	506	5	4	443	5	7
9	419	4	7	411	5	4
In	3228	36		3072	37	
Total	6456	72		6144	74	
Rating	70.0			73.8		
Slope	114			121		

EMILY GREENS GOLF COURSE

9 Executive Public

HCR 1, P.O. Box 24
Emily, Minnesota 56447
218/763-2169 Clubhouse/Proshop

HOURS	7 am to Dusk
SEASON	April to October

RESERVATIONS	218/763-2169	
	Walk-on: good/good	
GREEN FEES	M-F	S-S
Adult	$12/7	$12/7
Senior	$12/7	$12/7
Junior	$12/7	$12/7
Twilight	NA	NA
	10 round passes available	
PAYMENT	No credit cards accepted	
	Non-local checks accepted	
LEAGUES	Men: T	
	Women: Th	
MEMBERSHIPS	None	
OWNER	Dan & Sandy Lingwall	

FEATURES		
Putting green	Y	
Driving range	Y	$2
Practice area	N	
Golf carts		
Power (gas)	Y	$8
Pull carts	Y	$2
Club rental	Y	$3
Club storage	N	
Caddies	N	
Proshop		
Regular	Y	
Refreshments		
Restaurant	N	
Lounge	N	
Snacks	Y	
Clubhouse		
Showers	N	
Lockers	N	
Lodging	N	

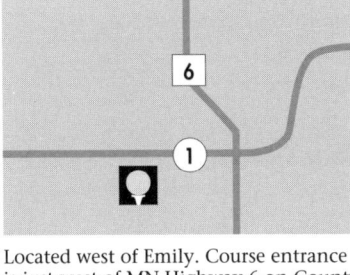

Located west of Emily. Course entrance is just west of MN Highway 6 on County Road 1.

	MEN			**WOMEN**		
	FRONT	PAR	HDCP	FRONT	PAR	HDCP
1	222	4	3	222	4	
2	160	3	2	160	3	
3	145	3	5	145	3	
4	259	4	9	192	4	
5	122	3	8	122	3	
6	137	3	7	137	3	
7	260	4	4	260	4	
8	245	4	6	245	4	
9	450	5	1	410	4	
Out	2000	33		1893	33	
1	222	4	3	222	4	
2	160	3	2	160	3	
3	145	3	5	145	3	
4	259	4	9	192	4	
5	122	3	8	122	3	
6	137	3	7	137	3	
7	260	4	4	260	4	
8	245	4	6	245	4	
9	450	5	1	410	4	
IN	2000	33		1893	33	
Total	4000	66		3786	66	
Rating	NA			NA		
Slope	NA			NA		

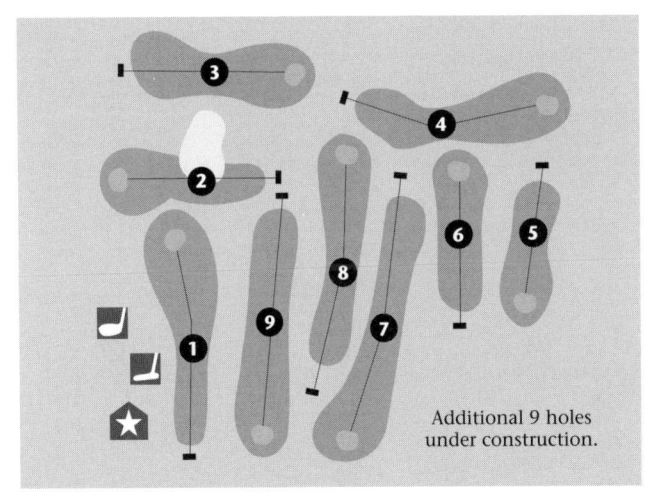

Additional 9 holes under construction.

ENGER PARK GOLF COURSE

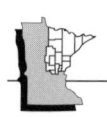

27 Regulation Public

1801 West Skyline Boulevard
Duluth, Minnesota 55439
218/723-3451 Clubhouse
218/723-3452 Proshop

RESERVATIONS	218/723-3452 2 days	
	Walk-on: good/fair	
GREEN FEES	M-F	S-S
Adult	$18/12	$18/12
Senior	$18/9	$18/9
Junior	$8/5	$8/5
Twilight	$7	$7
PAYMENT	No credit cards accepted	
	Non-local checks accepted	
LEAGUES	Men: Various	
	Women: Various	
MEMBERSHIPS	USGA, NGF, GCSAA, MGA	
OWNER	City of Duluth	
SUPERINTENDENT	Mike Netzel	

HOURS 7 am to Dusk
SEASON April-November

FEATURES

Putting green	Y	
Driving range	Y	$1.50
Practice area	Y	
Golf carts		
Power	Y	$18/10
Pull carts	Y	$2
Club rental	Y	
Club storage	N	
Caddies	N	
Proshop		
Extended	Y	
Refreshments		
Restaurant	N	
Lounge	N	
Snacks	Y	
Clubhouse		
Showers	N	
Lockers	Y	
Lodging	N	

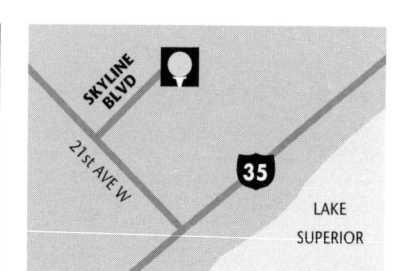

Located in Duluth. Course is west of I-35 on 21st Ave, then north on Skyline Dr.

	MEN				**WOMEN**		
	BACK	FRONT	PAR	HDCP	FRONT	PAR	HDCP
1	383	347	4	5	325	4	5
2	520	477	5	2	440	5	2
3	405	367	4	1	325	4	1
4	375	332	4	8	287	4	8
5	355	335	4	3	313	4	3
6	141	129	3	9	106	3	9
7	393	373	4	6	288	4	6
8	182	155	3	7	134	3	7
9	550	529	5	4	512	5	4
FRONT	3304	3044	36		2730	36	
1	495	454	5	4	413	5	4
2	365	327	4	9	291	4	9
3	337	301	4	5	269	4	5
4	412	383	4	1	334	4	1
5	374	348	4	3	286	4	3
6	140	114	3	8	101	3	8
7	333	272	4	7	249	4	7
8	193	174	3	6	121	3	6
9	481	460	5	2	453	5	2
MIDDLE	3130	2833	36		2517	36	
1	470	430	5	3	383	5	3
2	329	324	4	5	319	4	5
3	310	300	4	6	282	4	6
4	332	310	4	7	303	4	7
5	428	397	4	2	389	4	1
6	405	393	4	2	337	4	2
7	399	393	4	4	389	4	4
8	194	183	3	9	169	3	9
9	328	322	4	8	310	4	0
BACK	3195	3052	36		2887	36	
F/M	6434	5877	72		5247	72	
Rating	71.8	69.3			70.6		
Slope	130	124			129		
M/B	6325	5885	72		5404	72	
Rating	70.9	69.4			71.5		
Slope	125	122			125		
B/F	6499	6096	72		5617	72	
Rating	71.3	69.9			72.7		
Slope	125	122			125		

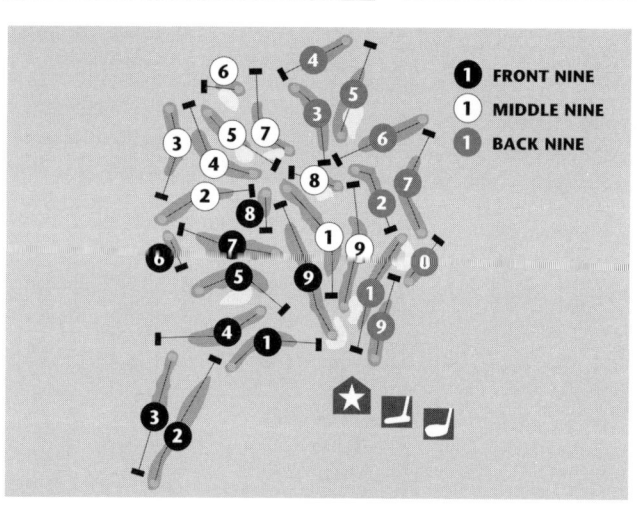

① FRONT NINE
① MIDDLE NINE
① BACK NINE

THE MINNESOTA ILLUSTRATED

ESHQUAGUMA CLUB

9 Regulation Private

Highway 53 South, P.O. Box 527
Virginia, Minnesota 55792
218/865-4263 Clubhouse
218/865-4706 Proshop

HOURS	Dawn to Dusk
SEASON	April-November

RESERVATIONS	218/865-4706
	Members only

GREEN FEES	M-F	S-S
Adult	Call	Call
Senior	Call	Call
Junior	Call	Call
Twilight	NA	NA
	Members and guests only	

PAYMENT	No credit cards accepted
	Non-local checks accepted

LEAGUES	Men: Various
	Women: Various

MEMBERSHIPS	USGA, PGA, GCSAA, MGA

PROFESSIONAL	Call

FEATURES	
Putting green	Y
Driving range	N
Practice area	N
Golf carts	
Power (gas)	Y
Pull carts	Y
Club rental	Y
Club storage	Y
Caddies	N
Proshop	
Extended	Y
Refreshments	
Restaurant	Y
Lounge	Y
Snacks	Y
Clubhouse	
Showers	Y
Lockers	Y
Lodging	N

Located southwest of Gilbert. Course is south of MN Highway 135 on County Road 4, then west on County Road 525.

	MEN			**WOMEN**		
	FRONT	PAR	HDCP	FRONT	PAR	HDCP
1	378	4	9	368	4	3
2	300	4	15	296	4	11
3	380	4	5	374	5	13
4	491	5	1	398	5	7
5	217	3	7	207	4	15
6	413	4	3	341	4	9
7	500	5	11	432	5	1
8	354	4	13	354	4	5
9	147	3	17	127	3	17
Out	3180	36		2897	38	
10	367	4	10	364	4	4
11	346	4	12	296	4	10
12	487	5	14	374	5	14
13	395	4	2	395	5	6
14	224	3	4	148	3	16
15	384	4	16	320	4	8
16	520	5	6	432	5	2
17	404	4	8	379	5	12
18	160	3	18	147	3	18
In	3287	36		2855	38	
Total	6467	72		5752	76	
Rating	70.7			73.1		
Slope	118			121		

Course layout map not provided.

GOLF COURSE DIRECTORY

EVELETH MUNICIPAL GOLF COURSE

9 Regulation Public

Highway 53 South, P.O. Box 649
Eveleth, Minnesota 55734
218/744-5943 Clubhouse/Proshop

HOURS 7:30 am to Dusk
SEASON April to October

RESERVATIONS	218/744-5943	
	Walk-on: good/fair	
GREEN FEES	M-F	S-S
Adult	$12/8	$12/12
Senior	$12/8	$12/12
Junior	$12/8	$12/12
Twilight	NA	NA
PAYMENT	No credit cards accepted	
	Non-local checks accepted	
LEAGUES	Men: M,T (5:30 pm)	
	Women: W (5:30 pm)	
MEMBERSHIPS	MGA	
GREENSKEEPER	Craig Homola	
PROFESSIONAL	Bill McKenzie	

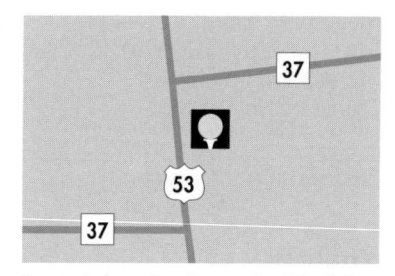

FEATURES		
Putting green	Y	
Driving range	N	
Practice area	N	
Golf carts		
Power (gas)	Y	$18/10
Pull carts	Y	$1.50
Club rental	Y	$4
Club storage	Y	
Caddies	N	
Proshop		
Extended	Y	
Refreshments		
Restaurant	Y	
Lounge	Y	
Snacks	Y	
Clubhouse		
Showers	Y	
Lockers	Y	
Lodging	N	

Located about 3 miles south of Eveleth. Course entrance is south of Highway 37 on U.S. Highway 53.

	MEN			WOMEN		
	FRONT	PAR	HDCP	FRONT	PAR	HDCP
1	325	4	5	325	4	5
2	508	5	1	508	5	1
3	335	4	7	335	4	7
4	400	4	3	400	4	3
5	379	4	4	379	4	4
6	332	4	8	332	4	8
7	128	3	9	128	3	9
8	406	4	2	406	4	2
9	305	4	6	305	4	6
Out	3118	36		3118	36	
1	325	4	5	325	4	5
2	508	5	1	508	5	1
3	335	4	7	335	4	7
4	400	4	3	400	4	3
5	379	4	4	379	4	4
6	332	4	8	332	4	8
7	128	3	9	128	3	9
8	406	4	2	406	4	2
9	305	4	6	305	4	6
In	3118	36		3118	36	
Total	6236	72		6236	72	
Rating	71.0			73.6		
Slope	125			125		

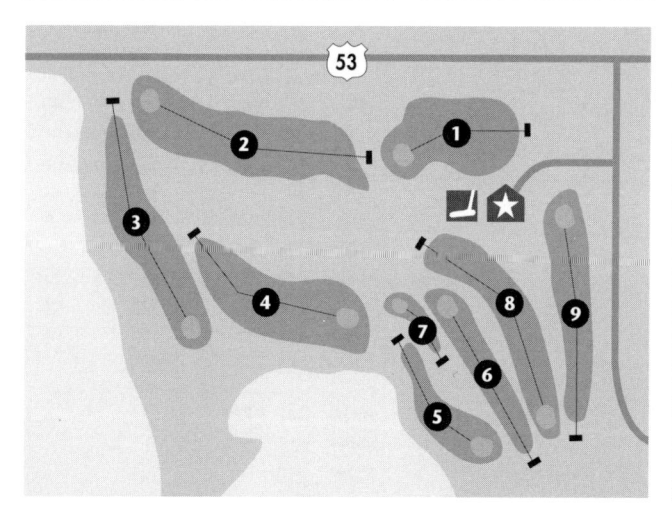

FAIR HILLS GOLF COURSE

WILDFLOWER COURSE/18 Regulation Public

Rural Route 1, Box 127A
Detroit Lakes, Minnesota 56501
218/439-3357 Clubhouse
218/532-3357 Proshop

HOURS	7 am to Dusk
SEASON	April–November

FEATURES		
Putting green	Y	
Driving range	Y	$1.75
Practice area	Y	
Golf carts		
Power (gas)	Y	$20
Pull carts	Y	$3
Club rental	Y	$7
Club storage	N	
Caddies	N	
Proshop		
Extended	Y	
Refreshments		
Restaurant	Y	
Lounge	Y	
Snacks	Y	
Clubhouse		
Showers	N	
Lockers	N	
Lodging/Resort	Y	Call

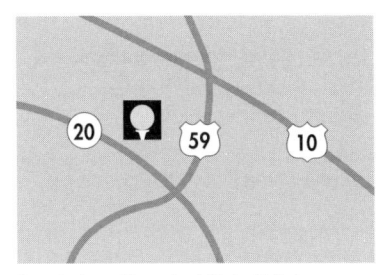

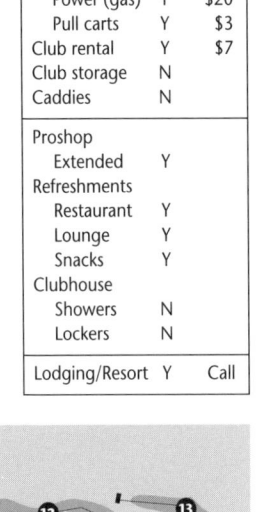

Located southwest of Detroit Lakes. Course entrance is 3 1/2 miles west of U.S. Highway 59 on County Road 20.

RESERVATIONS	218/532-3357 1 week
	Walk-on: fair/poor

GREEN FEES	M-F	S-S
Adult	$20/12	$25/15
Senior	$20/12	$25/15
Junior	$9/5	$9/5
Twilight	$16	$16

PAYMENT	Credit: Visa® MC® AmEx®
	Non-local checks accepted

LEAGUES	None

MEMBERSHIPS	USGA, NGF, PGA, GCSAA, MGA

OWNER	Dave Kaldahl
SUPERINTENDENT	Pete Bortenum
PROFESSIONAL	Dave Walters

	MEN				WOMEN		
	BACK	FRONT	PAR	HDCP	FRONT	PAR	HDCP
1	348	326	4	15	272	4	15
2	523	495	5	11	413	5	11
3	422	391	4	9	314	4	9
4	423	394	4	1	309	4	1
5	473	449	4	5	371	4	5
6	428	384	4	7	313	4	7
7	172	161	3	17	120	3	17
8	535	509	5	3	426	5	3
9	192	178	3	13	140	3	13
Out	3516	3287	36		2678	36	
10	426	406	4	2	331	4	2
11	165	154	3	16	100	3	16
12	548	524	5	6	431	5	6
13	402	359	4	12	296	4	12
14	566	540	5	4	460	5	4
15	328	302	4	18	223	4	18
16	410	376	4	10	293	4	10
17	208	201	3	14	163	3	14
18	422	402	4	8	324	4	8
In	3475	3264	36		2621	36	
Total	6991	6551	72		5299	72	
Rating	74.8	72.8			71.8		
Slope	136	132			124		

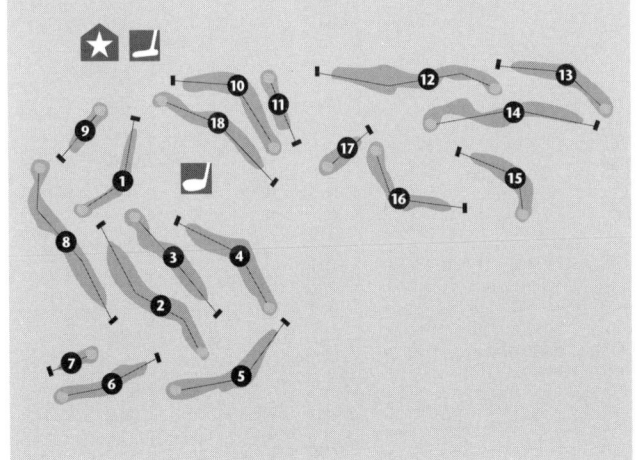

GOLF COURSE DIRECTORY

FAIR HILLS GOLF COURSE

EXECUTIVE COURSE/9 Executive Public

Rural Route 1, Box 127A
Detroit Lakes, Minnesota 56501
218/439-3357 Clubhouse
218/532-3357 Proshop

HOURS	7 am to Dusk
SEASON	April–November

FEATURES		
Putting green	Y	
Driving range	Y	$1.75
Practice area	Y	
Golf carts		
Power (gas)	Y	$20
Pull carts	Y	$3
Club rental	Y	$7
Club storage	N	
Caddies	N	
Proshop		
Extended	Y	
Refreshments		
Restaurant	Y	
Lounge	Y	
Snacks	Y	
Clubhouse		
Showers	N	
Lockers	N	
Lodging/Resort	Y	Call

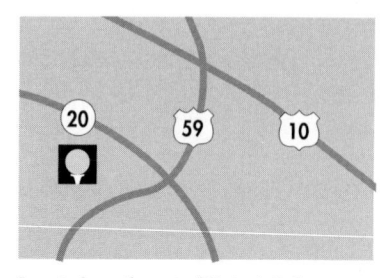

RESERVATIONS	218/532-3357 1 week
	Walk-on: fair/poor

GREEN FEES	M-F	S-S
Adult	$20/12	$25/15
Senior	$20/12	$25/15
Junior	$9/5	$9/5
Twilight	$16	$16

PAYMENT	Credit: Visa® MC® AmEx®
	Non-local checks accepted

LEAGUES	None

MEMBERSHIPS	USGA, NGF, PGA, GCSAA, MGA

OWNER	Dave Kaldahl
SUPERINTENDENT	Pete Bortenum
PROFESSIONAL	Dave Walters

Located southwest of Detroit Lakes. Course entrance is 3 1/2 miles west of U.S. Highway 59 on County Road 20.

	MEN			**WOMEN**		
	FRONT	PAR	HDCP	FRONT	PAR	HDCP
1	229	4		229	5	
2	222	4		152	4	
3	345	5		345	5	
4	140	3		140	4	
5	133	3		133	4	
6	292	4		292	5	
7	152	3		152	3	
8	107	3		107	3	
9	137	3		137	3	
Out	1757	32		1687	36	
1	229	4		229	5	
2	222	4		152	4	
3	345	5		345	5	
4	140	3		140	4	
5	133	3		133	4	
6	292	4		292	5	
7	152	3		152	3	
8	107	3		107	3	
9	137	3		137	3	
In	1757	32		1687	36	
Total	3514	64		3374	72	
Rating	56.8			60.0		
Slope	89			99		

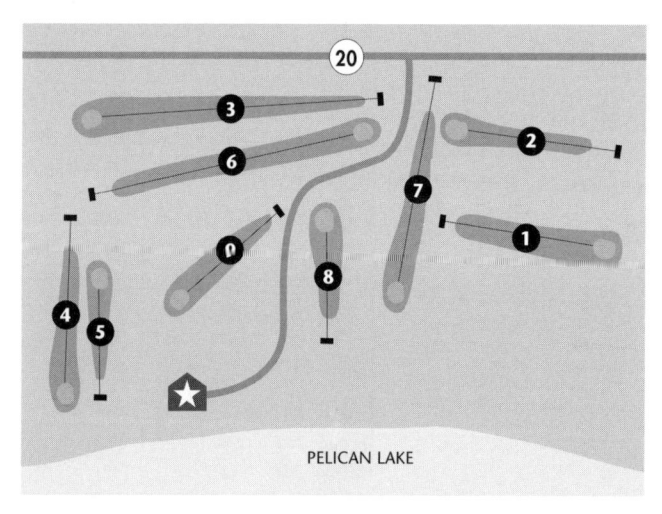

PELICAN LAKE

FALCON RIDGE GOLF COURSE   REGULATION COURSE/18 Regulation Public

33942 Falcon Avenue North
Stacy, Minnesota 55079
612/462-5797 Clubhouse/Proshop

HOURS	6:30 am - Dusk
SEASON	April-November

RESERVATIONS	612/462-5797	
	Walk-on: good/fair	

GREEN FEES	M-F	S-S
Adult	Call	Call
Senior	Call	Call
Junior	Call	Call
Twilight	NA	NA

PAYMENT	Credit: Visa® MasterCard®
	Non-local checks accepted

LEAGUES	Various

MEMBERSHIPS	MGA

MANAGER	Lynn Johnson
SUPERINTENDENT	James Kleven

FEATURES	
Putting green	Y
Driving range	Y
Practice area	N
Golf carts	
Power	Y
Pull carts	Y
Club rental	Y
Club storage	N
Caddies	N
Proshop	Y
Regular	Y
Refreshments	
Restaurant	N
Lounge	N
Snacks	Y
Clubhouse	
Showers	N
Lockers	N
Lodging	N

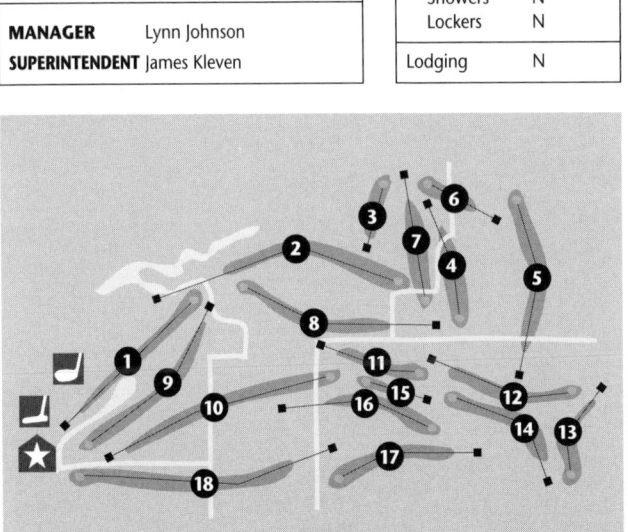

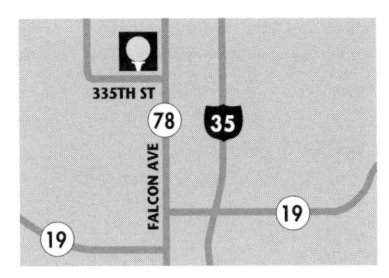

Located in Stacy. Course entrance is west of I-35 on County Road 19, then 3 miles north on Falcon Avenue.

	MEN				WOMEN		
	BACK	FRONT	PAR	HDCP	FRONT	PAR	HDCP
1	334	328	4	15	310	4	15
2	481	465	5	7	421	5	7
3	193	179	3	11	159	3	11
4	287	283	4	17	275	4	17
5	465	456	5	1	356	5	1
6	147	141	3	9	127	3	9
7	318	306	4	5	299	4	5
8	409	397	4	13	352	4	13
9	400	383	4	3	371	4	3
Out	3034	2938	36		2670	36	
10	481	471	5	2	375	5	8
11	221	213	3	12	197	3	12
12	293	287	4	16	278	4	4
13	234	226	4	4	214	4	6
14	303	295	4	10	281	4	16
15	164	158	3	18	138	3	18
16	299	293	4	6	285	4	14
17	292	286	4	14	276	4	2
18	466	460	5	8	356	5	10
In	2753	2689	36		2400	36	
Total	5787	5627	72		5070	72	
Rating	67.7	67.1			69.6		
Slope	106	104			117		

GOLF COURSE DIRECTORY

FALCON RIDGE GOLF COURSE

EXECUTIVE COURSE/9 Executive Public

33942 Falcon Avenue North
Stacy, Minnesota 55079
612/462-5797 Clubhouse/Proshop

HOURS	6:30 am - Dusk
SEASON	April-November

RESERVATIONS	612/462-5797
	Walk-on: good/fair

GREEN FEES	M-F	S-S
Adult	Call	Call
Senior	Call	Call
Junior	Call	Call
Twilight	NA	NA

PAYMENT	Credit: Visa® MasterCard®
	Non-local checks accepted

LEAGUES	Various

MEMBERSHIPS	MGA

MANAGER	Lynn Johnson
SUPERINTENDENT	James Kleven

FEATURES	
Putting green	Y
Driving range	Y
Practice area	N
Golf carts	
Power	Y
Pull carts	Y
Club rental	Y
Club storage	N
Caddies	N
Proshop	
Regular	Y
Refreshments	
Restaurant	N
Lounge	N
Snacks	Y
Clubhouse	
Showers	N
Lockers	N
Lodging	N

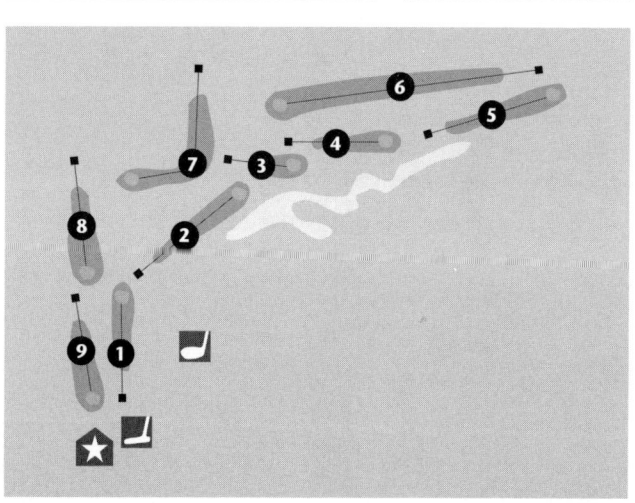

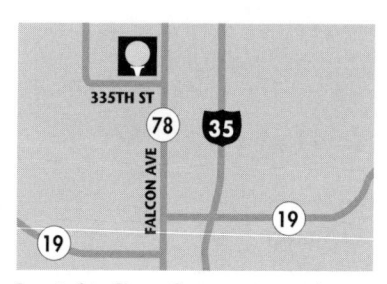

Located in Stacy. Course entrance is west of I-35 on County Road 19, then 3 miles north on Falcon Avenue.

	MEN			WOMEN		
	FRONT	PAR	HDCP	FRONT	PAR	HDCP
1	170	3		162	3	
2	143	3		132	3	
3	91	3		76	3	
4	144	3		137	3	
5	129	3		121	3	
6	302	4		281	4	
7	242	4		231	4	
8	149	3		145	3	
9	175	3		166	3	
Out	1545	29		1451	29	
1	170	3		162	3	
2	143	3		132	3	
3	91	3		76	3	
4	144	3		137	3	
5	129	3		121	3	
6	302	4		281	4	
7	242	4		231	4	
8	149	3		145	3	
9	175	3		166	3	
In	1545	29		1451	29	
Total	3090	58		2902	58	
Rating	54.0			55.6		
Slope	70			80		

FALLS COUNTRY CLUB

9 Regulation Semi-Private

County Road 106, P.O. Box 673
International Falls, Minnesota 56649
218/283-4491 Clubhouse/Proshop

HOURS	Dawn to Dusk
SEASON	April to October

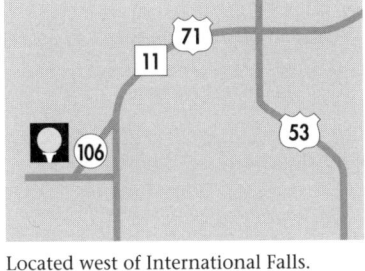

Located west of International Falls. Course entrance is about 1/2 mile west of U.S. Highway 71 on County Rd 106.

RESERVATIONS	218/283-4491	
	Walk-on: good/fair	

GREEN FEES	M-F	S-S
Adult	Call	Call
Senior	Call	Call
Junior	Call	Call
Twilight	NA	NA

PAYMENT	No credit cards accepted
	Non-local checks accepted

LEAGUES	Men: Various
	Women: Various

MEMBERSHIPS	MGA

PROFESSIONAL	Call

FEATURES		
Putting green	Y	
Driving range	N	
Practice area	N	
Golf carts		
Power (gas)	Y	$20
Pull carts	Y	$2.50
Club rental	Y	$7
Club storage	N	
Caddies	N	
Proshop		
Regular	Y	
Refreshments		
Restaurant	N	
Lounge	N	
Snacks	Y	
Clubhouse		
Showers	N	
Lockers	N	
Lodging	N	

	MEN			WOMEN		
	FRONT	PAR	HDCP	FRONT	PAR	HDCP
1	380	4	7	380	4	7
2	224	3	3	224	4	3
3	485	5	11	402	5	11
4	424	4	1	404	5	1
5	347	4	9	347	4	9
6	384	4	5	384	5	5
7	297	4	13	241	4	13
8	295	4	15	295	4	15
9	136	3	17	114	3	17
Out	2972	35		2791	38	
1	380	4	8	380	4	8
2	224	3	4	224	4	4
3	485	5	12	402	5	12
4	424	4	2	404	5	2
5	347	4	10	347	4	10
6	384	4	6	384	5	6
7	297	4	14	241	4	14
8	295	4	16	295	4	16
9	136	3	18	114	3	18
In	2972	35		2791	38	
Total	5944	70		5582	76	
Rating	68.0			71.2		
Slope	112			120		

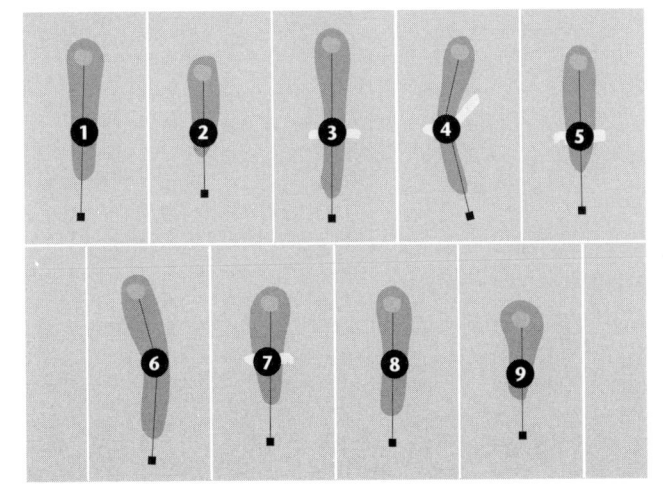

GOLF COURSE DIRECTORY

FARIBAULT GOLF & COUNTRY CLUB

18 Regulation Private

1700 N.W. 17th Street, P.O. Box 632
Faribault, Minnesota 55021
507/334-5559 Clubhouse
507/334-3810 Proshop

HOURS 6:30 am - Dusk

SEASON April-November

FEATURES

Putting green	Y
Driving range	Y
Practice area	Y

| RESERVATIONS | 507/334-3810 1 week |
| | Walk-on: fair/fair |

Golf carts		
Power (gas)	Y	$20
Pull carts	Y	$2
Club rental	Y	$6
Club storage	Y	
Caddies	N	

GREEN FEES	M-F	S-S
Adult	$20/11	$23/12
Senior	$20/11	$23/12
Junior	$10/6	$10/6
Twilight	NA	NA

| PAYMENT | No credit cards accepted |
| | Non-local checks accepted |

Proshop	
Extended	Y
Refreshments	
Restaurant	Y
Lounge	Y
Snacks	Y
Clubhouse	
Showers	Y
Lockers	Y

| LEAGUES | None |

| MEMBERSHIPS | USGA, PGA, GCSAA, MGA |

| Lodging | N |

| SUPERINTENDENT | Paul Eckholm |
| PROFESSIONAL | Ken Gorg, Jeff Ordal |

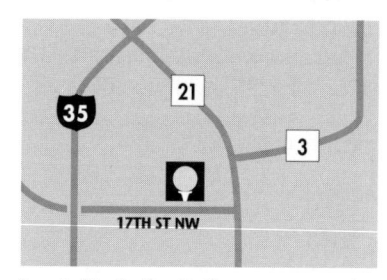

Located in Faribault. Course entrance is about 1 mile south of I-35 (Exit #59) on Highway 21, then west on 17th Street.

	MEN				WOMEN		
	BACK	FRONT	PAR	HDCP	FRONT	PAR	HDCP
1	285	280	4	15	274	4	15
2	373	364	4	5	279	4	5
3	477	472	5	3	430	5	3
4	354	348	4	7	338	4	7
5	348	337	4	13	327	4	13
6	367	360	4	9	274	4	9
7	381	356	4	11	341	4	11
8	158	144	3	17	125	3	17
9	572	564	5	1	506	5	1
Out	3315	3225	37		2894	37	
10	156	145	3	6	133	3	6
11	427	420	4	2	352	5	2
12	357	354	4	10	349	4	10
13	366	341	4	16	328	4	16
14	136	130	3	18	114	3	18
15	530	520	5	12	393	5	12
16	389	385	4	4	332	4	4
17	174	160	3	14	151	3	14
18	555	535	5	8	454	5	8
In	3090	2990	35		2606	36	
Total	6405	6215	72		5500	73	
Rating	70.2	69.4			71.6		
Slope	121	119			113		

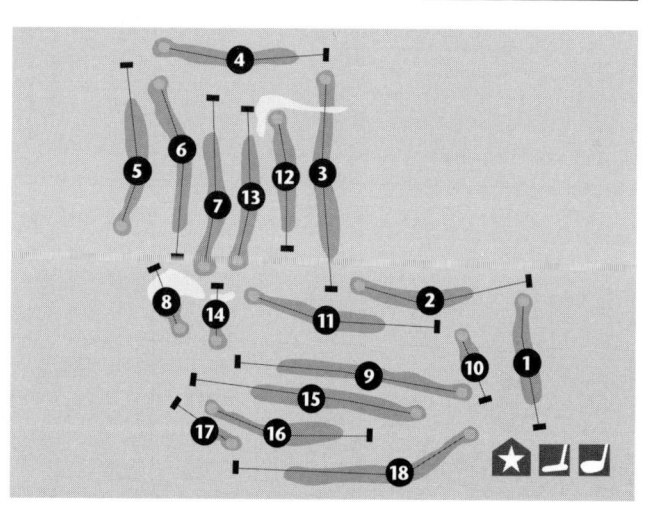

FARMERS GOLF & HEALTH CLUB

9 Regulation Public

County Road 15
Sanborn, Minnesota 56083
507/648-3629 Clubhouse/Proshop

HOURS	7 am to Dusk
SEASON	April to October

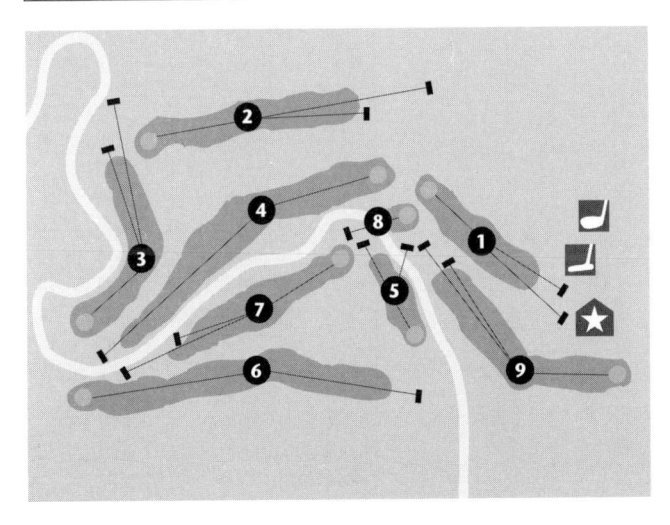

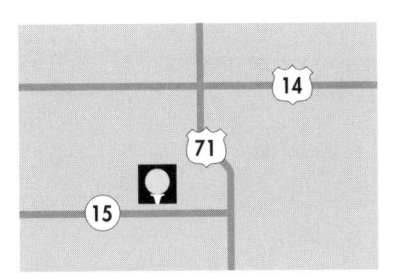

Located in Sanborn. Course entrance is about 1/2 mile west of U.S. Highway 71 on County Road 15.

RESERVATIONS	507/648-3629	
	Walk-on: good/good	
GREEN FEES	M-F	S-S
Adult	$12/8	$15/10
Senior	$12/8	$15/10
Junior	$12/8	$15/10
Twilight	NA	NA
PAYMENT	No credit cards accepted	
	Non-local checks accepted	
LEAGUES	Men: None	
	Women: None	
MEMBERSHIPS	USGA, MGA	
OWNER	Richard Meyers	
SUPERINTENDENT	Richard Meyers	

FEATURES	
Putting green	Y
Driving range	Y
Practice area	Y
Golf carts	
Power (gas)	Y
Pull carts	Y
Club rental	Y
Club storage	Y
Caddies	N
Proshop	
Extended	Y
Refreshments	
Restaurant	Y
Lounge	Y
Snacks	Y
Clubhouse	
Showers	Y
Lockers	Y
Lodging	N

	MEN			WOMEN		
	FRONT	PAR	HDCP	FRONT	PAR	HDCP
1	315	4	7	282	4	7
2	399	4	5	299	4	5
3	316	4	2	246	4	2
4	476	5	1	433	5	1
5	152	3	8	134	3	8
6	504	5	3	464	5	3
7	380	4	6	263	4	6
8	103	3	9	64	3	9
9	381	4	4	349	4	4
Out	3026	36		2534	36	
1	315	4	7	282	4	7
2	399	4	5	299	4	5
3	316	4	2	246	4	2
4	476	5	1	433	5	1
5	152	3	8	134	3	8
6	504	5	3	464	5	3
7	380	4	6	263	4	6
8	103	3	9	64	3	9
9	381	4	4	349	4	4
In	3026	36		2534	36	
Total	6052	72		5068	72	
Rating	70.2			69.8		
Slope	123			124		

FERNDALE COUNTRY CLUB

9 Regulation Public

Rural Route 2, Box 85A
Rushford, Minnesota 55971
507/864-7626 Clubhouse/Proshop

RESERVATIONS	507/864-7626 1 week	
	Walk-on: good/fair	
GREEN FEES	M-F	S-S
Adult	$15.95/8.95	$16.95/9.95
Junior	$15.95/8.95	$16.95/9.95
Senior	$15.95/8.95	$16.95/9.95
Twilight	NA	NA
PAYMENT	No credit cards accepted	
	Local checks only	
LEAGUES	Men: Th (noon-dusk)	
	Women: T (3-6 pm)	
MEMBERSHIPS	USGA, GCSAA, MGA	
PROFESSIONAL	Barry Johnson	

HOURS	Dawn to Dusk	
SEASON	April to October	

FEATURES		
Putting green	Y	
Driving range	N	
Practice area	N	
Golf carts		
Power (gas)	Y	$15/8
Pull carts	Y	$1.50
Club rental	Y	$8/4
Club storage	Y	
Caddies	N	
Proshop		
Extended	Y	
Refreshments		
Restaurant	N	
Lounge	Y	
Snacks	Y	
Clubhouse		
Showers	Y	
Lockers	Y	
Lodging	N	

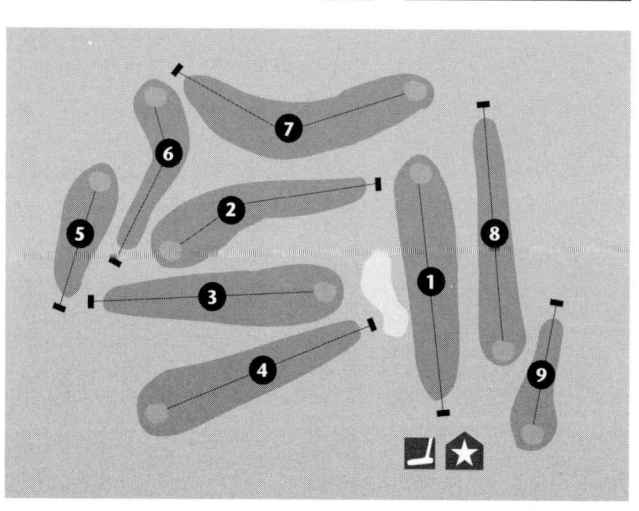

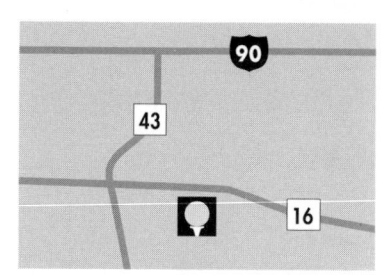

Located east of Rushford. Course is about 2 1/2 miles east of Highway 43 on Highway 16.

	MEN				**WOMEN**		
	BACK	FRONT	PAR	HDCP	FRONT	PAR	HDCP
1	392	387	4	9	382	5	7
2	527	514	5	7	439	5	3
3	413	403	4	3	389	5	5
4	376	366	4	1	346	4	1
5	172	144	3	17	130	3	17
6	374	358	4	11	334	4	11
7	530	513	5	15	493	5	9
8	396	378	4	5	310	4	13
9	180	165	3	13	155	3	15
Out	3360	3228	36		2978	38	
1	392	387	4	10	382	5	8
2	527	514	5	8	439	5	4
3	413	403	4	4	389	5	6
4	376	366	4	2	346	4	2
5	172	144	3	18	130	3	18
6	374	358	4	12	334	4	12
7	530	513	5	16	493	5	10
8	396	378	4	6	310	4	14
9	180	165	3	14	155	3	16
In	3360	3228	36		2978	38	
Total	6720	6456	72		5956	76	
Rating	71.8	70.4			73.4		
Slope	125	122			126		

FIDDLESTIX GOLF COURSE

18 Regulation Public

39155 Highway 47, P.O. Box 23
Isle, Minnesota 56342
612/676-3636 Clubhouse/Proshop

HOURS	7 am to Dusk
SEASON	April to October

RESERVATIONS	612/676-3636
	Walk-on: good/fair

GREEN FEES	M-F	S-S
Adult	$16/12	$18/13
Senior	$16/12	$18/13
Junior	$16/12	$18/13
Twilight	$11	$11 (Sun)

PAYMENT	Credit cards not accepted
	Non-local checks accepted

LEAGUES	Men: M-W (pm)
	Women: W (am), Th (pm)

MEMBERSHIPS	USGA, PGA, GCSAA, MGA

OWNER	Harley & Tama Exsted
SUPERINTENDENT	Dennis Peterson

FEATURES

Putting green	Y	
Driving range	Y	$3
Practice area	N	
Golf carts		
Power (gas)	Y	$20
Pull carts	Y	$2
Club rental	Y	$5
Club storage	N	
Caddies	N	
Proshop		
Extended	Y	
Refreshments		
Restaurant	N	
Lounge	N	
Snacks	Y	
Clubhouse		
Showers	N	
Lockers	N	
Lodging	N	

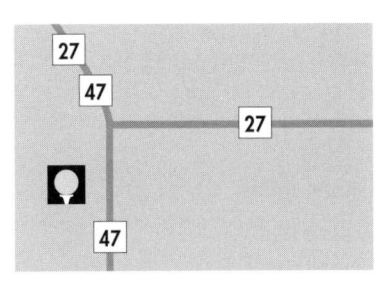

Located south of Isle. Course entrance is about 3 miles south of MN Highway 27 on MN Highway 47.

	MEN				**WOMEN**		
	BACK	FRONT	PAR	HDCP	FRONT	PAR	HDCP
1	365	336	4	3	316	4	3
2	340	333	4	13	306	4	13
3	485	475	5	15	375	5	15
4	339	331	4	7	296	4	7
5	422	412	4	1	375	4	1
6	193	163	3	8	137	3	8
7	355	315	4	12	270	4	12
8	156	136	3	17	116	3	17
9	383	363	4	4	355	4	4
Out	3038	2864	35		2546	35	
10	446	433	5	18	410	5	18
11	195	157	3	11	135	3	11
12	327	307	4	5	288	4	5
13	490	470	5	14	403	5	14
14	325	313	4	6	284	4	6
15	335	315	4	9	287	4	9
16	149	139	3	16	129	3	16
17	476	447	5	2	353	5	2
18	333	310	4	10	293	4	10
In	3076	2891	37		2582	37	
Total	6114	5755	72		5128	72	
Rating	69.3	67.9			69.5		
Slope	119	116			121		

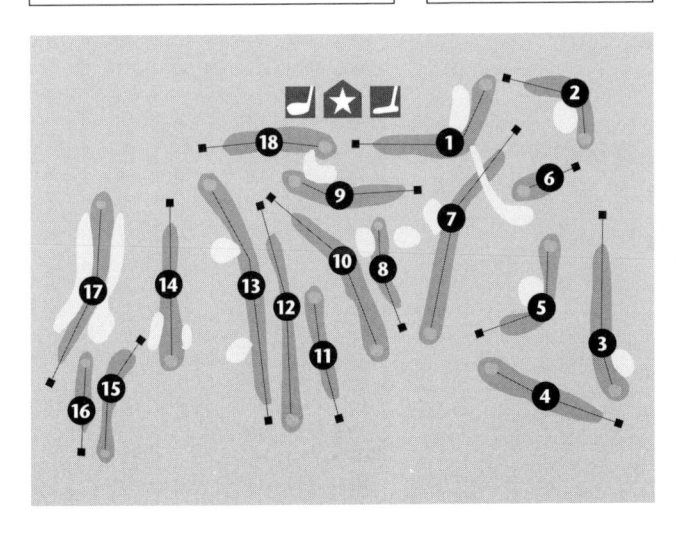

GOLF COURSE DIRECTORY

FOREST HILLS GOLF CLUB

18 Regulation Private

7530 North 210th Street
Forest Lake, Minnesota 55025
612/464-3097 Clubhouse
612/464-4514 Proshop

RESERVATIONS	612/464-4514	
	Members only	
GREEN FEES	M-F	S-S
Adult	$27/18	$30/22
Senior	$27/18	$30/22
Junior	$27/18	$30/22
Twilight	NA	NA
	Members and guests only	
PAYMENT	No credit cards accepted	
	Non-local checks accepted	
LEAGUES	None	
MEMBERSHIPS	USGA, PGA, GCSAA, MGA	
SUPERINTENDENT	Marlow Hansen	
PROFESSIONAL	Doug Gustafson	

HOURS	7 am to Dusk	
SEASON	April-November	
FEATURES		
Putting green	Y	
Driving range	Y	$3
Practice area	Y	
Golf carts		
Power (gas)	Y	$20
Pull carts	Y	
Club rental	Y	$3
Club storage	Y	$60/yr
Caddies	Y	
Proshop		
Extended	Y	
Refreshments		
Restaurant	Y	
Lounge	Y	
Snacks	Y	
Clubhouse		
Showers	Y	
Lockers	Y	
Lodging	N	

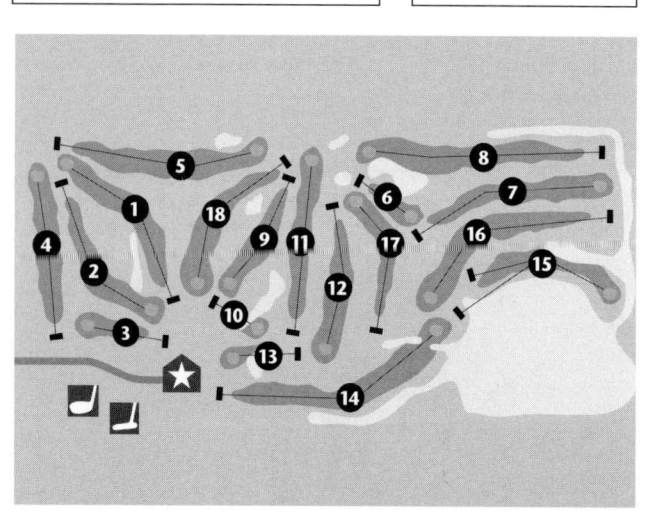

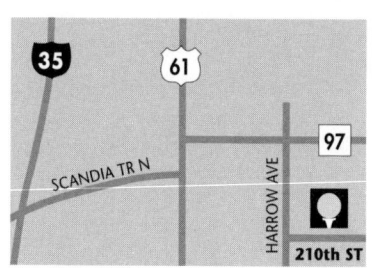

Located in Forest Lake. Course is east of U.S. Highway 61 on Highway 97, south on Harrow Ave N, then east on 210th St.

	MEN				**WOMEN**		
	BACK	FRONT	PAR	HDCP	FRONT	PAR	HDCP
1	447	427	4	5	370	5	13
2	373	363	4	9	350	4	1
3	201	194	3	7	171	3	11
4	357	354	4	13	334	4	3
5	486	466	5	15	439	5	9
6	183	164	3	11	138	3	17
7	452	440	4	1	360	4	5
8	542	520	5	3	385	5	7
9	292	284	4	17	268	4	15
Out	3333	3212	36		2815	37	
10	137	126	3	18	101	3	16
11	363	358	4	12	341	4	12
12	345	337	4	10	302	4	10
13	166	162	3	14	117	3	14
14	560	551	5	2	194	5	2
15	395	370	4	4	302	4	6
16	506	492	5	6	420	5	4
17	328	306	4	16	247	4	18
18	366	348	4	8	268	4	8
In	3166	3050	36		2592	36	
Total	6499	6262	72		5407	73	
Rating	71.3	70.1			71.6		
Slope	129	127			125		

THE MINNESOTA ILLUSTRATED

FORT RIDGELY STATE PARK GOLF COURSE

9 Regulation Public

Route 1, Box 65
Fairfax, Minnesota 55332
507/426-7840 Clubhouse

HOURS 8 am to Dusk

SEASON April to October

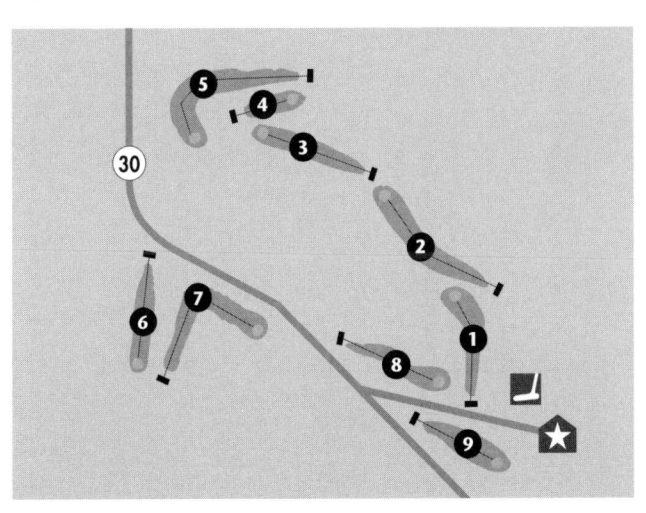

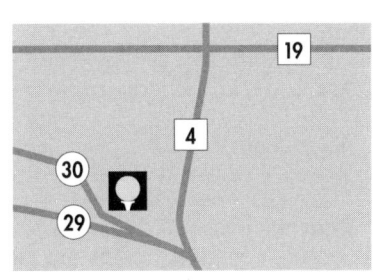

Located 6 miles south of Fairfax or 12 miles north of Sleepy Eye. Course is 1/4 mile west of Hwy 4 on County Road 29.

RESERVATIONS	No reservations accepted Walk-on: good/good

GREEN FEES	M-F	S-S
Adult	$5	$7
Senior	$5	$7
Junior	$5	$7
Twilight	NA	NA
	Group discounts available Mon-Sat $1 off green fee (20 or more required)	

PAYMENT	Credit: Visa® MC® Discover® Non-local checks accepted

LEAGUES	None

MEMBERSHIPS	MGA

MANAGERS	Mark Tjosaas

FEATURES

Putting green	Y	
Driving range	N	
Practice area	N	
Golf carts		
Power	N	
Pull carts	Y	$1
Club rental	Y	$2
Club storage	N	
Caddies	N	
Proshop		
Basic	Y	
Refreshments		
Restaurant	N	
Lounge	N	
Snacks	Y	
Clubhouse		
Showers	Y	
Lockers	N	
Lodging/camp	Y	$12.50

	MEN			**WOMEN**		
	FRONT	PAR	HDCP	FRONT	PAR	HDCP
1	291	4	3	290	4	3
2	408	4	2	361	4	2
3	305	4	4	300	4	4
4	176	3	8	168	3	8
5	457	5	6	384	5	6
6	221	3	5	217	3	5
7	349	4	1	308	4	1
8	281	4	7	275	4	7
9	269	4	9	257	4	9
Out	2757	35		2560	35	
1	291	4	3	290	4	3
2	408	4	2	361	4	2
3	305	4	4	300	4	4
4	176	3	8	168	3	8
5	457	5	6	384	5	6
6	221	3	5	217	3	5
7	349	4	1	308	4	1
8	281	4	7	275	4	7
9	269	4	9	257	4	9
In	2757	35		2560	35	
Total	5514	70		5120	70	
Rating	64.2			70.4		
Slope	109			114		

GOLF COURSE DIRECTORY

FORT SNELLING GOLF COURSE

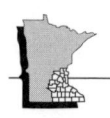

9 Regulation Public

Building 175
St. Paul, Minnesota 55111
612/726-6222 Clubhouse/Proshop

HOURS	Dawn to Dusk
SEASON	April to October

RESERVATIONS	No reservations accepted Walk-on: good/good	
GREEN FEES	M-F	S-S
Adult	$11.50	$11.50
Senior	$7.50[1]	$7.50[2]
Junior	$7.50[1]	$7.50[2]
Twilight	$8 (6:30pm)	$8 (6:30pm)
	[1] Before 11 am	
	[2] After 4 pm	
PAYMENT	Credit: Visa® MasterCard® Non-local checks accepted	
LEAGUES	Various	
MEMBERSHIPS	USGA, NGF, GCSAA, MGA	
MANAGER	Steve Skaar	
SUPERINTENDENT	Bill Jaunty	

FEATURES		
Putting green	Y	
Driving range	N	
Practice area	N	
Golf carts		
Power (gas)	Y	$9
Pull carts	Y	$1.50
Club rental	Y	$3.50
Club storage	N	
Caddies	N	
Proshop		
Basic	Y	
Refreshments		
Restaurant	N	
Lounge	N	
Snacks	Y	
Clubhouse		
Showers	N	
Lockers	N	
Lodging	N	

Located 1/2 mile south of Hwy 55 on Bloomington Rd, east on Minnehaha Ave., south on Taylor Ave. Follow signs.

	MEN			**WOMEN**		
	FRONT	PAR	HDCP	FRONT	PAR	HDCP
1	410	4	1	410	5	3
2	280	4	9	280	4	9
3	375	4	4	375	4	2
4	200	3	2	200	3	6
5	313	4	6	313	4	5
6	461	5	5	461	5	1
7	228	4	8	228	4	8
8	270	4	7	270	4	4
9	145	3	3	145	3	7
Out	2682	35		2682	36	
1	410	4	1	410	5	3
2	280	4	9	280	4	9
3	375	4	4	375	4	2
4	200	3	2	200	3	6
5	313	4	6	313	4	5
6	461	5	5	461	5	1
7	228	4	8	228	4	8
8	270	4	7	270	4	4
9	145	3	3	145	3	7
In	2682	35		2682	36	
Total	5364	70		5364	72	
Rating	65.0			67.8		
Slope	102			109		

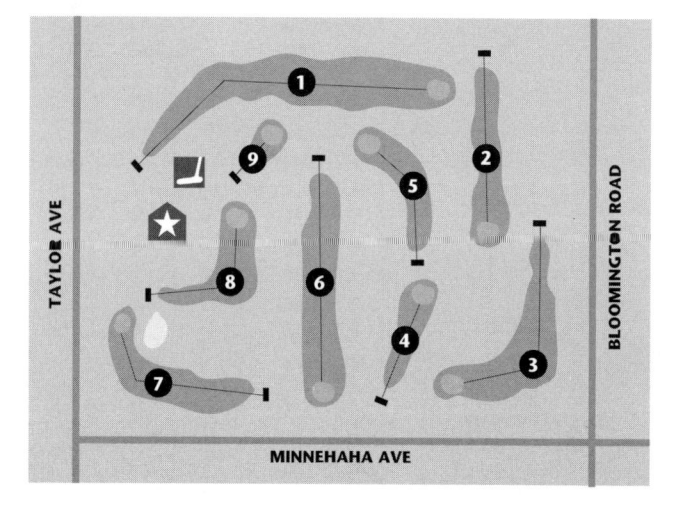

FOSSTON GOLF CLUB

9 Regulation Semi-Private

Highway 2 West, P.O. Box 483
Fosston, Minnesota 56542
218/435-6535 Clubhouse/Proshop

HOURS	7 am to Dusk
SEASON	April to October

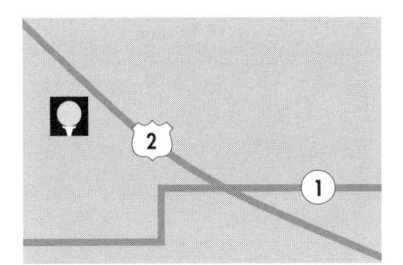

RESERVATIONS	218/435-6535
	Walk-on: good/fair

GREEN FEES	M-F	S-S
Adult	$8.50/6.50	$9.50/7.50
Senior	$8.50/6.50	$9.50/7.50
Junior	$4	$5
Twilight	NA	NA

PAYMENT	No credit cards accepted
	Non-local checks accepted

LEAGUES	None

MEMBERSHIPS	None

OWNER	Ernest Michelsen

FEATURES	
Putting green	Y
Driving range	Y
Practice area	Y
Golf carts	
Power (gas)	Y $7
Pull carts	Y $1.50
Club rental	Y $3
Club storage	N
Caddies	N
Proshop	
Regular	Y
Refreshments	
Restaurant	N
Lounge	N
Snacks	Y
Clubhouse	
Showers	N
Lockers	N
Lodging	N

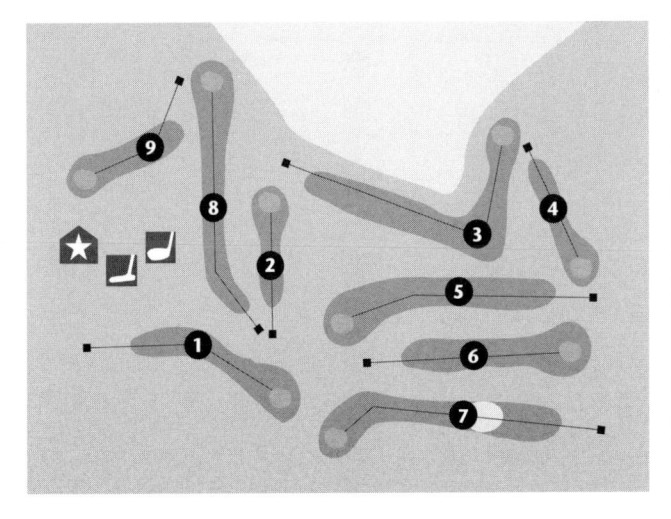

Located northwest of Fosston. Course is about 2 miles north of County Road 1 on U.S. Highway 2.

	MEN			WOMEN		
	FRONT	PAR	HDCP	FRONT	PAR	HDCP
1	405	4	3	401	5	3
2	160	3	8	134	3	8
3	345	4	5	286	4	5
4	215	3	4	172	3	4
5	480	5	7	382	4	7
6	438	4	1	401	5	1
7	512	5	2	456	5	2
8	380	4	6	286	4	6
9	280	4	9	256	4	9
Out	3215	36		2774	37	
1	405	4	3	401	5	3
2	160	3	8	134	3	8
3	345	4	5	286	4	5
4	215	3	4	172	3	4
5	480	5	7	382	4	7
6	438	4	1	401	5	1
7	512	5	2	456	5	2
8	380	4	6	286	4	6
9	280	4	9	256	4	9
In	3215	36		2774	37	
Total	6430	72		5548	74	
Rating	69.2			72.0		
Slope	NA			NA		

GOLF COURSE DIRECTORY

FOUNTAIN VALLEY GOLF CLUB

18 Regulation Public

2830 220th Street West
Farmington, Minnesota 55024
612/463-2121 Clubhouse/Proshop

RESERVATIONS	612/463-2121 1 week	
	Walk-on: fair/poor	
GREEN FEES	M-F	S-S
Adult	$17/10	$20/13
Senior	$10*	$20/13
Junior	$17/10	$20/13
Twilight	NA	NA
	* Before 12 pm	
PAYMENT	Credit: Visa® MasterCard®	
	Non-local checks accepted	
LEAGUES	Men: T (6 pm)	
	Women: W (6 pm)	
MEMBERSHIPS	LPGA, MGA	
OWNER	Bryce & Carole Olson	
SUPERINTENDENT	Mark Dischinger	
PROFESSIONAL	Sue Bremer	

HOURS	6 am to Dusk	
SEASON	April - October	
FEATURES		
Putting green	Y	
Driving range	Y	$2-4.50
Practice area	N	
Golf carts		
Power (gas)	Y	$18/10
Pull carts	Y	
Club rental	Y	$5
Club storage	N	
Caddies	N	
Proshop		
Extended	Y	
Refreshments		
Restaurant	N	
Lounge	N	
Snacks	Y	
Clubhouse		
Showers	N	
Lockers	N	
Lodging	N	

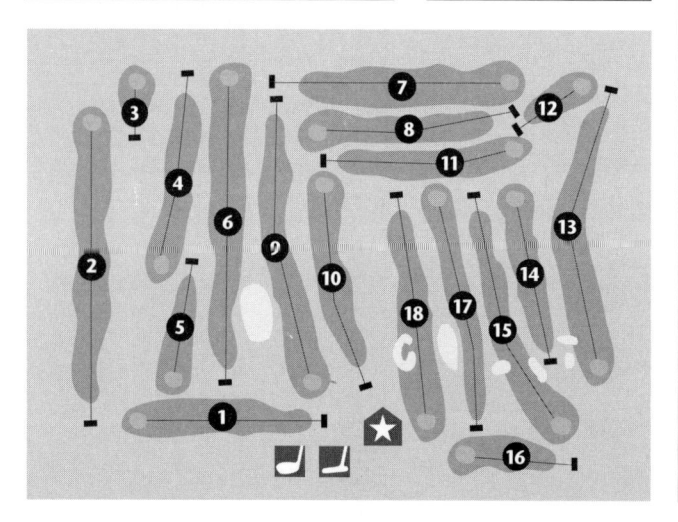

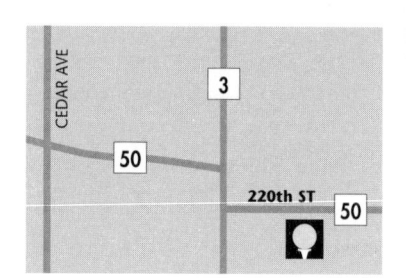

Located south of Farmington. Course entrance is one mile east of Highway 3 on 220th St./Highway 50.

	MEN				**WOMEN**		
	BACK	FRONT	PAR	HDCP	FRONT	PAR	HDCP
1	385	375	4	8	370	4	8
2	438	433	4	2	360	4	12
3	125	115	3	18	100	3	18
4	360	351	4	14	345	4	14
5	150	139	3	16	129	3	16
6	520	507	5	10	430	5	6
7	400	385	4	4	375	4	2
8	350	341	4	12	335	4	10
9	560	551	5	6	465	5	4
Out	3288	3197	36		2909	36	
10	370	365	4	5	360	4	9
11	365	353	4	7	345	4	11
12	165	155	3	17	145	3	17
13	485	477	5	11	470	5	1
14	350	288	4	13	288	4	13
15	562	550	5	3	460	5	3
16	200	175	3	15	170	3	15
17	425	417	4	1	370	4	5
18	350	341	4	9	335	4	7
In	3272	3121	36		2943	36	
Total	6560	6318	72		5852	72	
Rating	70.9	69.8			72.8		
Slope	117	115			120		

116

THE MINNESOTA ILLUSTRATED

FOX HOLLOW GOLF CLUB

18 Regulation Semi-Private

4780 Palmgren Avenue
Rogers, Minnesota 55374
612/428-8703 Clubhouse
612/428-4468 Proshop

HOURS	6:30 am to Dusk
SEASON	April-November

FEATURES

Putting green	Y	
Driving range	Y	$2.50
Practice area	Y	

Golf carts		
Power (gas)	Y	$22/11
Pull carts	Y	$3
Club rental	Y	$7.50/5
Club storage	N	
Caddies	N	

Proshop	
Extended	Y
Refreshments	
Restaurant	Y
Lounge	Y
Snacks	Y
Clubhouse	
Showers	Y
Lockers	N

Lodging	N

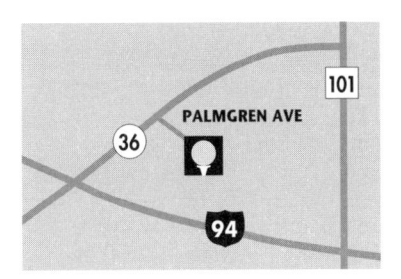

RESERVATIONS	612/428-4468 3 days
	Walk-on: good/fair

GREEN FEES	M-F	S-S
Adult	$20/14	$25/14
Senior	$12/12	$25/14
Junior	$11/11	$25/14
Twilight	NA	NA

PAYMENT	Credit: Visa® MC® AmEx®
	Non-local checks accepted

LEAGUES	Men: W,Sat
	Women: T,Sat

MEMBERSHIPS	USGA, NGF, PGA, GCSAA,
	CMAA, MGA

MANAGER	Doug Dieter
SUPERINTENDENT	Chuck Wolinari
PROFESSIONAL	Mark Sverkerson

Located northwest of Rogers. Course entrance is one mile east of I-94 (exit #205) on County Road 36.

	MEN				WOMEN		
	BACK	FRONT	PAR	HDCP	FRONT	PAR	HDCP
1	396	383	4	11	317	4	11
2	350	304	4	13	248	4	9
3	170	156	3	5	97	3	5
4	515	457	5	9	407	5	3
5	513	497	5	7	427	5	1
6	428	405	4	3	327	4	15
7	413	397	4	1	333	4	7
8	192	161	3	15	138	3	17
9	375	365	4	17	295	4	13
Out	3352	3125	36		2589	36	
10	406	389	4	12	330	4	14
11	501	490	5	14	410	5	4
12	179	158	3	16	129	3	16
13	459	417	4	2	329	4	10
14	541	523	5	4	420	5	2
15	156	131	3	18	88	3	18
16	353	330	4	6	297	4	8
17	326	301	4	8	258	4	6
18	394	380	4	10	311	4	12
In	3374	3169	36		2572	36	
Total	6726	6294	72		5161	72	
Rating	72.7	70.9			70.8		
Slope	129	125			122		

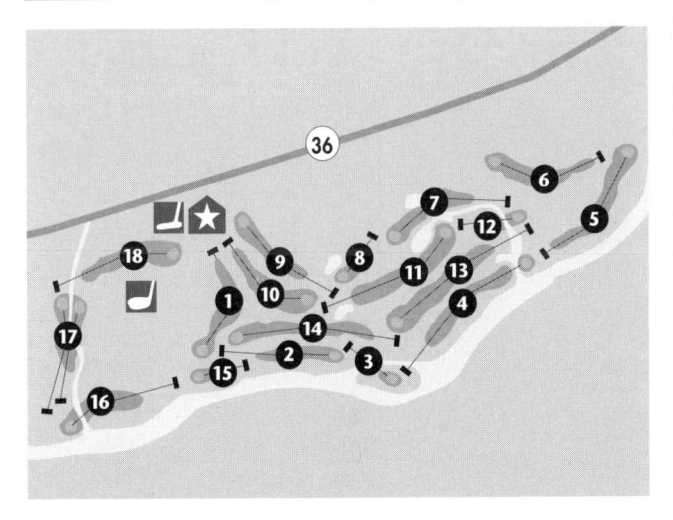

GOLF COURSE DIRECTORY

FOX LAKE GOLF CLUB

9 Regulation Semi-Private

P.O. Box 247
Sherburn, Minnesota 56171
507/764-8381 Clubhouse/Proshop

RESERVATIONS	507/764-8381	
	Walk-on: good/good	
GREEN FEES	M-F	S-S
Adult	$10/8	$11/9
Senior	$10/8	$11/9
Junior	$10/8	$11/9
Twilight	NA	NA
PAYMENT	No credit cards accepted	
	Non-local checks accepted	
LEAGUES	Men: Th (pm)	
	Women: W (pm)	
MEMBERSHIPS	GCSAA, MGA	
MANAGER	Jeff Ross	
SUPERINTENDENT	Monte Swift, Jim Studer	
PROFESSIONAL	Jeff Ross	

HOURS	Dawn to Dusk	
SEASON	April to October	
FEATURES		
Putting green	Y	
Driving range	N	
Practice area	N	
Golf carts		
Power (gas)	Y	$20
Pull carts	Y	$2.50
Club rental	Y	$7
Club storage	N	
Caddies	N	
Proshop		
Extended	Y	
Refreshments		
Restaurant	N	
Lounge	N	
Snacks	Y	
Clubhouse		
Showers	Y	
Lockers	N	
Lodging	N	

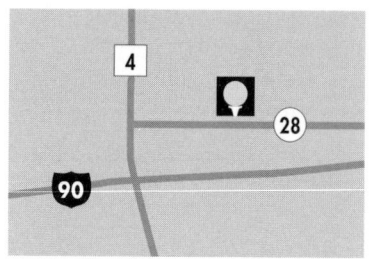

Located in Sherburn. Course entrance is east of Highway 4 on the north side of County Road 28.

	MEN				**WOMEN**		
	BACK	FRONT	PAR	HDCP	FRONT	PAR	HDCP
1	320	318	4	4	298	5	4
2	463	443	5	2	364	5	2
3	285	274	4	7	208	4	7
4	166	156	3	6	148	3	6
5	183	172	3	5	157	4	5
6	317	302	4	3	242	4	3
7	376	363	4	1	283	4	1
8	269	263	4	9	227	4	9
9	335	281	4	8	260	4	8
Out	2714	2572	35		2187	37	
1	320	318	4	4	298	5	4
2	463	443	5	2	364	5	2
3	285	274	4	7	208	4	7
4	166	156	3	6	148	3	6
5	183	172	3	5	157	4	5
6	317	302	4	3	242	4	3
7	376	363	4	1	283	4	1
8	269	263	4	9	227	4	9
9	335	281	4	8	260	4	8
In	2714	2572	35		2187	37	
Total	5428	5144	70		4374	74	
Rating	66.4	65.2			65.6		
Slope	120	118			114		

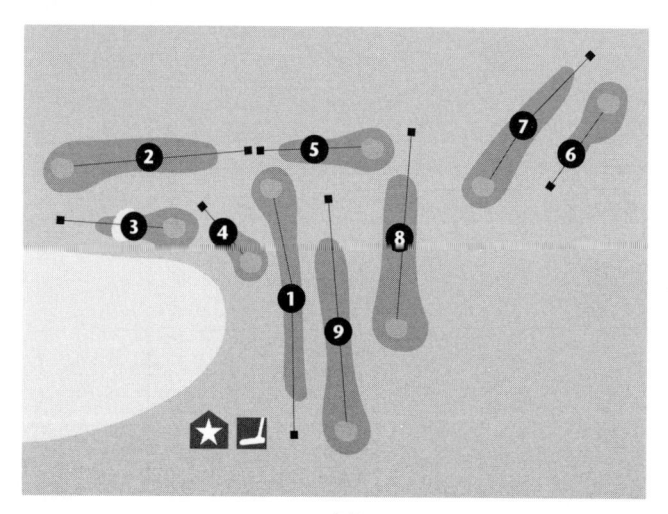

FRAZEE GOLF COURSE

9 Regulation Public

Highway 87, P.O. Box 291
Frazee, Minnesota 56544
218/334-3831 Clubhouse/Proshop

HOURS	8 am to Dusk
SEASON	April to October

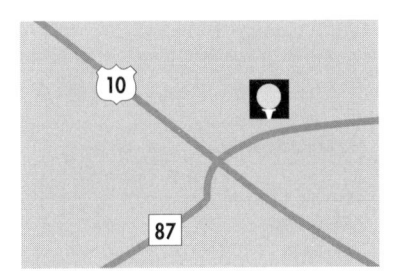

Located east of Frazee. Course entrance is about 1 mile east of U.S. Highway 10 on the north side of Highway 87.

RESERVATIONS	218/334-3831	
	Walk-on: good/fair	
GREEN FEES	M-F	S-S
Adult	$15/9.50	$15/9.50
Senior	$15/9.50	$15/9.50
Junior	$15/9.50	$15/9.50
Twilight	NA	NA
PAYMENT	No credit cards accepted	
	Non-local checks accepted	
LEAGUES	Men: Th (4-Dusk pm)	
	Women: W (4-5:30 pm)	
MEMBERSHIPS	USGA, GCSAA, MGA	
PRESIDENT	Vern Korsendorfer	
MANAGER	Bob Miller	

FEATURES

Putting green	Y	
Driving range	N	
Practice area	N	
Golf carts		
Power (gas)	Y	$14
Pull carts	Y	$3
Club rental	Y	
Club storage	Y	
Caddies	N	
Proshop		
Regular	Y	
Refreshments		
Restaurant	N	
Lounge	Y	
Snacks	Y	
Clubhouse		
Showers	Y	
Lockers	Y	
Lodging	N	

	MEN			**WOMEN**		
	FRONT	PAR	HDCP	FRONT	PAR	HDCP
1	309	4	4	309	4	4
2	185	3	6	168	3	6
3	245	4	7	237	4	7
4	410	5	2	396	5	2
5	320	3	8	320	3	8
6	156	3	8	145	3	8
7	350	4	1	295	4	1
8	120	3	9	120	3	9
9	409	5	3	357	5	3
Out	2504	35		2347	35	
1	309	4	4	309	4	4
2	185	3	6	168	3	6
3	245	4	7	237	4	7
4	410	5	2	396	5	2
5	320	3	8	320	3	8
6	156	3	8	145	3	8
7	350	4	1	295	4	1
8	120	3	9	120	3	9
9	409	5	3	357	5	3
In	2504	35		2347	35	
Total	5008	70		4694	70	
Rating	64.2			67.2		
Slope	104			109		

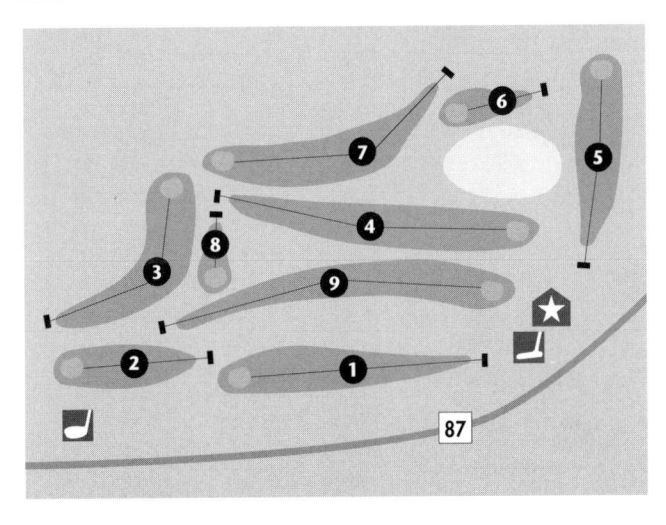

GOLF COURSE DIRECTORY

FRENCH LAKE OPEN GOLF COURSE

9 Executive Public

17500 County Road 81
Osseo, Minnesota 55369
612/428-4544 Clubhouse/Proshop

HOURS 6:30 am to Dusk
SEASON April to October

RESERVATIONS	612/428-4544 1 week	
	Walk-on: fair/poor	
GREEN FEES	M-F	S-S
Adult	$8	$9
Senior	$5.50	$9
Junior	$5.50	$9
Twilight	NA	NA
	Season tickets available	
	$5.50 second round	
PAYMENT	No credit cards accepted	
	Non-local checks accepted	
LEAGUES	Men: Various	
	Women: Various	
MEMBERSHIPS	PGA, MGA	
OWNER	LeLan & Lyden Moe	
PROFESSIONAL	Bob Mann, Aaron McClay	

FEATURES		
Putting green	Y	
Driving range	Y	
Practice area	N	
Golf carts		
Power (gas)	Y	$10
Pull carts	Y	$1
Club rental	Y	
Club storage	N	
Caddies	N	
Proshop		
Basic	Y	
Refreshments		
Restaurant	N	
Lounge	Y	
Snacks	Y	
Clubhouse		
Showers	N	
Lockers	N	
Lodging	N	

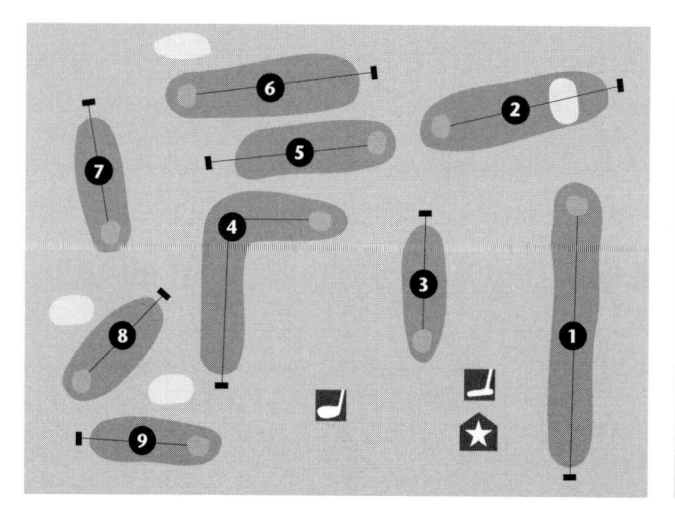

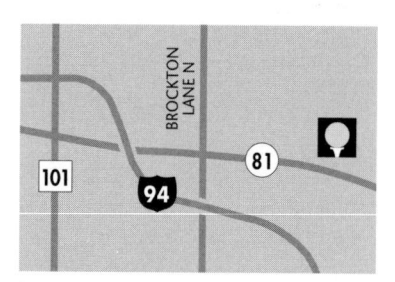

Located in Maple Grove. Course is four miles east of MN Highway 101 on County Road 81.

	MEN			WOMEN		
	FRONT	PAR	HDCP	FRONT	PAR	HDCP
1	243	4	5	233	4	5
2	145	3	9	100	3	9
3	155	3	3	145	3	3
4	277	4	4	260	4	4
5	132	3	7	101	3	7
6	135	3	8	105	3	8
7	121	3	6	111	3	6
8	139	3	2	129	3	2
9	160	3	1	123	3	1
Out	1507	29		1307	29	
1	243	4	5	233	4	5
2	145	3	9	100	3	9
3	155	3	3	145	3	3
4	277	4	4	260	4	4
5	132	3	7	101	3	7
6	135	3	8	105	3	8
7	121	3	6	111	3	6
8	139	3	2	129	3	2
9	160	3	1	123	3	1
In	1507	29		1307	29	
Total	3014	58		2614	58	
Rating	53.6			53.6		
Slope	74			79		

THE MINNESOTA ILLUSTRATED

FRITZ'S RESORT & GOLF COURSE

9 Par-3 Public

P.O. Box 803
Nisswa, Minnesota 56468
218/568-8988 Clubhouse/Proshop

HOURS	8 am to Dusk
SEASON	May to October

RESERVATIONS	218/568-8988 24 hours
	Walk-on: good/poor

GREEN FEES	M-F	S-S
Adult	$7.50/5	$7.50/5
Senior	$7.50/5	$7.50/5
Junior	$7.50/5	$7.50/5
Twilight	NA	NA

PAYMENT	Credit: Visa® MasterCard®
	Non-local checks accepted

LEAGUES	Men: None
	Women: None

MEMBERSHIPS	None

OWNER	Richard & Jane Geike
MANAGER	Richard & Jane Geike

FEATURES		
Putting green	N	
Driving range	N	
Practice area	N	
Golf carts		
Power	N	
Pull carts	Y	$1
Club rental	Y	$2.50
Club storage	N	
Caddies	N	
Proshop		
Regular	Y	
Refreshments		
Restaurant	N	
Lounge	N	
Snacks	Y	
Clubhouse		
Showers	N	
Lockers	N	
Lodging	Y	

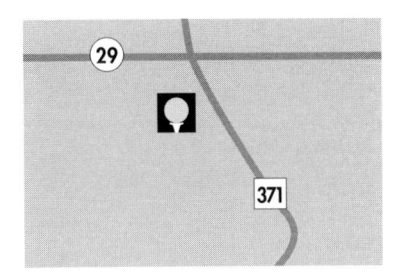

Located about one mile north of Nisswa. Course entrance is south of County Road 29 on MN Highway 371.

	MEN			**WOMEN**		
	FRONT	PAR	HDCP	FRONT	PAR	HDCP
1	139	4		139	4	
2	89	3		89	3	
3	84	3		84	3	
4	81	3		81	3	
5	123	3		123	3	
6	187	3		187	3	
7	135	4		135	4	
8	187	4		187	4	
9	97	3		97	3	
Out	1122	30		1122	30	
1	139	4		139	4	
2	89	3		89	3	
3	84	3		84	3	
4	81	3		81	3	
5	123	3		123	3	
6	187	3		187	3	
7	135	4		135	4	
8	187	4		187	4	
9	97	3		97	3	
In	1122	30		1122	30	
Total	2244	60		2244	60	
Rating	NA			NA		
Slope	NA			NA		

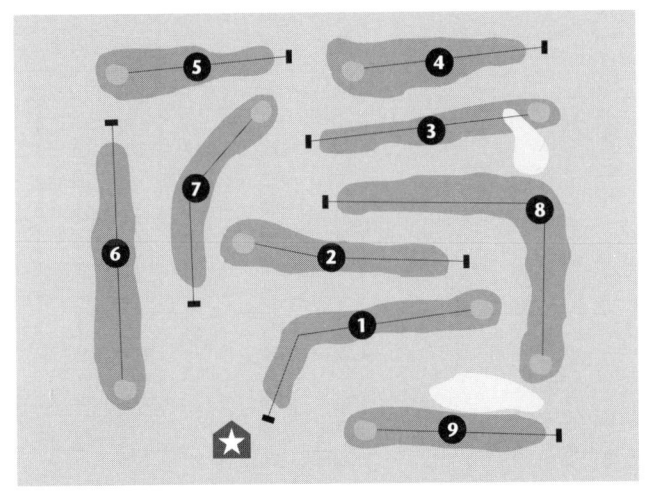

GOLF COURSE DIRECTORY

GARRISON CREEK GOLF COURSE

9 Regulation Public

Highway 169, P.O. Box 434
Garrison, Minnesota 56550
612/692-4922 Clubhouse/Proshop

HOURS	Dawn to Dusk
SEASON	April to October

RESERVATIONS	612/692-4922	
	Walk-on: good/fair	

GREEN FEES	M-F	S-S
Adult	$11/7	$12/7.50
Senior	$10/6	$12/7.50
Junior	$10/6	$12/7.50
Twilight	NA	NA

PAYMENT	No credit cards accepted
	Non-local checks accepted

LEAGUES	None

MEMBERSHIPS	None

OWNER	Wally & Jack Ashmore

FEATURES		
Putting green	Y	
Driving range	Y	
Practice area	N	
Golf carts		
Power (gas)	Y	$8
Pull carts	Y	$1.50
Club rental	Y	
Club storage	N	
Caddies	N	
Proshop		
Regular	Y	
Refreshments		
Restaurant	N	
Lounge	N	
Snacks	Y	
Clubhouse		
Showers	N	
Lockers	N	
Lodging	N	

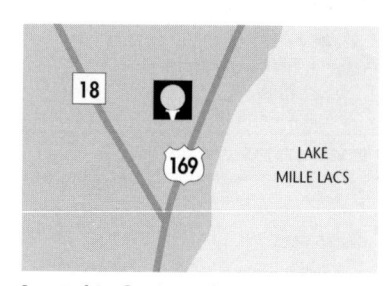

LAKE MILLE LACS

Located in Garrison. Course entrance is 3 blocks north of the U.S. Hwy 169/ MN Hwy 18 "Y" on U.S. Highway 169.

	MEN			**WOMEN**		
	FRONT	PAR	HDCP	FRONT	PAR	HDCP
1	309	4	4	309	4	4
2	185	3	6	168	3	6
3	245	4	7	237	4	7
4	410	5	2	396	5	2
5	320	3	8	320	3	8
6	156	3	8	145	3	8
7	350	4	1	295	4	1
8	120	3	9	120	3	9
9	409	5	3	357	5	3
Out	2504	35		2347	35	
1	309	4	4	309	4	4
2	185	3	6	168	3	6
3	245	4	7	237	4	7
4	410	5	2	396	5	2
5	320	3	8	320	3	8
6	156	3	8	145	3	8
7	350	4	1	295	4	1
8	120	3	9	120	3	9
9	409	5	3	357	5	3
In	2504	35		2347	35	
Total	5008	70		4694	70	
Rating	64.2			67.2		
Slope	104			109		

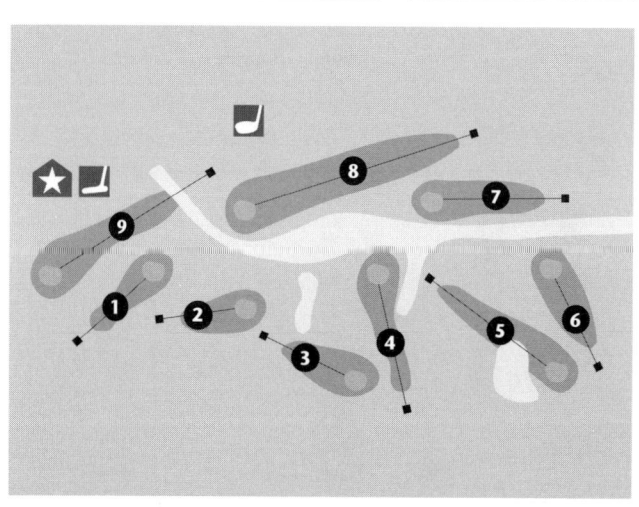

GEM LAKE HILLS GOLF COURSE

9 Par-3/9 Executive Public

4039 Scheuneman Road
White Bear Lake, Minnesota 55110
612/429-8715 Clubhouse/Proshop

HOURS	7 am to Dusk
SEASON	April to October

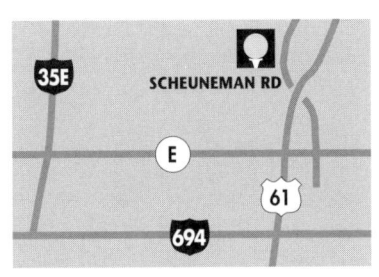

Located in White Bear Lake. Course is east of U.S. Highway 61 on County Road E, then north on Scheuneman Road.

RESERVATIONS	612/429-8715 1 day
	Walk-on: fair/fair
GREEN FEES	M-F	S-S
Adult–18	$14	$15
Exec/Par-3	$8.50/7.50	$9/8
Sr/Jr–18	$14	$15
Exec/Par-3	$8.50/7.50	$9/8
Twilight	NA	NA
	Sr/Jr cards available
PAYMENT	No credit cards accepted
	Non-local checks accepted
LEAGUES	Men: Various
	Women: Various
MEMBERSHIPS	USGA, GCSAA, MGA
MANAGER	Tony Carlson
PROFESSIONAL	Paul Mample

FEATURES		
Putting green	Y	
Driving cage	Y	$1.25
Practice area	N	
Golf carts		
Power	N	
Pull carts	Y	$1.75
Club rental	Y	$5.50
Club storage	N	
Caddies	N	
Proshop		
Basic	N	
Refreshments		
Restaurant	N	
Lounge	Y	
Snacks	Y	
Clubhouse		
Showers	N	
Lockers	N	
Lodging	N	

	MEN			**WOMEN**		
	FRONT	PAR	HDCP	FRONT	PAR	HDCP
1	182	3	8	167	3	3
2	216	3	1	214	4	9
3	144	3	5	124	3	5
4	163	3	7	157	3	6
5	196	3	2	175	3	1
6	180	3	4	170	3	4
7	154	3	3	146	3	2
8	160	3	9	155	3	8
9	174	3	6	159	3	7
Out	1569	27		1467	28	
10	163	3	8	148	3	4
11	280	4	9	215	4	7
12	132	3	7	122	3	9
13	140	3	6	133	3	8
14	315	4	2	252	4	3
15	161	3	4	126	3	5
16	308	4	5	300	4	6
17	163	3	1	121	3	2
18	141	3	3	134	3	1
In	1803	30		1551	30	
Total	3372	57		3018	58	
Rating	55.3			56.1		
Slope	77			80		

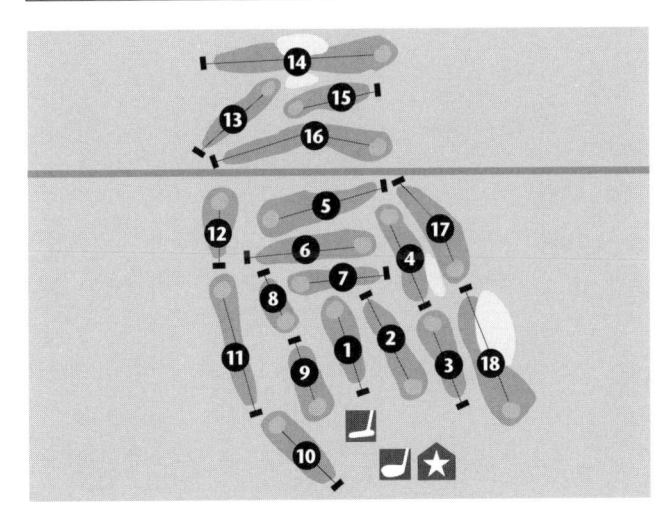

GOLF COURSE DIRECTORY

GLENCOE COUNTRY CLUB

18 Regulation Semi-Private

1221 10th Street East, P.O. Box 57
Glencoe, Minnesota 55336
612/864-3023 Clubhouse/Proshop

HOURS	7 am to Dusk
SEASON	Mar-November

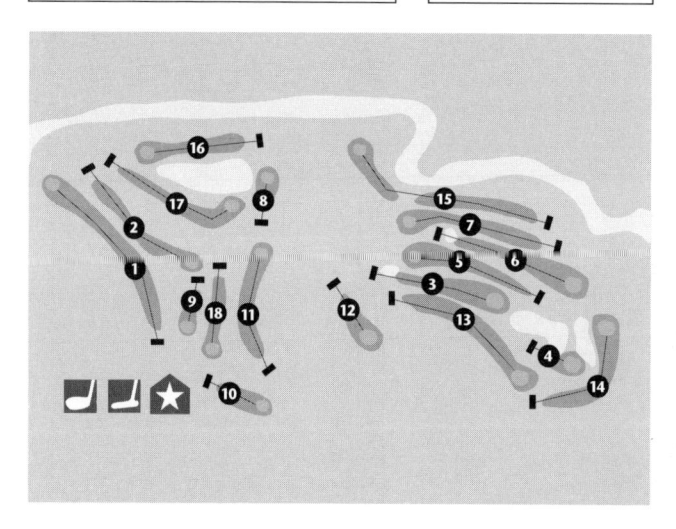

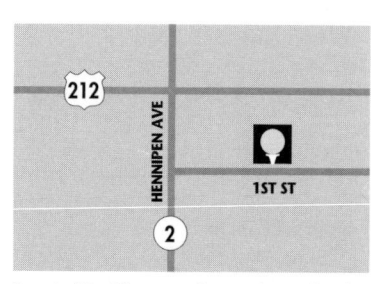

Located in Glencoe. Course is south of U.S. Highway 212 on Hennipen Avenue/County Road 2, then east on 1st Street.

RESERVATIONS	612/864-3023 3 days
	Walk-on: good/fair

GREEN FEES	M-F	S-S
Adult	$18/12	$22/14
Senior	$18/12	$22/14
Junior	$18/12	$22/14
Twilight	NA	NA

PAYMENT	Credit: Visa® MasterCard®
	Non-local checks accepted

LEAGUES	Men: Various
	Women: Various

MEMBERSHIPS	USGA, NGF, PGA, MGA

MANAGER	Bryan Koepp
PROFESSIONAL	Benny Menton

FEATURES

Putting green	Y	
Driving range	Y	$2
Practice area	Y	

Golf carts		
Power (gas)	Y	$18/12
Pull carts	Y	$2
Club rental	Y	$4
Club storage	Y	
Caddies	N	

Proshop	
Extended	Y
Refreshments	
Restaurant	Y
Lounge	Y
Snacks	Y
Clubhouse	
Showers	Y
Lockers	Y

Lodging	N

	MEN					**WOMEN**		
	BACK	FRONT	PAR	HDCP	FRONT	PAR	HDCP
1	505	485	5	3	420	5	3
2	403	393	4	1	345	4	1
3	358	326	4	15	237	4	15
4	160	141	3	7	120	3	7
5	351	333	4	11	303	4	11
6	491	470	5	5	408	5	5
7	394	372	4	13	338	4	13
8	115	110	3	17	100	3	17
9	284	274	4	9	242	4	9
Out	3061	2904	36		2513	36	
10	208	173	3	12	152	3	12
11	354	336	4	14	325	4	14
12	178	161	3	10	134	3	10
13	436	410	4	4	310	4	4
14	399	368	4	8	294	4	8
15	559	538	5	2	411	5	2
16	371	362	4	6	314	4	6
17	475	464	5	16	311	4	16
18	301	290	4	18	278	4	18
In	3281	3102	36		2251	35	
Total	6342	6006	72		4764	71	
Rating	69.7	67.1			69.0		
Slope	117	114			115		

124

THE MINNESOTA ILLUSTRATED

GOLDEN VALLEY COUNTRY CLUB

18 Regulation Private

7001 Golden Valley Road
Golden Valley, Minnesota 55427
612/545-2511 Clubhouse
612/545-0266 Proshop

HOURS	7 am to Dusk
SEASON	April-November

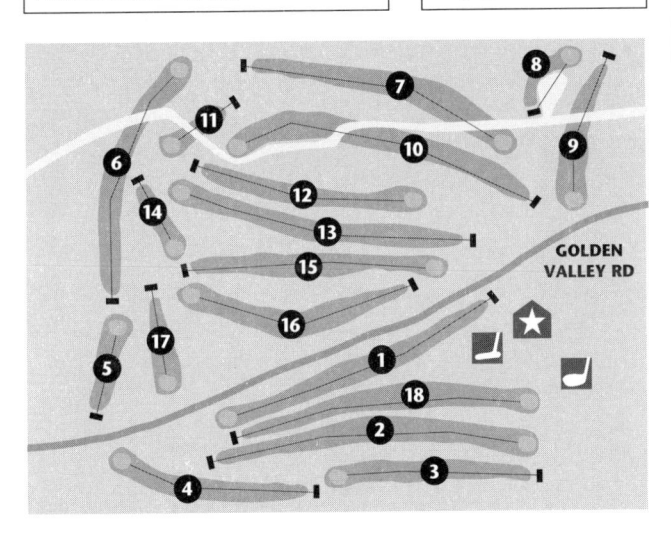

FEATURES

Putting green	Y
Driving range	Y
Practice area	Y
Golf carts	
Power (elec)	Y
Pull carts	Y
Club rental	Y
Club storage	Y
Caddies	Y
Proshop	
Extended	Y
Refreshments	
Restaurant	Y
Lounge	Y
Snacks	Y
Clubhouse	
Showers	Y
Lockers	Y
Lodging	N

Located in Golden Valley. Course is west of MN Highway 100 on Golden Valley Road.

RESERVATIONS	612/545-0266 3 days Members only

GREEN FEES	M-F	S-S
Adult	$55/37	$65/42
Senior	$55/37	$65/42
Junior	$12	$15
Twilight	$30	$30
	Members and guests only	

PAYMENT	Fees billed to members
LEAGUES	Men: Various Women: Various
MEMBERSHIPS	USGA, PGA, GCSAA, CMAA, MGA
SUPERINTENDENT	Mike Olson
PROFESSIONAL	Don Fink

	\multicolumn{4}{c}{MEN}	\multicolumn{3}{c}{WOMEN}
	BACK	FRONT	PAR	HDCP	FRONT	PAR	HDCP
1	486	465	5	13	444	5	3
2	549	525	5	3	465	5	1
3	378	357	4	7	335	4	9
4	336	320	4	11	298	4	13
5	174	161	3	17	153	3	17
6	490	470	5	9	382	5	5
7	430	390	4	1	312	4	7
8	179	163	3	15	159	3	15
9	383	335	4	5	325	4	11
Out	3405	3186	37		2873	37	
10	512	505	5	6	440	5	2
11	168	133	3	18	110	3	18
12	400	379	4	8	330	4	12
13	490	450	5	14	408	5	8
14	176	157	3	12	149	3	14
15	415	398	4	4	370	4	6
16	422	402	4	2	318	4	10
17	173	142	3	16	135	3	16
18	533	512	5	10	459	5	4
In	3289	3078	36		2719	36	
Total	6694	6264	73		5592	73	
Rating	73.0	71.1			73.3		
Slope	138	134			134		

GOLF COURSE DIRECTORY

GOODRICH GOLF COURSE

18 Regulation Public

1820 North Van Dyke Avenue
Maplewood, Minnesota 55109
612/777-7355 Clubhouse/Proshop

RESERVATIONS	612/777-7355 4 days	
	Walk-on: good/fair	
GREEN FEES	M-F	S-S
Adult	$18/12.50	$18/12.50
Senior	$18/12.50	$18/12.50
Junior	$9	$9
Twilight	$12.50	$12.50
PAYMENT	No credit cards accepted	
	No checks accepted	
LEAGUES	Various	
MEMBERSHIPS	PGA, MGA	
SUPERINTENDENT	Gerald Bibbey	
PROFESSIONAL	Michael Diebel	

HOURS	6 am to Dusk	
SEASON	March-November	
FEATURES		
Putting green	Y	
Driving range	N	
Practice area	N	
Golf carts		
Power (gas)	Y	$20/12
Pull carts	Y	$2
Club rental	Y	$8
Club storage	N	
Caddies	N	
Proshop		
Extended	Y	
Refreshments		
Restaurant	N	
Lounge	N	
Snacks	Y	
Clubhouse		
Showers	Y	
Lockers	Y	
Lodging	N	

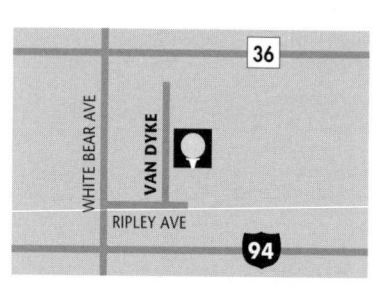

Located in Maplewood. Course is east of White Bear Avenue on Ripley Avenue, then north on Van Dyke Street.

	MEN			**WOMEN**		
	FRONT	PAR	HDCP	FRONT	PAR	HDCP
1	484	5	11	478	5	11
2	368	4	9	357	4	9
3	111	3	17	107	3	17
4	406	4	7	381	5	7
5	385	4	3	342	4	3
6	490	5	1	482	5	1
7	195	3	15	172	3	15
8	193	3	13	173	3	13
9	388	4	5	375	4	5
Out	3020	35		2877	36	
10	190	3	14	170	3	14
11	246	3	4	231	4	4
12	315	4	6	304	4	6
13	395	4	2	383	4	2
14	469	5	12	458	5	12
15	345	4	18	336	4	18
16	497	5	10	485	5	10
17	158	3	16	151	3	16
18	372	4	8	325	4	8
In	2987	35		2843	36	
Total	6007	70		5720	72	
Rating	67.9			71.2		
Slope	110			114		

GRACEVILLE GOLF CLUB

9 Regulation Semi-Private

Toqua Lake Road, P.O. Box 248
Graceville, Minnesota 56240
612/748-7557 Clubhouse/Proshop

HOURS	7 am to Dusk
SEASON	April-November

RESERVATIONS	612/748-7557	
	Walk-on: good/good	

GREEN FEES	M-F	S-S
Adult	$10/7	$12/8
Senior	$10/7	$12/8
Junior	$10/7	$12/8
Twilight	NA	NA

PAYMENT	No credit cards accepted
	Non-local checks accepted

LEAGUES	Men: W
	Women: Th

MEMBERSHIPS	PGA, MGA

PROFESSIONAL	None

FEATURES		
Putting green	Y	
Driving range	N	
Practice area	N	
Golf carts		
Power (gas)	Y	$15/9
Pull carts	Y	$1
Club rental	N	
Club storage	Y	
Caddies	N	
Proshop		
Basic	Y	
Refreshments		
Restaurant	N	
Lounge	Y	
Snacks	Y	
Clubhouse		
Showers	Y	
Lockers	N	
Lodging	N	

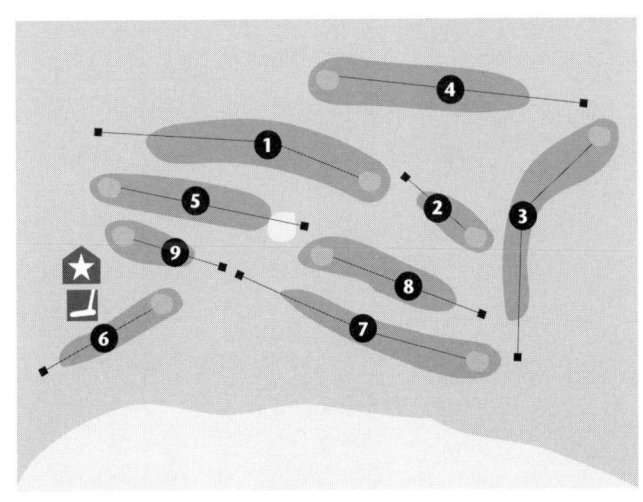

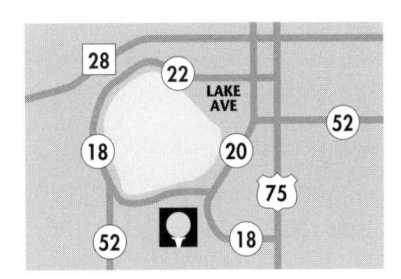

Located in Graceville. Course entrance is about 1/4 mile west of U.S. Highway 75 on County Road 18.

	MEN			**WOMEN**		
	FRONT	PAR	HDCP	FRONT	PAR	HDCP
1	491	5	7	401	5	7
2	162	3	15	162	3	15
3	345	4	13	291	4	13
4	499	5	9	398	5	9
5	341	4	5	341	4	5
6	210	3	1	110	3	1
7	475	5	3	427	5	3
8	346	4	11	346	4	11
9	160	3	17	160	3	17
Out	3029	36		2636	36	
1	491	5	8	401	5	8
2	162	3	16	162	3	16
3	345	4	14	291	4	14
4	499	5	10	398	5	10
5	341	4	6	341	4	6
6	210	3	2	110	3	2
7	475	5	4	427	5	4
8	346	4	12	346	4	12
9	160	3	18	160	3	18
In	3029	36		2636	36	
Total	6058	72		5272	72	
Rating	68.6			70.0		
Slope	112			110		

GOLF COURSE DIRECTORY

GRAND NATIONAL GOLF CLUB
18 Regulation Public

300 Ladyluck Drive
Hinckley, Minnesota 55037
612/384-7427 Clubhouse/Proshop

RESERVATIONS	612/384-7427 1 week	
	Walk-on: good/fair	
GREEN FEES	M-F	S-S
Adult	$21/15	$24/16
Senior	$21/15	$24/16
Junior	$21/15	$24/16
Twilight	NA	NA
PAYMENT	Credit: Visa® MasterCard®	
	Local checks only	
LEAGUES	Men: None	
	Women: None	
MEMBERSHIPS	GCSAA, MGA	
OWNER	Roger Parkin	
SUPERINTENDENT	Tom Haugnon	
PROFESSIONAL	Bill Manahan	

HOURS	7 am to Dusk	
SEASON	April-November	
FEATURES		
Putting green	Y	
Driving range	Y	
Practice area	Y	
Golf carts		
Power (elec)	Y	$21
Pull carts	Y	$2.50
Club rental	Y	$10
Club storage	N	
Caddies	N	
Proshop		
Extended	Y	
Refreshments		
Restaurant	N	
Lounge	Y	
Snacks	Y	
Clubhouse		
Showers	Y	
Lockers	N	
Lodging	Y	

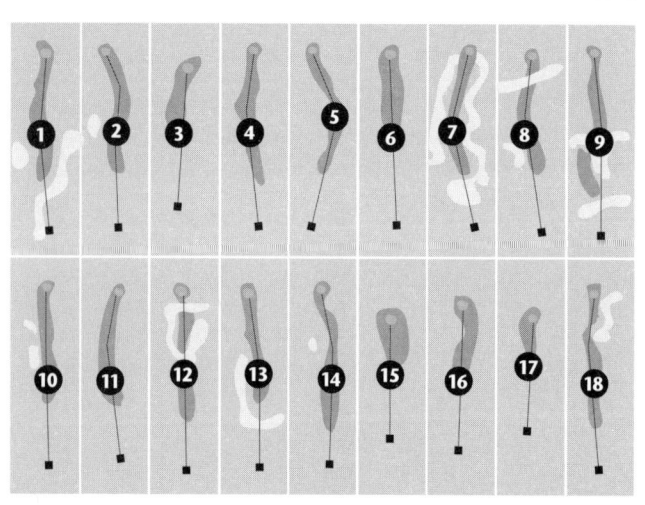

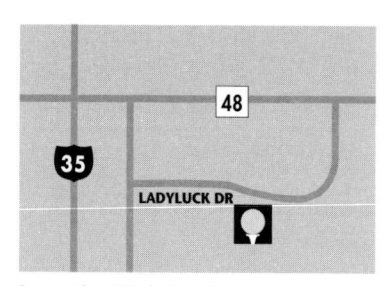

Located in Hinkcley. Course entrance is east of Interstate 35 on MN Highway 48 then south on Ladyluck Drive.

	MEN				**WOMEN**		
	BACK	FRONT	PAR	HDCP	FRONT	PAR	HDCP
1	409	368	4	9	320	4	15
2	369	322	4	15	258	4	13
3	180	140	3	13	124	3	11
4	391	342	4	7	282	4	9
5	416	371	4	1	334	4	5
6	161	125	3	17	104	3	17
7	503	465	5	11	391	5	7
8	412	358	4	5	291	4	1
9	577	531	5	3	455	5	3
Out	3418	3022	36		2559	36	
10	419	375	4	8	287	4	14
11	432	397	4	10	311	4	16
12	551	522	5	4	423	5	6
13	391	348	4	14	289	4	10
14	439	366	4	2	328	4	12
15	203	169	3	12	155	3	18
16	341	300	4	18	245	4	4
17	188	144	3	16	100	3	2
18	512	506	5	6	403	5	6
In	3476	3127	36		2541	36	
Total	6894	6149	72		5100	72	
Rating	72.0	68.7			68.7		
Slope	123	116			117		

THE MINNESOTA ILLUSTRATED

GRAND VIEW LODGE

PINES COURSE/27 Regulation Public

South 134 Nokomis
Nisswa, Minnesota 55369
218/963-2234 Clubhouse/Proshop

HOURS	7:30 am to Dusk
SEASON	April-November

RESERVATIONS	218/963-2234
	Walk-on: fair/fair

GREEN FEES	M-Th	F-S
Adult	$43.50	$49.50
Senior	$43.50	$49.50
Junior	$43.50	$49.50
Twilight	$25.50	$30.50

PAYMENT	Credit: Visa® MC® AmEx®
	Non-local checks accepted

LEAGUES	Men: Various
	Women: Various

MEMBERSHIPS	USGA, PGA, GCSAA, MGA

SUPERINTENDENT	Tom Kientzle
PROFESSIONAL	Kevin Cashman

FEATURES		
Putting green	Y	
Driving range	Y	$4
Practice area	Y	
Golf carts		
Power (gas)	Y	$29
Pull carts	N	
Club rental	Y	$20
Club storage	Y	$65
Caddies	N	
Proshop		
Extended	Y	
Refreshments		
Restaurant	Y	
Lounge	Y	
Snacks	Y	
Clubhouse		
Showers	Y	
Lockers	Y	
Lodging	Y	Call

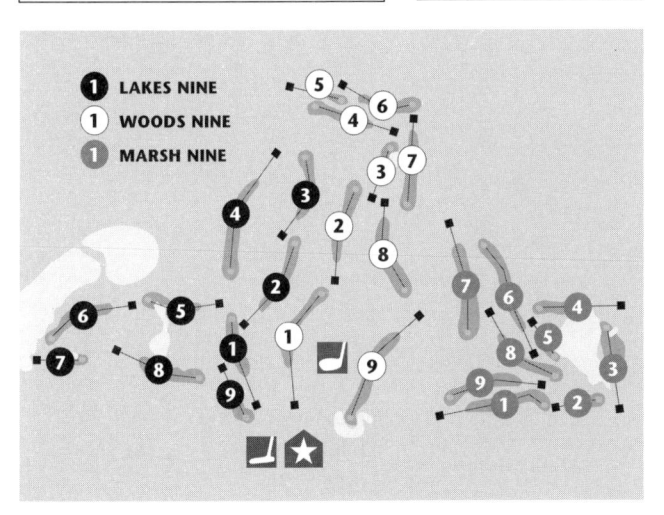

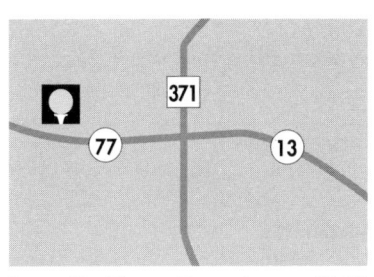

Located in Nisswa. Course is west of MN Highway 371 on County Road 77.

		MEN			WOMEN		
	BACK	FRONT	PAR	HDCP	FRONT	PAR	HDCP
1	402	380	4	9	286	4	7
2	454	390	4	1	352	4	3
3	406	330	4	15	274	4	11
4	547	496	5	3	417	5	5
5	356	320	4	7	291	4	1
6	475	460	5	17	370	5	15
7	152	130	3	13	100	3	9
8	410	366	4	5	297	4	17
9	212	194	3	11	131	3	13
LAKES	3414	3222	36		2518	36	
1	533	515	5	9	390	5	5
2	433	395	4	1	338	4	3
3	174	134	3	13	110	3	15
4	397	348	4	11	300	4	17
5	189	152	3	15	139	3	11
6	345	316	4	17	271	4	13
7	400	347	4	5	301	4	7
8	448	389	4	3	328	4	9
9	541	490	5	7	439	5	1
WOODS	3460	3086	36		2616	36	
1	501	475	5	1	413	5	1
2	204	166	3	11	147	3	13
3	370	346	4	13	274	4	7
4	351	302	4	9	267	4	9
5	175	131	3	17	101	3	17
6	527	501	5	15	447	5	5
7	451	396	4	5	317	4	11
8	418	381	4	3	318	4	3
9	426	375	4	7	310	4	15
MARSH	3423	3073	36		2594	36	
L/W Rating Slope	6874 74.2 137	6152 71.0 131	72		5134 70.6 128	72	
W/M Rating Slope	6883 73.9 139	6159 70.7 133	72		5210 71.3 129	72	
M/L Rating Slope	6837 74.3 141	6139 71.3 135	72		5112 70.7 132	72	

- **LAKES NINE**
- **WOODS NINE**
- **MARSH NINE**

GOLF COURSE DIRECTORY

GRAND VIEW LODGE

GARDEN COURSE/9 Executive Public

South 134 Nokomis
Nisswa, Minnesota 55369
218/963-2234 Clubhouse/Proshop

HOURS 7:30 am to Dusk

SEASON April-November

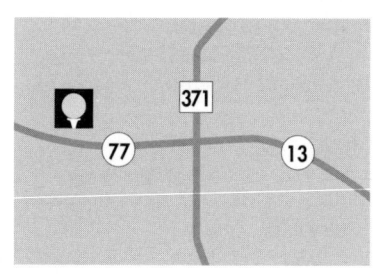

Located in Nisswa. Course entrance is west of MN Highway 371 on County Road 77.

RESERVATIONS	218/963-2234		
	Walk-on: fair/fair		
GREEN FEES	M-Th	F-S	
Adult	Call	Call	
Senior	Call	Call	
Junior	Call	Call	
Twilight	NA	NA	
PAYMENT	Credit: Visa® MC® AmEx®		
	Non-local checks accepted		
LEAGUES	Men: Various		
	Women: Various		
MEMBERSHIPS	USGA, PGA, GCSAA, MGA		
SUPERINTENDENT	Tom Kientzle		
PROFESSIONAL	Kevin Cashman		

FEATURES

Putting green	Y	
Driving range	Y	$4
Practice area	Y	
Golf carts		
Power (gas)	Y	
Pull carts	N	
Club rental	Y	$20
Club storage	Y	$65
Caddies	N	
Proshop		
Extended	Y	
Refreshments		
Restaurant	Y	
Lounge	Y	
Snacks	Y	
Clubhouse		
Showers	Y	
Lockers	Y	
Lodging	Y	Call

	MEN			WOMEN		
	FRONT	PAR	HDCP	FRONT	PAR	HDCP
1	338	4	1	315	4	1
2	384	5	7	351	5	7
3	426	5	5	379	5	5
4	186	3	4	173	3	4
5	229	4	9	166	4	9
6	295	4	3	270	4	3
7	184	3	2	170	3	2
8	305	4	6	275	4	6
9	155	3	8	146	3	8
Out	2502	35		2245	35	
1	338	4	1	315	4	1
2	384	5	7	351	5	7
3	426	5	5	379	5	5
4	186	3	4	173	3	4
5	229	4	9	166	4	9
6	295	4	3	270	4	3
7	184	3	2	170	3	2
8	305	4	6	275	4	6
9	155	3	8	146	3	8
In	2502	35		2245	35	
Total	5004	70		4490	70	
Rating	65.2			66.8		
Slope	116			110		

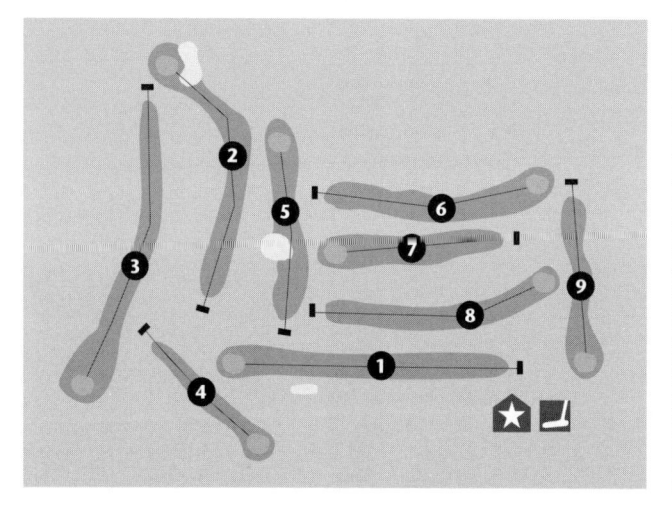

THE MINNESOTA ILLUSTRATED

GRANDVIEW GOLF CLUB

9 Regulation Public

5665 Grandview Road
Duluth, Minnesota 55810
218/624-3452 Clubhouse/Proshop

RESERVATIONS	No reservations accepted
	Walk-on: good/good

GREEN FEES	M-F	S-S
Adult	$8/6	$8/6
Senior	$7/5	$7/5
Junior	$7/5	$7/5
Twilight	NA	NA

PAYMENT	No credit cards accepted
	Local checks only

LEAGUES	Men: Various
	Women: Various

MEMBERSHIPS	None

OWNER	Pete Hendrickson
MANAGER	Pete Hendrickson

HOURS	7 am to Dusk
SEASON	April to October

FEATURES	
Putting green	N
Driving range	N
Practice area	N
Golf carts	
Power (gas)	Y $18/9
Pull carts	Y $2
Club rental	Y $3
Club storage	N
Caddies	N
Proshop	
Regular	Y
Refreshments	
Restaurant	N
Lounge	N
Snacks	Y
Clubhouse	
Showers	N
Lockers	N
Lodging	N

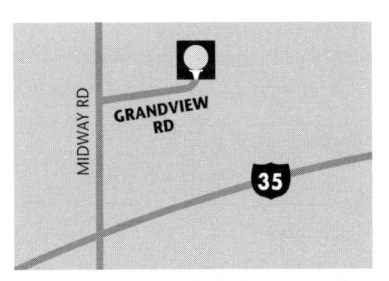

Located south of Duluth. Course is 1/2 mile north of I-35 on Midway Road, then east on Grandview Road.

	MEN			**WOMEN**		
	FRONT	PAR	HDCP	FRONT	PAR	HDCP
1	122	3	1	122	3	1
2	313	4	5	313	4	5
3	344	4	3	344	4	3
4	256	4	9	256	4	9
5	329	4	2	329	4	2
6	300	4	7	300	4	7
7	471	5	8	471	5	8
8	302	4	6	302	4	6
9	305	4	4	305	4	4
Out	2742	36		2742	36	
1	122	3	1	122	3	1
2	313	4	5	313	4	5
3	344	4	3	344	4	3
4	256	4	9	256	4	9
5	329	4	2	329	4	2
6	300	4	7	300	4	7
7	471	5	8	471	5	8
8	302	4	6	302	4	6
9	305	4	4	305	4	4
In	2742	36		2742	36	
Total	5484	71		5484	71	
Rating	NA			NA		
Slope	NA			NA		

Course layout map not provided.

GOLF COURSE DIRECTORY

GRANDY NINE GOLF COURSE

9 Regulation Public

Route 2, County Road 6
Stanchfield, Minnesota 5580
612/689-1417 Clubhouse/Proshop

RESERVATIONS	612/689-1417	
	Walk-on: good/fair	
GREEN FEES	M-F	S-S
Adult	Call	Call
Senior	Call	Call
Junior	Call	Call
Twilight	NA	NA
PAYMENT	No credit cards accepted	
	Non-local checks accepted	
LEAGUES	Men:	Various
	Women:	Various
MEMBERSHIPS	MGA	
PROFESSIONAL	Call	

HOURS	Dawn to Dusk
SEASON	April to October

FEATURES	
Putting green	Y
Driving range	N
Practice area	N
Golf carts	
Power (gas)	Y
Pull carts	Y
Club rental	Y
Club storage	N
Caddies	N
Proshop	
Extended	Y
Refreshments	
Restaurant	N
Lounge	N
Snacks	Y
Clubhouse	
Showers	N
Lockers	N
Lodging	N

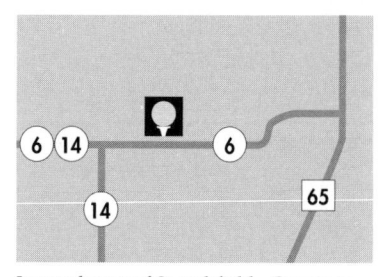

Located west of Stanchfield. Course is three miles west of MN Highway 65 on County Road 6.

	MEN			**WOMEN**		
	FRONT	PAR	HDCP	FRONT	PAR	HDCP
1	340	4	4	340	4	4
2	302	4	6	302	5	6
3	360	4	3	360	5	3
4	470	5	2	470	6	2
5	400	4	1	400	5	1
6	260	4	9	260	4	9
7	175	3	5	175	3	5
8	270	4	7	270	5	7
9	135	3	8	135	3	8
Out	2615	35		2615	40	
1	340	4	13	340	4	13
2	302	4	15	302	5	15
3	360	4	12	360	5	12
4	470	5	11	470	6	11
5	400	4	10	400	5	10
6	260	4	18	260	4	18
7	175	3	14	175	3	14
8	270	4	16	270	5	16
9	135	3	17	135	3	17
In	2615	35		2615	40	
Total	5230	70		5230	80	
Rating	65.6			69.4		
Slope	113			125		

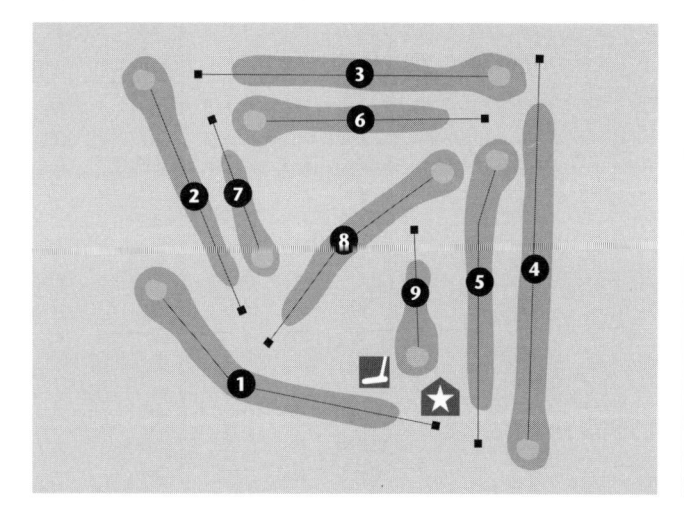

THE MINNESOTA ILLUSTRATED

GRANITE FALLS GOLF CLUB

9 Regulation Semi-Private

Highway 67 South
Granite Falls, Minnesota 56241
612/564-4141 Clubhouse
612/564-4755 Proshop

HOURS	7 am to Dusk
SEASON	April to October

RESERVATIONS	612/564-4755 1 day
	Walk-on: good/good

GREEN FEES	M-F	S-S
Adult	$15/10	$19/12
Senior	$15/10	$19/12
Junior	$15/10	$19/12
Twilight	NA	NA

PAYMENT	No credit cards accepted
	Non-local checks accepted

LEAGUES	None

MEMBERSHIPS	USGA, PGA, MGA

MANAGER	Odell Rude

FEATURES

Putting green	Y	
Driving range	N	
Practice area	Y	

Golf carts		
Power (gas)	Y	$10
Pull carts	Y	$2
Club rental	Y	$3.50
Club storage	Y	
Caddies	N	

Proshop	
Extended	Y
Refreshments	
Restaurant	Y
Lounge	Y
Snacks	Y
Clubhouse	
Showers	Y
Lockers	Y

Lodging	N

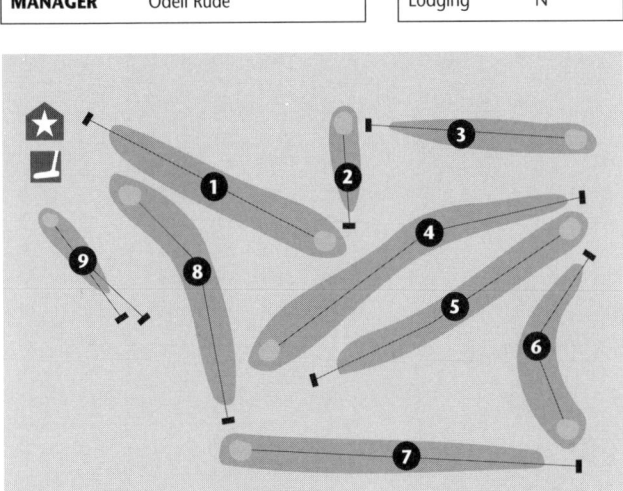

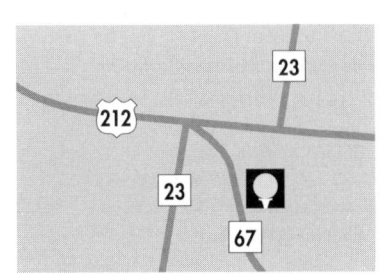

Located in Granite Falls. Course is two blocks south of U.S. Hwy 212 on Hwy 23, then one mile east on Hwy 67.

		MEN			WOMEN		
	BACK	FRONT	PAR	HDCP	FRONT	PAR	HDCP
1	388	377	4	2	327	4	6
2	129	122	3	9	112	3	9
3	281	275	4	6	270	4	4
4	491	479	5	4	458	5	3
5	414	405	4	1	360	4	1
6	290	278	4	7	273	4	7
7	485	481	5	3	478	5	2
8	349	341	4	5	314	4	5
9	140	122	3	8	115	3	8
Out	2967	2880	36		2757	36	
1	388	377	4	2	327	4	6
2	129	122	3	9	112	3	9
3	281	275	4	6	270	4	4
4	491	479	5	4	458	5	3
5	414	405	4	1	360	4	1
6	290	278	4	7	273	4	7
7	485	481	5	3	478	5	2
8	349	341	4	5	314	4	5
9	140	122	3	8	115	3	8
In	2967	2880	36		2757	36	
Total	5934	5760	72		5514	72	
Rating	67.8	67.0			71.4		
Slope	110	109			121		

GOLF COURSE DIRECTORY

GREEN LEA GOLF COURSE

18 Regulation Public

101 Richway Drive
Albert Lea, Minnesota 56007
507/373-1061 Clubhouse/Proshop

HOURS	Dawn to Dusk
SEASON	April-November

RICHWAY DR

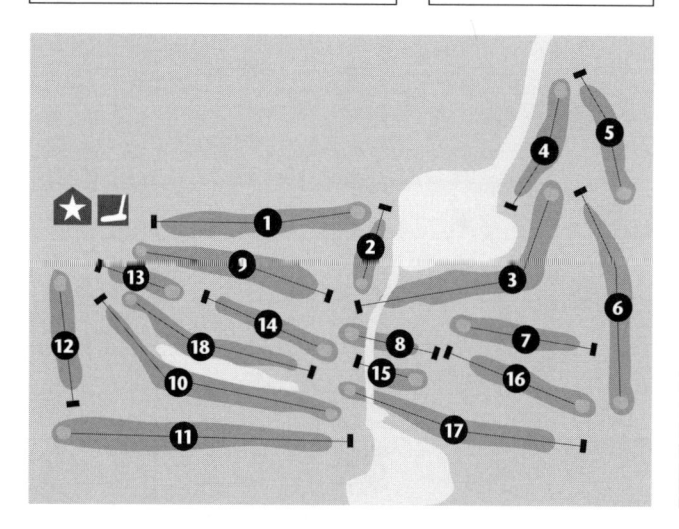

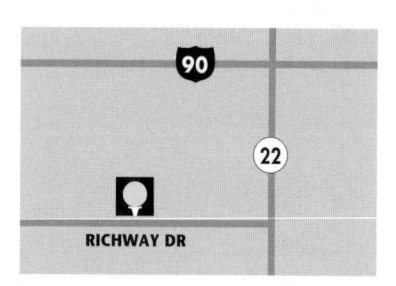

Located near Albert Lea. Course is about 1 1/2 miles south of I-90 on Cty Rd 22, then 3/4 mile west on Richway Drive.

RESERVATIONS	507/373-1061 3 days
	Walk-on: good/good

GREEN FEES	M-F	S-S
Adult	$15/9	$17/10
Senior	$12/8	$17/10
Junior	$12/8	$17/10
Twilight	NA	NA
	Group packages available	

PAYMENT	Credit: Visa® MasterCard®
	Non-local checks accepted

LEAGUES	Men: T,W (pm)
	Women: Th (am)

MEMBERSHIPS	USGA, GCSAA, MGA

MANAGER	Jeff Elseth
SUPERINTENDENT	Roger Hanson

FEATURES	
Putting green	Y
Driving range	N
Practice area	Y
Golf carts	
Power (gas)	Y $18/10
Pull carts	Y $2
Club rental	Y
Club storage	Y
Caddies	N
Proshop	
Extended	Y
Refreshments	
Restaurant	Y
Lounge	Y
Snacks	Y
Clubhouse	
Showers	N
Lockers	N
Lodging	N

	MEN				**WOMEN**		
	BACK	FRONT	PAR	HDCP	FRONT	PAR	HDCP
1	401	391	4	3	379	5	17
2	183	171	3	9	163	3	9
3	534	516	5	7	430	5	11
4	302	294	4	13	261	4	5
5	364	356	4	5	316	4	3
6	452	437	5	17	388	5	13
7	343	328	4	11	315	4	1
8	155	144	3	15	136	3	15
9	389	379	4	1	373	5	7
Out	3123	3016	36		2761	38	
10	533	525	5	4	382	5	12
11	477	461	5	10	366	5	6
12	249	238	4	18	238	4	16
13	148	131	3	16	119	3	10
14	278	273	4	14	250	4	4
15	131	123	3	12	119	3	8
16	334	330	4	6	326	5	18
17	508	494	5	8	476	5	2
18	385	379	4	2	367	5	14
In	3043	2954	37		2643	39	
Total	6166	5970	73		5404	77	
Rating	70.2	69.3			71.4		
Slope	122	120			126		

THE MINNESOTA ILLUSTRATED

GREEN VALLEY GOLF COURSE

9 Executive Public

Rural Route 2, P.O. Box 62
Lake Park, Minnesota 56554
218/532-7447 Clubhouse/Proshop

HOURS	7 am to Dusk
SEASON	April to October

RESERVATIONS	218/532-7447
	Walk-on: good/fair

GREEN FEES	M-F	S-S
Adult	$9/8	$9/8
Senior	$9/6	$9/6
Junior	$9/6	$9/6
Twilight	$6	$6
	20 game cards available	

PAYMENT	No credit cards accepted
	Non-local checks accepted

LEAGUES	Men: Th (pm)
	Women: T (pm)

MEMBERSHIPS	USGA, NGF, MGA

OWNER/MGR	Mike Lezin

FEATURES	
Putting green	Y
Driving range	N
Practice area	Y
Golf carts	
Power (gas)	Y
Pull carts	Y
Club rental	Y
Club storage	N
Caddies	N
Proshop	
Regular	Y
Refreshments	
Restaurant	N
Lounge	N
Snacks	Y
Clubhouse	
Showers	N
Lockers	N
Lodging	N

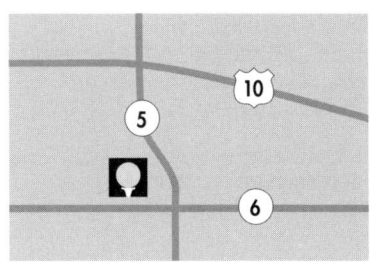

Located south of Lake Park. Course is about 6 miles south of U.S. Highway 10 on County Road 5.

		MEN			WOMEN		
	BACK	FRONT	PAR	HDCP	FRONT	PAR	HDCP
1	363	349	4		273	4	
2	329	306	4		246	4	
3	238	203	3		153	3	
4	165	159	3		159	3	
5	309	310	4		268	4	
6	192	200	3		125	3	
7	324	323	4		278	4	
8	561	550	5		440	5	
9	384	328	4		275	4	
Out	2865	2728	34		2217	34	
1	363	349	4		273	4	
2	329	306	4		246	4	
3	238	203	3		153	3	
4	165	159	3		159	3	
5	309	310	4		268	4	
6	192	200	3		125	3	
7	324	323	4		278	4	
8	561	550	5		440	5	
9	384	328	4		275	4	
In	2865	2728	34		2217	34	
Total	5730	5456	68		4434	68	
Rating	NA	65.2			64.2		
Slope	NA	100			100		

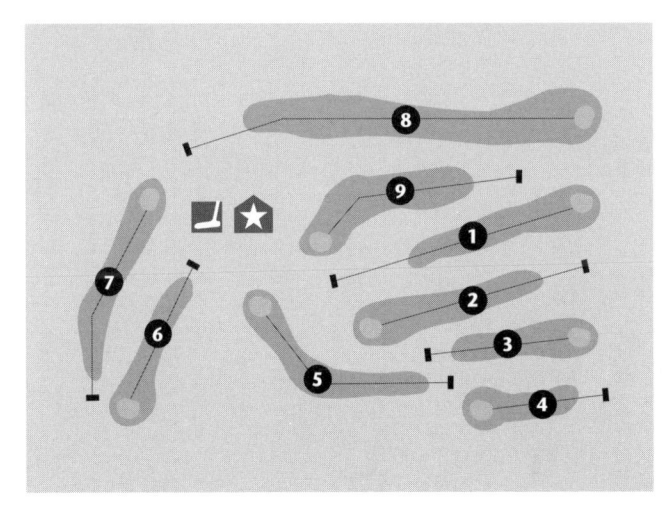

GOLF COURSE DIRECTORY

GREENHAVEN GOLF COURSE

18 Regulation Public

2800 Greenhaven Road
Anoka, Minnesota 55303
612/422-8161 Clubhouse
612/427-3180 Proshop

RESERVATIONS	612/427-3180 2 days
	Walk-on: fair/poor

GREEN FEES	M-F	S-S
Adult	$19/11.50	$22/11.50
Senior	$19/11.50	$22/11.50
Junior	$19/11.50	$22/11.50
Twilight	NA	NA

PAYMENT	No credit cards accepted
	Non-local checks accepted

LEAGUES	Men: Various
	Women: Various

MEMBERSHIPS	USGA, NGF, PGA, GCSAA, MGA

PROFESSIONAL	Jon Bendix

HOURS	7 am to Dusk
SEASON	April-November

FEATURES

Putting green	Y	
Driving range	Y	$1.50
Practice area	N	
Golf carts		
Power (gas)	Y	$20/11
Pull carts	Y	$2
Club rental	Y	$7/5
Club storage	Y	
Caddies	N	
Proshop		
Extended	Y	
Refreshments		
Restaurant	Y	
Lounge	Y	
Snacks	Y	
Clubhouse		
Showers	Y	
Lockers	Y	
Lodging	N	

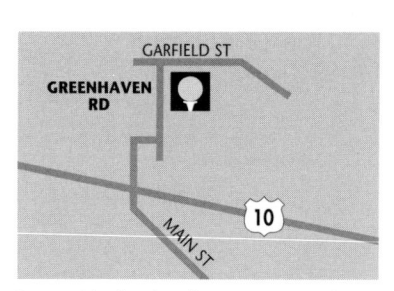

Located in Anoka. Course entrance is 1/4 mile north of U.S. Highway 10 on Greenhaven Road.

	MEN			WOMEN		
	FRONT	PAR	HDCP	FRONT	PAR	HDCP
1	422	4	5	401	5	3
2	346	4	13	319	4	11
3	165	3	17	150	3	17
4	522	5	3	416	5	1
5	425	4	1	402	5	5
6	377	4	11	336	4	9
7	486	5	7	416	5	7
8	158	3	9	136	3	15
9	345	4	15	335	4	13
Out	3246	36		2911	38	
10	352	4	16	325	4	8
11	182	3	10	158	3	18
12	304	4	18	231	4	16
13	479	5	2	436	5	4
14	167	3	6	160	3	10
15	359	4	12	348	4	6
16	494	5	4	426	5	2
17	197	3	8	187	3	14
18	340	4	14	242	4	12
In	2874	35		2513	35	
Total	6120	71		5424	73	
Rating	68.7			70.8		
Slope	122			122		

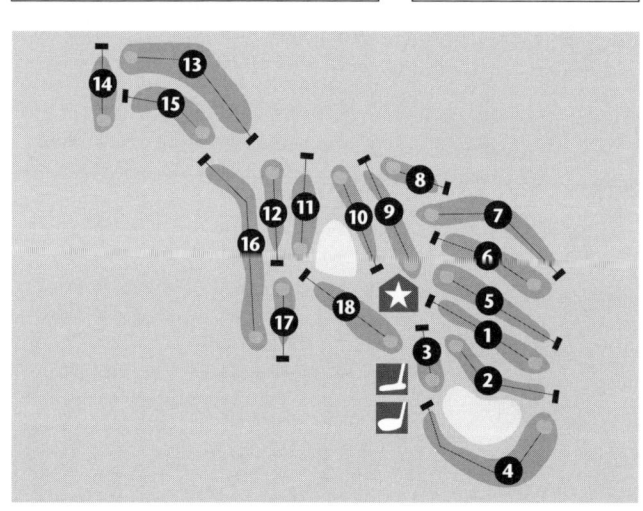

GREENWOOD GOLF COURSE

18 Executive Public

1361 Swenson Road N.E.
Bemidji, Minnesota 56601
218/751-3875 Clubhouse/Proshop

HOURS	8 am to Dusk
SEASON	April to October

| RESERVATIONS | No reservations accepted |
| | Walk-on: good/good |

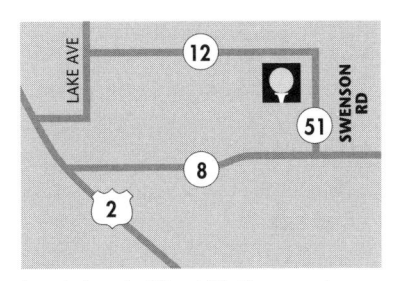

GREEN FEES	M-F	S-S
Adult	$10/7	$10/7
Senior	$10/7	$10/7
Junior	$10/7	$10/7
Twilight	NA	NA

| PAYMENT | No credit cards accepted |
| | Non-local checks accepted |

LEAGUES	None
MEMBERSHIPS	None
OWNER	Alice, Mark & Robert Arndt

FEATURES		
Putting green	Y	
Driving range	Y	$2-3
Practice area	N	
Golf carts		
Power	N	
Pull carts	Y	$2
Club rental	Y	$2.75
Club storage	N	
Caddies	N	
Proshop		
Extended	Y	
Refreshments		
Restaurant	N	
Lounge	N	
Snacks	Y	
Clubhouse		
Showers	N	
Lockers	N	
Lodging	N	

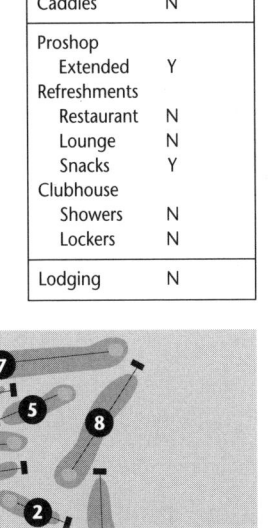

Located east of Bemidji. Course entrance is about 6 miles east of Lake Avenue on County Road 12.

	MEN			WOMEN		
	FRONT	PAR	HDCP	FRONT	PAR	HDCP
1	169	3	7	169	3	7
2	110	3	10	110	3	10
3	124	3	15	124	3	15
4	143	3	16	143	3	16
5	91	3	18	91	3	18
6	200	3	1	200	3	1
7	254	4	9	254	4	9
8	159	3	4	159	3	4
9	302	4	6	302	4	6
Out	1552	29		1552	29	
10	105	3	17	105	3	17
11	147	3	11	147	3	11
12	297	4	5	297	4	5
13	108	3	8	108	3	8
14	140	3	14	140	3	14
15	118	3	12	118	3	12
16	164	3	3	164	3	3
17	264	4	2	264	4	2
18	113	3	13	113	3	3
In	1454	29		1454	29	
Total	3008	58		3008	58	
Rating	NA			NA		
Slope	NA			NA		

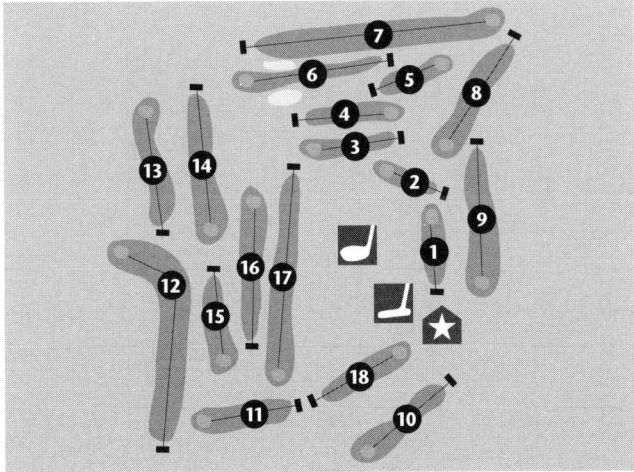

GOLF COURSE DIRECTORY

GREENWOOD GOLF LINKS

18 Regulation Public

4520 East Viking Boulevard
Wyoming, Minnesota 55092
612/462-4653 Clubhouse/Proshop

RESERVATIONS	612/462-4653 2 days	
	Walk-on: good/fair	
GREEN FEES	M-F	S-S
Adult	$16/9	$17.50/11
Senior	$13.50/7.75	$17.50/11
Junior	$13/7.25	$17.50/11
Twilight	NA	NA
PAYMENT	No credit cards accepted	
	Local checks only	
LEAGUES	Men:	T,Th (6 pm)
		W (4 pm)
	Women: W (6 pm)	
	Couples: M (6 pm)	
	Juniors: Th (9 am)	
MEMBERSHIPS	USGA, NGF, MGA	
OWNER	Johnson Family	
MANAGER	RR Johnson, CM Johnson	

HOURS	7 am to Dusk	
SEASON	April to October	
FEATURES		
Putting green	Y	
Driving range	N	
Practice area	Y	
Golf carts		
Power (gas)	Y	$18/9
Pull carts	Y	$3/2
Club rental	Y	$6/4
Club storage	N	
Caddies	N	
Proshop		
Extended	Y	
Refreshments		
Restaurant	N	
Lounge	Y	
Snacks	Y	
Clubhouse		
Showers	N	
Lockers	N	
Lodging (B&B)	Y	$85 up

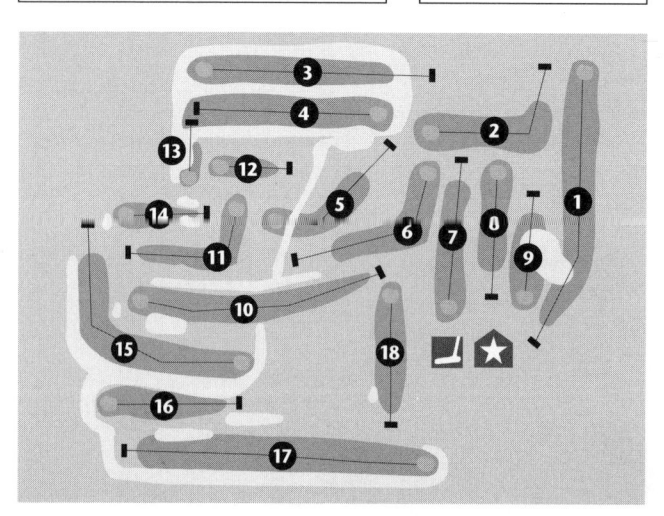

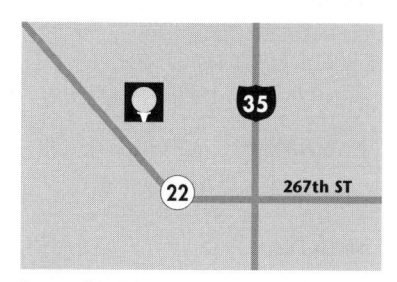

Located in Wyoming. Course entrance is about 1/2 mile west of I-35 on County Road 22 (East Viking Blvd).

	MEN				**WOMEN**		
	BACK	FRONT	PAR	HDCP	FRONT	PAR	HDCP
1	490	490	5	3	470	5	3
2	280	280	4	5	248	4	5
3	475	475	5	4	441	5	4
4	340	340	4	1	307	4	1
5	311	311	4	7	271	4	7
6	297	297	4	8	277	4	8
7	275	275	4	9	260	4	9
8	206	206	3	2	186	3	2
9	228	228	3	6	147	3	6
Out	2902	2902	36		2607	36	
10	472	465	5	6	426	5	6
11	251	234	4	12	191	4	12
12	91	86	3	14	82	3	14
13	112	107	3	10	78	3	10
14	111	97	3	18	90	3	18
15	471	464	5	2	382	5	2
16	299	294	4	16	265	4	16
17	581	571	5	4	481	5	4
18	228	218	4	8	189	4	8
In	2616	2536	36		2184	36	
Total	5518	5438	72		4791	72	
Rating	67.2	66.2			67.3		
Slope	105	101			112		

FRANCIS A. GROSS GOLF COURSE

18 Regulation Public

2201 St. Anthony Boulevard
St. Anthony, Minnesota 55418
612/789-2542 Clubhouse/Proshop

HOURS	6 am to Dusk
SEASON	April-November

RESERVATIONS	612/789-2542 4 days
	Weekends only $2 fee
	Walk-on: fair/poor

GREEN FEES	M-F	S-S
Adult	$18/13	$18/13
Senior	$18/13	$18/13
Junior	$18/13	$18/13
Twilight	NA	NA

PAYMENT	No credit cards accepted
	Local checks accepted

LEAGUES	Men: Various
	Women: Various

MEMBERSHIPS	USGA, PGA, GCSAA, MGA

PROFESSIONAL	Steve Walters

FEATURES	
Putting green	Y
Driving range	N
Practice area	Y
Golf carts	
Power (elec)	Y $20/12
Pull carts	Y $2.50
Club rental	Y
Club storage	N
Caddies	N
Proshop	
Basic	Y
Refreshments	
Restaurant	Y
Lounge	Y
Snacks	Y
Clubhouse	
Showers	Y
Lockers	Y
Lodging	N

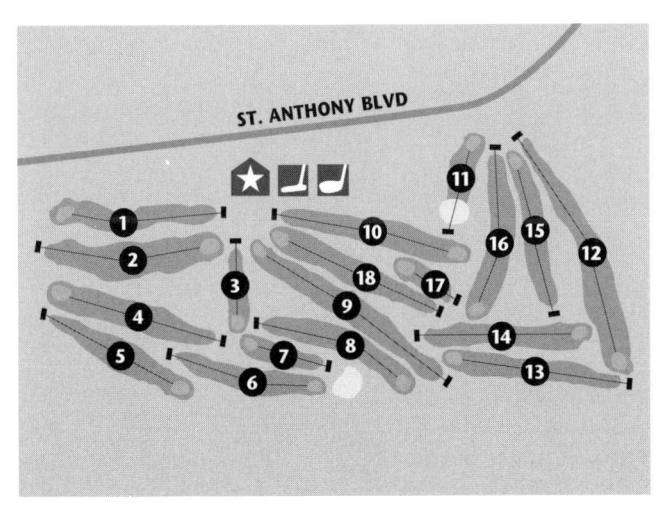

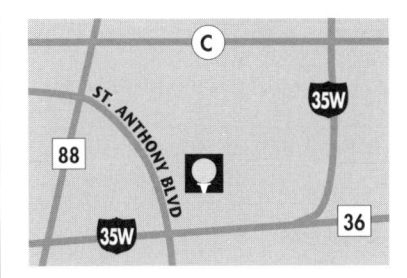

Located in St. Anthony. Course entrance is about 1/2 mile north of I-35W on St. Anthony Blvd.

	MEN				**WOMEN**		
	BACK	FRONT	PAR	HDCP	FRONT	PAR	HDCP
1	359	351	4	13	329	4	7
2	415	386	4	5	280	4	9
3	191	179	3	9	116	3	17
4	413	405	4	3	385	5	3
5	354	347	4	17	340	4	11
6	385	365	4	11	220	4	15
7	208	198	3	15	174	3	13
8	384	378	4	7	361	4	5
9	532	520	5	1	508	5	1
Out	3241	3129	35		2713	35	
10	497	491	4	8	436	5	4
11	214	186	3	12	180	3	16
12	580	566	5	2	431	5	2
13	395	380	4	6	275	4	8
14	404	396	4	4	284	4	6
15	360	356	4	14	352	4	12
16	377	357	4	10	341	4	10
17	164	159	3	18	123	3	18
18	343	328	4	16	320	4	14
In	3328	3221	36		2442	36	
Total	6569	6350	71		5155	71	
Rating	70.8	69.7			71.1		
Slope	120	118			117		

GOLF COURSE DIRECTORY

GUNFLINT HILLS GOLF CLUB

9 Executive Public

P.O. Box 820
Grand Marais, Minnesota 55604
218/387-9988 Clubhouse/Proshop

RESERVATIONS	218/387-9988	
	Walk-on: good/good	
GREEN FEES	M-F	S-S
Adult	$16/11	$18/13
Senior	$16/11	$18/13
Junior	$8/6	$9/7
Twilight	NA	NA
PAYMENT	No credit cards accepted	
	Non-local checks accepted	
LEAGUES	Men:	Th (12-5 pm)
	Women:	T,W (am)
MEMBERSHIPS	NGF, GCSAA, MGA	
OWNER	City of Grand Marais	
MANAGER	Michael Kunshier	

HOURS	7 am to Dusk
SEASON	May to October
FEATURES	
Putting green	Y
Driving range	Y
Practice area	Y
Golf carts	
Power (gas)	Y $18/11
Pull carts	Y $3
Club rental	Y
Club storage	N
Caddies	N
Proshop	
Extended	Y
Refreshments	
Restaurant	N
Lounge	N
Snacks	Y
Clubhouse	
Showers	N
Lockers	Y
Lodging	N

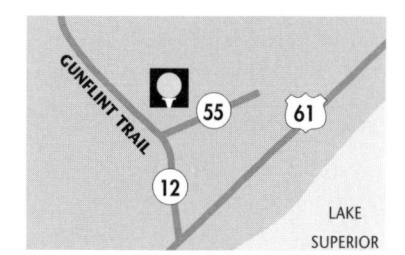

Located north of Grand Marais. Course is 4 miles north of Hwy 61 on Gunflint Trail, then 1/4 miles east on Cty Rd 55.

	MEN			**WOMEN**		
	FRONT	PAR	HDCP	FRONT	PAR	HDCP
1	190	3	11	190	4	13
2	270	4	1	270	4	7
3	155	3	15	155	3	15
4	354	4	7	259	4	5
5	351	4	9	299	4	9
6	178	3	17	178	3	17
7	303	4	13	303	4	11
8	443	5	3	443	5	3
9	400	4	5	400	5	1
Out	2644	34		2497	36	
1	190	3	12	190	4	14
2	270	4	2	270	4	8
3	155	3	16	155	3	16
4	354	4	8	259	4	6
5	351	4	10	299	4	10
6	178	3	18	178	3	18
7	303	4	14	303	4	12
8	443	5	4	443	5	4
9	400	4	6	400	5	2
In	2644	34		2497	35	
Total	5288	68		4994	72	
Rating	66.0			69.6		
Slope	118			119		

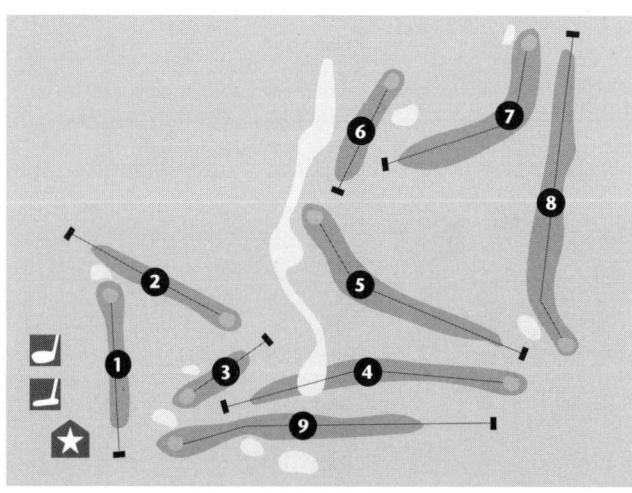

THE MINNESOTA ILLUSTRATED

HAMPTON HILLS GOLF COURSE

18 Regulation Public

5313 North Juneau Lane
Plymouth, Minnesota 55446
612/559-9800 Clubhouse/Proshop

HOURS	Dawn to Dusk
SEASON	April-November

| **RESERVATIONS** | 612/559-9800 5 days |
| | Walk-on: good/fair |

GREEN FEES	M-F	S-S
Adult	$16/11	$18/13
Senior	$8/6*	$18/13
Junior	$8/6*	$18/13
Twilight	NA	$7 (5 pm)
	*Before 2 pm	

| **PAYMENT** | No credit cards accepted |
| | Local checks only |

| **LEAGUES** | Men: Various |
| | Women: Various |

| **MEMBERSHIPS** | MGA |

OWNER	Ken Hampton
MANAGER	John Hampton, Dian Whelen
PROFESSIONAL	Karl Hathaway, Mike Svendahl

FEATURES		
Putting green	Y	
Driving cage	Y	$3
Practice area	N	
Golf carts		
Power (gas)	Y	$20/11
Pull carts	Y	$2
Club rental	Y	
Club storage	N	
Caddies	N	
Proshop		
Regular	Y	
Refreshments		
Restaurant	N	
Lounge	N	
Snacks	Y	
Clubhouse		
Showers	N	
Lockers	N	
Lodging	N	

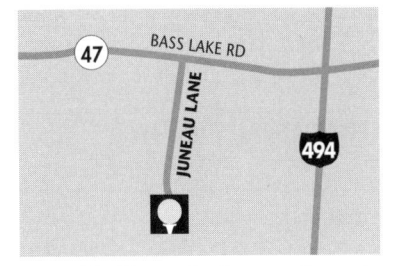

Located in Plymouth. Course entrance is 1 mile west of I-494 on Bass Lake Road, then 3/4 mile south on Juneau Lane.

	MEN			**WOMEN**		
	FRONT	PAR	HDCP	FRONT	PAR	HDCP
1	463	5	12	463	5	5
2	157	3	16	157	3	18
3	409	4	5	409	4	9
4	539	5	9	539	5	1
5	206	3	3	206	3	13
6	298	4	17	298	4	14
7	501	5	2	501	5	2
8	381	4	8	381	4	8
9	384	4	1	384	5	3
Out	3338	37		3338	38	
10	261	4	18	261	4	15
11	340	4	6	340	4	11
12	478	5	11	478	5	10
13	168	3	14	168	3	12
14	402	4	4	402	4	4
15	489	5	10	489	5	6
16	170	3	15	170	3	16
17	153	3	13	153	3	17
18	421	4	7	421	5	7
In	2882	35		2882	36	
Total	6220	72		6220	74	
Rating	68.2			73.2		
Slope	104			121		

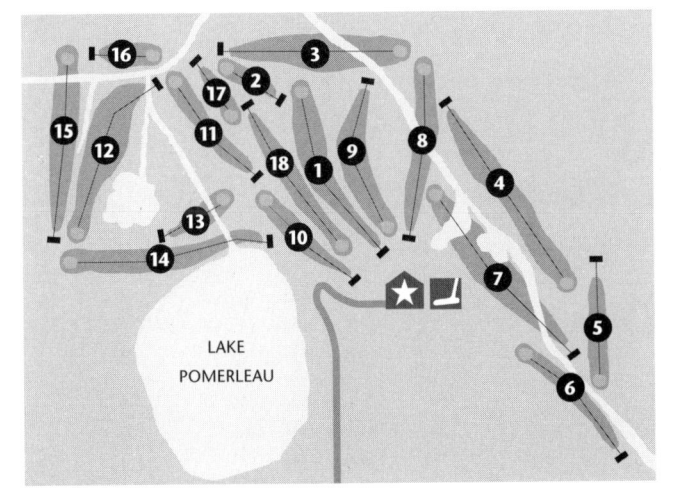

LAKE POMERLEAU

GOLF COURSE DIRECTORY

HARMONY GOLF CLUB

9 Regulation Semi-Private

535 Fourth Street NE, P.O. Box 538
Harmony, Minnesota 55939
507/886-5622 Clubhouse/Proshop

HOURS	Dawn to Dusk
SEASON	April-November

RESERVATIONS	507/886-5622
	Walk-on: good/fair

GREEN FEES	M-F	S-S
Adult	$12.50/7	$15/9
Senior	$12.50/7	$15/9
Junior	$12.50/7	$15/9
Twilight	NA	NA

PAYMENT	No credit cards accepted
	Non-local checks accepted

LEAGUES	Men: W (am), Th (pm)
	Women: T (pm)

MEMBERSHIPS	USGA, MGA

MANAGER	Jim Taubert
SUPERINTENDENT	Don Moren

FEATURES		
Putting green	Y	
Driving range	N	
Practice area	Y	
Golf carts		
Power (gas)	Y	$16/8
Pull carts	Y	$1
Club rental	Y	$3
Club storage	N	
Caddies	N	
Proshop		
Extended	Y	
Refreshments		
Restaurant	Y	
Lounge	Y	
Snacks	Y	
Clubhouse		
Showers	N	
Lockers	N	
Lodging	N	

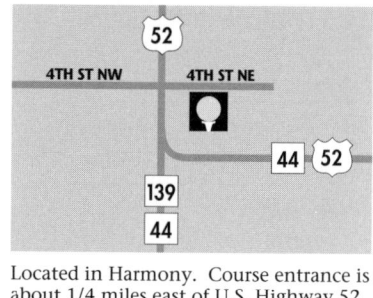

Located in Harmony. Course entrance is about 1/4 miles east of U.S. Highway 52 on 4th Street NE.

	MEN				**WOMEN**		
	BACK	FRONT	PAR	HDCP	FRONT	PAR	HDCP
1	348	328	4	9	284	4	9
2	284	272	4	13	272	4	13
3	129	119	3	17	119	3	17
4	356	342	4	3	332	4	3
5	519	509	5	1	428	5	1
6	360	350	4	5	295	4	5
7	168	150	3	7	138	3	7
8	495	485	5	11	457	5	11
9	155	145	3	15	140	3	15
Out	2814	2700	35		2465	35	
1	348	328	4	9	284	4	9
2	284	272	4	13	272	4	13
3	129	119	3	17	119	3	17
4	356	342	4	3	332	4	3
5	519	509	5	1	428	5	1
6	360	350	4	5	295	4	5
7	168	150	3	7	138	3	7
8	495	485	5	11	457	5	11
9	155	145	3	15	140	3	15
In	2814	2700	35		2465	35	
Total	5628	5400	70		4930	70	
Rating	NA	68.6			70.8		
Slope	NA	111			122		

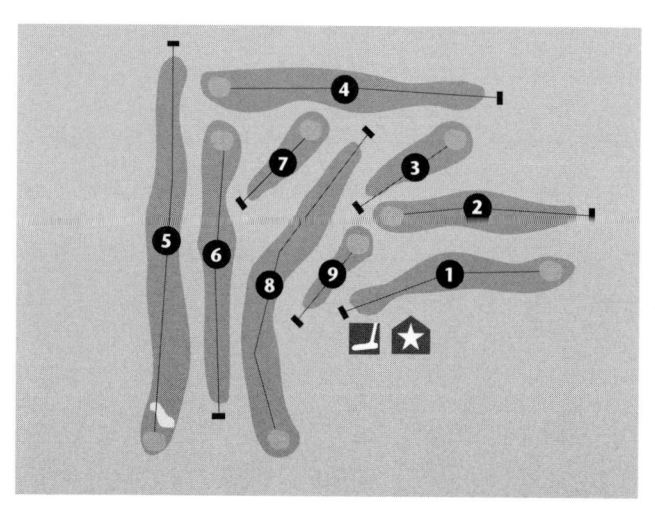

HASTINGS COUNTRY CLUB

18 Regulation Private

2015 Westview Drive
Hastings, Minnesota 55033
612/437-4612 Clubhouse
612/437-6483 Proshop

RESERVATIONS	612/437-6483	2 days
	Members only	
GREEN FEES	M-F	S-S
Adult	$30/18	$30/18
Senior	$30/18	$30/18
Junior	$30/18	$30/18
Twilight	NA	NA
	Members and guests only	
PAYMENT	Credit: Visa® MasterCard®	
	Non-local checks accepted	
LEAGUES	None	
MEMBERSHIPS	USGA, PGA, GCSAA,	
	CMAA, MGA	
SUPERINTENDENT	Tom Feriancek	
PROFESSIONAL	Brad Schmierer	

HOURS	8 am to 8 pm	
SEASON	April to October	
FEATURES		
Putting green	Y	
Driving range	Y	$4
Practice area	Y	
Golf carts		
Power (gas)	Y	$22
Pull carts	Y	$3
Club rental	Y	$3
Club storage	Y	$60/yr
Caddies	N	
Proshop		
Extended	Y	
Refreshments		
Restaurant	Y	
Lounge	Y	
Snacks	Y	
Clubhouse		
Showers	Y	
Lockers	Y	
Lodging	N	

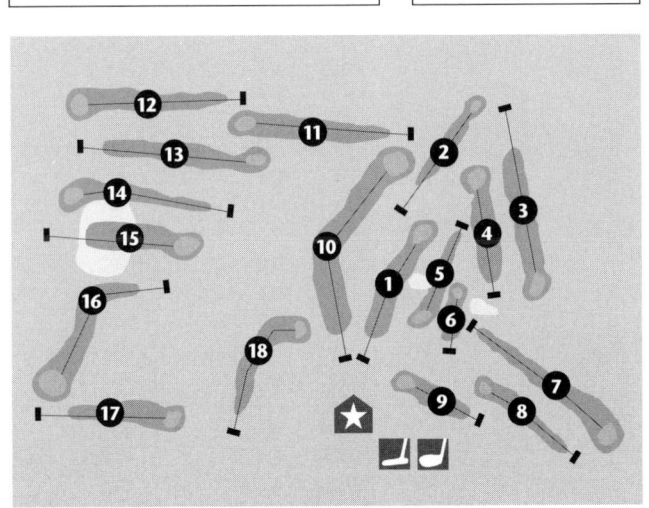

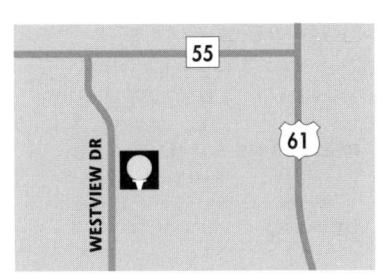

Located in Hastings. Course entrance is south of MN Highway 55 on Westview Drive.

	\multicolumn{4}{c}{**MEN**}	\multicolumn{3}{c}{**WOMEN**}
	BACK	FRONT	PAR	HDCP	FRONT	PAR	HDCP
1	413	400	4	5	382	4	3
2	310	300	4	17	280	4	17
3	525	497	5	9	450	5	9
4	425	405	4	7	340	4	7
5	410	395	4	3	350	4	5
6	190	180	3	11	150	3	11
7	480	460	5	13	405	5	13
8	439	420	4	1	345	4	1
9	162	155	3	15	140	3	15
Out	3354	3212	36		2842	36	
10	520	510	5	10	450	5	6
11	400	380	4	6	310	4	14
12	334	318	4	16	310	4	12
13	421	407	4	2	400	5	16
14	410	387	4	4	322	4	2
15	195	180	3	12	135	3	10
16	470	450	5	8	405	5	4
17	200	175	3	14	119	3	18
18	340	325	4	18	300	4	8
In	3290	3132	36		2751	37	
Total	6644	6344	72		5593	73	
Rating	72.6	71.5			73.0		
Slope	129	126			130		

GOLF COURSE DIRECTORY

HAVANA HILLS GOLF COURSE

9 Par-3 Public

Route 4, P.O. Box 14
Owatonna, Minnesota 55060
507/451-2577 Clubhouse/Proshop

HOURS	8 am to Dusk
SEASON	April-November

RESERVATIONS	507/451-2577 1 week
	Walk-on: good/good
GREEN FEES	M-F	S-S
Adult	$7/6	$9/6
Senior	$7/5	$8/5
Junior	$7/5	$8/5
Twilight	NA	NA
	Special: M-F $7 all day	
PAYMENT	Credit: Visa® MasterCard®
	Non-local checks accepted
LEAGUES	Women: T (pm)
MEMBERSHIPS	USGA, PGA, GCSAA
OWNERS	Dean Hartle & Glen Edin
MANAGER	Jim Deutsch
SUPERINTENDENT	Randy Nelson
PROFESSIONAL	Jim Deutsch

FEATURES		
Putting green	Y	
Driving range	Y	$3-5
Practice area	Y	
Golf carts		
Power (elec)	Y	$6
Pull carts	Y	$2
Club rental	Y	$3
Club storage	N	
Caddies	N	
Proshop		
Regular	Y	
Refreshments		
Restaurant	N	
Lounge	N	
Snacks	Y	
Clubhouse		
Showers	N	
Lockers	N	
Lodging	N	

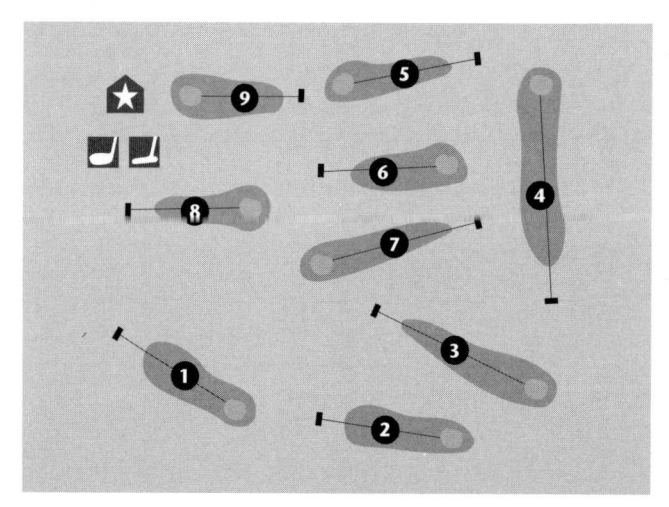

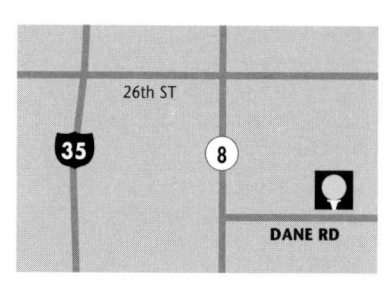

Located in Owatonna. Course is 2 1/2 miles east of I-35 on 26th Street, south on Cty Road 8, then east on Dane Road.

	MEN			**WOMEN**		
	FRONT	PAR	HDCP	FRONT	PAR	HDCP
1	125	3		125	3	
2	163	3		163	3	
3	125	3		125	3	
4	216	3		216	3	
5	159	3		159	3	
6	106	3		106	3	
7	218	3		218	3	
8	90	3		171	3	
9	90	3		331	3	
Out	1292	27		1292	27	
1	125	3		125	3	
2	163	3		163	3	
3	125	3		125	3	
4	216	3		216	3	
5	159	3		159	3	
6	106	3		106	3	
7	218	3		218	3	
8	90	3		171	3	
9	90	3		331	3	
In	1292	27		1292	27	
Total	2584	54		2584	54	
Rating	NA			NA		
Slope	NA			NA		

HAWLEY GOLF & COUNTRY CLUB

18 Regulation Public

Highway 10, P.O. Box 734
Hawley, Minnesota 56549
218/483-4808 Clubhouse/Proshop

HOURS	Dawn to Dusk
SEASON	April to October

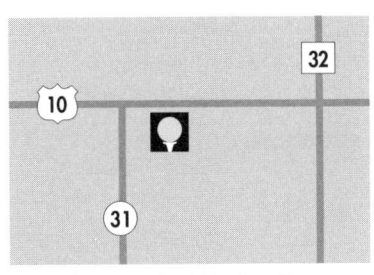

RESERVATIONS	218/483-4808	
	Walk-on: good/fair	
GREEN FEES	M-F	S-S
Adult	Call	Call
Senior	Call	Call
Junior	Call	Call
Twilight	NA	NA
PAYMENT	No credit cards accepted	
	Non-local checks accepted	
LEAGUES	Men: Various	
	Women: Various	
MEMBERSHIPS	USGA, MGA	
PROFESSIONAL	Call	

FEATURES		
Putting green	Y	
Driving range	N	
Practice area	Y	
Golf carts		
Power (gas)	Y	
Pull carts	Y	
Club rental	Y	
Club storage	N	
Caddies	N	
Proshop		
Regular	Y	
Refreshments		
Restaurant	N	
Lounge	Y	
Snacks	Y	
Clubhouse		
Showers	N	
Lockers	N	
Lodging	N	

Located just south of Hawley. Course entrance is west of MN Highway 32 on U.S. Highway 10.

	MEN				WOMEN		
	BACK	FRONT	PAR	HDCP	FRONT	PAR	HDCP
1	320	303	4	13	303	4	9
2	340	330	4	11	293	4	7
3	198	198	3	5	158	3	17
4	430	423	4	1	363	4	1
5	299	276	4	15	256	4	11
6	182	171	3	9	142	3	13
7	394	388	4	3	388	5	5
8	310	298	4	17	298	4	15
9	508	503	5	7	403	5	3
Out	2981	2890	35		2604	36	
10	172	158	3	12	158	3	10
11	327	277	4	18	277	4	16
12	373	353	4	6	300	4	8
13	145	134	3	16	134	3	18
14	512	496	5	2	447	5	2
15	374	362	4	8	320	4	6
16	186	176	3	14	176	3	12
17	471	471	5	4	451	5	4
18	336	330	4	10	330	4	14
In	2896	2757	35		2593	35	
Total	5877	5647	70		5197	71	
Rating	68.2	67.1			69.5		
Slope	115	113			115		

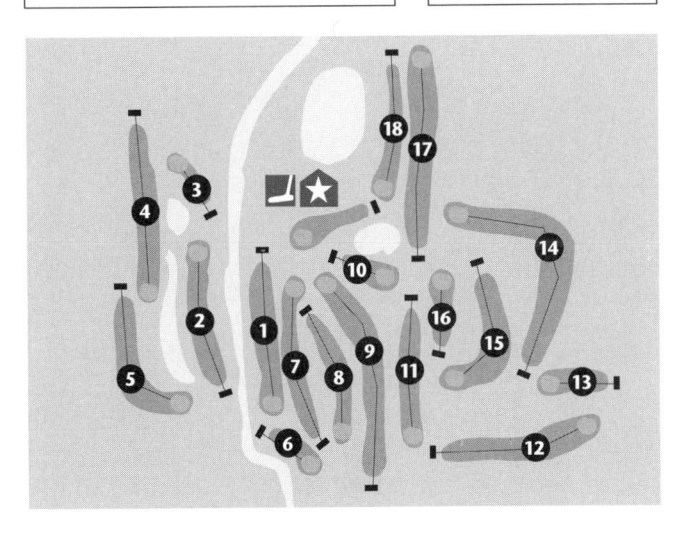

GOLF COURSE DIRECTORY

HAYDEN HILLS EXECUTIVE GOLF COURSE
18 Executive Public

13150 Deerwood Lane
Dayton, Minnesota 55327
612/421-0060 Clubhouse/Proshop

RESERVATIONS	612/421-0060	
	Walk-on: fair/poor	
GREEN FEES	M-F	S-S
Adult	$13.50/8.50	$15.50/9.50
Senior	$11/7*	$15.50/9.50
Junior	$13.50/8.50	$15.50/9.50
Twilight	NA	NA
	*Before 3 pm	
PAYMENT	No credit cards accepted	
	Non-local checks accepted	
LEAGUES	Men: T,W (pm)	
	Women: T,W (am)	
	Senior: M (am)	
MEMBERSHIPS	MGA	
OWNER	Donald Chapman	
MANAGER	Judi Chapman, Cathy Kessler	
SUPERINTENDENT	John Kessler	

HOURS	Dawn to Dusk
SEASON	April-November

FEATURES		
Putting green	Y	
Driving range	N	
Practice area	N	
Golf carts		
Power (gas)	Y	$15.50
Pull carts	Y	$2
Club rental	Y	$3
Club storage	N	
Caddies	N	
Proshop		
Basic	Y	
Refreshments		
Restaurant	N	
Lounge	Y	
Snacks	Y	
Clubhouse		
Showers	N	
Lockers	N	
Lodging	N	

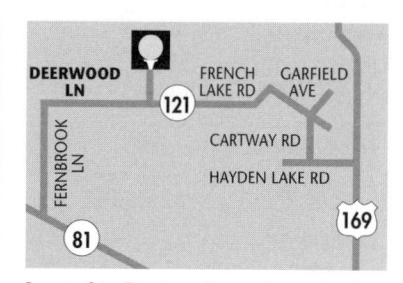

Located in Dayton. Course is north of Cty Rd 81 on Fernbrook Ln, east on Cty Rd 121, then north on Deerwood Ln.

	MEN			**WOMEN**		
	FRONT	PAR	HDCP	FRONT	PAR	HDCP
1	193	4	5	193	4	5
2	149	3	9	149	3	9
3	208	4	3	208	4	3
4	93	3	17	93	3	17
5	127	3	15	127	3	15
6	130	3	13	130	3	13
7	158	3	7	158	3	7
8	133	3	11	133	3	11
9	230	4	1	230	4	1
Out	1421	30		1421	30	
10	187	4	10	187	4	10
11	124	3	16	124	3	16
12	137	3	14	137	3	14
13	233	4	6	233	4	6
14	132	3	12	132	3	12
15	176	3	8	176	3	8
16	120	3	18	120	3	18
17	251	4	4	251	4	4
18	468	5	2	468	5	2
In	1848	32		1848	32	
Total	3269	62		3269	62	
Rating	54.0			56.7		
Slope	71			78		

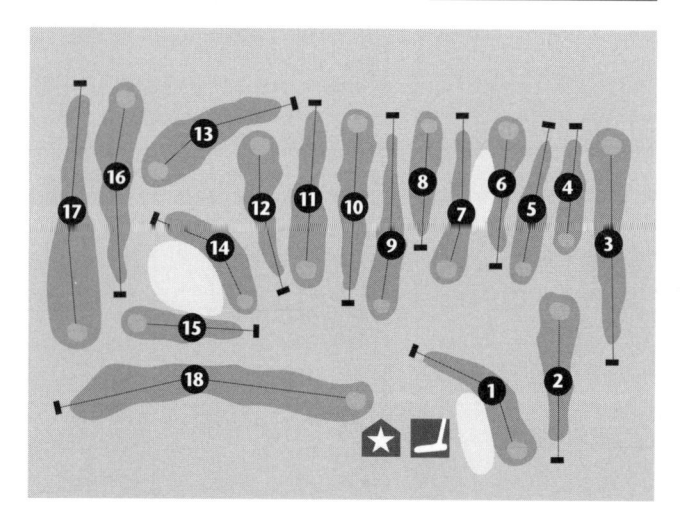

HAZELTINE NATIONAL GOLF CLUB

18 Regulation Private

1900 Hazeltine Blvd
Chaska, Minnesota 55318
612/448-4929 Clubhouse
612/448-4500 Proshop

HOURS	Dawn to Dusk
SEASON	April-November

FEATURES	
Putting green	Y
Driving range	Y
Practice area	Y
Golf carts	
Power (gas)	Y
Pull carts	Y
Club rental	Y
Club storage	Y
Caddies	Y
Proshop	
Extended	Y
Refreshments	
Restaurant	Y
Lounge	Y
Snacks	Y
Clubhouse	
Showers	Y
Lockers	Y
Lodging	N

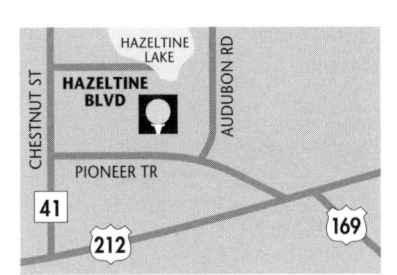

Located in Chaska west of I-494 on Hwy 212. Exit north on Hwy 41. Go east on Hazeltine Blvd. Course south of road.

RESERVATIONS	612/448-4500
	Members only

GREEN FEES	M-F	S-S
Adult	$60	$70
Senior	$60	$70
Junior	$12	$12
Twilight	NA	NA
	Members and guests only	

PAYMENT	Fees billed to members

LEAGUES	Men: None
	Women: None

MEMBERSHIPS	USGA, NGF, PGA, LPGA, GCSAA, CMAA, NCA, MGA

PROFESSIONAL	Mike Schultz

	MEN			WOMEN		
	BACK	FRONT	PAR	HDCP	FRONT	PAR	HDCP
1	440	390	4	11	378	4	7
2	430	374	4	5	364	4	5
3	580	510	5	1	468	5	1
4	196	160	3	17	142	3	17
5	396	362	4	3	350	4	11
6	380	345	4	7	338	4	13
7	518	474	5	9	406	5	9
8	166	124	3	15	108	3	15
9	425	380	4	13	326	4	3
Out	3531	3119	36		2880	36	
10	402	376	4	6	368	4	12
11	560	515	5	4	464	5	2
12	418	378	4	10	373	4	6
13	192	164	3	18	144	3	18
14	352	310	4	14	303	4	14
15	584	517	5	2	492	5	4
16	370	312	4	8	240	4	8
17	182	135	3	16	112	3	16
18	432	358	4	12	348	4	10
In	3492	3065	36		2844	36	
Total	7023	6184	72		5724	72	
Rating	74.7	70.8			74.7		
Slope	137	130			133		

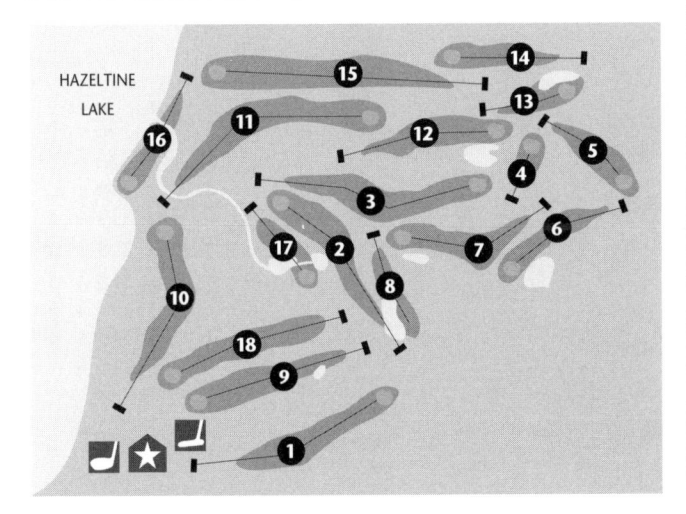

GOLF COURSE DIRECTORY

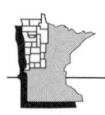

HEADWATERS COUNTRY CLUB

18 Regulation Semi-Private

P.O. Box 9
Park Rapids, Minnesota 56470
218/732-4832 Clubhouse/Proshop

HOURS	6 am to Dusk
SEASON	April-November

RESERVATIONS	218/732-4832 1 week	
	Walk-on: good/fair	
GREEN FEES	M-F	S-S
Adult	$20/12	$20/12
Senior	$20/12	$20/12
Junior	$20/12	$20/12
Twilight	NA	NA
PAYMENT	Credit: Visa®	
	Non-local checks accepted	
LEAGUES	Men: Th	
	Women: T	
	Couples: Sun	
MEMBERSHIPS	USGA, NGF, PGA, GCSAA, MGA	
MANAGER	Mark Fossum	
PROFESSIONAL	Jeff Anderson	

FEATURES		
Putting green	Y	
Driving range	Y	$2
Practice area	Y	
Golf carts		
Power (gas)	Y	$20/12
Pull carts	Y	$2
Club rental	Y	$7.50
Club storage	Y	$15/yr
Caddies	N	
Proshop		
Extended	Y	
Refreshments		
Restaurant	Y	
Lounge	Y	
Snacks	Y	
Clubhouse		
Showers	Y	
Lockers	Y	
Lodging	N	

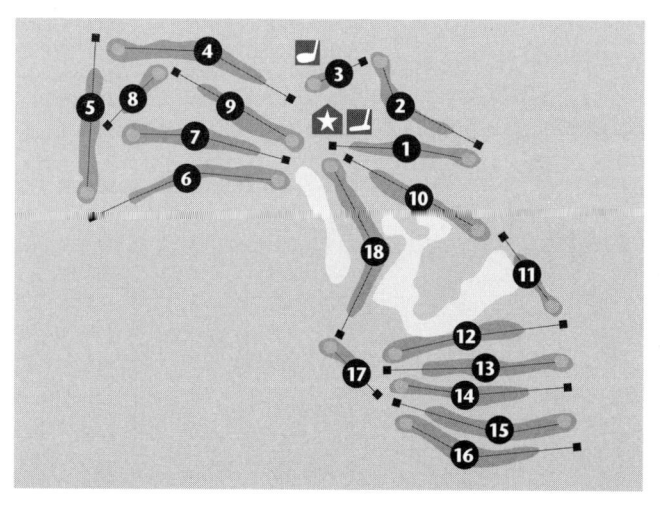

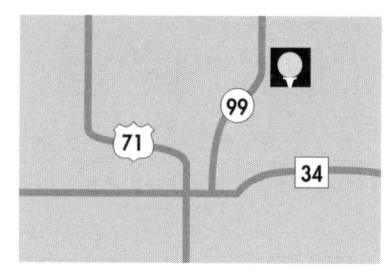

Located north of Park Rapids. Course is east of U.S. Highway 71 on Highway 34, then 2 miles north on County Road 99.

	MEN					**WOMEN**		
	BACK	FRONT	PAR	HDCP		FRONT	PAR	HDCP
1	321	306	4	14		296	4	16
2	348	340	4	10		305	4	10
3	127	123	3	18		111	3	18
4	505	497	5	6		395	5	4
5	397	387	4	4		305	4	12
6	486	480	5	16		413	5	14
7	423	413	4	2		346	4	2
8	177	173	3	8		165	3	8
9	358	353	4	12		343	4	6
Out	3142	3072	36			2679	36	
10	381	375	4	15		304	4	9
11	197	160	3	13		138	3	15
12	387	375	4	1		334	4	1
13	389	385	4	7		276	4	13
14	393	387	4	9		320	4	7
15	490	475	5	17		408	5	17
16	398	382	4	3		329	4	3
17	197	190	3	5		182	3	5
18	481	478	5	11		392	5	11
In	3313	3207	36			2683	36	
Total	6455	6279	72			5362	72	
Rating	70.9	70.1				71.0		
Slope	120	119				118		

HEART OF THE VALLEY GOLF CLUB

9 Regulation Public

P.O. Box 68
Ada, Minnesota 56510
218/784-4746 Clubhouse/Proshop

HOURS	8 am to Dusk
SEASON	April to October

RESERVATIONS	No reservations accepted
	Walk-on: good/good

GREEN FEES	M-F	S-S
Adult	$10/7	$13/9
Senior	$10/7	$13/9
Junior	$10/7	$13/9
Twilight	$3 (7 pm)	NA

PAYMENT	No credit cards accepted
	Non-local checks accepted

LEAGUES	Men: M,Th (5:45 pm)
	Women: T (9 am)

MEMBERSHIPS	USGA, MGA

MANAGER	Delford Johnson

FEATURES	
Putting green	Y
Driving range	N
Practice area	Y
Golf carts	
Power (gas)	Y $14
Pull carts	Y $1
Club rental	Y $3
Club storage	Y
Caddies	N
Proshop	
Basic	Y
Refreshments	
Restaurant	N
Lounge	Y
Snacks	Y
Clubhouse	
Showers	N
Lockers	N
Lodging	N

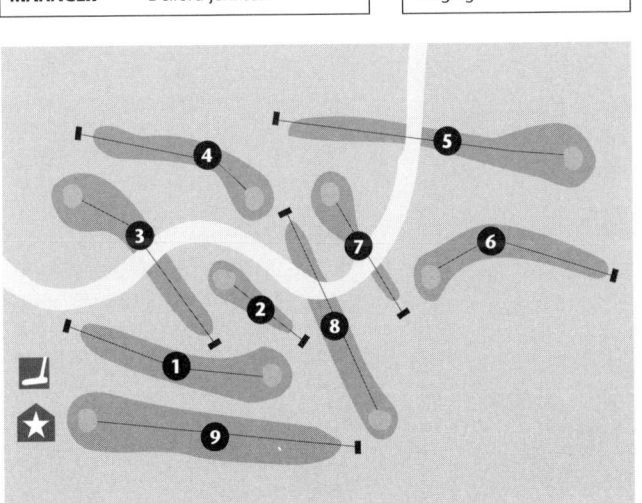

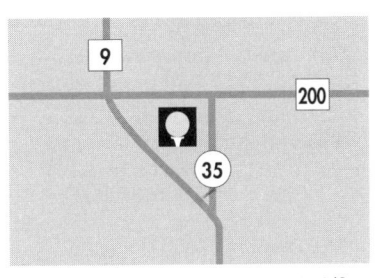

Located in Ada. Course entrance is 1/2 mile south of Highway 200 or 1/2 mile north of Highway 9 on County Road 35.

	MEN			WOMEN		
	FRONT	PAR	HDCP	FRONT	PAR	HDCP
1	427	5	9	388	5	9
2	137	3	7	137	3	7
3	319	4	4	246	4	4
4	338	4	3	288	4	3
5	505	5	1	433	5	1
6	295	4	8	262	4	8
7	161	3	5	143	3	5
8	325	4	2	226	4	2
9	481	5	6	426	5	6
Out	2985	37		2549	37	
1	427	5	9	388	5	9
2	137	3	7	137	3	7
3	319	4	4	246	4	4
4	338	4	3	288	4	3
5	505	5	1	433	5	1
6	295	4	8	262	4	8
7	161	3	5	143	3	5
8	325	4	2	226	4	2
9	481	5	6	426	5	6
In	2985	37		2549	37	
Total	5970	74		5098	74	
Rating	68.6			69.4		
Slope	116			120		

GOLF COURSE DIRECTORY

HIAWATHA GOLF COURSE   18 Regulation Public

4553 Longfellow Avenue South
Minneapolis, Minnesota 55407
612/724-7715 Clubhouse/Proshop

HOURS	6 am to Dusk
SEASON	April-November

RESERVATIONS	612/724-7715 4 days
	Weekends only $2 fee
	Walk-on: good/fair

GREEN FEES	M-F	S-S
Adult	$18/13	$18/18
Senior	$18/13	$18/18
Junior	$18/13	$18/18
Twilight	$13 (4pm)	$10.50 (4pm)

PAYMENT	Credit: Visa® MasterCard®
	Local checks only

LEAGUES	Men: Various
	Women: Various

MEMBERSHIPS	USGA, MGA

MANAGER	Bob Nordstrom, Dan Stoneberg
SUPERINTENDENT	Rick Randall
PROFESSIONAL	Bob Nordstrom

FEATURES			
Putting green	Y		
Driving range	Y	$2.50	
Practice area	Y		
Golf carts			
Power (elec)	Y	$18	
Pull carts	Y	$2.50	
Club rental	Y	$7	
Club storage	N		
Caddies	N		
Proshop			
Basic	Y		
Refreshments			
Restaurant	N		
Lounge	N		
Snacks	Y		
Clubhouse			
Showers	Y		
Lockers	Y	$25/yr	
Lodging	N		

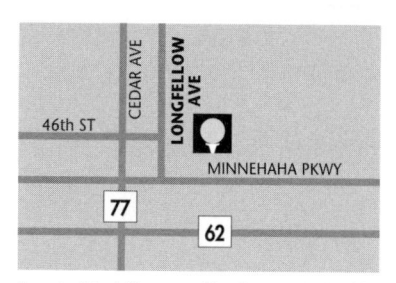

Located in Minneapolis. Course is 1 1/2 miles north of Highway 62 on Highway 77 (Cedar Ave), then east on 46th Street.

	MEN				**WOMEN**		
	BACK	FRONT	PAR	HDCP	FRONT	PAR	HDCP
1	480	450	5	15	425	5	11
2	520	510	5	9	428	5	13
3	126	114	3	17	93	3	17
4	317	287	4	13	263	4	15
5	422	402	4	3	392	4	3
6	352	335	4	11	318	4	7
7	540	526	5	7	511	5	1
8	200	190	3	5	180	3	5
9	438	429	4	1	420	5	9
Out	3395	3243	37		3030	38	
10	510	471	5	18	440	5	12
11	395	383	4	6	325	4	8
12	168	151	3	8	136	3	14
13	485	470	5	10	440	5	4
14	350	302	4	16	289	4	16
15	164	155	3	12	130	3	18
16	412	362	4	2	350	4	2
17	405	393	4	4	328	4	6
18	361	349	4	14	328	4	10
In	3250	3036	36		2766	36	
Total	6645	6279	73		5796	74	
Rating	70.6	68.3			71.7		
Slope	114	112			123		

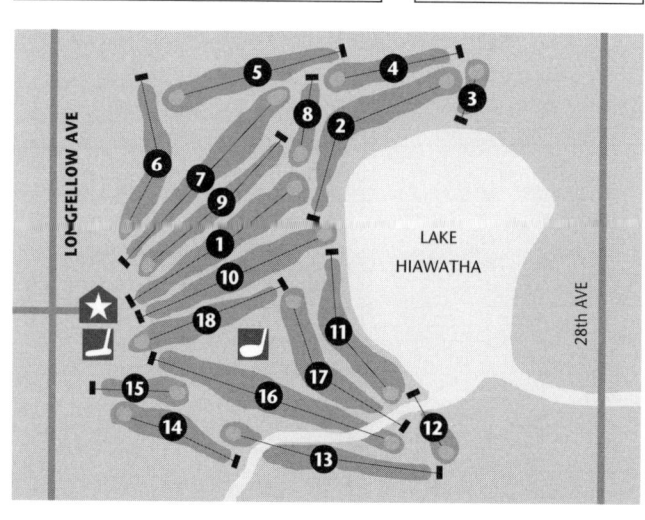

HIBBING MUNICIPAL GOLF COURSE

9 Executive Public

7th Avenue East and 16th Street
Hibbing, Minnesota 55746
218/263-4720 Clubhouse/Proshop

RESERVATIONS	218/263-4720 1 day
	Walk-on: good/fair

GREEN FEES	M-F	S-S
Adult	$10/7	$13/10
Senior	$10/7	$13/10
Junior	$10/7	$13/10
Twilight	$5	$5

PAYMENT	Credit: Visa® MasterCard®
	Non-local checks accepted

LEAGUES	Men: W (3-6:30 pm)
	Women: Th (4-6:30 pm)
	Seniors: M,T (am)

MEMBERSHIPS	USGA, NGF, GCSAA, MGA

MANAGER	Cindy Hyduke
SUPERINTENDENT	Kraig Stolhammer

HOURS	8 am to Dusk
SEASON	April to October

FEATURES	
Putting green	Y
Driving range	N
Practice area	N
Golf carts	
Power	N
Pull carts	Y $1
Club rental	Y $3
Club storage	N
Caddies	N
Proshop	
Extended	Y
Refreshments	
Restaurant	N
Lounge	Y
Snacks	Y
Clubhouse	
Showers	N
Lockers	N
Lodging	N

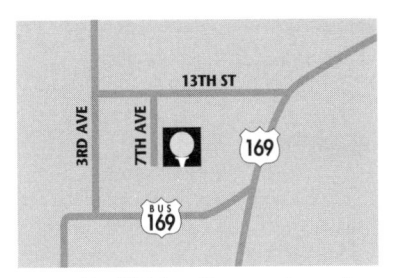

Located in Hibbing. Course entrance is about 1/2 mile west of U.S. Highway 169 on 13th Street, then south on 7th Ave.

		MEN			WOMEN		
		FRONT	PAR	HDCP	FRONT	PAR	HDCP
1		411	4	1	411	5	1
2		336	4	4	336	4	4
3		311	4	7	311	4	8
4		191	3	3	191	3	3
5		300	4	5	300	4	7
6		304	4	6	304	4	5
7		287	4	8	287	4	6
8		147	3	9	147	3	9
9		370	4	2	370	5	2
Out		2657	34		2657	36	
1		411	4	1	411	5	1
2		336	4	4	336	4	4
3		311	4	7	311	4	8
4		191	3	3	191	3	3
5		300	4	5	300	4	7
6		304	4	6	304	4	5
7		287	4	8	287	4	6
8		147	3	9	147	3	9
9		370	4	2	370	5	2
In		2657	34		2657	36	
Total		5314	68		5314	72	
Rating		64.6			70.0		
Slope		107			112		

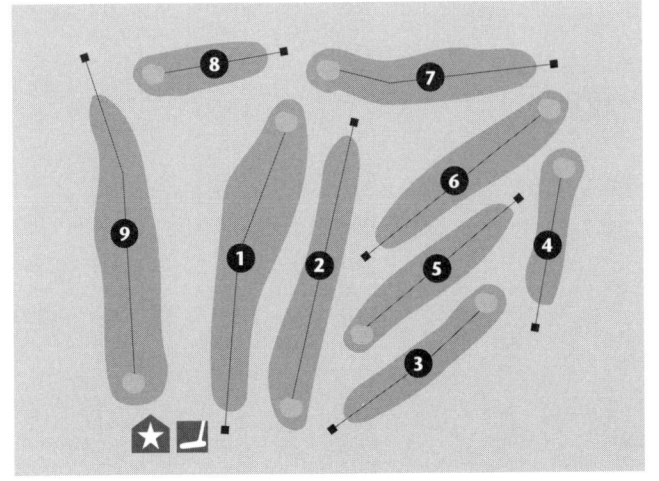

HIDDEN CREEK GOLF CLUB

18 Regulation Public

East Rose Street, Route 4 Box 14
Owatonna, Minnesota 55060
507/444-9229 Clubhouse/Proshop

RESERVATIONS	507/444-9229 1 week	
	Walk-on: good/fair	
GREEN FEES	M-F	S-S
Adult	$20/13	$24/13
Senior	$20/13	$24/13
Junior	$20/13	$24/13
Twilight	NA	NA
PAYMENT	Credit: Visa® MC® Discover®	
	Non-local checks accepted	
LEAGUES	None	
MEMBERSHIPS	USGA, PGA, GCSAA, MGA, PGAM	
SUPERINTENDENT	Randy Nelson	
PROFESSIONAL	Jim Deutsch	

HOURS	Dawn to Dusk	
SEASON	April-November	
FEATURES		
Putting green	Y	
Driving range	Y	$3-6
Practice area	Y	
Golf carts		
Power	Y	$20
Pull carts	Y	$3
Club rental	Y	$6
Club storage	N	
Caddies	N	
Proshop		
Extended	Y	
Refreshments		
Restaurant	Y	
Lounge	Y	
Snacks	Y	
Clubhouse		
Showers	Y	
Lockers	Y	
Lodging	N	

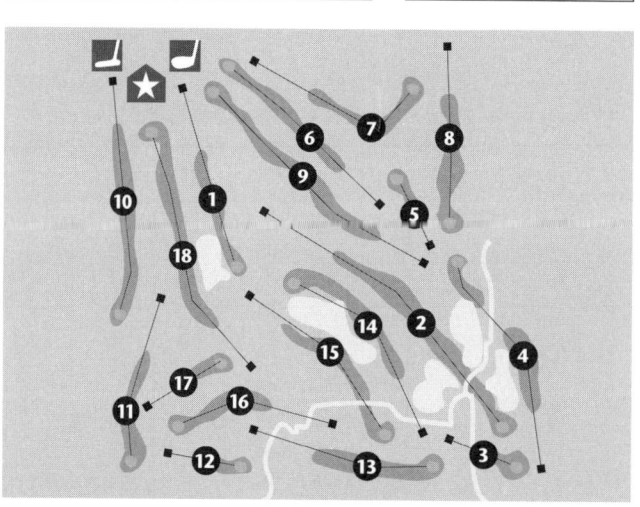

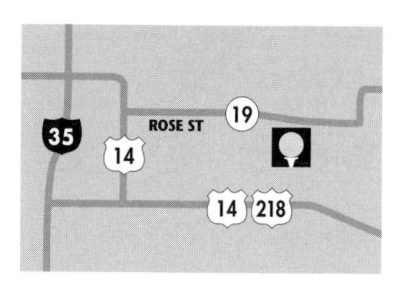

Located in Owatonna. Course entrance is about three miles east of U.S. Highway 14 on Rose Street (County Road 19).

	MEN				**WOMEN**		
	BACK	FRONT	PAR	HDCP	FRONT	PAR	HDCP
1	395	358	4	9	243	4	9
2	625	533	5	5	446	5	5
3	177	154	3	13	118	3	13
4	426	393	4	1	227	4	1
5	183	165	3	7	114	3	7
6	405	353	4	17	255	4	17
7	365	318	4	11	224	4	11
8	395	331	4	3	230	4	3
9	572	510	5	15	415	5	15
Out	3543	3115	36		2272	36	
10	515	493	5	10	384	5	10
11	383	321	4	4	265	4	4
12	206	180	3	18	146	3	18
13	426	396	4	12	243	4	12
14	426	336	4	2	284	4	2
15	400	353	4	8	270	4	8
16	370	345	4	14	196	4	14
17	160	146	3	16	116	3	16
18	573	531	5	6	406	5	6
In	3459	3101	36		2310	36	
Total	7002	6216	72		4582	72	
Rating	73.6	70.2			66.2		
Slope	126	119			116		

152

THE MINNESOTA ILLUSTRATED

HIDDEN GREENS GOLF COURSE

18 Regulation Public

12977 200th Street East
Hastings, Minnesota 55033
612/437-3085 Clubhouse/Proshop

HOURS	7 am to Dusk
SEASON	April-November

RESERVATIONS	612/437-3085 4 days
	Walk-on: good/poor

GREEN FEES	M-F	S-S
Adult	$14/9	$16/11
Senior	$14/9	$16/11
Junior	$14/9	$16/11
Twilight	NA	NA

PAYMENT	No credit cards accepted
	Non-local checks accepted

LEAGUES	Men: Various
	Women: Various

MEMBERSHIPS	MGA

OWNER	Dorothy Swanson

FEATURES	
Putting green	Y
Driving range	N
Practice area	Y
Golf carts	
Power (gas)	Y $16/9
Pull carts	Y $2
Club rental	Y $2
Club storage	N
Caddies	N
Proshop	
Basic	Y
Refreshments	
Restaurant	N
Lounge	N
Snacks	Y
Clubhouse	
Showers	N
Lockers	N
Lodging	N

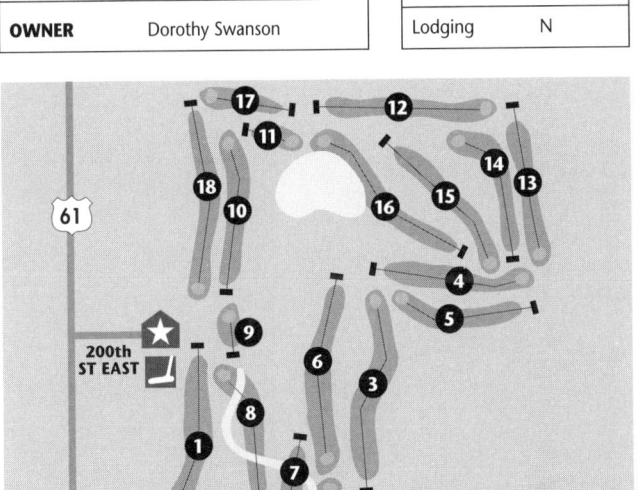

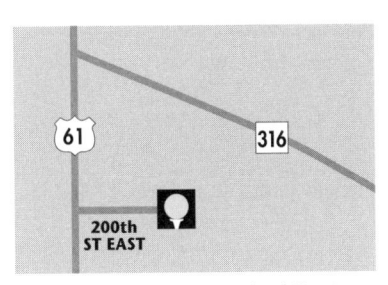

Located about 5 miles south of Hastings. Course entrance is east of U.S. Highway 61 on 200th Street East.

	MEN			**WOMEN**		
	FRONT	PAR	HDCP	FRONT	PAR	HDCP
1	369	4	8	351	4	8
2	290	4	10	257	4	10
3	527	5	4	516	5	4
4	372	4	12	347	4	12
5	331	4	14	311	4	14
6	501	5	6	481	5	6
7	142	3	18	132	3	18
8	281	4	2	262	4	2
9	164	3	16	146	3	16
Out	2977	36		2803	36	
10	476	5	5	466	5	5
11	158	3	17	148	3	17
12	391	4	3	356	4	3
13	336	4	11	318	4	11
14	295	4	9	273	4	9
15	293	4	13	283	4	13
16	395	4	1	349	4	1
17	153	3	15	133	3	15
18	480	5	7	470	5	7
In	2977	36		2796	36	
Total	5954	72		5599	72	
Rating	68.8			72.2		
Slope	118			127		

GOLF COURSE DIRECTORY

HIDDEN HAVEN COUNTRY CLUB

9 Regulation Public

20520 Polk Street Northeast
Cedar, Minnesota 55011
612/434-4626 Clubhouse
612/434-6867 Proshop

HOURS	Dawn to Dusk
SEASON	April-November

RESERVATIONS	612/434-6867 4 days
	Walk-on: fair/poor

GREEN FEES	M-F	S-S
Adult	$9.50	$10
Senior	$8.50	$9
Junior	$8.50	$9
Twilight	$5	$5

PAYMENT	Credit: Visa® MasterCard®
	Local checks only

LEAGUES	Various

MEMBERSHIPS	USGA, MGA

MANAGER	Deanna Lee, Bob McFarlane
SUPERINTENDENT	Mike Krogstad

FEATURES

Putting green	Y	
Driving range	N	
Practice area	N	
Golf carts		
Power (gas)	Y	$10
Pull carts	Y	$2
Club rental	Y	$5
Club storage	N	
Caddies	N	
Proshop		
Extended	Y	
Refreshments		
Restaurant	Y	
Lounge	Y	
Snacks	Y	
Clubhouse		
Showers	N	
Lockers	N	
Lodging	N	

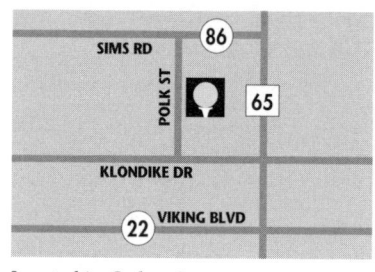

Located in Cedar. Course entrance is west of MN Highway 65 on Klondike Drive, then north on Polk Street NE.

	MEN			WOMEN		
	FRONT	PAR	HDCP	FRONT	PAR	HDCP
1	377	4	5	316	4	5
2	137	3	9	132	3	9
3	308	4	8	268	4	8
4	447	5	6	406	5	6
5	361	4	3	341	4	2
6	311	4	7	276	4	7
7	446	5	2	414	5	1
8	223	3	1	180	3	4
9	328	4	4	298	4	3
Out	2938	36		2631	36	
1	377	4	5	316	4	5
2	137	3	9	132	3	9
3	308	4	8	268	4	8
4	447	5	6	406	5	6
5	361	4	3	341	4	2
6	311	4	7	276	4	7
7	446	5	2	414	5	1
8	223	3	1	180	3	4
9	328	4	4	298	4	3
In	2938	36		2631	36	
Total	5876	72		5262	72	
Rating	69.2			70.6		
Slope	115			121		

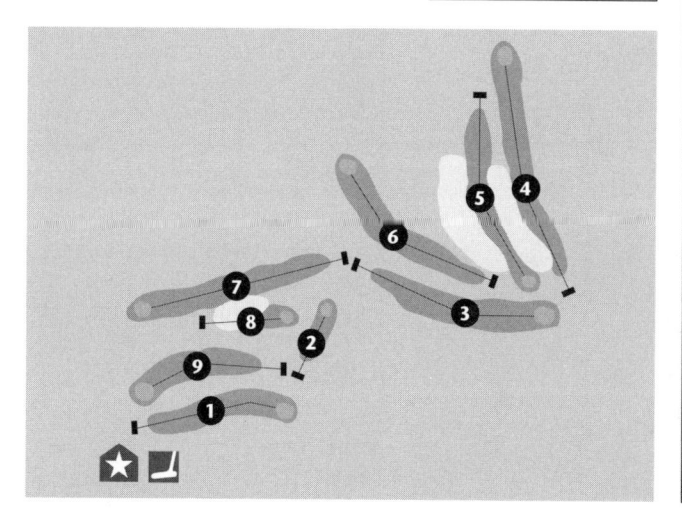

HIGHLAND PARK GOLF COURSE

18 Regulation Public

1403 Montreal Avenue
St. Paul, Minnesota 55116
612/699-3650 Clubhouse
612/699-5825 Proshop

HOURS	6 am to Dusk
SEASON	April-November

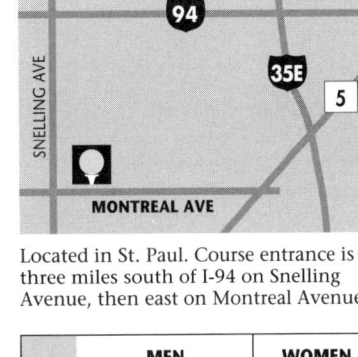

FEATURES	
Putting green	Y
Driving range	Y
Practice area	N
Golf carts	
Power (gas)	Y $20/12
Pull carts	Y
Club rental	Y
Club storage	N
Caddies	N
Proshop	
Extended	Y
Refreshments	
Restaurant	N
Lounge	N
Snacks	Y
Clubhouse	
Showers	Y
Lockers	Y
Lodging	N

RESERVATIONS	612/699-5825 2 days
	$2 reservation fee
	Walk-on: fair/fair

GREEN FEES	M-F	S-S
Adult	$18.50/13	$18.50/13
Senior	$18.50/13	$18.50/13
Junior	$18.50/13	$18.50/13
Twilight	$13 (4 pm)	$13 (4 pm)

PAYMENT	Credit: Visa® MasterCard®
	No checks accepted

LEAGUES	Men: Various
	Women: Various

MEMBERSHIPS	USGA, NGF, PGA, GCSAA,
	CMAA, MGA

PROFESSIONAL	Bobby Cotie

Located in St. Paul. Course entrance is three miles south of I-94 on Snelling Avenue, then east on Montreal Avenue.

	MEN				**WOMEN**		
	BACK	FRONT	PAR	HDCP	FRONT	PAR	HDCP
1	489	479	5	9	464	5	1
2	195	182	3	11	177	3	13
3	409	404	4	1	344	4	5
4	519	513	5	3	504	5	3
5	164	155	3	17	131	3	11
6	472	472	5	5	407	5	9
7	298	288	4	13	280	4	15
8	324	311	4	15	302	4	7
9	181	165	3	7	137	3	17
Out	3051	2969	36		2746	36	
10	414	410	4	2	348	4	2
11	136	130	3	14	124	3	16
12	383	378	4	12	372	4	8
13	320	308	4	6	296	4	4
14	404	374	4	4	303	4	14
15	494	489	5	16	438	5	10
16	329	324	4	18	316	4	6
17	236	236	3	10	217	4	18
18	498	495	5	8	440	5	12
In	3214	3144	36		2854	37	
Total	6265	6113	72		5600	73	
Rating	69.9	69.3			71.8		
Slope	119	118			120		

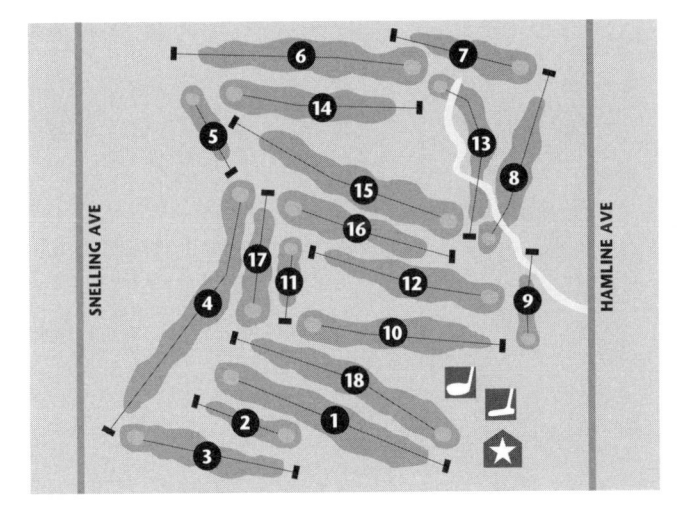

GOLF COURSE DIRECTORY

HIGHLAND PARK NINE HOLE GOLF COURSE
9 Regulation Public

1797 Edgcumbe Road
St. Paul, Minnesota 55116
612/699-6082 Clubhouse/Proshop

HOURS	6 am to 9 pm
SEASON	April-November

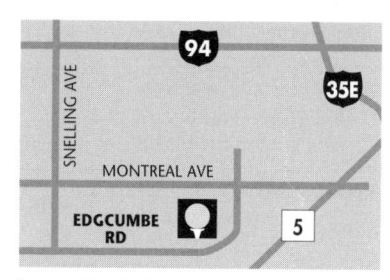

Located in St. Paul. Course entrance is 3 miles south of I-94 on Snelling Avenue, then east on Montreal Avenue.

RESERVATIONS	No reservations accepted Walk-on: good/good

GREEN FEES	M-F	S-S
Adult	$12	$12
Senior	$12	$12
Junior	$12	$12
Twilight	$9.25(6 pm)	$9.25(6 pm)
	Sr/Jr discount pass available	

PAYMENT	Credit: Visa® MasterCard® Local checks only

LEAGUES	Women: M-Th (7:30 am) M-Th (3:30 pm)

MEMBERSHIPS	USGA, NGF, GCSAA, MGA

MANAGER	Joseph Yannarelly
SUPERINTENDENT	Thomas Stelter

FEATURES	
Putting green	Y
Driving range	N
Practice area	N
Golf carts	
Power (gas)	Y $12
Pull carts	Y $2.50
Club rental	Y $5
Club storage	N
Caddies	N
Proshop	
Basic	Y
Refreshments	
Restaurant	N
Lounge	N
Snacks	Y
Clubhouse	
Showers	N
Lockers	N
Lodging	N

	MEN				WOMEN		
	BACK	FRONT	PAR	HDCP	FRONT	PAR	HDCP
1	477	467	5	3	438	5	3
2	185	175	3	4	111	3	9
3	320	306	4	9	306	4	8
4	384	371	4	2	371	4	1
5	316	306	4	7	306	4	7
6	397	362	4	1	335	4	2
7	170	160	3	5	160	3	6
8	345	330	4	6	330	4	4
9	328	317	4	8	317	4	5
Out	2922	2794	35		2674	35	
1	477	467	5	3	438	5	3
2	185	175	3	4	111	3	9
3	320	306	4	9	306	4	8
4	384	371	4	2	371	4	1
5	316	306	4	7	306	4	7
6	397	362	4	1	335	4	2
7	170	160	3	5	160	3	6
8	345	330	4	6	330	4	4
9	328	317	4	8	317	4	5
In	2922	2794	35		2674	35	
Total	5844	5588	70		5348	70	
Rating	66.5	64.4			68.4		
Slope	105	103			109		

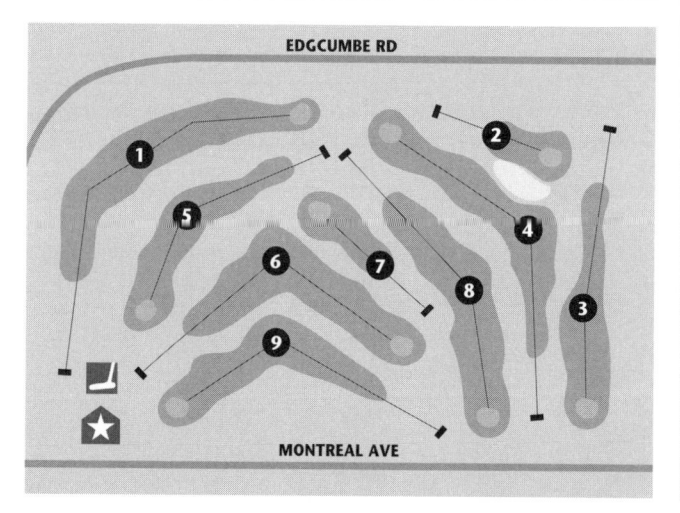

THE MINNESOTA ILLUSTRATED

HILLCREST COUNTRY CLUB

18 Regulation Private

2200 East Larpenteur Avenue
St. Paul, Minnesota 55109
612/774-6088 Clubhouse
612/771-1515 Proshop

HOURS	8 am to Dusk
SEASON	April-November

RESERVATIONS	612/771-1515 3 days
	Members only

GREEN FEES	M-F	S-S
Adult	$35	$35
Senior	$35	$35
Junior	$35	$35
Twilight	NA	NA
	Members and guests only	

PAYMENT	No credit cards accepted
	Local checks only

LEAGUES	None

MEMBERSHIPS	PGA, LPGA, GCSAA, CMAA, MGA

SUPERINTENDENT	George Ostler
PROFESSIONAL	Jay Norman

FEATURES

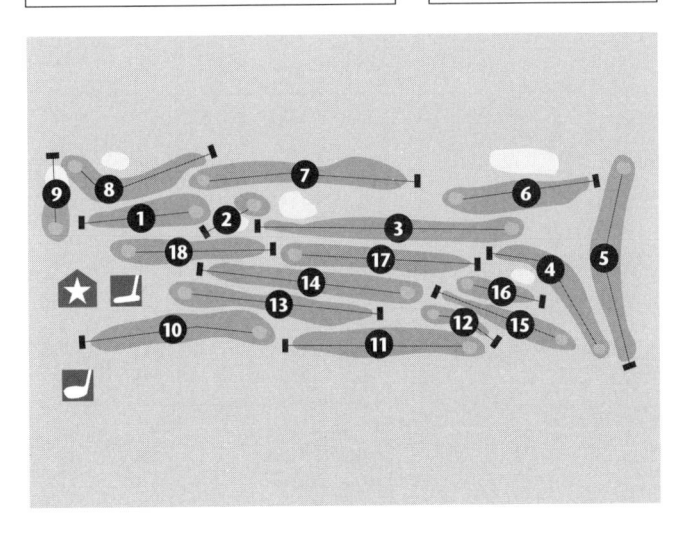

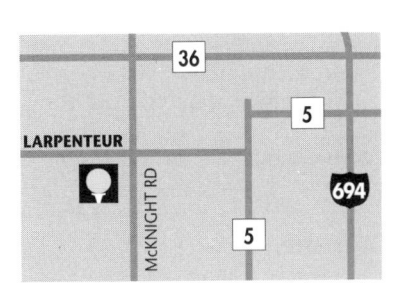

Putting green	Y
Driving range	Y
Practice area	Y
Golf carts	
Power (elec)	Y
Pull carts	Y
Club rental	Y
Club storage	Y
Caddies	Y
Proshop	
Extended	Y
Refreshments	
Restaurant	Y
Lounge	Y
Snacks	Y
Clubhouse	
Showers	Y
Lockers	Y
Lodging	N

Located in St. Paul. Course is about 1 1/2 miles south of Highway 36 on McKnight Road, then west on Larpenteur Avenue.

	MEN			**WOMEN**		
	FRONT	PAR	HDCP	FRONT	PAR	HDCP
1	278	4	17	271	4	13
2	134	3	13	118	3	17
3	564	5	1	492	5	1
4	339	4	7	335	4	7
5	396	4	3	385	4	5
6	348	4	9	288	4	11
7	476	5	11	404	5	3
8	339	4	5	316	4	9
9	144	3	15	118	3	15
Out	3018	36		2674	36	
10	354	4	6	278	4	12
11	410	4	4	404	5	8
12	145	3	10	118	3	18
13	425	4	2	419	5	4
14	474	5	14	466	5	2
15	312	4	16	307	4	14
16	180	3	8	174	3	16
17	424	5	18	407	5	6
18	367	4	12	361	4	10
In	3091	36		2934	38	
Total	6109	72		5608	74	
Rating	70.8			74.1		
Slope	133			138		

HOLIDAY PARK GOLF COURSE

9 Par-3 Public

Route 3, P.O. Box 15
Hayward, Minnesota 56043
507/373-3886 Clubhouse/Proshop

HOURS	8 am to Dusk
SEASON	April-November

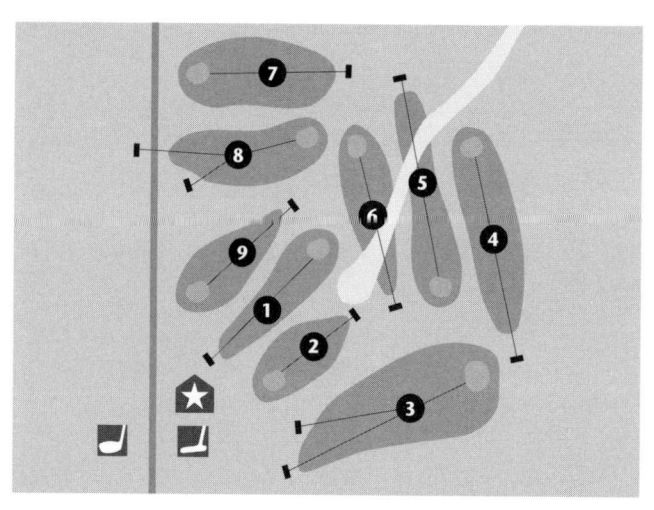

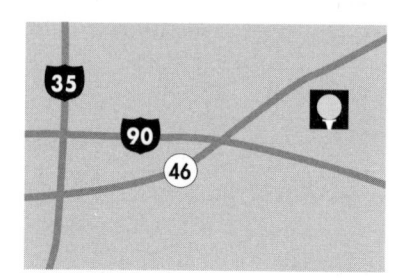

Located in Hayward. Course entrance is north of Interstate-90 (Exit #166) on County Road 46.

RESERVATIONS	No reservations accepted
	Walk-on: good/fair

GREEN FEES	M-F	S-S
Adult	$8.50/5.50	$8.50/5.50
Senior	$5.50/4.00	$8.50/5.50
Junior	$6.00/4.50	$6.00/4.00
Twilight	NA	NA

PAYMENT	No credit cards accepted
	Local checks only

LEAGUES	None

MEMBERSHIPS	USGA, NGF, PGA, GCSAA

OWNER	American Holiday Inc.
MANAGER	John Worlein
PROFESSIONAL	Harlan Hinrichs

FEATURES		
Putting green	Y	
Driving range	Y	$4.50
Practice area	N	
Golf carts		
Power (gas)	Y	
Pull carts	Y	$1
Club rental	Y	$2.50
Club storage	N	
Caddies	N	
Proshop		
Regular	Y	
Refreshments		
Restaurant	N	
Lounge	N	
Snacks	Y	
Clubhouse		
Showers	N	
Lockers	N	
Lodging	N	

	MEN			**WOMEN**		
	FRONT	PAR	HDCP	FRONT	PAR	HDCP
1	138	3	7	138	3	7
2	110	3	2	110	3	2
3	210	3	9	210	3	9
4	175	3	18	175	3	18
5	140	3	5	140	3	5
6	118	3	12	118	3	12
7	128	3	15	128	3	15
8	105	3	3	105	3	3
9	112	3	10	112	3	10
Out	1236	27		1236	27	
1	138	3	8	138	3	8
2	110	3	14	110	3	14
3	169	3	1	169	3	1
4	175	3	13	175	3	13
5	140	3	16	140	3	16
6	118	3	6	118	3	6
7	128	3	4	128	3	4
8	135	3	11	135	3	11
9	112	3	17	112	3	17
In	1225	27		1225	27	
Total	2461	54		2461	54	
Rating	NA			NA		
Slope	NA			NA		

HOLLYDALE GOLF CLUB

18 Regulation Public

4710 Holly Lane North
Plymouth, Minnesota 55446
612/559-9847 Clubhouse/Proshop

HOURS	Dawn to Dusk
SEASON	April to October

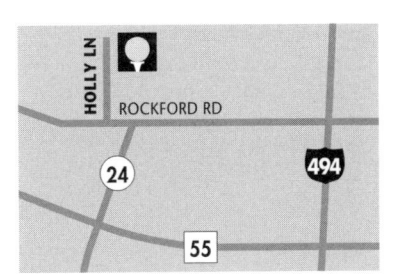

Located in Plymouth. Course entrance is west of I-494 on Rockford Road, then north on Holly Lane.

RESERVATIONS	612/559-9847 4 days
	Weekends & holidays only
	Walk-on: good/poor

GREEN FEES	M-F	S-S
Adult	$17/12	$19/13
Senior	$12/9*	$19/13
Junior	$12/9*	$19/13
Twilight	NA	NA
	* Before 11 am	

PAYMENT	No credit cards accepted
	Local checks accepted

LEAGUES	Men: Various
	Women: Various

MEMBERSHIPS	MGA

MANAGER	Bill Deziel

FEATURES

Putting green	Y	
Driving range	N	
Practice area	N	
Golf carts		
Power (gas)	Y	$20/11
Pull carts	Y	$2
Club rental	Y	$4
Club storage	N	
Caddies	N	
Proshop		
Extended	Y	
Refreshments		
Restaurant	N	
Lounge	N	
Snacks	Y	
Clubhouse		
Showers	N	
Lockers	N	
Lodging	N	

	MEN				**WOMEN**		
	BACK	FRONT	PAR	HDCP	FRONT	PAR	HDCP
1	392	377	4	9	357	4	5
2	382	377	4	3	352	4	1
3	183	176	3	5	136	3	11
4	484	474	5	13	464	5	3
5	167	155	3	15	125	3	17
6	539	531	5	7	443	5	9
7	333	323	4	11	305	4	7
8	421	415	4	1	403	5	13
9	301	291	4	17	271	4	15
Out	3202	3082	36		2856	37	
10	342	330	4	8	304	4	6
11	425	415	4	2	402	5	10
12	219	204	3	4	142	3	18
13	296	292	4	18	242	4	16
14	158	153	3	14	146	3	8
15	504	494	5	16	438	5	2
16	349	328	4	6	278	4	12
17	472	452	5	12	417	5	4
18	148	135	3	10	119	3	14
In	2913	2803	35		2488	36	
Total	6115	5922	71		5344	73	
Rating	68.7	67.9			68.1		
Slope	108	107			111		

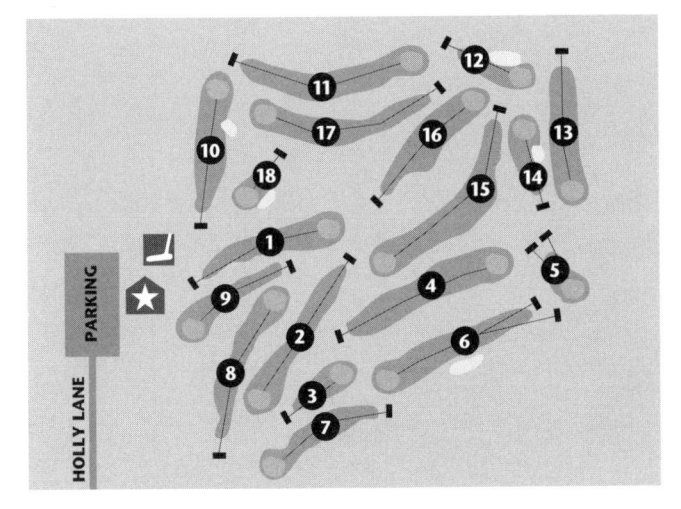

GOLF COURSE DIRECTORY

HOWARD LAKE GREENS

9 Regulation Public

5055 County Road 7 S.W.
Howard Lake, Minnesota 55349
612/543-3330 Clubhouse/Proshop

HOURS	Dawn to Dusk
SEASON	April to October

RESERVATIONS	612/543-3330	
	Walk-on: good/fair	
GREEN FEES	M-F	S-S
Adult	$16/10	$17/11
Senior	$16/10	$17/11
Junior	$16/10	$17/11
Twilight	NA	NA
PAYMENT	Credit: Visa® MasterCard®	
	Non-local checks accepted	
LEAGUES	None	
MEMBERSHIPS	None	
OWNER	The Lahr Family	

FEATURES	
Putting green	Y
Driving range	Y
Practice area	N
Golf carts	
Power (gas)	Y
Pull carts	Y
Club rental	Y
Club storage	N
Caddies	N
Proshop	
Basic	Y
Refreshments	
Restaurant	N
Lounge	N
Snacks	Y
Clubhouse	
Showers	N
Lockers	N
Lodging	N

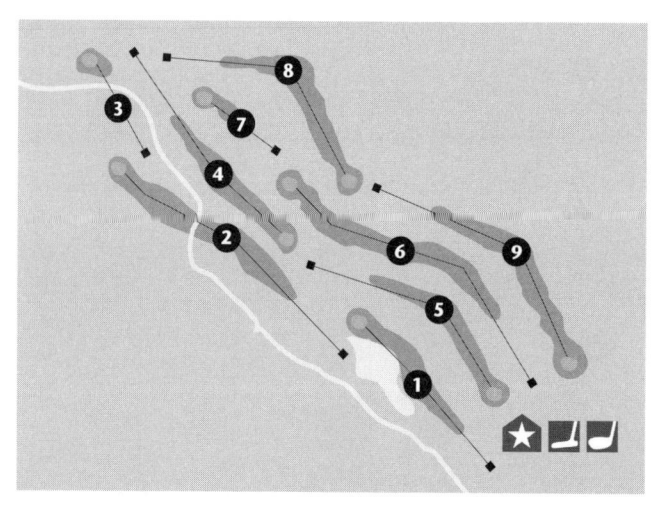

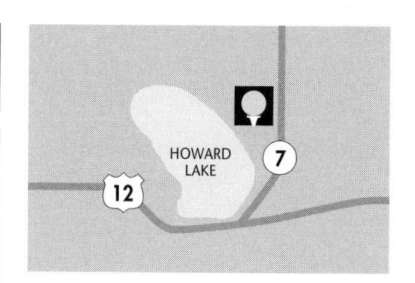

Located in Howard Lake. Course is 1/2 mile north of U.S. Highway 12 on the west side of County Road 7.

	MEN				**WOMEN**		
	BACK	FRONT	PAR	HDCP	FRONT	PAR	HDCP
1	350	325	4		275	4	
2	500	475	5		405	5	
3	200	175	3		75	3	
4	375	350	4		300	4	
5	400	375	4		325	4	
6	550	525	5		450	5	
7	150	125	3		100	3	
8	425	400	4		350	4	
9	450	425	4		375	4	
Out	3400	3175	36		2655	36	
1	350	325	4		275	4	
2	500	475	5		405	5	
3	200	175	3		75	3	
4	375	350	4		300	4	
5	400	375	4		325	4	
6	550	525	5		450	5	
7	150	125	3		100	3	
8	425	400	4		350	4	
9	450	425	4		375	4	
In	3400	3175	36		2655	36	
Total	6800	6350	72		5310	72	
Rating	NA	NA			NA		
Slope	NA	NA			NA		

THE MINNESOTA ILLUSTRATED

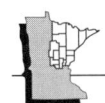

HOWARD'S BARN/FIFTY LAKES GOLF CENTER

9 Executive Public

Cty Rd 3 & Hwy 1, P.O. Box 85
Fifty Lakes, Minnesota 56448
218/763-2038 Clubhouse/Proshop

HOURS	8 am to Dusk
SEASON	April to October

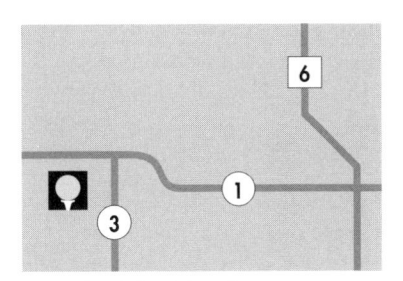

RESERVATIONS	No reservations accepted
	Walk-on: good/fair

GREEN FEES	M-F	S-S
Adult	$8.50/5.50	$8.50/5.50
Senior	$8.50/5.50	$8.50/5.50
Junior	$8.50/5.50	$8.50/5.50
Twilight	NA	NA

PAYMENT	Credit: Visa® MasterCard®
	Non-local checks accepted

LEAGUES	Men: Various
	Women: Various

MEMBERSHIPS	None

OWNER	Richard & Vernice Henderson

FEATURES	
Putting green	N
Driving range	Y
Practice area	N
Golf carts	
Power (gas)	Y
Pull carts	Y
Club rental	Y $2.50
Club storage	N
Caddies	N
Proshop	
Extended	Y
Refreshments	
Restaurant	N
Lounge	N
Snacks	Y
Clubhouse	
Showers	N
Lockers	N
Lodging	N

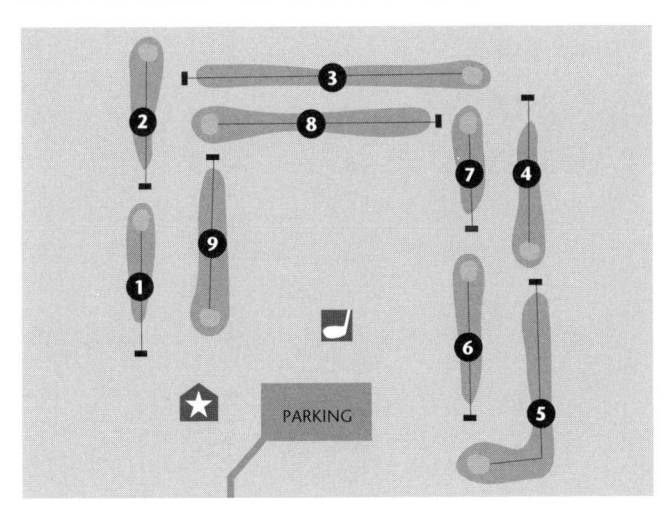

Located in Fifty Lakes. Course entrance is just west of County Road 3 on County Road 1.

	MEN			WOMEN		
	FRONT	PAR	HDCP	FRONT	PAR	HDCP
1	133	3	7	133	3	7
2	168	3	6	168	3	6
3	259	4	2	259	4	2
4	135	3	8	135	3	8
5	219	4	3	219	4	3
6	187	3	5	187	3	5
7	129	3	9	129	3	9
8	170	3	4	170	3	4
9	258	4	1	258	4	1
Out	1664	30		1664	30	
1	133	3	7	133	3	7
2	168	3	6	168	3	6
3	259	4	2	259	4	2
4	135	3	8	135	3	8
5	219	4	3	219	4	3
6	187	3	5	187	3	5
7	129	3	9	129	3	9
8	170	3	4	170	3	4
9	258	4	1	258	4	1
In	1664	30		1664	30	
Total	3328	60		3328	60	
Rating	NA			NA		
Slope	NA			NA		

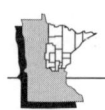

HOYT LAKES COUNTRY CLUB

9 Regulation Public

P.O. Box 209
Hoyt Lakes, Minnesota 55750
218/225-2841 Clubhouse/Proshop

HOURS	7 am to Dusk
SEASON	April-September

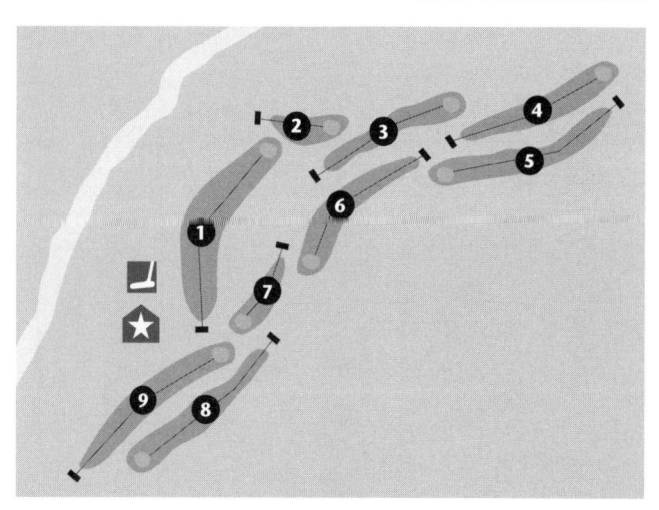

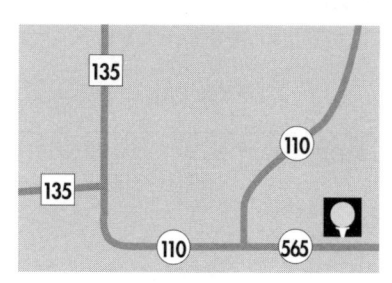

Located in Hoyt Lakes. Course entrance is about two miles east of County Road 110 on County Road 565.

RESERVATIONS	No reservations accepted
	Walk-on: good/fair

GREEN FEES	M-F	S-S
Adult	$11	$11
Senior	$11	$11
Junior	$11	$11
Twilight	NA	NA

PAYMENT	No credit cards accepted
	Non-local checks accepted

LEAGUES	Men:	Various
	Women:	Various

MEMBERSHIPS	USGA, MGA

OWNER	City of Hoyt Lakes
MANAGER	Beth Anderson

FEATURES	
Putting green	Y
Driving range	N
Practice area	Y
Golf carts	
Power	Y
Pull carts	N
Club rental	N
Club storage	Y
Caddies	N
Proshop	
Basic	Y
Refreshments	
Restaurant	N
Lounge	Y
Snacks	Y
Clubhouse	
Showers	Y
Lockers	N
Lodging	N

	MEN			**WOMEN**		
	FRONT	PAR	HDCP	FRONT	PAR	HDCP
1	512	5	5	512	5	5
2	166	3	9	166	3	9
3	371	4	6	371	4	6
4	410	4	2	410	5	2
5	471	5	7	471	5	7
6	399	4	3	399	5	3
7	208	3	8	208	4	8
8	427	4	1	427	5	1
9	394	4	4	394	4	4
Out	3358	36		3358	40	
1	512	5	5	512	5	5
2	166	3	9	166	3	9
3	371	4	6	371	4	6
4	410	4	2	410	5	2
5	471	5	7	471	5	7
6	399	4	3	399	5	3
7	208	3	8	208	4	8
8	427	4	1	427	5	1
9	394	4	4	394	4	4
In	3358	36		3358	40	
Total	6716	72		6716	80	
Rating	70.1			76.3		
Slope	107			122		

HYLAND GREENS GOLF COURSE — 18 Par-3 Public

10200 102nd Street
Bloomington, Minnesota 55437
612/887-9668 Clubhouse/Proshop

RESERVATIONS	612/887-9668 1 week	
	Outside nine only	
	Walk-on: good/fair	
GREEN FEES	M-F	S-S
Adult	$7/6	$7/6
Senior	$7/6	$7/6
Junior	$7/6	$7/6
Twilight	NA	NA
	Fees for outside/inside nine	
	Season tickets available	
PAYMENT	No credit cards accepted	
	Local checks only	
LEAGUES	Men: Various	
	Women: Various	
MEMBERSHIPS	None	
MANAGER	Bob Allison	
PROFESSIONAL	Mike Berry	

HOURS Dawn to Dusk
SEASON April to October

FEATURES

Putting green	Y
Driving range	Y
Practice area	N
Golf carts	
Power	Y $10
Pull carts	Y $1
Club rental	Y $4.50
Club storage	N
Caddies	N
Proshop	
Basic	Y
Refreshments	
Restaurant	N
Lounge	N
Snacks	Y
Clubhouse	
Showers	N
Lockers	N
Lodging	N

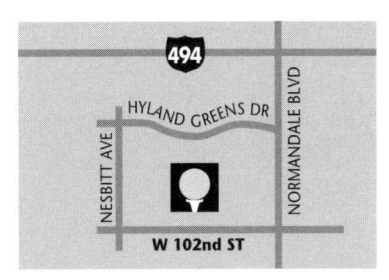

Located in Bloomington. Course is south of Normandale Blvd, then 1/8 mile west on 102nd Street.

	MEN			WOMEN		
	FRONT	PAR	HDCP	FRONT	PAR	HDCP
1	175	3	3	175	3	3
2	170	3	5	170	3	5
3	160	3	9	160	3	9
4	220	3	1	220	3	1
5	170	3	4	170	3	4
6	195	3	6	195	3	6
7	150	3	8	150	3	8
8	165	3	2	165	3	2
9	155	3	7	155	3	7
Out	1560	27		1560	27	
1	110	3	8	110	3	8
2	165	3	3	165	3	3
3	150	3	4	150	3	4
4	120	3	6	120	3	6
5	200	3	1	200	3	1
6	85	3	9	85	3	9
7	170	3	2	170	3	2
8	110	3	7	110	3	7
9	150	3	5	150	3	5
In	1260	27		1260	27	
Total	2820	54		2820	54	
Rating	NA			NA		
Slope	NA			NA		

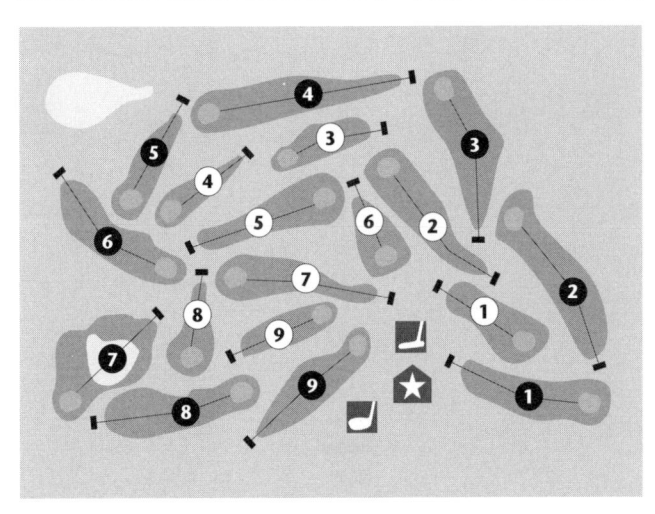

INDIAN HILLS GOLF CLUB — 18 Regulation Private

6667 Keats Avenue North
Stillwater, Minnesota 55082
612/770-2301 Clubhouse
612/770-2366 Proshop

RESERVATIONS	612/770-2366	
	Members only	
GREEN FEES	M-F	S-S
Adult	$27/14	$27/14
Senior	$27/14	$27/14
Junior	$27/14	$27/14
Twilight	$6	$6
	Members and guests only	
PAYMENT	No credit cards accepted	
	Non-local checks accepted	
LEAGUES	Various	
MEMBERSHIPS	USGA, PGA, GCSAA, MGA	
MANAGER	Michael Regan	
SUPERINTENDENT	Richard Grundstrom	
PROFESSIONAL	Richard Nelson	

HOURS 7 am to Dusk
SEASON April-November

FEATURES

Putting green	Y	
Driving range	Y	$2.50
Practice area	Y	
Golf carts		
Power (elec)	Y	$20
Pull carts	Y	$3
Club rental	Y	
Club storage	Y	
Caddies	Y	
Proshop		
Extended	Y	
Refreshments		
Restaurant	Y	
Lounge	N	
Snacks	Y	
Clubhouse		
Showers	Y	
Lockers	Y	
Lodging	N	

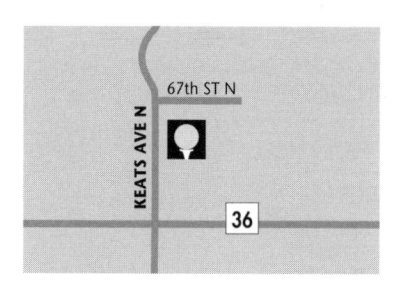

Located in Stillwater. Course entrance is about one mile north of MN Highway 36 on Keats Avenue.

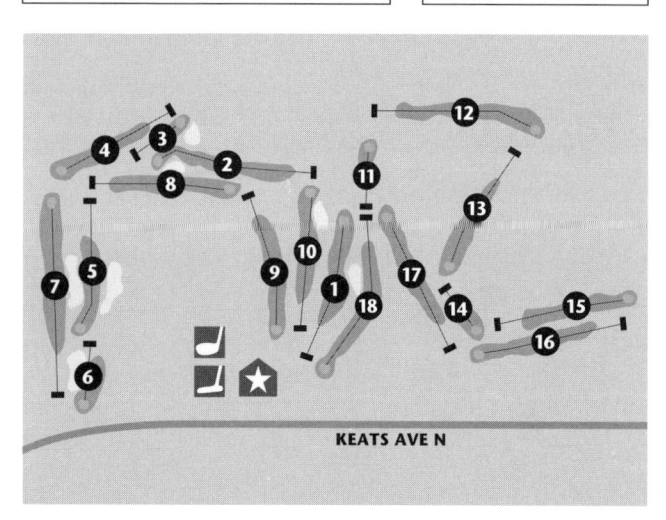

	MEN				**WOMEN**		
	BACK	FRONT	PAR	HDCP	FRONT	PAR	HDCP
1	383	370	4	9	352	4	7
2	538	490	5	11	451	5	1
3	163	140	3	17	131	3	15
4	376	349	4	15	331	4	11
5	365	346	4	5	316	4	9
6	167	167	3	13	98	3	17
7	554	527	5	1	430	5	5
8	436	425	4	3	412	5	13
9	407	390	4	7	377	4	3
Out	3389	3204	36		2898	37	
10	373	354	4	8	337	4	4
11	193	170	3	10	156	3	14
12	486	475	5	12	453	5	8
13	371	352	4	16	336	4	10
14	173	157	3	14	144	3	18
15	415	401	4	2	390	4	2
16	438	421	4	4	401	5	16
17	433	410	4	6	395	4	6
18	480	472	5	18	438	5	12
In	3362	3212	36		3050	37	
Total	6751	6416	72		5948	74	
Rating	72.6	71.3			74.8		
Slope	126	123			131		

INTERLACHEN COUNTRY CLUB

18 Regulation Private

6200 Interlachen Boulevard
Edina, Minnesota 55436
612/929-1661 Clubhouse
612/929-3641 Proshop

HOURS	Dawn to Dusk
SEASON	April to October

FEATURES	
Putting green	Y
Driving range	Y
Practice area	Y
Golf carts	
Power (gas)	Y
Pull carts	Y
Club rental	Y
Club storage	Y
Caddies	Y
Proshop	
Extended	Y
Refreshments	
Restaurant	Y
Lounge	Y
Snacks	Y
Clubhouse	
Showers	Y
Lockers	Y
Lodging	N

RESERVATIONS	612/929-3641
	Members only

GREEN FEES	M-F	S-S
Adult	Call	Call
Senior	Call	Call
Junior	Call	Call
Twilight	NA	NA
	Members and guests only	

PAYMENT	Credit: Visa® MC® Discover®
	Non-local checks accepted

LEAGUES	None

MEMBERSHIPS	USGA, PGA, GCSAA, MGA

PROFESSIONAL	Call

Located in Edina. Course entrance is east of U.S. Hwy 169 on Cty Rd 3, south on Blake Rd then east in Interlachen Blvd.

	MEN				**WOMEN**		
	BACK	FRONT	PAR	HDCP	FRONT	PAR	HDCP
1	531	526	5	3	496	5	5
2	351	336	4	13	308	4	11
3	203	179	3	9	150	3	15
4	530	493	5	5	478	5	3
5	175	153	3	17	130	3	17
6	250	338	4	7	317	4	9
7	346	337	4	15	306	4	13
8	430	400	4	1	300	4	7
9	520	508	5	11	438	5	1
Out	3436	3270	37		2923	37	
10	341	335	4	10	329	4	4
11	476	470	5	16	450	5	8
12	541	536	5	2	441	5	2
13	187	181	3	12	169	3	18
14	440	427	4	4	411	5	16
15	414	409	4	8	399	5	14
16	318	313	4	18	251	4	10
17	226	206	3	14	186	3	12
18	400	381	4	6	337	4	6
In	3458	3258	36		3005	38	
Total	6804	6528	73		5928	75	
Rating	72.9	71.9			76.8		
Slope	134	132			137		

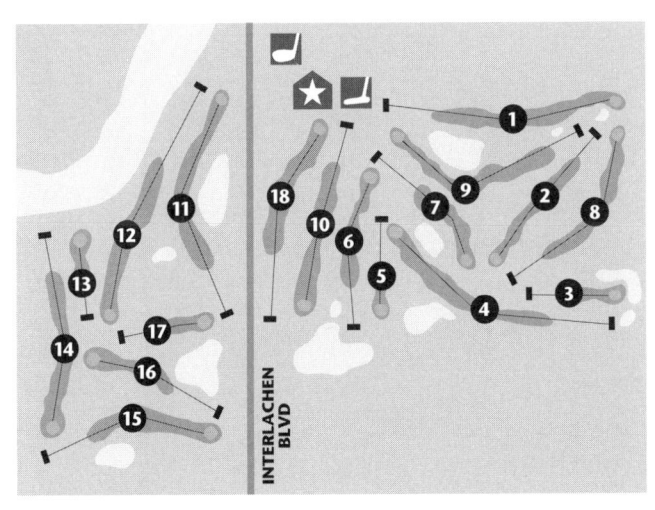

GOLF COURSE DIRECTORY

INTERLAKEN GOLF CLUB

18 Regulation Private

277 Amber Lake Drive
Fairmont, Minnesota 56031
507/235-5145 Clubhouse
507/238-1693 Proshop

HOURS	7 am to Dusk
SEASON	April to October

RESERVATIONS	507/238-1693 1 week
	Members only

GREEN FEES	M-F	S-S
Adult	$21	$21
Senior	$21	$21
Junior	$21	$21
Twilight	NA	NA
	Members and guests only	

PAYMENT	No credit cards accepted
	Non-local checks accepted

LEAGUES	Men: Various
	Women: Various

MEMBERSHIPS	USGA, NGF, PGA, MGA

PROFESSIONAL	Paul Baldus

FEATURES		
Putting green	Y	
Driving range	Y	$2
Practice area	Y	
Golf carts		
Power (gas)	Y	$16
Pull carts	Y	$1.50
Club rental	Y	$5
Club storage	Y	
Caddies	N	
Proshop		
Extended	Y	
Refreshments		
Restaurant	Y	
Lounge	Y	
Snacks	Y	
Clubhouse		
Showers	Y	
Lockers	N	
Lodging	N	

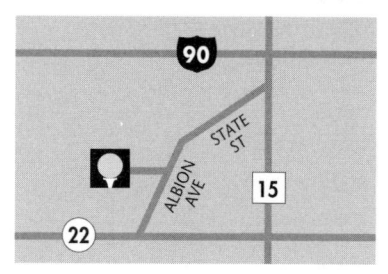

Located in Fairmont. Course is west of MN Highway 15 on State Street/Albion Avenue, then west on Amber Lake Road.

		MEN			**WOMEN**		
	BACK	FRONT	PAR	HDCP	FRONT	PAR	HDCP
1	368	327	4	9	319	4	11
2	487	477	5	17	467	5	5
3	179	168	3	7	155	3	15
4	405	378	4	1	364	4	9
5	154	146	3	15	132	3	17
6	565	524	5	5	487	5	1
7	490	482	5	11	420	5	3
8	409	397	4	3	352	4	7
9	300	275	4	13	246	4	13
Out	3357	3174	37		2942	37	
10	352	345	4	6	337	4	12
11	432	387	4	4	357	4	8
12	409	386	4	2	327	4	4
13	170	150	3	14	130	3	18
14	291	276	4	18	257	4	16
15	402	354	4	12	343	4	6
16	191	184	3	10	154	3	14
17	480	466	5	16	376	5	2
18	352	345	4	8	336	4	10
In	3079	2893	35		2617	35	
Total	6436	6067	72		5559	72	
Rating	70.6	69.5			73.0		
Slope	124	121			126		

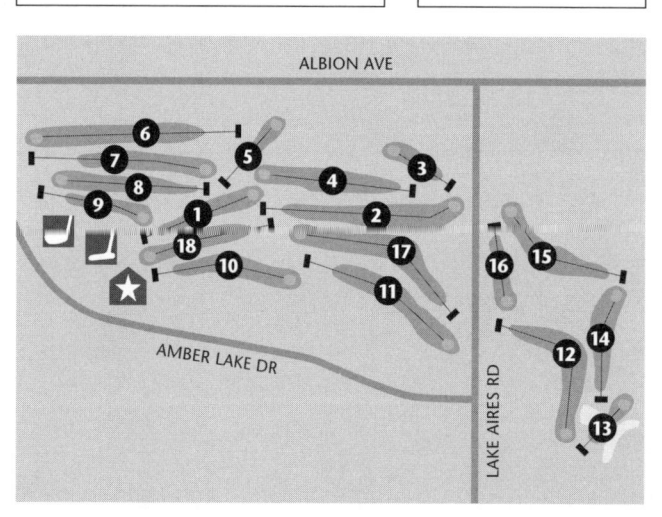

INVER WOOD GOLF COURSE

18 Regulation Public

1850 70th Street East
Inver Grove Heights, MN 55077
612/457-3667 Clubhouse/Proshop

RESERVATIONS	612/457-3667 3 days	
	Walk-on: fair/poor	
GREEN FEES	M-F	S-S
Adult	$22/12	$22/12
Senior	$22/12	$22/12
Junior	$17/9	$22/12
Twilight	NA	NA
PAYMENT	Credit: Visa® MasterCard®	
	Local checks accepted	
LEAGUES	Men: W (pm)	
	Women: M (pm)	
MEMBERSHIPS	USGA, NGF, PGA, GCSAA, MGA	
OWNER	City of Inver Grove Heights	
MANAGER	Al McMurchie	
SUPERINTENDENT	Glen Lentner	
PROFESSIONAL	Leon Otness	

HOURS	6 am to Dusk
SEASON	April to October

FEATURES		
Putting green	Y	
Driving range	Y	$1.50-5
Practice area	Y	
Golf carts		
Power (gas)	Y	$20/12
Pull carts	Y	
Club rental	Y	$6-12
Club storage	N	
Caddies	N	
Proshop		
Extended	Y	
Refreshments		
Restaurant	Y	
Lounge	N	
Snacks	Y	
Clubhouse		
Showers	N	
Lockers	Y	
Lodging	N	

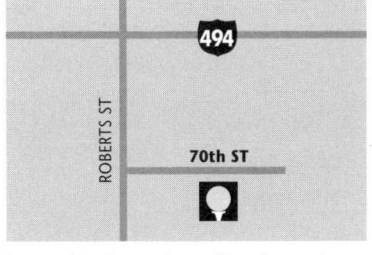

Located in Inver Grove Hts. Course is 2 1/2 miles south of I-494 on Roberts Street, then 3/4 mile east on 70th St.

	MEN				WOMEN		
	BACK	FRONT	PAR	HDCP	FRONT	PAR	HDCP
1	536	526	5	7	444	5	5
2	349	334	4	11	259	4	13
3	363	334	4	9	285	4	9
4	352	328	4	15	282	4	11
5	409	383	4	5	326	4	7
6	206	160	3	13	118	3	15
7	537	512	5	3	450	5	3
8	453	428	4	1	368	4	1
9	167	134	3	17	114	3	17
Out	3372	3139	36		2646	36	
10	512	484	5	2	416	5	2
11	351	325	4	14	276	4	10
12	240	176	3	8	123	3	16
13	351	305	4	12	228	4	18
14	540	512	5	4	434	5	4
15	389	361	4	6	308	4	6
16	385	359	4	18	307	4	14
17	190	172	3	16	134	3	12
18	394	361	4	10	303	4	8
In	3352	3055	36		2529	36	
Total	6724	6194	72		5175	72	
Rating	72.5	70.3			70.3		
Slope	135	131			124		

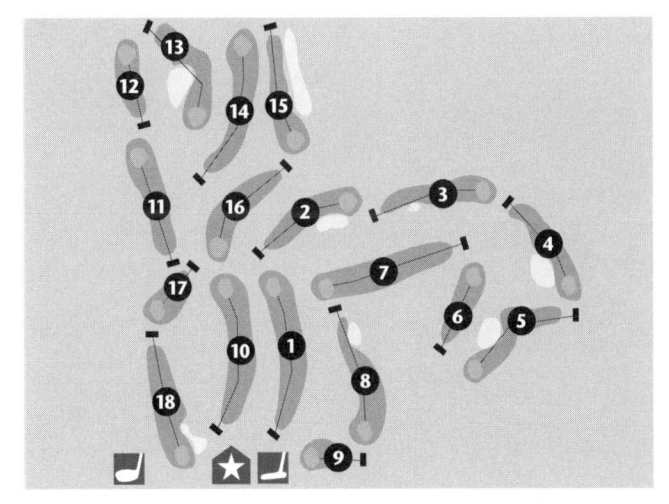

GOLF COURSE DIRECTORY

INVER WOOD GOLF COURSE

9 Executive Public

1850 70th Street East
Inver Grove Heights, MN 55077
612/457-3667 Clubhouse/Proshop

RESERVATIONS	612/457-3667	3 days
	Walk-on: good/fair	

GREEN FEES	M-F	S-S
Adult	$17/9	$17/9
Senior	$17/9	$17/9
Junior	$9	$17/9
Twilight	NA	NA

PAYMENT	Credit: Visa® MasterCard®
	Local checks accepted

LEAGUES	Men: W (pm)
	Women: M (pm)

MEMBERSHIPS	USGA, NGF, PGA, GCSAA, MGA

OWNER	City of Inver Grove Heights
MANAGER	Al McMurchie
SUPERINTENDENT	Glen Lentner
PROFESSIONAL	Leon Otness

HOURS	6 am to Dusk
SEASON	April to October

FEATURES		
Putting green	Y	
Driving range	Y	$1.50-5
Practice area	Y	
Golf carts		
Power (gas)	Y	$20/12
Pull carts	Y	
Club rental	Y	$6-12
Club storage	N	
Caddies	N	
Proshop		
Extended	Y	
Refreshments		
Restaurant	Y	
Lounge	N	
Snacks	Y	
Clubhouse		
Showers	N	
Lockers	Y	
Lodging	N	

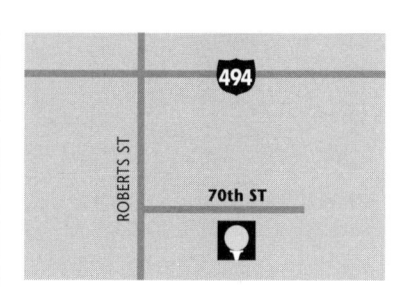

Located in Inver Grove Hts. Course is 2 1/2 miles south of I-494 on Roberts Street, then 3/4 mile east on 70th St.

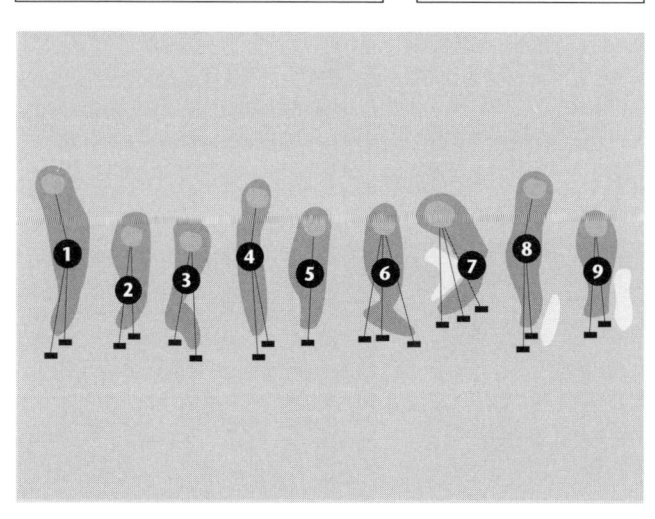

	MEN				**WOMEN**		
	BACK	FRONT	PAR	HDCP	FRONT	PAR	HDCP
1	384	353	4	4	305	4	1
2	139	108	3	8	89	3	8
3	125	105	3	7	102	3	5
4	308	289	4	1	266	4	3
5	149	136	3	9	121	3	6
6	116	101	3	6	92	3	7
7	121	92	3	3	75	3	9
8	365	329	4	3	286	4	2
9	150	118	3	5	108	3	4
Out	1857	1631	30		1444	30	
1	384	353	4	4	305	4	1
2	139	108	3	8	89	3	8
3	125	105	3	7	102	3	5
4	308	289	4	1	266	4	3
5	149	136	3	9	121	3	6
6	116	101	3	6	92	3	7
7	121	92	3	3	75	3	9
8	365	329	4	3	286	4	2
9	150	118	3	5	108	3	4
In	1857	1631	30		1444	30	
Total	3714	3262	60		2888	60	
Rating	56.6	54.6			55.2		
Slope	82	78			80		

IRISH HILLS GOLF COURSE

9 Regulation Public

McGuire's Piney Ridge Lodge
Route 1, Box 315
Pine River, Minnesota 56474
218/587-2296 Clubhouse/Proshop

HOURS	7 am to Dusk
SEASON	April-November

FEATURES		
Putting green	Y	
Driving range	N	
Practice area	N	
Golf carts		
Power (gas)	Y	$20/12
Pull carts	Y	$3
Club rental	Y	$5
Club storage	Y	
Caddies	N	
Proshop		
Extended	Y	
Refreshments		
Restaurant	Y	
Lounge	N	
Snacks	Y	
Clubhouse		
Showers	Y	
Lockers	Y	
Lodging	Y	Call

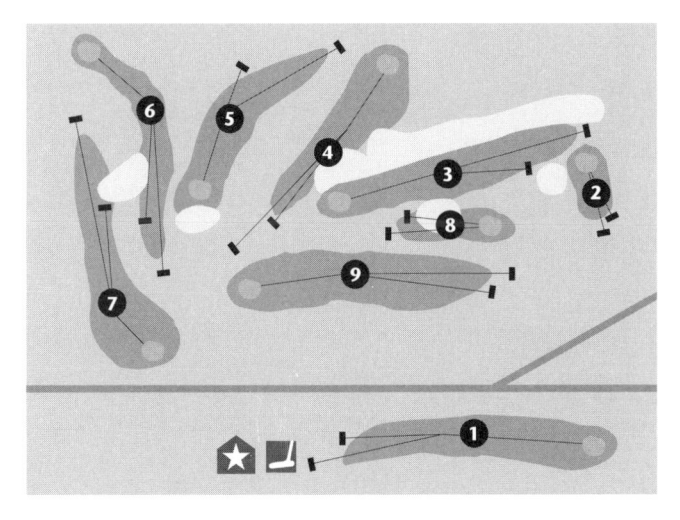

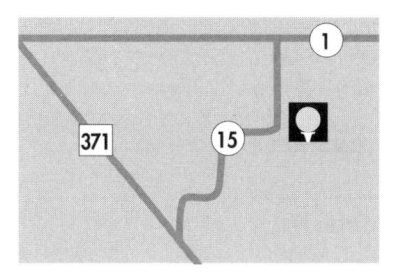

Located east of Pine River. Course is about 6 miles east of MN Highway 371 on County Road 15.

RESERVATIONS	218/587-2296 1 day
	Walk-on: good/fair

GREEN FEES	M-F	S-S
Adult	$19/13	$19/13
Senior	$15*	$19/13
Junior	$19/13	$19/13
Twilight	NA	NA
	* M-Th (7-9 am) with cart	

PAYMENT	Credit: Visa® MasterCard®
	Non-local checks accepted

LEAGUES	Various

MEMBERSHIPS	USGA, GCSAA, MGA

OWNER	Mark & Debra Sisson
PROFESSIONAL	Mark Sisson

	MEN			WOMEN		
	FRONT	PAR	HDCP	FRONT	PAR	HDCP
1	330	4	9	300	4	9
2	166	3	17	148	3	17
3	370	4	7	320	4	7
4	380	4	1	340	4	1
5	320	4	3	285	4	3
6	476	5	5	405	5	5
7	427	5	15	405	5	15
8	181	3	11	147	3	11
9	385	4	13	350	4	13
Out	3035	36		2700	36	
1	330	4	10	300	4	10
2	166	3	18	148	3	18
3	370	4	8	320	4	8
4	380	4	2	340	4	2
5	320	4	4	285	4	4
6	476	5	6	405	5	6
7	427	5	16	405	5	16
8	181	3	12	147	3	12
9	385	4	14	350	4	14
In	3035	36		2700	36	
Total	6070	72		5400	72	
Rating	70.8			75.0		
Slope	120			125		

GOLF COURSE DIRECTORY

IRONMAN GOLF COURSE

18 Par-3 Public

Route 2, Box 254A
Detroit Lakes, Minnesota 56501
218/847-5592 Clubhouse/Proshop

HOURS	Dawn to Dusk
SEASON	April to October

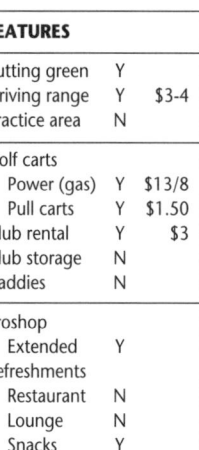

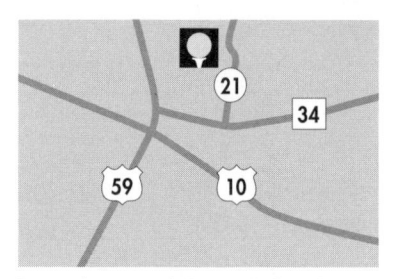

Located just north Detroit Lakes. Course entrance is about 3 1/2 miles north of MN Highway 34 on County Road 21.

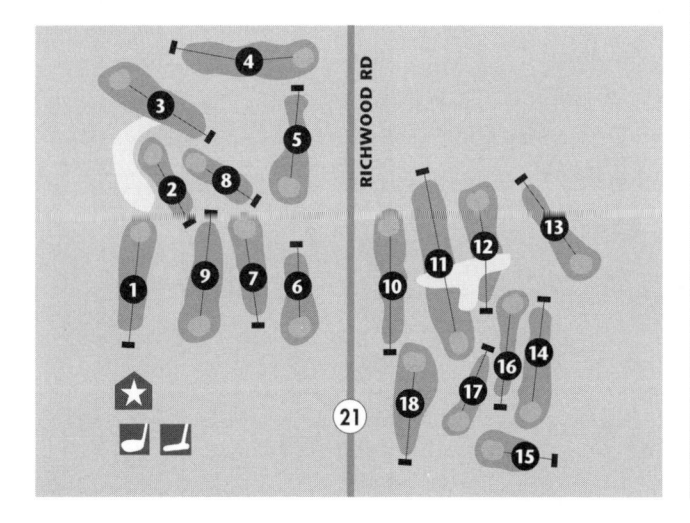

RESERVATIONS	218/847-5592	
	Walk-on: good/fair	
GREEN FEES	M-F	S-S
Adult	$12/8	$12/8
Senior	$11/7	$11/7
Junior	$11/7	$11/7
Twilight	$8	$8
	Weekday junior discounts	
PAYMENT	Credit: Visa® MC® AmEx®	
	Non-local checks accepted	
LEAGUES	None	
MEMBERSHIPS	MGA	
OWNER/MGR	Ford & Patricia Hermanson	
SUPERINTENDENT	Ford Hermanson	
PROFESSIONAL	Dean Hermanson	

FEATURES		
Putting green	Y	
Driving range	Y	$3-4
Practice area	N	
Golf carts		
Power (gas)	Y	$13/8
Pull carts	Y	$1.50
Club rental	Y	$3
Club storage	N	
Caddies	N	
Proshop		
Extended	Y	
Refreshments		
Restaurant	N	
Lounge	N	
Snacks	Y	
Clubhouse		
Showers	N	
Lockers	Y	
Lodging	N	

	MEN			**WOMEN**		
	FRONT	PAR	HDCP	FRONT	PAR	HDCP
1	176	3	9	156	3	9
2	150	3	3	141	3	3
3	170	3	11	163	3	11
4	121	3	15	103	3	15
5	210	3	1	157	3	1
6	174	3	7	161	3	5
7	136	3	13	127	3	13
8	125	3	17	113	3	17
9	198	3	3	158	3	7
Out	1460	27		1279	27	
10	145	3	10	138	3	8
11	208	3	2	167	3	2
12	170	3	8	117	3	12
13	142	3	12	129	3	6
14	193	3	4	175	3	4
15	108	3	18	100	3	18
16	174	3	6	138	3	10
17	103	3	16	95	3	16
18	151	3	14	138	3	14
In	1394	27		1197	27	
Total	2854	54		2476	54	
Rating	53.4			53.5		
Slope	79			74		

ISLAND FALLS COUNTRY CLUB

18 Regulation Public

212 West 7th Street
Atwater, Minnesota 56209
612/974-8886 Clubhouse/Proshop

RESERVATIONS	612/974-8886 1 day	
	Walk-on: good/fair	
GREEN FEES	M-Th	F-S
Adult	$16/10	$18/11
Senior	$13/8	$18/11
Junior	$11/7	$13/8
Twilight	NA	NA
PAYMENT	Credit: Visa® MasterCard®	
	Non-local checks accepted	
LEAGUES	Men: M,Th	
	Women: W (pm)	
	Couples: F (pm)	
	Seniors: W (am)	
MEMBERSHIPS	GCSAA, MGA	
MANAGER	Charlie Zaeska	
SUPERINTENDENT	Jim Brown	

HOURS	6 am to Dusk
SEASON	April-November

FEATURES		
Putting green	Y	
Driving range	N	
Practice area	Y	
Golf carts		
Power (gas)	Y	$18/10
Pull carts	Y	$2
Club rental	Y	$5
Club storage	N	
Caddies	N	
Proshop		
Extended	Y	
Refreshments		
Restaurant	N	
Lounge	Y	
Snacks	Y	
Clubhouse		
Showers	N	
Lockers	N	
Lodging	N	

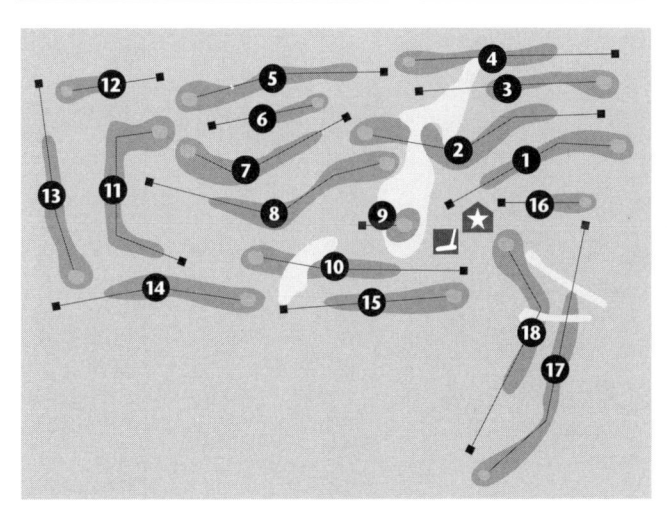

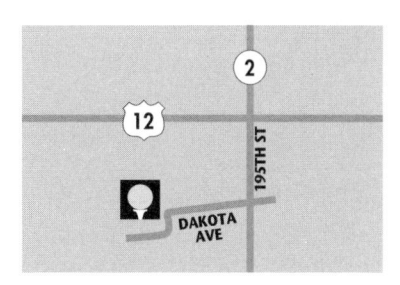

Located in Atwater. Course entrance is south of U.S. Highway 12 on 195th Street, then west on Dakota Avenue.

		MEN				WOMEN		
	BACK	FRONT	PAR	HDCP		FRONT	PAR	HDCP
1	373	336	4	15		280	4	15
2	525	464	5	3		421	5	3
3	433	389	4	7		223	4	7
4	410	375	4	11		315	4	11
5	430	395	4	5		323	4	5
6	203	177	3	17		149	3	17
7	419	381	4	9		334	4	9
8	526	462	5	1		422	5	1
9	144	137	3	13		124	3	13
Out	3463	3116	36			2591	36	
10	410	389	4	6		356	4	6
11	587	541	5	2		445	5	2
12	177	160	3	16		112	3	16
13	352	314	4	10		282	4	10
14	415	368	4	8		322	4	8
15	333	309	4	14		260	4	14
16	146	139	3	18		115	3	18
17	457	437	5	4		372	5	4
18	346	304	4	12		263	4	12
In	3223	2961	36			2527	36	
Total	6686	6077	72			5118	72	
Rating	71.9	69.1				69.0		
Slope	117	111				114		

GOLF COURSE DIRECTORY

ISLAND VIEW GOLF CLUB

18 Regulation Semi-Private

9150 Island View Road
Waconia, Minnesota 55387
612/442-2956 Clubhouse
612/442-6116 Proshop

HOURS	7 am to Dusk
SEASON	April-November

FEATURES

Putting green	Y
Driving range	Y
Practice area	N
Golf carts	
Power (gas)	Y
Pull carts	Y
Club rental	Y
Club storage	N
Caddies	N
Proshop	
Extended	Y
Refreshments	
Restaurant	Y
Lounge	Y
Snacks	Y
Clubhouse	
Showers	N
Lockers	Y
Lodging	N

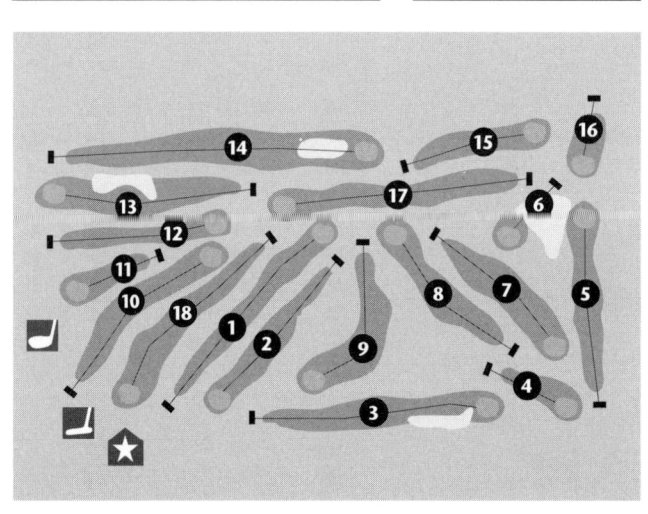

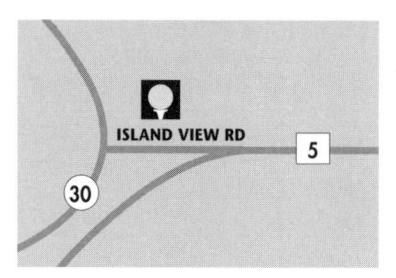

Located east of Waconia. Course is about 1/2 mile west of MN Highway 5 on Island View Road.

RESERVATIONS	612/442-6116	
	Walk-on: poor/poor	
GREEN FEES	M-Th	F-S
Adult	$26	$32
Senior	$26	$32
Junior	$26	$32
Twilight	$16	$14
PAYMENT	No credit cards accepted	
	Local checks accepted	
LEAGUES	None	
MEMBERSHIPS	USGA, NGF, PGA, GCSAA,	
	CMAA, MGA	
SUPERINTENDENT	Mark Poppitz	
PROFESSIONAL	Ross Stevens	

	MEN				WOMEN		
	BACK	FRONT	PAR	HDCP	FRONT	PAR	HDCP
1	486	465	5	15	448	5	5
2	398	382	4	1	335	4	3
3	520	509	5	3	486	5	1
4	161	151	3	17	131	3	17
5	394	382	4	11	357	4	7
6	189	176	3	9	133	3	15
7	400	357	4	5	290	4	11
8	384	355	4	13	292	4	13
9	401	384	4	7	310	4	9
Out	3333	3161	36		2782	36	
10	364	355	4	6	338	4	6
11	180	172	3	16	157	3	14
12	322	310	4	14	285	4	12
13	345	329	4	12	263	4	10
14	571	558	5	2	445	5	2
15	336	325	4	10	302	4	8
16	145	131	3	18	126	3	18
17	554	543	5	4	334	4	4
18	402	392	4	8	350	5	16
In	3219	3115	36		2600	36	
Total	6552	6276	72		5382	72	
Rating	71.4	70.3			71.4		
Slope	128	126			124		

IZATYS GOLF & YACHT CLUB

18 Regulation Public

40005 85th Avenue
Onamia, Minnesota 56359
800/533-1728 Clubhouse
612/532-4575 Proshop

HOURS 7:30 am to Dusk

SEASON April to October

FEATURES

Putting green	Y	
Driving range	Y	$3
Practice area	Y	
Golf carts		
Power (gas)	Y	$25
Pull carts	Y	$5
Club rental	Y	$15
Club storage	Y	$2/day
Caddies	N	
Proshop		
Extended	Y	
Refreshments		
Restaurant	Y	
Lounge	Y	
Snacks	Y	
Clubhouse		
Showers	Y	
Lockers	N	
Lodging	Y	Call

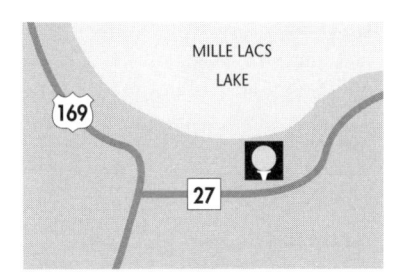

RESERVATIONS	612/532-4575 3 days	
	Walk-on: good/good	
GREEN FEES	M-Th	F-S
Adult	$35/25	$50
Senior	$35/25	$50
Junior	$35/25	$50
Twilight	$20	$30
PAYMENT	Credit: Visa® MC® AmEx®	
	Non-local checks accepted	
LEAGUES	Men: T	
	Women: Th	
MEMBERSHIPS	USGA, NGF, PGA, GCSAA,	
	CMAA, MGA	
SUPERINTENDENT	Steve Schumacher	
PROFESSIONAL	Steve Whillock	

Located east of Onamia. Course is about 3 miles east of U.S. Highway 169 on MN Highway 27, then north on Izatys Road.

	MEN				WOMEN		
	BACK	FRONT	PAR	HDCP	FRONT	PAR	HDCP
1	366	336	4	8	278	4	6
2	528	508	5	2	456	5	2
3	363	348	4	10	307	4	10
4	176	164	3	18	131	3	18
5	351	310	4	16	282	4	16
6	163	154	3	6	110	3	8
7	369	293	4	12	260	4	14
8	500	473	5	4	416	5	4
9	343	306	4	14	286	4	12
Out	3159	2892	36		2526	36	
10	386	344	4	13	279	4	15
11	612	586	5	1	457	5	1
12	125	114	3	15	84	3	13
13	477	449	5	5	319	5	3
14	310	290	4	17	248	4	17
15	429	409	4	7	322	4	7
16	217	161	3	9	120	3	11
17	433	416	4	3	320	4	5
18	333	300	4	11	264	4	9
In	3322	3069	36		2413	36	
Total	6481	5961	72		4939	72	
Rating	72.1	69.7			69.7		
Slope	132	127			128		

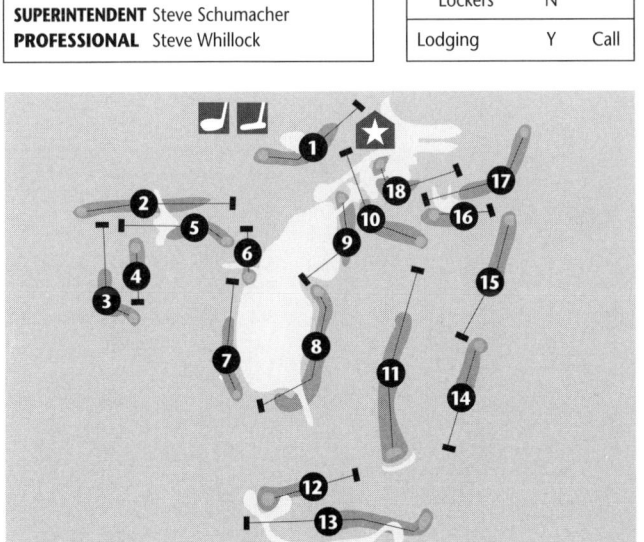

GOLF COURSE DIRECTORY

JACKSON GOLF CLUB
9 Regulation Semi-Private

North Highway 71, P.O. Box 82
Jackson, Minnesota 56143
507/847-2660 Clubhouse/Proshop

HOURS	Dawn to Dusk
SEASON	April to October

RESERVATIONS	507/847-2660	
	Walk-on: good/fair	

GREEN FEES	M-F	S-S
Adult	Call	Call
Senior	Call	Call
Junior	Call	Call
Twilight	NA	NA

PAYMENT	No credit cards accepted
	Non-local checks accepted

LEAGUES	Men: Various
	Women: Various

MEMBERSHIPS	USGA, MGA

PROFESSIONAL	Call

FEATURES	
Putting green	Y
Driving range	N
Practice area	N
Golf carts	
Power (gas)	Y
Pull carts	Y
Club rental	Y
Club storage	N
Caddies	N
Proshop	
Regular	Y
Refreshments	
Restaurant	N
Lounge	N
Snacks	Y
Clubhouse	
Showers	N
Lockers	N
Lodging	N

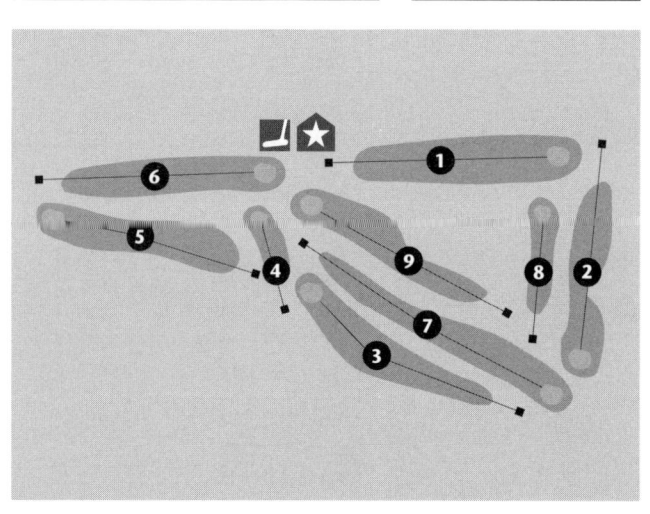

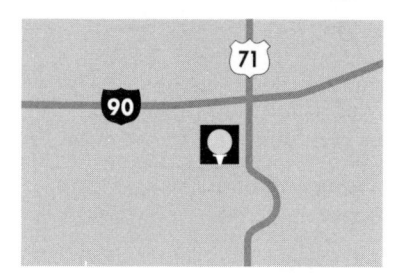

Located just north of Jackson. Course entrance is about 1/2 mile south of I-90 on U.S. Highway 71.

	MEN			**WOMEN**		
	FRONT	PAR	HDCP	FRONT	PAR	HDCP
1	341	4	6	341	4	4
2	315	4	7	315	4	5
3	365	4	1	255	4	9
4	140	3	8	130	3	8
5	355	4	3	325	4	1
6	360	4	4	340	4	3
7	475	5	9	410	5	6
8	190	3	2	155	3	2
9	350	4	5	350	5	7
Out	2891	35		2621	36	
1	341	4	6	341	4	4
2	315	4	7	315	4	5
3	365	4	1	255	4	9
4	140	3	8	130	3	8
5	355	4	3	325	4	1
6	360	4	4	340	4	3
7	475	5	9	410	5	6
8	190	3	2	155	3	2
9	350	4	5	350	5	7
In	2891	35		2621	36	
Total	5782	70		5242	72	
Rating	68.8			71.4		
Slope	130			119		

KATE HAVEN GOLF COURSE

9 Executive Public

8791 Lexington Avenue Northeast
Circle Pines, Minnesota 55014
612/786-2945 Clubhouse/Proshop

HOURS	Dawn to Dusk
SEASON	April to October

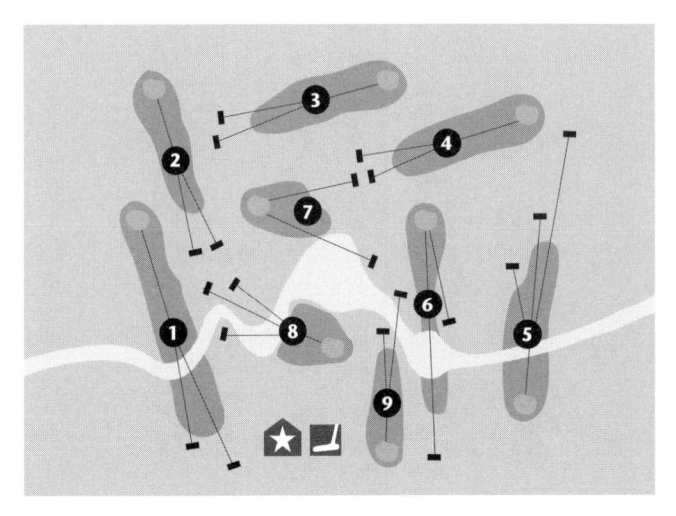

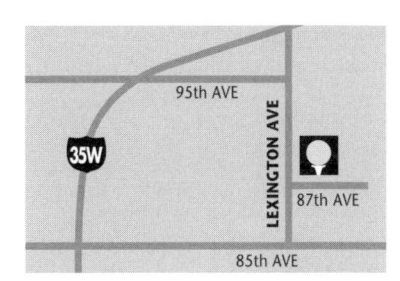

Located in Circle Pines. Course entrance is east of I-35W on 85th Avenue, then 1/4 mile south on Lexington Avenue.

RESERVATIONS	612/786-2945 6 days
	Walk-on: poor/poor

GREEN FEES	M-F	S-S
Adult	$15/8	$17/9
Senior	$11/6*	$17/9
Junior	$11/6*	$17/9
Twilight	NA	NA

*Before 3:30 pm

PAYMENT	No credit cards accepted
	Non-local checks accepted

LEAGUES	Men: Various
	Women: Various
	Youth: T,Th

MEMBERSHIPS	GCSAA, MGA

OWNER	Harley & Carlotta Flor
MANAGER	Carlotta Flor
SUPERINTENDENT	Tom Lundgren

FEATURES	
Putting green	Y
Driving range	N
Practice area	N
Golf carts	
Power (gas)	Y $9
Pull carts	Y $2
Club rental	Y $3
Club storage	N
Caddies	N
Proshop	
Regular	Y
Refreshments	
Restaurant	N
Lounge	N
Snacks	Y
Clubhouse	
Showers	N
Lockers	N
Lodging	N

	MEN				**WOMEN**		
	BACK	FRONT	PAR	HDCP	FRONT	PAR	HDCP
1	245	178	4/3	3	150	3	3
2	121	121	3	9	121	3	9
3	165	165	3	6	142	3	6
4	167	167	3	5	113	3	5
5	261	155	4/3	1	140	3	1
6	222	109	4/3	2	99	3	2
7	146	146	3	8	130	3	8
8	160	113	3	7	82	3	7
9	176	176	3	4	117	3	4
Out	1663	1330	30/27		1094	27	
1	245	178	4/3	3	150	3	3
2	121	121	3	9	121	3	9
3	165	165	3	6	142	3	6
4	167	167	3	5	113	3	5
5	261	155	4/3	1	140	3	1
6	222	109	4/3	2	99	3	2
7	146	146	3	8	130	3	8
8	160	113	3	7	82	3	7
9	176	176	3	4	117	3	4
In	1663	1330	30/27		1094	27	
Total	3326	2660	60/54		2188	54	
Rating	55.4	55.4			53.2		
Slope	79	78			76		

GOLF COURSE DIRECTORY

KELLER GOLF COURSE

18 Regulation Public

2166 Maplewood Drive
St. Paul, Minnesota 55109
612/482-9717 Clubhouse
612/484-3011 Proshop

RESERVATIONS	612/484-3011 4 days	
	Walk-on: good/good	

GREEN FEES	M-F	S-S
Adult	$20	$20
Senior	$10.50	$10.50
Junior	$10	$10
Twilight	$13 (5 pm)	$13 (5 pm)

PAYMENT	No credit cards accepted
	Local checks only

LEAGUES	Men: Various
	Women: Various

MEMBERSHIPS	USGA, NGF, PGA, GCSAA, MGA

MANAGER	Allison Young
SUPERINTENDENT	Dave Bauer
PROFESSIONAL	Thomas Purcell

HOURS	6 am to Dusk	
SEASON	April-November	

FEATURES		
Putting green	Y	
Driving range	Y	$4
Practice area	Y	
Golf carts		
Power (gas)	Y	$20/12
Pull carts	Y	$3
Club rental	Y	$10
Club storage	N	
Caddies	N	
Proshop		
Extended	Y	
Refreshments		
Restaurant	Y	
Lounge	Y	
Snacks	Y	
Clubhouse		
Showers	Y	
Lockers	Y	
Lodging	N	

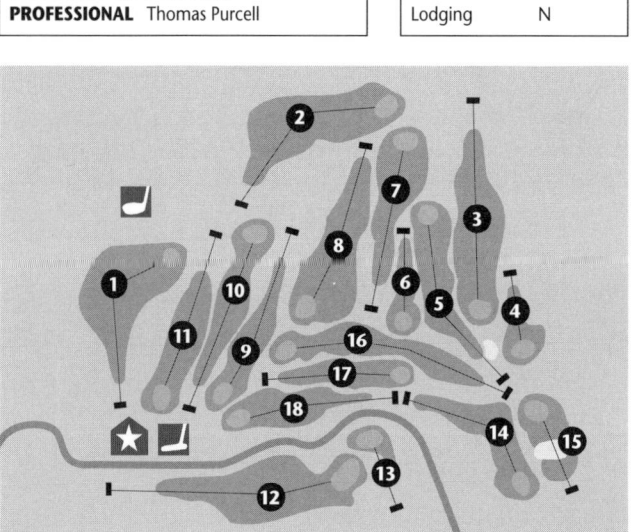

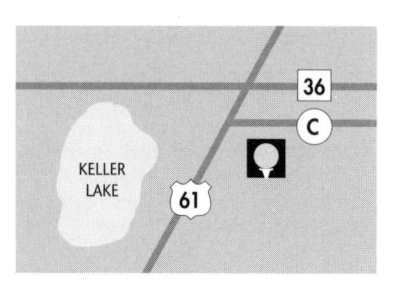

Located in St. Paul. Course entrance is just east of U.S. Highway 61 on County Road C.

	MEN				WOMEN		
	BACK	FRONT	PAR	HDCP	FRONT	PAR	HDCP
1	332	310	4	15	290	4	7
2	373	334	4	9	287	4	11
3	505	485	5	11	425	5	1
4	150	130	3	13	110	3	15
5	380	371	4	7	300	4	9
6	210	190	3	5	134	3	17
7	420	400	4	3	314	4	13
8	396	382	4	1	340	4	3
9	462	437	5	17	422	5	5
Out	3228	3132	36		2622	36	
10	445	426	4	2	403	5	8
11	392	346	4	10	323	4	8
12	510	475	5	14	430	5	2
13	147	137	3	18	127	3	16
14	350	332	4	12	282	4	4
15	177	155	3	8	125	3	18
16	550	431	5/4	4	411	5	10
17	362	320	4	16	300	4	14
18	405	380	4	6	350	5	12
In	3338	3002	36/35		2751	37	
Total	6566	6041	72/71		5597	73	
Rating	71.7	69.6			71.4		
Slope	127	123			124		

THE MINNESOTA ILLUSTRATED

KENYON COUNTRY CLUB

9 Regulation Semi-Private

Highway 56 North, P.O. Box K
Kenyon, Minnesota 55946
507/789-6307 Clubhouse/Proshop

HOURS	8 am to Dusk
SEASON	April to October

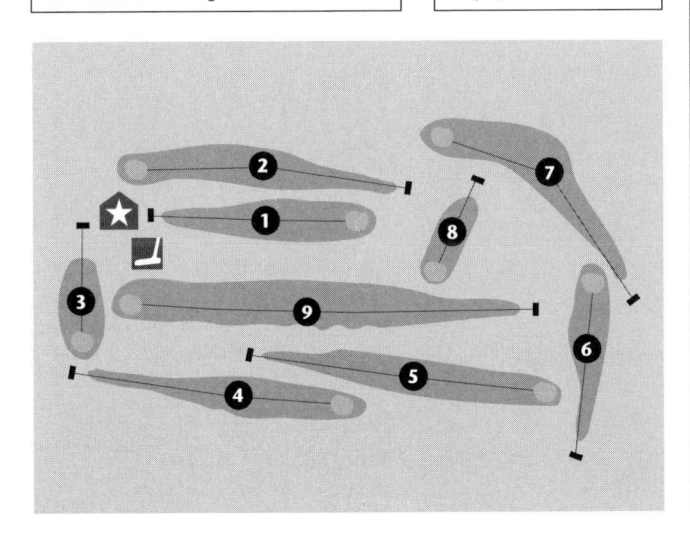

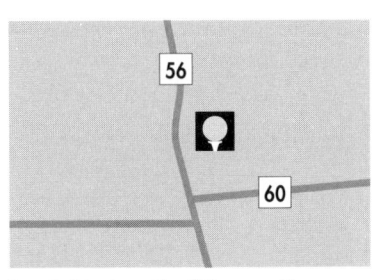

Located just north of Kenyon. Course entrance is north of MN Highway 60 on MN Highwayy 56.

RESERVATIONS	507/789-6307
	Walk-on: good/fair

GREEN FEES	M-F	S-S
Adult	$12	$16
Senior	$11	$16
Junior	$11	$16
Twilight	$8	$8

PAYMENT	No credit cards accepted
	Non-local checks accepted

LEAGUES	Men:	Th (12pm - Dusk)
	Women:	W (8 am - 4 pm)
	Couples:	M (5 pm - Dusk)

MEMBERSHIPS	USGA, MGA

OWNER	Kenyon Realty Company
MANAGER	Pam Angelstad
SUPERINTENDENT	Greg Canton

FEATURES	
Putting green	Y
Driving range	N
Practice area	N
Golf carts	
Power (gas)	Y $15/11
Pull carts	Y $1
Club rental	N
Club storage	Y $25/yr
Caddies	N
Proshop	
Basic	Y
Refreshments	
Restaurant	Y
Lounge	Y
Snacks	Y
Clubhouse	
Showers	N
Lockers	Y $25/yr
Lodging	N

	MEN			**WOMEN**		
	FRONT	PAR	HDCP	FRONT	PAR	HDCP
1	259	4	9	259	4	9
2	411	4	1	411	5	1
3	165	3	6	145	3	6
4	288	4	7	288	4	7
5	397	4	2	397	5	2
6	182	3	3	153	3	3
7	309	4	4	309	4	4
8	138	3	8	138	3	8
9	477	5	5	398	5	5
Out	2626	34		2498	36	
1	259	4	9	259	4	9
2	411	4	1	411	5	1
3	165	3	6	145	3	6
4	288	4	7	288	4	7
5	397	4	2	397	5	2
6	182	3	3	153	3	3
7	309	4	4	309	4	4
8	138	3	8	138	3	8
9	477	5	5	398	5	5
In	2626	34		2498	36	
Total	5252	68		4996	72	
Rating	65.2			68.8		
Slope	107			118		

KIMBALL GOLF CLUB

9 Regulation Public

11823 County Road 150, P.O. Box 188
Kimball, Minnesota 55353
612/398-2285 Clubhouse/Proshop

HOURS	6 am to Dusk
SEASON	April-November

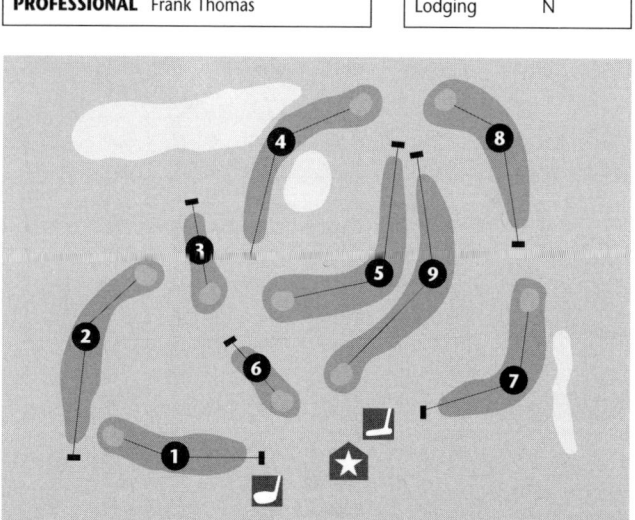

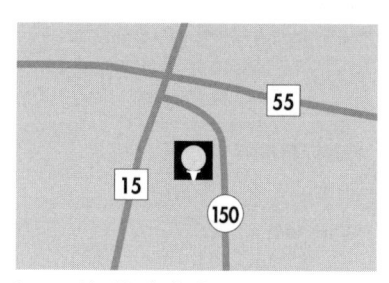

Located in Kimball. Couse entrance is about one mile east of MN Highway 15 on County Road 150.

RESERVATIONS	612/398-2285 1 week
	Walk-on: good/poor

GREEN FEES	M-F	S-S
Adult	$14/9.50	$17/10.50
Senior	$10/7*	$17/10.50
Junior	$14/9.50	$17/10.50
Twilight	NA	NA
	* Thursday's after 9 am	

PAYMENT	No credit cards accepted
	Non-local checks accepted

LEAGUES	Men: T (12 pm - dusk)
	Women: W (2-7 pm)
	Seniors: Th (9 am)

MEMBERSHIPS	USGA, PGA, GCSAA, MGA

SUPERINTENDENT	Curt Erickson
PROFESSIONAL	Frank Thomas

FEATURES		
Putting green	Y	
Driving range	Y	$3
Practice area	N	
Golf carts		
Power (gas)	Y	$19
Pull carts	N	
Club rental	Y	$5
Club storage	Y	$15
Caddies	N	
Proshop		
Extended	Y	
Refreshments		
Restaurant	N	
Lounge	Y	
Snacks	Y	
Clubhouse		
Showers	N	
Lockers	N	
Lodging	N	

	MEN			WOMEN		
	FRONT	PAR	HDCP	FRONT	PAR	HDCP
1	420	4	4	405	5	4
2	359	4	6	349	4	6
3	119	3	8	102	3	8
4	384	4	5	371	4	5
5	444	5	9	435	5	9
6	221	3	2	203	4	2
7	398	4	3	356	4	3
8	314	4	7	301	4	7
9	537	5	1	441	5	1
Out	3196	36		2963	38	
1	420	4	4	405	5	4
2	359	4	6	349	4	6
3	119	3	8	102	3	8
4	384	4	5	371	4	5
5	444	5	9	435	5	9
6	221	3	2	203	4	2
7	398	4	3	356	4	3
8	314	4	7	301	4	7
9	537	5	1	441	5	1
In	3196	36		2963	38	
Total	6392	72		5926	76	
Rating	70.8			74.0		
Slope	118			124		

LAFAYETTE CLUB

9 Executive Private

2800 Northview Road
Minnetonka Beach, Minnesota 55361
612/471-8493 Clubhouse
612/471-9600 Proshop

RESERVATIONS	612/471-9600	
	Members only	

GREEN FEES	M-F	S-S
Adult	Call	Call
Senior	Call	Call
Junior	Call	Call
Twilight	NA	NA
	Members and guests only	

PAYMENT	Credit: Visa® MC® Discover®
	Non-local checks accepted

LEAGUES	Men: None
	Women: None

MEMBERSHIPS	USGA, PGA, GCSAA, MGA

PROFESSIONAL	Call

HOURS Dawn to Dusk
SEASON April to October

FEATURES

Putting green	Y
Driving range	N
Practice area	N

Golf carts	
Power (gas)	Y
Pull carts	Y
Club rental	Y
Club storage	Y
Caddies	N

Proshop	
Extended	Y
Refreshments	
Restaurant	Y
Lounge	Y
Snacks	Y
Clubhouse	
Showers	Y
Lockers	Y

Lodging	N

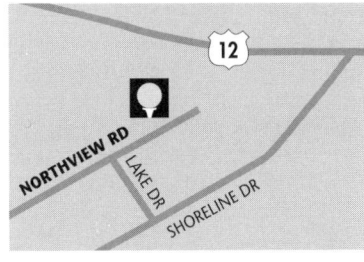

Located in Minnetonka Beach. Course is north of Shoreline Drive on Lake Drive, then east on Northview Road.

	MEN			WOMEN		
	FRONT	PAR	HDCP	FRONT	PAR	HDCP
1	180	3	11	180	3	11
2	312	4	7	312	4	5
3	362	4	3	362	4	1
4	237	4	17	237	4	9
5	161	3	9	161	3	7
6	181	3	13	181	3	13
7	212	3	1	212	4	15
8	165	3	15	165	3	17
9	341	4	5	341	4	3
Out	2151	31		2151	32	
10	166	3	12	166	3	10
11	306	4	8	306	4	6
12	325	4	4	325	4	2
13	227	4	18	227	4	8
14	121	3	16	121	3	18
15	181	3	10	181	3	12
16	202	3	2	202	4	14
17	165	3	14	165	3	16
18	316	4	6	316	4	4
In	2009	31		2009	32	
Total	4160	62		4160	64	
Rating	61.0			64.6		
Slope	99			100		

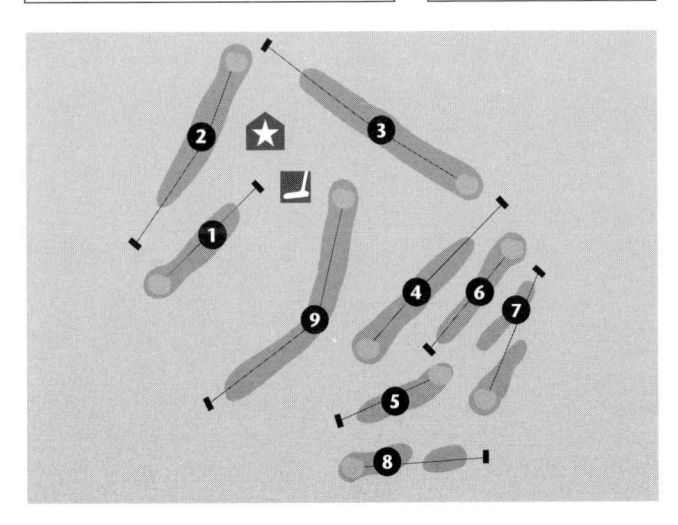

GOLF COURSE DIRECTORY

LAKE CITY COUNTRY CLUB

9 Regulation Semi-Private

Route 2, P.O. Box 119
Lake City, Minnesota 55041
612/345-3221 Clubhouse/Proshop

HOURS	8 am to Dusk
SEASON	April to October

RESERVATIONS	612/345-3221 2 days
	Course closed Wed & Thurs
	Walk-on: good/fair

GREEN FEES	M-F	S-S
Adult	$14/10	$17/12
Senior	$14/10	$17/12
Junior	$14/10	$17/12
Twilight	NA	NA

PAYMENT	No credit cards accepted
	Non-local checks accepted

LEAGUES	None

MEMBERSHIPS	USGA, NGF, GCSAA, MGA

MANAGER	Mike Schmidt
SUPERINTENDENT	Cliff Reynolds

FEATURES		
Putting green	Y	
Driving range	Y	$2
Practice area	Y	
Golf carts		
Power (gas)	Y	$15/9
Pull carts	Y	$1.50
Club rental	N	
Club storage	N	
Caddies	N	
Proshop		
Extended	Y	
Refreshments		
Restaurant	N	
Lounge	N	
Snacks	Y	
Clubhouse		
Showers	Y	
Lockers	Y	
Lodging	N	

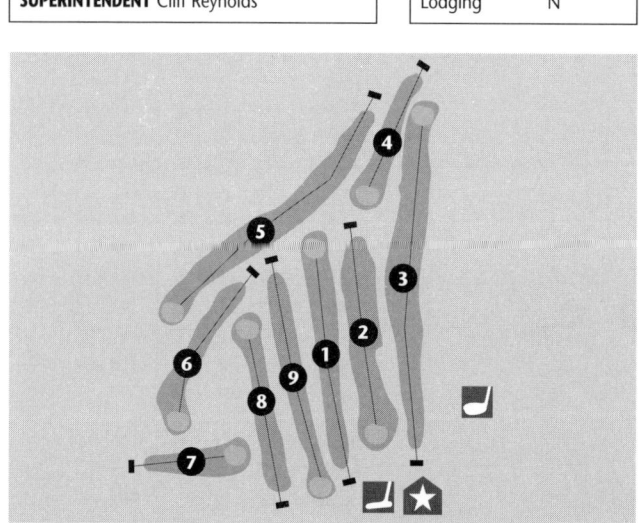

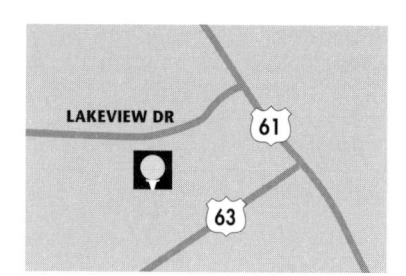

Located north of Lake City. Course entrance is west of U.S. Highway 61 on Lakeview Drive.

	MEN			**WOMEN**		
	FRONT	PAR	HDCP	FRONT	PAR	HDCP
1	365	4	3	355	5	3
2	375	4	8	355	4	8
3	530	5	2	510	6	2
4	170	3	13	137	3	13
5	490	5	6	476	5	6
6	305	4	17	254	4	17
7	173	3	12	156	3	12
8	275	4	15	254	4	15
9	340	4	10	275	4	10
Out	3023	36		2772	38	
1	365	4	4	355	5	4
2	375	4	7	355	4	7
3	530	5	1	510	6	1
4	170	3	14	137	3	14
5	490	5	5	476	5	5
6	305	4	18	254	4	18
7	173	3	11	156	3	11
8	275	4	16	254	4	16
9	340	4	9	275	4	9
In	3023	36		2772	38	
Total	6046	72		5544	76	
Rating	68.6			70.4		
Slope	126			124		

THE MINNESOTA ILLUSTRATED

LAKE HENDRICKS COUNTRY CLUB

9 Regulation Semi-Private

P.O. Box 31, W. Lincoln Cty Hwy 17
Hendricks, Minnesota 56136
507/275-3852 Clubhouse/Proshop

HOURS	8 am to Dusk
SEASON	April-November

RESERVATIONS	507/275-3852 1 day	
	Walk-on: good/fair	
GREEN FEES	M-F	S-S
Adult	$11/8	$13/9
Senior	$11/8	$13/9
Junior	$11/8	$13/9
Twilight	NA	NA
PAYMENT	Credit cards not accepted	
	Non-local checks accepted	
LEAGUES	Men: W (pm)	
	Women: T (pm)	
MEMBERSHIPS	MGA	
MANAGER	Kim & Duwayne Buseth	
SUPERINTENDENT	Eric Pitzl	

FEATURES

Putting green	Y	
Driving range	N	
Practice area	N	
Golf carts		
Power (gas)	Y	$12/8
Pull carts	Y	$2
Club rental	Y	$3
Club storage	N	
Caddies	N	
Proshop		
Basic	Y	
Refreshments		
Restaurant	Y	
Lounge	Y	
Snacks	Y	
Clubhouse		
Showers	Y	
Lockers	N	
Lodging	N	

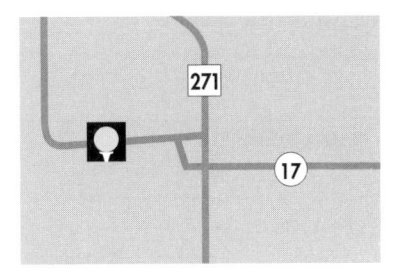

Located west of Hendricks. Course is about one mile west of MN Highway 271 on County Road 17.

		MEN				WOMEN		
	BACK	FRONT	PAR	HDCP		FRONT	PAR	HDCP
1	318	313	4	5		305	4	4
2	185	160	3	6		150	3	6
3	392	392	4	1		305	4	3
4	354	319	4	8		319	4	8
5	310	295	4	9		295	4	9
6	436	426	5	7		427	5	7
7	348	338	4	2		328	4	1
8	353	343	4	4		335	4	5
9	407	400	4	3		324	4	2
Out	3103	2918	36			2788	36	
1	318	313	4	5		305	4	4
2	185	160	3	6		150	3	6
3	392	392	4	1		305	4	3
4	354	319	4	8		319	4	8
5	310	295	4	9		295	4	9
6	436	426	5	7		427	5	7
7	348	338	4	2		328	4	1
8	353	343	4	4		335	4	5
9	407	400	4	3		324	4	2
In	3103	2918	36			2788	36	
Total	6206	5836	72			5576	72	
Rating	NA	67.6				70.2		
Slope	NA	101				107		

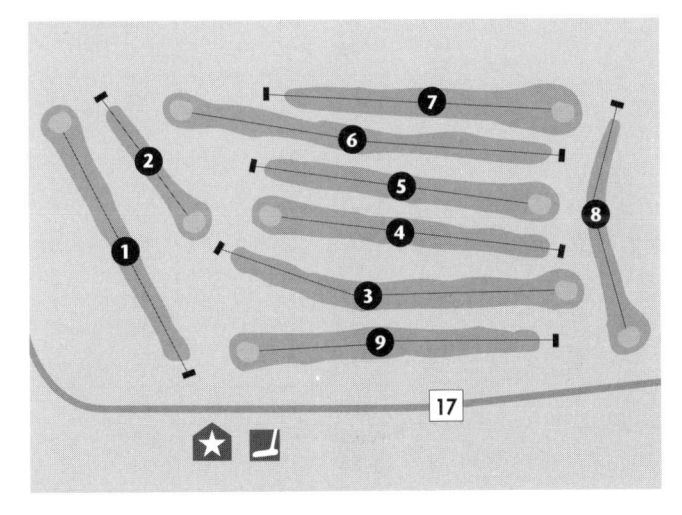

GOLF COURSE DIRECTORY

LAKE MILTONA GOLF CLUB

9 Regulation Public

P.O. Box 164
Miltona, Minnesota 56354
218/943-2901 Clubhouse/Proshop

HOURS	Dawn to Dusk
SEASON	April to October

| **RESERVATIONS** | 218/943-2901 2 days |
| | Walk-on: good/fair |

GREEN FEES	M-F	S-S
Adult	$19/12	$21/13
Senior	$19/12	$21/13
Junior	$19/12	$21/13
Twilight	NA	NA

| **PAYMENT** | No credit cards accepted |
| | Non-local checks accepted |

LEAGUES	Men: Th (4-6 pm)
	Women: W (9-10 am)
	Senior: T (9-10 am)

| **MEMBERSHIPS** | USGA, NGF, GCSAA, MGA |

| **OWNER** | Robert & Jeanne Shields |

FEATURES	
Putting green	Y
Driving range	N
Practice area	N
Golf carts	
Power	Y
Pull carts	Y
Club rental	Y
Club storage	N
Caddies	N
Proshop	
Basic	Y
Refreshments	
Restaurant	N
Lounge	N
Snacks	Y
Clubhouse	
Showers	N
Lockers	N
Lodging	N

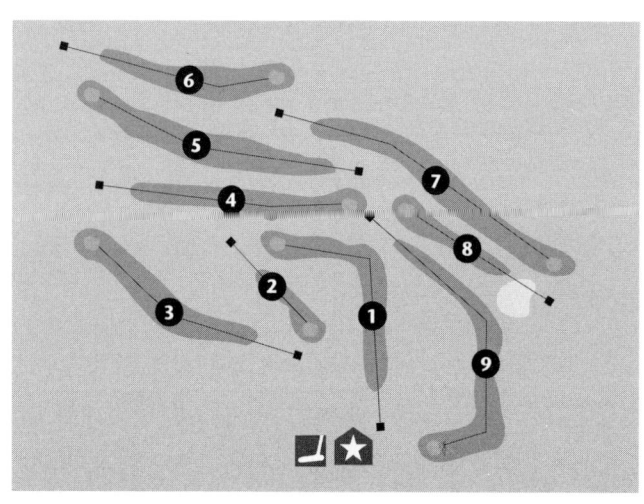

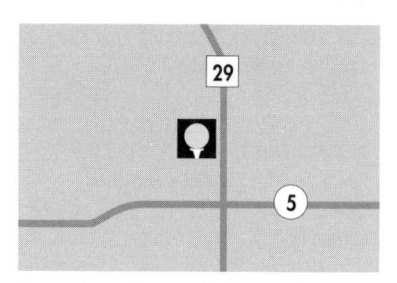

Located southwest of Miltona. Course entrance is just north of County Road 5 on MN Highway 29.

	MEN			**WOMEN**		
	FRONT	PAR	HDCP	FRONT	PAR	HDCP
1	370	5	2	352	4	2
2	154	3	9	154	3	9
3	352	4	7	320	4	7
4	345	4	6	345	4	6
5	400	5	1	388	4	1
6	316	4	8	300	4	8
7	506	5	4	435	5	4
8	214	4	5	200	3	5
9	439	5	3	430	5	3
Out	3102	39		2852	36	
1	370	5	2	352	4	2
2	154	3	9	154	3	9
3	352	4	7	320	4	7
4	345	4	6	345	4	6
5	400	5	1	388	4	1
6	316	4	8	300	4	8
7	506	5	4	435	5	4
8	214	4	5	200	3	5
9	439	5	3	430	5	3
In	3102	39		2852	36	
Total	6204	78		5704	72	
Rating	69.6			72.0		
Slope	117			124		

LINKS AT LAKE PLACE

9 Par-3 Public

5585 Golfview Avenue North
Oakdale, Minnesota 55128
612/773-3494 Clubhouse/Proshop

HOURS	Dawn to Dusk
SEASON	Mar-November

RESERVATIONS	612/773-3494	
	Walk-on: fair/good	
GREEN FEES	M-F	S-S
Adult	$7.25	$7.75
Senior	$5	$7.75
Junior	$5	$7.75
Twilight	NA	NA
	Season pass available	
PAYMENT	No credit cards accepted	
	Non-local checks accepted	
LEAGUES	Men: Th	
	Seniors: W	
MEMBERSHIPS	None	
OWNER	Ryan Helgeson	

FEATURES		
Putting green	Y	
Driving range	N	
Practice area	Y	
Golf carts		
Power (elec)	Y	$7
Pull carts	Y	$1.50
Club rental	Y	$3
Club storage	N	
Caddies	N	
Proshop		
Basic	Y	
Refreshments		
Restaurant	Y	
Lounge	Y	
Snacks	Y	
Clubhouse		
Showers	N	
Lockers	N	
Lodging	N	

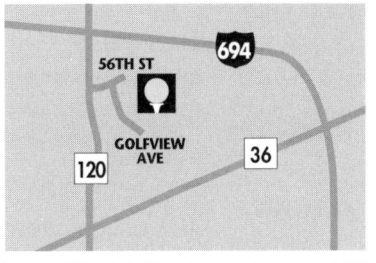

Located in Oakdale. Course is east of MN Highway 120 on 56th Avenue North, then south on Golfview Avenue North.

	MEN			WOMEN		
	FRONT	PAR	HDCP	FRONT	PAR	HDCP
1	180	3		136	3	
2	159	3		150	3	
3	117	3		112	3	
4	169	3		151	3	
5	164	3		155	3	
6	155	3		145	3	
7	147	3		139	3	
8	174	3		129	3	
9	146	3		140	3	
Out	1411	27		1257	27	
1	180	3		136	3	
2	159	3		150	3	
3	117	3		112	3	
4	169	3		151	3	
5	164	3		155	3	
6	155	3		145	3	
7	147	3		139	3	
8	174	3		129	3	
9	146	3		140	3	
In	1411	27		1257	27	
Total	2822	54		2514	54	
Rating	NA			NA		
Slope	NA			NA		

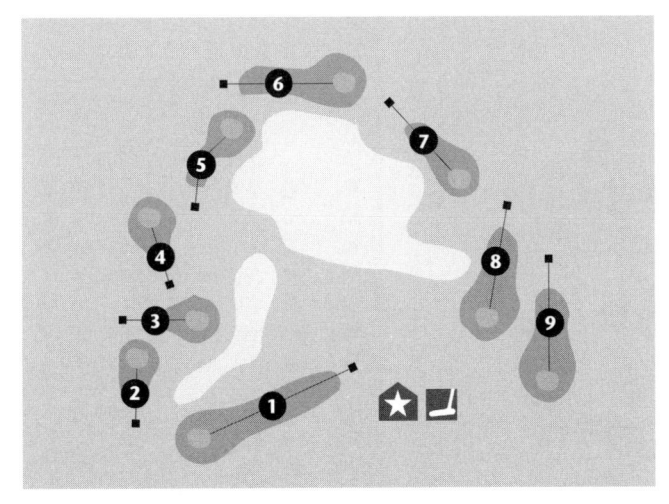

GOLF COURSE DIRECTORY

LAKEVIEW GOLF COURSE   18 Regulation Public

405 North Arm Drive
Mound, Minnesota 55364
612/472-3459 Clubhouse/Proshop

HOURS	5:30 am to Dusk
SEASON	Mar-November

RESERVATIONS	612/472-3459 3 days
	Walk-on: fair/poor

GREEN FEES	M-F	S-S
Adult	$18/12	$20/13
Senior	$13/8.50	$20/13
Junior	$13/8.50	$20/13
Twilight	NA	$10 (6 pm)

PAYMENT	Credit: Visa® MC® AmEx®
	Non-local checks accepted

LEAGUES	Men: M-Th
	Women: M-Th

MEMBERSHIPS	USGA, GCSAA, CMAA, MGA

OWNER	Grant & Vicky Wenkstern
MANAGER	David Eidahl
SUPERINTENDENT	Curt Norton

FEATURES	
Putting green	Y
Driving range	N
Practice area	N
Golf carts	
Power	Y $18/10
Pull carts	Y $2
Club rental	Y $10/7
Club storage	N
Caddies	N
Proshop	
Basic	Y
Refreshments	
Restaurant	N
Lounge	N
Snacks	Y
Clubhouse	
Showers	N
Lockers	N
Lodging	N

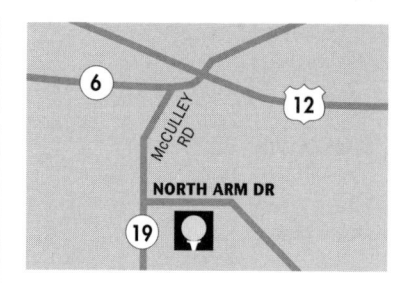

Located in Mound. Course is west of U.S. Hwy 12 on Cty 6, south on McCulley Rd (Cty 19), then east on North Arm Drive.

	MEN				WOMEN		
	BACK	FRONT	PAR	HDCP	FRONT	PAR	HDCP
1	295	295	4	8	295	4	3
2	354	349	4	14	338	4	13
3	155	145	3	10	133	3	5
4	324	312	4	6	298	4	11
5	163	155	3	12	146	3	15
6	330	323	4	16	313	4	9
7	500	479	5	2	457	5	1
8	303	296	4	4	270	4	7
9	152	152	3	18	152	3	17
Out	2576	2506	34		2402	34	
10	180	180	3	9	180	3	14
11	510	490	5	1	430	5	2
12	264	251	4	13	236	4	16
13	273	259	4	11	248	4	10
14	231	222	4	15	213	4	12
15	370	359	4	5	334	4	8
16	391	363	4	3	330	4	4
17	156	132	3	17	123	3	18
18	473	462	5	7	398	5	6
In	2848	2718	36		2492	36	
Total	5424	5224	70		4894	70	
Rating	66.3	65.3			68.2		
Slope	107	104			112		

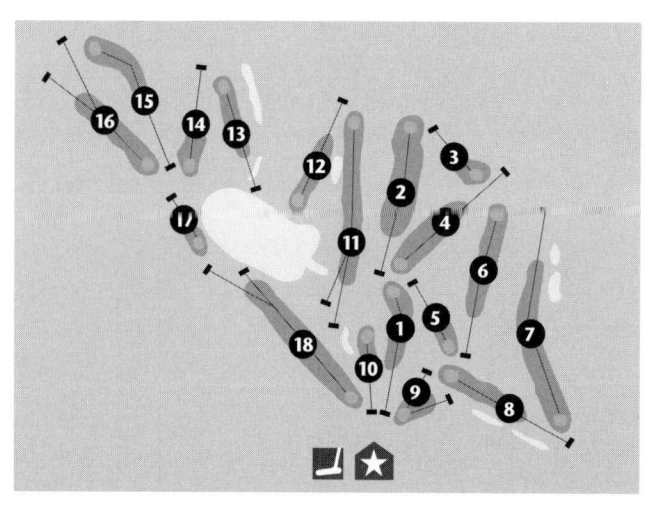

THE MINNESOTA ILLUSTRATED

LAKEWAY GOLF COURSE

9 Regulation Public

Route 1, P.O. Box 129
Dalton, Minnesota 56324
218/589-8591 Clubhouse/Proshop

HOURS	7 am to Dusk
SEASON	April to October

RESERVATIONS	218/589-8591
	Walk-on: good/poor

GREEN FEES	M-F	S-S
Adult	$15/9	$17/10
Senior	$15/9	$17/10
Junior	$15/9	$17/10
Twilight	NA	NA

PAYMENT	No credit cards accepted
	Non-local checks accepted

LEAGUES	Men: T (4:30 pm)
	Women: Th

MEMBERSHIPS	MGA

OWNER	Robert & Nancy Purdon
PROFESSIONAL	Robert Purdon

FEATURES	
Putting green	N
Driving range	N
Practice area	N
Golf carts	
Power (gas)	Y
Pull carts	Y
Club rental	Y
Club storage	Y
Caddies	N
Proshop	
Extended	Y
Refreshments	
Restaurant	N
Lounge	N
Snacks	Y
Clubhouse	
Showers	N
Lockers	Y
Lodging	N

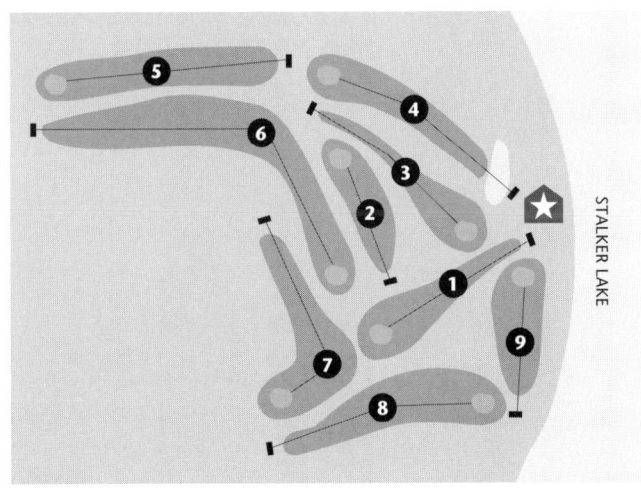

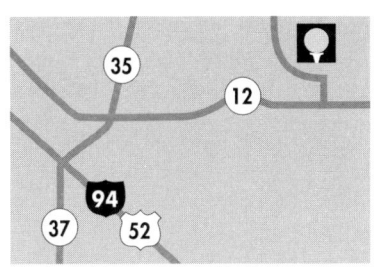

Located east of Dalton. Course is east of County Road 35 on County Road 12, then north on gravel road. Follow signs.

	MEN			**WOMEN**		
	FRONT	PAR	HDCP	FRONT	PAR	HDCP
1	245	4	7	245	4	7
2	170	3	9	170	3	9
3	320	4	8	320	4	8
4	290	4	3	290	4	3
5	305	4	6	305	4	6
6	485	5	1	485	5	1
7	300	4	2	300	4	2
8	290	4	4	290	4	4
9	175	3	5	175	3	5
Out	2580	35		2580	35	
1	245	4	7	245	4	7
2	170	3	9	170	3	9
3	320	4	8	320	4	8
4	290	4	3	290	4	3
5	305	4	6	305	4	6
6	485	5	1	485	5	1
7	300	4	2	300	4	2
8	290	4	4	290	4	4
9	175	3	5	175	3	5
In	2580	35		2580	35	
Total	5160	70		5160	70	
Rating	64.4			68.6		
Slope	106			109		

GOLF COURSE DIRECTORY

LANESBORO GOLF CLUB

9 Executive Semi-Private

Box 10
Lanesboro, Minnesota 55949
507/467-3742 Clubhouse/Proshop

HOURS	Dawn to Dusk
SEASON	April to October

RESERVATIONS	507/467-3742 1 day	
	Walk-on: good/good	
GREEN FEES	M-F	S-S
Adult	$12/7	$14/7
Senior	$12/7	$14/7
Junior	$12/7	$14/7
Twilight	NA	NA
PAYMENT	No credit cards accepted	
	Non-local checks accepted	
LEAGUES	Men: W	
	Women: T	
MEMBERSHIPS	USGA, MGA	
MANAGER	Dennis Albright	

FEATURES	
Putting green	Y
Driving range	N
Practice area	N
Golf carts	
Power (gas)	Y $13/6.5
Pull carts	Y $1
Club rental	N
Club storage	N
Caddies	N
Proshop	
Basic	Y
Refreshments	
Restaurant	Y
Lounge	Y
Snacks	Y
Clubhouse	
Showers	N
Lockers	N
Lodging	N

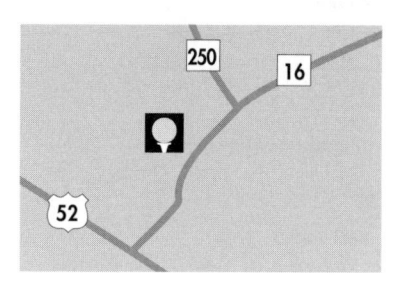

Located south of Lanesboro. Course is about five miles east of U.S. Highway 52 on MN Highway 16.

	MEN			**WOMEN**		
	FRONT	PAR	HDCP	FRONT	PAR	HDCP
1	471	5	1	366	5	2
2	172	3	4	172	3	5
3	300	4	8	300	4	6
4	471	5	3	471	5	1
5	152	3	7	94	3	9
6	302	4	9	302	4	8
7	202	3	2	202	4	7
8	331	4	5	331	4	3
9	328	4	6	328	4	4
Out	2729	35		2566	36	
1	471	5	1	366	5	2
2	172	3	4	172	3	5
3	300	4	8	300	4	6
4	471	5	3	471	5	1
5	152	3	7	94	3	9
6	302	4	9	302	4	8
7	202	3	2	202	4	7
8	331	4	5	331	4	3
9	328	4	6	328	4	4
In	2729	35		2566	36	
Total	5458	70		5132	72	
Rating	66.6			69.8		
Slope	111			113		

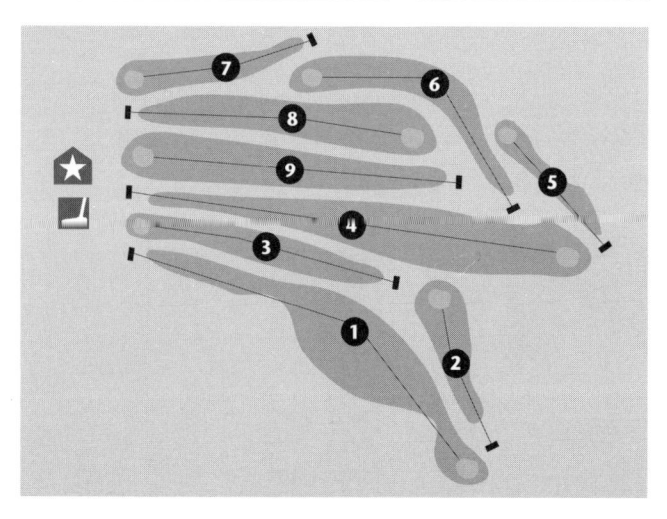

LE SUEUR COUNTRY CLUB

18 Regulation Semi-Private

Rural Route 1, Box 163
Le Sueur, Minnesota 56058
612/665-2291 Clubhouse
612/665-6292 Proshop

HOURS	7 am to Dusk
SEASON	April to October

FEATURES	
Putting green	Y
Driving range	Y
Practice area	Y
Golf carts	
Power (gas)	Y
Pull carts	Y
Club rental	N
Club storage	Y
Caddies	N
Proshop	
Extended	Y
Refreshments	
Restaurant	Y
Lounge	Y
Snacks	Y
Clubhouse	
Showers	Y
Lockers	Y
Lodging	N

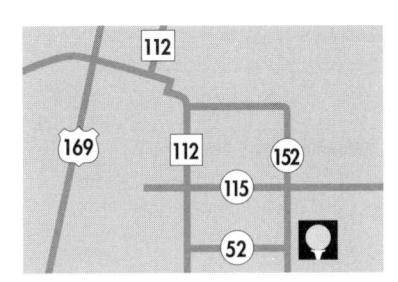

Located southeast of Le Sueur. Course is east of Highway 112 on County Road 115, then south on County Road 152.

RESERVATIONS	612/665-6292 3 days
	Walk-on: fair/poor

GREEN FEES	M-F	S-S
Adult	$20/10	$26/13
Senior	$20/10	$26/13
Junior	$20/10	$26/13
Twilight	NA	NA

PAYMENT	Credit: Visa® MasterCard®
	Credit for merchandise only
	Non-local checks accepted

LEAGUES	Men:	Th (10 am-dusk)
	Women:	W (9 am)
		W (3:30-5:30 pm)

MEMBERSHIPS	USGA, PGA, GCSAA, MGA

SUPERINTENDENT	Rick Hoffman
PROFESSIONAL	Rick Ellefson

	MEN				**WOMEN**		
	BACK	FRONT	PAR	HDCP	FRONT	PAR	HDCP
1	514	471	5	3	384	5	5
2	202	191	3	7	182	3	7
3	388	378	4	11	333	4	9
4	366	310	4	13	240	4	11
5	449	490	4/5	5	410	5	3
6	346	336	4	15	306	4	13
7	163	148	3	17	138	3	17
8	414	405	4	9	339	4	15
9	471	438	4	1	353	4	1
Out	3313	3167	35/36		2685	36	
10	170	145	3	18	89	3	18
11	374	347	4	10	244	4	10
12	510	486	5	6	407	5	6
13	415	400	4	4	347	4	2
14	210	303	3/4	14	210	4	14
15	173	156	3	16	147	3	12
16	471	471	5	2	401	5	4
17	347	327	4	8	243	4	16
18	336	336	4	12	328	4	8
In	3006	2971	35/36		2416	36	
Total	6319	6138	70/72		5101	72	
Rating	69.4	68.6			69.7		
Slope	118	116			118		

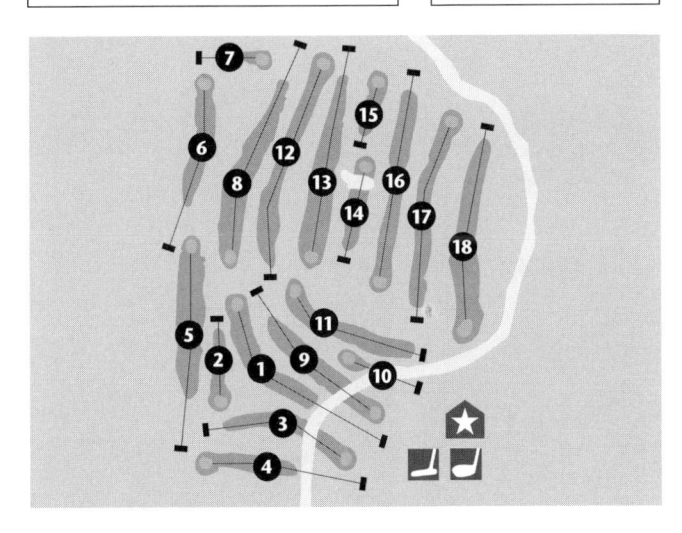

LESTER PARK GOLF COURSE

27 Regulation Public

1860 Lester Park Road
Duluth, Minnesota 55804
218/525-1400 Clubhouse/Proshop

HOURS	6:30 am to Dusk
SEASON	May-November

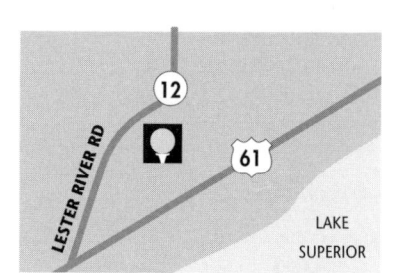

Located in Duluth. Course is west of U.S. Highway 61 on Lester River Road.

RESERVATIONS	218/525-1400
	Reservations required
	Walk-on: good/fair

GREEN FEES	M-F	S-S
Adult	$18/12	$18/12
Senior	$18/9	$18/9
Junior	$8/5	$8/5
Twilight	$7	NA

PAYMENT	Credit: Visa® MasterCard®
	Local checks only

LEAGUES	Men: W (pm)
	Women: T (am)

MEMBERSHIPS	USGA, GCSAA, MGA

OWNER	City of Duluth
SUPERINTENDENT	Jeff Anderson

FEATURES		
Putting green	Y	
Driving range	Y	$1.50
Practice area	Y	
Golf carts		
Power	Y	$14
Pull carts	Y	$1
Club rental	Y	
Club storage	Y	
Caddies	N	
Proshop		
Extended	Y	
Refreshments		
Restaurant	Y	
Lounge	N	
Snacks	Y	
Clubhouse		
Showers	N	
Lockers	N	
Lodging	N	

	MEN				**WOMEN**		
	BACK	FRONT	PAR	HDCP	FRONT	PAR	HDCP
1	406	399	4	1	353	4	1
2	464	439	5	4	381	5	4
3	377	368	4	3	360	4	3
4	338	330	4	6	295	4	6
5	313	308	4	8	300	4	8
6	167	159	3	7	139	3	7
7	418	410	4	2	400	5	2
8	213	184	3	5	125	3	5
9	486	464	5	9	458	5	9
FRONT	3182	3061	36		2811	37	
1	475	465	5	4	455	5	4
2	171	152	3	6	109	3	6
3	487	444	5	5	382	5	5
4	383	340	4	8	316	4	8
5	373	365	4	1	358	4	1
6	141	127	3	9	109	3	9
7	415	399	4	3	385	4	3
8	306	271	4	7	235	4	7
9	438	438	4	2	422	5	2
BACK	3189	3001	36		2771	37	
1	394	369	4	5	316	4	5
2	538	516	5	1	442	5	1
3	375	350	4	6	286	4	6
4	387	345	4	2	307	4	2
5	197	176	3	7	135	3	7
6	316	303	4	9	271	4	9
7	574	552	5	4	476	5	4
8	169	143	3	8	115	3	8
9	437	414	4	3	345	4	3
LAKE	3417	3168	36		2693	36	
F/B	6371	6062	72		5582	74	
Rating	70.8	69.4			72.6		
Slope	118	115			122		
B/L	6606	6169	72		5464	73	
Rating	72.6	70.6			72.5		
Slope	129	125			126		
L/F	6599	6229	72		5504	73	
Rating	72.6	71.0			73.1		
Slope	129	125			127		

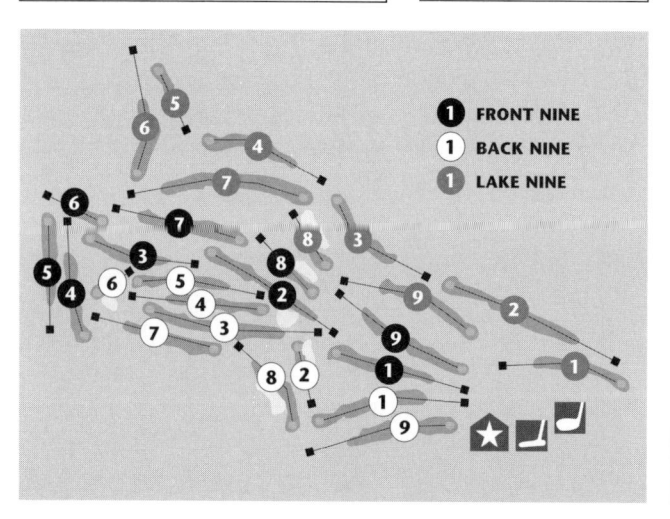

1 FRONT NINE
1 BACK NINE
1 LAKE NINE

LEWISTON COUNTRY CLUB

9 Regulation Public

Route 2, Highway 14
Lewiston, Minnesota 55952
507/523-9000 Clubhouse/Proshop

HOURS	Dawn to Dusk
SEASON	April to October

RESERVATIONS	507/523-9000	
	Walk-on: good/fair	
GREEN FEES	M-F	S-S
Adult	$6.25	$7.25
Senior	$6.25	$7.25
Junior	$6.25	$7.25
Twilight	NA	NA
PAYMENT	No credit cards accepted	
	Non-local checks accepted	
LEAGUES	Men: Various	
	Women: Various	
MEMBERSHIPS	MGA	
MANAGER	Terry Cramer	
PROFESSIONAL	Bruce Johnson	

FEATURES		
Putting green	Y	
Driving range	Y	$2.95
Practice area	N	
Golf carts		
Power (gas)	Y	$7.50
Pull carts	Y	$1
Club rental	Y	$3
Club storage	N	
Caddies	N	
Proshop		
Basic	Y	
Refreshments		
Restaurant	N	
Lounge	N	
Snacks	Y	
Clubhouse		
Showers	Y	
Lockers	Y	
Lodging	N	

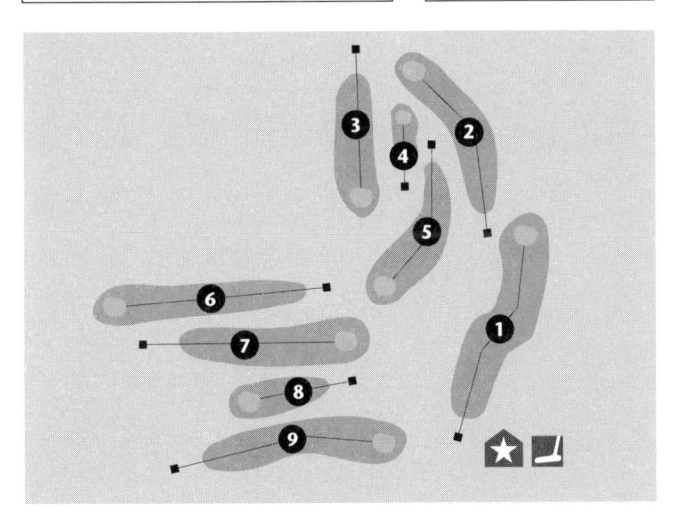

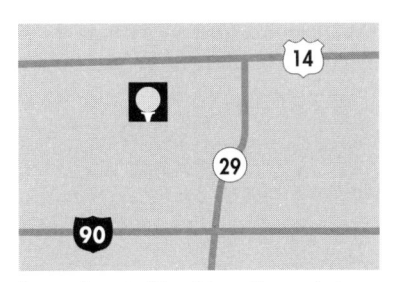

Located west of Lewiston. Course is two miles west of County Road 29 on U.S. Highway 14.

	MEN			**WOMEN**		
	FRONT	PAR	HDCP	FRONT	PAR	HDCP
1	513	5	3	513	5	3
2	313	4	15	313	4	15
3	363	4	13	363	4	13
4	200	3	7	200	3	7
5	383	4	5	383	4	5
6	510	5	1	510	5	1
7	410	4	9	410	5	9
8	160	3	17	160	3	17
9	377	4	11	377	4	11
Out	3229	36		3229	37	
1	513	5	4	513	5	4
2	313	4	16	313	4	16
3	363	4	14	363	4	14
4	200	3	8	200	3	8
5	383	4	6	383	4	6
6	510	5	2	510	5	2
7	410	4	10	410	5	10
8	160	3	18	160	3	18
9	377	4	12	377	4	12
Out	3229	36		3229	37	
Total	6458	72		6458	72	
Rating	69.4			75.0		
Slope	111			122		

GOLF COURSE DIRECTORY

LITCHFIELD GOLF CLUB 18 Regulation Public

West Pleasure Drive, P.O. Box 706
Litchfield, Minnesota 55355
612/693-6425 Clubhouse
612/693-6059 Proshop

HOURS	7 am to Dusk
SEASON	April-November

FEATURES	
Putting green	Y
Driving range	N
Practice area	Y
Golf carts	
Power (gas)	Y
Pull carts	Y
Club rental	Y
Club storage	Y
Caddies	N
Proshop	
Extended	Y
Refreshments	
Restaurant	Y
Lounge	Y
Snacks	Y
Clubhouse	
Showers	Y
Lockers	Y
Lodging	N

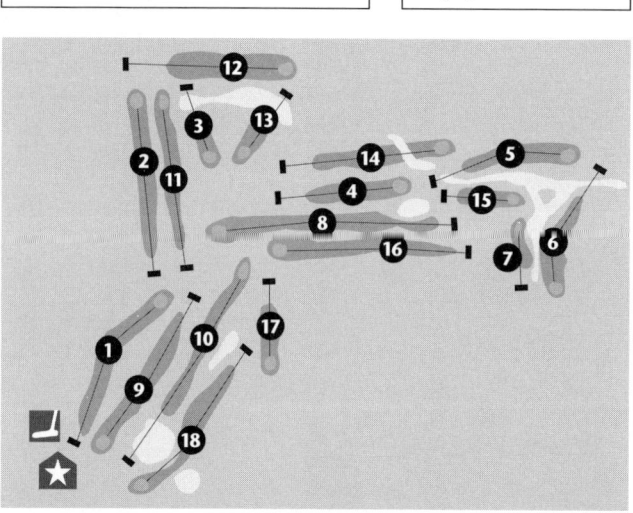

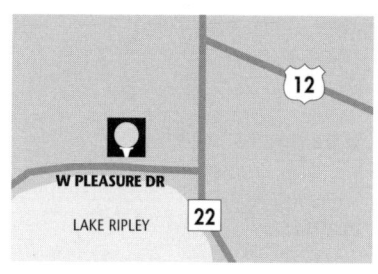

Located in Litchfield. Course entrance is 2 blocks west of MN Highway 22/Sibley Avenue on West Pleasure Drive.

RESERVATIONS	612/693-6059 3 days
	Walk-on: good/good

GREEN FEES	M-F	S-S
Adult	$12/9	$16/12
Senior	$12/9	$16/12
Junior	$12/9	$16/12
Twilight	NA	NA

PAYMENT	Credit: Visa® MasterCard®
	Non-local checks accepted

LEAGUES	Men: W
	Women: T
	Seniors: Th

MEMBERSHIPS	USGA, MGA

MANAGER	John Streed
SUPERINTENDENT	John Streed

	MEN				WOMEN		
	BACK	FRONT	PAR	HDCP	FRONT	PAR	HDCP
1	454	437	4	3	367	4	3
2	400	390	4	5	335	4	7
3	174	165	3	17	129	3	17
4	350	337	4	15	265	4	15
5	315	305	4	11	233	4	11
6	370	332	4	13	259	4	13
7	172	162	3	9	128	3	9
8	560	547	5	1	473	5	1
9	404	392	4	7	336	4	5
Out	3199	3067	35		2525	35	
10	497	479	5	10	415	5	10
11	381	365	4	8	317	4	8
12	307	295	4	14	241	4	14
13	178	168	3	18	104	3	18
14	434	422	4	2	354	4	2
15	181	166	3	16	145	3	16
16	486	473	5	4	398	5	4
17	203	186	3	12	148	3	12
18	428	416	4	6	364	4	6
In	3095	2970	35		2486	35	
Total	6294	6037	70		5011	70	
Rating	69.3	68.4			68.4		
Slope	116	113			115		

LITTLE CROW COUNTRY CLUB

18 Regulation Semi-Private

Highway 23, P.O. Box 219
Spicer, Minnesota 56288
612/354-2296 Clubhouse/Proshop

HOURS	7 am to Dusk
SEASON	April to October

RESERVATIONS	612/354-2296 1 day
	Walk-on: fair/poor

GREEN FEES	M-F	S-S
Adult	$15/9	$18/11
Senior	$15/9	$18/11
Junior	$15/9	$18/11
Twilight	NA	NA

PAYMENT	Credit: Visa® MasterCard®
	Non-local checks accepted

LEAGUES	Men: T,W
	Women: T
	Senior: Th

MEMBERSHIPS	USGA, PGA, GCSAA, MGA

MANAGER	Judd Bonham
SUPERINTENDENT	Dave Lohn
PROFESSIONAL	Judd Bonham

FEATURES	
Putting green	Y
Driving range	Y $2.50
Practice area	N
Golf carts	
Power (gas)	Y $18/10
Pull carts	Y $1.50
Club rental	Y $10
Club storage	N
Caddies	N
Proshop	
Extended	Y
Refreshments	
Restaurant	Y
Lounge	N
Snacks	N
Clubhouse	
Showers	Y
Lockers	Y
Lodging	N

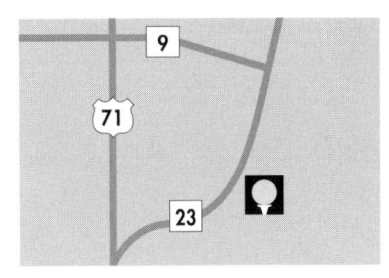

Located between New London and Spicer. Course entrance is north of U.S. Highway 71 on MN Highway 23.

	MEN				**WOMEN**		
	BACK	FRONT	PAR	HDCP	FRONT	PAR	HDCP
1	400	395	4	4	320	4	6
2	150	135	3	18	120	3	18
3	585	570	5	2	475	5	4
4	375	365	4	10	355	4	10
5	195	165	3	16	150	3	16
6	350	305	4	14	290	4	14
7	375	345	4	12	330	4	12
8	535	500	5	6	410	5	2
9	360	350	4	8	335	4	8
Out	3325	3130	36		2785	36	
10	420	400	4	1	307	4	3
11	515	495	5	5	475	5	1
12	190	170	3	15	155	3	15
13	385	355	4	13	340	4	13
14	400	385	4	9	375	4	9
15	490	485	5	7	415	5	5
16	410	395	4	3	300	4	7
17	230	215	3	17	160	3	17
18	370	360	4	11	350	4	11
In	3415	3260	36		2877	36	
Total	6740	6390	72		5662	72	
Rating	72.3	70.5			73.1		
Slope	123	119			125		

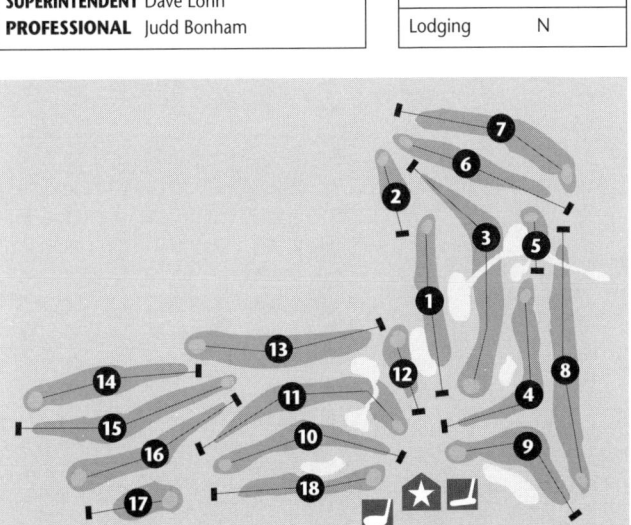

GOLF COURSE DIRECTORY

LITTLE FALLS COUNTRY CLUB   18 Regulation Public

1 Edgewater Drive
Little Falls, Minnesota 56345
612/632-3584 Clubhouse/Proshop

HOURS	6:30 am - Dusk
SEASON	April-November

| RESERVATIONS | 612/632-3584 1 week |
| | Walk-on: good/poor |

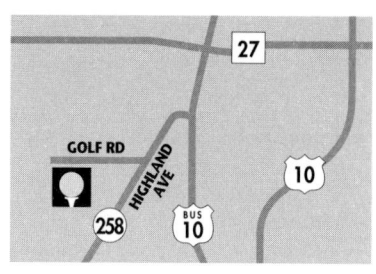

GREEN FEES	M-F	S-S
Adult	$17/11	$17/11
Senior	$17/11	$17/11
Junior	$17/11	$17/11
Twilight	NA	NA
	Five play cards available	

| PAYMENT | Credit cards not accepted |
| | Non-local checks accepted |

LEAGUES	Men: W
	Women: T
	Seniors: Th (am)

| MEMBERSHIPS | GCSAA, MGA |

| SUPERINTENDENT | Doug Veillette |
| PROFESSIONAL | Doug Veillette |

FEATURES		
Putting green	Y	
Driving range	Y	$1-3
Practice area	Y	
Golf carts		
Power	Y	$17/11
Pull carts	Y	$3/2
Club rental	Y	$5/4
Club storage	Y	$25/yr
Caddies	N	
Proshop		
Extended	Y	
Refreshments		
Restaurant	Y	
Lounge	Y	
Snacks	Y	
Clubhouse		
Showers	N	
Lockers	N	
Lodging	N	

Located in Little Falls. Course is west of U.S. Hwy 10 on Highland Avenue, then west on Golf Road.

	MEN			WOMEN		
	FRONT	PAR	HDCP	FRONT	PAR	HDCP
1	310	4	14	305	4	13
2	339	4	12	329	4	11
3	139	3	18	130	3	15
4	366	4	2	355	4	5
5	347	4	10	340	4	9
6	150	3	16	140	3	17
7	471	5	6	460	5	1
8	370	4	4	350	4	7
9	489	5	8	465	5	3
Out	2981	36		2874	36	
10	387	4	3	377	5	8
11	293	4	17	280	4	14
12	448	5	7	419	5	6
13	184	3	15	176	3	18
14	374	4	5	367	4	4
15	331	4	9	303	4	10
16	186	3	11	137	3	16
17	554	5	1	480	5	2
18	313	4	13	300	4	12
In	3070	36		2839	37	
Total	6051	72		5713	73	
Rating	69.0			72.6		
Slope	121			125		

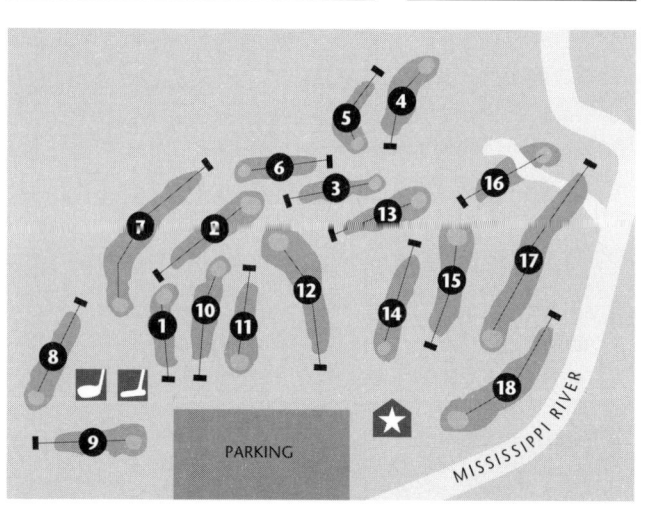

LONE PINE COUNTRY CLUB

18 Executive Public

15451 Howard Lake Road
Shakopee, Minnesota 55379
612/445-3575 Clubhouse/Proshop

HOURS	Dawn to Dusk
SEASON	April to October

FEATURES	
Putting green	Y
Driving range	Y
Practice area	N
Golf carts	
Power (gas)	Y $18/10
Pull carts	Y $2
Club rental	Y $5
Club storage	N
Caddies	N
Proshop	
Basic	Y
Refreshments	
Restaurant	N
Lounge	Y
Snacks	Y
Clubhouse	
Showers	N
Lockers	N
Lodging	N

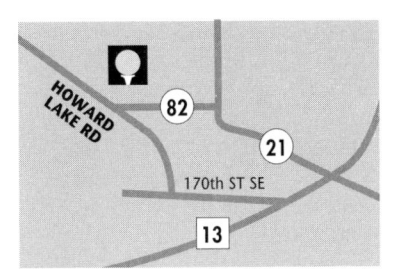

RESERVATIONS	612/445-3575 1 week
	Walk-on: fair/fair

GREEN FEES	M-F	S-S
Adult	$15/10	$18/11
Senior	$12/8*	$18/11
Junior	$15/10	$18/11
Twilight	NA	NA
	* Before 3 pm	

PAYMENT	No credit cards accepted
	Local checks accepted

LEAGUES	Men: Various
	Women: Various

MEMBERSHIPS	MGA

MANAGER	Betty McKush
PROFESSIONAL	Greg McKush

Located in Shakopee. Course is west of MN Highway 13 on County Road 21, then west on County Road 82.

	MEN			WOMEN		
	FRONT	PAR	HDCP	FRONT	PAR	HDCP
1	265	4	9	240	4	7
2	145	3	15	130	3	15
3	315	4	7	270	4	5
4	490	5	1	430	5	1
5	330	4	5	220	4	9
6	450	5	3	430	5	3
7	185	3	11	140	3	11
8	175	3	13	130	3	13
9	120	3	17	115	3	17
Out	2475	34		2105	34	
10	175	3	14	150	3	14
11	325	4	10	275	4	12
12	125	3	18	110	3	18
13	305	4	12	285	4	10
14	415	4	4	410	5	4
15	335	4	8	315	4	8
16	380	4	6	350	4	6
17	505	5	2	460	5	2
18	140	3	16	130	3	16
In	2705	34		2485	35	
Total	5180	68		4590	69	
Rating	65.3			66.3		
Slope	108			115		

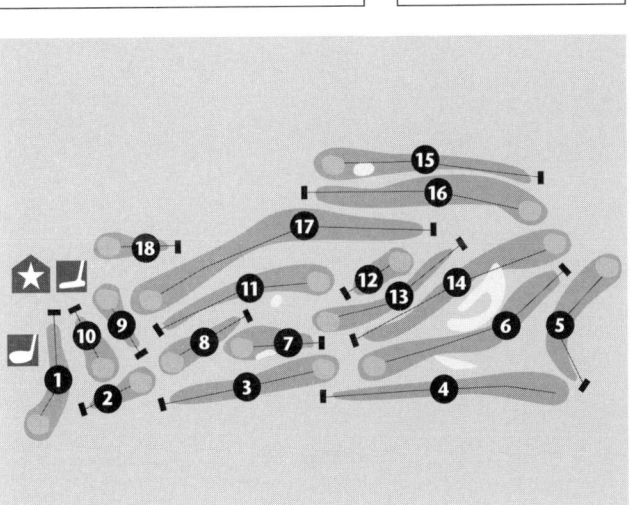

GOLF COURSE DIRECTORY

LONG PRAIRIE COUNTRY CLUB

9 Regulation Semi-Private

405 6th Street Southeast
Long Prairie, Minnesota 56347
612/732-3312 Clubhouse/Proshop

HOURS	8 am to 10 pm
SEASON	April-November

RESERVATIONS	612/732-3312 3 days
	Walk-on: good/good

GREEN FEES	M-F	S-S
Adult	$10	$14.50
Senior	$10	$14.50
Senior	$10	$14.50
Twilight	NA	NA

PAYMENT	No credit cards accepted
	Non-local checks accepted

LEAGUES	Men: W (11 am-Dusk)
	Women: Th (12 pm-Dusk)

MEMBERSHIPS	USGA, GCSAA, MGA

MANAGER	Fred Dinkel
SUPERINTENDENT	John Monson

FEATURES		
Putting green	Y	
Driving range	N	
Practice area	Y	
Golf carts		
Power (gas)	Y	$13/8
Pull carts	Y	$2
Club rental	Y	$5
Club storage	N	
Caddies	N	
Proshop		
Extended	Y	
Refreshments		
Restaurant	N	
Lounge	Y	
Snacks	Y	
Clubhouse		
Showers	N	
Lockers	N	
Lodging	N	

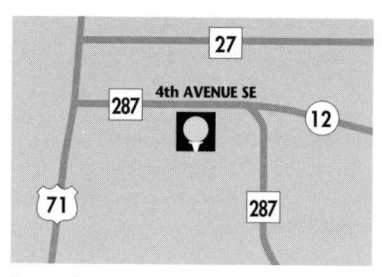

Located in Long Prairie. Course entrance is 1/2 mile east of U.S. Highway 71 on MN Highway 287/4th Avenue SE.

	MEN			**WOMEN**		
	FRONT	PAR	HDCP	FRONT	PAR	HDCP
1	473	5	6	438	5	6
2	343	4	5	340	4	5
3	367	4	1	342	4	1
4	162	3	8	158	3	8
5	442	5	9	430	5	9
6	217	3	2	213	4	2
7	370	4	3	300	4	3
8	277	4	7	267	4	7
9	356	4	4	340	4	4
Out	3007	36		2828	37	
1	473	5	6	438	5	6
2	343	4	5	340	4	5
3	367	4	1	342	4	1
4	162	3	8	158	3	8
5	442	5	9	430	5	9
6	217	3	2	213	4	2
7	370	4	3	300	4	3
8	277	4	7	267	4	7
9	356	4	4	340	4	4
In	3007	36		2828	37	
Total	6014	72		5656	74	
Rating	69.4			73.2		
Slope	118			125		

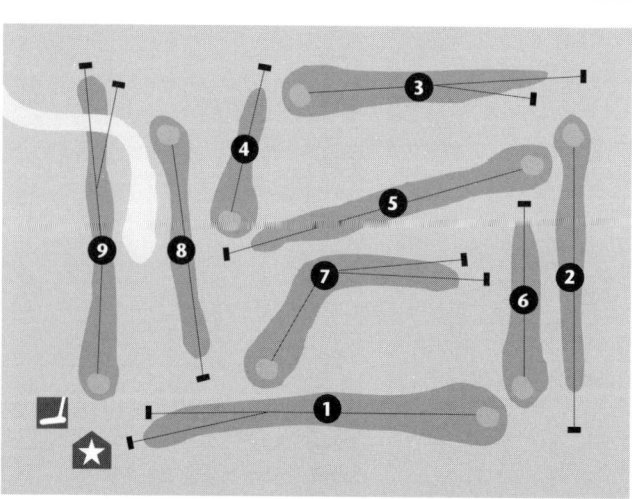

THE MINNESOTA ILLUSTRATED

LOON LAKE GOLF CLUB   9 Regulation Public

Rural Route 3, P.O. Box 203A
Jackson, Minnesota 56143
507/847-4036 Clubhouse/Proshop

HOURS 6:30 am to Dusk
SEASON April to October

RESERVATIONS	507/847-4036 1 day
	Walk-on: good/fair

GREEN FEES	M-F	S-S
Adult	Call	Call
Senior	Call	Call
Junior	Call	Call
Twilight	NA	NA

PAYMENT	No credit cards accepted
	Non-local checks accepted

LEAGUES	Men: Various
	Women: Various

MEMBERSHIPS	MGA

OWNER	Kevin & Sally Farrington
MANAGER	Kevin & Sally Farrington

FEATURES

Putting green	Y
Driving range	N
Practice area	N
Golf carts	
Power (gas)	Y
Pull carts	Y
Club rental	Y
Club storage	Y
Caddies	N
Proshop	
Extended	Y
Refreshments	
Restaurant	N
Lounge	Y
Snacks	Y
Clubhouse	
Showers	Y
Lockers	Y
Lodging	N

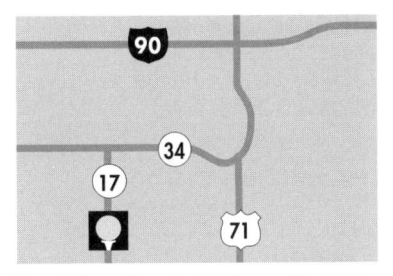

Located southwest of Jackson. Course is south of I-90 on US Hwy 71, west of Cty Road 34, then south on Cty Road 17.

	MEN				WOMEN		
	BACK	FRONT	PAR	HDCP	FRONT	PAR	HDCP
1	240	238	4	9	182	4	9
2	441	421	4	1	323	4	1
3	472	468	5	2	412	5	2
4	390	358	4	7	300	4	7
5	303	290	4	8	290	4	8
6	330	322	4	6	250	4	6
7	382	369	4	3	315	4	3
8	365	360	4	5	301	4	5
9	169	165	3	4	141	3	4
Out	3092	2991	36		2514	36	
1	240	238	4	9	182	4	9
2	441	421	4	1	323	4	1
3	472	468	5	2	412	5	2
4	390	358	4	7	300	4	7
5	303	290	4	8	290	4	8
6	330	322	4	6	250	4	6
7	382	369	4	3	315	4	3
8	365	360	4	5	301	4	5
9	169	165	3	4	141	3	4
In	3092	2991	36		2514	36	
Total	6184	5982	72		5028	72	
Rating	69.8	68.8			68.4		
Slope	117	115			110		

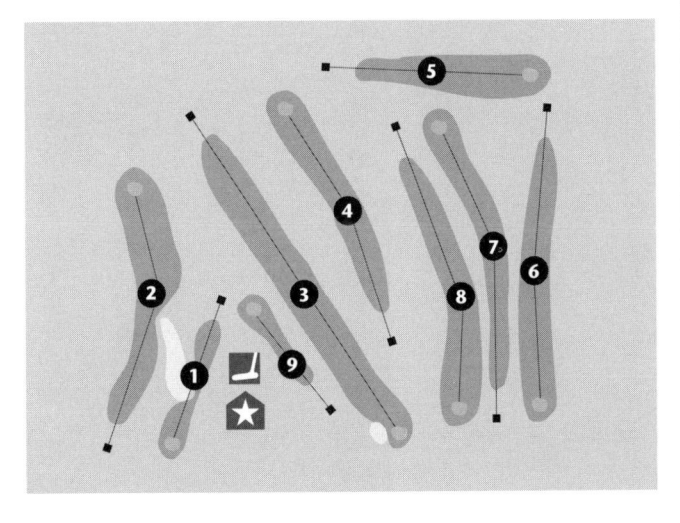

GOLF COURSE DIRECTORY

LOST SPUR COUNTRY CLUB

9 Executive Private

2750 Sibley Highway
Eagan, Minnesota 55121
612/454-2330 Clubhouse
612/454-5681 Proshop

RESERVATIONS	612/454-5681	
	Members only	
GREEN FEES	M-F	S-S
Adult	Call	Call
Senior	Call	Call
Junior	Call	Call
Twilight	NA	NA
	Members and guests only	
PAYMENT	Credit: Visa® MC® Discover®	
	Non-local checks accepted	
LEAGUES	Men: None	
	Women: None	
MEMBERSHIPS	MGA	
PROFESSIONAL	Rob Stitzer	

HOURS Dawn to Dusk
SEASON April to October

FEATURES

Putting green	Y
Driving range	Y
Practice area	N
Golf carts	
Power (gas)	Y
Pull carts	Y
Club rental	Y
Club storage	N
Caddies	N
Proshop	
Extended	Y
Refreshments	
Restaurant	Y
Lounge	Y
Snacks	Y
Clubhouse	
Showers	N
Lockers	N
Lodging	N

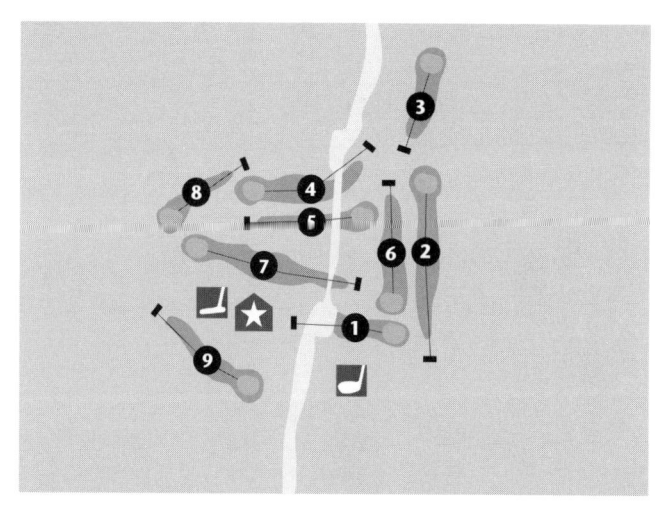

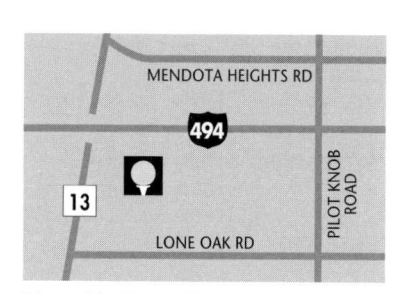

Located in Eagan. Course is south of I-494 on Pilot Knob Road, west on Lone Oak Road, then north on Highway 13.

	\multicolumn{3}{c	}{MEN}	\multicolumn{3}{c	}{WOMEN}
	FRONT	PAR	HDCP	FRONT	PAR	HDCP
1	346	4	6	338	4	4
2	253	4	8	246	4	8
3	157	3	16	144	3	16
4	276	4	4	271	4	6
5	302	4	12	254	4	10
6	212	3	10	208	4	14
7	435	5	2	418	5	2
8	145	3	14	136	3	18
9	255	4	18	225	4	12
Out	2381	34		2240	35	
10	352	4	5	346	4	3
11	260	4	7	253	4	7
12	161	3	15	157	3	15
13	296	4	3	296	4	5
14	303	4	11	302	4	9
15	216	3	9	212	4	13
16	440	5	1	421	5	1
17	165	3	13	165	3	17
18	260	4	17	255	4	11
In	2455	34		2407	35	
Total	4836	68		4647	70	
Rating	62.6			65.0		
Slope	102			115		

LUVERNE COUNTRY CLUB

9 Regulation Semi-Private

Rural Route 3, P.O. Box 853
Luverne, Minnesota 56156
507/283-4383 Clubhouse/Proshop

HOURS	8 am to Dusk
SEASON	April to October

| **RESERVATIONS** | 507/283-4383 1 day |
| | Walk-on: fair/poor |

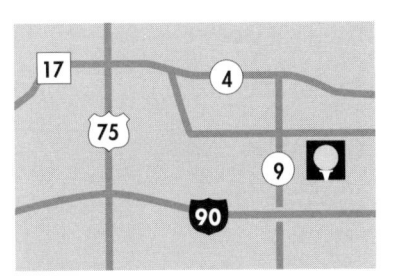

GREEN FEES	M-F	S-S
Adult	$15/10	$20/12
Senior	$15/10	$20/12
Junior	$15/10	$20/12
Twilight	NA	NA

| **PAYMENT** | No credit cards accepted |
| | Non-local checks accepted |

| **LEAGUES** | Men: W |
| | Women: T |

| **MEMBERSHIPS** | MGA |

MANAGER	Sherri Thompson
SUPERINTENDENT	Mike Kunkel
PROFESSIONAL	Jerilyn Britz

FEATURES		
Putting green	Y	
Driving range	Y	$2.50
Practice area	Y	
Golf carts		
Power (elec)	Y	$18/9
Pull carts	Y	$1.50
Club rental	Y	$5
Club storage	N	
Caddies	N	
Proshop		
Extended	Y	
Refreshments		
Restaurant	Y	
Lounge	Y	
Snacks	Y	
Clubhouse		
Showers	Y	
Lockers	Y	
Lodging	N	

Located southeast of Luverne. Course is east of Hwy 75 on Cty Rd 4, south 1/2 mile on Cty Rd 9, then east to course.

	MEN				WOMEN		
	BACK	FRONT	PAR	HDCP	FRONT	PAR	HDCP
1	404	392	4	3	304	4	3
2	496	489	5	9	379	5	9
3	172	152	3	17	96	3	17
4	434	414	4	1	349	4	1
5	424	402	4	5	298	4	5
6	333	321	4	11	250	4	11
7	175	157	3	13	140	3	13
8	547	525	5	7	413	5	7
9	354	346	4	15	287	4	15
Out	3339	3198	36		2516	36	
1	404	392	4	4	304	4	4
2	496	489	5	10	379	5	10
3	172	152	3	18	96	3	18
4	434	414	4	2	349	4	2
5	424	402	4	6	298	4	6
6	333	321	4	12	250	4	12
7	175	157	3	14	140	3	14
8	547	525	5	8	413	5	8
9	354	346	4	16	287	4	16
In	3339	3198	36		2516	36	
Total	6678	6396	72		5032	72	
Rating	72.4	71.0			69.4		
Slope	129	126			122		

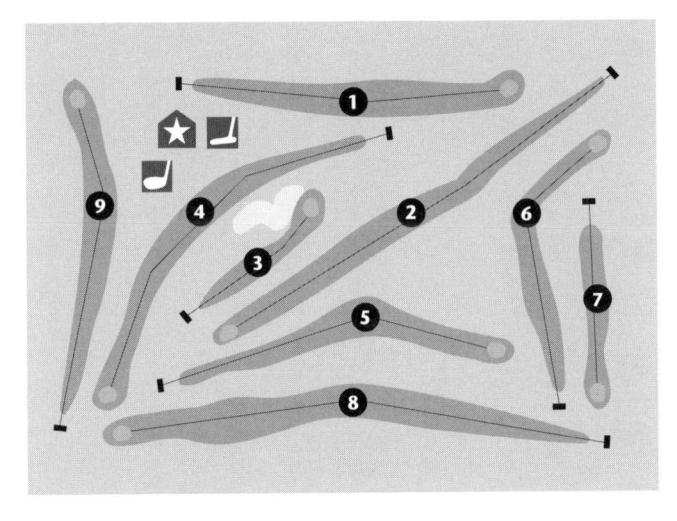

GOLF COURSE DIRECTORY

MA-CAL-GROVE COUNTRY CLUB

9 Regulation Semi-Private

Highway 44, P.O. Box 407
Caledonia, Minnesota 55921
507/724-2733 Clubhouse/Proshop

HOURS	7 am to Dusk
SEASON	April to October

RESERVATIONS	507/724-2733 3 days
	Walk-on: good/fair

GREEN FEES	M-F	S-S
Adult	$14.50/8.25	$16.50/9.25
Senior	$14.50/8.25	$16.50/9.25
Junior	$14.50/8.25	$16.50/9.25
Twilight	NA	NA

PAYMENT	No credit cards accepted
	Non-local checks accepted

LEAGUES	Men: T (pm)
	Women: M (pm)

MEMBERSHIPS	NGF, GCSAA, MGA

MANAGER	Carlene Boone
SUPERINTENDENT	Darren Armstrong

FEATURES	
Putting green	Y
Driving range	Y
Practice area	N
Golf carts	
Power (gas)	Y
Pull carts	Y
Club rental	Y
Club storage	Y
Caddies	N
Proshop	
Extended	Y
Refreshments	
Restaurant	N
Lounge	Y
Snacks	Y
Clubhouse	
Showers	Y
Lockers	Y
Lodging	N

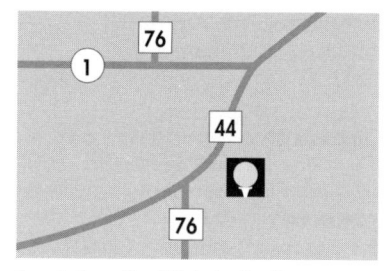

Located south of Caledonia. Course entrance is about 1 1/2 miles south of County Road 1 on MN Highways 44/76.

	MEN				**WOMEN**		
	BACK	FRONT	PAR	HDCP	FRONT	PAR	HDCP
1	532	526	5	1	485	5	1
2	319	312	4	9	306	4	4
3	184	177	3	3	155	3	7
4	405	385	4	2	361	5	3
5	314	302	4	8	290	4	9
6	182	177	3	7	172	3	8
7	361	349	4	5	263	4	6
8	506	490	5	6	453	5	2
9	400	393	4	4	383	5	5
Out	3203	3111	36		2868	38	
1	532	526	5	1	485	5	1
2	319	312	4	9	306	4	4
3	184	177	3	3	155	3	7
4	405	385	4	2	361	5	3
5	314	302	4	8	290	4	9
6	182	177	3	7	172	3	8
7	361	349	4	5	263	4	6
8	506	490	5	6	453	5	2
9	400	393	4	4	383	5	5
In	3203	3111	36		2868	38	
Total	6406	6222	72		5736	76	
Rating	70.0	69.2			72.4		
Slope	121	120			123		

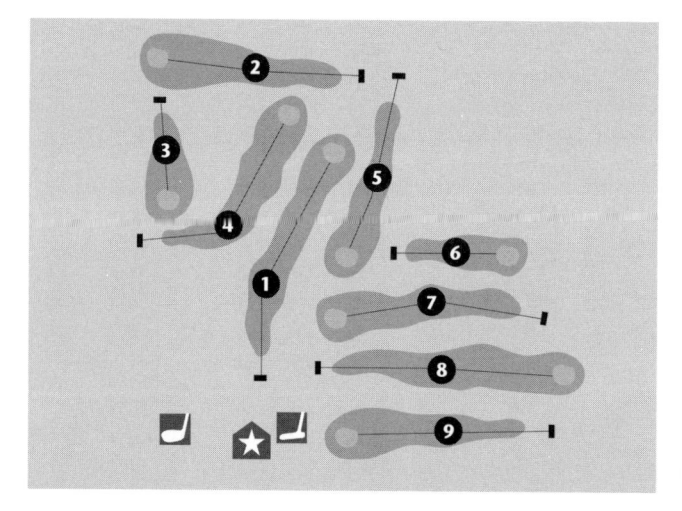

MADDEN'S ON GULL LAKE

PINE BEACH EAST/18 Regulation Public

8001 Pine Beach Peninsula
Brainerd, Minnesota 56401
218/829-2811 Clubhouse/Proshop

RESERVATIONS	218/829-2811 1 day	
	Walk-on: good/fair	
GREEN FEES	M-F	S-S
Adult	$26.95	$27.95
Senior	$26.95	$27.95
Junior	$26.95	$27.95
Twilight	$16	$16
PAYMENT	Credit: Visa® MasterCard®	
	Non-local checks accepted	
LEAGUES	None	
MEMBERSHIPS	USGA, NGF, GCSAA, MGA, CMAA	
OWNER	Jim Madden, John Arnold & Brian Thuringer	
SUPERINTENDENT	Scott Hoffmann	
PROFESSIONAL	Ken Lubke	

HOURS	8 am to Dusk	
SEASON	April to October	
FEATURES		
Putting green	Y	
Driving range	Y	$4.75
Practice area	Y	
Golf carts		
Power (gas)	Y	$25/18
Pull carts	Y	$4
Club rental	Y	$13
Club storage	N	
Caddies	N	
Proshop		
Extended	Y	
Refreshments		
Restaurant	Y	
Lounge	Y	
Snacks	Y	
Clubhouse		
Showers	N	
Lockers	Y	
Lodging	Y	Call

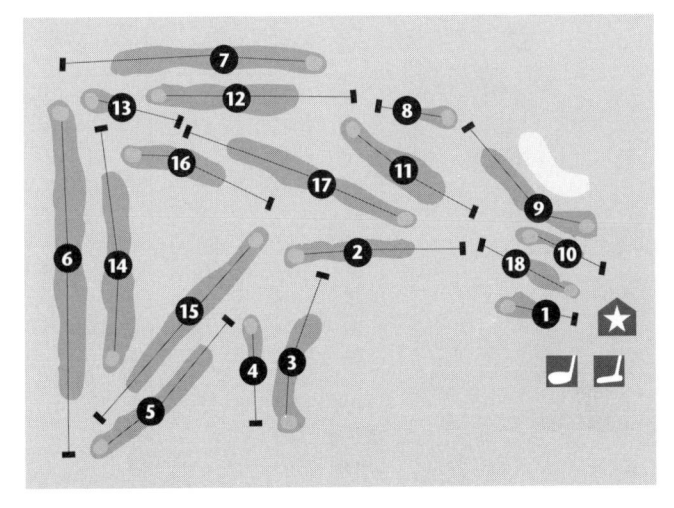

Located north of Brainerd. Course is west of MN Highway 371 on County Road 77.

	MEN			WOMEN		
	FRONT	PAR	HDCP	FRONT	PAR	HDCP
1	160	3	7	140	3	13
2	343	4	11	330	4	9
3	331	4	13	331	4	15
4	176	3	5	160	3	7
5	365	4	9	314	4	5
6	618	6	15	502	6	11
7	519	5	1	467	5	1
8	118	3	17	108	3	17
9	347	4	3	337	4	3
Out	2977	36		2689	36	
10	172	3	8	172	3	8
11	315	4	14	305	4	16
12	398	4	2	382	4	2
13	172	3	4	149	3	4
14	460	5	16	440	5	14
15	475	5	12	375	5	6
16	306	4	18	276	4	18
17	482	5	6	422	5	12
18	175	3	10	152	3	10
In	2955	36		2673	36	
Total	5932	72		5362	72	
Rating	67.9			70.9		
Slope	111			116		

GOLF COURSE DIRECTORY

MADDEN'S ON GULL LAKE

PINE BEACH WEST/18 Regulation Public

8001 Pine Beach Peninsula
Brainerd, Minnesota 56401
218/829-2811 Clubhouse/Proshop

HOURS	8 am to Dusk
SEASON	April to October

RESERVATIONS	218/829-2811 1 day	
	Walk-on: good/fair	
GREEN FEES	M-F	S-S
Adult	$26.95	$27.95
Senior	$26.95	$27.95
Junior	$26.95	$27.95
Twilight	$16	$16
PAYMENT	Credit: Visa® MasterCard®	
	Non-local checks accepted	
LEAGUES	None	
MEMBERSHIPS	USGA, NGF, GCSAA, MGA, CMAA	
OWNER	Jim Madden, John Arnold & Brian Thuringer	
SUPERINTENDENT	Scott Hoffmann	
PROFESSIONAL	Ken Lubke	

FEATURES		
Putting green	Y	
Driving range	Y	$4.75
Practice area	Y	
Golf carts		
Power (gas)	Y	$25/18
Pull carts	Y	$4
Club rental	Y	$13
Club storage	N	
Caddies	N	
Proshop		
Extended	Y	
Refreshments		
Restaurant	Y	
Lounge	Y	
Snacks	Y	
Clubhouse		
Showers	N	
Lockers	Y	
Lodging	Y	Call

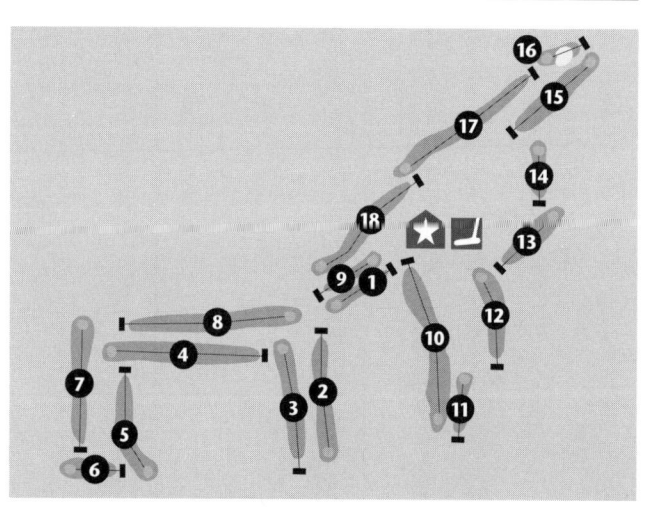

Located north of Brainerd. Course is west of MN Highway 371 on County Road 77.

	MEN			**WOMEN**		
	FRONT	PAR	HDCP	FRONT	PAR	HDCP
1	180	3	7	164	3	3
2	318	4	5	318	4	14
3	340	4	15	340	4	11
4	409	4	1	409	5	1
5	335	4	11	335	4	9
6	131	3	17	141	3	17
7	314	4	13	314	4	13
8	489	5	3	386	4	4
9	163	3	9	174	3	7
Out	2679	34		2581	34	
10	425	4	2	366	4	2
11	145	3	14	123	3	10
12	251	4	16	235	4	16
13	186	3	4	185	3	5
14	155	3	8	153	3	12
15	295	4	6	285	4	8
16	126	3	18	90	3	18
17	456	5	12	339	5	6
18	331	4	10	305	4	15
In	2370	33		2081	33	
Total	5049	67		4662	67	
Rating	64.0			66.7		
Slope	103			107		

THE MINNESOTA ILLUSTRATED

MADDEN'S ON GULL LAKE

SOCIAL NINE/9 Executive Public

8001 Pine Beach Peninsula
Brainerd, Minnesota 56401
218/829-2811 Clubhouse/Proshop

RESERVATIONS	218/829-2811 1 day	
	Walk-on: good/fair	
GREEN FEES	M-F	S-S
Adult	Call	Call
Senior	Call	Call
Junior	Call	Call
Twilight	NA	NA
PAYMENT	Credit: Visa® MasterCard®	
	Non-local checks accepted	
LEAGUES	None	
MEMBERSHIPS	USGA, NGF, GCSAA, MGA, CMAA	
OWNER	Jim Madden, John Arnold & Brian Thuringer	
SUPERINTENDENT	Scott Hoffmann	
PROFESSIONAL	Ken Lubke	

HOURS	8 am to Dusk	
SEASON	April to October	
FEATURES		
Putting green	Y	
Driving range	Y	$4.75
Practice area	Y	
Golf carts		
Power (gas)	Y	$25/18
Pull carts	Y	$4
Club rental	Y	$13
Club storage	N	
Caddies	N	
Proshop		
Extended	Y	
Refreshments		
Restaurant	Y	
Lounge	Y	
Snacks	Y	
Clubhouse		
Showers	N	
Lockers	Y	
Lodging	Y	Call

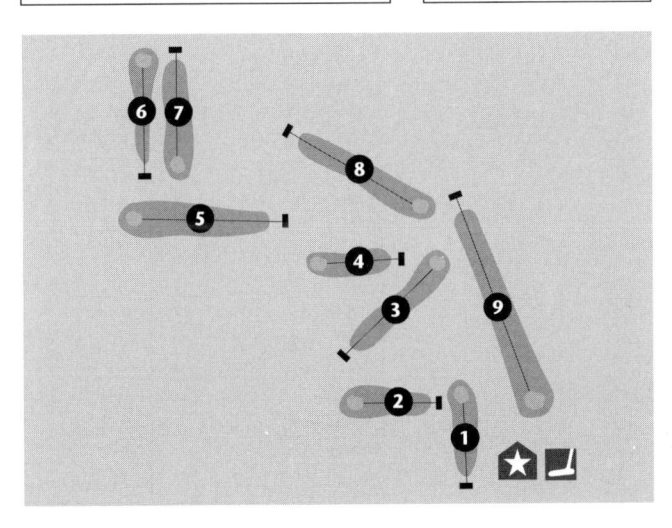

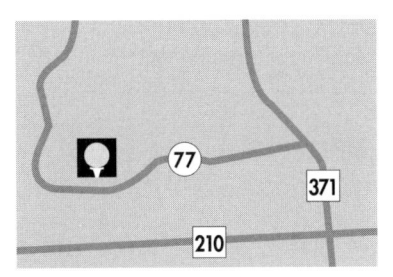

Located north of Brainerd. Course is west of MN Highway 371 on County Road 77.

	MEN			WOMEN		
	FRONT	PAR	HDCP	FRONT	PAR	HDCP
1	126	3		126	3	
2	92	3		92	3	
3	140	3		140	3	
4	123	3		123	3	
5	170	3		170	3	
6	126	3		126	3	
7	146	3		146	3	
8	173	3		173	3	
9	245	4		245	4	
Out	1341	28		1341	28	
1	126	3		126	3	
2	92	3		92	3	
3	140	3		140	3	
4	123	3		123	3	
5	170	3		170	3	
6	126	3		126	3	
7	146	3		146	3	
8	173	3		173	3	
9	245	4		245	4	
In	1341	28		1341	28	
Total	2682	56		2682	56	
Rating	NA			NA		
Slope	NA			NA		

GOLF COURSE DIRECTORY

MADELIA GOLF COURSE

9 Regulation Public

116 West Main Street
Madelia, Minnesota 56062
507/642-3608 Clubhouse/Proshop

HOURS	7 am to Dusk
SEASON	April-November

RESERVATIONS	507/642-3608 3 days
	Walk-on: fair/poor

GREEN FEES	M-F	S-S
Adult	$13/9	$17/11
Senior	$13/9	$17/11
Junior	$13/9	$17/11
Twilight	NA	NA

PAYMENT	No credit cards accepted
	Non-local checks accepted

LEAGUES	Men:	Th (5:30 pm)

MEMBERSHIPS	MGA

MANAGER	Harold Davis
SUPERINTENDENT	Harold Davis

FEATURES		
Putting green	Y	
Driving range	Y	$1.50
Practice area	N	
Golf carts		
Power (elec)	Y	$12/7
Pull carts	Y	$1
Club rental	Y	$2
Club storage	N	
Caddies	N	
Proshop		
Regular	Y	
Refreshments		
Restaurant	N	
Lounge	N	
Snacks	Y	
Clubhouse		
Showers	N	
Lockers	N	
Lodging	N	

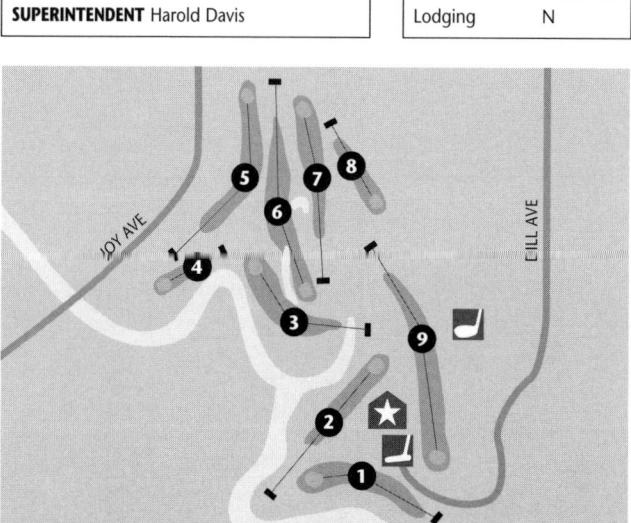

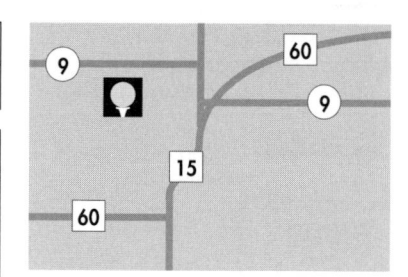

Located in Madelia. Course is west of MN Hwy 60 on Cty Rd 9. Turn into Watona Park. Follow signs to course.

		MEN				WOMEN		
	BACK	FRONT	PAR	HDCP		FRONT	PAR	HDCP
1	346	337	4	7		286	4	7
2	332	329	4	8		277	4	8
3	360	353	4	2		269	4	2
4	155	144	3	9		113	3	9
5	392	384	4	1		330	4	1
6	476	471	5	6		371	5	6
7	378	367	4	4		279	4	4
8	212	206	3	3		154	3	3
9	490	481	5	5		418	5	5
Out	3141	3072	36			2497	36	
1	346	337	4	7		286	4	7
2	332	329	4	8		277	4	8
3	360	353	4	2		269	4	2
4	155	144	3	9		113	3	9
5	392	384	4	1		330	4	1
6	476	471	5	6		371	5	6
7	378	367	4	4		279	4	4
8	212	206	3	3		154	3	3
9	490	481	5	5		418	5	5
In	3141	3072	36			2497	36	
Total	6282	6144	72			4994	72	
Rating	70.0	69.0				68.2		
Slope	109	107				110		

MADISON COUNTRY CLUB

9 Regulation Semi-Private

MN Highway 40, P.O. Box 154
Madison, Minnesota 56526
612/598-7587 Clubhouse/Proshop

HOURS	8 am to Dusk
SEASON	April-November

RESERVATIONS	No reservations accepted
	Walk-on: good/fair

GREEN FEES	M-F	S-S
Adult	$8/5	$10/7
Senior	$8/5	$10/7
Junior	$8/5	$10/7
Twilight	NA	NA

PAYMENT	No credit cards accepted
	Non-local checks accepted

LEAGUES	Men: Various
	Women: Various

MEMBERSHIPS	GCSAA, MGA

MANAGER	Donn Larson

FEATURES		
Putting green	Y	
Driving range	N	
Practice area	Y	
Golf carts		
Power (gas)	Y	$10
Pull carts	Y	$2/1
Club rental	Y	$4/2
Club storage	Y	
Caddies	N	
Proshop		
Extended	Y	
Refreshments		
Restaurant	N	
Lounge	Y	
Snacks	Y	
Clubhouse		
Showers	Y	
Lockers	Y	
Lodging	N	

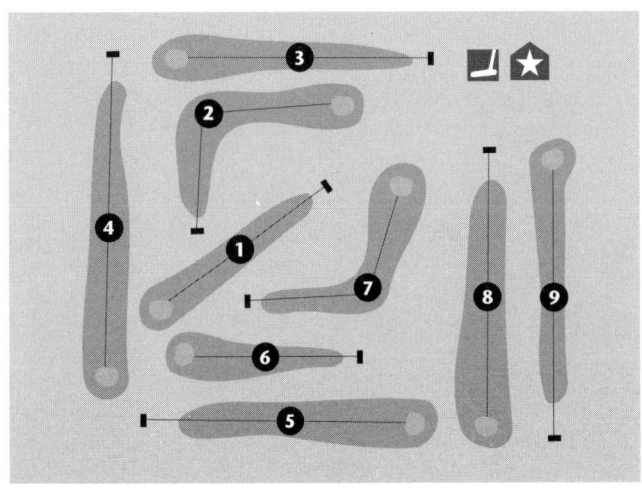

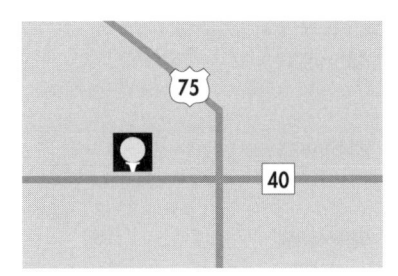

Located west of Madison. Course is 1/4 mile west of U.S. Highway 75 on MN Highway 40.

	MEN			**WOMEN**		
	FRONT	PAR	HDCP	FRONT	PAR	HDCP
1	340	4	4	340	4	4
2	353	4	1	353	4	1
3	317	4	6	317	4	6
4	368	4	2	368	4	2
5	284	4	9	284	4	9
6	150	3	5	150	3	5
7	344	4	3	344	4	3
8	317	4	7	317	4	7
9	329	4	8	329	4	8
Out	2802	35		2802	35	
1	340	4	4	340	4	4
2	353	4	1	353	4	1
3	317	4	6	317	4	6
4	368	4	2	368	4	2
5	284	4	9	284	4	9
6	150	3	5	150	3	5
7	344	4	3	344	4	3
8	317	4	7	317	4	7
9	329	4	8	329	4	8
In	2802	35		2802	35	
Total	5604	70		5604	70	
Rating	67.4			72.4		
Slope	119			119		

GOLF COURSE DIRECTORY

MAHNOMEN COUNTRY CLUB

9 Regulation Public

Route 2, P.O. Box 58
Mahnomen, Minnesota 56557
218/935-5188 Clubhouse/Proshop

HOURS	8 am to Dusk
SEASON	April to October

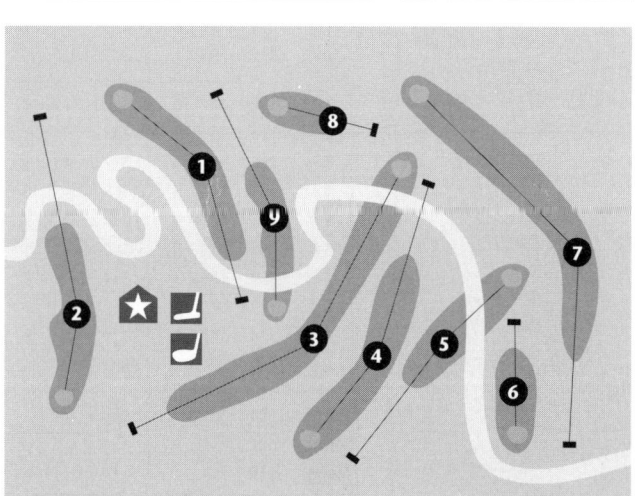

Located south of Mahnomen. Course is about one mile east of U.S. Highway 59 on County Road 125.

RESERVATIONS	218/935-5188 2 weeks	
	Walk-on: good/fair	
GREEN FEES	M-F	S-S
Adult	$12/8	$14/10
Senior	$12/8	$14/10
Junior	$12/8	$12/8
Twilight	$6 for 9-holes	NA
PAYMENT	No credit cards accepted	
	Non-local checks accepted	
LEAGUES	Men: Th (6 pm)	
	Women: T (3 pm)	
MEMBERSHIPS	USGA, MGA	
MANAGER	Gloria Tranka	
SUPERINTENDENT	Tom Wiebolt	

FEATURES		
Putting green	Y	
Driving range	Y	$3
Practice area	N	
Golf carts		
Power(gas)	Y	$14
Pull carts	Y	$1.50
Club rental	Y	$3.50
Club storage	N	
Caddies	N	
Proshop		
Basic	Y	
Refreshments		
Restaurant	N	
Lounge	N	
Snacks	Y	
Clubhouse		
Showers	N	
Lockers	N	
Lodging	N	

	MEN			**WOMEN**		
	FRONT	PAR	HDCP	FRONT	PAR	HDCP
1	319	4	13	248	4	11
2	327	4	1	228	4	13
3	489	5	5	408	5	3
4	359	4	9	280	4	9
5	318	4	15	318	4	5
6	204	3	11	132	3	17
7	504	5	3	445	5	1
8	174	3	17	174	3	15
9	285	4	7	285	4	7
Out	2979	36		2518	36	
1	319	4	14	248	4	12
2	327	4	2	228	4	14
3	489	5	6	408	5	4
4	359	4	10	280	4	10
5	318	4	16	318	4	6
6	204	3	12	132	3	18
7	504	5	4	445	5	2
8	174	3	18	174	3	16
9	285	4	8	285	4	8
In	2979	36		2518	36	
Total	5958	72		5036	72	
Rating	69.6			68.2		
Slope	125			121		

MAJESTIC OAKS GOLF CLUB — GOLD COURSE/18 Regulation Public

701 Bunker Lake Boulevard
Ham Lake, Minnesota 55304
612/755-2140 Clubhouse
612/755-2142 Proshop

HOURS	6 am to Dusk
SEASON	April-November

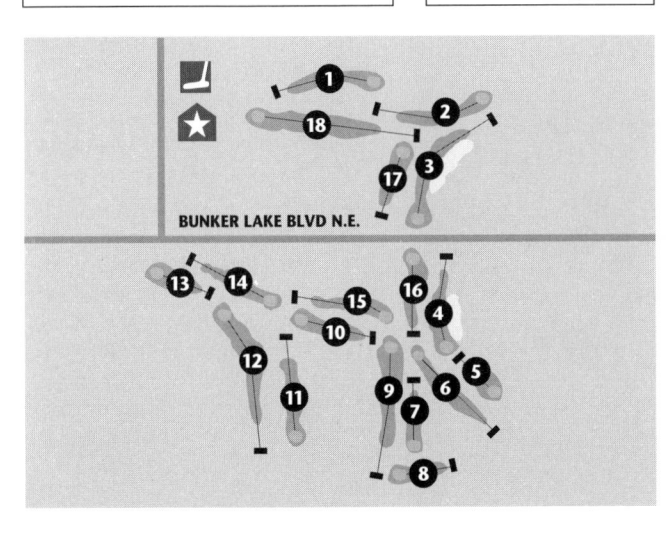

FEATURES

Putting green	Y	
Driving range	Y	$2.5-4
Practice area	Y	
Golf carts		
Power (gas)	Y	$20
Pull carts	Y	$3
Club rental	Y	$5-15
Club storage	Y	$20
Caddies	N	
Proshop		
Extended	Y	
Refreshments		
Restaurant	Y	
Lounge	Y	
Snacks	Y	
Clubhouse		
Showers	Y	
Lockers	Y	
Lodging	N	

RESERVATIONS	612/755-2142 4 days	
	Walk-on: good/fair	
GREEN FEES	M-F	S-S
Adult	$16/8	$20/10
Senior	$14/7	$14/7
Junior	$14/7	$14/7
Twilight	$9 (6 pm)	$9 (6 pm)
PAYMENT	Credit: Visa® MC® AmEx®	
	Non-local checks accepted	
LEAGUES	Various	
MEMBERSHIPS	USGA, NGF, PGA, LPGA, GCSAA, MGA	
OWNER	Lary Carlson	
MANAGER	Al Schecher	
SUPERINTENDENT	John Christenson	
PROFESSIONAL	Bill Folkes, Paul Oster	

Located in Ham Lake. Course entrance is 1/2 mile west of MN Highway 65 on Bunker Lake Blvd (County Road 116).

	MEN				WOMEN		
	BACK	FRONT	PAR	HDCP	FRONT	PAR	HDCP
1	376	351	4	9	283	4	5
2	433	404	4	1	321	4	1
3	489	463	5	3	395	5	9
4	310	285	4	15	266	4	13
5	157	140	3	17	117	3	17
6	336	299	4	11	259	4	11
7	379	342	4	5	289	4	3
8	176	150	3	13	119	3	15
9	509	472	5	7	406	5	7
Out	3165	2906	36		2455	36	
10	335	305	4	10	256	4	12
11	352	328	4	6	282	4	8
12	516	486	5	4	394	5	6
13	204	174	3	12	135	3	14
14	412	387	4	2	263	4	2
15	365	336	4	18	284	4	10
16	324	285	4	14	244	4	18
17	195	170	3	16	145	3	16
18	528	502	5	8	390	5	4
In	3231	2973	36		2393	36	
Total	6396	5879	72		4848	72	
Rating	71.2	68.8			68.4		
Slope	123	118			120		

MAJESTIC OAKS GOLF CLUB

PLATINUM COURSE/18 Regulation Public

701 Bunker Lake Boulevard
Ham Lake, Minnesota 55304
612/755-2140 Clubhouse
612/755-2142 Proshop

HOURS	6 am to Dusk
SEASON	April-November

FEATURES		
Putting green	Y	
Driving range	Y	$2.5-4
Practice area	Y	
Golf carts		
Power (gas)	Y	$20
Pull carts	Y	$3
Club rental	Y	$5-15
Club storage	Y	$20
Caddies	N	
Proshop		
Extended	Y	
Refreshments		
Restaurant	Y	
Lounge	Y	
Snacks	Y	
Clubhouse		
Showers	Y	
Lockers	Y	
Lodging	N	

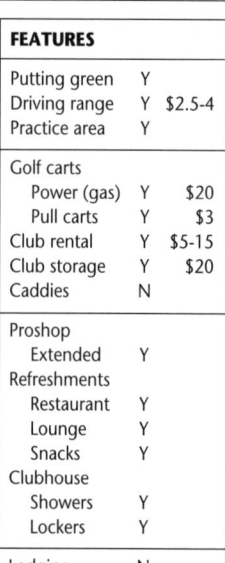

Located in Ham Lake. Course entrance is 1/2 mile west of MN Highway 65 on Bunker Lake Blvd (County Road 116).

RESERVATIONS	612/755-2142 4 days	
	Walk-on: good/fair	
GREEN FEES	M-F	S-S
Adult	$18/10	$22/12
Senior	$14/7	$14/7
Junior	$14/7	$14/7
Twilight	$9 (6 pm)	$9 (6 pm)
PAYMENT	Credit: Visa® MC® AmEx®	
	Non-local checks accepted	
LEAGUES	Various	
MEMBERSHIPS	USGA, NGF, PGA, LPGA,	
	GCSAA, MGA	
OWNER	Lary Carlson	
MANAGER	Al Schecher	
SUPERINTENDENT	John Christenson	
PROFESSIONAL	Bill Folkes, Paul Oster	

	MEN				WOMEN		
	BACK	FRONT	PAR	HDCP	FRONT	PAR	HDCP
1	540	506	5	7	430	5	3
2	375	353	4	15	302	4	11
3	415	395	4	9	315	4	9
4	220	175	3	11	130	3	15
5	396	376	4	13	310	4	5
6	545	537	5	1	480	5	1
7	422	389	4	3	300	4	7
8	150	139	3	17	95	3	17
9	420	401	4	5	278	4	13
Out	3483	3271	36		2640	36	
10	415	389	4	2	325	4	8
11	427	400	4	14	325	4	10
12	200	174	3	18	142	3	16
13	509	475	5	6	402	5	4
14	412	390	4	10	284	4	12
15	188	164	3	16	132	3	18
16	550	525	5	4	425	5	2
17	400	377	4	12	256	4	14
18	429	396	4	8	337	4	6
In	3530	3290	36		2628	36	
Total	7013	6561	72		5268	72	
Rating	73.9	71.4			71.6		
Slope	129	125			126		

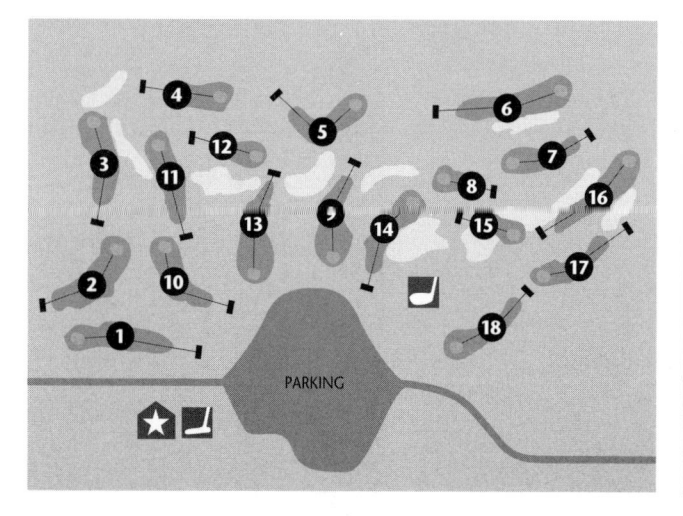

MAJESTIC OAKS GOLF CLUB

9 Executive Public

701 Bunker Lake Boulevard
Ham Lake, Minnesota 55304
612/755-2140 Clubhouse
612/755-2142 Proshop

HOURS	6 am to Dusk
SEASON	April-November

FEATURES

Putting green	Y	
Driving range	Y	$2.5-4
Practice area	Y	
Golf carts		
Power (gas)	Y	$20
Pull carts	Y	$3
Club rental	Y	$5-15
Club storage	Y	$20
Caddies	N	
Proshop		
Extended	Y	
Refreshments		
Restaurant	Y	
Lounge	Y	
Snacks	Y	
Clubhouse		
Showers	Y	
Lockers	Y	
Lodging	N	

BUNKER LAKE BLVD N.E. 65

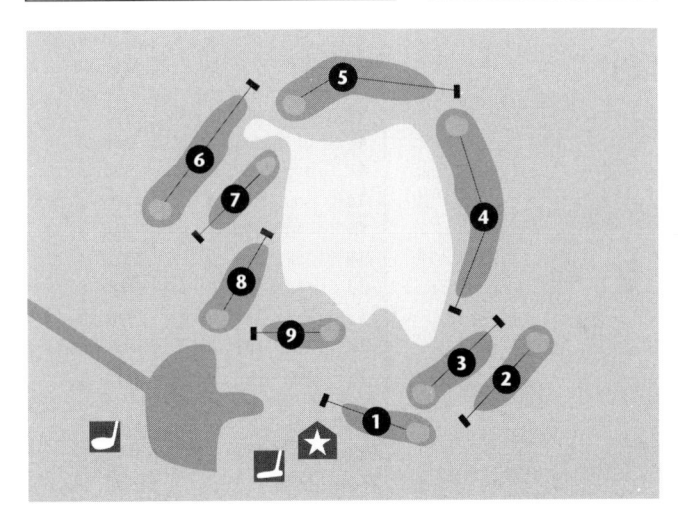

Located in Ham Lake. Course entrance is 1/2 mile west of MN Highway 65 on Bunker Lake Blvd (County Road 116).

RESERVATIONS	612/755-2142 4 days
	Walk-on: good/fair

GREEN FEES	M-F	S-S
Adult	Call	Call
Senior	Call	Call
Junior	Call	Call
Twilight	NA	NA

PAYMENT	Credit: Visa® MC® AmEx®
	Non-local checks accepted

LEAGUES	Various
MEMBERSHIPS	USGA, NGF, PGA, LPGA, GCSAA, MGA
OWNER	Lary Carlson
MANAGER	Al Schecher
SUPERINTENDENT	John Christenson
PROFESSIONAL	Bill Folkes, Paul Oster

	MEN			WOMEN		
	FRONT	PAR	HDCP	FRONT	PAR	HDCP
1	180	3	4	175	3	4
2	190	3	2	185	3	2
3	170	3	5	165	3	5
4	325	4	3	320	4	1
5	305	4	8	300	4	3
6	235	3	1	225	4	8
7	160	3	6	155	3	6
8	140	3	7	135	3	7
9	90	3	9	90	3	9
Out	1795	29		1750	30	
1	180	3	4	175	3	4
2	190	3	2	185	3	2
3	170	3	5	165	3	5
4	325	4	3	320	4	1
5	305	4	8	300	4	3
6	235	3	1	225	4	8
7	160	3	6	155	3	6
8	140	3	7	135	3	7
9	90	3	9	90	3	9
In	1795	29		1750	30	
Total	3590	58		3500	60	
Rating	56.2			59.0		
Slope	73			81		

MANITOU RIDGE GOLF COURSE

18 Regulation Public

3200 North McKnight Road
White Bear Lake, Minnesota 55110
612/777-2987 Clubhouse/Proshop

HOURS	Dawn to Dusk
SEASON	Mar-November

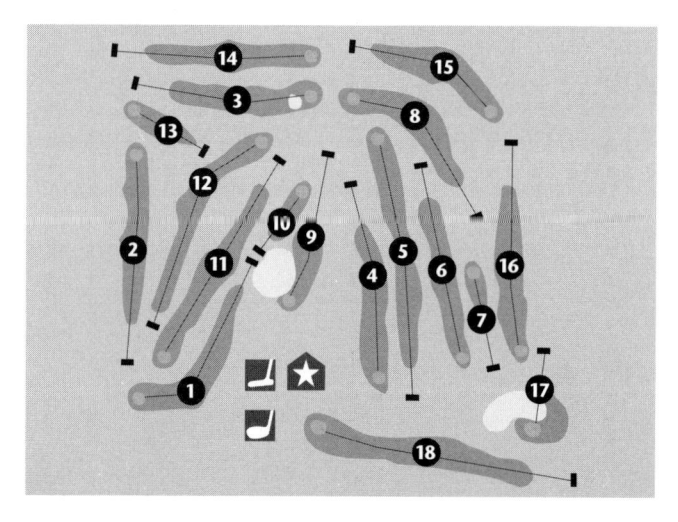

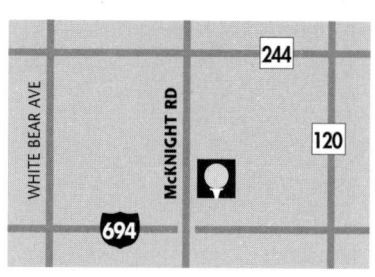

Located in White Bear Lake. Course entrance is south of MN Highway 244 on McKnight Road.

RESERVATIONS	612/777-2987 4 days
	Walk-on: good/good

GREEN FEES	M-F	S-S
Adult	$18	$18
Senior	$10	$10
Junior	$9	$9
Twilight	$12.50	$12.50

PAYMENT	Credit: Visa® MasterCard®
	Non-local checks accepted

LEAGUES	Men: M-Th (pm)
	Women: M-Th

MEMBERSHIPS	USGA, PGA, GCSAA, MGA

OWNER	Ramsey County
MANAGER	Greg Hubbard
SUPERINTENDENT	Greg Hubbard
PROFESSIONAL	Mark Foley

FEATURES		
Putting green	Y	
Driving range	Y	$2.25
Practice area	N	
Golf carts		
Power (gas)	Y	$20
Pull carts	Y	$2
Club rental	Y	
Club storage	N	
Caddies	N	
Proshop		
Extended	Y	
Refreshments		
Restaurant	N	
Lounge	Y	
Snacks	Y	
Clubhouse		
Showers	N	
Lockers	N	
Lodging	N	

	MEN				**WOMEN**		
	BACK	FRONT	PAR	HDCP	FRONT	PAR	HDCP
1	325	312	4	10	307	4	10
2	397	380	4	4	365	4	4
3	368	353	4	2	338	4	2
4	382	357	4	6	333	4	6
5	503	472	5	16	445	5	8
6	420	405	4	8	389	4	12
7	158	143	3	18	125	3	18
8	361	335	4	14	310	4	14
9	302	280	4	12	255	4	16
Out	3216	3037	36		2867	36	
10	211	204	3	9	105	3	17
11	425	404	4	1	385	4	5
12	389	382	4	17	375	4	7
13	189	174	3	13	166	3	15
14	368	358	4	5	339	4	1
15	368	358	4	15	338	4	9
16	529	504	5	3	420	5	3
17	189	157	3	7	141	3	13
18	538	500	5	11	406	5	11
In	3206	3041	35		2675	35	
Total	6422	6078	71		5542	71	
Rating	70.7	69.3			71.9		
Slope	120	117			120		

THE MINNESOTA ILLUSTRATED

MAPLE HILLS GOLF CENTER

9 Par-3 Public

905 Parkway Drive
St. Paul, Minnesota 55106
612/776-2226 Clubhouse/Proshop

HOURS	7 am to Dusk
SEASON	May to October

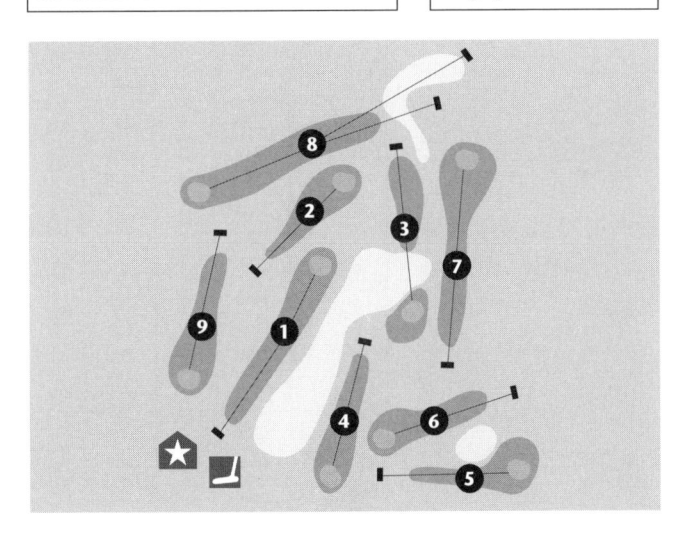

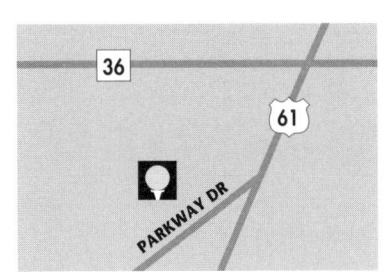

Located in St. Paul. Course is one mile south of MN Hwy 36 on U.S. Hwy 61, then one block west on Parkway Drive.

RESERVATIONS	No reservations accepted
	Walk-on: good/good

GREEN FEES	M-F	S-S
Adult	$6.75	$7.25
Senior	$5.25	$7.25
Junior	$5.25	$7.25
Twilight	NA	NA

PAYMENT	No credit cards accepted
	Local checks only

LEAGUES	Various

MEMBERSHIPS	GCSAA

OWNER	Robert Mogren
MANAGER	Darlene Mogren
SUPERINTENDENT	Arthur Cosello

FEATURES	
Putting green	Y
Driving range	N
Practice area	N
Golf carts	
Power	Y $10
Pull carts	Y $1.50
Club rental	Y $2.25
Club storage	N
Caddies	N
Proshop	
Basic	Y
Refreshments	
Restaurant	N
Lounge	N
Snacks	Y
Clubhouse	
Showers	N
Lockers	N
Lodging	N

	MEN			**WOMEN**		
	FRONT	PAR	HDCP	FRONT	PAR	HDCP
1	167	3	3	142	3	3
2	102	3	6	102	3	6
3	126	3	1	126	3	1
4	108	3	9	108	3	9
5	110	3	8	110	3	8
6	105	3	5	105	3	5
7	150	3	2	150	3	2
8	220	3	4	179	3	4
9	113	3	7	113	3	7
Out	1191	27		1125	27	
1	167	3	3	142	3	3
2	102	3	6	102	3	6
3	126	3	1	126	3	1
4	108	3	9	108	3	9
5	110	3	8	110	3	8
6	105	3	5	105	3	5
7	150	3	2	150	3	2
8	220	3	4	179	3	4
9	113	3	7	113	3	7
In	1191	27		1125	27	
Total	2382	54		2250	54	
Rating	NA			NA		
Slope	NA			NA		

GOLF COURSE DIRECTORY

MAPLE HILLS GOLF CLUB
9 Regulation Public

Route 4, P.O. Box 433
Frazee, Minnesota 56544
218/847-9532 Clubhouse/Proshop

HOURS	7 am to Dusk
SEASON	April to October

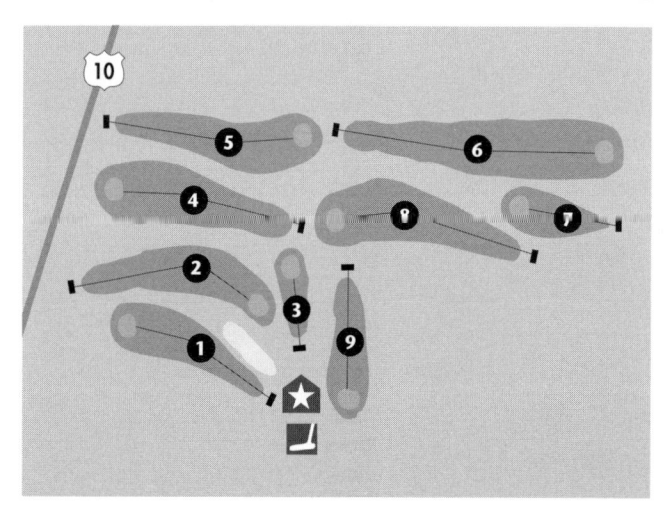

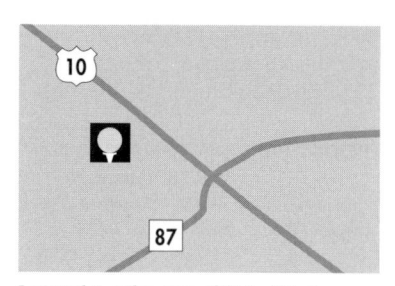

Located 4 miles east of Detroit Lakes. Course entrance is west of MN Highway 87 on U.S. Highway 10.

RESERVATIONS	218/847-9532 1 day
	Walk-on: good/fair

GREEN FEES	M-F	S-S
Adult	$15/10	$15/10
Senior	$15/10	$15/10
Junior	$15/10	$15/10
Twilight	$10	$10

PAYMENT	No credit cards accepted
	Non-local checks accepted

LEAGUES	Men: W (3-6 pm)
	Women: Th (5-6 pm)

MEMBERSHIPS	GCSAA, MGA

OWNER	Les & Pat Kertscher
SUPERINTENDENT	Ron Kertscher, Russ Kertscher

FEATURES	
Putting green	Y
Driving range	N
Practice area	N
Golf carts	
Power (gas)	Y $15/10
Pull carts	Y $2
Club rental	Y $3
Club storage	Y $10
Caddies	N
Proshop	
Extended	Y
Refreshments	
Restaurant	N
Lounge	N
Snacks	Y
Clubhouse	
Showers	N
Lockers	N
Lodging	N

	MEN				**WOMEN**		
	BACK	FRONT	PAR	HDCP	FRONT	PAR	HDCP
1	325	310	4	6	255	4	6
2	367	340	4	2	300	4	2
3	154	154	3	8	142	3	8
4	340	320	4	5	245	4	5
5	376	365	4	3	300	4	3
6	498	424	5	1	304	4	1
7	169	158	3	9	128	3	9
8	486	465	5	4	377	5	4
9	308	288	4	7	282	4	7
Out	3023	2824	36		2333	35	
1	325	310	4	6	255	4	6
2	367	340	4	2	300	4	2
3	154	154	3	8	142	3	8
4	340	320	4	5	245	4	5
5	376	365	4	3	300	4	3
6	498	424	5	1	304	4	1
7	169	158	3	9	128	3	9
8	486	465	5	4	377	5	4
9	308	288	4	7	282	4	7
In	3023	2824	36		2333	35	
Total	6046	5648	72		4666	70	
Rating	68.6	66.8			66.2		
Slope	112	108			111		

THE MINNESOTA ILLUSTRATED

MAPLE VALLEY GOLF & COUNTRY CLUB

18 Regulation Semi-Private

8600 Maple Valley Road Southeast
Rochester, Minnesota 55904
507/285-9100 Clubhouse/Proshop

RESERVATIONS	507/285-9100 5 days	
	Walk-on: fair/poor	
GREEN FEES	M-F	S-S
Adult	$17/10.50	$17/10.50
Senior	$17/10.50	$17/10.50
Junior	$17/10.50	$17/10.50
Twilight	NA	NA
PAYMENT	Credit: Visa® MasterCard®	
	Non-local checks accepted	
LEAGUES	Men: Th	
	Women: T	
MEMBERSHIPS	USGA, NGF, PGA, MGA	
OWNER	Wayne & Suzanne Idso	
MANAGER	Suzanne Idso	
SUPERINTENDENT	Eric Idso	
PROFESSIONAL	Jeff Gorman	

HOURS	6 am to Dusk	
SEASON	Mar–November	
FEATURES		
Putting green	Y	
Driving range	N	
Practice area	N	
Golf carts		
Power	Y	$17
Pull carts	Y	$1.75
Club rental	Y	$5
Club storage	N	
Caddies	N	
Proshop		
Extended	Y	
Refreshments		
Restaurant	Y	
Lounge	Y	
Snacks	Y	
Clubhouse		
Showers	N	
Lockers	N	
Lodging	N	

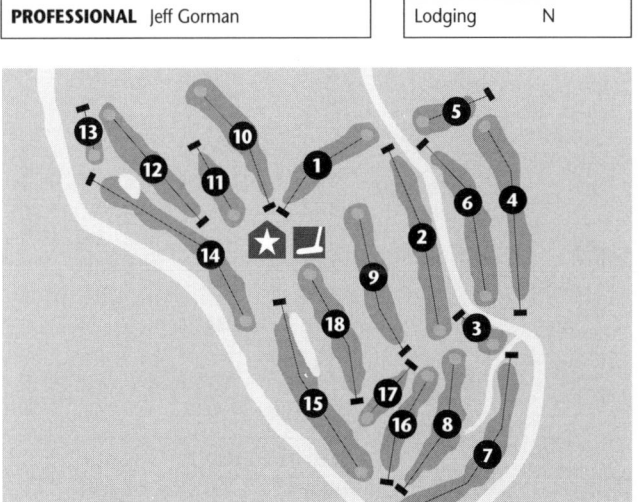

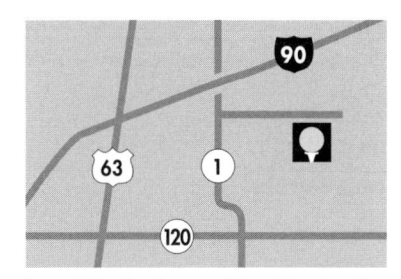

Located in Rochester. Course is east of U.S. Hwy 63 on Cty Rd 120, north on Cty Rd 1, then east on Maple Valley Rd.

	MEN				WOMEN		
	BACK	FRONT	PAR	HDCP	FRONT	PAR	HDCP
1	325	320	4	15	290	4	13
2	430	395	4	3	335	4	5
3	155	145	3	11	115	3	15
4	535	515	5	1	450	5	1
5	135	125	3	17	110	3	17
6	430	380	4	5	320	4	11
7	500	480	5	7	415	5	3
8	400	380	4	9	330	4	7
9	360	340	4	13	330	4	9
Out	3270	3100	36		2695	36	
10	380	370	4	4	345	4	4
11	190	175	3	10	160	3	12
12	375	365	4	12	340	4	8
13	165	150	3	18	145	3	16
14	525	520	5	2	490	5	2
15	500	490	5	6	400	5	6
16	325	320	4	14	290	4	14
17	155	145	3	16	125	3	18
18	385	375	4	8	340	4	10
In	3000	2910	35		2635	35	
Total	6270	5990	71		5330	71	
Rating	70.5	69.1			71.1		
Slope	121	118			120		

GOLF COURSE DIRECTORY

MARSHALL GOLF CLUB   18 Regulation Semi-Private

800 Country Club Dr., P.O. Box 502
Marshall, Minnesota 56258
507/532-2278 Clubhouse
507/537-1622 Proshop

RESERVATIONS	507/537-1622 1 week	
	Walk-on: fair/fair	
GREEN FEES	M-F	S-S
Adult	$22/13	$26/15
Senior	$22/13	$26/15
Junior	$22/13	$26/15
Twilight	NA	NA
PAYMENT	No credit cards accepted	
	Non-local checks accepted	
LEAGUES	Men: Th	
	Women: T	
MEMBERSHIPS	USGA, PGA, GCSAA, MGA	
MANAGER	Phyllis Taveirne	
SUPERINTENDENT	Drew Demorest	
PROFESSIONAL	Allen Lucht	

HOURS	7 am to Dusk
SEASON	April-November

FEATURES		
Putting green	Y	
Driving range	Y	
Practice area	Y	
Golf carts		
Power (gas)	Y	$22/15
Pull carts	Y	$2.50
Club rental	Y	$10
Club storage	Y	$50/yr
Caddies	N	
Proshop		
Extended	Y	
Refreshments		
Restaurant	Y	
Lounge	Y	
Snacks	Y	
Clubhouse		
Showers	Y	
Lockers	Y	
Lodging	N	

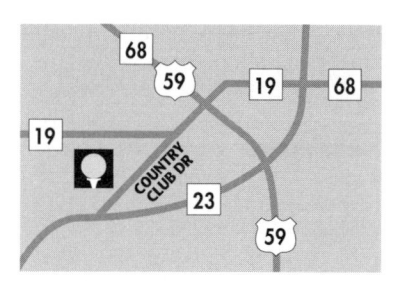

Located in Marshall. Course entrance is about 1/2 mile south of MN Highway 19 on Country Club Drive.

	MEN				WOMEN		
	BACK	FRONT	PAR	HDCP	FRONT	PAR	HDCP
1	552	513	5	5	430	5	9
2	515	479	5	7	421	5	7
3	303	288	4	13	254	4	11
4	168	158	3	11	124	3	13
5	370	355	4	3	285	4	5
6	203	178	3	15	149	3	17
7	544	523	5	1	416	5	3
8	418	403	4	9	332	4	1
9	170	163	3	17	150	3	15
Out	3243	3060	36		2561	36	
10	200	182	3	16	152	3	16
11	426	390	4	12	326	4	8
12	400	392	4	4	300	4	10
13	380	350	4	10	263	4	4
14	465	456	5	8	381	5	14
15	363	354	4	6	310	4	6
16	168	160	3	18	141	3	18
17	384	365	4	14	294	4	12
18	536	513	5	2	408	5	2
In	3322	3162	36		2575	36	
Total	6565	6222	72		5136	72	
Rating	71.6	70.0			69.5		
Slope	123	120			120		

MAYFLOWER COUNTRY CLUB

9 Regulation Public

RR 1, Box 131H
Fairfax, Minnesota 55332
507/426-9964 Clubhouse/Proshop

RESERVATIONS	507/426-9964 2 days	
	Walk-on: good/poor	
GREEN FEES	M-F	S-S
Adult	$8	$12
Senior	$8	$12
Junior	$8	$12
Twilight	NA	NA
PAYMENT	No credit cards accepted	
	Non-local checks accepted	
LEAGUES	Men: Th	
	Women: W	
MEMBERSHIPS	MGA	
MANAGER	Donald Beilke	
SUPERINTENDENT	Orville Blackwell	

HOURS	8 am to Dusk	
SEASON	April to October	
FEATURES		
Putting green	Y	
Driving range	Y	
Practice area	N	
Golf carts		
Power (gas)	Y	$9
Pull carts	Y	$1
Club rental	Y	$4
Club storage	Y	$8/yr
Caddies	N	
Proshop		
Extended	Y	
Refreshments		
Restaurant	N	
Lounge	N	
Snacks	Y	
Clubhouse		
Showers	Y	
Lockers	Y	
Lodging	N	

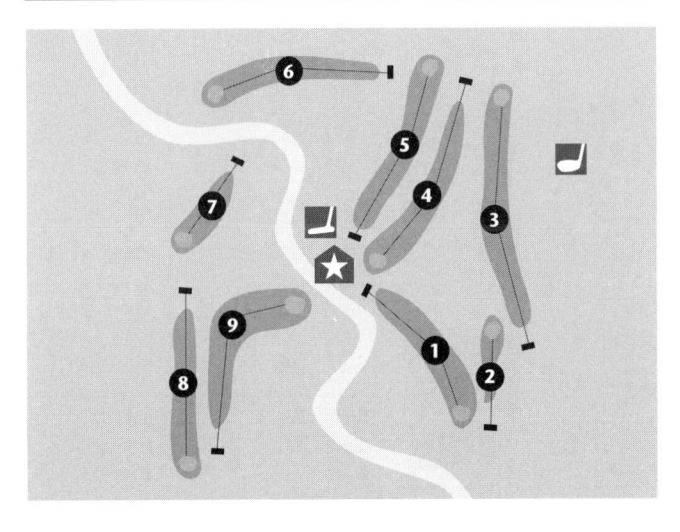

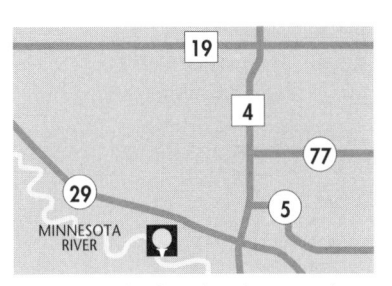

Located south of Fairfax. Course is about three miles south of MN Hwy 19 on MN Hwy 4, then 1 mile west on Cty Rd 29.

	MEN			**WOMEN**		
	FRONT	PAR	HDCP	FRONT	PAR	HDCP
1	331	4	6	244	4	6
2	170	3	8	155	3	8
3	501	5	3	445	5	3
4	400	4	5	308	4	5
5	382	4	4	283	4	4
6	392	4	1	311	4	1
7	167	3	9	155	3	9
8	354	4	7	345	4	7
9	365	4	2	353	5	2
Out	3062	35		2599	36	
1	331	4	6	244	4	6
2	170	3	8	155	3	8
3	501	5	3	445	5	3
4	400	4	5	308	4	5
5	382	4	4	283	4	4
6	392	4	1	311	4	1
7	167	3	9	155	3	9
8	354	4	7	345	4	7
9	365	4	2	353	5	2
In	3062	35		2599	36	
Total	6124	70		5198	72	
Rating	68.4			68.6		
Slope	107			104		

MEADOW GREENS GOLF COURSE

9 Executive Public

Route 1, Box 157
Austin, Minnesota 55912
507/433-4878 Clubhouse/Proshop

| **HOURS** | Dawn to Dusk |
| **SEASON** | April-November |

RESERVATIONS	507/433-4878	
	Walk-on: good/fair	
GREEN FEES	M-F	S-S
Adult	Call	Call
Senior	Call	Call
Junior	Call	Call
Twilight	NA	NA
PAYMENT	No credit cards accepted	
	Non local checks accepted	
LEAGUES	Men: Various	
	Women: Various	
MEMBERSHIPS	MGA	
OWNER	Larry, Barb & Mike Grinstead	

FEATURES	
Putting green	Y
Driving range	N
Practice area	N
Golf carts	
Power	Y
Pull carts	Y
Club rental	Y
Club storage	N
Caddies	N
Proshop	
Basic	Y
Refreshments	
Restaurant	N
Lounge	N
Snacks	Y
Clubhouse	
Showers	N
Lockers	N
Lodging	N

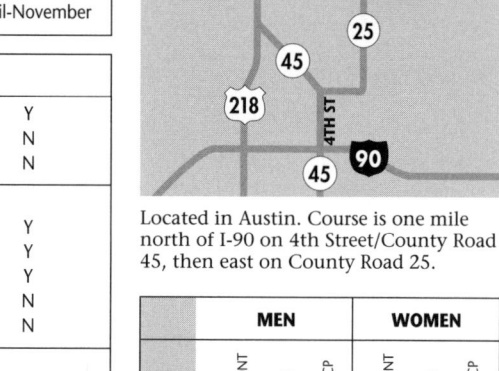

Located in Austin. Course is one mile north of I-90 on 4th Street/County Road 45, then east on County Road 25.

	MEN			**WOMEN**		
	FRONT	PAR	HDCP	FRONT	PAR	HDCP
1	132	3		121	3	
2	255	4		250	4	
3	261	4		256	4	
4	450	5		382	5	
5	87	3		82	3	
6	250	4		218	4	
7	152	3		147	3	
8	133	3		114	3	
9	277	4		272	4	
Out	1997	33		1842	33	
1	132	3		121	3	
2	255	4		250	4	
3	261	4		256	4	
4	450	5		382	5	
5	87	3		82	3	
6	250	4		218	4	
7	152	3		147	3	
8	133	3		114	3	
9	277	4		272	4	
In	1997	33		1842	33	
Total	3994	66		3684	66	
Rating	59.6			61.2		
Slope	90			100		

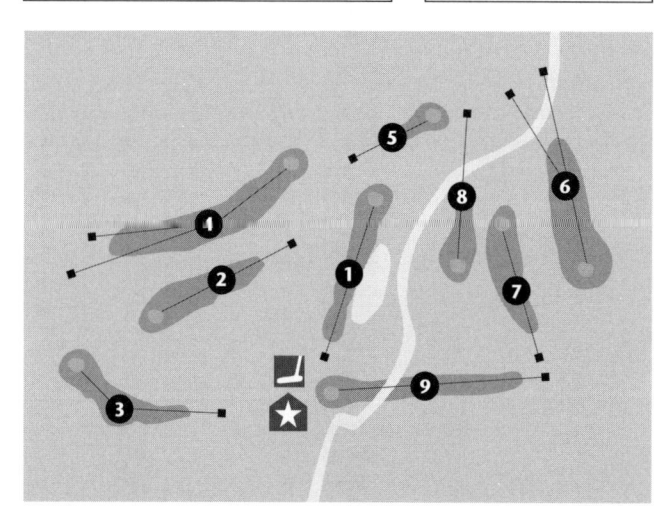

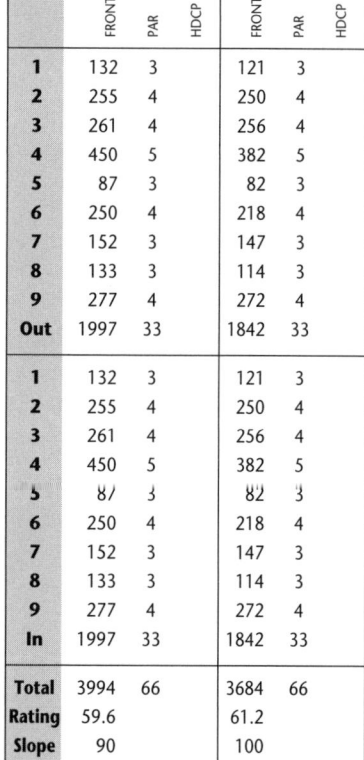

MEADOWBROOK COUNTRY CLUB

9 Regulation Public

Route 2, Highway 44
Mabel, Minnesota 55954
507/493-5708 Clubhouse/Proshop

HOURS	7 am to Dusk
SEASON	April to October

RESERVATIONS	507/493-5708
	Walk-on: good/good

GREEN FEES	M-F	S-S
Adult	$13/8	$13/8
Senior	$13/8	$13/8
Junior	$13/8	$13/8
Twilight	NA	NA

PAYMENT	No credit cards accepted
	Non-local checks accepted

LEAGUES	Men: Th
	Women: T

MEMBERSHIPS	MGA

MANAGER	James Gunderson
SUPERINTENDENT	James Gunderson

FEATURES		
Putting green	Y	
Driving range	N	
Practice area	N	
Golf carts		
Power	Y	$7
Pull carts	Y	$1
Club rental	Y	$2
Club storage	Y	
Caddies	N	
Proshop		
Basic	Y	
Refreshments		
Restaurant	N	
Lounge	Y	
Snacks	Y	
Clubhouse		
Showers	N	
Lockers	N	
Lodging	N	

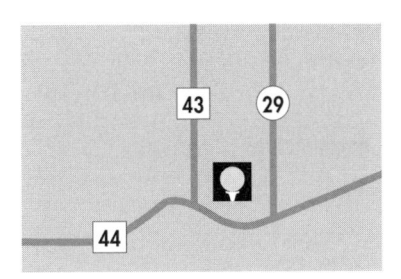

Located north of Mabel. Course entrance is just east of MN Highway 43 on MN Highway 44.

	MEN			**WOMEN**		
	FRONT	PAR	HDCP	FRONT	PAR	HDCP
1	213	4	17	207	4	17
2	304	4	7	300	4	7
3	102	3	3	90	3	3
4	266	4	11	258	4	11
5	485	5	13	415	5	13
6	489	5	5	419	5	5
7	268	4	15	159	3	15
8	175	3	1	134	3	1
9	254	4	9	250	4	9
Out	2556	36		2232	35	
1	213	4	18	207	4	18
2	304	4	8	300	4	8
3	102	3	4	90	3	4
4	266	4	12	258	4	12
5	485	5	14	415	5	14
6	489	5	6	419	5	6
7	268	4	16	159	3	16
8	175	3	2	134	3	2
9	254	4	10	250	4	10
In	2556	36		2232	35	
Total	5112	72		4464	70	
Rating	65.6			66.0		
Slope	104			105		

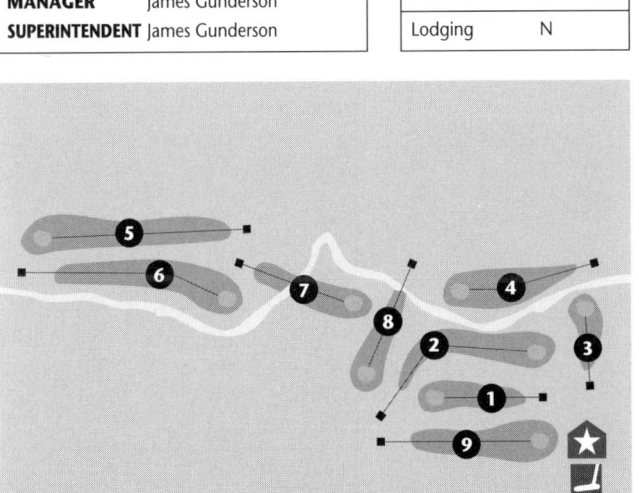

GOLF COURSE DIRECTORY

MEADOWBROOK GOLF CLUB

18 Regulation Public

201 Meadowbrook Road
Hopkins, Minnesota 55343
612/929-2077 Clubhouse/Proshop

HOURS	Dawn to Dusk
SEASON	April–November

RESERVATIONS	612/929-2077 3 days
	$2 fee for weekends
	Walk-on: fair/poor

GREEN FEES	M-F	S-S
Adult	$18/13	$18/13
Senior	$18/13	$18/13
Junior	$18/13	$18/13
Twilight	NA	NA

| **PAYMENT** | No credit cards accepted |
| | Local checks only |

| **LEAGUES** | Men: Various |
| | Women: Various |

| **MEMBERSHIPS** | USGA, PGA, GCSAA, MGA |

| **PROFESSIONAL** | Wayne Wojack |

FEATURES	
Putting green	Y
Driving range	N
Practice area	Y
Golf carts	
Power (gas)	Y $20/12
Pull carts	Y $2.50
Club rental	Y $6/3
Club storage	N
Caddies	N
Proshop	
Basic	Y
Refreshments	
Restaurant	Y
Lounge	N
Snacks	Y
Clubhouse	
Showers	Y
Lockers	Y
Lodging	N

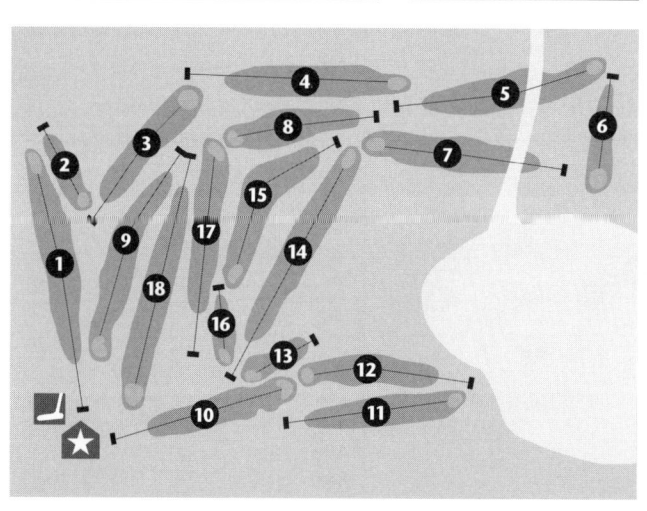

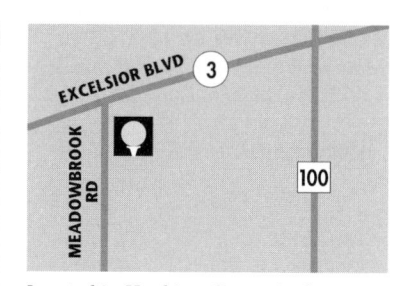

Located in Hopkins. Course is about one mile west of MN Hwy 100 on Excelsior Blvd, then south on Meadowbrook Rd.

	MEN				**WOMEN**		
	BACK	FRONT	PAR	HDCP	FRONT	PAR	HDCP
1	518	508	5	7	491	5	1
2	168	158	3	17	119	3	17
3	328	313	4	13	305	4	11
4	466	454	5	9	408	5	3
5	452	410	4	1	401	5	5
6	185	175	3	15	165	3	15
7	405	390	4	5	307	4	9
8	365	331	4	11	321	4	13
9	460	450	4	3	354	4	7
Out	3347	3189	36		2871	37	
10	400	367	4	6	322	4	10
11	370	362	4	12	321	4	8
12	350	340	4	14	324	4	12
13	127	121	3	18	117	3	18
14	497	491	5	10	431	5	4
15	407	390	4	2	340	4	6
16	135	115	3	16	108	3	16
17	417	407	4	4	321	4	14
18	543	533	5	8	455	5	2
In	3246	3126	36		2739	36	
Total	6593	6315	72		5610	73	
Rating	69.9	68.7			71.1		
Slope	113	111			114		

MEADOWLARK COUNTRY CLUB

9 Regulation Public

837 Country Club Drive, Box 68
Melrose, Minnesota 56352
612/256-4989 Clubhouse/Proshop

HOURS	7 am to Dusk	
SEASON	April-November	

RESERVATIONS	612/256-4989 1 day	
	Walk-on: good/fair	
GREEN FEES	M-F	S-S
Adult	$13/10	$15.50/12.50
Senior	$13/10	$15.50/12.50
Junior	$12/9	$14.50/11.50
Twilight	NA	NA
	Group discount available	
PAYMENT	No credit cards accepted	
	Non-local checks accepted	
LEAGUES	Men: W	
	Women: T	
MEMBERSHIPS	MGA	
MANAGER	Dave Anderson	
SUPERINTENDENT	Tom Spaeth	

FEATURES		
Putting green	Y	
Driving range	Y	
Practice area	Y	
Golf carts		
Power	Y	$15/10
Pull carts	Y	$2
Club rental	Y	$4
Club storage	Y	$25/yr
Caddies	N	
Proshop		
Extended	Y	
Refreshments		
Restaurant	N	
Lounge	N	
Snacks	Y	
Clubhouse		
Showers	N	
Lockers	N	
Lodging	N	

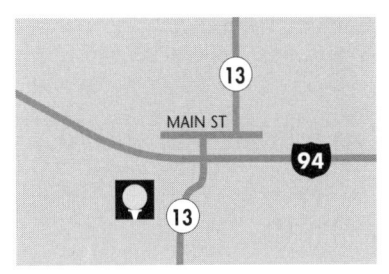

Located just south of Melrose. Course entrance is about 1/2 mile south of I-94 on County Road 13

	MEN				**WOMEN**		
	BACK	FRONT	PAR	HDCP	FRONT	PAR	HDCP
1	398	390	4	1	380	4	1
2	520	513	5	15	405	5	9
3	370	367	4	11	362	4	3
4	180	176	3	9	167	3	15
5	355	351	4	5	286	4	11
6	332	322	4	7	315	4	7
7	162	154	3	17	149	3	17
8	480	473	5	13	410	5	5
9	410	402	4	3	400	5	13
Out	3207	3148	36		2874	37	
1	398	390	4	2	380	4	2
2	520	513	5	16	405	5	10
3	370	367	4	12	362	4	4
4	180	176	3	10	167	3	16
5	355	351	4	6	286	4	12
6	332	322	4	8	315	4	8
7	162	154	3	18	149	3	18
8	480	473	5	14	410	5	6
9	410	402	4	4	400	5	14
In	3207	3148	36		2874	37	
Total	6414	6296	72		5748	74	
Rating	NA	69.4			72.4		
Slope	NA	114			118		

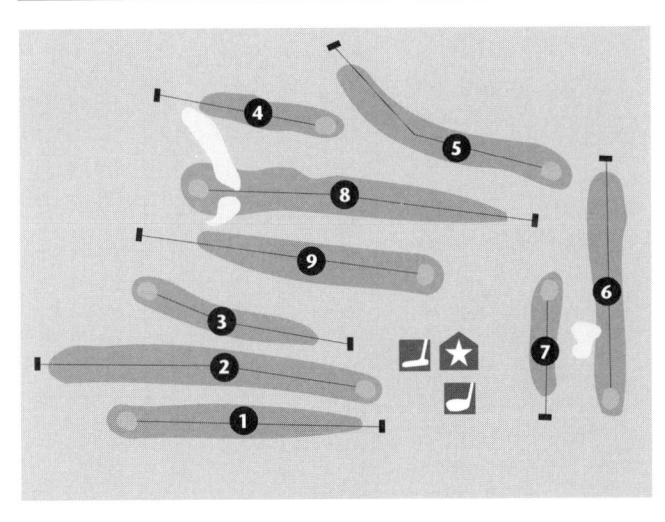

GOLF COURSE DIRECTORY

MEADOWS GOLF COURSE

18 Regulation Public

401 34th Street South
Moorhead, Minnesota 56560
218/299-5244 Clubhouse/Proshop

RESERVATIONS	218/299-5244 1 day	
	Walk-on: good/fair	
GREEN FEES	M-F	S-S
Adult	$15/8	$17/10
Senior	$12/7	$12/8
Junior	$12/7	$12/8
Twilight	NA	NA
	Punch cards available	
PAYMENT	Credit: Visa® MasterCard®	
	Non-local checks accepted	
LEAGUES	Men: W (pm)	
	Women: T (pm)	
MEMBERSHIPS	USGA, PGA, GCSAA, MGA	
SUPERINTENDENT	Todd Grimm	
PROFESSIONAL	Bill Iverson	

HOURS	7 am to Dusk	
SEASON	April to October	
FEATURES		
Putting green	Y	
Driving range	Y	$3
Practice area	Y	
Golf carts		
Power (gas)	Y	$18/10
Pull carts	Y	$2
Club rental	Y	$5
Club storage	N	
Caddies	N	
Proshop		
Extended	Y	
Refreshments		
Restaurant	Y	
Lounge	Y	
Snacks	Y	
Clubhouse		
Showers	N	
Lockers	N	
Lodging	N	

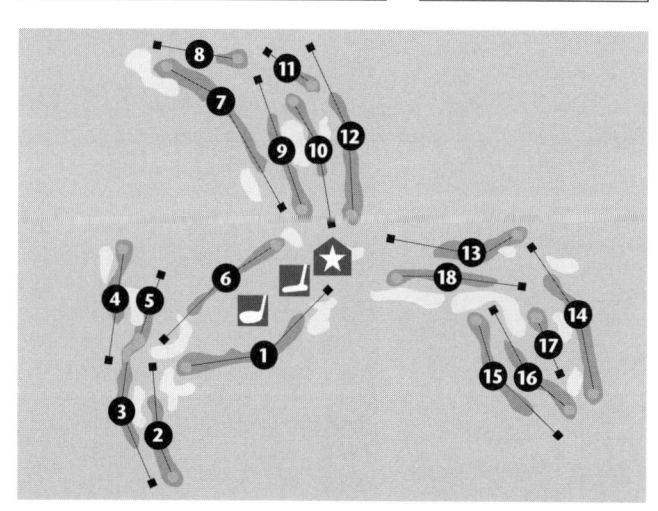

Located in Moorhead. Course entrance is north of I-94 on Highway 231, east on 12th Avenue, then north on 34th Street.

	MEN				WOMEN		
	BACK	FRONT	PAR	HDCP	FRONT	PAR	HDCP
1	514	504	5	4	406	5	4
2	368	338	4	16	257	4	16
3	417	392	4	7	307	4	7
4	332	303	4	13	228	4	13
5	205	196	3	14	147	3	14
6	440	422	4	2	344	4	2
7	563	538	5	8	448	5	8
8	201	187	3	11	132	3	11
9	437	400	4	5	332	4	5
Out	3477	3280	36		2601	36	
10	386	361	4	12	277	4	12
11	136	125	3	17	84	3	17
12	512	496	5	15	415	5	15
13	385	370	4	10	292	4	10
14	513	496	5	6	414	5	6
15	454	426	4	1	351	4	1
16	408	384	4	9	293	4	9
17	184	163	3	18	116	3	18
18	407	389	4	3	307	4	3
In	3385	3210	36		2549	36	
Total	6862	6490	72		5150	72	
Rating	72.1	70.4			69.1		
Slope	120	117			113		

MEADOWWOODS GOLF COURSE

9 Executive Public

18300 Ridgewood Road
Minnetonka, Minnesota 55345
612/470-4000 Clubhouse/Proshop

HOURS	Dawn to Dusk
SEASON	April–November

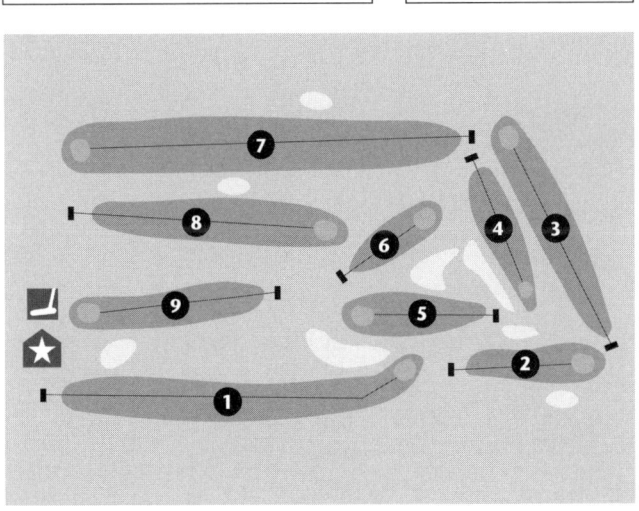

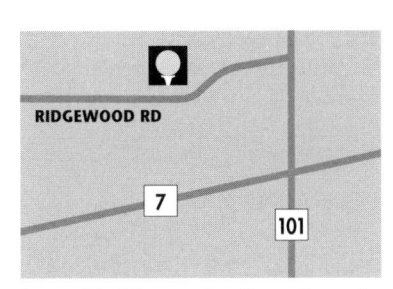

Located in Minnetonka. Course is north of MN Highway 7 on MN Highway 101, then west on Ridgewood Road.

RESERVATIONS	612/470-4000 4 days	
	Walk-on: good/fair	
GREEN FEES	M-F	S-S
Adult	$7.25	$7.75
Senior	$5.75	$7.75
Junior	$6	$7.75
Twilight	NA	NA
PAYMENT	Credit: Visa® MC® AmEx®	
	Non-local checks accepted	
LEAGUES	Men: Various	
	Women: Various	
MEMBERSHIPS	MGA	
MANAGER	Tim Peterson	
PROFESSIONAL	Bob Goodrich	

FEATURES		
Putting green	Y	
Driving range	N	
Practice area	Y	
Golf carts		
Power	Y	$7.75
Pull carts	Y	$2
Club rental	Y	$4
Club storage	Y	
Caddies	N	
Proshop		
Extended	Y	
Refreshments		
Restaurant	N	
Lounge	Y	
Snacks	Y	
Clubhouse		
Showers	N	
Lockers	N	
Lodging	N	

	MEN			WOMEN		
	FRONT	PAR	HDCP	FRONT	PAR	HDCP
1	253	4	3	228	4	3
2	157	3	7	145	3	7
3	190	3	1	160	3	1
4	133	3	6	122	3	6
5	169	3	5	147	3	5
6	133	3	8	123	3	8
7	295	4	2	273	4	2
8	175	3	4	161	3	4
9	136	3	9	107	3	9
Out	1641	29		1466	29	
1	253	4	3	228	4	3
2	157	3	7	145	3	7
3	190	3	1	160	3	1
4	133	3	6	122	3	6
5	169	3	5	147	3	5
6	133	3	8	123	3	8
7	295	4	2	273	4	2
8	175	3	4	161	3	4
9	136	3	9	107	3	9
In	1641	29		1466	29	
Total	3282	58		2932	58	
Rating	55.6			55.8		
Slope	86			91		

MENDAKOTA COUNTRY CLUB

18 Regulation Private

2075 Mendakota Drive
Mendota Heights, Minnesota 55120
612/454-2822 Clubhouse
612/454-4200 Proshop

RESERVATIONS	612/454-4200	
	Members only	
GREEN FEES	M-F	S-S
Adult	$38	$38
Senior	$38	$38
Junior	$38	$38
Twilight	NA	NA
	Members and guests only	
PAYMENT	Credit: Visa® MC® AmEx®	
	Non-local checks accepted	
LEAGUES	Various	
MEMBERSHIPS	USGA, PGA, GCSAA,	
	CMAA, MGA	
SUPERINTENDENT	Bob McKinney	
PROFESSIONAL	Dale Jones, Jr.	

HOURS	7 am to 6 pm	
SEASON	April-November	
FEATURES		
Putting green	Y	
Driving range	Y	$5
Practice area	N	
Golf carts		
Power (gas)	Y	$24/12
Pull carts	Y	$2.50
Club rental	Y	
Club storage	Y	$75/yr
Caddies	Y	$15
Proshop		
Extended	Y	
Refreshments		
Restaurant	Y	
Lounge	Y	
Snacks	Y	
Clubhouse		
Showers	Y	
Lockers	Y	
Lodging	N	

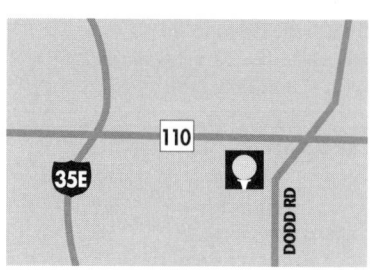

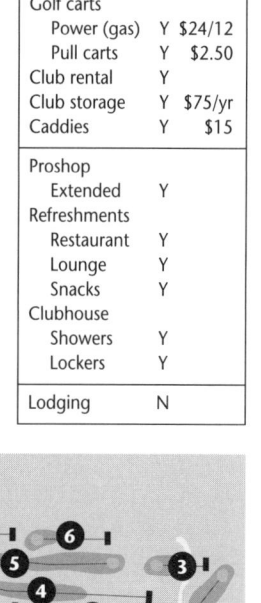

Located in Mendota Heights. Course is 1/2 mile east of I-35E on Highway 110, then south on Dodd Road.

	MEN			**WOMEN**		
	BACK	FRONT	PAR HDCP	FRONT	PAR	HDCP
1	531	502	5 11	462	5	5
2	372	360	4 3	302	4	11
3	180	170	3 13	136	3	13
4	547	545	5 5	422	5	9
5	396	390	4 1	379	4	1
6	172	143	3 17	122	3	15
7	192	185	3 9	170	3	17
8	331	312	4 15	306	4	7
9	522	509	5 7	488	5	3
Out	3243	3116	36	2787	36	
10	314	312	4 17	305	4	13
11	345	340	4 15	314	4	9
12	563	530	5 9	501	5	3
13	534	528	5 3	504	5	1
14	189	164	3 13	143	3	17
15	425	420	4 1	328	4	5
16	400	379	4 5	311	4	11
17	164	156	3 7	109	3	15
18	370	340	4 11	305	4	7
In	3305	3169	36	2820	36	
Total	6548	6285	72	5607	72	
Rating	71.1	70.3		72.8		
Slope	128	126		126		

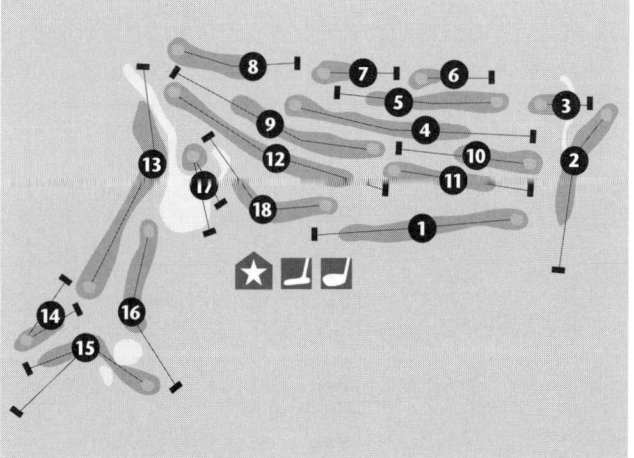

MENDOTA HEIGHTS PAR-3

9 Par-3 Public

1695 Dodd Road
Mendota Heights, Minnesota 55150
612/454-9822 Clubhouse/Proshop

RESERVATIONS	612/454-9822	
	Walk-on: good/fair	

GREEN FEES	M-F	S-S
Adult	$12/7.55	$12/7.55
Senior	$10.95/6.50	$10.95/6.50
Junior	$10.95/6.50	$10.95/6.50
Twilight	NA	NA

PAYMENT	No credit cards accepted
	Non–local checks accepted

LEAGUES	Men: Various
	Women: Various

MEMBERSHIPS	None

PROFESSIONAL	None

HOURS	Dawn to Dusk
SEASON	April-November

FEATURES

Putting green	Y	
Driving range	N	
Practice area	N	
Golf carts		
Power	N	
Pull carts	Y	$1
Club rental	Y	$3.75
Club storage	N	
Caddies	N	
Proshop		
Basic	Y	
Refreshments		
Restaurant	N	
Lounge	N	
Snacks	Y	
Clubhouse		
Showers	N	
Lockers	N	
Lodging	N	

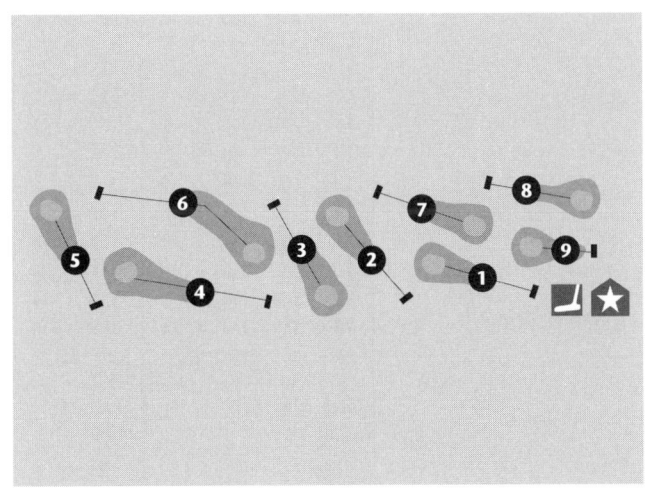

Located in Mendota Heights. Course is north of MN Highway 110 on Dodd Road, then west on Bachelor Avenue.

	MEN			WOMEN		
	FRONT	PAR	HDCP	FRONT	PAR	HDCP
1	150	3	4	150	3	4
2	130	3	6	130	3	6
3	105	3	9	105	3	9
4	170	3	2	170	3	2
5	125	3	7	125	3	7
6	180	3	1	180	3	1
7	140	3	5	140	3	5
8	167	3	3	167	3	3
9	110	3	8	110	3	8
Out	1277	27		1277	27	
1	150	3	4	150	3	4
2	130	3	6	130	3	6
3	105	3	9	105	3	9
4	170	3	2	170	3	2
5	125	3	7	125	3	7
6	180	3	1	180	3	1
7	140	3	5	140	3	5
8	167	3	3	167	3	3
9	110	3	8	110	3	8
In	1277	27		1277	27	
Total	2554	54		2554	54	
Rating	NA			NA		
Slope	NA			NA		

GOLF COURSE DIRECTORY

MESABA COUNTRY CLUB

18 Regulation Private

415 East 51st Street
Hibbing, Minnesota 55746
218/263-2851 Clubhouse
218/263-4826 Proshop

RESERVATIONS	218/263-4826	
	Members only	

GREEN FEES	M-F	S-S
Adult	$25/15	$30/20
Senior	$25/15	$30/20
Junior	$25/15	$30/20
Twilight	NA	NA
	Members and guests only	

PAYMENT	No credit cards accepted
	Local checks only

LEAGUES	Various

MEMBERSHIPS	USGA, NGF, PGA, GCSAA, MGA

SUPERINTENDENT John Kuusinen
PROFESSIONAL Gary Yeager

HOURS 8 am to Dusk
SEASON April to October

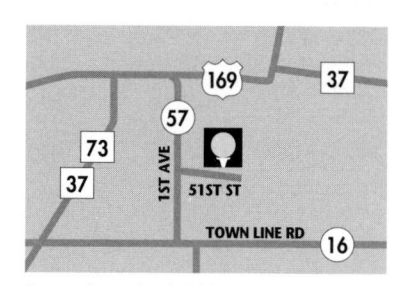

FEATURES

Putting green	Y	
Driving range	Y	$2.50
Practice area	Y	

Golf carts		
Power (gas)	Y	$17.50
Pull carts	Y	$2
Club rental	Y	$10
Club storage	Y	
Caddies	N	

Proshop	
Extended	Y
Refreshments	
Restaurant	Y
Lounge	Y
Snacks	Y
Clubhouse	
Showers	Y
Lockers	Y

Lodging	N

Located south of Hibbing. Course is south of U.S. Highway 169 on County Road 57, then east on 51st Street.

	MEN				WOMEN		
	BACK	FRONT	PAR	HDCP	FRONT	PAR	HDCP
1	492	486	5	15	465	5	3
2	425	412	4	1	372	4	1
3	369	359	4	11	300	4	5
4	433	429	4	3	357	4	7
5	434	419	4	7	102	5	9
6	371	359	4	9	295	4	13
7	247	228	3	5	208	4	17
8	167	157	3	17	133	3	15
9	486	480	5	13	397	5	11
Out	3424	3329	36		2929	38	
10	371	367	4	16	353	4	10
11	211	205	3	6	95	3	12
12	555	549	5	4	491	5	4
13	400	360	4	10	255	4	8
14	410	396	4	8	378	4	6
15	159	144	3	18	119	3	18
16	557	542	5	2	481	5	2
17	362	345	4	12	327	4	14
18	343	336	4	14	319	4	16
In	3368	3244	36		2818	36	
Total	6792	6573	72		5747	74	
Rating	73.1	72.0			74.1		
Slope	131	129			130		

Course layout map not provided.

MIDLAND HILLS COUNTRY CLUB

18 Regulation Private

2001 Fulham Street
Roseville, Minnesota 55113
612/631-0440 Clubhouse
612/631-2017 Proshop

RESERVATIONS	612/631-2017	
	Members only	
GREEN FEES	M-F	S-S
Adult	$45	$55
Senior	$45	$55
Junior	$45	$55
Twilight	NA	NA
	Members and guests only	
PAYMENT	Credit: Visa® MasterCard®	
	Non-local checks accepted	
LEAGUES	None	
MEMBERSHIPS	USGA, PGA, GCSAA, CMAA, MGA	
SUPERINTENDENT	Scott Austin	
PROFESSIONAL	Jim Manthis	

HOURS	7 am to Dusk
SEASON	April-November

FEATURES	
Putting green	Y
Driving range	Y
Practice area	Y
Golf carts	
Power (gas)	Y
Pull carts	Y
Club rental	Y
Club storage	Y
Caddies	Y
Proshop	
Extended	Y
Refreshments	
Restaurant	Y
Lounge	N
Snacks	Y
Clubhouse	
Showers	Y
Lockers	Y
Lodging	N

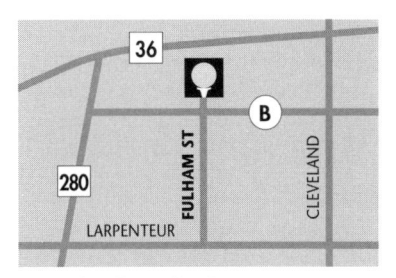

Located in Roseville. Course entrance is south of MN Hwy 36 on Cleveland, west on Cty Rd B, then north on Fulham St.

	MEN				WOMEN		
	BACK	FRONT	PAR	HDCP	FRONT	PAR	HDCP
1	329	323	4	14	300	4	13
2	367	333	4	8	327	4	11
3	420	412	4	10	411	5	5
4	147	138	3	16	128	3	17
5	485	477	5	4	468	5	1
6	539	524	5	2	464	5	3
7	160	152	3	18	143	3	15
8	327	331	4	6	270	4	7
9	371	360	4	12	346	4	9
Out	3145	3050	36		2857	37	
10	570	559	5	3	491	5	2
11	425	415	4	1	400	5	10
12	177	171	3	17	160	3	16
13	390	384	4	7	375	4	6
14	424	389	4	9	335	4	8
15	373	345	4	11	333	4	12
16	203	191	3	15	140	3	18
17	508	500	5	5	440	5	4
18	345	340	4	13	300	4	14
In	3415	3294	36		2974	37	
Total	6560	6344	72		5831	74	
Rating	72.4	71.5			75.1		
Slope	134	131			137		

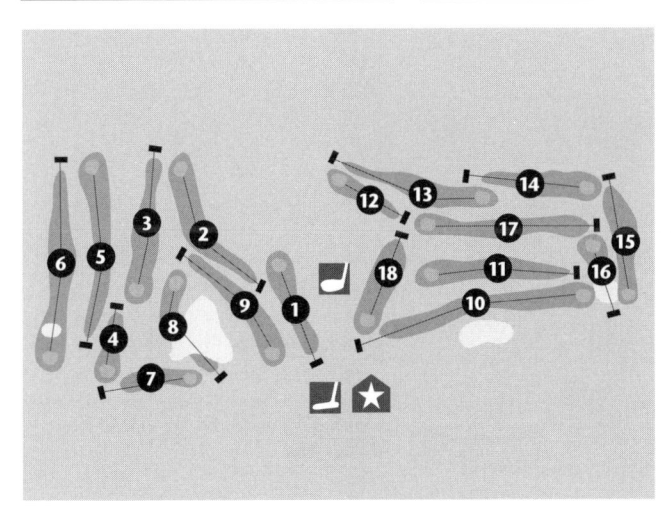

GOLF COURSE DIRECTORY

MILACA GOLF CLUB

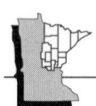

9 Regulation Semi-Private

P.O. Box 175
Milaca, Minnesota 56353
612/983-2110 Clubhouse/Proshop

RESERVATIONS	612/983-2110 5 days	
	Walk-on: good/poor	

GREEN FEES	M-F	S-S
Adult	$13/9	$14/11
Senior	$9/6.50	$14/11
Junior	$9/6.50	$11/8
Twilight	NA	NA

PAYMENT	No credit cards accepted
	Non-local checks accepted

LEAGUES	Men: W (12 pm - Dusk)
	Women: T (12 pm - Dusk)

MEMBERSHIPS MGA

MANAGER Nancy Wilken
SUPERINTENDENT Dick Becker

HOURS	8 am to Dusk
SEASON	April to October

FEATURES	
Putting green	Y
Driving range	Y
Practice area	N
Golf carts	
Power (gas)	Y
Pull carts	Y
Club rental	Y
Club storage	Y
Caddies	N
Proshop	
Extended	Y
Refreshments	
Restaurant	N
Lounge	N
Snacks	Y
Clubhouse	
Showers	N
Lockers	N
Lodging	N

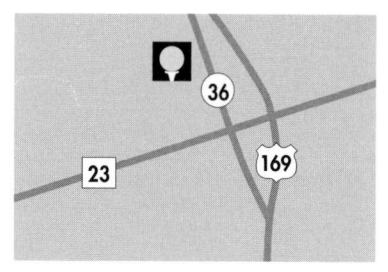

Located north of Milaca. Course is west of U.S. Highway 169 on Highway 23, then 1 mile north on County Road 36.

	MEN			WOMEN		
	BACK	FRONT	PAR	HDCP	FRONT	PAR	HDCP
1	411	411	4	1	411	5	1
2	464	454	5	8	404	5	2
3	356	356	4	5	351	4	6
4	180	169	3	4	132	3	4
5	262	252	4	9	244	4	9
6	405	395	4	2	390	5	3
7	370	370	4	3	355	4	5
8	174	166	3	7	166	3	8
9	341	326	4	6	326	4	7
Out	2963	2899	35		2779	37	
1	411	411	4	1	411	5	1
2	464	454	5	8	404	5	2
3	356	356	4	5	351	4	6
4	180	169	3	4	132	3	4
5	262	252	4	9	244	4	9
6	405	395	4	2	390	5	3
7	370	370	4	3	355	4	5
8	174	166	3	7	166	3	8
9	341	326	4	6	326	4	7
In	2963	2899	35		2779	37	
Total	5926	5798	70		5558	74	
Rating	68.2	67.8			71.8		
Slope	112	111			121		

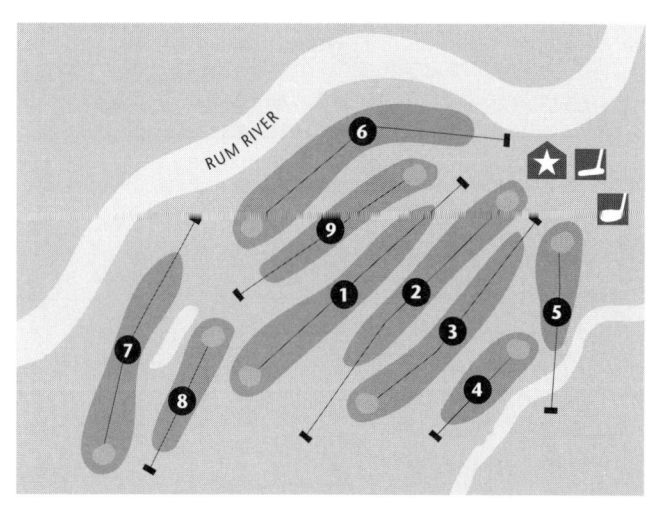

MILLE LACS LAKE GOLF RESORT

18 Regulation Public

Highway 169 South, P.O. Box 163A
Garrison, Minnesota 56450
800/435-8720 Clubhouse/Proshop

HOURS	7 am to Dusk
SEASON	April-November

RESERVATIONS	800/435-8720 2 weeks
	Walk-on: good/fair

GREEN FEES	M-F	S-S
Adult	$24/14	$24/14
Senior	$24/14	$24/14
Junior	$10/6	$10/6
Twilight	NA	NA
	2-day golf package available	

PAYMENT	Credit: Visa® MasterCard®
	Non-local checks accepted

LEAGUES	Men: T, Th (am)
	Women: W (am)

MEMBERSHIPS	USGA, NGF, PGA, GCSAA, MGA

OWNER	R.J. Smiley
SUPERINTENDENT	Bob Weston
PROFESSIONAL	Mike Gearman

FEATURES		
Putting green	Y	
Driving range	Y	$3-5
Practice area	Y	
Golf carts		
Power (gas)	Y	
Pull carts	Y	
Club rental	Y	
Club storage	N	
Caddies	N	
Proshop		
Extended	Y	
Refreshments		
Restaurant	Y	
Lounge	Y	
Snacks	Y	
Clubhouse		
Showers	N	
Lockers	N	
Lodging	Y	

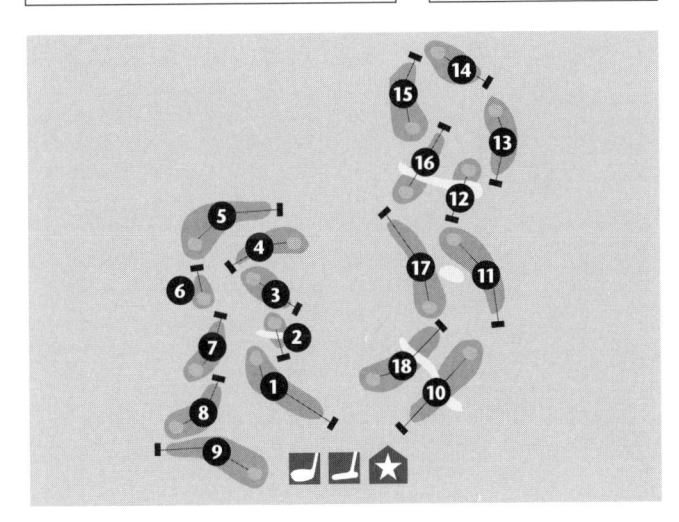

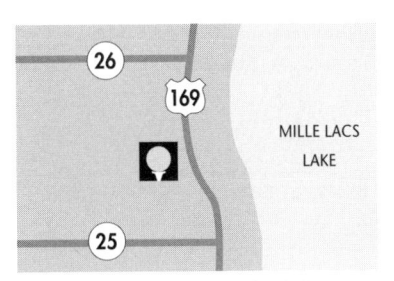

Located about 4 miles south of Garrison. Course is south of Cty Road 26 & north of Cty Road 25 on U.S. Highway 169.

		MEN			WOMEN		
	BACK	FRONT	PAR	HDCP	FRONT	PAR	HDCP
1	361	353	4	16	318	4	14
2	135	128	3	18	118	3	18
3	276	276	4	10	214	4	12
4	334	319	4	14	270	4	16
5	458	458	5	2	404	5	2
6	161	153	3	12	143	3	8
7	369	364	4	6	274	4	4
8	362	357	4	4	263	4	10
9	483	473	5	8	411	5	6
Out	2939	2881	36		2415	36	
10	375	350	4	11	325	4	3
11	446	446	4	3	351	4	5
12	172	172	3	13	172	3	9
13	439	409	4	5	294	4	13
14	240	205	3	1	230	4	1
15	402	387	4	15	307	4	15
16	337	327	4	17	269	4	17
17	529	510	5	9	413	5	7
18	412	390	4	7	330	4	11
In	3352	3196	35		2691	36	
Total	6291	6077	71		5106	72	
Rating	69.7	69.2			68.7		
Slope	119	115			113		

GOLF COURSE DIRECTORY

MINAKWA GOLF & RACQUETBALL CLUB
9 Regulation Semi-Private

Fisher Avenue, P.O. Box 633
Crookston, Minnesota 56716
218/281-1773 Clubhouse
218/281-1774 Proshop

HOURS	8 am to Dusk
SEASON	April to October

FEATURES

Putting green	Y	
Driving range	Y	$2
Practice area	Y	
Golf carts		
Power (gas)	Y	$9
Pull carts	Y	$3
Club rental	Y	$3
Club storage	Y	$20/yr
Caddies	N	
Proshop		
Extended	Y	
Refreshments		
Restaurant	Y	
Lounge	Y	
Snacks	Y	
Clubhouse		
Showers	Y	
Lockers	Y	
Lodging	N	

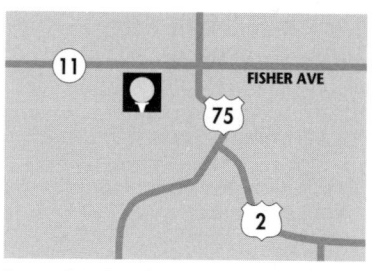

RESERVATIONS	218/281-1774 1 week
	Walk-on: fair/fair

GREEN FEES	M-F	S-S
Adult	$13/9	$14/10
Senior	$13/9	$14/10
Junior	$13/9	$14/10
Twilight	NA	NA

PAYMENT	Credit: Visa® MasterCard®
	Non-local checks accepted

LEAGUES	None

MEMBERSHIPS	USGA, NGF, MGA

MANAGER	Kyle Pearson
SUPERINTENDENT	Ralph Pester, Bill Loff

Located in Crookston. Course entrance is 2 blocks west of of U.S. Highways 2/75 on Fisher Avenue (County Road 11).

	MEN				WOMEN		
	BACK	FRONT	PAR	HDCP	FRONT	PAR	HDCP
1	252	245	4	15	228	4	15
2	357	336	4	1	316	4	1
3	301	286	4	13	273	4	13
4	137	129	3	17	120	3	17
5	330	313	4	11	296	4	11
6	213	202	3	5	194	4	5
7	313	305	4	9	263	4	9
8	475	464	5	3	432	5	3
9	447	427	5	7	355	5	7
Out	2825	2707	36		2477	37	
1	252	245	4	16	228	4	16
2	357	336	4	2	316	4	2
3	301	286	4	14	273	4	14
4	137	129	3	18	120	3	18
5	330	313	4	12	296	4	12
6	213	202	3	6	194	4	6
7	313	305	4	10	263	4	10
8	475	464	5	4	432	5	4
9	447	427	5	8	355	5	8
In	2825	2707	36		2477	37	
Total	5650	5414	72		4954	74	
Rating	67.0	66.0			68.4		
Slope	114	112			117		

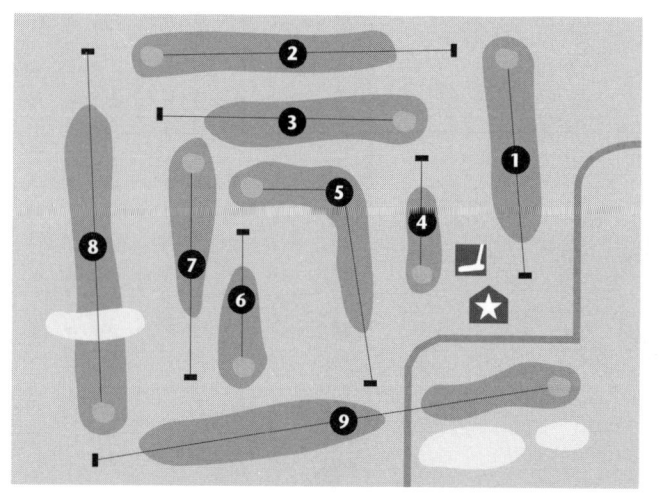

MINIKAHDA CLUB

18 Regulation Private

3205 Excelsior Boulevard
Minneapolis, Minnesota 55416
612/926-1601 Clubhouse
612/924-1667 Proshop

HOURS	8 am to Dusk
SEASON	April-November

FEATURES	
Putting green	Y
Driving range	Y
Practice area	Y

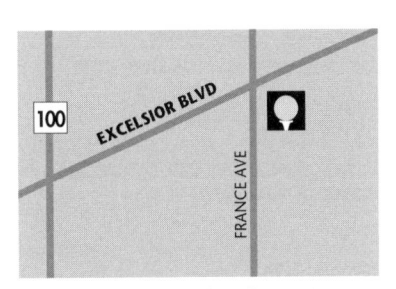

Located in Minneapolis. Course is east of MN Highway 100 on Excelsior Blvd, then south on France Avenue.

RESERVATIONS	Reservations not accepted
	Members only

GREEN FEES	M-F	S-S
Adult	$55	$55
Senior	$55	$55
Junior	$55	$55
Twilight	NA	NA
	Members and guests only	

Golf carts		
Power (elec)	Y	$28
Pull carts	Y	$4
Club rental	Y	$15
Club storage	Y	
Caddies	Y	

PAYMENT	Fees charged to member
LEAGUES	None
MEMBERSHIPS	USGA, NGF, PGA, LPGA, GCSAA, CMAA, MGA
SUPERINTENDENT	Doug Mahal
PROFESSIONAL	Paul Purtzer

Proshop	
Extended	Y
Refreshments	
Restaurant	Y
Lounge	Y
Snacks	Y
Clubhouse	
Showers	Y
Lockers	Y
Lodging	N

	MEN				**WOMEN**		
	BACK	FRONT	PAR	HDCP	FRONT	PAR	HDCP
1	310	304	4	16	280	4	12
2	432	432	4	4	339	4	6
3	160	160	3	18	115	3	18
4	500	492	5	10	438	5	2
5	310	305	4	14	277	4	10
6	190	183	3	12	152	3	14
7	512	490	5	2	353	5	8
8	216	205	3	8	174	3	16
9	535	500	5	6	424	5	4
Out	3165	3050	36		2552	36	
10	436	420	4	3	337	4	3
11	174	165	3	17	160	3	17
12	390	375	4	5	310	4	9
13	540	530	5	1	426	5	1
14	475	465	5	9	425	5	7
15	375	370	4	11	287	4	11
16	398	350	4	7	284	4	5
17	335	330	4	13	275	4	15
18	362	355	4	15	297	4	13
In	3485	3360	37		2801	37	
Total	6650	6410	73		5353	73	
Rating	72.7	71.6			72.8		
Slope	139	137			131		

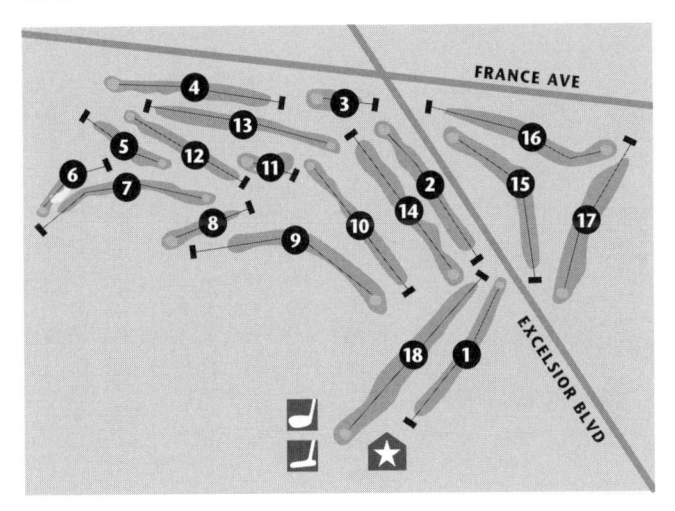

GOLF COURSE DIRECTORY

MINNEAPOLIS GOLF CLUB

18 Regulation Private

2001 Flag Avenue South
Minneapolis, Minnesota 55426
612/544-4471 Clubhouse
612/544-0021 Proshop

RESERVATIONS	612/544-3961
	Members only

GREEN FEES	M-F	S-S
Adult	$50	$75
Senior	$50	$75
Junior	$50	$75
Twilight	NA	NA
	Members and guests only	

PAYMENT	Credit: Visa® MasterCard®
	Non-local checks accepted

LEAGUES	None

MEMBERSHIPS	USGA, NGF, GCSAA, CMAA, MGA

MANAGER	Steve Pedersen
PROFESSIONAL	Dave Haberle

HOURS	7 am to Dusk
SEASON	April–November

FEATURES	
Putting green	Y
Driving range	Y
Practice area	Y
Golf carts	
Power (elec)	Y
Pull carts	Y
Club rental	Y
Club storage	Y
Caddies	Y
Proshop	
Extended	Y
Refreshments	
Restaurant	Y
Lounge	Y
Snacks	Y
Clubhouse	
Showers	Y
Lockers	Y
Lodging	N

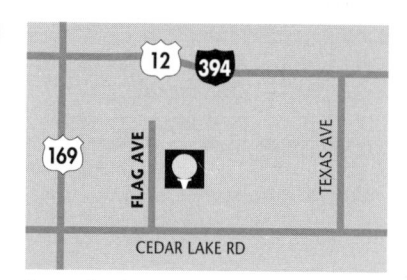

Located in Minneapolis. Course is east of U.S. Highway 169 on Cedar Lake Road, then five blocks north on Flag Avenue.

	MEN				WOMEN		
	BACK	FRONT	PAR	HDCP	FRONT	PAR	HDCP
1	474	471	5	15	443	5	5
2	379	359	4	9	284	4	13
3	562	529	5	7	475	5	1
4	140	132	3	17	112	3	15
5	431	387	4	3	310	4	7
6	211	196	3	13	122	3	17
7	452	422	4	1	401	5	11
8	412	396	4	5	306	4	9
9	351	338	4	11	335	4	3
Out	3412	3230	36		2788	37	
10	230	216	3	4	170	3	12
11	408	391	4	8	296	4	8
12	488	471	5	18	451	5	2
13	403	385	4	10	324	4	6
14	338	322	4	12	244	4	16
15	543	509	5	16	405	5	10
16	213	183	3	14	164	3	18
17	420	400	4	6	345	4	4
18	427	410	4	2	403	5	14
In	3470	3287	36		2802	37	
Total	6882	6517	72		5590	74	
Rating	74.3	72.7			73.4		
Slope	137	133			133		

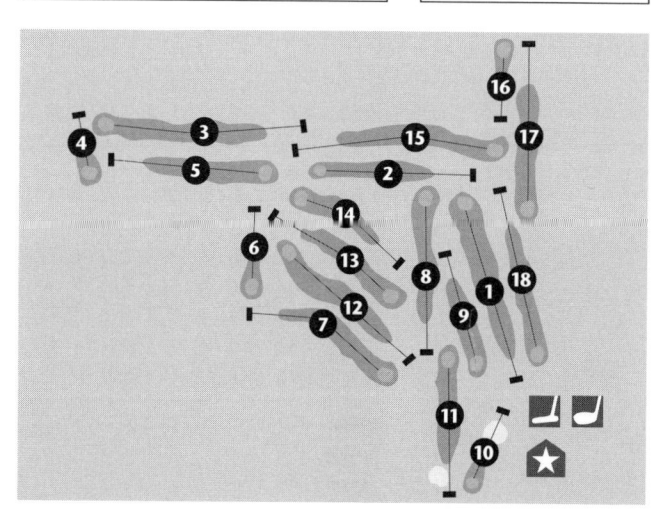

MINNEOPA GOLF CLUB

9 Executive Public

Route 9, P.O. Box 133
Mankato, Minnesota 56001
507/625-5777 Clubhouse/Proshop

RESERVATIONS	507/625-5777 1 week
	Walk-on: good/fair

GREEN FEES	M-F	S-S
Adult	$12.50/7.50	$13.50/8
Senior	$10.50/5.50*	$13.50/8
Junior	$9/4.50*	$13.50/8
Twilight	NA	NA
	* Before 1 pm	
	Season tickets available	

PAYMENT	No credit cards accepted
	Non-local checks accepted

LEAGUES	Men: W (pm)
	Women: W (am)

MEMBERSHIPS	USGA, NGF, MGA

OWNER	Ken & Donna Bohks
SUPERINTENDENT	Kyle Bohks

HOURS	6 am to Dusk
SEASON	April to October

FEATURES	
Putting green	Y
Driving range	N
Practice area	Y
Golf carts	
Power (gas)	Y $15/8
Pull carts	Y $1.50
Club rental	Y $3.50
Club storage	Y $8.50/yr
Caddies	N
Proshop	
Extended	Y
Refreshments	
Restaurant	N
Lounge	Y
Snacks	Y
Clubhouse	
Showers	Y
Lockers	Y
Lodging	N

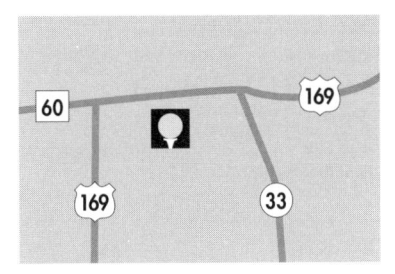

Located south of Mankato. Course is one mile west of County Road 33 on MN Highway 60/U.S. Highway 169.

	MEN			WOMEN		
	FRONT	PAR	HDCP	FRONT	PAR	HDCP
1	367	4	1	367	4	1
2	352	4	3	352	4	3
3	344	4	2	344	4	2
4	205	3	8	205	4	8
5	215	3	7	215	4	7
6	261	4	6	261	4	6
7	166	3	9	103	3	9
8	259	4	5	259	4	5
9	316	4	4	316	4	4
Out	2488	33		2425	35	
1	367	4	1	367	4	1
2	352	4	3	352	4	3
3	344	4	2	344	4	2
4	205	3	8	205	4	8
5	215	3	7	215	4	7
6	261	4	6	261	4	6
7	166	3	9	103	3	9
8	259	4	5	259	4	5
9	316	4	4	316	4	4
In	2488	33		2425	35	
Total	4976	66		4850	70	
Rating	63.2			67.6		
Slope	102			107		

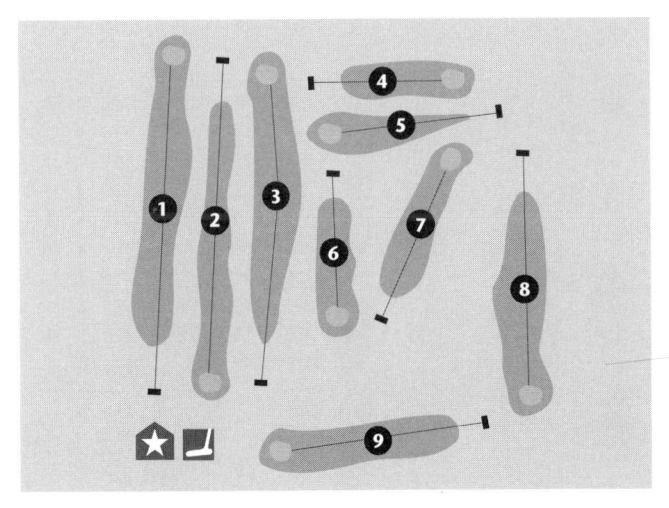

GOLF COURSE DIRECTORY

MINNESOTA VALLEY COUNTRY CLUB

18 Regulation Private

6300 Auto Club Road
Bloomington, Minnesota 55438
612/884-2409 Clubhouse
612/884-1744 Proshop

RESERVATIONS	612/884-1744	
	Members only	
GREEN FEES	M-F	S-S
Adult	$40	$40
Senior	$40	$40
Junior	$12	$12
Twilight	$20	$20
	Members and guests only	
PAYMENT	Fees charged to member	
LEAGUES	None	
MEMBERSHIPS	USGA, NGF, PGA, GCSAA, CMAA, MGA	
MANAGER	Glenn Baldwin	
SUPERINTENDENT	Larry Mueller	
PROFESSIONAL	Rob Hary	

HOURS	7 am to Dusk
SEASON	April–November

FEATURES	
Putting green	Y
Driving range	Y
Practice area	Y
Golf carts	
Power (gas)	Y
Pull carts	Y
Club rental	Y
Club storage	Y
Caddies	Y
Proshop	
Extended	Y
Refreshments	
Restaurant	Y
Lounge	Y
Snacks	Y
Clubhouse	
Showers	Y
Lockers	Y
Lodging	N

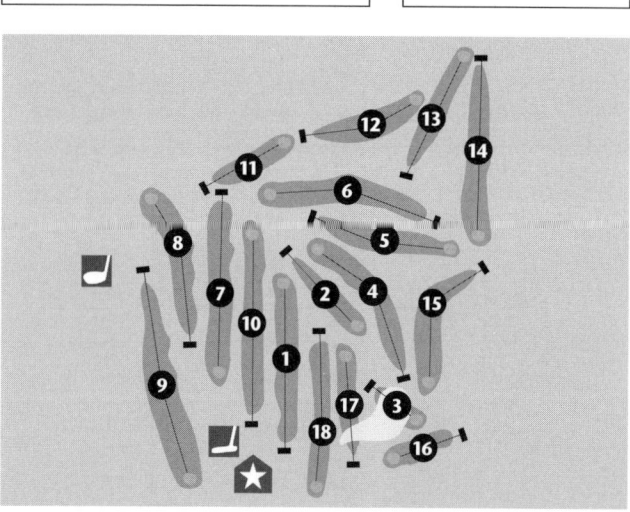

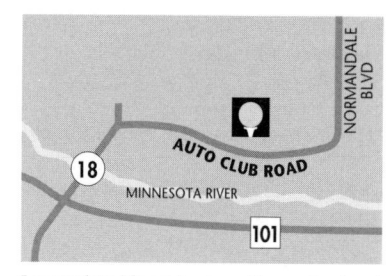

Located in Bloomington. Course is about five blocks west of Normandale Blvd/MN Highway 100 on Auto Club Road.

	MEN			WOMEN		
	BACK	FRONT	PAR	HDCP	FRONT	PAR	HDCP
1	489	476	5	5	405	5	3
2	239	193	3	15	144	3	17
3	142	130	3	17	100	3	15
4	397	360	4	9	222	4	5
5	413	398	4	7	302	4	13
6	552	537	5	1	410	5	9
7	367	351	4	13	302	4	7
8	432	400	4	3	320	4	11
9	593	489	5	11	369	5	1
Out	3624	3334	37		2574	37	
10	504	488	5	6	400	5	4
11	172	157	3	18	123	3	18
12	346	329	4	12	298	4	14
13	350	332	4	14	292	4	12
14	549	510	5	10	416	5	2
15	349	344	4	2	207	4	10
16	158	149	3	16	140	3	16
17	299	290	4	8	235	4	6
18	450	432	4	4	429	5	8
In	3177	3031	36		2540	37	
Total	6801	6365	73		5114	74	
Rating	72.7	70.7			71.0		
Slope	127	123			130		

MINNETONKA COUNTRY CLUB

18 Regulation Private

24575 Smithtown Rd., P.O. Box 360
Excelsior, Minnesota 55331
612/474-5222 Clubhouse
612/474-9571 Proshop

HOURS 7:30 am to Dusk

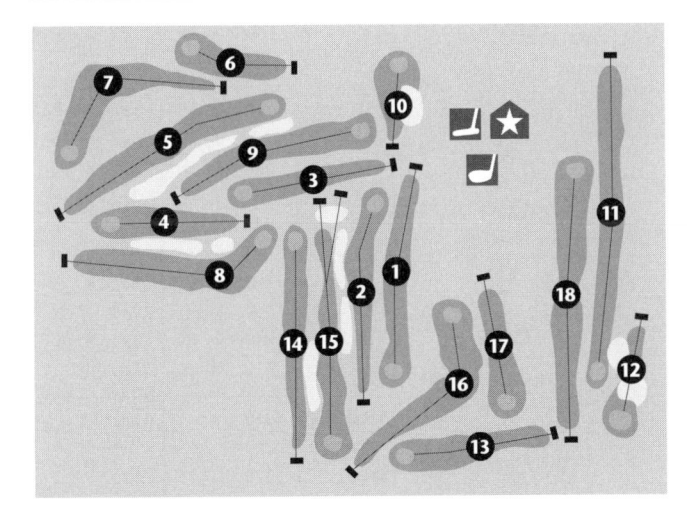

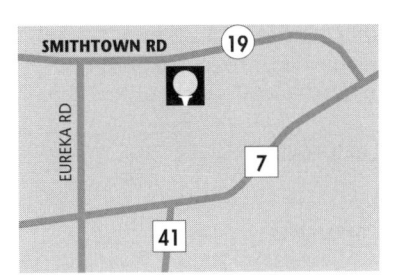

SEASON April-November

Located in Excelsior. Course entrance is north 1 1/4 miles of MN Highway 7 on County Road 19.

RESERVATIONS	612/474-9571 2 days
	Members only

GREEN FEES	M-F	S-S
Adult	$45/22.50	$55/27.50
Senior	$45/22.50	$55/27.50
Junior	$15/15	$15/15
Twilight	$22.50	$27.50

PAYMENT	No credit cards accepted
	Local checks only

LEAGUES	Various

MEMBERSHIPS	USGA, NGF, PGA, GCSAA, MGA

OWNER	B. Witrak
MANAGER	B. Witrak
SUPERINTENDENT	Max Olson
PROFESSIONAL	Bob Olds

FEATURES

Putting green	Y	
Driving range	Y	
Practice area	Y	
Golf carts		
Power (gas)	Y	$28/14
Pull carts	Y	$3
Club rental	Y	$15
Club storage	Y	
Caddies	N	
Proshop		
Extended	Y	
Refreshments		
Restaurant	Y	
Lounge	Y	
Snacks	Y	
Clubhouse		
Showers	Y	
Lockers	Y	
Lodging	N	

		MEN			WOMEN		
	BACK	FRONT	PAR	HDCP	FRONT	PAR	HDCP
1	415	406	4	3	401	5	13
2	370	364	4	7	320	4	1
3	367	359	4	9	342	4	3
4	289	284	4	17	270	4	15
5	438	432	4	1	410	5	11
6	170	160	3	15	134	3	17
7	351	347	4	11	313	4	9
8	392	347	4	13	274	4	7
9	525	509	5	5	419	5	5
Out	3317	3208	36		2883	38	
10	196	180	3	10	156	3	12
11	540	521	5	2	441	5	10
12	150	141	3	16	119	3	18
13	285	281	4	14	266	4	14
14	369	359	4	8	344	4	4
15	468	468	5	4	414	5	8
16	352	343	4	6	334	4	6
17	151	146	3	18	133	3	16
18	470	470	5	12	427	5	2
In	2981	2909	36		2634	36	
Total	6298	6117	72		5517	74	
Rating	72.3	71.6			74.8		
Slope	138	137			140		

GOLF COURSE DIRECTORY

MINNEWASKA GOLF CLUB

18 Regulation Semi-Private

29 Golf Course Road, P.O. Box 110
Glenwood, Minnesota 56334
612/634-3680 Clubhouse/Proshop

HOURS	7 am to Dusk
SEASON	April to October

| **RESERVATIONS** | 612/634-3680 1 week |
| | Walk-on: good/good |

GREEN FEES	M-F	S-S
Adult	$18.95/11.95	$19.95/11.95
Senior	$18.95/11.95	$19.95/11.95
Junior	$8/5*	$19.95/11.95
Twilight	NA	NA

* Wednesday's before 11 am

| **PAYMENT** | Credit: Visa® MasterCard® |
| | Non-local checks accepted |

| **LEAGUES** | Various |

| **MEMBERSHIPS** | USGA, PGA, GCSAA, MGA |

MANAGER	Michael Pearson
SUPERINTENDENT	Dennis Schoenfeldt
PROFESSIONAL	Michael Pearson

FEATURES	
Putting green	Y
Driving range	Y
Practice area	Y
Golf carts	
Power (gas)	Y
Pull carts	Y
Club rental	Y
Club storage	N
Caddies	N
Proshop	
Extended	Y
Refreshments	
Restaurant	Y
Lounge	Y
Snacks	Y
Clubhouse	
Showers	Y
Lockers	N
Lodging	N

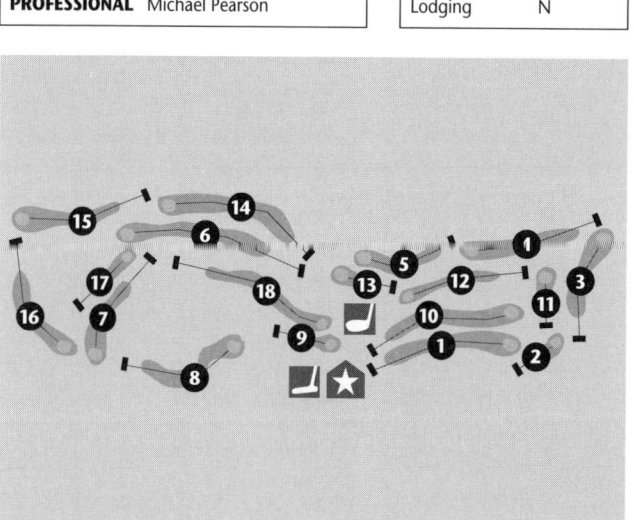

Located in Glenwood. Course is west of MN Highway 55 on MN Highway 28/29, then north on Golf Course Road.

	\multicolumn{4}{c	}{**MEN**}	\multicolumn{3}{c	}{**WOMEN**}
	BACK	FRONT	PAR	HDCP	FRONT	PAR	HDCP
1	481	476	5	11	476	5	1
2	200	181	3	9	140	3	17
3	357	324	4	7	268	4	15
4	412	409	4	1	395	5	9
5	341	334	4	13	284	4	13
6	524	517	5	5	421	3	3
7	384	367	4	15	282	5	11
8	397	366	4	3	308	3	5
9	122	118	3	17	72	5	7
Out	3219	3092	36		2646	37	
10	476	471	5	16	385	5	2
11	152	148	3	10	146	3	16
12	396	391	4	8	360	4	10
13	149	139	3	18	112	3	18
14	536	528	5	14	461	5	4
15	382	362	4	6	286	4	12
16	439	405	4	2	353	4	8
17	223	197	3	4	148	3	14
18	486	479	5	12	395	5	6
In	3239	3120	36		2646	36	
Total	6457	6212	72		5292	73	
Rating	70.7	69.7			71.7		
Slope	122	120			123		

MINNIOWA GOLF CLUB

9 Regulation Public

North Highway 169
Elmore, Minnesota 56027
507/943-3149 Clubhouse/Proshop

HOURS	Dawn to Dusk
SEASON	April to October

RESERVATIONS	507/943-3149
	Walk-on: good/fair

GREEN FEES	M-F	S-S
Adult	$11/6.50	$12/7.50
Senior	$11/6.50	$12/7.50
Junior	$11/6.50	$12/7.50
Twilight	NA	NA

PAYMENT	No credit cards accepted
	Non-local checks accepted

LEAGUES	Men: Various
	Women: Various

MEMBERSHIPS	MGA

PROFESSIONAL	Call

FEATURES	
Putting green	Y
Driving range	Y
Practice area	N
Golf carts	
Power	Y
Pull carts	Y
Club rental	Y
Club storage	N
Caddies	N
Proshop	
Basic	Y
Refreshments	
Restaurant	N
Lounge	N
Snacks	Y
Clubhouse	
Showers	N
Lockers	N
Lodging	N

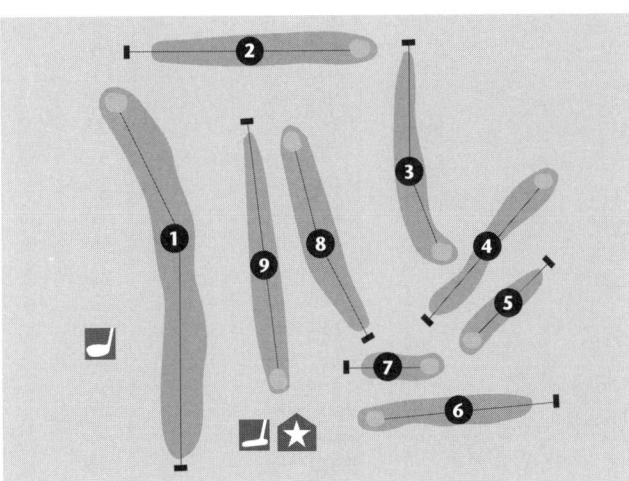

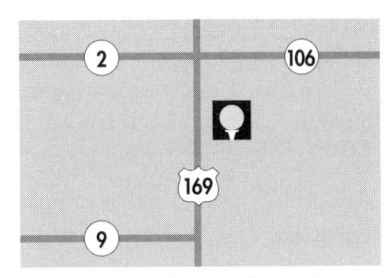

Located north of Elmore. Course is one mile north of County Road 9 on U.S. Highway 169.

	MEN				**WOMEN**		
	BACK	FRONT	PAR	HDCP	FRONT	PAR	HDCP
1	466	455	5	18	446	5	18
2	345	337	4	16	327	4	6
3	406	400	4	4	391	5	14
4	383	377	4	6	293	4	16
5	195	190	3	12	127	3	12
6	418	413	4	2	404	5	8
7	175	167	3	14	157	3	10
8	351	347	4	10	337	4	2
9	372	363	4	8	354	4	4
Out	3111	3049	35		2836	37	
1	466	455	5	17	446	5	17
2	345	337	4	15	327	4	5
3	406	400	4	3	391	5	13
4	383	377	4	5	293	4	15
5	195	190	3	11	127	3	11
6	418	413	4	1	404	5	7
7	175	167	3	13	157	3	9
8	351	347	4	9	337	4	1
9	372	363	4	7	354	4	3
In	3111	3049	35		2836	37	
Total	6222	6098	70		5672	74	
Rating	69.6	69.0			72.0		
Slope	113	111			117		

GOLF COURSE DIRECTORY

MISSISSIPPI DUNES GOLF LINKS

18 Regulation Public

10351 Grey Cloud Trail
Cottage Grove, Minnesota 55016
612/768-7611 Clubhouse/Proshop

HOURS	Dawn to Dusk
SEASON	April-November

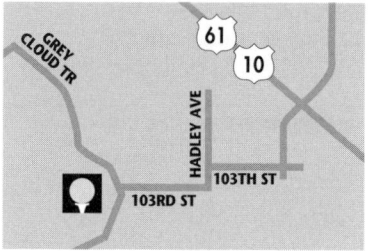

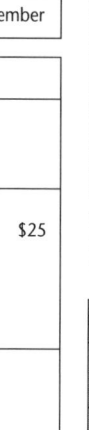

Located in Cottage Grove. Course is west of Hwy 61 on Jamaica, north on 100th, west on Hadley, south on Grey Cloud.

RESERVATIONS	612/768-7611 5 days	
	Walk-on: good/fair	
GREEN FEES	M-F	S-S
Adult	$25	$30
Senior	$25	$30
Junior	$25	$30
Twilight	$15	$15
PAYMENT	No credit cards accepted	
	Non-local checks accepted	
LEAGUES	Men: Various	
	Women: Various	
MEMBERSHIPS	USGA, PGA, GCSAA, MGA	
PROFESSIONAL	Dave Tentis	

FEATURES		
Putting green	Y	
Driving range	Y	
Practice area	Y	
Golf carts		
Power (gas)	Y	$25
Pull carts	Y	
Club rental	Y	
Club storage	N	
Caddies	N	
Proshop		
Extended	Y	
Refreshments		
Restaurant	Y	
Lounge	Y	
Snacks	Y	
Clubhouse		
Showers	Y	
Lockers	Y	
Lodging	N	

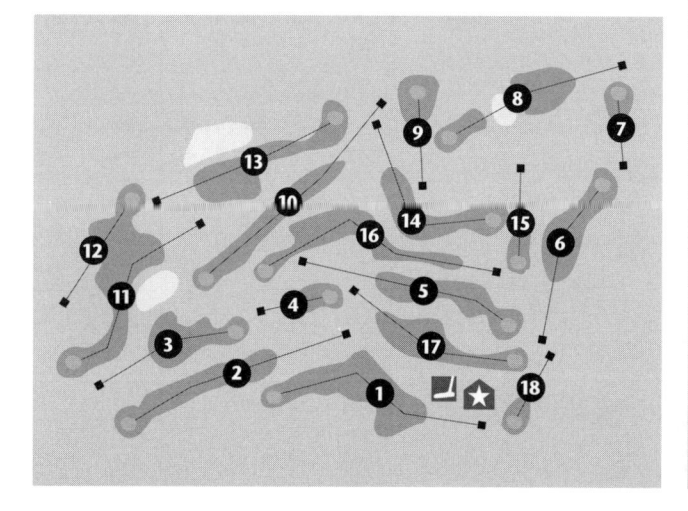

	MEN			**WOMEN**		
	BACK	FRONT	PAR	HDCP	FRONT	PAR	HDCP
1	440	410	4	2	330	4	2
2	425	360	4	16	320	4	16
3	320	280	4	13	200	4	13
4	225	180	3	9	130	3	9
5	525	485	5	7	370	5	7
6	300	300	4	5	280	4	5
7	145	125	3	17	115	3	17
8	510	475	5	15	405	5	15
9	225	180	3	11	140	3	11
Out	3115	2795	35		2290	35	
10	585	510	5	1	440	5	1
11	400	310	4	3	280	4	3
12	220	175	3	14	130	3	14
13	545	475	5	6	385	5	6
14	410	360	4	10	325	4	10
15	190	170	3	12	150	3	12
16	575	520	5	8	475	5	8
17	440	410	4	4	340	4	4
18	125	105	3	18	80	3	18
In	3490	3035	36		2605	36	
Total	6605	5830	71		4895	71	
Rating	NA	NA			NA		
Slope	NA	NA			NA		

MISSISSIPPI NATIONAL GOLF LINKS

27 Regulation Public

409 Golf Links Drive
Red Wing, Minnesota 55066
612/388-1874 Clubhouse/Proshop

HOURS	6 am to Dusk
SEASON	April-November

FEATURES		
Putting green	Y	
Driving range	Y	$2.75
Practice area	Y	
Golf carts		
Power (gas)	Y	$24/16
Pull carts	Y	
Club rental	Y	$8
Club storage	N	
Caddies	N	
Proshop		
Extended	Y	
Refreshments		
Restaurant	Y	
Lounge	Y	
Snacks	Y	
Clubhouse		
Showers	Y	
Lockers	Y	
Lodging	N	

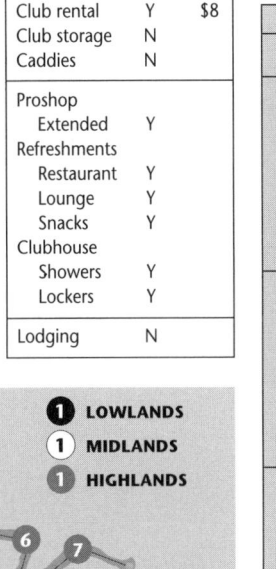

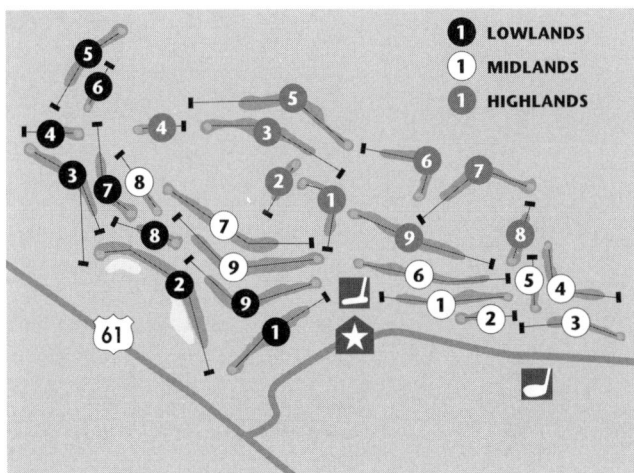

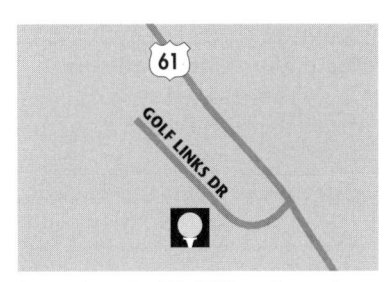

Located south of Red Wing. Course is west of U.S. Hwy 61 on Golf Links Drive.

RESERVATIONS	612/388-1874 1 week
	Walk-on: good/poor
GREEN FEES	M-F S-S
Adult	$22.50/14.50 $24.50/16.50
Senior	$22.50/14.50 $24.50/16.50
Junior	$22.50/14.50 $24.50/16.50
Twilight	NA NA
PAYMENT	Credit: Visa® MasterCard®
	Non-local checks accepted
LEAGUES	Men: M (pm)
	Women: W
	Senior: T (am)
MEMBERSHIPS	USGA, NGF, PGA, GCSAA, MGA
OWNER	Wendell Pittenger
SUPERINTENDENT	Randy Juliar
PROFESSIONAL	Sam Drodofsky

	MEN				**WOMEN**		
	BACK	FRONT	PAR	HDCP	FRONT	PAR	HDCP
1	405	395	4	3	335	4	3
2	540	529	5	1	455	5	1
3	420	413	4	4	353	4	4
4	163	153	3	9	147	3	9
5	380	370	4	5	355	4	5
6	195	180	3	7	129	3	7
7	360	322	4	6	302	4	6
8	165	157	3	8	147	3	8
9	511	501	5	2	481	5	2
LOW	3139	3020	35		2704	35	
1	454	447	4	1	388	5	1
2	184	153	3	9	143	3	9
3	352	337	4	5	271	4	5
4	401	386	4	2	368	4	2
5	180	141	3	7	115	3	7
6	540	525	5	4	437	5	4
7	498	488	5	6	438	5	6
8	217	205	3	8	168	3	8
9	508	496	5	3	433	5	3
MID	3334	3178	36		2761	37	
1	318	286	4	2	263	4	2
2	164	152	3	8	124	3	8
3	428	414	4	1	286	4	1
4	103	84	3	9	70	3	9
5	504	494	5	4	413	5	4
6	327	308	4	6	284	4	6
7	378	360	4	3	312	4	3
8	171	149	3	7	129	3	7
9	488	475	5	5	443	5	5
HIGH	2881	2722	35		2324	35	
L/M	6473	6198	71		5465	72	
Rating	71.5	70.2			71.9		
Slope	128	125			126		
M/H	6215	5900	71		5085	72	
Rating	71.1	69.7			70.8		
Slope	130	127			127		
H/L	6020	5742	70		5028	70	
Rating	70.0	68.7			70.1		
Slope	125	123			125		

● LOWLANDS
● MIDLANDS
● HIGHLANDS

GOLF COURSE DIRECTORY

MONTEVIDEO COUNTRY CLUB

9 Regulation Semi-Private

West Highway 212, P.O. Box 231
Montevideo, Minnesota 56265
612/269-8600 Clubhouse
612/269-6828 Proshop

RESERVATIONS	612/269-6828 1 week	
	Walk-on: good/fair	
GREEN FEES	M-F	S-S
Adult	$15/10	$18/12
Senior	$15/10	$18/12
Junior	$15/10	$18/12
Twilight	$8	$10
PAYMENT	Credit: Visa®	
	Non-local checks accepted	
LEAGUES	Men:	Th (2:30 - 7 pm)
MEMBERSHIPS	USGA, NGF, GCSAA, MGA	
MANAGER	Tom Blank	
SUPERINTENDENT	Gerry Quast	
PROFESSIONAL	Tom Blank	

HOURS	7 am to Dusk
SEASON	April to October

FEATURES

Putting green	Y	
Driving range	Y	
Practice area	Y	
Golf carts		
Power (gas)	Y	$16
Pull carts	Y	$1
Club rental	Y	$5
Club storage	Y	
Caddies	N	
Proshop		
Extended	Y	
Refreshments		
Restaurant	Y	
Lounge	Y	
Snacks	Y	
Clubhouse		
Showers	Y	
Lockers	N	
Lodging	N	

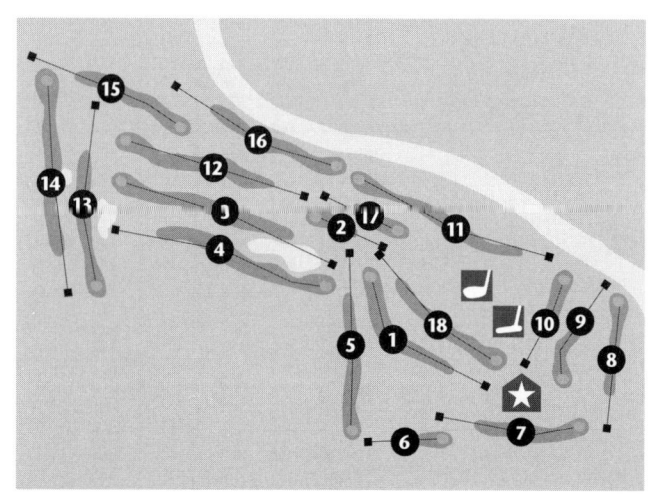

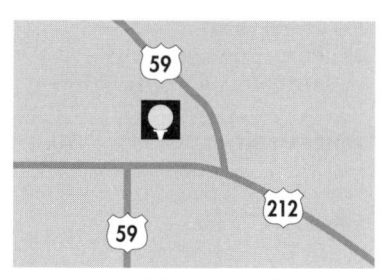

Located west of Montevideo. Course is 1/4 mile west of north U.S. Highway 59 on U.S. Highway 212.

	MEN				**WOMEN**		
	BACK	FRONT	PAR	HDCP	FRONT	PAR	HDCP
1	405	366	4	3	354	4	3
2	206	156	3	17	129	3	17
3	487	426	5	9	416	5	13
4	511	490	5	1	422	5	1
5	365	356	4	15	301	4	15
6	158	146	3	13	135	3	7
7	342	334	4	5	295	4	5
8	262	257	4	11	250	4	9
9	240	231	4	7	225	4	11
Out	2976	2762	36		2527	36	
10	211	206	3	4	186	3	8
11	468	455	5	10	390	5	12
12	433	397	4	2	354	4	2
13	367	342	4	6	251	4	14
14	459	445	5	16	402	5	6
15	332	320	4	14	263	4	16
16	369	322	4	8	304	4	4
17	143	131	3	18	119	3	18
18	396	355	4	12	267	4	10
In	3178	2973	36		2536	36	
Total	6118	5936	72		5374	72	
Rating	68.2	67.3			69.3		
Slope	107	105			109		

THE MINNESOTA ILLUSTRATED

MONTGOMERY GOLF CLUB

18 Regulation Public

900 Rogers Drive
Montgomery, Minnesota 56069
612/364-5602 Clubhouse/Proshop

HOURS 7 am to Dusk

SEASON April-November

RESERVATIONS	612/364-5602 1 day	
	Walk-on: good/fair	
GREEN FEES	M-F	S-S
Adult	$14/9	$16/12
Senior	$14/9	$16/12
Junior	$14/9	$16/12
Twilight	$10/6	NA
	Special rates available	
PAYMENT	No credit cards accepted	
	Non-local checks accepted	
LEAGUES	Men: W	
	Women: Th	
MEMBERSHIPS	USGA, NGF, GCSAA, MGA	
MANAGER	John LaFramboise	
SUPERINTENDENT	James Reiter	

FEATURES		
Putting green	Y	
Driving range	Y	$2
Practice area	N	
Golf carts		
Power	Y	$17/12
Pull carts	Y	$4/2
Club rental	Y	$5
Club storage	Y	$20
Caddies	N	
Proshop		
Extended	Y	
Refreshments		
Restaurant	N	
Lounge	Y	
Snacks	Y	
Clubhouse		
Showers	Y	
Lockers	Y	$20
Lodging	N	

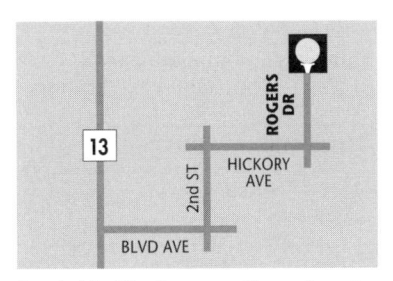

Located in Montgomery. Course is east of Hwy 13 on Blvd Ave, north on 2nd St, east on Hickory, then north Rogers Dr.

	MEN				WOMEN		
	BACK	FRONT	PAR	HDCP	FRONT	PAR	HDCP
1	350	345	4	13	305	4	13
2	483	469	5	3	397	5	5
3	184	170	3	15	160	3	15
4	392	370	4	9	290	4	11
5	378	370	4	1	346	4	3
6	361	340	4	7	250	4	9
7	173	150	3	17	118	3	17
8	524	513	5	5	424	5	1
9	406	391	4	11	268	4	7
Out	3251	3118	36		2558	36	
10	415	398	4	12	330	4	10
11	398	354	4	10	269	4	12
12	301	283	4	6	225	4	4
13	352	332	4	4	260	4	6
14	171	141	3	18	110	3	14
15	498	488	5	8	401	5	8
16	390	341	4	16	292	4	16
17	216	198	3	14	159	3	18
18	548	540	5	2	425	5	2
In	3289	3075	36		2471	36	
Total	6540	6193	72		5029	72	
Rating	71.5	69.9			68.9		
Slope	125	122			125		

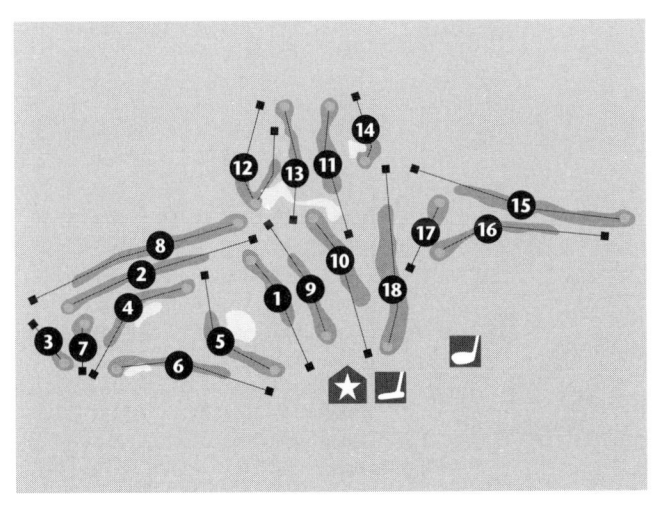

GOLF COURSE DIRECTORY

MONTICELLO COUNTRY CLUB

18 Regulation Public

1209 Golf Course Road
Monticello, Minnesota 55362
612/295-4653 Clubhouse/Proshop

HOURS	7 am to Dusk
SEASON	April-November

RESERVATIONS	612/295-4653
	Walk-on: good/fair
GREEN FEES	M-F S-S
Adult	$16/11 $22/14
Senior	$16/11 $22/14
Junior	$16/11 $22/14
Twilight	NA NA
	M-Th 18 hole special before 1 pm, $12 without power cart or $18 with power cart
PAYMENT	Credit: Visa® MasterCard® Non-local checks accepted
LEAGUES	Various
MEMBERSHIPS	USGA, GCSAA, MGA
MANAGER	Rick Traver
SUPERINTENDENT	Rick Traver, Dave Reif
PROFESSIONAL	Jon Foulauct, Scott Allen

FEATURES	
Putting green	Y
Driving range	Y
Practice area	Y
Golf carts	
Power	Y
Pull carts	Y
Club rental	Y
Club storage	N
Caddies	N
Proshop	
Extended	Y
Refreshments	
Restaurant	Y
Lounge	Y
Snacks	Y
Clubhouse	
Showers	Y
Lockers	Y
Lodging	N

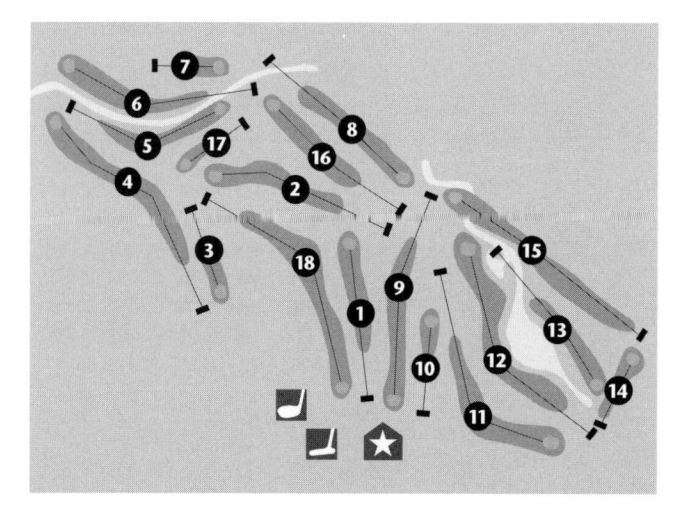

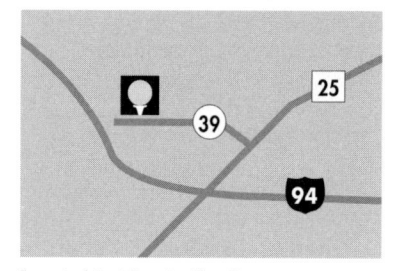

Located in Monticello. Course entrance is north of I-94 on MN Highway 25, west on County Road 39/Hart Blvd.

	MEN				WOMEN		
	BACK	FRONT	PAR	HDCP	FRONT	PAR	HDCP
1	335	324	4	13	276	4	13
2	395	385	4	7	375	4	5
3	227	175	3	15	165	3	11
4	530	514	5	3	500	5	1
5	371	371	4	5	295	4	3
6	352	313	4	9	266	4	7
7	166	158	3	17	134	3	15
8	380	364	4	11	317	4	9
9	444	434	4	1	375	5	17
Out	3200	3038	35		2723	36	
10	185	177	3	18	167	3	16
11	433	383	4	8	340	4	8
12	487	470	5	6	418	5	6
13	343	335	4	10	293	4	12
14	170	143	3	14	111	3	10
15	515	500	5	4	403	5	2
16	358	348	4	12	271	4	14
17	167	162	3	16	157	3	18
18	516	506	5	2	435	5	4
In	3174	3024	36		2595	36	
Total	6374	6062	71		5318	72	
Rating	70.4	69.0			70.8		
Slope	118	116			119		

THE MINNESOTA ILLUSTRATED

MOORHEAD COUNTRY CLUB

18 Regulation Private

2101 North River Drive, Box 255
Moorhead, Minnesota 56560
218/236-0100 Clubhouse
218/236-0200 Proshop

HOURS 7:30 to Dusk

SEASON April-November

| **RESERVATIONS** | 218/236-0200 1 week |
| | Members only |

GREEN FEES	M-F	S-S
Adult	$22/12	$22/12
Senior	$22/12	$22/12
Junior	$22/12	$22/12
Twilight	NA	NA
	Members and guests only	

| **PAYMENT** | Credit: Visa® MasterCard® |
| | Non-local checks accepted |

| **LEAGUES** | Men: None |
| | Women: None |

| **MEMBERSHIPS** | USGA, NGF, PGA, GCSAA, |
| | CMAA, MGA |

| **PROFESSIONAL** | Larry Murphy |

FEATURES

Putting green	Y	
Driving range	Y	$3
Practice area	Y	
Golf carts		
Power	Y	
Pull carts	Y	
Club rental	Y	
Club storage	Y	
Caddies	N	
Proshop		
Extended	Y	
Refreshments		
Restaurant	Y	
Lounge	Y	
Snacks	Y	
Clubhouse		
Showers	Y	
Lockers	Y	
Lodging	N	

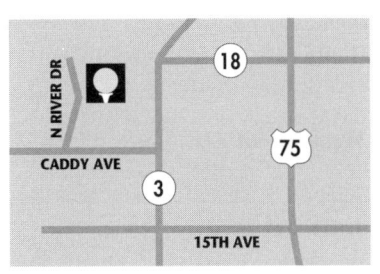

Located in Moorhead. Course is west of Hwy 75 on 15th Ave, north on Cty Rd 3, west on Caddy Ave, north on River Dr.

	MEN				**WOMEN**		
	BACK	FRONT	PAR	HDCP	FRONT	PAR	HDCP
1	480	468	5	15	453	5	1
2	405	393	4	1	305	4	9
3	316	310	4	13	253	4	11
4	177	167	3	9	124	3	13
5	533	505	5	7	406	5	5
6	200	176	3	11	150	3	15
7	501	472	5	3	410	5	3
8	415	380	4	5	405	5	7
9	164	144	3	17	102	3	17
Out	3191	3015	36		2608	37	
10	366	308	4	8	283	4	6
11	151	141	3	18	116	3	18
12	334	320	4	10	309	4	8
13	525	475	5	2	420	5	4
14	509	500	5	6	409	5	2
15	201	172	3	4	80	3	16
16	362	342	4	14	229	4	14
17	341	333	4	16	266	4	12
18	394	376	4	12	303	4	10
In	3183	2967	36		2415	36	
Total	6374	5982	72		5023	73	
Rating	71.5	69.8			69.7		
Slope	125	122			120		

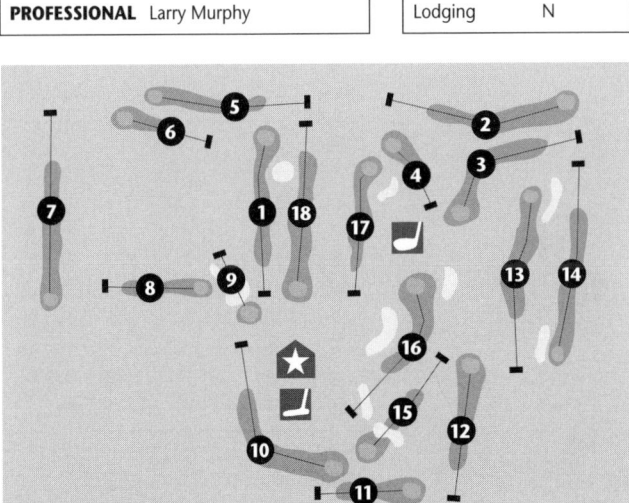

GOLF COURSE DIRECTORY

MOOSE LAKE GOLF CLUB

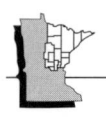

9 Executive Public

Highway 61, P.O. Box 2
Moose Lake, Minnesota 55767
218/485-4886 Clubhouse/Proshop

HOURS	7 am to Dusk
SEASON	April to October

RESERVATIONS	218/485-4886 3 days	
	Walk-on: good/fair	
GREEN FEES	M-F	S-S
Adult	$13/8.50	$16/11.50
Senior	$13/8.50	$16/11.50
Senior	$13/8.50	$16/11.50
Twilight	NA	NA
PAYMENT	No credit cards accepted	
	Non-local checks accepted	
LEAGUES	Men: Th (pm)	
	Women: T (am)	
MEMBERSHIPS	USGA, MGA	
MANAGER	Dawn Thomas	
SUPERINTENDENT	Dave Hambly, Don Bisch	

FEATURES		
Putting green	Y	
Driving range	N	
Practice area	N	
Golf carts		
Power (gas)	Y	$15/10
Pull carts	Y	$3
Club rental	Y	$5
Club storage	Y	$10
Caddies	N	
Proshop		
Extended	Y	
Refreshments		
Restaurant	N	
Lounge	Y	
Snacks	Y	
Clubhouse		
Showers	N	
Lockers	N	
Lodging	N	

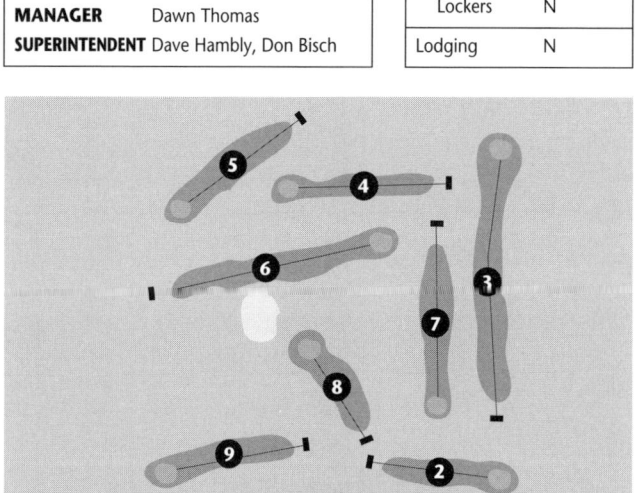

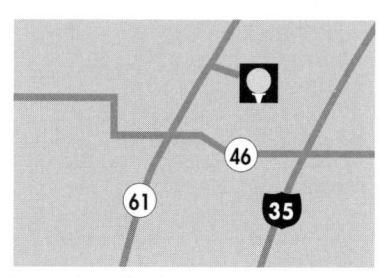

Located south of Moose Lake. Course is west of I-35 on Cty Rd 46, north on Cty Road 61, then east on Golf Course Road.

	MEN			WOMEN		
	FRONT	PAR	HDCP	FRONT	PAR	HDCP
1	293	4	3	280	4	5
2	124	3	9	116	3	9
3	431	5	1	410	5	1
4	295	4	6	270	4	4
5	175	3	8	163	3	7
6	413	5	2	393	5	2
7	330	4	5	310	4	3
8	183	3	7	175	3	8
9	203	3	4	178	3	6
Out	2447	34		2295	34	
1	293	4	3	280	4	5
2	124	3	9	116	3	9
3	431	5	1	410	5	1
4	295	4	6	270	4	4
5	175	3	8	163	3	7
6	413	5	2	393	5	2
7	330	4	5	310	4	3
8	183	3	7	175	3	8
9	203	3	4	178	3	6
In	2447	34		2295	34	
Total	4894	68		4590	68	
Rating	64.0			66.8		
Slope	106			111		

MOUNT FRONTENAC GOLF CLUB

18 Regulation Public

Highway 61, Box 119
Frontenac, Minnesota 55026
612/388-5826 Clubhouse
612/345-3504 Proshop

HOURS Dawn to Dusk

SEASON April to October

RESERVATIONS	800/488-5826 10 days
	Walk on: fair/poor

GREEN FEES	M-Th	F-S
Adult	$15/10	$18/12
Senior	$14/9	$18/12
Junior	$15/10	$18/12
Twilight	NA	$12 (4 pm)

PAYMENT	Credit: Visa® MasterCard®
	Non-local checks accepted

LEAGUES	Men: T,W (pm)

MEMBERSHIPS	NGF, MGA

OWNER	Darrell Boyd, Bill Webster
MANAGER	Todd Fuller
SUPERINTENDENT	Mike Hoeft, Jess Edelbach

FEATURES

Putting green	Y
Driving range	N
Practice area	N
Golf carts	
Power (gas)	Y $18/12
Pull carts	N
Club rental	Y $6
Club storage	N
Caddies	N
Proshop	
Basic	Y
Refreshments	
Restaurant	N
Lounge	Y
Snacks	Y
Clubhouse	
Showers	N
Lockers	N
Lodging	N

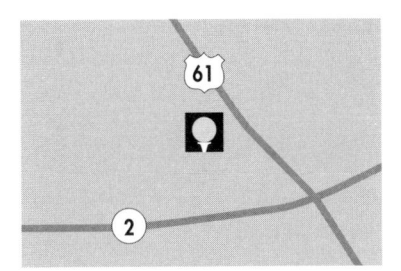

Located west of Frontenac. Course is about one mile north of County Road 2 on U.S. Highway 61.

	MEN			**WOMEN**		
	BACK	FRONT	PAR	HDCP	FRONT	PAR	HDCP
1	400	390	4	5	372	4	5
2	289	281	4	15	236	4	11
3	173	163	3	13	143	3	15
4	395	380	4	7	324	4	7
5	212	180	3	11	162	3	17
6	530	525	5	1	426	5	1
7	394	372	4	9	275	4	9
8	526	516	5	3	431	5	3
9	291	283	4	17	215	4	13
Out	3210	3090	36		2584	36	
10	355	352	4	10	322	4	6
11	174	164	3	18	131	3	14
12	398	388	4	4	373	4	4
13	375	350	4	8	278	4	10
14	290	281	4	16	218	4	12
15	216	170	3	12	128	3	16
16	374	364	4	6	299	4	8
17	176	171	3	14	110	3	18
18	482	472	5	2	389	5	2
In	2840	2712	34		2248	34	
Total	6039	5802	70		4832	70	
Rating	69.2	68.1			67.7		
Slope	119	117			117		

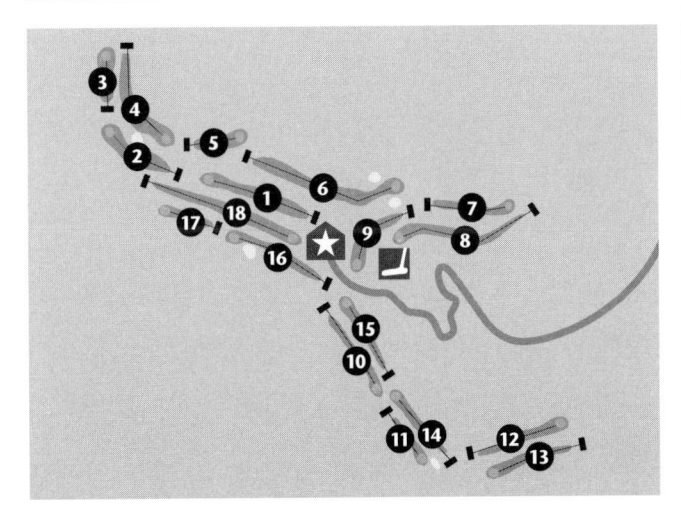

GOLF COURSE DIRECTORY

MOUNTAIN LAKE GOLF CLUB

9 Regulation Public

South Lakeshore Drive, P.O. Box 227
Mountain Lake, Minnesota 56159
507/427-3869 Clubhouse/Proshop

HOURS	8 am to Dusk
SEASON	April to October

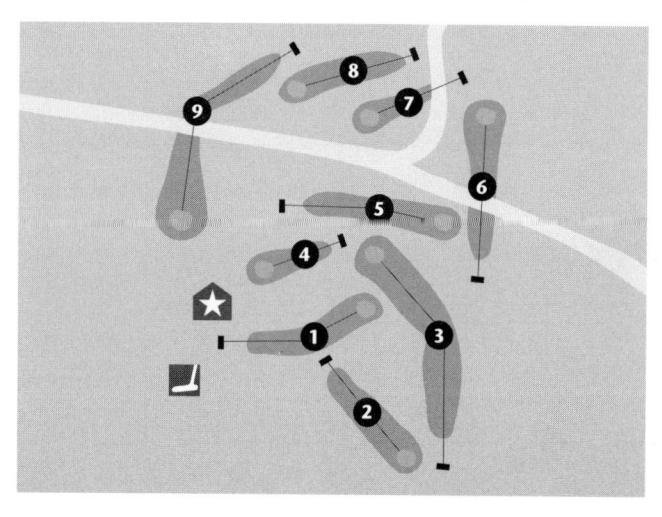

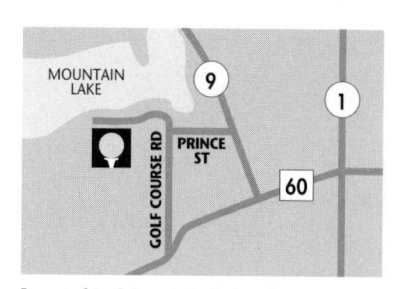

Located in Mountain Lake. Course is north of Highway 60 on Golf Course Road, then west on Lake Shore Drive.

RESERVATIONS	No reservations accepted
	Walk-on: good/good

GREEN FEES	M-F	S-S
Adult	$10/8	$11/9
Senior	$10/8	$11/9
Junior	$10/8	$11/9
Twilight	NA	NA

PAYMENT	No credit cards accepted
	Non-local checks accepted

LEAGUES	None

MEMBERSHIPS	MGA

MANAGER	Wendy Voshage
SUPERINTENDENT	Willis Krahn

FEATURES	
Putting green	Y
Driving range	N
Practice area	N
Golf carts	
Power (elec)	Y $18/10
Pull carts	Y $1
Club rental	Y $1
Club storage	Y
Caddies	N
Proshop	
Extended	Y
Refreshments	
Restaurant	N
Lounge	Y
Snacks	Y
Clubhouse	
Showers	N
Lockers	N
Lodging	N

		MEN				WOMEN		
	BACK	FRONT	PAR	HDCP		FRONT	PAR	HDCP
1	379	359	4	4		345	4	4
2	319	304	4	7		282	4	7
3	490	465	5	5		443	5	5
4	177	157	3	8		147	3	8
5	406	386	4	1		371	4	1
6	494	469	5	3		381	5	3
7	167	142	3	6		131	3	6
8	367	336	4	9		324	4	9
9	429	401	4	2		379	4	2
Out	3228	3019	36			2803	36	
1	379	359	4	4		345	4	4
2	319	304	4	7		282	4	7
3	490	465	5	5		443	5	5
4	177	157	3	8		147	3	8
5	406	386	4	1		371	4	1
6	494	469	5	3		381	5	3
7	167	142	3	6		131	3	6
8	367	336	4	9		324	4	9
9	429	401	4	2		379	4	2
In	3228	3019	36			2803	36	
Total	6456	6038	72			5606	72	
Rating	72.0	70.2				73.2		
Slope	126	123				126		

NEW HOPE VILLAGE GOLF COURSE

9 Par-3 Public

8130 Bass Lake Road
New Hope, Minnesota 55428
612/531-5178 Clubhouse/Proshop

RESERVATIONS	612/531-5178 1 week	
	Walk-on: poor/fair	
GREEN FEES	M-F	S-S
Adult	$12.50/7.50	$12.50/7.50
Senior	$11.50/6.50	$11.50/6.50
Junior	$11.50/6.50	$11.50/6.50
Twilight	NA	NA
PAYMENT	Credit: Visa® MasterCard®	
	Non-local checks accepted	
LEAGUES	Men: M (pm)	
	Women: T (am), W,Th	
	Seniors: M,F (am)	
	Juniors: M,T (pm)	
MEMBERSHIPS	USGA, NGF, GCSAA, MGA	
MANAGER	Mark Severson	
SUPERINTENDENT	Mark Severson	

HOURS	6 am to Dusk
SEASON	April–November

FEATURES		
Putting green	Y	
Driving range	N	
Practice area	N	
Golf carts		
Power (gas)	Y	$8
Pull carts	Y	$1
Club rental	Y	$2
Club storage	N	
Caddies	N	
Proshop		
Extended	Y	
Refreshments		
Restaurant	N	
Lounge	N	
Snacks	Y	
Clubhouse		
Showers	N	
Lockers	N	
Lodging	N	

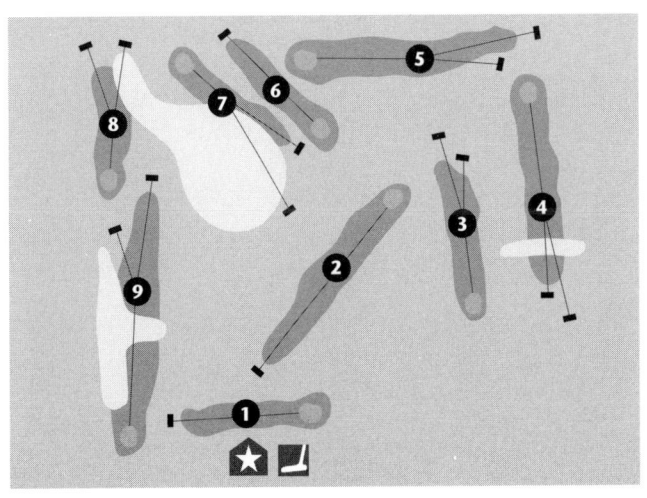

Located in New Hope. Course is on Cty Rd 10 (Bass Lake Road) between Boone Ave N and Winnetka Ave N.

	MEN			**WOMEN**		
	FRONT	PAR	HDCP	FRONT	PAR	HDCP
1	124	3	9	124	3	8
2	169	3	3	169	3	1
3	130	3	7	118	3	9
4	171	3	4	153	3	2
5	159	3	5	142	3	6
6	128	3	6	128	3	7
7	169	3	2	127	3	4
8	108	3	8	108	3	5
9	231	3	1	143	3	3
Out	1389	27		1212	27	
1	124	3	9	124	3	8
2	169	3	3	169	3	1
3	130	3	7	118	3	9
4	171	3	4	153	3	2
5	159	3	5	142	3	6
6	128	3	6	128	3	7
7	169	3	2	127	3	4
8	108	3	8	108	3	5
9	231	3	1	143	3	3
In	1389	27		1212	27	
Total	2778	54		2424	54	
Rating	53.4			53.2		
Slope	74			71		

GOLF COURSE DIRECTORY

NEW PRAGUE GOLF CLUB

18 Regulation Public

400 Lexington Ave S., P.O. Box 107
New Prague, Minnesota 56071
612/758-3126 Clubhouse/Proshop

HOURS	6 am to Dusk
SEASON	April-November

RESERVATIONS	612/758-3126 4 days	
	Walk-on: fair/poor	
GREEN FEES	M-F	S-S
Adult	$22/12	$25/14
Senior	$16/8	$16/8
Junior	$12/6	$12/6
Twilight	NA	NA
PAYMENT	Credit: Visa® MasterCard®	
	Non-local checks accepted	
LEAGUES	Men: Th (9:30am-7pm)	
	Women: T (8-9:30 am)	
	Couples: W (6-9 pm)	
MEMBERSHIPS	USGA, NGF, GCSAA, MGA	
MANAGER	W. Scott Proshek, Jim Kobout	
SUPERINTENDENT	Bob Adam, Bob Porter	

FEATURES		
Putting green	Y	
Driving range	Y	$3.50
Practice area	N	
Golf carts		
Power (gas)	Y	$20-25
Pull carts	Y	$2.50
Club rental	N	
Club storage	N	
Caddies	N	
Proshop		
Extended	Y	
Refreshments		
Restaurant	Y	
Lounge	Y	
Snacks	Y	
Clubhouse		
Showers	Y	
Lockers	Y	
Lodging	N	

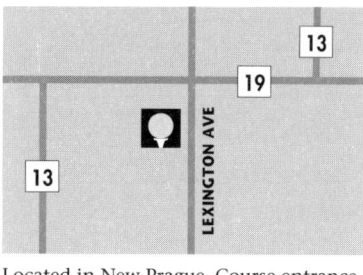

Located in New Prague. Course entrance is 4 blocks south of MN Highway 19 on Lexington Avenue.

	MEN				**WOMEN**		
	BACK	FRONT	PAR	HDCP	FRONT	PAR	HDCP
1	456	443	5	4	372	5	14
2	295	277	4	8	233	4	16
3	396	363	4	10	319	4	4
4	351	351	4	6	315	4	8
5	201	187	3	16	148	3	12
6	505	489	5	2	402	5	2
7	151	140	3	18	132	3	18
8	336	312	4	12	272	4	10
9	356	345	4	14	306	4	6
Out	3047	2907	36		2499	36	
10	345	322	4	9	299	4	9
11	550	536	5	1	408	5	3
12	164	145	3	17	131	3	15
13	536	524	5	3	420	5	5
14	196	178	3	15	115	3	17
15	335	325	4	7	280	4	1
16	355	343	4	11	260	4	13
17	400	385	4	5	282	4	11
18	407	365	4	13	338	4	7
In	3288	3123	36		2533	36	
Total	6335	6030	72		5032	72	
Rating	69.5	68.1			68.3		
Slope	121	118			116		

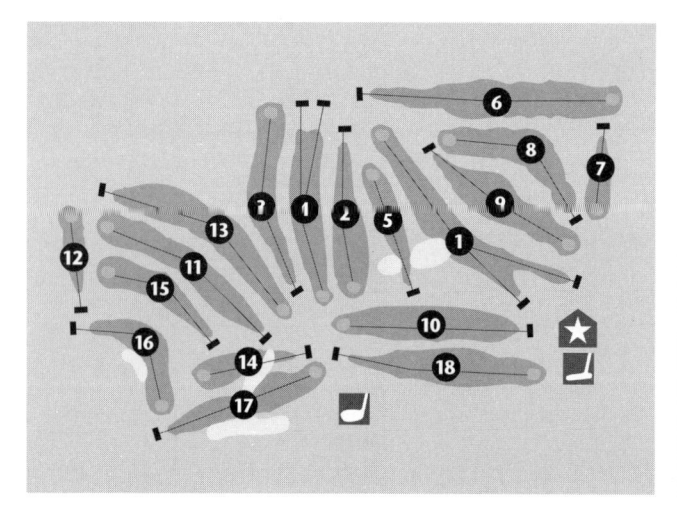

NEW ULM COUNTRY CLUB

18 Regulation Semi-Public

1 Golf Drive, P.O. Box 576
New Ulm, Minnesota 56073
507/354-8896 Clubhouse
507/359-4410 Proshop

HOURS	7 am to Dusk
SEASON	April-November

FEATURES		
Putting green	Y	
Driving range	Y	$3.50
Practice area	Y	
Golf carts		
Power (gas)	Y	$21.25
Pull carts	Y	$2
Club rental	Y	$10
Club storage	Y	
Caddies	N	
Proshop		
Extended	Y	
Refreshments		
Restaurant	Y	
Lounge	Y	
Snacks	Y	
Clubhouse		
Showers	Y	
Lockers	Y	
Lodging	N	

RESERVATIONS	507/359-4410	3 days	
	Walk-on: good/fair		
GREEN FEES	M-F	S-S	
Adult	$21.25/15	$23.50/16	
Senior	$21.25/15	$23.50/16	
Senior	$21.25/15	$23.50/16	
Twilight	NA	NA	
PAYMENT	No credit cards accepted		
	Non-local checks accepted		
LEAGUES	Men: W		
	Women: Th		
MEMBERSHIPS	USGA, PGA, GCSAA,		
	CMAA, MGA		
SUPERINTENDENT	Johnny Helget		
PROFESSIONAL	Gary Christenson, Jr.		

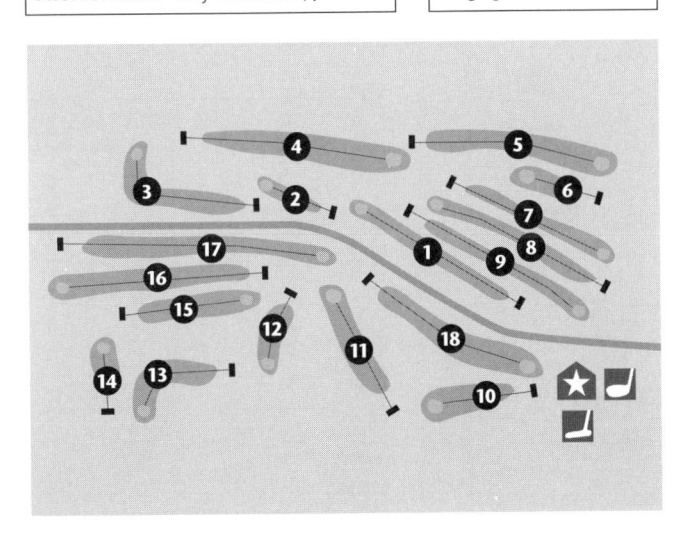

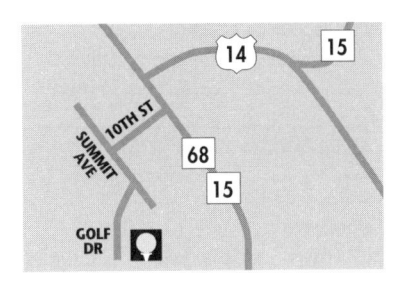

Located in New Ulm. Course entrance is west of MN Hwy 15/68 on 10th St, south on Summit Ave, then west on Golf Dr.

	MEN				**WOMEN**		
	BACK	FRONT	PAR	HDCP	FRONT	PAR	HDCP
1	506	494	5	13	480	5	7
2	176	160	3	15	108	3	15
3	324	301	4	17	281	4	17
4	365	355	4	9	345	4	3
5	416	398	4	1	379	5	13
6	227	200	3	7	160	3	11
7	353	343	4	5	331	4	5
8	381	365	4	3	351	4	1
9	515	502	5	11	453	5	9
Out	3263	3118	36		2888	37	
10	180	170	3	10	159	3	12
11	420	411	4	4	401	5	10
12	177	170	3	6	145	3	2
13	451	441	5	14	430	5	4
14	180	176	3	16	164	3	14
15	395	388	4	2	381	5	8
16	300	285	4	18	254	4	18
17	341	330	4	8	265	4	16
18	496	485	5	12	474	5	6
In	2940	2856	35		2673	37	
Total	6203	5974	71		5561	74	
Rating	70.3	69.2			72.2		
Slope	120	118			124		

GOLF COURSE DIRECTORY

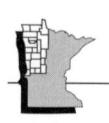

NORDIC TRAILS GOLF COURSE

9 Executive Public

4343 County Road 20 NE
Alexandria, Minnesota 56308
612/762-5420 Clubhouse/Proshop

HOURS	7 am to Dusk
SEASON	April-November

RESERVATIONS	612/762-5420	
	Walk-on: good/good	
GREEN FEES	M-Th	F-S
Adult	$13.50/8.50	$13.50/8.50
Senior	$10/6	$13.50/8.50
Junior	$10/6	$13.50/8.50
Twilight	NA	NA
PAYMENT	Credit: Visa® MasterCard®	
	Non-local checks accepted	
LEAGUES	Men: Th	
	Women: M (pm), W (am)	
MEMBERSHIPS	None	
OWNER	Grant Wenkstern, Dave Krupp	
MANAGER	Mark Vendell	
SUPERINTENDENT	Toby Wiebye	

FEATURES	
Putting green	Y
Driving range	N
Practice area	Y
Golf carts	
Power	Y
Pull carts	Y
Club rental	Y
Club storage	N
Caddies	N
Proshop	
Regular	Y
Refreshments	
Restaurant	N
Lounge	Y
Snacks	Y
Clubhouse	
Showers	N
Lockers	N
Lodging	N

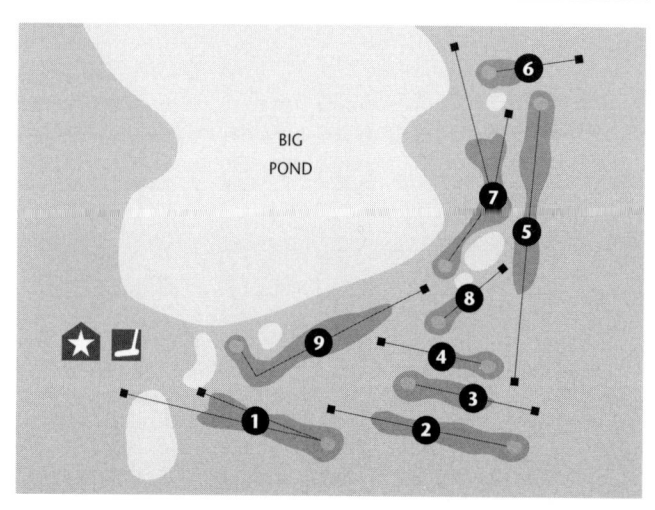

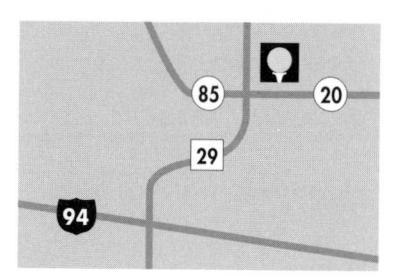

Located in Alexandria. Course entrance is about 1/4 mile east of MN Highway 29 on County Road 20.

	MEN			**WOMEN**		
	FRONT	PAR	HDCP	FRONT	PAR	HDCP
1	311	4	3	213	4	3
2	263	4	5	263	4	5
3	176	3	6	176	3	6
4	137	3	7	137	3	7
5	394	4	2	321	4	2
6	95	3	9	95	3	9
7	306	4	1	248	4	1
8	111	3	8	111	3	8
9	321	4	4	321	4	4
Out	2114	32		1885	32	
1	311	4	3	213	4	3
2	263	4	5	263	4	5
3	176	3	6	176	3	6
4	137	3	7	137	3	7
5	394	4	2	321	4	2
6	95	3	9	95	3	9
7	306	4	1	248	4	1
8	111	3	8	111	3	8
9	321	4	4	321	4	4
In	2114	32		1885	32	
Total	4228	64		3770	64	
Rating	NA			NA		
Slope	NA			NA		

NORMANDALE EXECUTIVE GOLF COURSE

9 Executive Public

7640 Parklawn Avenue
Edina, Minnesota 55435
612/927-9335 Clubhouse/Proshop

| **HOURS** | Dawn to Dusk |
| **SEASON** | April-November |

| **RESERVATIONS** | 612/927-9335 1 day |
| | Walk-on: good/fair |

GREEN FEES	M-F	S-S
Adult	$9	$9
Senior	$9	$9
Junior	$6	$6
Twilight	NA	NA

| **PAYMENT** | No credit cards accepted |
| | Non-local checks accepted |

| **LEAGUES** | Men: Various |
| | Women: Various |

| **MEMBERSHIPS** | MGA |

| **PROFESSIONAL** | None |

FEATURES	
Putting green	Y
Driving range	N
Practice area	N
Golf carts	
Power	Y $10
Pull carts	Y $1.75
Club rental	Y
Club storage	N
Caddies	N
Proshop	
Basic	Y
Refreshments	
Restaurant	N
Lounge	N
Snacks	Y
Clubhouse	
Showers	N
Lockers	N
Lodging	N

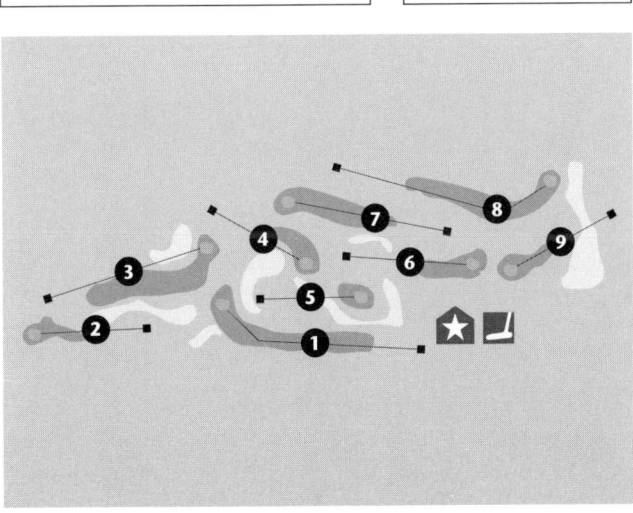

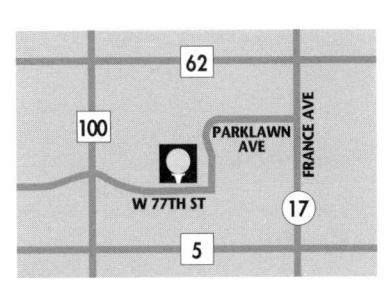

Located in Edina. Course is east of MN Highway 100 on West 77th Street, then north on Parklawn Avenue.

	MEN				**WOMEN**		
	BACK	FRONT	PAR	HDCP	FRONT	PAR	HDCP
1	294	282	4	2	262	4	2
2	164	137	3	8	112	3	8
3	298	254	4	3	210	4	3
4	147	130	3	9	100	3	9
5	150	142	3	7	129	3	7
6	200	168	3	5	134	3	5
7	175	175	3	4	170	3	4
8	320	299	4	1	275	4	1
9	182	158	3	6	105	3	6
Out	1930	1745	30		1497	30	
1	294	282	4	2	262	4	2
2	164	137	3	8	112	3	8
3	298	254	4	3	210	4	3
4	147	130	3	9	100	3	9
5	150	142	3	7	129	3	7
6	200	168	3	5	134	3	5
7	175	175	3	4	170	3	4
8	320	299	4	1	275	4	1
9	182	158	3	6	105	3	6
In	1930	1745	30		1497	30	
Total	3860	3490	60		2994	60	
Rating	58.6	56.8			57.0		
Slope	86	82			90		

GOLF COURSE DIRECTORY

NORTH BRANCH GOLF COURSE

9 Regulation Public

1256 Forest Blvd., P.O. Box 387
North Branch, Minnesota 55056
612/674-9989 Clubhouse/Proshop

HOURS	6 am to Dusk
SEASON	April to October

RESERVATIONS	612/674-9989
	Walk-on: good/fair

GREEN FEES	M-F	S-S
Adult	$14.25/9.50	$15.75/10.50
Senior	$9.25/6.25	$15.75/10.50
Junior	$9/5.50	$15.75/10.50
Twilight	NA	NA

PAYMENT	No credit cards accepted
	Non-local checks accepted

LEAGUES	Men:	M (3:45, 6 pm)
		W (6 pm)
	Women:	T (6 pm)

MEMBERSHIPS	GCSAA, MGA

MANAGER	Donna White
SUPERINTENDENT	Michael McDougall

FEATURES		
Putting green	Y	
Driving range	N	
Practice area	N	
Golf carts		
Power (gas)	Y	$16
Pull carts	Y	$2
Club rental	Y	$6
Club storage	N	
Caddies	N	
Proshop		
Regular	Y	
Refreshments		
Restaurant	N	
Lounge	N	
Snacks	Y	
Clubhouse		
Showers	N	
Lockers	N	
Lodging	N	

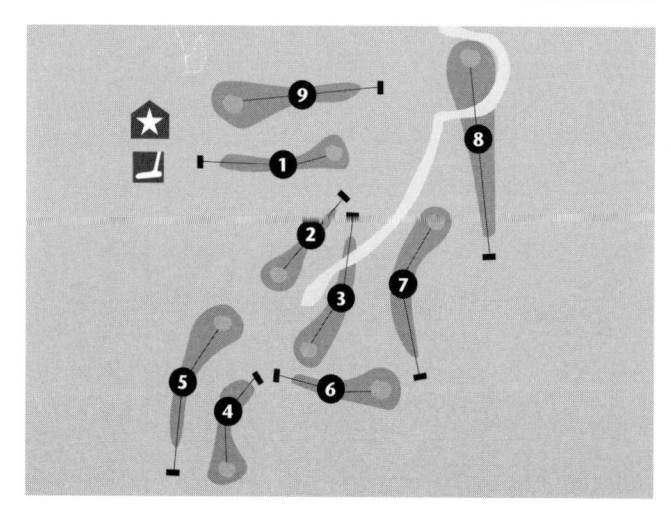

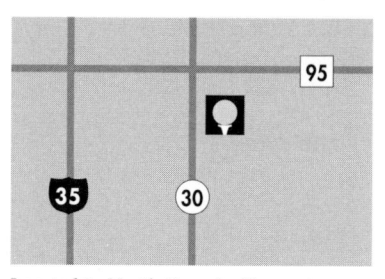

Located in North Branch. Course is one mile east of I-35 on MN Highway 95, then 3 blocks south on County Road 30.

		MEN			WOMEN	
	FRONT	PAR	HDCP	FRONT	PAR	HDCP
1	477	5	9	454	5	2
2	186	3	3	145	3	9
3	335	4	4	308	4	1
4	334	4	6	321	4	6
5	305	4	7	297	4	7
6	193	3	2	185	3	3
7	353	4	5	270	4	4
8	275	4	8	257	4	5
9	440	4	1	383	5	8
Out	2898	35		2620	36	
1	477	5	9	454	5	2
2	186	3	3	145	3	9
3	335	4	4	308	4	1
4	334	4	6	321	4	6
5	305	4	7	297	4	7
6	193	3	2	185	3	3
7	353	4	5	270	4	4
8	275	4	8	257	4	5
9	440	4	1	383	5	8
In	2898	35		2620	36	
Total	5796	70		5240	72	
Rating	66.6			68.8		
Slope	113			113		

THE MINNESOTA ILLUSTRATED

NORTH LINKS GOLF COURSE

18 Regulation Public

RFD 2
North Mankato, Minnesota 56003
507/947-3355 Clubhouse/Proshop

RESERVATIONS	507/947-3355 1 week	
	Walk-on: good/fair	
GREEN FEES	M-F	S-S
Adult	$17.50/10	$19.50/12.50
Senior	$11/6.50*	$19.50/12.50
Junior	$11/6.50*	$19.50/12.50
Twilight	$8.50 (Friday)	$8.50
	*Before 1 pm	
PAYMENT	Credit: Visa® MC® AmEx®	
	Non-local checks accepted	
LEAGUES	Various	
MEMBERSHIPS	USGA, PGA, GCSAA, MGA	
OWNER	Banc-One	
MANAGER	Evergreen Alliance Golf Ltd.	
SUPERINTENDENT	Jerry Storjohann	
PROFESSIONAL	Mike Thomas	

HOURS	7 am to Dusk
SEASON	April–November

FEATURES		
Putting green	Y	
Driving range	Y	$3.75
Practice area	Y	
Golf carts		
Power (gas)	Y	$17/11
Pull carts	Y	$3/2.25
Club rental	Y	$7.50
Club storage	N	
Caddies	N	
Proshop		
Extended	Y	
Refreshments		
Restaurant	Y	
Lounge	Y	
Snacks	Y	
Clubhouse		
Showers	Y	
Lockers	N	
Lodging	N	

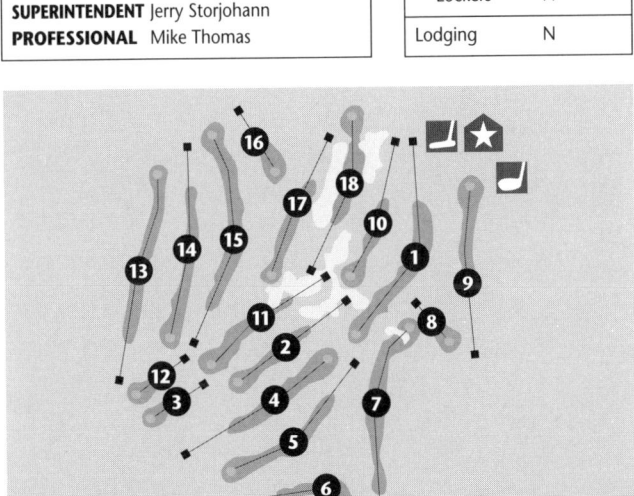

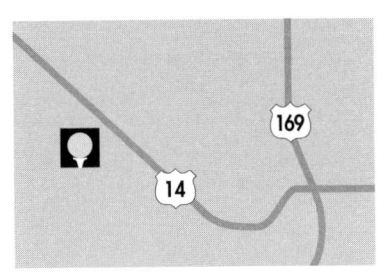

Located in North Mankato. Course is about five miles west of U.S. Highway 169 on U.S. Highway 14.

	MEN				WOMEN		
	BACK	FRONT	PAR	HDCP	FRONT	PAR	HDCP
1	479	452	5	5	399	5	3
2	318	298	4	13	233	4	5
3	151	126	3	15	95	3	17
4	377	351	4	7	304	4	13
5	386	361	4	9	306	4	11
6	352	328	4	11	280	4	9
7	497	472	5	1	410	5	1
8	108	92	3	17	67	3	15
9	365	337	4	3	288	4	7
Out	3033	2817	36		2382	36	
10	307	278	4	12	223	4	10
11	327	312	4	14	242	4	14
12	154	135	3	16	103	3	16
13	487	460	5	2	403	5	2
14	414	377	4	4	291	4	12
15	497	472	5	8	423	5	8
16	164	137	3	18	94	3	18
17	338	312	4	10	258	4	4
18	352	324	4	6	240	4	6
In	3040	2807	36		2277	36	
Total	6073	5624	72		4659	72	
Rating	69.5	67.4			66.9		
Slope	117	113			114		

GOLF COURSE DIRECTORY

249

NORTH OAKS GOLF CLUB

18 Regulation Private

54 East Oaks Road
North Oaks, Minnesota 55127
612/484-6311 Clubhouse
612/484-1635 Proshop

RESERVATIONS	612/484-1635	
	Members only	
GREEN FEES	M-F	S-S
Adult	Call	Call
Senior	Call	Call
Junior	Call	Call
Twilight	NA	NA
	Members and guests only	
PAYMENT	Fees billed to members	
LEAGUES	Men: None	
	Women: None	
MEMBERSHIPS	USGA, NGF, PGA, LPGA, GCSAA, CMAA, MGA	
SUPERINTENDENT	Jack McKenzie	
PROFESSIONAL	Don Powers	

HOURS	Dawn to Dusk
SEASON	April-November

FEATURES	
Putting green	Y
Driving range	Y
Practice area	Y
Golf carts	
Power	Y
Pull carts	Y
Club rental	N
Club storage	Y
Caddies	Y
Proshop	
Extended	Y
Refreshments	
Restaurant	Y
Lounge	Y
Snacks	Y
Clubhouse	
Showers	Y
Lockers	Y
Lodging	N

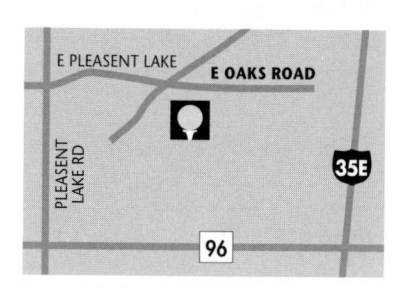

Located in North Oaks. Course is north of MN Hwy 96 on Pleasant Lake Road, east on E. Pleasant Lake/E. Oaks Road.

	MEN				WOMEN		
	BACK	FRONT	PAR	HDCP	FRONT	PAR	HDCP
1	531	511	5	13	461	5	1
2	462	462	4	1	430	5	9
3	420	415	4	5	375	4	5
4	358	340	4	17	340	4	13
5	194	194	3	9	160	3	15
6	405	395	4	7	380	4	3
7	447	423	4	3	405	5	11
8	190	180	3	11	170	3	17
9	528	503	5	15	420	5	7
Out	3535	3423	36		3141	38	
10	349	335	4	18	305	4	14
11	179	164	3	10	145	3	16
12	368	353	4	12	340	4	10
13	155	138	3	16	130	3	18
14	409	404	4	2	401	5	8
15	228	218	3	4	170	3	12
16	521	511	5	6	450	5	2
17	371	356	4	8	345	4	6
18	507	481	5	14	435	5	4
In	3087	2960	35		2721	36	
Total	6622	6383	71		5862	74	
Rating	73.0	71.9			75.1		
Slope	136	134			138		

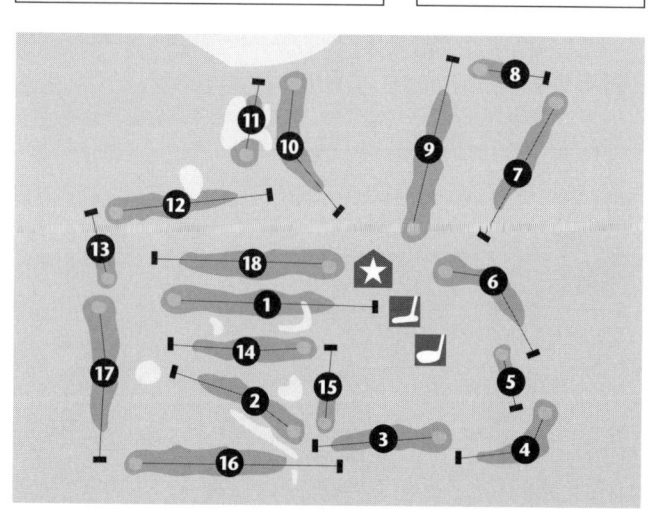

NORTHERN HILLS GOLF CLUB

18 Regulation Public

4805 Northwest 41st Avenue
Rochester, Minnesota 55901
507/281-6170 Clubhouse/Proshop

HOURS	6 am to Dusk
SEASON	April–November

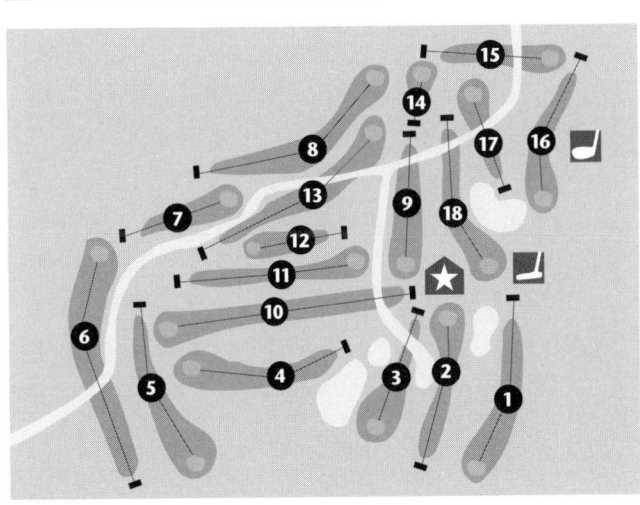

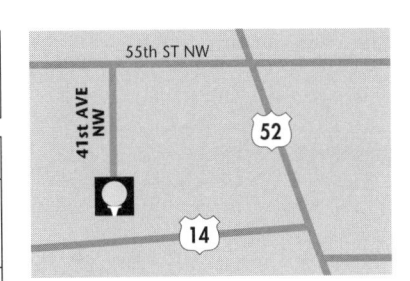

Located in Rochester. Course entrance is west of U.S. Highway 52 on 55th Steet, then south on 41st Avenue.

RESERVATIONS	507/281-6170 2 days
	Walk-on: fair/poor

GREEN FEES	M-F	S-S
Adult	$18/11.50	$18/11.50
Senior	$18/11.50	$18/11.50
Junior	$18/11.50	$18/11.50
Twilight	NA	NA

PAYMENT	Credit: Visa® MasterCard®
	Non-local checks accepted

LEAGUES	Men: W
	Women: T

MEMBERSHIPS	USGA, MGA

MANAGER	Jake Manahan
SUPERINTENDENT	Harvey Boyser
PROFESSIONAL	Jake Manahan, Bill Watson, Brad Pederson

FEATURES		
Putting green	Y	
Driving range	Y	$3
Practice area	Y	
Golf carts		
Power (gas)	Y	$16
Pull carts	Y	$2
Club rental	Y	$5
Club storage	N	
Caddies	N	
Proshop		
Extended	Y	
Refreshments		
Restaurant	N	
Lounge	N	
Snacks	Y	
Clubhouse		
Showers	N	
Lockers	N	
Lodging	N	

	MEN				WOMEN		
	BACK	FRONT	PAR	HDCP	FRONT	PAR	HDCP
1	381	357	4	2	336	4	2
2	365	320	4	16	292	4	16
3	173	152	3	12	130	3	12
4	338	326	4	18	298	4	18
5	340	310	4	8	295	4	8
6	504	484	5	4	417	5	4
7	175	165	3	14	153	3	14
8	520	485	5	6	435	5	6
9	386	374	4	10	350	4	10
Out	3157	2963	36		2696	36	
10	486	478	5	9	430	5	9
11	418	396	4	3	371	4	3
12	185	163	3	13	155	3	13
13	393	371	4	5	349	4	5
14	144	124	3	17	103	3	17
15	333	316	4	11	307	4	11
16	346	336	4	7	318	4	7
17	342	334	4	15	326	4	15
18	506	490	5	1	467	5	1
In	3153	3008	36		2826	36	
Total	6310	5971	72		5522	72	
Rating	70.4	68.8			71.6		
Slope	123	120			123		

GOLF COURSE DIRECTORY

NORTHFIELD GOLF CLUB

18 Regulation Semi-Private

707 Prairie Street
Northfield, Minnesota 55057
507/645-4026 Clubhouse/Proshop

HOURS	Dawn to Dusk
SEASON	April–November

RESERVATIONS	507/645-4026 2 days
	Walk-on: good/poor

GREEN FEES	M-F	S-S
Adult	$28/19	$36/22
Senior	$28/19	$36/22
Junior	$28/19	$36/22
Twilight	NA	NA

PAYMENT	Credit: Visa® MC® AmEx®
	Non-local checks accepted

LEAGUES	Men: T (pm)
	Women: W (pm)

MEMBERSHIPS	USGA, PGA, LPGA, GCSAA, MGA

SUPERINTENDENT	Bill Whitworth
PROFESSIONAL	Dan Dols

FEATURES	
Putting green	Y
Driving range	N
Practice area	Y
Golf carts	
Power (gas)	Y $23/17
Pull carts	Y $2
Club rental	Y
Club storage	Y
Caddies	N
Proshop	
Extended	Y
Refreshments	
Restaurant	Y
Lounge	Y
Snacks	Y
Clubhouse	
Showers	Y
Lockers	Y
Lodging	N

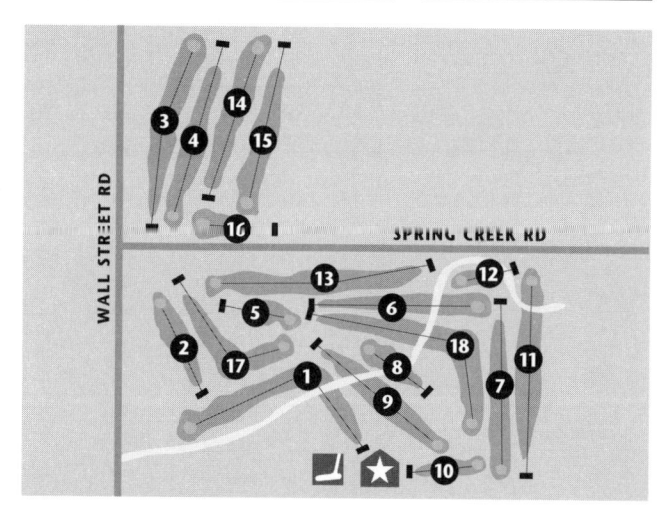

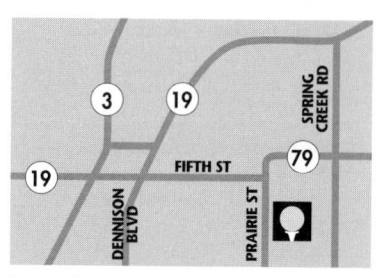

Located in Northfield. Course entrance is east of MN Highway 3/19 on 5th St, then south on Prairie Street.

		MEN				WOMEN		
	BACK	FRONT	PAR	HDCP		FRONT	PAR	HDCP
1	515	488	5	5		431	5	3
2	198	185	3	9		165	3	13
3	404	384	4	3		410	5	1
4	385	372	4	13		356	4	11
5	146	134	3	17		114	3	17
6	404	400	4	1		400	5	5
7	352	328	4	11		298	4	9
8	195	171	3	15		145	3	15
9	350	340	4	7		260	4	7
Out	2949	2802	34			2579	36	
10	146	130	3	18		105	3	18
11	377	369	4	4		361	4	2
12	168	146	3	12		118	3	14
13	488	473	5	10		422	5	8
14	316	335	4	0		330	4	0
15	348	336	4	6		316	4	10
16	160	147	3	16		120	3	16
17	339	331	4	14		307	4	12
18	535	535	5	2		445	5	4
In	2907	2802	35			2524	35	
Total	5856	5604	69			5103	71	
Rating	68.7	67.7				70.4		
Slope	128	126				126		

THE LINKS AT NORTHFORK

18 Regulation Public

9333 153rd Avenue Northwest
Ramsey, Minnesota 55303
612/241-0506 Clubhouse/Proshop

HOURS	6:30 am–Dusk
SEASON	April-November

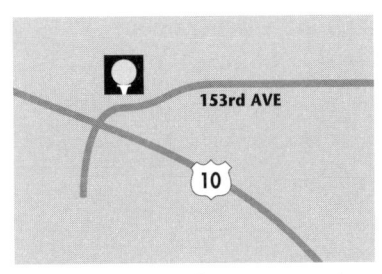

RESERVATIONS	612/241-0506 3 days
	Walk-on: good/fair

GREEN FEES	M-F	S-S
Adult	$35	$35
Senior	$23*	$23*
Junior	$18	$18 (2 pm)
Twilight	$23*	$23*
	*Includes cart	

PAYMENT	Credit: Visa® MC® AmEx®
	Non-local checks accepted

LEAGUES	None

MEMBERSHIPS	USGA, NGF, PGA, GCSAA, CMAA, MGA

MANAGER	Doyle Ricks
SUPERINTENDENT	Mitch Fossey
PROFESSIONAL	Doyle Ricks, Joel Gohlmann

FEATURES	
Putting green	Y
Driving range	Y
Practice area	Y
Golf carts	
Power (gas)	Y
Pull carts	Y
Club rental	Y
Club storage	N
Caddies	N
Proshop	
Extended	Y
Refreshments	
Restaurant	Y
Lounge	Y
Snacks	Y
Clubhouse	
Showers	N
Lockers	N
Lodging	N

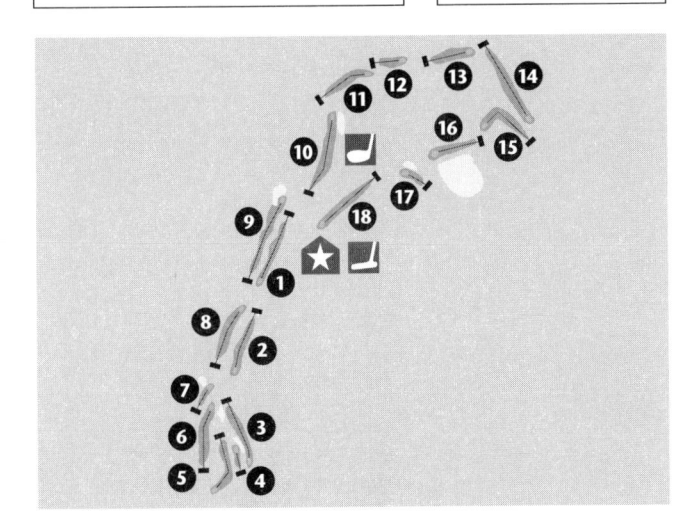

Located in Ramsey. Course entrance is north of U.S. Highway 10 on 153rd Avenue.

	MEN				**WOMEN**		
	BACK	FRONT	PAR	HDCP	FRONT	PAR	HDCP
1	525	494	5	4	457	5	4
2	428	385	4	10	324	4	10
3	420	381	4	8	296	4	8
4	190	160	3	16	109	3	16
5	371	335	4	14	266	4	14
6	429	375	4	12	318	4	12
7	155	125	3	18	79	3	18
8	446	415	4	6	340	4	6
9	514	479	5	2	403	5	2
Out	3478	3149	36		2592	36	
10	490	471	5	3	425	5	3
11	426	384	4	9	318	4	9
12	206	184	3	15	153	3	15
13	380	338	4	13	264	4	13
14	557	512	5	1	416	5	1
15	403	362	4	11	304	4	11
16	440	381	4	7	316	4	7
17	176	153	3	17	109	4	17
18	432	406	4	5	344	4	5
In	3510	3195	36		2649	36	
Total	6988	6344	72		5241	72	
Rating	73.7	71.0			70.5		
Slope	127	121			117		

GOLF COURSE DIRECTORY

NORTHLAND COUNTRY CLUB

18 Regulation Private

3901 East Superior Street
Duluth, Minnesota 55804
218/525-1941 Clubhouse
218/525-1970 Proshop

HOURS	7 am to Dusk
SEASON	April–November

FEATURES

Putting green	Y
Driving range	Y
Practice area	Y
Golf carts	
Power (gas)	Y
Pull carts	N
Club rental	Y
Club storage	Y
Caddies	Y
Proshop	
Extended	Y
Refreshments	
Restaurant	Y
Lounge	Y
Snacks	Y
Clubhouse	
Showers	Y
Lockers	Y
Lodging	N

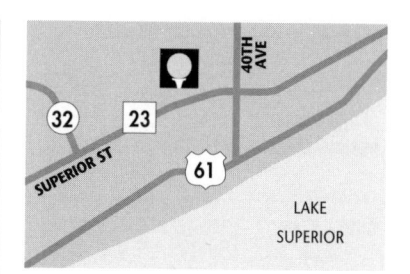

Located in Duluth. Course entrance is about 1/4 mile north of County Road 32 on MN Highway 23/East Superior Street.

RESERVATIONS	218/525-1970
	Members only

GREEN FEES	M-F	S-S
Adult	$35	$40
Senior	$35	$40
Junior	$35	$40
Twilight	NA	NA
	Members and guests only	

PAYMENT	No credit cards accepted
	Non-local checks accepted

LEAGUES	None

MEMBERSHIPS	USGA, NGF, PGA, GCSAA, CMAA, NCA, MGA

SUPERINTENDENT	David Kohlbry
PROFESSIONAL	Joe O'Connor

		MEN			WOMEN		
	BACK	FRONT	PAR	HDCP	FRONT	PAR	HDCP
1	428	418	4	7	418	5	11
2	324	315	4	15	239	4	15
3	376	361	4	1	346	4	1
4	498	458	5	9	428	5	5
5	150	135	3	17	122	3	17
6	382	367	4	13	352	4	9
7	434	418	4	3	402	5	7
8	230	216	3	11	191	3	13
9	561	544	5	5	463	5	3
Out	3383	3232	36		2961	38	
10	409	391	4	2	345	4	2
11	485	468	5	6	406	5	8
12	205	180	3	14	160	3	16
13	421	409	4	10	384	4	4
14	453	404	3	18	387	5	14
15	411	396	4	12	373	4	12
16	415	402	4	8	349	4	10
17	175	155	3	18	135	3	18
18	428	401	4	4	396	5	6
In	3402	3266	36		2935	37	
Total	6785	6498	72		5896	75	
Rating	73.2	71.9			74.6		
Slope	132	129			132		

Course layout map not provided.

OAK GLEN COUNTRY CLUB — 18 Regulation Public

1599 McKusick Road
Stillwater, Minnesota 55082
612/439-6981 Clubhouse
612/439-6963 Proshop

RESERVATIONS	612/439-6963 2 days
	Walk-on: good/fair

GREEN FEES	M-F	S-S
Adult	$20/13	$26/15
Senior	$20/13	$25/15
Junior	$20/13	$25/15
Twilight	$15	NA

PAYMENT	Credit: Visa® MasterCard®
	Non-local checks accepted
LEAGUES	None
MEMBERSHIPS	USGA, PGA, GCSAA, MGA
MANAGER	Greg Stang
SUPERINTENDENT	Peter Mogren
PROFESSIONAL	Greg Stang

HOURS	7 am to Dusk
SEASON	April–November

FEATURES		
Putting green	Y	
Driving range	Y	$2
Practice area	N	
Golf carts		
Power (gas)	Y	$20
Pull carts	Y	$2
Club rental	Y	$12
Club storage	N	
Caddies	N	
Proshop		
Extended	Y	
Refreshments		
Restaurant	Y	
Lounge	Y	
Snacks	Y	
Clubhouse		
Showers	Y	
Lockers	Y	
Lodging	N	

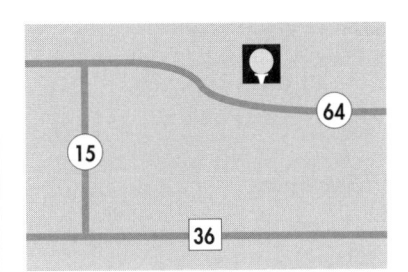

Located in Stillwater. Course entrance is north of MN Hwy 36 on Cty Rd 15, then east 2 miles on Cty Rd 64/McKusick Rd.

		MEN				WOMEN		
	BACK	FRONT	PAR	HDCP		FRONT	PAR	HDCP
1	368	348	4	6		334	4	6
2	488	480	5	2		455	5	2
3	140	130	3	16		105	5	2
4	328	323	4	14		290	4	14
5	408	395	4	8		340	4	10
6	136	126	3	18		106	3	18
7	441	416	4	4		353	4	12
8	501	490	5	10		433	5	4
9	406	388	4	12		365	4	8
Out	3216	3096	36			2781	36	
10	406	388	4	1		353	4	7
11	498	486	5	7		464	5	3
12	183	175	3	17		150	3	17
13	356	350	4	13		335	4	11
14	509	502	5	3		447	5	1
15	420	370	4	11		300	4	13
16	218	185	3	5		155	3	5
17	358	358	4	15		306	4	15
18	410	400	4	9		335	4	9
In	3358	3214	36			2845	36	
Total	6574	6310	72			5626	72	
Rating	72.4	71.3				73.4		
Slope	131	128				130		

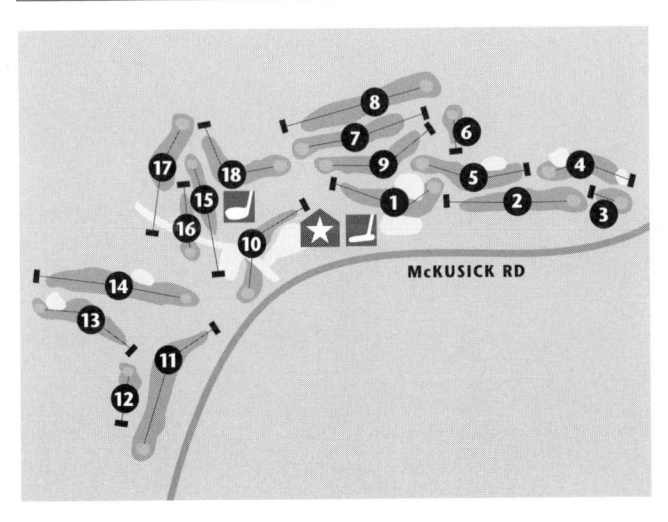

GOLF COURSE DIRECTORY

OAK GLEN COUNTRY CLUB

9 Executive Public

1599 McKusick Road
Stillwater, Minnesota 55082
612/439-6981 Clubhouse
612/439-6963 Proshop

RESERVATIONS	612/439-6981	2 days
	Walk-on: good/fair	

GREEN FEES	M-F	S-S
Adult	$8.50	$8.50
Senior	$8.50	$8.50
Junior	$8.50	$8.50
Twilight	NA	NA

PAYMENT	Credit: Visa® MasterCard®
	Non-local checks accepted

LEAGUES	None

MEMBERSHIPS	USGA, PGA, GCSAA, MGA

MANAGER	Greg Stang
SUPERINTENDENT	Peter Mogren
PROFESSIONAL	Greg Stang

HOURS	7 am to Dusk
SEASON	April–November

FEATURES		
Putting green	Y	
Driving range	Y	$2
Practice area	N	
Golf carts		
Power (gas)	Y	$20
Pull carts	Y	$2
Club rental	Y	$12
Club storage	N	
Caddies	N	
Proshop		
Extended	Y	
Refreshments		
Restaurant	Y	
Lounge	Y	
Snacks	Y	
Clubhouse		
Showers	Y	
Lockers	Y	
Lodging	N	

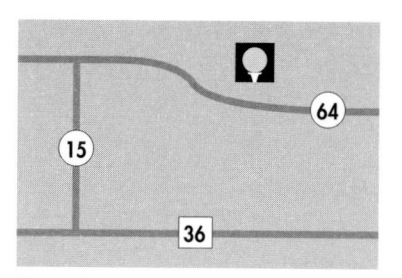

Located in Stillwater. Course entrance is north of MN Hwy 36 on Cty Rd 15, then east 2 miles on Cty Rd 64/McKusick Rd.

	MEN			WOMEN		
	FRONT	PAR	HDCP	FRONT	PAR	HDCP
1	163	3	5	128	3	5
2	163	3	4	153	3	4
3	160	3	6	135	3	6
4	344	4	1	320	4	1
5	165	3	3	139	3	3
6	169	3	7	159	3	7
7	130	3	8	111	3	8
8	336	4	2	316	4	2
9	108	3	9	99	3	9
Out	1738	29		1560	29	
1	163	3	5	128	3	5
2	163	3	4	153	3	4
3	160	3	6	135	3	6
4	344	4	1	320	4	1
5	165	3	3	139	3	3
6	169	3	7	159	3	7
7	130	3	8	111	3	8
8	336	4	2	316	4	2
9	108	3	9	99	3	9
In	1738	29		1560	29	
Total	3476	58		3120	58	
Rating	56.5			56.5		
Slope	82			82		

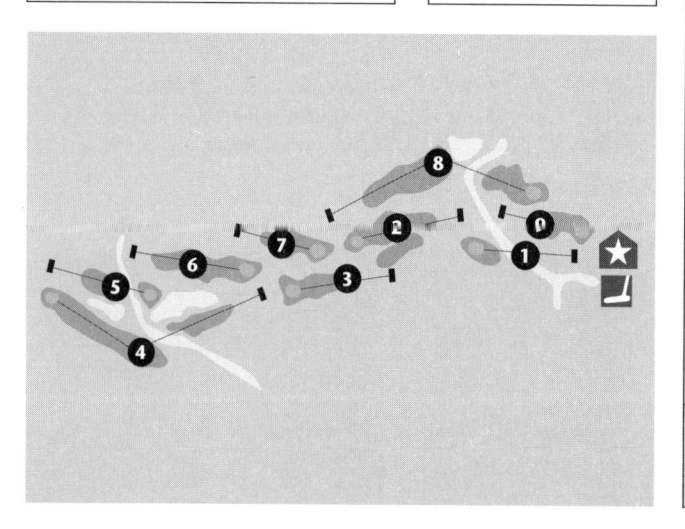

THE MINNESOTA ILLUSTRATED

OAK HARBOR GOLF CLUB

9 Regulation Semi-Private

Rural Route 1, P.O. Box 102A
Baudette, Minnesota 56623
218/634-9939 Clubhouse/Proshop

HOURS	8 am to Dusk
SEASON	April to October

RESERVATIONS	218/634-9939 1 week
	Walk-on: good/fair

GREEN FEES	M-F	S-S
Adult	$15/10	$17/12
Senior	$15/10	$17/12
Junior	$6/4	$8/6
Twilight	NA	NA

PAYMENT	No credit cards accepted
	Non-local checks accepted

LEAGUES	Men: W (pm)
	Women: T

MEMBERSHIPS	USGA, NGF, PGA, MGA

MANAGER	Steve Timm
SUPERINTENDENT	Jeff Lacoursuere
PROFESSIONAL	Steve Timm

FEATURES	
Putting green	Y
Driving range	Y
Practice area	N
Golf carts	
Power	Y
Pull carts	Y
Club rental	Y
Club storage	N
Caddies	N
Proshop	
Extended	Y
Refreshments	
Restaurant	Y
Lounge	Y
Snacks	Y
Clubhouse	
Showers	Y
Lockers	Y
Lodging	N

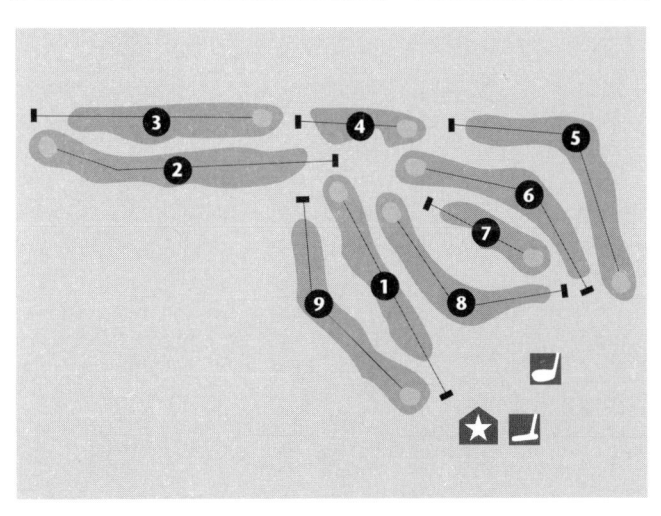

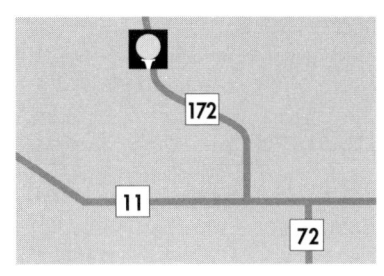

Located north of Baudette. Course is about 10 miles north of MN Highway 11 on MN Highway 172.

	MEN			WOMEN		
	FRONT	PAR	HDCP	FRONT	PAR	HDCP
1	391	4	2	356	4	2
2	471	5	9	401	5	9
3	371	4	6	306	4	6
4	181	3	5	129	3	5
5	481	5	7	416	5	7
6	378	4	4	324	4	4
7	167	3	8	127	3	8
8	410	4	1	335	4	1
9	391	4	3	339	5	3
Out	3241	36		2733	37	
1	391	4	2	356	4	2
2	471	5	9	401	5	9
3	371	4	6	306	4	6
4	181	3	5	129	3	5
5	481	5	7	416	5	7
6	378	4	4	324	4	4
7	167	3	8	127	3	8
8	410	4	1	335	4	1
9	391	4	3	339	5	3
In	3241	36		2733	37	
Total	6482	72		5466	74	
Rating	70.8			70.6		
Slope	115			115		

GOLF COURSE DIRECTORY

OAK HILL GOLF CLUB

9 Regulation Public

9000 Highway 10 N.W.
Rice, Minnesota 56367
612/259-8969 Clubhouse/Proshop

HOURS	6 am to Dusk
SEASON	April–November

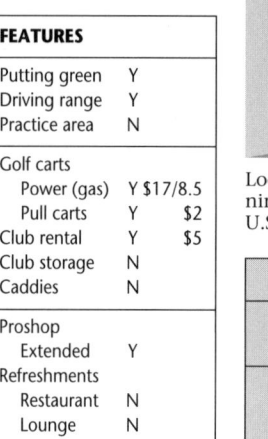

RESERVATIONS	612/259-8969 1 week
	Walk-on: good/poor

GREEN FEES	M-F	S-S
Adult	$11/8	$13/10
Senior	$9/6	$11/8
Junior	$9/6	$11/8
Twilight	NA	NA

PAYMENT	No credit cards accepted
	Non-local checks accepted

LEAGUES	Men: Various
	Women: Various

MEMBERSHIPS	NGF, MGA

OWNER	Jim Dahl, Roger Peterson
MANAGER	Jim Dahl, Roger Peterson

FEATURES	
Putting green	Y
Driving range	Y
Practice area	N
Golf carts	
Power (gas)	Y $17/8.5
Pull carts	Y $2
Club rental	Y $5
Club storage	N
Caddies	N
Proshop	
Extended	Y
Refreshments	
Restaurant	N
Lounge	N
Snacks	Y
Clubhouse	
Showers	N
Lockers	N
Lodging	N

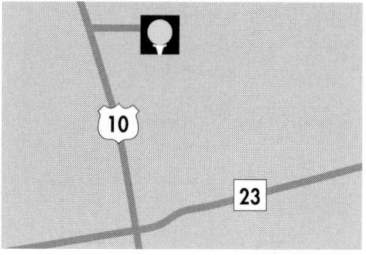

Located south of Rice. Course is about nine miles north of MN Highway 23 on U.S. Highway 10.

	MEN			**WOMEN**		
	FRONT	PAR	HDCP	FRONT	PAR	HDCP
1	318	4	7	284	4	7
2	495	5	9	405	5	9
3	175	3	5	139	3	5
4	310	4	8	276	4	8
5	335	4	3	275	4	3
6	139	3	6	115	3	6
7	451	5	1	370	5	1
8	291	4	4	272	4	4
9	371	4	2	348	4	2
Out	2885	36		2484	36	
1	318	4	7	284	4	7
2	495	5	9	405	5	9
3	175	3	5	139	3	5
4	310	4	8	276	4	8
5	335	4	3	275	4	3
6	139	3	6	115	3	6
7	451	5	1	370	5	1
8	291	4	4	272	4	4
9	371	4	2	348	4	2
In	2885	36		2484	36	
Total	5770	72		4968	72	
Rating	68.4			69.4		
Slope	123			129		

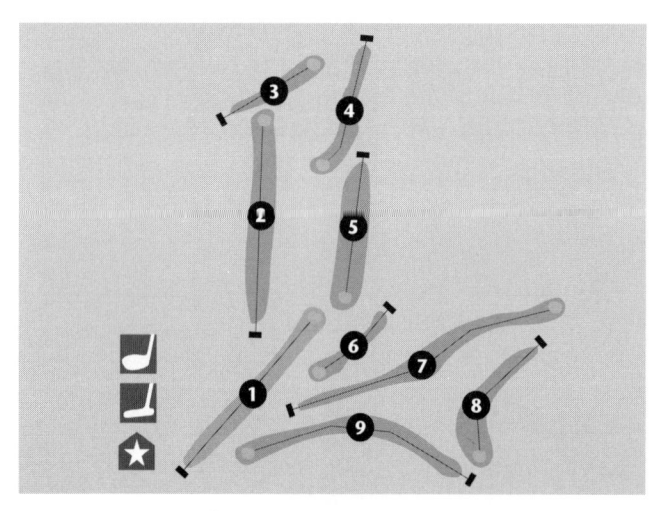

OAK KNOLLS GOLF CLUB

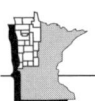

9 Regulation Public

Highway 32 South, P.O. Box 208
Red Lake Falls, Minnesota 56750
218/253-4423 Clubhouse/Proshop

HOURS	Dawn to Dusk
SEASON	May–September

RESERVATIONS	No reservations accepted
	Walk-on: good/fair

GREEN FEES	M-F	S-S
Adult	$9/6	$11/8
Senior	$9/6	$11/8
Junior	$9/6	$11/8
Twilight	NA	NA

PAYMENT	No credit cards accepted
	Non-local checks accepted

LEAGUES	Men: Various
	Women: Various

MEMBERSHIPS	MGA

MANAGER	Vern Knnack

FEATURES	
Putting green	Y
Driving range	N
Practice area	N
Golf carts	
Power (gas)	Y $12/6
Pull carts	Y $4/2
Club rental	Y $2-3
Club storage	N
Caddies	N
Proshop	
Extended	Y
Refreshments	
Restaurant	N
Lounge	N
Snacks	Y
Clubhouse	
Showers	N
Lockers	N
Lodging	N

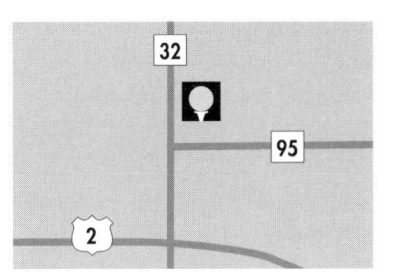

Located in Red Lake Falls. Course is just north of MN Highway 95 on MN Highway 32.

	MEN			**WOMEN**		
	FRONT	PAR	HDCP	FRONT	PAR	HDCP
1	444	5	5	358	5	6
2	392	4	1	377	5	1
3	180	3	4	170	3	5
4	273	4	7	262	4	8
5	416	5	8	416	5	2
6	325	4	2	312	4	3
7	187	3	3	187	4	4
8	125	3	9	117	3	9
9	429	5	6	327	5	7
Out	2771	36		2526	38	
1	444	5	5	358	5	6
2	392	4	1	377	5	1
3	180	3	4	170	3	5
4	273	4	7	262	4	8
5	416	5	8	416	5	2
6	325	4	2	312	4	3
7	187	3	3	187	4	4
8	125	3	9	117	3	9
9	429	5	6	327	5	7
In	2771	36		2526	38	
Total	5542	72		5052	76	
Rating	66.4			68.6		
Slope	107			112		

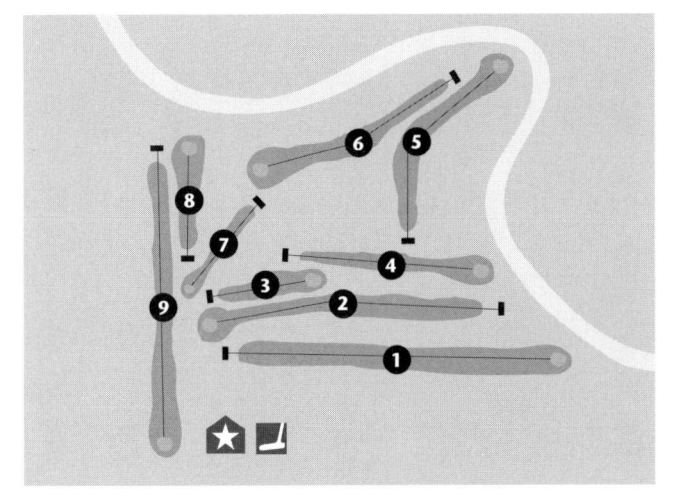

OAK RIDGE COUNTRY CLUB

18 Regulation Private

700 Oak Ridge Road
Hopkins, Minnesota 55343
612/935-7721 Clubhouse/Proshop

HOURS	Dawn to Dusk
SEASON	April to October

RESERVATIONS	612/935-7721	
	Members only	
GREEN FEES	M-F	S-S
Adult	Call	Call
Senior	Call	Call
Junior	Call	Call
Twilight	NA	NA
	Members and guests only	
PAYMENT	Fees billed to members	
LEAGUES	Men: None	
	Women: None	
MEMBERSHIPS	MGA	
SUPERINTENDENT	Keith Scott	
PROFESSIONAL	Chuck Hanson	

FEATURES	
Putting green	Y
Driving range	Y
Practice area	Y
Golf carts	
Power	Y
Pull carts	Y
Club rental	Y
Club storage	Y
Caddies	N
Proshop	
Extended	Y
Refreshments	
Restaurant	Y
Lounge	Y
Snacks	Y
Clubhouse	
Showers	Y
Lockers	Y
Lodging	N

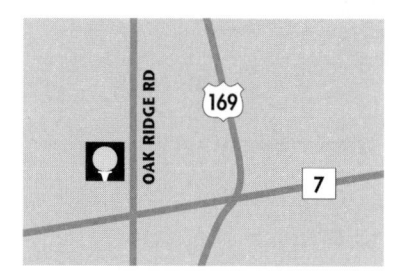

Located in Hopkins. Course entrance is north of MN Highway 7 on Oak Ridge Road.

	MEN				**WOMEN**		
	BACK	FRONT	PAR	HDCP	FRONT	PAR	HDCP
1	403	349	4	7	346	4	9
2	412	330	4	3	328	4	13
3	184	158	3	15	135	3	17
4	394	374	4	11	371	4	3
5	494	480	5	5	469	5	1
6	374	356	4	13	352	4	7
7	199	176	3	17	173	3	15
8	457	419	4	9	417	5	5
9	409	391	4	1	389	5	11
Out	3326	3033	35		2980	37	
10	336	320	4	10	293	4	10
11	217	208	3	14	206	4	18
12	418	103	4	6	400	5	8
13	350	261	4	12	259	4	16
14	540	514	5	2	512	5	2
15	362	346	4	16	344	4	12
16	170	158	3	18	143	3	14
17	387	360	4	8	340	4	4
18	436	427	4	4	424	5	6
In	3216	2997	35		2921	38	
Total	6542	6030	70		5901	75	
Rating	72.1	69.7			74.6		
Slope	132	127			131		

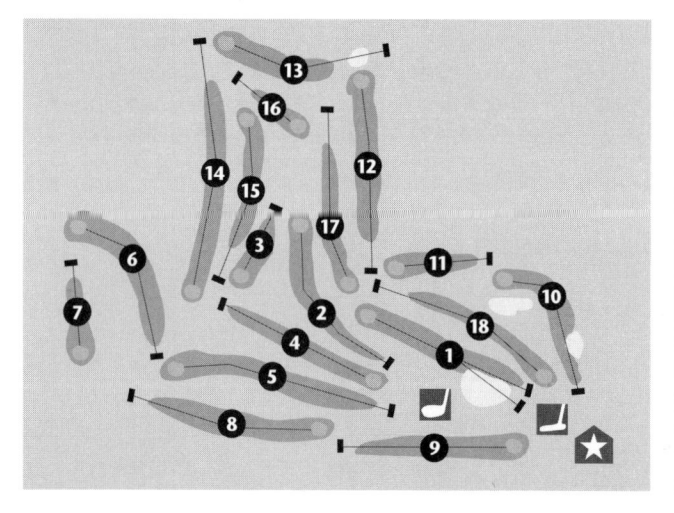

OAK SUMMIT GOLF COURSE

18 Regulation Public

2751 County Road 16 SW
Rochester, Minnesota 55902
507/252-1808 Clubhouse/Proshop

HOURS	6 am to Dusk
SEASON	Mar-November

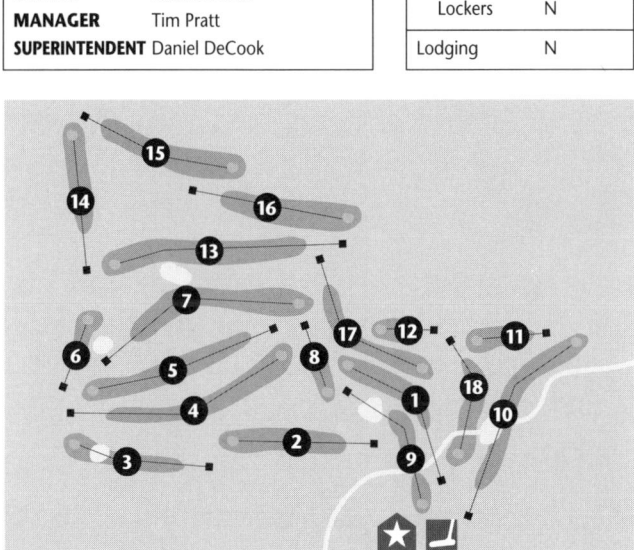

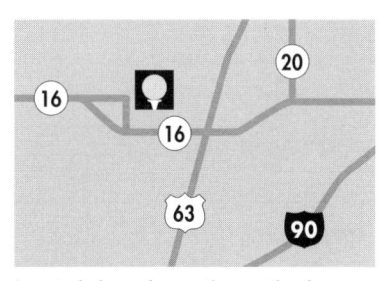

Located about four miles south of Rochester. Course entrance is west of U.S. Highway 63 on County Road 16.

RESERVATIONS	507/252-1808 5 days
	Walk-on: good/fair

GREEN FEES	M-F	S-S
Adult	$13/8	$15/9
Senior	$13/8	$15/9
Junior	$13/8	$15/9
Twilight	NA	NA
	Mondays green fees $10/5	

PAYMENT	Credit: Visa® MasterCard®
	Non-local checks accepted

LEAGUES	Men: W (6 pm)

MEMBERSHIPS	USGA, GCSAA, MGA

OWNER	Leon DeCook
MANAGER	Tim Pratt
SUPERINTENDENT	Daniel DeCook

FEATURES	
Putting green	Y
Driving range	N
Practice area	N
Golf carts	
Power	Y $16/10
Pull carts	Y $2
Club rental	Y $5
Club storage	N
Caddies	N
Proshop	
Extended	Y
Refreshments	
Restaurant	N
Lounge	Y
Snacks	Y
Clubhouse	
Showers	N
Lockers	N
Lodging	N

	MEN				WOMEN		
	BACK	FRONT	PAR	HDCP	FRONT	PAR	HDCP
1	380	377	4	3	248	4	3
2	340	332	4	13	294	4	13
3	311	304	4	7	297	4	7
4	524	518	5	11	484	5	11
5	463	449	4	5	435	5	5
6	182	173	3	15	164	3	15
7	516	512	5	9	449	5	9
8	184	167	3	17	150	3	17
9	340	332	4	1	324	4	1
Out	3240	3164	36		2845	37	
10	498	481	5	2	464	5	2
11	185	171	3	16	157	3	16
12	127	123	3	18	119	3	18
13	525	519	5	4	504	5	4
14	328	324	4	14	294	4	14
15	371	362	4	12	353	4	12
16	365	361	4	10	339	4	10
17	397	393	4	6	373	4	6
18	328	322	4	8	267	4	8
In	3124	3056	36		2870	36	
Total	6364	6220	72		5715	73	
Rating	69.4	68.7			71.8		
Slope	113	112			118		

GOLF COURSE DIRECTORY

OAK VIEW GOLF CLUB

9 Regulation Public

County Road 8, Box 73
Freeborn, Minnesota 56032
507/863-2288 Clubhouse/Proshop

HOURS Dawn to Dusk

SEASON April to October

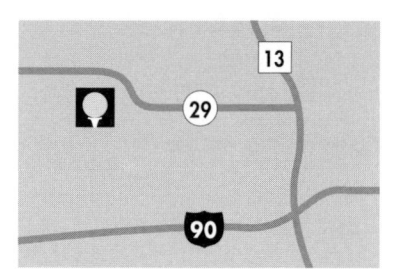

Located near Freeborn. Course entrance is five miles west of MN Highway 13 on County Road 29.

RESERVATIONS	507/863-2288	
	Walk on: good/good	

GREEN FEES	M-F	S-S
Adult	$11/8	$14/10
Senior	$11/8	$14/10
Junior	$11/8	$14/10
Twilight	NA	NA

PAYMENT	No credit cards accepted
	Non-local checks accepted

LEAGUES	Men: Various
	Women: Various

MEMBERSHIPS GCSAA, MGA

MANAGER Sam Nelson
SUPERINTENDENT John Sheedy

FEATURES		
Putting green	Y	
Driving range	N	
Practice area	N	
Golf carts		
Power (gas)	Y	$14/8
Pull carts	Y	$1.50
Club rental	Y	$2.50
Club storage	Y	
Caddies	N	
Proshop		
Regular	Y	
Refreshments		
Restaurant	N	
Lounge	N	
Snacks	Y	
Clubhouse		
Showers	Y	
Lockers	Y	
Lodging	N	

		MEN			WOMEN	
	FRONT	PAR	HDCP	FRONT	PAR	HDCP
1	477	5	15	457	5	15
2	411	4	5	401	5	5
3	279	4	17	269	4	17
4	291	4	13	281	4	13
5	479	5	11	459	5	11
6	165	3	9	155	3	9
7	367	4	3	360	4	3
8	171	3	7	156	3	7
9	362	4	1	352	4	1
Out	3002	36		2890	37	
1	477	5	16	457	5	16
2	411	4	6	401	5	6
3	279	4	18	269	4	18
4	291	4	14	281	4	14
5	479	5	12	459	5	12
6	165	3	10	155	3	10
7	367	4	4	360	4	4
8	171	3	8	156	3	8
9	362	4	2	352	4	2
In	3002	36		2890	37	
Total	6004	72		5780	74	
Rating	68.8			73.2		
Slope	115			125		

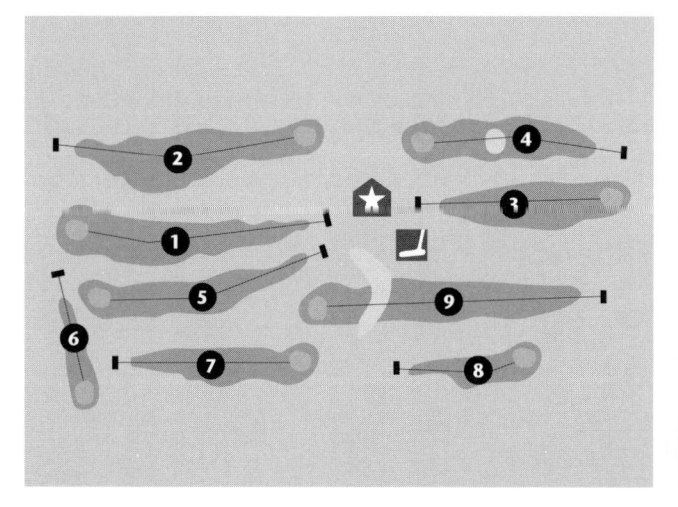

OAK VIEW GOLF COURSE

9 Regulation Public

Highway 11 West, P.O. Box 2
Greenbush, Minnesota 56726
218/782-2380 Clubhouse/Proshop

HOURS	8 am to Dusk
SEASON	May–September

RESERVATIONS	218/782-2380	
	Walk-on: good/good	
GREEN FEES	M-F	S-S
Adult	$10/7	$12/8
Senior	$10/7	$12/8
Junior	$10/7	$12/8
Twilight	NA	NA
PAYMENT	No credit cards accepted	
	Non-local checks accepted	
LEAGUES	Men: W (5 pm)	
	Women: T (5 pm)	
MEMBERSHIPS	MGA	
OWNER	Greenbush Golf Association	
MANAGER	Bernard Nelson	

FEATURES		
Putting green	Y	
Driving range	N	
Practice area	N	
Golf carts		
Power	N	
Pull carts	Y	$1.50
Club rental	Y	$5
Club storage	Y	
Caddies	N	
Proshop		
Basic	Y	
Refreshments		
Restaurant	N	
Lounge	N	
Snacks	Y	
Clubhouse		
Showers	N	
Lockers	N	
Lodging	N	

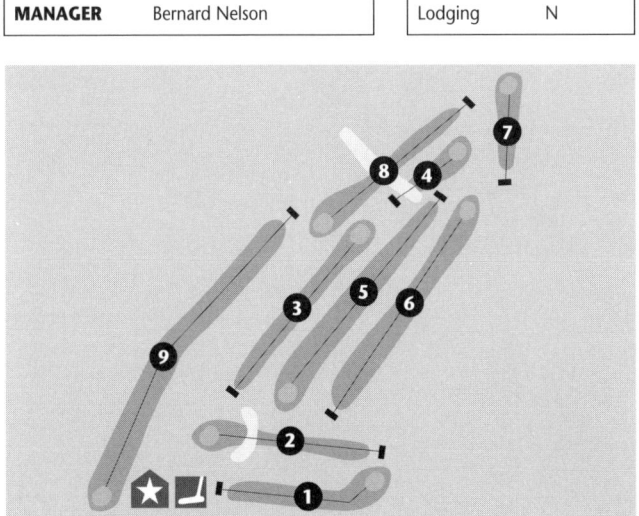

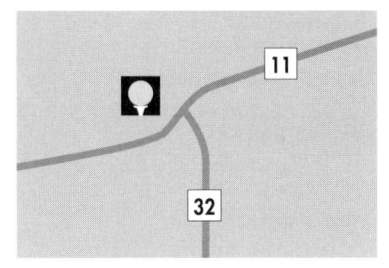

Located in Greenbush. Course entrance is west of MN Highway 32 on MN Highway 11..

	MEN			WOMEN		
	FRONT	PAR	HDCP	FRONT	PAR	HDCP
1	269	4	7	269	4	7
2	299	4	5	299	4	5
3	359	4	2	350	4	2
4	142	3	9	142	3	9
5	347	4	6	347	4	6
6	306	4	4	306	4	4
7	173	3	8	173	3	8
8	315	4	3	267	4	3
9	482	5	1	425	5	1
Out	2692	35		2578	35	
1	269	4	7	269	4	7
2	299	4	5	299	4	5
3	359	4	2	350	4	2
4	142	3	9	142	3	9
5	347	4	6	347	4	6
6	306	4	4	306	4	4
7	173	3	8	173	3	8
8	315	4	3	267	4	3
9	482	5	1	425	5	1
In	2692	35		2578	35	
Total	5384	70		5156	70	
Rating	65.2			68.6		
Slope	108			117		

GOLF COURSE DIRECTORY

OAKCREST GOLF COURSE

9 Executive Public

5th Street Southeast, Box 69
Roseau, Minnesota 56751
218/463-3016 Clubhouse/Proshop

HOURS	8 am to Dusk
SEASON	April to October

| **RESERVATIONS** | 218/463-3016 |
| | Walk on: good/good |

GREEN FEES	M-F	S-S
Adult	$14/9	$15/10
Senior	$14/9	$15/10
Junior	$14/9	$15/10
Twilight	NA	NA

| **PAYMENT** | Credit: Visa® MasterCard® |
| | Non-local checks accepted |

| **LEAGUES** | Men: Various |
| | Women: Various |

| **MEMBERSHIPS** | MGA |

| **SUPERINTENDENT** | Carson Headlund |
| **PROFESSIONAL** | Dan Fabian |

FEATURES	
Putting green	Y
Driving range	N
Practice area	N
Golf carts	
Power	Y $8
Pull carts	Y $2
Club rental	Y $2.50
Club storage	N
Caddies	N
Proshop	
Extended	Y
Refreshments	
Restaurant	N
Lounge	Y
Snacks	Y
Clubhouse	
Showers	N
Lockers	N
Lodging	N

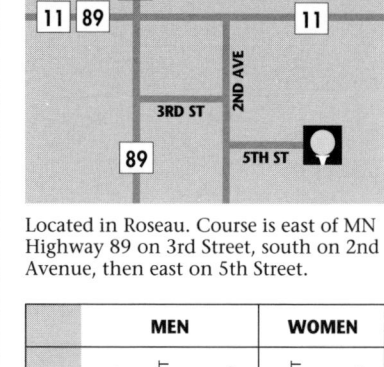

Located in Roseau. Course is east of MN Highway 89 on 3rd Street, south on 2nd Avenue, then east on 5th Street.

	MEN				**WOMEN**		
	BACK	FRONT	PAR	HDCP	FRONT	PAR	HDCP
1	340	335	4	9	330	4	9
2	307	307	4	15	307	4	15
3	401	395	4	3	344	4	3
4	162	147	3	17	130	3	17
5	311	290	4	11	248	4	11
6	199	180	3	13	159	3	13
7	355	340	4	5	285	4	5
8	435	365	4	1	310	4	1
9	350	342	4	7	300	4	7
Out	2860	2699	34		2413	34	
1	340	335	4	10	330	4	10
2	307	307	4	16	307	4	16
3	401	395	4	4	344	4	4
4	162	147	3	18	130	3	18
5	311	290	4	12	248	4	12
6	199	180	3	14	159	3	14
7	355	340	4	6	285	4	6
8	435	365	4	2	310	4	2
9	350	342	4	8	300	4	8
In	2860	2699	34		2413	34	
Total	5720	5298	68		4826	68	
Rating	67.2	63.6			67.6		
Slope	112	109			111		

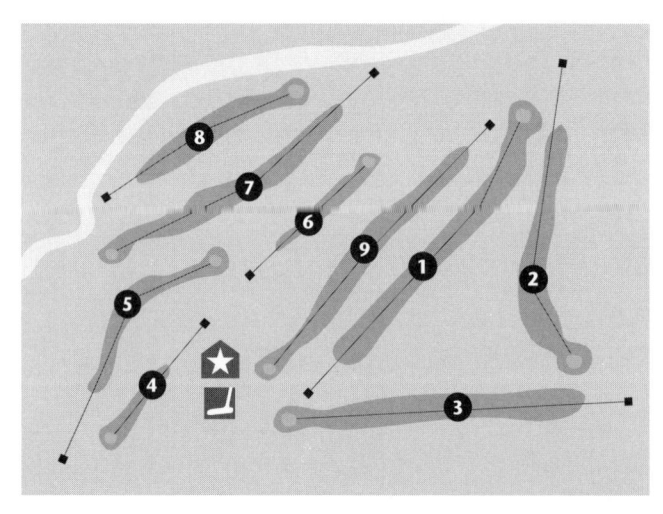

OAKDALE COUNTRY CLUB

18 Regulation Semi-Private

Route 2, P.O. Box 136
Buffalo Lake, Minnesota 55314
612/833-5518 Clubhouse/Proshop

HOURS	Dawn to Dusk
SEASON	April–November

RESERVATIONS	612/833-5518 2 days	
	Walk-on: fair/fair	
GREEN FEES	M-F	S-S
Adult	$15/10	$18/12
Senior	$15/10	$18/12
Junior	$15/10	$18/12
Twilight	NA	NA
PAYMENT	No credit cards accepted	
	Non-local checks accepted	
LEAGUES	Men: T (pm)	
	Women: W (pm)	
MEMBERSHIPS	USGA, GCSAA, MGA	
MANAGER	Richard Loftness	
SUPERINTENDENT	Warren Haugen	

FEATURES	
Putting green	Y
Driving range	Y
Practice area	Y
Golf carts	
Power (elec)	Y
Pull carts	Y
Club rental	Y
Club storage	Y
Caddies	N
Proshop	
Regular	Y
Refreshments	
Restaurant	N
Lounge	N
Snacks	Y
Clubhouse	
Showers	Y
Lockers	Y
Lodging	N

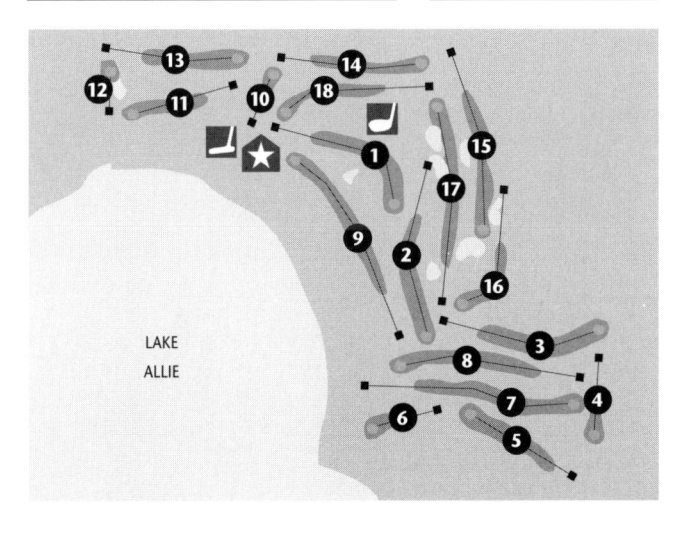

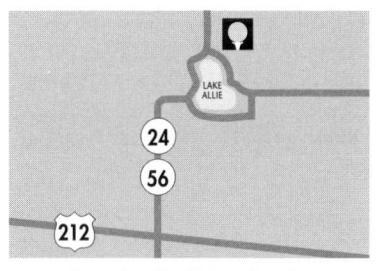

Located north of Buffalo Lake. Course is north of U.S. Highway 212 on County Road 24/56.

	MEN			WOMEN	
	BACK	FRONT	PAR HDCP	FRONT	PAR HDCP
1	388	378	4	369	4
2	432	422	4	338	4
3	397	387	4	272	4
4	203	191	3	145	3
5	374	364	4	271	4
6	163	140	3	113	3
7	498	486	5	409	5
8	441	429	4	312	4
9	559	546	5	452	5
Out	3455	3343	36	2681	36
10	173	163	3	154	3
11	294	284	4	270	4
12	134	119	3	92	3
13	361	335	4	329	4
14	399	381	4	302	4
15	489	479	5	404	5
16	368	357	4	268	4
17	557	545	5	453	5
18	397	366	4	280	4
In	3172	3029	36	2552	36
Total	6627	6372	72	5233	72
Rating	69.7	69.1		68.4	
Slope	111	110		112	

GOLF COURSE DIRECTORY

OAKS GOLF CLUB

18 Regulation Public

Country Club Road, P.O. Box 86
Hayfield, Minnesota 55940
507/477-3233 Clubhouse/Proshop

HOURS	7:30 am to Dusk
SEASON	April to October

RESERVATIONS	507/477-3233 5 days
	Walk-on: good/fair

GREEN FEES	M-F	S-S
Adult	$15.50/10.25	$15.50/10.25
Senior	$15.50/10.25	$15.50/10.25
Junior	$15.50/10.25	$15.50/10.25
Twilight	NA	NA

PAYMENT	Credit: Visa® MasterCard®
	Non-local checks accepted

LEAGUES	Men: Various
	Women: Various

MEMBERSHIPS	PGA, GCSAA, CMAA, MGA

MANAGER	Dennis Gavin
SUPERINTENDENT	Jeff Wendler
PROFESSIONAL	Dennis Gavin

FEATURES		
Putting green	Y	
Driving range	Y	$2.75
Practice area	Y	
Golf carts		
Power (gas)	Y	$16
Pull carts	Y	$3/2
Club rental	Y	$8/5
Club storage	N	
Caddies	N	
Proshop		
Extended	Y	
Refreshments		
Restaurant	Y	
Lounge	Y	
Snacks	Y	
Clubhouse		
Showers	Y	
Lockers	Y	
Lodging	N	

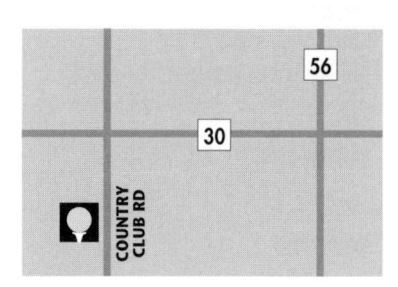

Located 2 1/2 miles west of Hayfield. Course is about 1/2 mile south of MN Highway 30 on Country Club Road.

	MEN				**WOMEN**		
	BACK	FRONT	PAR	HDCP	FRONT	PAR	HDCP
1	385	367	4	5	348	4	5
2	354	344	4	11	332	4	11
3	166	148	3	7	130	3	7
4	480	471	5	3	453	5	3
5	309	295	4	17	278	4	17
6	191	175	3	9	165	3	9
7	321	311	4	15	301	4	15
8	521	487	5	1	474	5	1
9	336	328	4	13	318	4	13
Out	3063	2926	36		2799	36	
10	491	471	5	8	445	5	8
11	332	317	4	18	306	4	18
12	400	339	4	10	322	4	10
13	388	374	4	12	362	4	12
14	200	170	3	14	129	3	14
15	402	387	4	6	371	4	6
16	155	118	3	16	102	3	16
17	445	427	4	4	374	4	4
18	528	516	5	2	453	5	2
In	3341	3119	36		2943	36	
Total	6404	6045	72		5742	72	
Rating	69.7	68.0			72.4		
Slope	114	111			120		

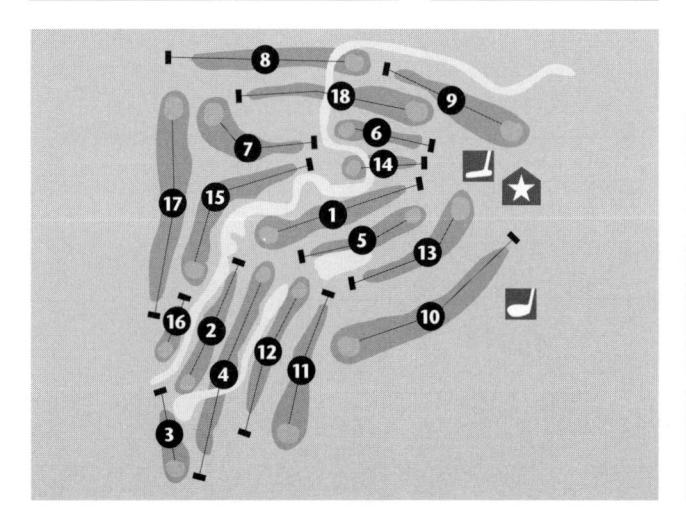

THE MINNESOTA ILLUSTRATED

OAKWOOD GOLF COURSE

9 Regulation Public

Route 1, P.O. Box 262A
Henning, Minnesota 56551
218/583-2127 Clubhouse/Proshop

HOURS Dawn to Dusk

SEASON April to October

RESERVATIONS	218/583-2127	
	Walk-on: good/good	
GREEN FEES	M-F	S-S
Adult	Call	Call
Senior	Call	Call
Junior	Call	Call
Twilight	NA	NA

PAYMENT	No credit cards accepted
	Non-local checks accepted
LEAGUES	Men: Various
	Women: Various
MEMBERSHIPS	MGA
PROFESSIONAL	Call

FEATURES	
Putting green	Y
Driving range	N
Practice area	N
Golf carts	
Power	N
Pull carts	Y
Club rental	Y
Club storage	N
Caddies	N
Proshop	
Basic	Y
Refreshments	
Restaurant	N
Lounge	N
Snacks	Y
Clubhouse	
Showers	N
Lockers	N
Lodging	N

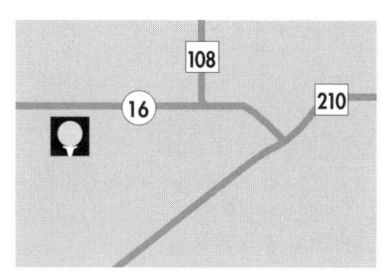

Located west of Henning. Course is just three miles west of MN Highway 108 on County Road 16.

	\multicolumn{3}{c}{**MEN**}	\multicolumn{3}{c}{**WOMEN**}
	FRONT	PAR	HDCP	FRONT	PAR	HDCP
1	360	4	2	323	4	2
2	525	5	1	425	5	1
3	354	4	3	291	4	3
4	289	4	8	276	4	8
5	165	5	3	157	5	3
6	360	4	6	303	4	6
7	118	3	9	96	3	9
8	335	4	4	328	4	4
9	434	5	7	434	5	7
Out	2942	36		2633	36	
1	360	4	2	323	4	2
2	525	5	1	425	5	1
3	354	4	3	291	4	3
4	289	4	8	276	4	8
5	165	5	3	157	5	3
6	360	4	6	303	4	6
7	118	3	9	96	3	9
8	335	4	4	328	4	4
9	434	5	7	434	5	7
In	2942	36		2633	36	
Total	5884	72		5266	72	
Rating	68.6			70.4		
Slope	122			121		

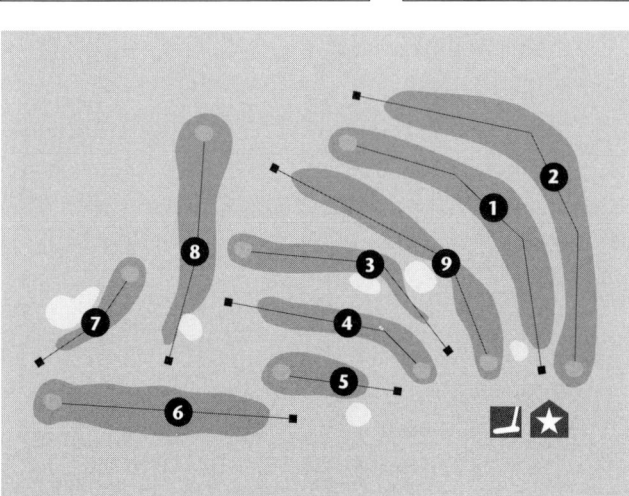

GOLF COURSE DIRECTORY

OLIVIA GOLF CLUB

9 Regulation Private

512 South 6th Street, P.O. Box 66
Olivia, Minnesota 56277
612/523-2313 Clubhouse/Proshop

HOURS	7 am to Dusk
SEASON	April to October

RESERVATIONS	612/523-2313	
	Walk-on: fair/poor	

GREEN FEES	M-F	S-S
Adult	$13/9	$17/12
Senior	$13/9	$17/12
Junior	$13/9	$17/12
Twilight	NA	NA

PAYMENT	No credit cards accepted
	Non-local checks accepted

LEAGUES	Various

MEMBERSHIPS	USGA, NGF, MGA

MANAGER	Keith Sharpe
SUPERINTENDENT	Rick Kelivington, Jerry Peterson

FEATURES		
Putting green	Y	
Driving range	N	
Practice area	Y	
Golf carts		
Power (gas)	Y	$15/10
Pull carts	Y	$2
Club rental	Y	
Club storage	N	
Caddies	N	
Proshop		
Extended	Y	
Refreshments		
Restaurant	N	
Lounge	Y	
Snacks	Y	
Clubhouse		
Showers	N	
Lockers	N	
Lodging	N	

Located in Olivia. Course entrance is south of U.S. Highway 212 on 7th Street, then east on Oak Street.

	MEN			**WOMEN**		
	BACK	FRONT	PAR	HDCP	FRONT	PAR	HDCP
1	511	501	5	5	437	5	3
2	237	227	3	3	202	3	5
3	393	383	4	2	383	4	2
4	359	349	4	7	349	4	6
5	155	145	3	9	145	3	9
6	420	410	4	1	362	4	4
7	381	371	4	6	333	4	7
8	525	512	5	4	391	5	1
9	316	305	4	8	210	4	8
Out	3297	3203	36		2812	36	
1	511	501	5	5	437	5	3
2	237	227	3	3	202	3	5
3	393	383	4	2	383	4	2
4	359	349	4	7	349	4	6
5	155	145	3	9	145	3	9
6	420	410	4	1	362	4	4
7	381	371	4	6	333	4	7
8	525	512	5	4	391	5	1
9	316	305	4	8	210	4	8
In	3297	3203	36		2812	36	
Total	6594	6406	72		5624	72	
Rating	70.5	70.5			72.2		
Slope	116	116			117		

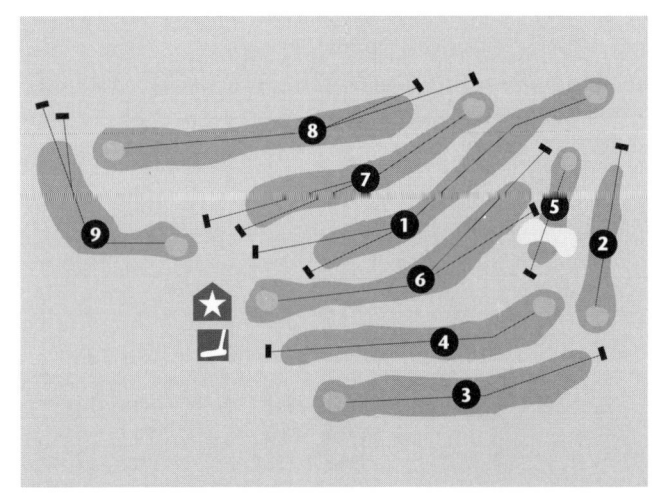

OLYMPIC HILLS GOLF CLUB

18 Regulation Private

10625 Mount Curve Road
Eden Prairie, Minnesota 55344
612/941-6262 Clubhouse
612/941-6265 Proshop

HOURS Dawn to Dusk

SEASON April to October

FEATURES

Putting green	Y
Driving range	Y
Practice area	Y
Golf carts	
Power	Y
Pull carts	Y
Club rental	Y
Club storage	Y
Caddies	N
Proshop	
Extended	Y
Refreshments	
Restaurant	Y
Lounge	Y
Snacks	Y
Clubhouse	
Showers	Y
Lockers	Y
Lodging	N

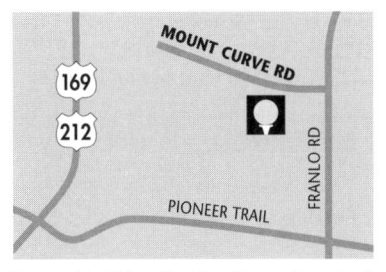

Located in Eden Prairie. Course is east of Hwy 169/212 on Pioneer Tr, north on Franlo Rd, then west on Mt. Curve Rd.

RESERVATIONS	612/941-6265 Members only		
GREEN FEES		M-F	S-S
Adult		Call	Call
Senior		Call	Call
Junior		Call	Call
Twilight		NA	NA
	Members and guests only		
PAYMENT	Credit: Visa® MasterCard® Non-local checks accepted		
LEAGUES	None		
MEMBERSHIPS	MGA		
MANAGER	Marv Segal, Kirk MacAllister		
SUPERINTENDENT	Orland Maenke		
PROFESSIONAL	Bill Brask		

	MEN					**WOMEN**		
	BACK	FRONT	PAR	HDCP		FRONT	PAR	HDCP
1	472	423	5	17		108	5	13
2	390	350	4	13		338	4	7
3	202	130	3	15		125	3	17
4	393	358	4	3		349	4	5
5	567	522	5	5		475	5	3
6	447	390	4	1		380	5	11
7	423	362	4	11		330	4	9
8	210	169	3	7		130	3	15
9	564	507	5	9		486	5	1
Out	3668	3211	37			3021	38	
10	540	507	5	6		500	5	10
11	385	353	4	10		345	4	6
12	399	350	4	8		334	4	8
13	173	135	3	16		112	3	18
14	316	293	4	18		220	4	12
15	566	513	5	2		474	5	2
16	190	147	3	14		140	3	16
17	370	335	4	12		320	4	4
18	458	386	4	4		380	5	14
In	3397	3019	36			2825	37	
Total	7065	6230	73			5846	75	
Rating	74.7	70.8				75.1		
Slope	144	137				138		

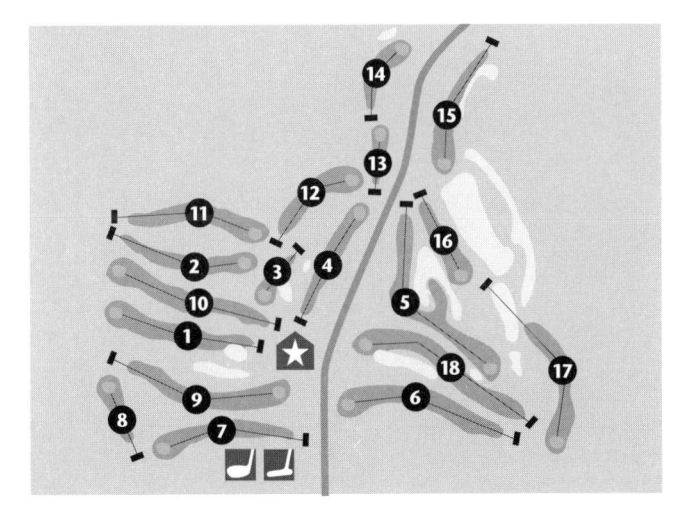

GOLF COURSE DIRECTORY

ONEKA RIDGE GOLF COURSE
18 Regulation Public

5610 120th Street North
White Bear Lake, Minnesota 55110
612/429-2390 Clubhouse/Proshop

RESERVATIONS	612/429-2390	
	Walk-on: good/fair	
GREEN FEES	M-F	S-S
Adult	$18/12	$18/12
Senior	$14/10	$16/12*
Junior	$14/10	$16/12*
Twilight	$14	NA
	* After 3 pm	
PAYMENT	Credit: Visa® MasterCard®	
	Non-local checks accepted	
LEAGUES	Various	
MEMBERSHIPS	PGA, GCSAA, CMAA, MGA	
MANAGER	Steve Venarchick	
SUPERINTENDENT	Kelly Johnson	
PROFESSIONAL	Steve Venarchick	

HOURS	6 am to Dusk	
SEASON	April-November	
FEATURES		
Putting green	Y	
Driving range	Y	$4.75
Practice area	N	
Golf carts		
Power (elec)	Y	$20
Pull carts	Y	$3
Club rental	Y	$9
Club storage	N	
Caddies	N	
Proshop		
Extended	Y	
Refreshments		
Restaurant	N	
Lounge	Y	
Snacks	Y	
Clubhouse		
Showers	N	
Lockers	N	
Lodging	N	

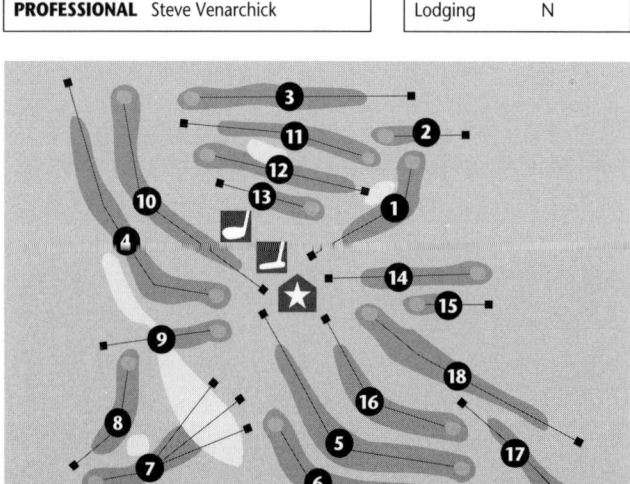

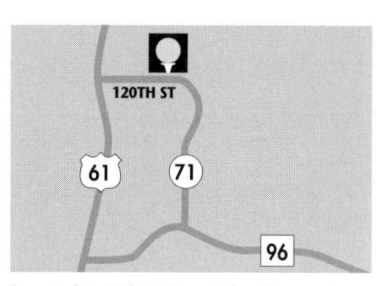

Located in White Bear Lake. Course is 1/2 mile east of U.S. Highway 61 on 120th Street North.

	MEN				**WOMEN**		
	BACK	FRONT	PAR	HDCP	FRONT	PAR	HDCP
1	310	298	4	16	229	4	12
2	185	174	3	6	112	3	18
3	410	399	4	2	294	4	6
4	497	486	5	12	408	5	8
5	489	481	5	14	445	5	4
6	424	416	4	4	371	4	2
7	324	289	4	8	240	4	14
8	343	334	4	10	317	4	10
9	141	135	3	18	121	3	16
Out	3123	3012	36		2536	36	
10	483	473	5	13	445	5	3
11	373	366	4	7	318	4	11
12	396	386	4	5	322	4	7
13	255	235	3	3	167	3	5
14	307	294	4	17	281	4	9
15	181	161	3	15	116	3	17
16	350	340	4	9	291	4	13
17	334	300	4	11	246	4	15
18	549	494	5	1	443	5	1
In	3228	3049	36		2629	36	
Total	6351	6061	72		5165	72	
Rating	69.8	68.8			68.2		
Slope	117	115			117		

ORCHARD GARDENS GOLF COURSE

9 Par-3 Public

1020 West 155th Street
Burnsville, Minnesota 55337
612/435-5771 Clubhouse/Proshop

HOURS	6 am to Dusk
SEASON	March-October

RESERVATIONS	612/435-5771 2 weeks
	Walk-on: good/poor
GREEN FEES	M-F	S-S
Adult	$14/9	$15/10
Senior	$13.50/8.50*	$15/10
Junior	$14/9	$15/10
Twilight	NA	NA
	* Before 4 pm	
PAYMENT	No credit cards accepted
	Non-local checks accepted
LEAGUES	Various
MEMBERSHIPS	NGF, GCSAA, MGA
OWNER	Mel & Joanne Henry
MANAGER	Sherri Henry
SUPERINTENDENT	Mel Henry
PROFESSIONAL	Jim Webber

FEATURES		
Putting green	Y	
Driving range	Y	$4
Practice area	Y	
Golf carts		
Power	N	
Pull carts	Y	
Club rental	Y	
Club storage	N	
Caddies	N	
Proshop		
Regular	Y	
Refreshments		
Restaurant	N	
Lounge	N	
Snacks	Y	
Clubhouse		
Showers	N	
Lockers	N	
Lodging	N	

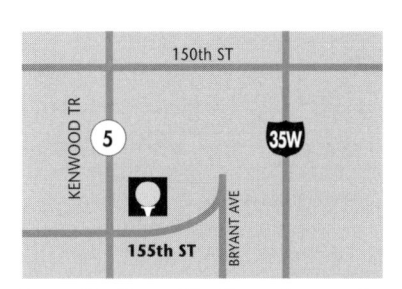

Located in Burnsville. Course is west of I-35W on 150th St, south on Kenwood Trail/Cty Road 5, then west on 55th St.

	MEN			**WOMEN**		
	FRONT	PAR	HDCP	FRONT	PAR	HDCP
1	140	3	9	140	3	9
2	227	3	5	227	4	5
3	228	3	1	128	4	1
4	160	3	2	160	3	2
5	130	3	7	130	3	7
6	160	3	6	160	3	6
7	200	3	4	200	3	4
8	100	3	8	100	3	8
9	225	3	3	225	4	3
Out	1570	27		1570	30	
1	140	3	9	140	3	9
2	227	3	5	227	4	5
3	228	3	1	128	4	1
4	160	3	2	160	3	2
5	130	3	7	130	3	7
6	160	3	6	160	3	6
7	200	3	4	200	3	4
8	100	3	8	100	3	8
9	225	3	3	225	4	3
In	1570	27		1570	30	
Total	3140	54		3140	60	
Rating	54.3			56.6		
Slope	74			81		

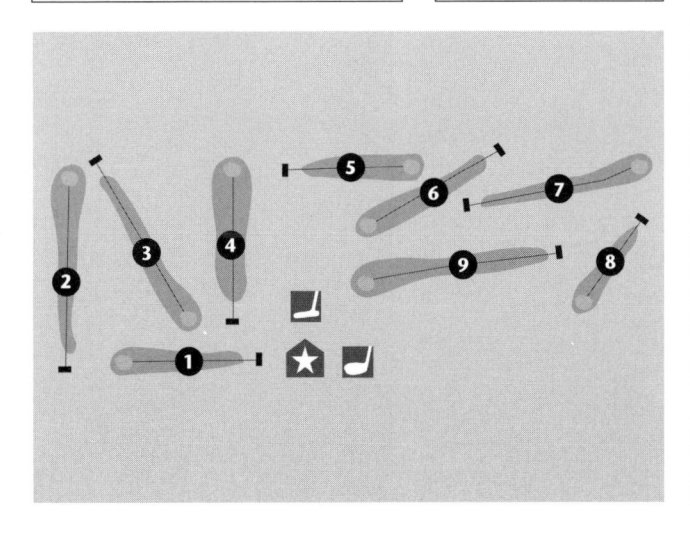

GOLF COURSE DIRECTORY

ORONO GOLF COURSE

9 Executive Public

265 Orono Orchard Road
Orono, Minnesota 55391
612/473-9904 Clubhouse
612/473-0876 Proshop

HOURS 6:30 am to Dusk

SEASON April-November

FEATURES

Putting green	N
Driving range	N
Practice area	N
Golf carts	
Power (gas)	Y $18/10
Pull carts	Y $2
Club rental	Y $2.50
Club storage	N
Caddies	N
Proshop	
Regular	Y
Refreshments	
Restaurant	N
Lounge	Y
Snacks	Y
Clubhouse	
Showers	N
Lockers	N
Lodging	N

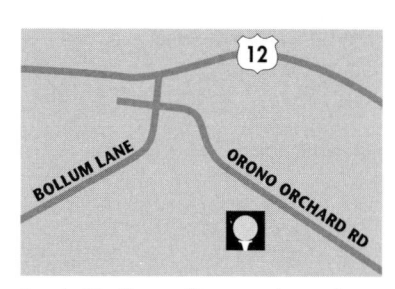

Located in Orono. Course entrance is south of U.S. Highway 12 on Bollum Lane, then east Orono Orchard Road.

RESERVATIONS	612/473-9904 3 days
	Walk-on: good/good

GREEN FEES	M-F*	S-S
Adult	$15/8.75	$15/8.75
Senior	$15/8.75	$15/8.75
Junior	$15/8.75	$15/8.75
Twilight	NA	NA
	M-F discounts before noon	

PAYMENT	No credit cards accepted
	Local checks only

LEAGUES	Men: Variuos
	Women: Various

MEMBERSHIPS	USGA, GCSAA, MGA

SUPERINTENDENT	Ron Steffenhagen
PROFESSIONAL	Doug Erickson, Bart Osborn

		MEN			WOMEN	
	FRONT	PAR	HDCP	FRONT	PAR	HDCP
1	224	4	7	224	4	7
2	231	4	4	231	4	4
3	124	3	9	124	3	9
4	345	4	1	345	4	1
5	183	3	8	183	3	8
6	248	4	5	248	4	5
7	249	4	6	249	4	6
8	190	3	3	190	3	3
9	345	4	2	345	4	2
Out	2139	33		2139	33	
1	224	4	7	224	4	7
2	231	4	4	231	4	4
3	124	3	9	124	3	9
4	345	4	1	345	4	1
5	183	3	8	183	3	8
6	248	4	5	248	4	5
7	249	4	6	249	4	6
8	190	3	3	190	3	3
9	345	4	2	345	4	2
In	2139	33		2139	33	
Total	4278	66		4278	66	
Rating	61.6			64.6		
Slope	101			104		

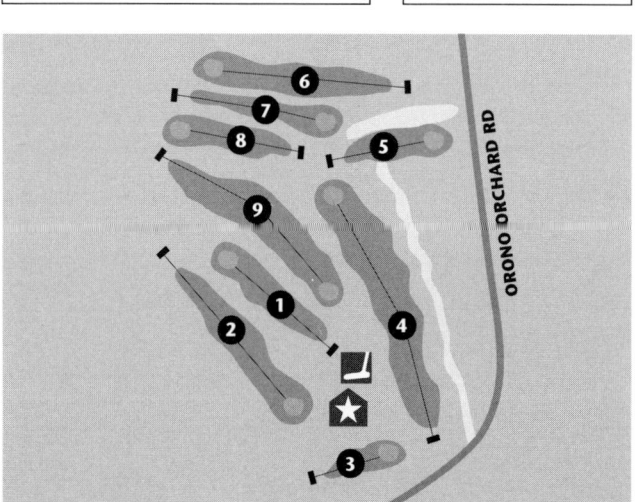

ORTONVILLE GOLF CLUB

18 Regulation Public

Highland Hwy & Golf Course Road
Ortonville, Minnesota 56278
612/839-3606 Clubhouse/Proshop

HOURS 8 am to Dusk

SEASON April-November

RESERVATIONS	612/839-3606 1 week	
	Walk-on: good/good	
GREEN FEES	M-F	S-S
Adult	$12/8	$13/9
Senior	$12/8	$13/9
Junior	$12/8	$13/9
Twilight	NA	NA
PAYMENT	Credit cards not accepted	
	Non-local checks accepted	
LEAGUES	Various	
MEMBERSHIPS	USGA, NGF, LPGA, GCSAA,	
	CMAA, MGA	
MANAGER	Donna Johnson	
SUPERINTENDENT	Paul Tinklenberg	

FEATURES		
Putting green	Y	
Driving range	N	
Practice area	Y	
Golf carts		
Power (gas)	Y	$15
Pull carts	Y	$1
Club rental	Y	$3
Club storage	N	
Caddies	N	
Proshop		
Extended	Y	
Refreshments		
Restaurant	Y	
Lounge	Y	
Snacks	Y	
Clubhouse		
Showers	Y	
Lockers	Y	
Lodging	N	

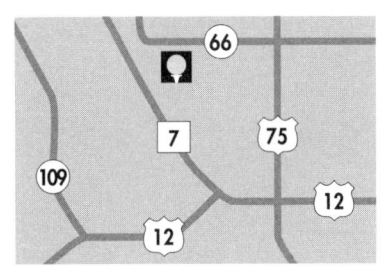

Located in Ortonville. Course entrance is about 1 1/2 miles west of U.S. Highway 75 on County Road 66.

	MEN			WOMEN		
	BACK	FRONT	PAR	HDCP	FRONT	PAR	HDCP
1	297	291	4	16	281	4	14
2	170	157	3	12	102	3	16
3	485	473	5	2	402	5	4
4	366	357	4	10	334	4	10
5	388	366	4	8	346	4	8
6	155	145	3	18	111	3	18
7	480	472	5	4	439	5	2
8	378	375	4	6	327	4	6
9	335	330	4	14	323	4	12
Out	3054	2966	36		2665	36	
10	567	550	5	1	443	5	1
11	487	479	5	3	428	5	3
12	364	354	4	9	340	4	5
13	340	324	4	13	308	4	13
14	366	350	4	7	334	4	9
15	166	154	3	15	142	3	15
16	349	344	4	5	290	4	11
17	129	127	3	17	123	3	17
18	360	353	4	11	346	4	7
In	3128	3035	36		2754	36	
Total	6182	6001	72		5419	72	
Rating	68.9	68.1			70.6		
Slope	112	111			115		

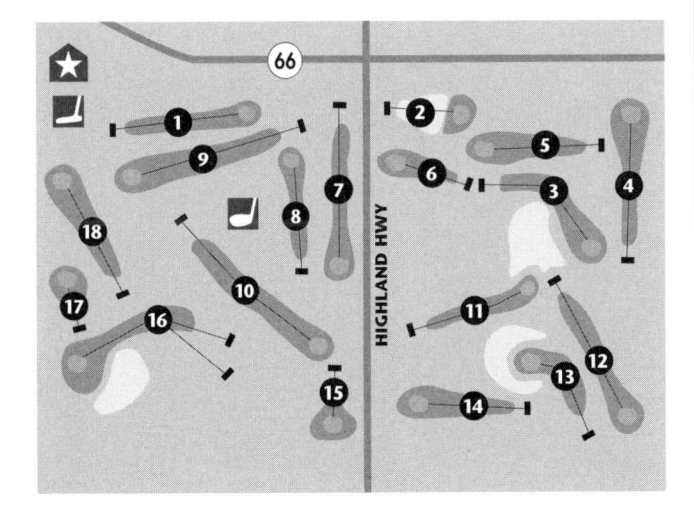

GOLF COURSE DIRECTORY

OSAKIS COUNTRY CLUB

9 Regulation Public

Highway 27 East, P.O. Box 388
Osakis, Minnesota 56360
612/859-2140 Clubhouse/Proshop

HOURS	7 am to Dusk
SEASON	April to October

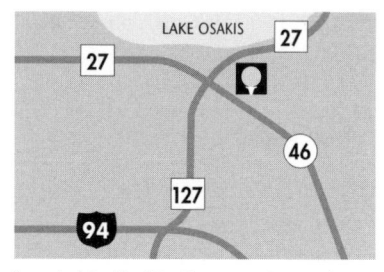

Located in Osakis. Course entrance is north of I-94 on MN Highway 127, then west on County Road 46.

RESERVATIONS	612/859-2140 1 day	
	Walk-on: good/fair	
GREEN FEES	M-F	S-S
Adult	$16/8.50	$18/9.50
Senior	$16/8.50	$18/9.50
Junior	$16/8.50	$18/9.50
Twilight	NA	NA
PAYMENT	No credit cards accepted	
	Non-local checks accepted	
LEAGUES	Men: Th (pm)	
	Women: T (pm)	
MEMBERSHIPS	MGA	
MANAGER	Ronald Boys	
SUPERINTENDENT	Mike Didier	

FEATURES		
Putting green	Y	
Driving range	N	
Practice area	N	
Golf carts		
Power (gas)	Y	$9
Pull carts	Y	$2
Club rental	Y	$3
Club storage	N	
Caddies	N	
Proshop		
Extended	Y	
Refreshments		
Restaurant	N	
Lounge	Y	
Snacks	Y	
Clubhouse		
Showers	N	
Lockers	N	
Lodging	N	

	MEN FRONT	PAR	HDCP	WOMEN FRONT	PAR	HDCP
1	347	4	3	310	4	3
2	146	3	8	138	3	8
3	275	4	5	261	4	5
4	370	4	1	285	4	1
5	284	4	9	279	4	9
6	450	5	7	319	5	7
7	185	3	6	178	3	6
8	443	5	4	332	5	4
9	378	4	2	371	5	2
Out	2878	36		2533	37	
1	347	4	3	310	4	3
2	146	3	8	138	3	8
3	275	4	5	261	4	5
4	370	4	1	285	4	1
5	284	4	9	279	4	9
6	450	5	7	319	5	7
7	185	3	6	178	3	6
8	443	5	4	332	5	4
9	378	4	2	371	5	2
In	2878	36		2533	37	
Total	5756	72		5066	74	
Rating	68.0			69.8		
Slope	119			121		

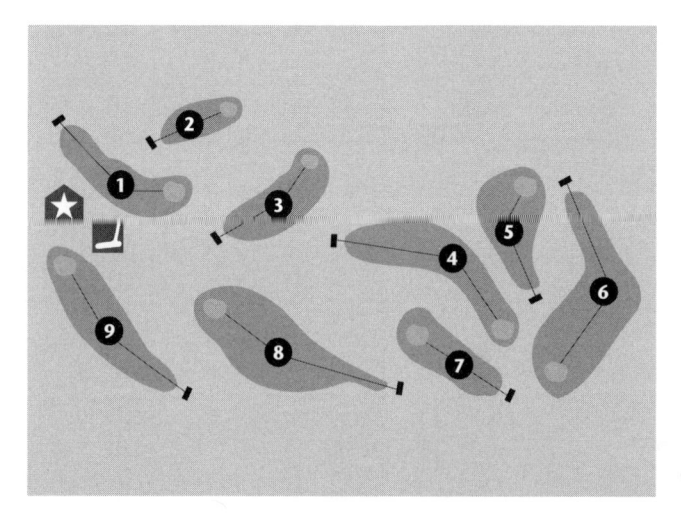

OWATONNA COUNTRY CLUB

18 Regulation Semi-Private

Lemond Road, P.O. Box 446
Owatonna, Minnesota 55060
507/451-6120 Clubhouse
507/451-1363 Proshop

RESERVATIONS	507/451-1363 2 days	
	Walk-on: fair/fair	
GREEN FEES	M-F	S-S
Adult	$35/20	$35/20
Senior	$35/20	$35/20
Junior	$35/20	$35/20
Twilight	NA	NA
PAYMENT	Credit: Visa® MasterCard®	
	Non-local checks accepted	
LEAGUES	Various	
MEMBERSHIPS	USGA, PGA, GCSAA, CMAA, MGA	
MANAGER	Roger Van Eman	
SUPERINTENDENT	Steve Van Natta	
PROFESSIONAL	John Hamilton	

HOURS	8 am to Dusk	
SEASON	April-November	
FEATURES		
Putting green	Y	
Driving range	Y	
Practice area	Y	
Golf carts		
Power (gas)	Y	
Pull carts	Y	
Club rental	Y	
Club storage	N	
Caddies	N	
Proshop		
Extended	Y	
Refreshments		
Restaurant	Y	
Lounge	Y	
Snacks	Y	
Clubhouse		
Showers	Y	
Lockers	N	
Lodging	N	

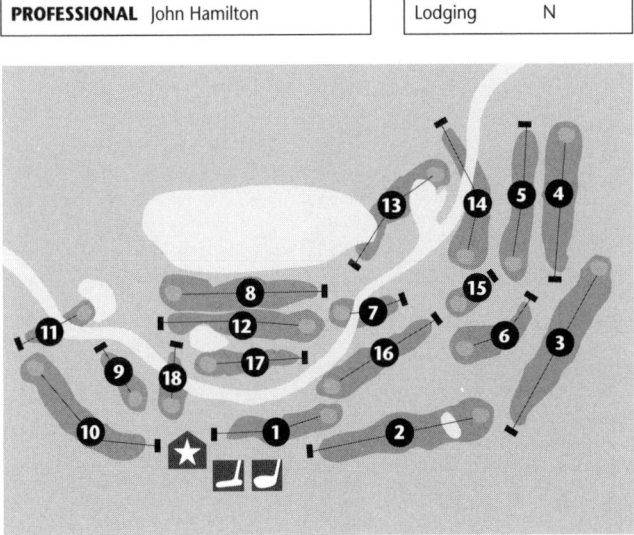

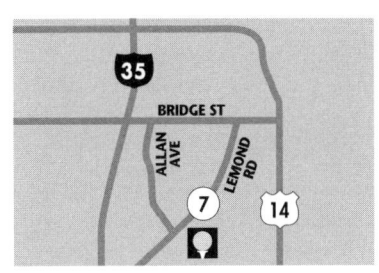

Located in Owatonna. Course is east of I-35 on Bridge Street, south on Allan Avenue, then west on Lemond Road.

	\multicolumn{4}{c	}{MEN}	\multicolumn{3}{c	}{WOMEN}
	BACK	FRONT	PAR	HDCP	FRONT	PAR	HDCP
1	330	326	4	9	315	4	11
2	497	485	5	5	420	5	1
3	417	406	4	1	377	4	5
4	386	377	4	13	349	4	13
5	369	364	4	11	346	4	9
6	401	396	4	3	318	4	7
7	175	144	3	15	106	3	17
8	514	503	5	7	454	5	3
9	198	172	3	17	160	3	15
Out	3287	3173	36		2845	36	
10	494	485	5	8	412	5	2
11	157	140	3	16	116	3	16
12	490	478	5	12	405	5	4
13	441	424	4	2	350	4	8
14	349	337	4	6	295	4	10
15	137	126	3	14	100	3	18
16	448	442	4	4	420	5	6
17	312	306	4	10	290	4	12
18	181	170	3	18	125	3	14
In	3009	2908	35		2513	36	
Total	6296	6081	71		5358	72	
Rating	70.8	69.9			71.8		
Slope	126	124			123		

GOLF COURSE DIRECTORY

PARKVIEW GOLF CLUB

18 Executive Public

1310 Cliff Road
Eagan, Minnesota 55123
612/454-9884 Clubhouse/Proshop

HOURS 6 am to Dusk
SEASON Mar-November

RESERVATIONS	612/454-9884 1 week	
	Walk-on: good/fair	
GREEN FEES	M-F	S-S
Adult	$16/10	$17/12
Senior	$11/7.50	$17/12
Junior	$12/8.50	$17/12
Twilight	NA	NA
	Season tickets available	
PAYMENT	No credit cards accepted	
	Non-local checks accepted	
LEAGUES	Men: Th (pm)	
	Women: M (pm), T (am)	
MEMBERSHIPS	USGA, NGF, MGA	
OWNER	Donald W. Larsen	
MANAGER	Ken Severson	
SUPERINTENDENT	Scott Held	

FEATURES

Putting green	Y	
Driving range	N	
Practice area	N	
Golf carts		
Power (gas)	Y	$18/11
Pull carts	Y	$2.25
Club rental	Y	$7
Club storage	N	
Caddies	N	
Proshop		
Basic	Y	
Refreshments		
Restaurant	N	
Lounge	N	
Snacks	Y	
Clubhouse		
Showers	N	
Lockers	N	
Lodging	N	

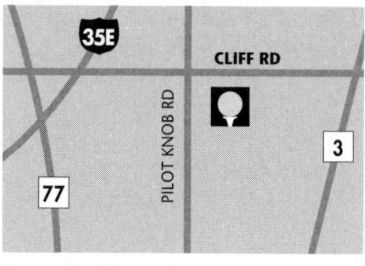

Located in Eagan. Course entrance is 3 miles east of MN Highway 77 and 2 1/2 miles east of I-35E on Cliff Road.

	MEN			**WOMEN**		
	FRONT	PAR	HDCP	FRONT	PAR	HDCP
1	378	4	6	368	4	2
2	200	3	9	188	3	4
3	157	3	14	152	3	7
4	148	3	18	136	3	16
5	276	4	10	270	4	5
6	362	4	3	251	4	13
7	218	3	2	209	4	17
8	191	3	11	171	3	6
9	339	4	5	331	4	3
Out	2269	31		2076	32	
10	327	4	8	265	4	12
11	156	3	15	144	3	10
12	208	3	4	200	4	18
13	521	5	7	431	5	9
14	160	3	13	144	3	8
15	332	4	16	322	4	11
16	110	3	17	98	3	14
17	166	3	12	115	3	15
18	319	4	1	313	4	1
In	2299	32		2032	33	
Total	4568	63		4210	65	
Rating	61.2			63.8		
Slope	96			99		

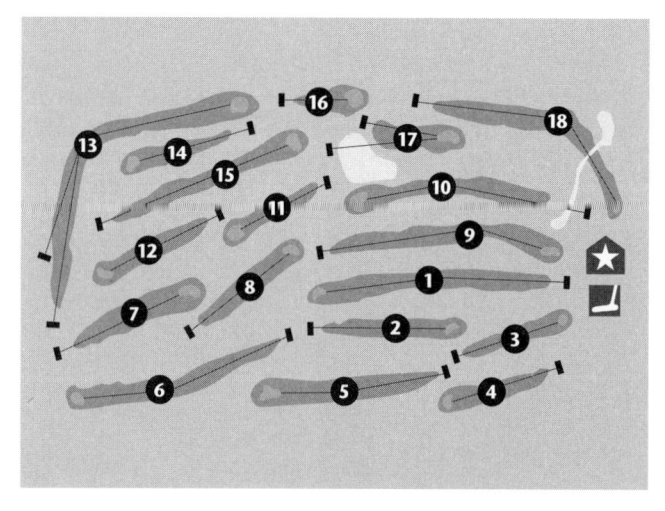

THE MINNESOTA ILLUSTRATED

PEBBLE CREEK COUNTRY CLUB

27 Regulation Public

14000 Club House Dr., P.O. Box 337
Becker, Minnesota 55308
612/261-4653 Clubhouse/Proshop

RESERVATIONS	612/261-4653 2 days	
	Walk-on: good/fair	
GREEN FEES	M-F	S-S
Adult	$20/13	$25
Senior	$12/8*	$25
Junior	$7	$25
Twilight	NA	NA
	* M-Th before 9:30 am	
PAYMENT	Credit: Visa® MasterCard®	
	Non-local checks accepted	
LEAGUES	Men: None	
	Women: None	
MEMBERSHIPS	USGA, NGF, PGA, GCSAA, CMAA, MGA	
OWNER	City of Becker	
SUPERINTENDENT	Cary Femrite	
PROFESSIONAL	Jim Resch	

HOURS	7 am to Dusk
SEASON	April-November

FEATURES		
Putting green	Y	
Driving range	Y	$3
Practice area	Y	
Golf carts		
Power (gas)	Y	$22
Pull carts	Y	$3
Club rental	Y	$10
Club storage	N	
Caddies	N	
Proshop		
Entended	Y	
Refreshments		
Restaurant	Y	
Lounge	Y	
Snacks	Y	
Clubhouse		
Showers	Y	
Lockers	Y	
Lodging	N	

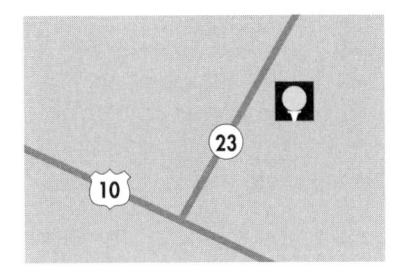

Located in Becker. Course is one mile north of U.S. Highway 10 on Cty Rd 23.

	MEN				**WOMEN**		
	BACK	FRONT	PAR	HDCP	FRONT	PAR	HDCP
1	405	375	4	3	345	4	3
2	365	345	4	15	315	4	15
3	165	150	3	17	125	3	17
4	420	400	4	5	350	4	5
5	530	500	5	7	425	5	7
6	400	365	4	13	320	4	13
7	550	535	5	1	460	5	1
8	210	190	3	9	165	3	9
9	415	345	4	11	330	4	11
RED	3460	3255	36		2835	36	
1	435	420	4	1	370	4	1
2	505	500	5	3	445	5	3
3	370	345	4	15	310	4	15
4	190	165	3	7	115	3	7
5	525	490	5	5	430	5	5
6	175	155	3	13	125	3	13
7	395	355	4	11	350	4	11
8	395	350	4	9	320	4	9
9	370	320	4	17	300	4	17
WHITE	3360	3100	36		2765	36	
1	328	286	4	13	251	4	13
2	408	370	4	5	295	4	5
3	360	320	4	11	280	4	11
4	202	165	3	9	136	3	9
5	490	452	5	7	416	5	7
6	366	331	4	15	285	4	15
7	129	113	3	17	93	3	17
8	466	432	4	1	361	4	1
9	548	500	5	3	422	5	3
BLUE	3297	2969	36		2539	36	
R/W	6820	6355	72		5600	72	
Rating	73.2	71.1			72.9		
Slope	129	125			126		
W/B	6657	6069	72		5304	72	
Rating	72.2	69.6			70.6		
Slope	126	121			126		
B/R	6757	6224	72		5374	72	
Rating	72.4	70.1			71.1		
Slope	129	124			125		

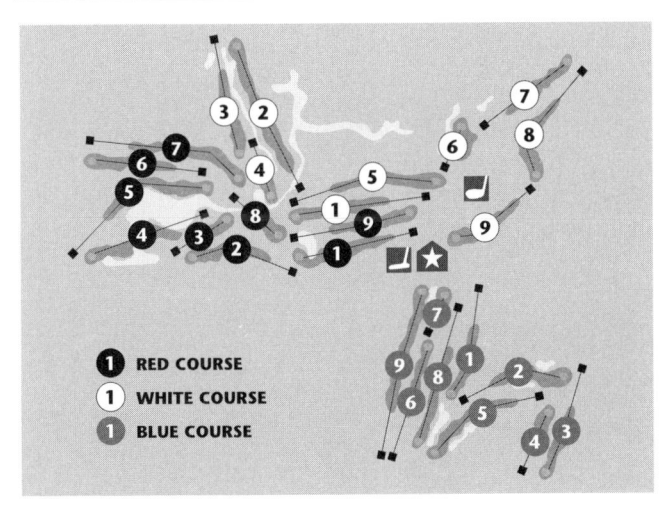

① RED COURSE
① WHITE COURSE
① BLUE COURSE

PEBBLE LAKE GOLF CLUB

18 Regulation Public

County Road 82 South
Fergus Falls, Minnesota 56537
218/739-4014 Clubhouse
218/736-7404 Proshop

HOURS	7 am to Dusk
SEASON	April to October

FEATURES		
Putting green	Y	
Driving range	Y	$2.50
Practice area	Y	
Golf carts		
Power (gas)	Y	$18/11
Pull carts	Y	$3/1.50
Club rental	Y	$5/2.50
Club storage	Y	$35/yr
Caddies	N	
Proshop		
Extended	Y	
Refreshments		
Restaurant	Y	
Lounge	Y	
Snacks	Y	
Clubhouse		
Showers	Y	
Lockers	Y	
Lodging	N	

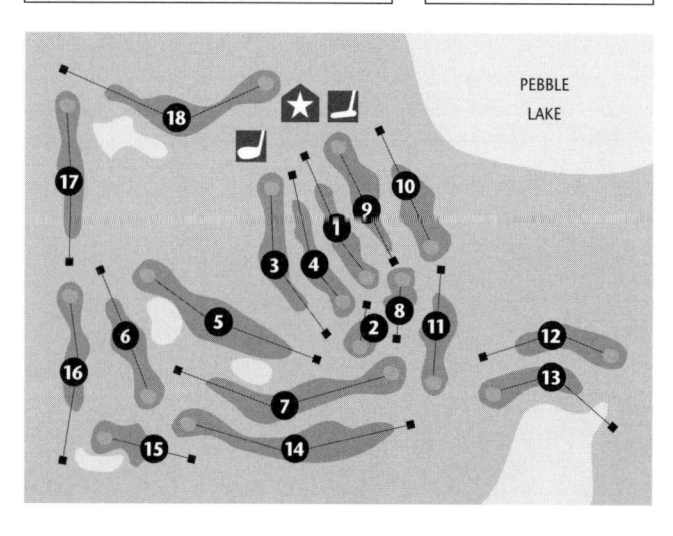

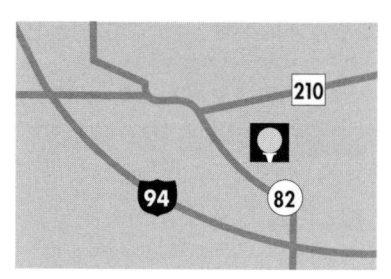

Located south of Fergus Falls. Course is about one mile south of MN Highway 210 on County Road 82.

RESERVATIONS	218/736-7404 1 week	
	Walk-on: good/fair	

GREEN FEES	M-F	S-S
Adult	$20.75/13.25	$20.75/13.25
Senior	$20.75/13.25	$20.75/13.25
Junior	$10/10	$10/10
Twilight	NA	NA

PAYMENT Credit: Visa® MasterCard®
Non-local checks accepted

LEAGUES Men: T (12-7 pm)
Women: W (8-12, 4-7 pm)

MEMBERSHIPS USGA, PGA, GCSAA, MGA

SUPERINTENDENT Rick Odden
PROFESSIONAL Greg J. Mireault

	MEN				WOMEN		
	BACK	FRONT	PAR	HDCP	FRONT	PAR	HDCP
1	399	395	4	7	382	5	13
2	142	137	3	17	132	3	15
3	500	492	5	5	372	5	11
4	423	418	4	3	403	5	9
5	522	514	5	9	426	5	5
6	383	354	4	13	334	4	3
7	518	508	5	1	439	5	1
8	176	171	3	15	135	3	17
9	388	378	4	11	363	4	7
Out	3457	3367	37		2986	39	
10	356	346	4	10	292	4	8
11	213	195	3	14	160	3	16
12	431	418	4	12	368	4	14
13	398	358	4	8	296	4	6
14	520	510	5	4	455	5	10
15	163	156	3	18	106	3	18
16	359	349	4	16	305	4	12
17	432	377	4	2	259	4	2
18	388	372	4	6	325	4	4
In	3254	3081	35		2545	35	
Total	6711	6448	72		5531	74	
Rating	72.3	71.1			72.7		
Slope	128	125			128		

THE MINNESOTA ILLUSTRATED

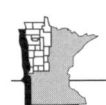

PERHAM LAKESIDE COUNTRY CLUB

18 Regulation Public

Rural Route 1, P.O. Box 313
Perham, Minnesota 56573
218/346-6070 Clubhouse/Proshop

HOURS	6 am to Dusk
SEASON	April-November

RESERVATIONS	218/346-6070 10 days	
	Walk-on: fair/poor	
GREEN FEES	M-F	S-S
Adult	$21/13	$21/13
Senior	$21/13	$21/13
Junior	$21/13	$21/13
Twilight	$8.50	$8.50
PAYMENT	Credit: Visa® MasterCard®	
	Non-local checks accepted	
LEAGUES	Men: T (1 pm)	
	Women: W (3 pm)	
MEMBERSHIPS	USGA, NGF, PGA, GCSAA, MGA	
MANAGER	Nick Anderson	
SUPERINTENDENT	Steve Shumansky	
PROFESSIONAL	Nick Anderson	

FEATURES	
Putting green	Y
Driving range	Y
Practice area	Y
Golf carts	
Power (gas)	Y
Pull carts	Y
Club rental	Y
Club storage	N
Caddies	N
Proshop	
Extended	Y
Refreshments	
Restaurant	N
Lounge	Y
Snacks	Y
Clubhouse	
Showers	N
Lockers	Y
Lodging	N

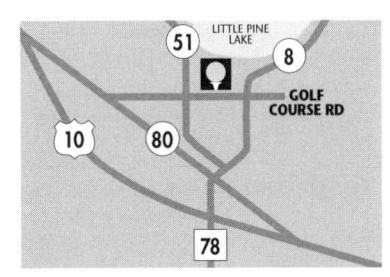

Located north of Perham. Course is north of U.S. Highway 10 on County Road 8, then north on County Road 51.

	MEN				**WOMEN**		
	BACK	FRONT	PAR	HDCP	FRONT	PAR	HDCP
1	467	460	5	17	417	5	7
2	180	174	3	9	124	3	17
3	385	362	4	7	285	4	15
4	385	376	4	5	323	4	3
5	510	502	5	13	426	5	11
6	183	160	3	15	153	3	9
7	517	484	5	11	404	5	13
8	435	421	4	3	419	5	5
9	417	409	4	1	374	4	1
Out	3479	3348	37		2925	38	
10	475	463	5	18	410	5	18
11	165	154	3	12	110	3	8
12	361	348	4	8	300	4	6
13	206	198	3	10	156	3	10
14	413	405	4	14	325	4	16
15	179	171	3	16	134	3	12
16	493	467	5	2	396	5	2
17	383	371	4	4	321	4	14
18	421	396	4	6	311	4	4
In	3096	2973	35		2463	35	
Total	6575	6321	72		5388	73	
Rating	72.5	71.3			71.1		
Slope	128	126			122		

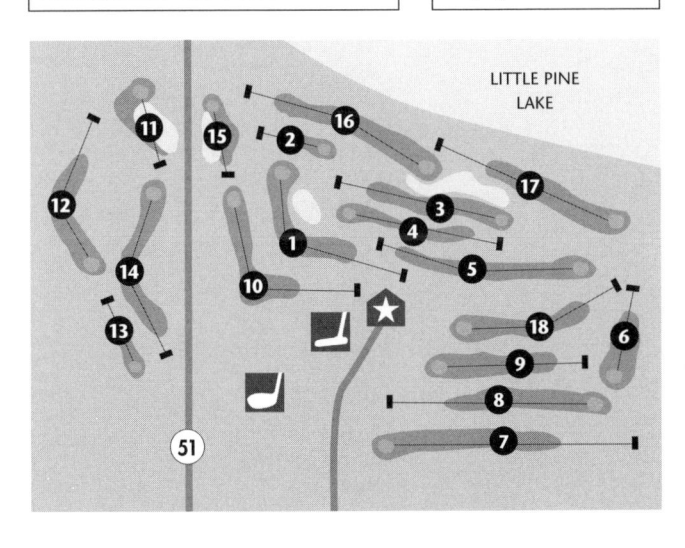

GOLF COURSE DIRECTORY

PEZHEKEE GOLF COURSE   18 Regulation Public

Peters' Sunset Beach Resort
2500 South Lakeshore Drive
Glenwood, Minnesota 56334
612/634-4501 Clubhouse/Proshop

RESERVATIONS	612/634-4501	
	Walk-on: good/good	

GREEN FEES	M-F	S-S
Adult	$22	$22
Senior	$22	$22
Junior	$12	$12
Twilight	$18	$18
	Guest packages available	

PAYMENT	Credit: Visa® MasterCard®
	Non-local checks accepted

LEAGUES	None

MEMBERSHIPS	USGA, PGA, MGA

OWNER	Bill, David & Jim Peters
SUPERINTENDENT	Brad & Jeff Rosten
PROFESSIONAL	Bill Peters

HOURS 6 am to Dusk
SEASON April to October

FEATURES

Putting green	Y
Driving range	N
Practice area	N

Golf carts		
Power (gas)	Y	$22
Pull carts	Y	$4
Club rental	Y	$8
Club storage	N	
Caddies	N	

Proshop	
Regular	Y
Refreshments	
Restaurant	Y
Lounge	Y
Snacks	Y
Clubhouse	
Showers	Y
Lockers	N
Lodging/resort	Y

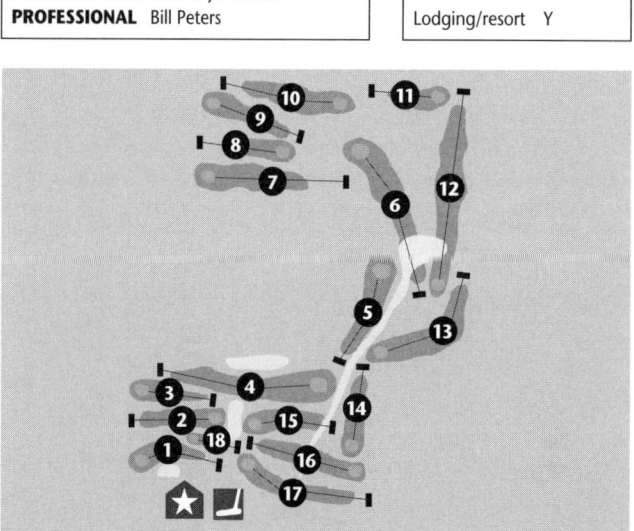

Located south of Glenwood. Course is south of MN Highway 55 on County Road 104, then west on Pezhekee Road.

	MEN				WOMEN		
	BACK	FRONT	PAR	HDCP	FRONT	PAR	HDCP
1	280	270	4	17	260	4	17
2	305	291	4	11	280	4	9
3	190	174	3	15	165	3	13
4	465	443	5	9	420	5	7
5	394	350	4	1	330	4	5
6	435	415	4	3	390	4	1
7	515	481	5	5	360	5	3
8	220	199	3	7	125	3	15
9	360	350	4	13	305	4	11
Out	3164	2973	36		2705	36	
10	495	478	5	8	384	5	6
11	240	185	3	6	150	3	12
12	565	554	5	4	505	6	2
13	405	381	4	12	365	4	10
14	215	197	3	10	185	4	16
15	330	319	4	16	280	4	14
16	430	423	4	2	410	5	4
17	465	450	5	14	420	5	8
18	145	140	3	18	130	3	18
In	3290	3127	36		2830	39	
Total	6454	6100	72		5465	75	
Rating	70.8	69.6			71.5		
Slope	119	116			122		

PHALEN PARK GOLF COURSE

18 Regulation Public

1615 Phalen Drive
St. Paul, Minnesota 55106
612/778-0424 Clubhouse
612/778-0413 Proshop

HOURS	Dawn to Dusk
SEASON	April-November

RESERVATIONS	612/488-9673
	$2 reservation fee
	Walk-on: fair/fair

GREEN FEES	M-F	S-S
Adult	$18.50/13	$18.50/13
Senior	$18.50/13	$18.50/13
Junior	$18.50/13	$18.50/13
Twilight	$13 (4 pm)	$13 (4 pm)

PAYMENT	Credit: Visa® MasterCard®
	Non-local checks accepted

LEAGUES	Men: Various
	Women: Various

MEMBERSHIPS	USGA, PGA, GCSAA, MGA

PROFESSIONAL	Nora McGuire

FEATURES

Putting green	Y	
Driving range	N	
Practice area	Y	
Golf carts		
Power (gas)	Y	$20/12
Pull carts	Y	$2.50
Club rental	Y	$6
Club storage	N	
Caddies	N	
Proshop		
Basic	Y	
Refreshments		
Restaurant	Y	
Lounge	Y	
Snacks	Y	
Clubhouse		
Showers	N	
Lockers	N	
Lodging	N	

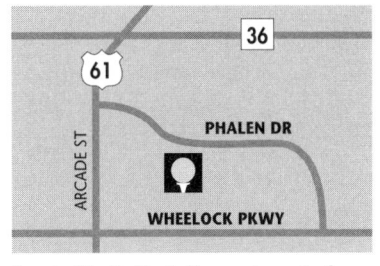

Located in St. Paul. Course is west of Arcade Street or north of Wheelock Parkway on Phalen Drive.

	MEN				WOMEN		
	BACK	FRONT	PAR	HDCP	FRONT	PAR	HDCP
1	361	349	4	11	325	4	11
2	351	344	4	13	322	4	5
3	209	195	3	9	165	3	15
4	510	495	5	3	468	5	1
5	345	333	4	15	281	4	13
6	370	358	4	7	333	4	9
7	415	408	4	1	406	5	3
8	152	144	3	17	122	3	17
9	337	325	4	5	299	4	7
Out	3050	2942	35		2721	36	
10	359	346	4	14	323	4	12
11	506	485	5	6	412	5	2
12	176	164	3	16	135	3	18
13	372	360	4	12	332	4	10
14	394	379	4	2	351	4	6
15	363	351	4	8	322	4	8
16	167	154	3	18	139	3	16
17	404	391	4	4	374	4	4
18	310	300	4	10	280	4	14
In	3051	2930	35		2668	35	
Total	6101	5872	70		5439	71	
Rating	68.7	67.7			70.7		
Slope	121	119			121		

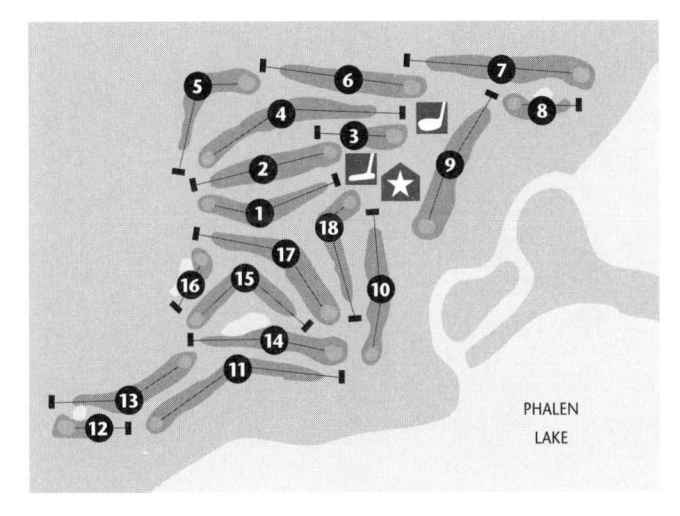

GOLF COURSE DIRECTORY

PHEASANT RUN GOLF CLUB
18 Regulation Public

10705 County Road 116
Corcoran, Minnesota 55374
612/428-8244 Clubhouse/Proshop

RESERVATIONS	612/428-8244 5 days	
	Walk-on: good/fair	
GREEN FEES	M-F	S-S
Adult	$17/13	$20/15
Senior	$10	$20/15
Junior	$7/7	$20/15
Twilight	$10 (6 pm)	$10 (6 pm)
PAYMENT	No credit cards accepted	
	Non-local checks accepted	
LEAGUES	Men: Various	
	Women: Various	
MEMBERSHIPS	USGA, PGA, GCSAA, MGA	
SUPERINTENDENT	Scott Weltzin	
PROFESSIONAL	Steve Fessler	

HOURS	Dawn to Dusk
SEASON	April-November

FEATURES			
Putting green	Y		
Driving range	Y		
Practice area	N		
Golf carts			
Power	Y	$20/13	
Pull carts	Y	$2	
Club rental	Y		
Club storage	N		
Caddies	N		
Proshop			
Extended	Y		
Refreshments			
Restaurant	N		
Lounge	Y		
Snacks	Y		
Clubhouse			
Showers	N		
Lockers	N		
Lodging	N		

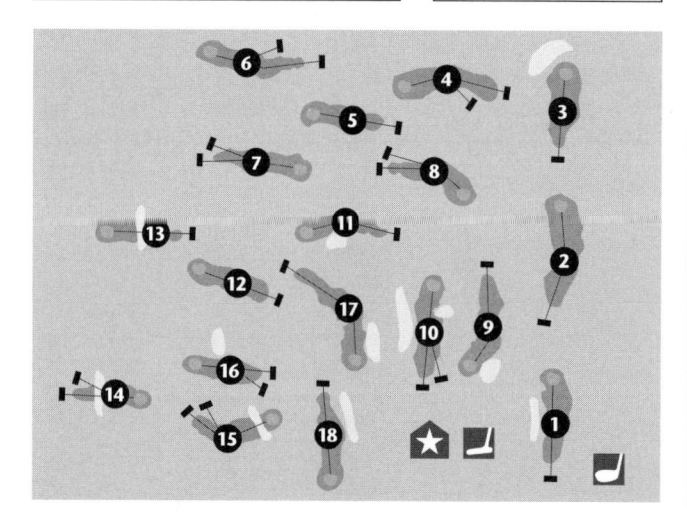

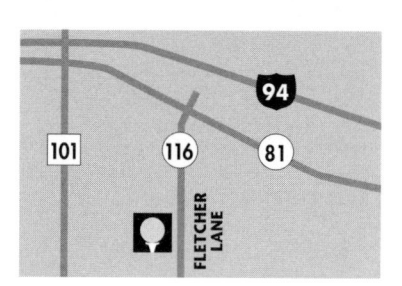

Located south of Rogers. Course is east of MN Highway 101 on County Road 81, then south on County Road 116.

	MEN				WOMEN		
	BACK	FRONT	PAR	HDCP	FRONT	PAR	HDCP
1	325	306	4	15	287	4	13
2	344	334	4	13	324	4	7
3	126	120	3	17	110	3	17
4	516	504	5	3	436	5	3
5	137	126	3	11	116	3	15
6	412	403	4	7	322	4	9
7	348	339	4	9	272	4	11
8	492	482	5	5	403	5	1
9	441	431	4	1	426	5	5
Out	3151	3055	36		2693	37	
10	390	380	4	6	305	4	6
11	400	384	4	2	292	4	4
12	339	331	4	18	238	4	16
13	205	195	3	8	160	3	8
14	341	336	4	10	247	4	10
15	505	495	5	4	412	5	2
16	206	196	3	12	137	3	18
17	385	376	4	14	289	4	14
18	343	333	4	16	323	4	12
In	3113	3020	35		2403	35	
Total	6264	6081	71		5096	72	
Rating	69.9	69.0			68.6		
Slope	117	116			115		

PIERZ GOLF COURSE

9 Regulation Public

P.O. Box 129
Pierz, Minnesota 56364
612/468-2662 Clubhouse/Proshop

HOURS	Dawn to Dusk
SEASON	April to October

RESERVATIONS	612/468-2662
	Walk-on: good/good

GREEN FEES	M-F	S-S
Adult	Call	Call
Senior	Call	Call
Junior	Call	Call
Twilight	NA	NA

PAYMENT	No credit cards accepted
	Non-local checks accepted

LEAGUES	Men: Various
	Women: Various

MEMBERSHIPS	MGA

PROFESSIONAL	Call

FEATURES	
Putting green	Y
Driving range	N
Practice area	N
Golf carts	
Power	Y
Pull carts	Y
Club rental	Y
Club storage	N
Caddies	N
Proshop	
Standard	Y
Refreshments	
Restaurant	N
Lounge	Y
Snacks	Y
Clubhouse	
Showers	N
Lockers	N
Lodging	N

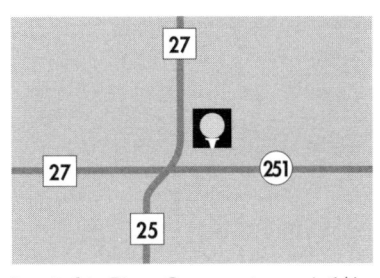

Located in Pierz. Course entrance is 1/4 mile north of MN Highway 27 on MN Highway 25.

	MEN				**WOMEN**		
	BACK	FRONT	PAR	HDCP	FRONT	PAR	HDCP
1	376	350	4	4	344	4	3
2	578	571	4	8	545	6	1
3	376	376	4	1	363	5	4
4	181	166	3	2	141	3	8
5	300	294	4	9	277	4	7
6	315	310	4	5	282	4	6
7	185	175	3	6	158	3	9
8	411	401	4	3	393	5	2
9	336	331	4	7	319	4	5
Out	3058	2974	35		2822	38	
1	376	350	4	4	344	4	3
2	578	571	4	8	545	6	1
3	376	376	4	1	363	5	4
4	181	166	3	2	141	3	8
5	300	294	4	9	277	4	7
6	315	310	4	5	282	4	6
7	185	175	3	6	158	3	9
8	411	401	4	3	393	5	2
9	336	331	4	7	319	4	5
In	3058	2974	35		2822	38	
Total	6116	5948	70		5644	76	
Rating	69.2	68.4			73.0		
Slope	110	109			116		

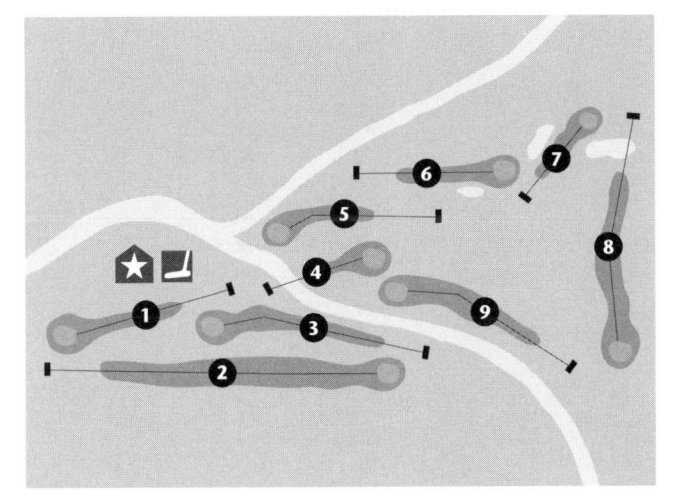

PIKE LAKE COUNTRY CLUB

9 Regulation Semi-Private

4895 East Pike Lake Road
Duluth, Minnesota 55811
218/729-8160 Clubhouse/Proshop

HOURS	Dawn to Dusk
SEASON	May-September

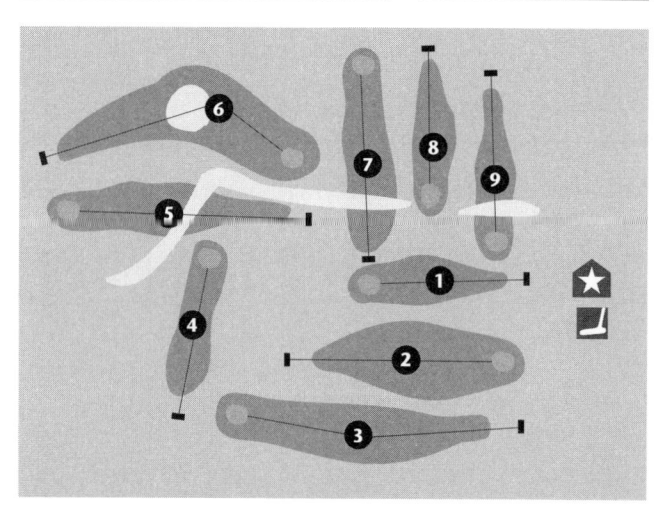

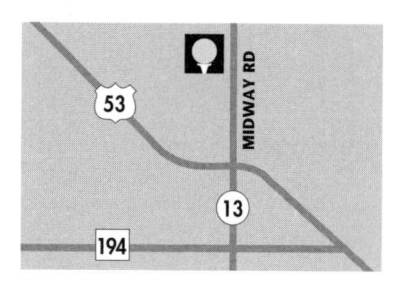

Located west of Duluth. Course entrance is about one mile north of U.S. Highway 53 on Midway Road/County Road 13.

RESERVATIONS	No reservations accepted
	Walk-on: good/fair

GREEN FEES	M-F	S-S
Adult	$11/8	$11/8
Senior	$8.50/6.50	$11/8
Junior	$8.50/6.50	$11/8
Twilight	NA	NA
	AAA members get $2 off	

PAYMENT	Credit: Visa® MasterCard®
	Non-local checks accepted

LEAGUES	Men: Various
	Women: Various

MEMBERSHIPS	None

OWNER	AAA Minnesota
MANAGER	Harold Burke

FEATURES

Putting green	Y	
Driving range	N	
Practice area	N	
Golf carts		
Power (gas)	Y	$14/9
Pull carts	Y	$2
Club rental	Y	$4
Club storage	N	
Caddies	N	
Proshop		
Basic	N	
Refreshments		
Restaurant	N	
Lounge	N	
Snacks	Y	
Clubhouse		
Showers	N	
Lockers	Y	
Lodging	N	

	MEN				**WOMEN**		
	BACK	FRONT	PAR	HDCP	FRONT	PAR	HDCP
1	121	113	3	9	105	3	9
2	177	172	3	6	165	3	6
3	229	222	3	4	210	4	4
4	123	111	3	8	108	3	8
5	428	418	4	1	354	4	1
6	374	369	4	2	369	4	2
7	296	280	4	3	280	4	3
8	153	153	3	5	153	3	5
9	146	110	3	7	97	3	7
Out	2047	1984	30		1841	31	
1	121	113	3	9	105	3	9
2	177	172	3	6	165	3	6
3	229	222	3	4	210	4	4
4	123	111	3	8	108	3	8
5	428	418	4	1	354	4	1
6	374	369	4	2	369	4	2
7	296	280	4	3	280	4	3
8	153	153	3	5	153	3	5
9	146	110	3	7	97	3	7
In	2047	1984	30		1841	31	
Total	4094	3968	60		3682	62	
Rating	59.0	58.2			60.1		
Slope	87	85			90		

PINE CITY COUNTRY CLUB

9 Regulation Public

Route 4, Box 6C
Pine City, Minnesota 55063
612/629-3848 Clubhouse/Proshop

| **HOURS** | Dawn to Dusk |
| **SEASON** | April to October |

| **RESERVATIONS** | 612/629-3848 |
| | Walk-on: good/fair |

GREEN FEES	M-F	S-S
Adult	Call	Call
Senior	Call	Call
Junior	Call	Call
Twilight	NA	NA

| **PAYMENT** | No credit cards accepted |
| | Non-local checks accepted |

| **LEAGUES** | Men: Various |
| | Women: Various |

| **MEMBERSHIPS** | PGA, MGA |

| **PROFESSIONAL** | Jim O'Leary |

FEATURES	
Putting green	Y
Driving range	Y
Practice area	Y
Golf carts	
Power	Y
Pull carts	Y
Club rental	Y
Club storage	N
Caddies	N
Proshop	
Standard	Y
Refreshments	
Restaurant	Y
Lounge	Y
Snacks	Y
Clubhouse	
Showers	N
Lockers	N
Lodging	N

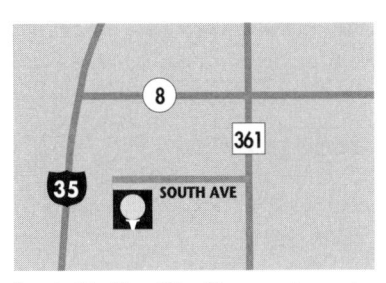

Located in Pine City. Course entrance is east of I-35 on County Road 8, south on Highway 361, then west on South Ave.

	MEN				**WOMEN**		
	BACK	FRONT	PAR	HDCP	FRONT	PAR	HDCP
1	485	475	5	9	425	5	9
2	360	350	4	11	325	4	11
3	185	180	3	15	170	3	15
4	505	500	5	5	450	5	5
5	410	405	4	3	400	5	3
6	330	325	4	13	315	4	13
7	165	155	3	17	145	3	17
8	370	365	4	7	300	4	7
9	430	425	4	1	415	5	1
Out	3240	3180	36		2945	38	
1	485	475	5	10	425	5	10
2	360	350	4	12	325	4	12
3	185	180	3	16	170	3	16
4	505	500	5	6	450	5	6
5	410	405	4	4	400	5	4
6	330	325	4	14	315	4	14
7	165	155	3	18	145	3	18
8	370	365	4	8	300	4	8
9	430	425	4	2	415	5	2
In	3240	3180	36		2945	38	
Total	6480	6360	72		5890	76	
Rating	71.0	70.2			74.0		
Slope	121	120			124		

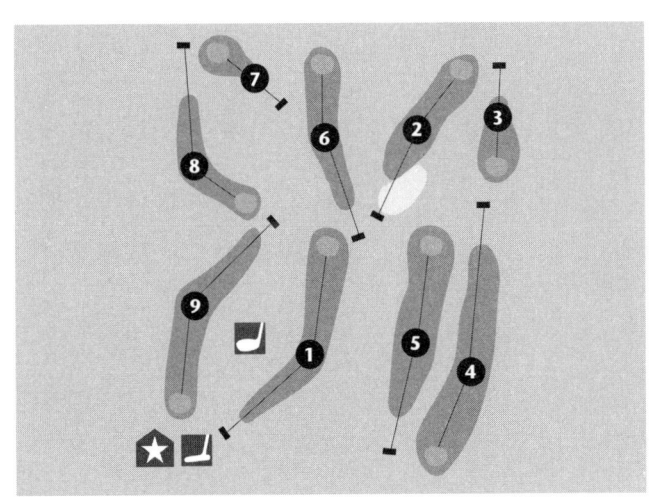

GOLF COURSE DIRECTORY

PINE CREEK GOLF COURSE

9 Regulation Public

3815 North Pine Creek Road
La Crescent, Minnesota 55947
507/895-2410 Clubhouse/Proshop

HOURS Dawn to Dusk
SEASON April to October

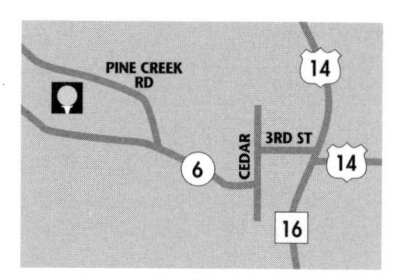

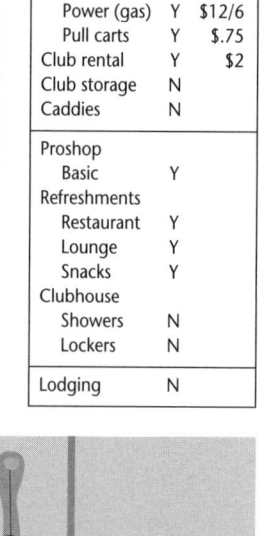

Located west of La Crescent. Course is west of Hwy 16 on 3rd St, west on Cty Road 6, then north on Pine Creek Road.

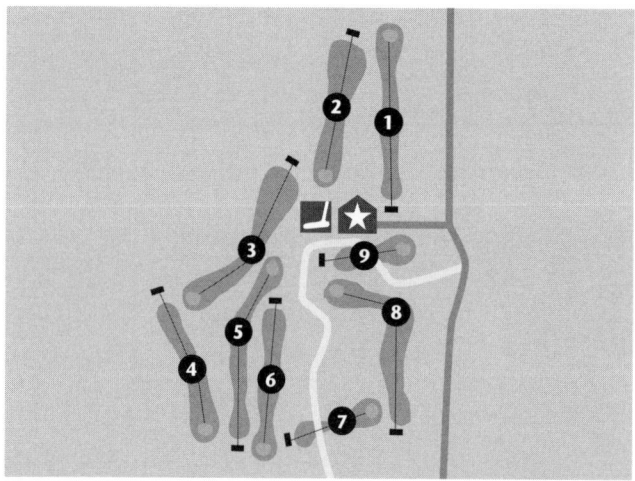

RESERVATIONS	507/895-2410	
	Walk-on: fair/poor	
GREEN FEES	M-F	S-S
Adult	$10/5	$11/5.50
Senior	$10/5	$11/5.50
Junior	$10/5	$11/5.50
Twilight	NA	NA
PAYMENT	No credit cards accepted	
	Non-local checks accepted	
LEAGUES	Men: Various	
	Women: Various	
MEMBERSHIPS	MGA	
MANAGER	Roy Lemke, Lisa Yahnke	

FEATURES		
Putting green	Y	
Driving range	N	
Practice area	N	
Golf carts		
Power (gas)	Y	$12/6
Pull carts	Y	$.75
Club rental	Y	$2
Club storage	N	
Caddies	N	
Proshop		
Basic	Y	
Refreshments		
Restaurant	Y	
Lounge	Y	
Snacks	Y	
Clubhouse		
Showers	N	
Lockers	N	
Lodging	N	

	MEN			WOMEN		
	FRONT	PAR	HDCP	FRONT	PAR	HDCP
1	347	4	4	347	4	4
2	281	4	6	281	4	6
3	503	5	1	503	6	1
4	355	4	5	355	4	5
5	385	4	3	385	5	3
6	344	4	7	277	4	7
7	170	3	8	143	3	8
8	395	4	2	395	5	2
9	169	3	9	125	3	9
Out	2949	35		2811	38	
1	347	4	4	347	4	4
2	281	4	6	281	4	6
3	503	5	1	503	6	1
4	355	4	5	355	4	5
5	385	4	3	385	5	3
6	344	4	7	277	4	7
7	170	3	8	143	3	8
8	395	4	2	395	5	2
9	169	3	9	125	3	9
In	2949	35		2811	38	
Total	5898	70		5622	76	
Rating	64.6			67.4		
Slope	98			109		

PINE HILL GOLF CLUB

9 Executive Public

215 Highway 61
Carlton, Minnesota 55718
218/384-3727 Clubhouse/Proshop

HOURS	8 am to Dusk
SEASON	May to October

RESERVATIONS	218/384-3727	
	Walk-on: good/good	
GREEN FEES	M-F	S-S
Adult	$10/7	$10/7
Senior	$9/6	$9/6
Junior	$9/6	$9/6
Twilight	NA	NA
PAYMENT	No credit cards accepted	
	Local checks only	
LEAGUES	Men: W (pm)	
	Women: W (am)	
MEMBERSHIPS	MGA	
OWNER	DaWay & Jean Johnson,	
	Cecil & Ardis Jons	
MANAGER	Mike McCorison	

FEATURES		
Putting green	N	
Driving range	N	
Practice area	N	
Golf carts		
Power	Y	$18/10
Pull carts	Y	$2/1
Club rental	Y	$5/3
Club storage	N	
Caddies	N	
Proshop		
Basic	Y	
Refreshments		
Restaurant	N	
Lounge	Y	
Snacks	Y	
Clubhouse		
Showers	N	
Lockers	N	
Lodging	N	

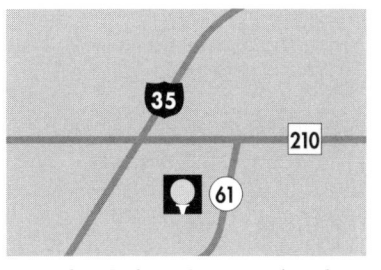

Located in Carlton. Course is 1/4 mile east of I-35 on MN Highway 210, then one mile south on County Road 61.

	MEN			**WOMEN**		
	FRONT	PAR	HDCP	FRONT	PAR	HDCP
1	140	3		130	3	
2	308	4		226	4	
3	280	4		266	4	
4	168	3		118	3	
5	291	4		190	4	
6	206	3		157	3	
7	155	3		121	3	
8	185	3		185	4	
9	167	3		120	3	
Out	1900	30		1513	31	
1	140	3		130	3	
2	308	4		226	4	
3	280	4		266	4	
4	168	3		118	3	
5	291	4		190	4	
6	206	3		157	3	
7	155	3		121	3	
8	185	3		185	4	
9	167	3		120	3	
In	1900	30		1513	31	
Total	3800	60		3026	62	
Rating	NA			NA		
Slope	NA			NA		

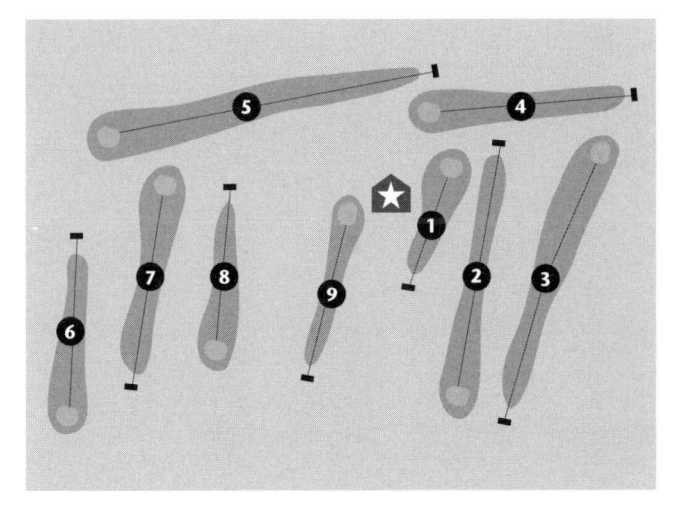

GOLF COURSE DIRECTORY

PINE ISLAND GOLF COURSE

9 Regulation Semi-Private

P.O. Box 341
Pine Island, Minnesota 55963
507/356-8252 Clubhouse/Proshop

HOURS	Dawn to Dusk
SEASON	April-November

RESERVATIONS	507/356-8252	
	Walk-on: good/fair	
GREEN FEES	M-F	S-S
Adult	Call	Call
Senior	Call	Call
Junior	Call	Call
Twilight	NA	NA
PAYMENT	No credit cards accepted	
	Non-local checks accepted	
LEAGUES	Men: Various	
	Women: Various	
MEMBERSHIPS	MGA	
MANAGER	Vince Fangman	

FEATURES	
Putting green	Y
Driving range	Y
Practice area	N
Golf carts	
Power (gas)	Y
Pull carts	Y
Club rental	Y
Club storage	N
Caddies	N
Proshop	
Regular	Y
Refreshments	
Restaurant	N
Lounge	Y
Snacks	Y
Clubhouse	
Showers	N
Lockers	N
Lodging	N

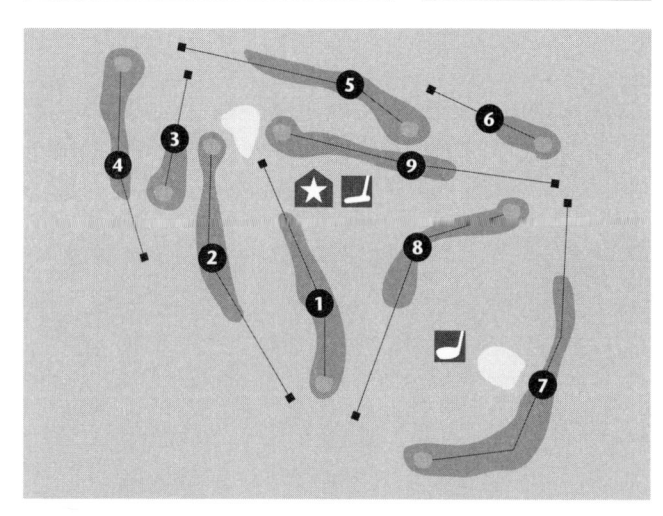

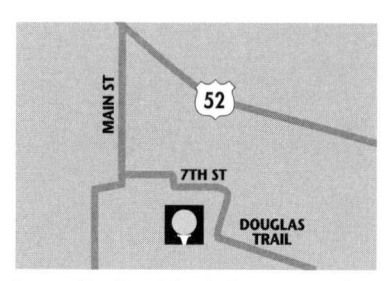

Located in Pine Island. Course is south of U.S. Hwy 52 on Main Street, east on 7th Street, then south on Douglas Trail.

	MEN				**WOMEN**		
	BACK	FRONT	PAR	HDCP	FRONT	PAR	HDCP
1	370	365	4		324	4	
2	513	469	5		348	5	
3	180	164	3		109	3	
4	313	296	4		233	4	
5	391	365	4		260	4	
6	198	158	3		144	3	
7	538	509	5		442	5	
8	411	364	4		294	4	
9	429	400	4		313	4	
Out	3343	3085	36		2467	36	
1	370	365	4		324	4	
2	513	469	5		348	5	
3	180	164	3		109	3	
4	313	296	4		233	4	
5	391	365	4		260	4	
6	198	158	3		144	3	
7	538	509	5		442	5	
8	411	364	4		294	4	
9	429	400	4		313	4	
In	3343	3085	36		2467	36	
Total	6686	6170	72		4934	72	
Rating	NA	NA			NA		
Slope	NA	NA			NA		

PINE MEADOWS AT BRAINERD

18 Regulation Semi-Private

500 Golf Course Drive
Brainerd, Minnesota 56401
218/829-5733 Clubhouse
800/368-2048 Proshop

HOURS	Dawn to Dusk
SEASON	April to October

FEATURES

Putting green	Y	
Driving range	Y	$3.50
Practice area	Y	
Golf carts		
Power (gas)	Y	$25/15
Pull carts	Y	$2.50
Club rental	Y	$5-15
Club storage	N	
Caddies	N	
Proshop		
Extended	Y	
Refreshments		
Restaurant	Y	
Lounge	Y	
Snacks	Y	
Clubhouse		
Showers	Y	
Lockers	Y	
Lodging	N	

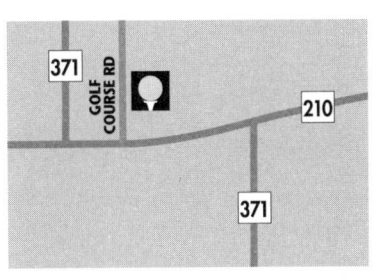

Located in Brainerd. Course entrance is north of MN Highway 371/210 on Golf Course Road.

RESERVATIONS	800/368-2048 1 week
	Walk-on: fair/poor

GREEN FEES	M-F	S-S
Adult	$25/15	$27/16
Senior	$25/15	$27/16
Junior	$25/15	$27/16
Twilight	$15	$16

PAYMENT	Credit: Visa® MC® AmEx®
	Non-local checks accepted

LEAGUES	Men: Th (pm)
	Women: Th (am)

MEMBERSHIPS	USGA, PGA, GCSAA, MGA

MANAGER	Mark Johnson
SUPERINTEDENT	Dick William
PROFESSIONAL	Mark Johnson, Keith Skelton

	MEN				WOMEN		
	BACK	FRONT	PAR	HDCP	FRONT	PAR	HDCP
1	500	480	5	6	352	5	2
2	347	335	4	14	275	4	12
3	131	121	3	18	102	3	18
4	411	400	4	2	306	4	10
5	524	490	5	4	385	5	4
6	216	150	3	12	122	3	16
7	340	321	4	8	295	4	6
8	307	289	4	10	235	4	8
9	348	295	4	16	195	4	14
Out	3124	2881	36		2267	36	
10	381	370	4	7	321	4	7
11	345	335	4	11	288	4	13
12	420	355	4	3	245	4	3
13	488	466	5	13	361	5	9
14	142	135	3	17	104	3	17
15	379	360	4	5	315	4	5
16	424	404	4	1	294	4	1
17	332	317	4	15	274	4	15
18	337	304	4	9	280	4	11
In	3248	3046	36		2482	36	
Total	6372	5927	72		4749	72	
Rating	70.7	NA			72.7		
Slope	129	NA			133		

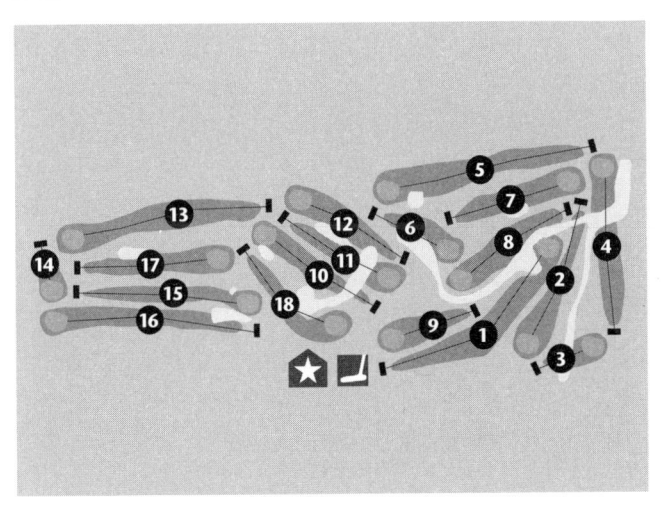

GOLF COURSE DIRECTORY

PINE RIDGE GOLF CLUB

9 Regulation Public

100 Hillcrest Road
Motley, Minnesota 56466
218/575-3300 Clubhouse/Proshop

HOURS 7 am to Dusk
SEASON April to October

RESERVATIONS	218/575-3300 5 days
	Walk-on: good/fair

GREEN FEES	M-F	S-S
Adult	$17/12	$18/13
Senior	$17/12	$18/13
Junior	$17/12	$18/13
Twilight	NA	NA

PAYMENT	Credit: Visa® MasterCard®
	Non-local checks accepted

LEAGUES	Men: Th (pm)
	Senior: T

MEMBERSHIPS	MGA

OWNER	Roger & Marge Pedley
MANAGER	Howard Houle
SUPERINTENDENT	Chris Vaseka

FEATURES

Putting green	Y	
Driving range	Y	$2.50
Practice area	N	
Golf carts		
Power (gas)	Y	$18/10
Pull carts	Y	$3
Club rental	Y	$10/7.5
Club storage	N	
Caddies	N	
Proshop		
Extended	Y	
Refreshments		
Restaurant	Y	
Lounge	Y	
Snacks	Y	
Clubhouse		
Showers	N	
Lockers	N	
Lodging	N	

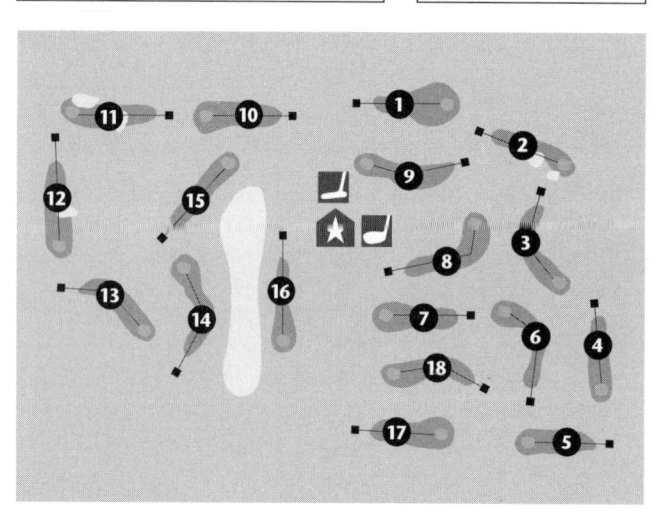

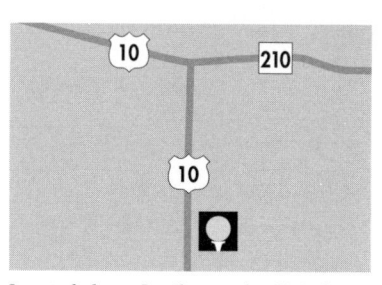

Located about 5 miles south of Motley. Course entrance is east of U.S. Highway 10 on Hillcreast Road.

	MEN				WOMEN		
	BACK	FRONT	PAR	HDCP	FRONT	PAR	HDCP
1	455	450	5	15	420	5	15
2	430	410	4	3	380	4	3
3	350	340	4	17	320	4	17
4	385	367	4	9	340	4	9
5	143	128	3	13	118	3	13
6	477	457	5	7	429	5	7
7	140	130	3	11	120	3	11
8	413	383	4	5	365	4	5
9	575	545	5	1	515	5	1
Out	3368	3210	37		3007	35	
10	143	130	3	16	122	3	16
11	535	510	5	4	480	5	4
12	340	325	4	8	310	4	8
13	310	300	4	14	285	4	14
14	315	302	4	18	280	4	18
15	175	160	3	6	150	3	6
16	355	340	4	10	325	4	10
17	400	375	4	2	355	4	2
18	465	450	5	12	430	5	12
In	3038	2892	36		2737	36	
Total	6406	6102	73		5744	73	
Rating	69.9	69.9			72.5		
Slope	121	121			130		

PINE RIVER COUNTRY CLUB

9 Regulation Public

P.O. Box 196
Pine River, Minnesota 56474
218/587-4774 Clubhouse/Proshop

HOURS	6:30 am to Dusk
SEASON	April to October

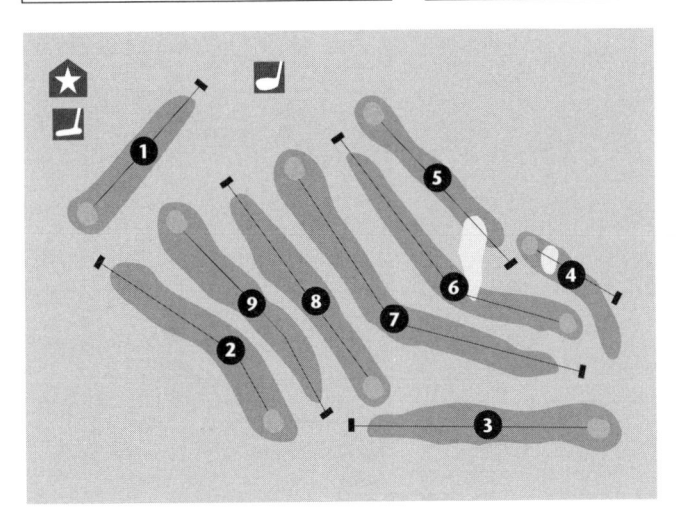

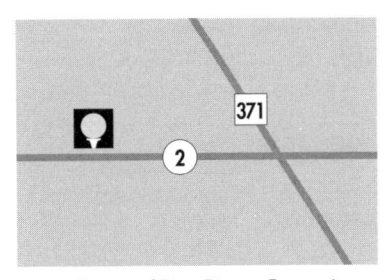

Located west of Pine River. Course is one mile west of MN Highway 371 on County Road 2.

| **RESERVATIONS** | 218/587-4774 |
| | Walk-on: fair/poor |

GREEN FEES	M-F	S-S
Adult	$17/11	$19/13
Senior	$17/11	$19/13
Junior	$17/11	$19/13
Twilight	$7.50 (5 pm)	NA

| **PAYMENT** | No credit cards accepted |
| | Non-local checks accepted |

LEAGUES	Men: W (5 pm)
	Women: Th (9 am)
	Sr Men: T (9 am)

| **MEMBERSHIPS** | USGA, GCSAA, MGA |

| **MANAGER** | John A. Lindstrom |
| **SUPERINTENDENT** | Chris Youngbauer |

FEATURES	
Putting green	Y
Driving range	Y $3.25
Practice area	Y
Golf carts	
Power (gas)	Y $20/14
Pull carts	Y $2.50
Club rental	Y $4.50
Club storage	Y $15/yr
Caddies	N
Proshop	
Extended	Y
Refreshments	
Restaurant	N
Lounge	N
Snacks	Y
Clubhouse	
Showers	N
Lockers	N
Lodging	N

		MEN			WOMEN		
	BACK	FRONT	PAR	HDCP	FRONT	PAR	HDCP
1	198	192	3	7	181	3	17
2	392	388	4	3	266	4	15
3	424	404	4	1	273	4	9
4	173	153	3	13	131	3	13
5	321	313	4	17	266	4	11
6	485	470	5	15	418	5	3
7	588	510	5	11	463	5	1
8	429	374	4	5	310	4	7
9	445	354	4	9	314	4	5
Out	3455	3158	36		2622	36	
1	198	192	3	7	181	3	17
2	392	388	4	3	266	4	15
3	424	404	4	1	273	4	9
4	173	153	3	13	131	3	13
5	321	313	4	17	266	4	11
6	485	470	5	15	418	5	3
7	588	510	5	11	463	5	1
8	429	374	4	5	310	4	7
9	445	354	4	9	314	4	5
In	3455	3158	36		2622	36	
Total	6910	6316	72		5244	72	
Rating	71.8	69.0			68.8		
Slope	119	113			112		

GOLF COURSE DIRECTORY

PINEWOOD GOLF COURSE

9 Executive Public

14000 182nd Avenue NW
Elk River, Minnesota 55330
612/441-3451 Clubhouse/Proshop

HOURS	7 am to Dusk
SEASON	April-November

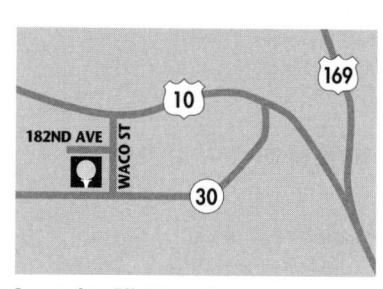

RESERVATIONS	612/441-3451	
	Walk-on: fair/poor	
GREEN FEES	M-F	S-S
Adult	$12/8	$14/9
Senior	$11/7	$13/8
Junior	$11/7	$13/8
Twilight	NA	NA
PAYMENT	No credit cards accepted	
	Local checks accepted	
LEAGUES	Men: Th (pm)	
	Women: T (pm)	
	Seniors: W (1 pm)	
MEMBERSHIPS	None	
OWNER	Paul & Pam Krause	
MANAGER	Jill Thomas	
SUPERINTENDENT	Bill Stevenson	
PROFESSIONAL	Paul Krause	

FEATURES		
Putting green	Y	
Driving range	Y	$2.50
Practice area	Y	
Golf carts		
Power (gas)	Y	$7
Pull carts	Y	$1
Club rental	Y	$3
Club storage	N	
Caddies	N	
Proshop		
Extended	Y	
Refreshments		
Restaurant	N	
Lounge	N	
Snacks	Y	
Clubhouse		
Showers	N	
Lockers	N	
Lodging	N	

Located in Elk River. Course entrance is south of U.S. Highway 10/52 on Waco Street, then west on 182nd Avenue.

	MEN			**WOMEN**		
	FRONT	PAR	HDCP	FRONT	PAR	HDCP
1	290	4	2	290	4	2
2	170	3	3	170	3	3
3	150	3	5	150	3	5
4	125	3	8	125	3	8
5	290	4	4	290	4	4
6	140	3	7	140	3	7
7	390	4	1	390	4	1
8	150	3	6	150	3	6
9	125	3	9	125	3	9
Out	1830	30		1830	30	
1	290	4	2	290	4	2
2	170	3	3	170	3	3
3	150	3	5	150	3	5
4	125	3	8	125	3	8
5	290	4	4	290	4	4
6	140	3	7	140	3	7
7	390	4	1	390	4	1
8	150	3	6	150	3	6
9	125	3	9	125	3	9
Out	1830	30		1830	30	
Total	3660	60		3660	60	
Rating	NA			NA		
Slope	NA			NA		

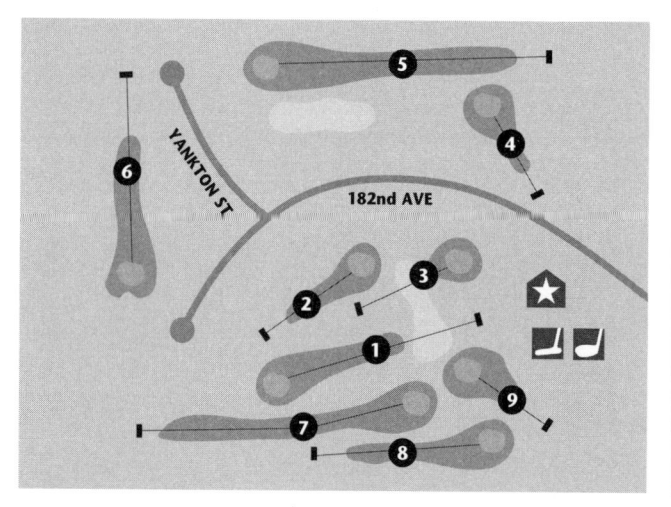

PIPER HILLS GOLF COURSE

9 Regulation Public

Highway 42 South, P.O. Box 535
Plainview, Minnesota 55964
507/534-2613 Clubhouse/Proshop

HOURS 7 am to Dusk
SEASON April-November

RESERVATIONS	507/534-2613	
	Walk-on: fair/fair	
GREEN FEES	M-F*	S-S
Adult	$14/8.50	$14/8.50
Senior	$14/8.50	$14/8.50
Junior	$14/8.50	$14/8.50
Twilight	NA	NA
	Special: M-F $12 for all day	
PAYMENT	No credit cards accepted	
	Non-local checks accepted	
LEAGUES	None	
MEMBERSHIPS	USGA, PGA, MGA	
SUPERINTENDENT	Chas Peluso	
PROFESSIONAL	Paul Pehler	

FEATURES		
Putting green	Y	
Driving range	Y	$2
Practice area	Y	
Golf carts		
Power	Y	$15/8.5
Pull carts	Y	$2
Club rental	Y	$3
Club storage	Y	$25
Caddies	N	
Proshop		
Extended	Y	
Refreshments		
Restaurant	Y	
Lounge	Y	
Snacks	Y	
Clubhouse		
Showers	N	
Lockers	N	
Lodging	N	

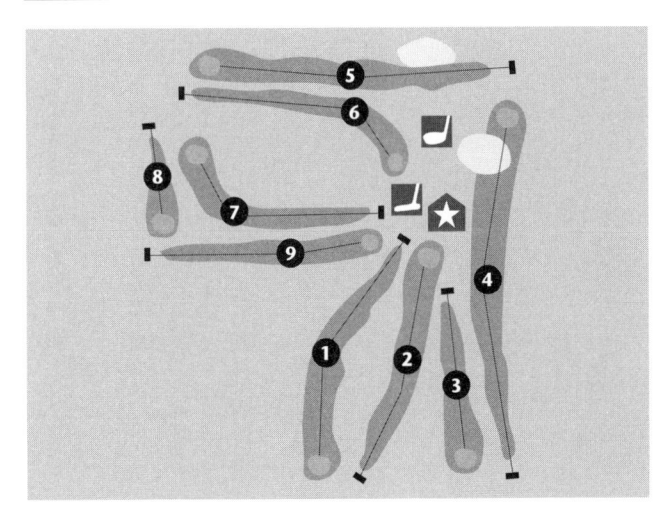

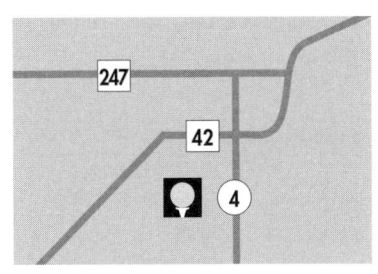

Located south of Plainview. Course entrance is about 1/4 mile south of MN Highway 42 on County Road 4.

	MEN			WOMEN		
	FRONT	PAR	HDCP	FRONT	PAR	HDCP
1	373	4	1	344	4	3
2	360	4	3	321	4	6
3	190	3	4	150	3	8
4	564	5	2	491	5	1
5	471	5	8	405	5	2
6	328	4	6	318	4	4
7	314	4	9	300	4	5
8	157	3	5	151	3	9
9	329	4	7	282	4	7
Out	3086	36		2762	36	
1	381	4	2	344	4	3
2	360	4	3	321	4	6
3	320	4	8	150	3	8
4	491	5	4	491	5	1
5	410	4	1	405	5	2
6	323	4	6	318	4	4
7	307	4	9	300	4	5
8	163	3	5	151	3	9
9	334	4	7	282	4	7
In	3091	36		2762	36	
Total	6177	72		5524	72	
Rating	68.4			71.0		
Slope	114			118		

GOLF COURSE DIRECTORY

PIPESTONE COUNTRY CLUB

9 Regulation Semi-Private

8th Avenue S.E., P.O. Box 462
Pipestone, Minnesota 56164
507/825-2592 Clubhouse/Proshop

HOURS	Dawn to Dusk
SEASON	April–September

RESERVATIONS	507/825-2592	
	Walk-on: good/good	

GREEN FEES	M-F	S-S
Adult	$10/8	$15/10
Senior	$10/8	$15/10
Junior	$10/8	$15/10
Twilight	NA	NA

PAYMENT	No credit cards accepted
	No checks accepted

LEAGUES	Men:	Various
	Women:	Various

MEMBERSHIPS	GCSAA, MGA

MANAGER	Blas Brual

FEATURES		
Putting green	Y	
Driving range	Y	$2
Practice area	N	
Golf carts		
Power (gas)	Y	$12/7
Pull carts	Y	$1
Club rental	Y	$4
Club storage	Y	
Caddies	N	
Proshop		
Basic	Y	
Refreshments		
Restaurant	N	
Lounge	N	
Snacks	N	
Clubhouse		
Showers	Y	
Lockers	N	
Lodging	N	

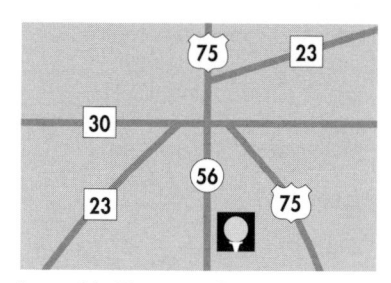

Located in Pipestone. Course entrance is about 1/4 mile south of MN Highway 30 on County Road 56.

	MEN			**WOMEN**		
	FRONT	PAR	HDCP	FRONT	PAR	HDCP
1	481	5	8	438	5	2
2	333	4	6	333	4	4
3	311	4	9	311	4	5
4	424	4	1	392	5	1
5	202	3	3	182	3	6
6	378	4	5	335	4	8
7	147	3	7	147	3	9
8	505	5	4	425	5	3
9	355	4	2	280	4	7
Out	3136	36		2853	37	
1	481	5	8	438	5	2
2	333	4	6	333	4	4
3	311	4	9	311	4	5
4	424	4	1	392	5	1
5	202	3	3	182	3	6
6	378	4	5	335	4	8
7	147	3	7	147	3	9
8	505	5	4	425	5	3
9	355	4	2	280	4	7
In	3136	36		2853	37	
Total	6272	72		5706	74	
Rating	69.0			71.6		
Slope	114			118		

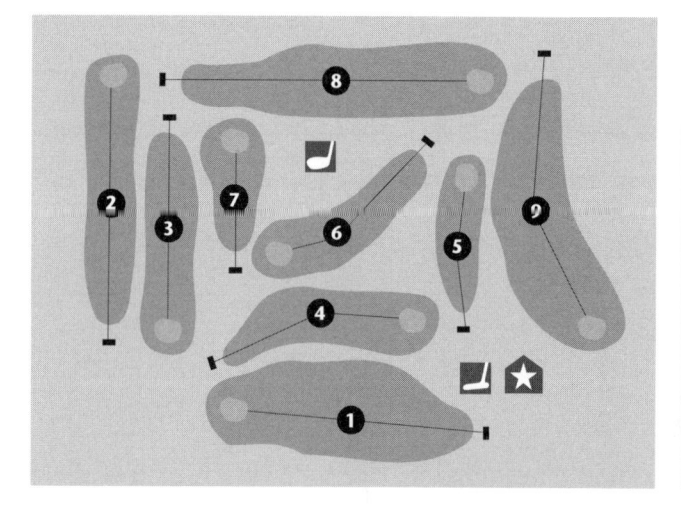

POKEGAMA GOLF COURSE

18 Regulation Public

3910 Golf Course Road
Grand Rapids, Minnesota 55744
218/326-3444 Clubhouse/Proshop

HOURS	7 am to Dusk
SEASON	April to October

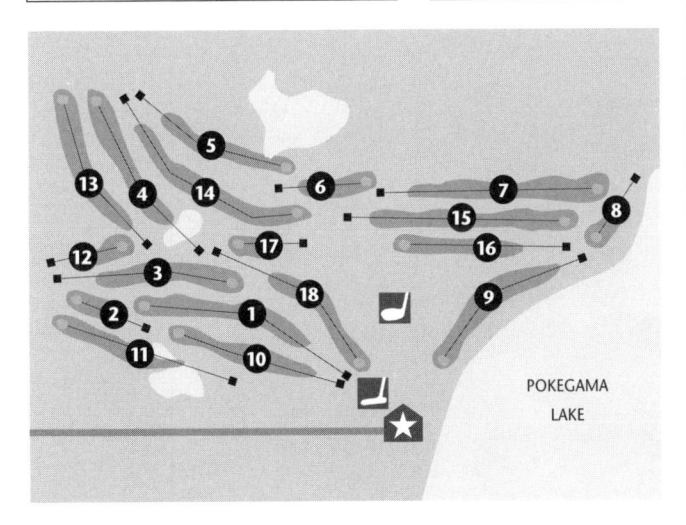

Located in Grand Rapids. Course is four miles west of U.S. Highway 169 on Golf Course Road/County Road 23.

RESERVATIONS	218/326-3444 1 week	
	Walk-on: fair/poor	
GREEN FEES	M-F	S-S
Adult	$18/12	$22/16
Senior	$18/12	$22/16
Junior	$18/12	$22/16
Twilight	$9	$9
PAYMENT	Credit: Visa® MasterCard®	
	Non-local checks accepted	
LEAGUES	Various	
MEMBERSHIPS	USGA, PGA, GCSAA, MGA	
SUPERINTEDENT	Dan Peluso	
PROFESSIONAL	Bob Cahill, Kelly Hain	

FEATURES		
Putting green	Y	
Driving range	Y	
Practice area	Y	
Golf carts		
Power (gas)	Y	$18/10
Pull carts	Y	$2
Club rental	Y	
Club storage	N	
Caddies	N	
Proshop		
Extended	Y	
Refreshments		
Restaurant	Y	
Lounge	Y	
Snacks	Y	
Clubhouse		
Showers	N	
Lockers	N	
Lodging	N	

	MEN				**WOMEN**		
	BACK	FRONT	PAR	HDCP	FRONT	PAR	HDCP
1	485	469	5	13	451	5	3
2	168	156	3	15	118	3	15
3	383	359	4	5	291	4	9
4	434	426	4	3	426	5	13
5	415	398	4	1	305	4	5
6	204	160	3	7	125	3	11
7	484	472	5	11	400	5	7
8	149	141	3	17	131	3	17
9	432	370	4	9	314	4	1
Out	3154	2951	35		2561	36	
10	362	348	4	6	336	4	2
11	391	372	4	2	270	4	12
12	159	146	3	18	132	3	14
13	386	372	4	8	292	4	8
14	520	498	5	4	401	5	6
15	524	509	5	16	436	5	4
16	386	354	4	12	282	4	10
17	189	170	3	14	100	3	16
18	410	385	4	10	236	4	18
In	3327	3154	36		2485	36	
Total	6481	6105	71		5046	72	
Rating	70.3	68.5			67.7		
Slope	121	117			116		

GOLF COURSE DIRECTORY

POMME DE TERRE GOLF CLUB

9 Regulation Semi-Private

South Highway 9, P.O. Box 306
Morris, Minnesota 56267
612/589-1009 Clubhouse/Proshop

HOURS	8 am to Dusk
SEASON	April-November

RESERVATIONS	612/589-1009 2 days
	Walk-on: good/fair

GREEN FEES	M-F	S-S
Adult	$15/9.50	$15/9.50
Senior	$15/9.50	$15/9.50
Junior	$15/9.50	$15/9.50
Twilight	NA	NA
	Punch card avalible	

PAYMENT	No credit cards accepted
	Non-local checks accepted

LEAGUES	Men: Th
	Women: W

MEMBERSHIPS	USGA, MGA

MANAGER	Jay Carlson

FEATURES		
Putting green	Y	
Driving range	Y	
Practice area	Y	
Golf carts		
Power (gas)	Y	
Pull carts	Y	$2.50
Club rental	Y	$5
Club storage	N	
Caddies	N	
Proshop		
Regular	Y	
Refreshments		
Restaurant	N	
Lounge	Y	
Snacks	Y	
Clubhouse		
Showers	N	
Lockers	N	
Lodging	N	

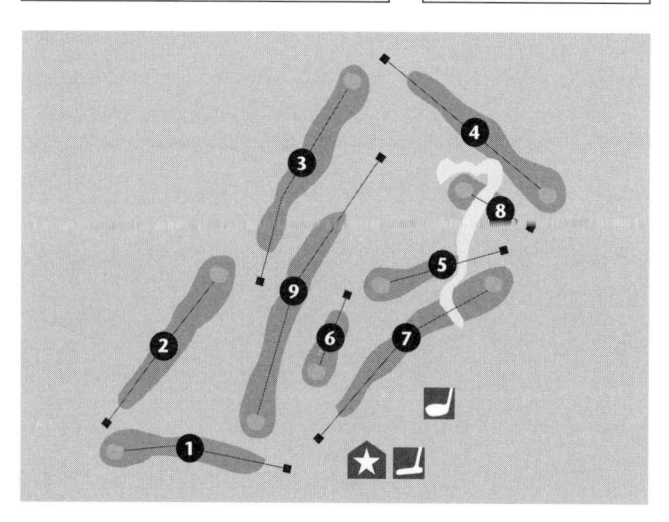

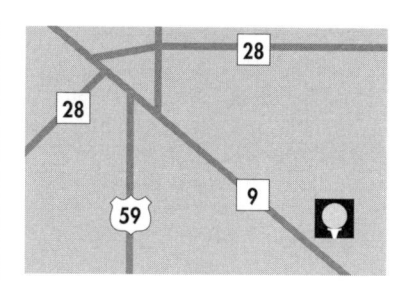

Located south of Morris. Course is about 2 1/2 miles south of U.S. Highway 59 on MN Highway 9.

	MEN			WOMEN		
	FRONT	PAR	HDCP	FRONT	PAR	HDCP
1	282	4	9	238	4	8
2	366	4	7	350	4	4
3	393	4	2	378	5	3
4	352	4	5	208	4	9
5	257	4	8	235	4	7
6	178	3	3	99	3	6
7	414	4	1	370	5	1
8	124	3	6	92	3	5
9	505	5	4	443	5	2
Out	2871	35		2413	37	
1	282	4	9	238	4	8
2	366	4	7	350	4	4
3	393	4	2	378	5	3
4	352	4	5	208	4	9
5	257	4	8	235	4	7
6	178	3	3	99	3	6
7	414	4	1	370	5	1
8	124	3	6	92	3	5
9	505	5	4	443	5	2
In	2871	35		2413	37	
Total	5742	70		4826	74	
Rating	68.2			68.4		
Slope	123			120		

THE MINNESOTA ILLUSTRATED

PONDEROSA GOLF CLUB

9 Regulation Public

Rural Route 2, P.O. Box 259
Glyndon, Minnesota 56547
218/498-2201 Clubhouse/Proshop

HOURS	7 am to Dusk
SEASON	April–November

RESERVATIONS	218/498-2201	
	Walk-on: good/fair	

GREEN FEES	M-F	S-S
Adult	$10/6	$13/7
Senior	$8/5	$13/7
Junior	$8/5	$13/7
Twilight	$5	NA
	Group packages available	

PAYMENT	No credit cards accepted
	Non-local checks accepted

LEAGUES	Men: W-F
	Women: T (am)

MEMBERSHIPS	USGA, NGF, GCSAA, MGA
OWNER	MSU Foundation
MANAGER	Phillip P. Sanders

FEATURES		
Putting green	Y	
Driving range	N	
Practice area	Y	
Golf carts		
Power (gas)	Y	$15/9
Pull carts	Y	$2
Club rental	Y	$2.50
Club storage	N	
Caddies	N	
Proshop		
Regular	Y	
Refreshments		
Restaurant	N	
Lounge	Y	
Snacks	Y	
Clubhouse		
Showers	Y	
Lockers	Y	
Lodging	N	

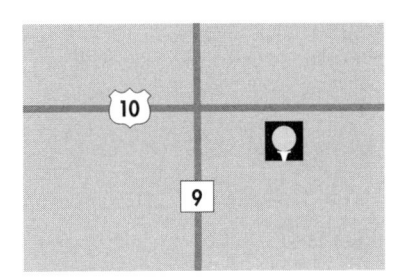

Located in Glyndon. Course entrance is about 1 3/4 miles east of MN Highway 9 on U.S. Highway 10.

	MEN				WOMEN		
	BACK	FRONT	PAR	HDCP	FRONT	PAR	HDCP
1	383	347	4	3	311	4	3
2	593	572	5	1	443	5	1
3	374	310	4	4	274	4	4
4	509	490	5	2	432	5	2
5	124	118	3	9	107	3	9
6	314	294	4	7	272	4	7
7	160	156	3	8	125	3	8
8	316	310	4	6	296	4	6
9	300	287	4	5	269	4	5
Out	3073	2884	36		2529	36	
1	383	347	4	3	311	4	3
2	593	572	5	1	443	5	1
3	374	310	4	4	274	4	4
4	509	490	5	2	432	5	2
5	124	118	3	9	107	3	9
6	314	294	4	7	272	4	7
7	160	156	3	8	125	3	8
8	316	310	4	6	296	4	6
9	300	287	4	5	269	4	5
In	3073	2884	36		2529	36	
Total	6146	5768	72		5058	72	
Rating	69.2	67.4			69.0		
Slope	122	118			119		

Course layout map not provided.

PRAIRIE VIEW MUNICIPAL GOLF COURSE

18 Regulation Public

Highway 266, P.O. Box 279
Worthington, Minnesota 56187
507/372-8670 Clubhouse/Proshop

HOURS	7 am to Dusk
SEASON	April-November

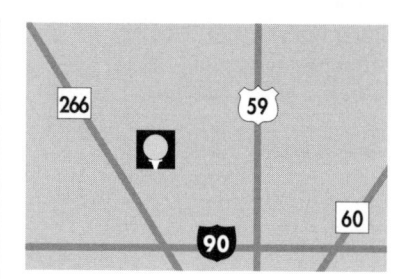

Located north of Worthington. Course entrance is 1/2 mile north of I-90 on MN Highway 266.

| **RESERVATIONS** | 507/372-7896 1 week |
| | Walk-on: good/fair |

GREEN FEES	M-F	S-S
Adult	$14/8	$16/10
Senior	$14/8	$16/10
Junior	$14/8	$16/10
Twilight	NA	$6 (6 pm)

| **PAYMENT** | No credit cards accepted |
| | Non-local checks accepted |

| **LEAGUES** | Men: T |
| | Women: Th (pm) |

| **MEMBERSHIPS** | NGF, PGA, GCSAA, MGA |

| **PROFESSIONAL** | Scott Larson |

FEATURES		
Putting green	Y	
Driving range	Y	$2.50
Practice area	Y	
Golf carts		
Power (gas)	Y	$15/9
Pull carts	Y	$1.50
Club rental	Y	$2.50
Club storage	Y	
Caddies	N	
Proshop		
Extended	Y	
Refreshments		
Restaurant	N	
Lounge	Y	
Snacks	Y	
Clubhouse		
Showers	N	
Lockers	N	
Lodging	N	

	MEN				**WOMEN**		
	BACK	FRONT	PAR	HDCP	FRONT	PAR	HDCP
1	503	491	5	3	439	5	3
2	166	141	3	15	126	3	15
3	377	361	4	6	294	4	6
4	348	322	4	9	261	4	9
5	156	134	3	17	90	3	17
6	326	307	4	13	259	4	13
7	375	358	4	7	338	4	7
8	530	511	5	10	475	5	10
9	215	196	3	11	164	3	11
Out	2994	2821	35		2444	35	
10	515	495	5	2	437	5	2
11	425	405	4	8	347	4	8
12	358	327	4	14	283	4	14
13	181	158	3	16	141	3	16
14	410	384	4	1	320	4	1
15	518	500	5	4	421	5	4
16	173	151	3	18	132	3	18
17	372	347	4	12	276	4	12
18	420	401	4	5	302	4	5
In	3372	3168	36		2659	36	
Total	6366	5989	71		5103	71	
Rating	69.9	68.2			68.3		
Slope	112	109			113		

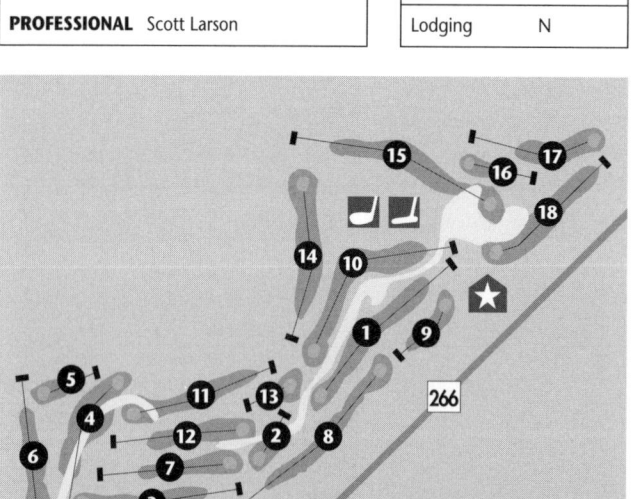

PRESTON GOLF & COUNTRY CLUB

9 Regulation Semi-Private

Highway 16 West
Preston, Minnesota 55965
507/765-4485 Clubhouse/Proshop

RESERVATIONS	507/765-4485	
	Walk-on: good/good	
GREEN FEES	M-F	S-S
Adult	$14/8	$16/9
Senior	$14/8	$16/9
Junior	$14/8	$16/9
Twilight	NA	NA
PAYMENT	No credit cards accepted	
	Non-local checks accepted	
LEAGUES	None	
MEMBERSHIPS	MGA	
MANAGER	Ken Denny	
PROFESSIONAL	Ken Denny	

HOURS	7 am to Dusk	
SEASON	April-November	
FEATURES		
Putting green	Y	
Driving range	N	
Practice area	N	
Golf carts		
Power	Y	$14/7
Pull carts	Y	$3/1.50
Club rental	Y	$4/2
Club storage	Y	$15/yr
Caddies	N	
Proshop		
Extended	Y	
Refreshments		
Restaurant	N	
Lounge	Y	
Snacks	Y	
Clubhouse		
Showers	Y	
Lockers	Y	$15/yr
Lodging	N	

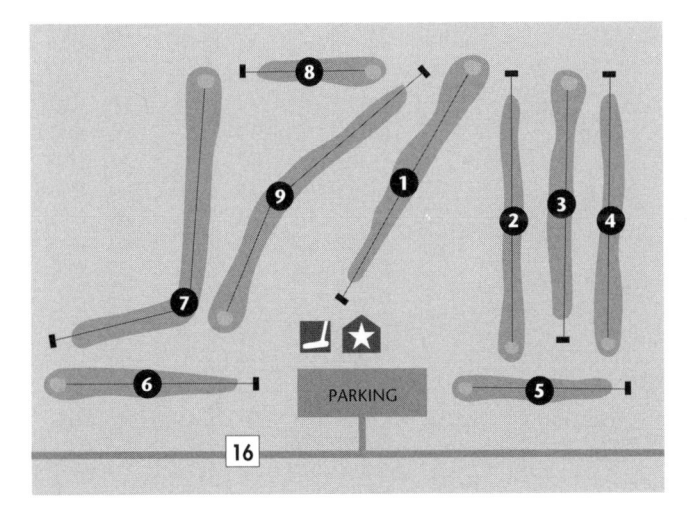

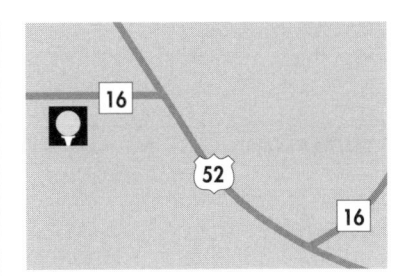

Located west of Preston. Course is 1/2 mile west of U.S. Highway 52 on MN Highway 16.

	MEN			WOMEN		
	FRONT	PAR	HDCP	FRONT	PAR	HDCP
1	360	4	2	360	5	2
2	364	4	4	364	4	4
3	328	4	8	328	4	8
4	362	4	5	362	4	5
5	185	3	3	185	3	3
6	327	4	7	327	4	7
7	505	5	9	505	5	9
8	161	3	6	161	3	6
9	391	4	1	391	5	1
Out	2983	35		2983	37	
1	360	4	2	360	5	2
2	364	4	4	364	4	4
3	328	4	8	328	4	8
4	362	4	5	362	4	5
5	185	3	3	185	3	3
6	327	4	7	327	4	7
7	505	5	9	505	5	9
8	161	3	6	161	3	6
9	391	4	1	391	5	1
In	2983	35		2983	37	
Total	5966	70		5966	74	
Rating	67.2			73.4		
Slope	106			116		

GOLF COURSE DIRECTORY

PRESTWICK GOLF CLUB

18 Regulation Semi-Private

9555 Wedgewood Drive
Woodbury, Minnesota 55125
612/731-4779 Clubhouse/Proshop

HOURS	Dawn to Dusk
SEASON	April-November

RESERVATIONS	612/731-4779 3 days
	Walk-on: good/good

GREEN FEES	M-Th	F-S
Adult	$30/18	$35/20
Senior	$30/18	$35/20
Junior	$30/18	$35/20
Twilight	$18 (5pm)	$20 (5 pm)

PAYMENT	Credit: Visa® MC® AmEx®
	Local checks only

LEAGUES	Men: Various
	Women: Various

MEMBERSHIPS	USGA, NGF, PGA, LPGA,
	GCSAA, MGA

SUPERINTENDENT	Jerry Weeb
PROFESSIONAL	Steve Dornfeld

FEATURES	
Putting green	Y
Driving range	Y
Practice area	Y
Golf carts	
Power (gas)	Y $25
Pull carts	Y
Club rental	Y
Club storage	N
Caddies	N
Proshop	
Extended	Y
Refreshments	
Restaurant	Y
Lounge	Y
Snacks	Y
Clubhouse	
Showers	Y
Lockers	Y
Lodging	N

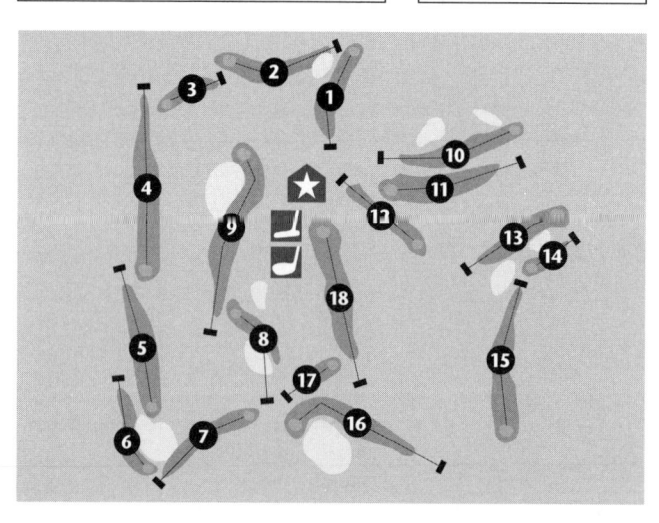

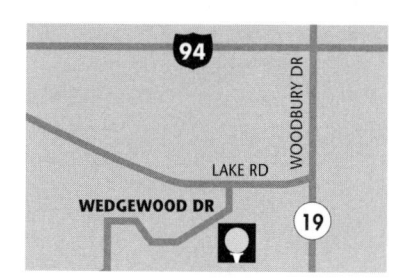

Located in Woodbury. Course is south of I-94 on County Road 19, west on Lake Road, then south on Wedgewood Drive.

	MEN				**WOMEN**		
	BACK	FRONT	PAR	HDCP	FRONT	PAR	HDCP
1	358	334	4	13	290	4	13
2	396	374	4	9	311	4	7
3	180	148	3	17	115	3	15
4	534	487	5	3	417	5	3
5	442	429	4	1	335	4	5
6	174	161	3	15	96	3	17
7	400	390	4	5	314	4	9
8	336	321	4	11	240	4	11
9	506	494	5	7	408	5	1
Out	3326	3138	36		2526	36	
10	409	392	4	10	328	4	10
11	389	378	4	8	310	4	8
12	331	307	4	14	266	4	16
13	408	386	4	2	334	4	6
14	161	147	3	18	135	3	18
15	419	409	4	4	327	4	2
16	569	519	5	6	428	5	4
17	205	178	3	16	173	3	14
18	500	480	5	12	440	5	12
In	3391	3196	36		2741	36	
Total	6717	6334	72		5267	72	
Rating	72.3	70.7			70.1		
Slope	120	116			121		

PRINCETON GOLF CLUB

18 Regulation Public

Golf Course Road, P.O. Box 326
Princeton, Minnesota 55371
612/389-5109 Clubhouse/Proshop

HOURS	7 am to Dusk
SEASON	April–November

RESERVATIONS	612/389-5109 7 days
	Walk-on: fair/fair

GREEN FEES	M-F	S-S
Adult	$16/12	$18/14
Senior	$12/9	$14/10
Junior	$7/7	$12/9
Twilight	$8 (6 pm)	$8 (6 pm)

PAYMENT	Credit: Visa® MasterCard®
	Non-local checks accepted

LEAGUES	Men: T,Th
	Women: M,W

MEMBERSHIPS	USGA, NGF, PGA, GCSAA, MGA

MANAGER	Tim Murphy
SUPERINTENDENT	Jim Sinkel
PROFESSIONAL	Tim Murphy

FEATURES		
Putting green	Y	
Driving range	Y	$3
Practice area	Y	
Golf carts		
Power (gas)	Y	$20/10
Pull carts	Y	$2
Club rental	Y	$5
Club storage	Y	
Caddies	N	
Proshop		
Extended	Y	
Refreshments		
Restaurant	Y	
Lounge	Y	
Snacks	Y	
Clubhouse		
Showers	Y	
Lockers	Y	
Lodging	N	

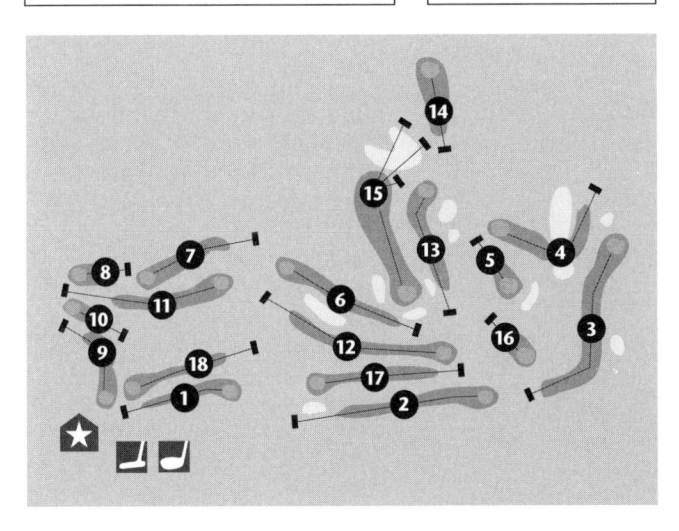

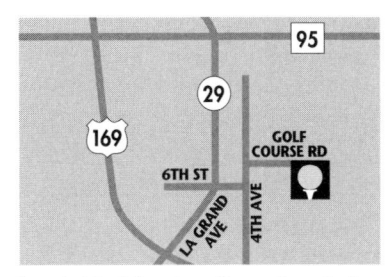

Located in Princeton. Course is east of U.S. Highway 169 on La Grand Ave, east on 4th Street, then north on 4th Ave.

	MEN				**WOMEN**		
	BACK	FRONT	PAR	HDCP	FRONT	PAR	HDCP
1	320	302	4	17	282	4	7
2	566	527	5	1	465	5	5
3	515	507	5	3	351	4	1
4	418	412	4	5	194	4	15
5	183	173	3	11	166	3	17
6	391	386	4	9	268	4	9
7	328	322	4	13	231	4	13
8	163	153	3	7	141	3	3
9	279	273	4	15	253	4	11
Out	3163	3055	36		2351	35	
10	150	147	3	18	132	3	18
11	397	390	4	10	313	4	14
12	510	499	5	6	402	5	4
13	327	322	4	12	231	4	2
14	182	174	3	14	146	3	16
15	488	451	5	4	362	5	10
16	170	166	3	16	143	3	12
17	435	414	4	8	360	4	6
18	401	387	4	2	375	5	8
In	3060	2950	35		2464	36	
Total	6223	6005	71		4815	71	
Rating	69.9	68.9			67.5		
Slope	117	115			112		

GOLF COURSE DIRECTORY

PURPLE HAWK COUNTRY CLUB

18 Regulation Semi-Private

North Highway 65, P.O. Box 528
Cambridge, Minnesota 55008
612/689-3433 Clubhouse
612/689-3800 Proshop

HOURS	7 am to Dusk
SEASON	April-November

FEATURES	
Putting green	Y
Driving range	Y $2-3.75
Practice area	Y
Golf carts	
Power (gas)	Y $22/11
Pull carts	Y $2.50
Club rental	Y $10
Club storage	N
Caddies	N
Proshop	
Extended	Y
Refreshments	
Restaurant	Y
Lounge	Y
Snacks	Y
Clubhouse	
Showers	N
Lockers	N
Lodging	N

RESERVATIONS	612/689-3800 5 days
	Walk-on: good/fair

GREEN FEES	M-F	S-S
Adult	$18/11	$22
Senior	$12/8*	$22
Junior	$12/8*	$22
Twilight	$8.50 (6 pm)	$12 (6 pm)
	* Before 11 am	

PAYMENT	Credit: Visa® MC® Discover® Non-local checks accepted

LEAGUES	Men: Th Women: M,W Seniors: T

MEMBERSHIPS	USGA, NGF, PGA, LPGA, GCSAA, MGA

PROFESSIONAL	Jon Swanson

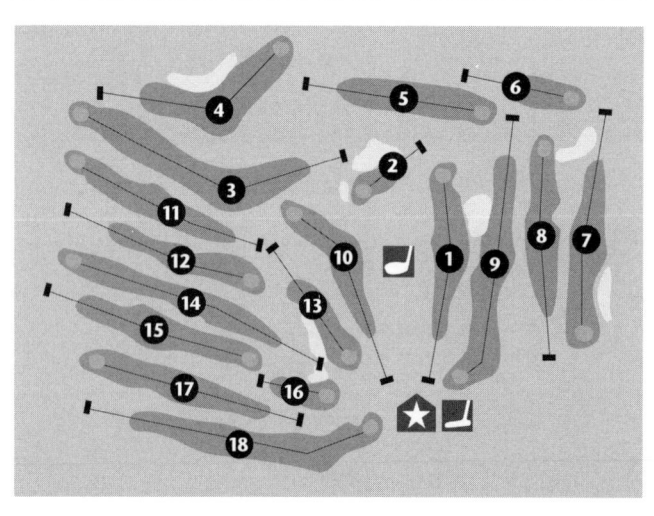

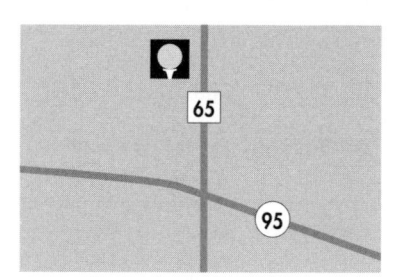

Located in Cambridge. Course entrance is 3 1/2 miles north of County Road 95 on MN Highway 65.

		MEN				**WOMEN**	
	BACK	FRONT	PAR	HDCP	FRONT	PAR	HDCP
1	372	356	4	4	340	4	12
2	150	142	3	18	131	3	18
3	528	507	5	12	412	5	2
4	350	333	4	8	263	4	10
5	366	330	4	14	300	4	14
6	193	182	3	10	170	3	16
7	435	396	4	2	384	5	8
8	384	364	4	6	361	4	4
9	486	472	5	16	451	5	6
Out	3263	3082	36		2812	37	
10	382	361	4	11	339	4	15
11	400	383	4	3	299	4	13
12	373	360	4	15	346	4	9
13	233	210	3	5	189	3	1
14	516	500	5	13	406	5	7
15	423	408	4	1	392	5	11
16	155	141	3	17	126	3	17
17	393	382	4	7	369	4	5
18	541	526	5	9	470	5	3
In	3416	3271	36		2936	37	
Total	6679	6353	72		5748	74	
Rating	72.3	70.9			73.5		
Slope	132	129			131		

QUADNA HILLS GOLF COURSE

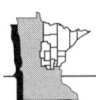

9 Regulation Public

100 Quadna Road
Hill City, Minnesota 55748
218/697-8444 Clubhouse/Proshop

HOURS	8 am to Dusk
SEASON	April-November

RESERVATIONS	218/697-8444 1 day
	Walk-on: good/good

GREEN FEES	M-F	S-S
Adult	$14/10	$16/12.50
Senior	$10/7.50	$13/10
Junior	$10/7.50	$13/10
Twilight	NA	NA

PAYMENT	Credit: Visa® MC® Am\Ex®
	Non-local checks accepted

LEAGUES	Mixed: T (pm)

MEMBERSHIPS	MGA

OWNER	Lou Jackson
MANAGER	Jim Salscheider
SUPERINTENDENT	Craig Thurlby

FEATURES		
Putting green	Y	
Driving range	N	
Practice area	N	
Golf carts		
Power (gas)	Y	$18/12
Pull carts	Y	$3
Club rental	Y	$6
Club storage	N	
Caddies	N	
Proshop		
Basic	Y	
Refreshments		
Restaurant	Y	
Lounge	N	
Snacks	Y	
Clubhouse		
Showers	N	
Lockers	N	
Lodging	Y	Call

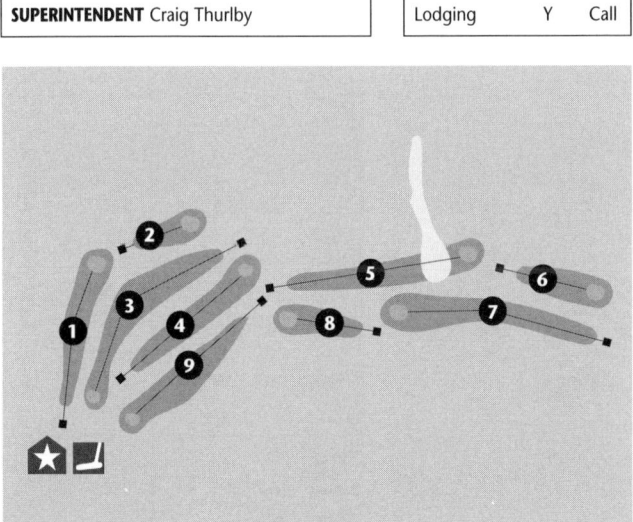

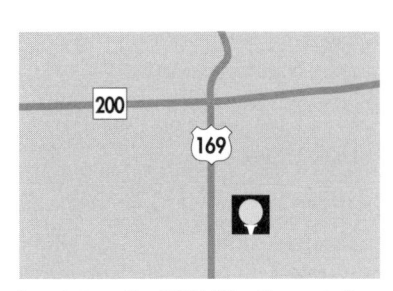

Located south of Hill City. Course is 2 miles south of MN Hwy 200 on U.S. Hwy 169, then east on Quadna Road.

	MEN			WOMEN		
	FRONT	PAR	HDCP	FRONT	PAR	HDCP
1	365	4	15	365	4	15
2	125	3	17	125	3	17
3	500	5	5	500	5	5
4	375	4	9	375	4	9
5	435	4	1	435	4	1
6	170	3	7	170	3	7
7	470	5	11	470	5	11
8	190	3	13	190	3	13
9	435	4	3	435	4	3
Out	3065	35		3065	35	
1	365	4	16	365	4	16
2	125	3	18	125	3	18
3	500	5	6	500	5	6
4	375	4	10	375	4	10
5	435	4	2	435	4	2
6	170	3	8	170	3	8
7	470	5	12	470	5	12
8	190	3	14	190	3	14
9	435	4	4	435	4	4
In	3065	35		3065	35	
Total	6130	70		6130	70	
Rating	NA			NA		
Slope	NA			NA		

GOLF COURSE DIRECTORY

RAMSEY GOLF CLUB

18 Regulation Public

Route 1
Austin, Minnesota 55912
507/433-9098 Clubhouse/Proshop

HOURS	Dawn to Dusk
SEASON	April-November

RESERVATIONS	507/433-9098	
	Walk-on: good/good	
GREEN FEES	M-F	S-S
Adult	$16/10	$16/10
Senior	$16/10	$16/10
Junior	$16/10	$16/10
Twilight	NA	NA
PAYMENT	No credit cards accepted	
	Non-local checks accepted	
LEAGUES	None	
MEMBERSHIPS	USGA, MGA	
OWNER	Giles Healy, Jim Vacura	
MANAGER	Roger Larson	
SUPERINTENDENT	Joe Bartholomew	

FEATURES		
Putting green	Y	
Driving range	N	
Practice area	Y	
Golf carts		
Power (gas)	Y	$16/9
Pull carts	Y	$2
Club rental	Y	$5
Club storage	Y	$15/yr
Caddies	N	
Proshop		
Extended	Y	
Refreshments		
Restaurant	Y	
Lounge	Y	
Snacks	Y	
Clubhouse		
Showers	N	
Lockers	N	
Lodging	N	

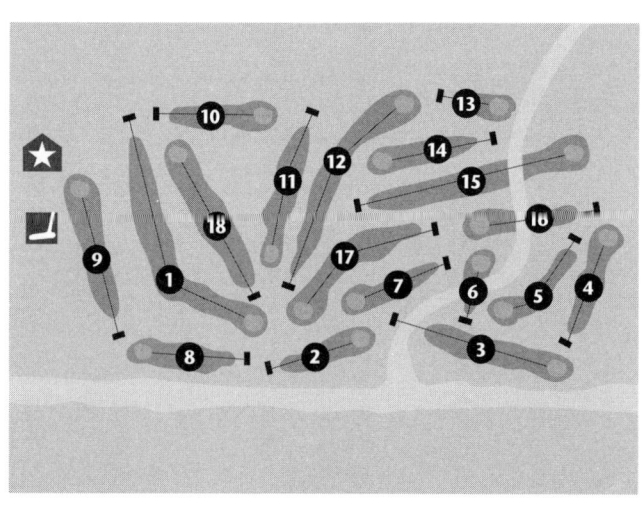

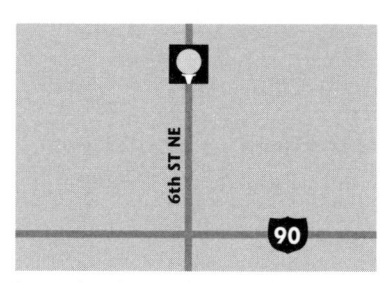

Located in Austin. Course entrance is about 2 1/4 miles north of I-90 on 6th Street N.E.

	MEN FRONT	PAR	HDCP	**WOMEN** FRONT	PAR	HDCP
1	492	5	4	492	5	1
2	128	3	18	100	3	17
3	511	5	2	387	4	3
4	297	4	12	297	4	9
5	347	4	6	347	4	5
6	144	3	16	121	3	15
7	315	4	8	315	4	7
8	206	3	10	206	4	13
9	288	4	14	288	4	11
Out	2728	35		2553	35	
10	193	3	17	193	3	12
11	342	4	13	319	4	10
12	524	5	5	464	5	4
13	179	3	11	132	3	18
14	354	4	7	248	4	16
15	595	5	1	498	5	2
16	307	4	15	254	4	14
17	363	4	9	363	4	6
18	402	4	3	402	5	8
In	3259	36		2873	37	
Total	5987	71		5426	72	
Rating	68.2			70.7		
Slope	120			117		

RED OAK GOLF COURSE

9 Par-3 Public

855 Red Oak Lane
Mound, Minnesota 55364
612/472-3999 Clubhouse/Proshop

HOURS 7 am to Dusk

SEASON April to October

RESERVATIONS	612/472-3999 1 week
	Walk-on: good/fair

GREEN FEES	M-F	S-S
Adult	$11/6.75	$12/7.50
Senior	$7.50/5.50	$12/7.50
Junior	$6.50/4	$12/7.50
Twilight	NA	NA

PAYMENT	No credit cards accepted
	Non-local checks accepted

LEAGUES	Men: M (am), W (pm)
	Women: M (pm), Th (am)

MEMBERSHIPS	USGA, GCSAA, CMAA

OWNER	Grant & Vicky Wenkstern
MANAGER	David Eidahl
SUPERINTENDENT	Curt Norton

FEATURES

Putting green	Y	
Driving range	N	
Practice area	N	
Golf carts		
Power	Y	$6
Pull carts	Y	$.50
Club rental	Y	$1.50
Club storage	N	
Caddies	N	
Proshop		
Basic	Y	
Refreshments		
Restaurant	N	
Lounge	Y	
Snacks	Y	
Clubhouse		
Showers	N	
Lockers	N	
Lodging	N	

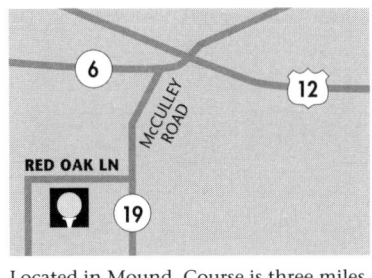

Located in Mound. Course is three miles south of U.S. Highway 12 on County Road 6/19, then west on Red Oak Lane.

		MEN			WOMEN	
	FRONT	PAR	HDCP	FRONT	PAR	HDCP
1	142	3	3	142	3	3
2	168	3	2	168	3	2
3	113	3	5	113	3	5
4	123	3	6	123	3	6
5	112	3	7	112	3	7
6	94	3	8	94	3	8
7	111	3	9	111	3	9
8	128	3	4	128	3	4
9	217	3	1	217	3	1
Out	1208	27		1208	27	
1	142	3	3	142	3	3
2	168	3	2	168	3	2
3	113	3	5	113	3	5
4	123	3	6	123	3	6
5	112	3	7	112	3	7
6	94	3	8	94	3	8
7	111	3	9	111	3	9
8	128	3	4	128	3	4
9	217	3	1	217	3	1
In	1208	27		1208	27	
Total	2416	54		2416	54	
Rating	50.5			50.4		
Slope	61			62		

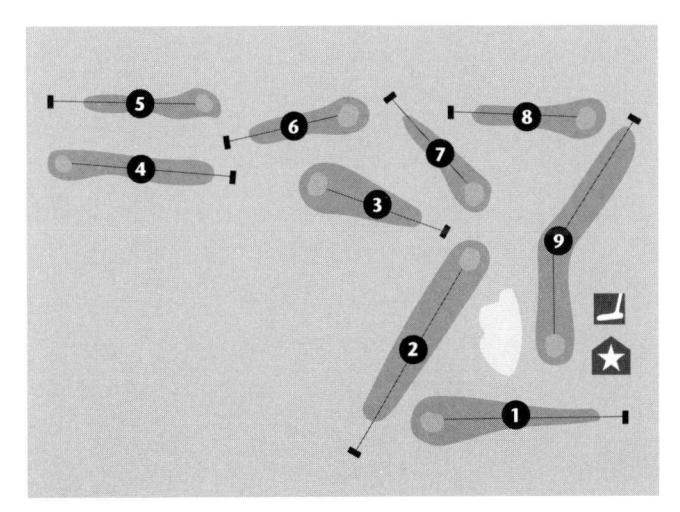

RED ROCK GOLF COURSE

9 Regulation Public

Hwy. 27 & Cty. Rd. 25 (P.O. Box 5)
Hoffman, Minnesota 56339
612/986-2342 Clubhouse/Proshop

HOURS	7 am to Dusk
SEASON	April to October

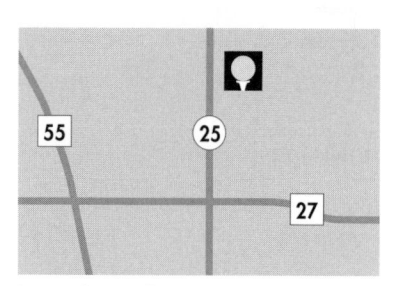

Located in Hoffman. Course is north of MN Highway 27 on Golf Course Road (County Road 25).

RESERVATIONS	612/986-2342	
	Walk-on: good/fair	
GREEN FEES	M-F	S-S
Adult	$12/7	$14/9
Senior	$12/7	$14/9
Junior	$12/7	$14/9
Twilight	NA	NA
PAYMENT	No credit cards accepted	
	Non-local checks accepted	
LEAGUES	Men: Th (5 pm)	
	Women: T (5 pm)	
MEMBERSHIPS	USGA, MGA	
OWNER	Jim & Pat Hanson	

FEATURES		
Putting green	Y	
Driving range	N	
Practice area	N	
Golf carts		
Power (gas)	Y	$13/6
Pull carts	Y	$1
Club rental	Y	$3
Club storage	Y	
Caddies	N	
Proshop		
Extended Refreshments	Y	
Restaurant	N	
Lounge	N	
Snacks	Y	
Clubhouse		
Showers	N	
Lockers	N	
Lodging	N	

	MEN			**WOMEN**		
	FRONT	PAR	HDCP	FRONT	PAR	HDCP
1	235	4	3	198	4	4
2	485	5	1	342	5	1
3	168	3	6	118	3	6
4	480	5	2	392	5	2
5	338	4	9	286	4	5
6	372	4	4	360	4	3
7	379	4	5	279	4	7
8	122	3	8	87	3	8
9	301	4	7	252	4	9
Out	2880	36		2314	36	
1	235	4	3	198	4	4
2	485	5	1	342	5	1
3	168	3	6	118	3	6
4	480	5	2	392	5	2
5	338	4	9	286	4	5
6	372	4	4	360	4	3
7	379	4	5	279	4	7
8	122	3	8	87	3	8
9	301	4	7	252	4	9
In	2880	36		2314	36	
Total	5760	72		4628	72	
Rating	68.0			67.0		
Slope	115			112		

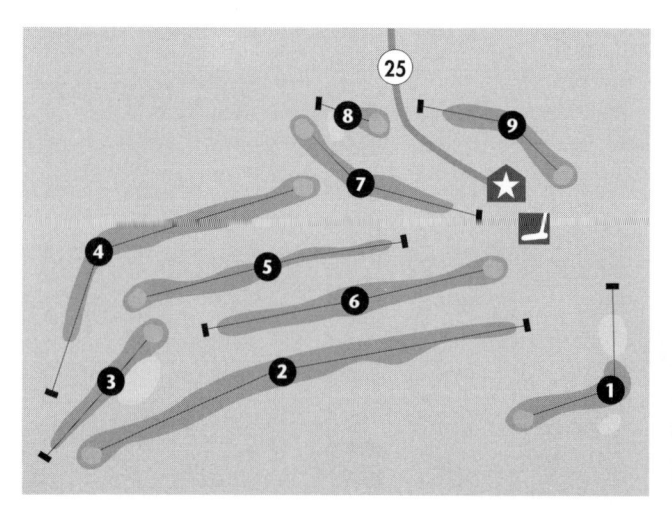

RED WING COUNTRY CLUB

18 Regulation Semi-Private

1311 West 6th Street
Red Wing, Minnesota 55066
612/388-9524 Clubhouse/Proshop

HOURS	8 am to Dusk
SEASON	April-November

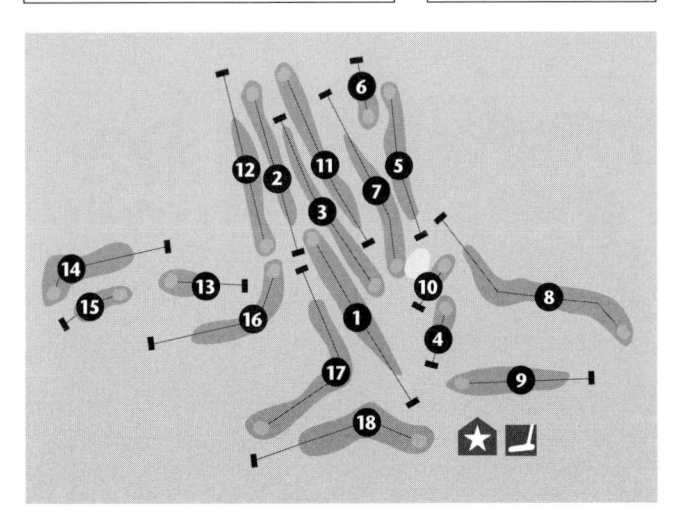

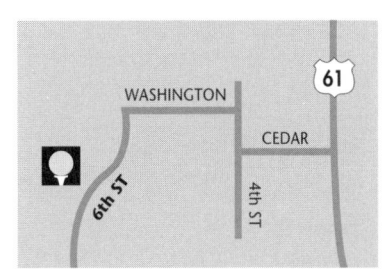

Located in Red Wing. Course is west of Hwy 61 on Cedar, north on 4th St, west on Washington, then south on 6th St.

RESERVATIONS	612/388-9524 3 days
	Walk-on: good/good

GREEN FEES	M-F	S-S
Adult	$27.50/20	$27.50/20
Senior	$27.50/20	$27.50/20
Junior	$27.50/20	$27.50/20
Twilight	NA	NA

PAYMENT	No credit cards accepted
	Non-local checks accepted

LEAGUES	Men: M (pm), W
	Women: T

MEMBERSHIPS	USGA, GCSAA, MGA

MANAGER	Dewey Hove
SUPERINTENDENT	Chuck Pelowski

FEATURES	
Putting green	Y
Driving range	N
Practice area	Y
Golf carts	
Power (gas)	Y $20/12
Pull carts	Y $2.50
Club rental	N
Club storage	Y $40/yr
Caddies	N
Proshop	
Extended	Y
Refreshments	
Restaurant	Y
Lounge	Y
Snacks	Y
Clubhouse	
Showers	Y
Lockers	Y
Lodging	N

	MEN				**WOMEN**		
	BACK	FRONT	PAR	HDCP	FRONT	PAR	HDCP
1	441	415	4	1	402	5	7
2	366	366	4	13	330	4	9
3	529	517	5	5	432	5	3
4	180	171	3	15	146	3	15
5	332	329	4	11	305	4	11
6	145	140	3	17	109	3	17
7	375	371	4	9	296	4	13
8	501	492	5	3	430	5	1
9	343	319	4	7	251	4	5
Out	3212	3120	36		2701	37	
10	177	155	3	16	148	3	16
11	494	478	5	10	370	5	6
12	390	384	4	2	315	4	4
13	177	170	3	14	106	3	14
14	320	315	4	12	206	4	12
15	150	127	3	18	108	3	18
16	386	379	4	8	292	4	8
17	482	470	5	4	368	5	2
18	420	406	4	6	219	4	10
In	2996	2884	35		2132	35	
Total	6208	6004	71		4833	72	
Rating	71.4	70.5			69.6		
Slope	132	130			123		

GOLF COURSE DIRECTORY

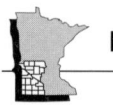

REDWOOD FALLS GOLF CLUB

9 Regulation Semi-Private

101 East Oak Street, P.O. Box 384
Redwood Falls, Minnesota 56283
507/637-8901 Clubhouse/Proshop

HOURS	7 am to Dusk
SEASON	April to October

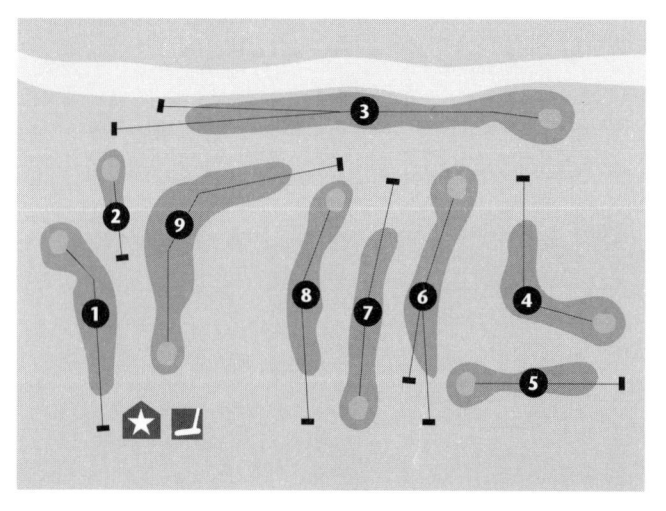

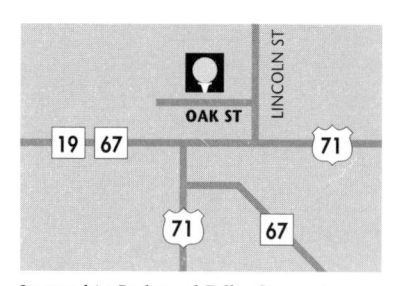

Located in Redwood Falls. Course is north of Hwy 71/19 on Lincoln Street, then west on Oak Street.

| **RESERVATIONS** | 507/637-8901 |
| | Walk-on: good/fair |

GREEN FEES	M-F	S-S
Adult	$16/11	$19/13
Senior	$16/11	$19/13
Junior	$16/11	$19/13
Twilight	NA	NA
	Punch cards available	

| **PAYMENT** | Credit: Visa® MastrCard® |
| | Non-local checks accepted |

| **LEAGUES** | Men: W (pm) |
| | Women: Th |

| **MEMBERSHIPS** | USGA, GCSAA, MGA |

| **MANAGER** | Lyn Redding |
| **SUPERINTENDENT** | Tom Balleo |

FEATURES	
Putting green	Y
Driving range	Y
Practice area	N
Golf carts	
Power (gas)	Y $16/11
Pull carts	Y $1
Club rental	Y $3
Club storage	Y $10
Caddies	N
Proshop	
Extended	Y
Refreshments	
Restaurant	N
Lounge	Y
Snacks	Y
Clubhouse	
Showers	Y
Lockers	Y
Lodging	N

		MEN			**WOMEN**	
	FRONT	PAR	HDCP	FRONT	PAR	HDCP
1	252	4	9	247	4	9
2	171	3	8	164	3	8
3	559	5	1	492	5	1
4	364	4	3	308	4	3
5	191	3	7	188	3	7
6	378	4	2	370	4	2
7	372	4	4	368	4	4
8	355	4	6	330	4	6
9	453	5	5	428	5	5
Out	3095	36		2895	36	
1	252	4	9	247	4	9
2	171	3	8	164	3	8
3	559	5	1	492	5	1
4	364	4	3	308	4	3
5	191	3	7	188	3	7
6	378	4	2	370	4	2
7	372	4	4	368	4	4
8	355	4	6	330	4	6
9	453	5	5	428	5	5
In	3095	36		2895	36	
Total	6190	72		5790	72	
Rating	71.0			73.0		
Slope	129			122		

THE MINNESOTA ILLUSTRATED

RICH ACRES GOLF COURSE

18 Regulation/9 Par-3 Public

2201 East 66th Street
Richfield, Minnesota 55423
612/861-9341 Clubhouse/Proshop

RESERVATIONS	612/861-9345 1 day
	Walk-on: fair/fair

GREEN FEES	M-F	S-S
Adult	$18/12	$20/13
Senior	$13.50/9	$13.50/9
Junior	$13.50/9	$13.50/9
Twilight	$11.25 (6pm)	$12.25 (5pm)
	Patron tickets available	

PAYMENT	Credit: Visa® MasterCard®
	Non-local checks accepted

LEAGUES	Various

MEMBERSHIPS	USGA, NGF, GCSAA, MGA

MANAGER	Darrel Harman
PROFESSIONAL	Paul Stande, Larry Nelson

HOURS	Dawn to Dusk
SEASON	April–November

FEATURES		
Putting green	Y	
Driving range	Y	$3-5
Practice area	N	
Golf carts		
Power (gas)	Y	$20/12
Pull carts	Y	$2
Club rental	Y	$9/7
Club storage	N	
Caddies	N	
Proshop		
Basic	Y	
Refreshments		
Restaurant	N	
Lounge	Y	
Snacks	Y	
Clubhouse		
Showers	N	
Lockers	N	
Lodging	N	

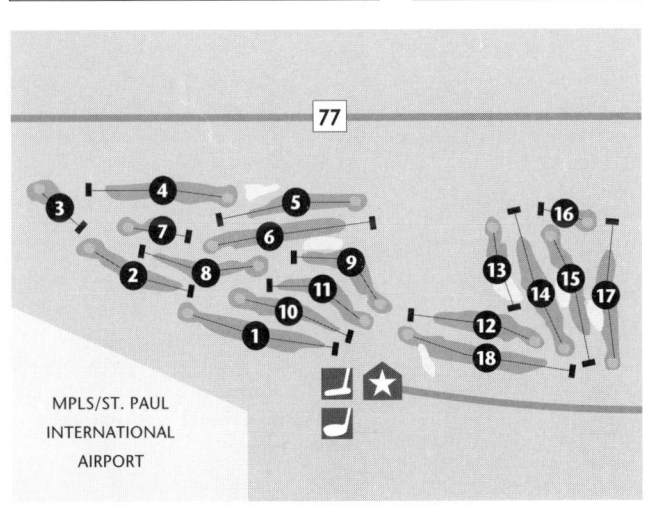

Located in Richfield. Course is 1/4 mile east of MN Hwy 77 on 66th Street. Next to Mpls/St. Paul International Airport.

	MEN				WOMEN		
	BACK	FRONT	PAR	HDCP	FRONT	PAR	HDCP
1	495	479	5	17	463	5	1
2	396	379	4	7	326	4	16
3	158	153	3	13	115	3	10
4	451	431	4	1	411	5	7
5	403	386	4	3	369	4	3
6	494	484	5	9	401	5	5
7	193	182	3	5	134	3	14
8	402	382	4	11	319	4	9
9	371	356	4	15	341	4	12
Out	3363	3233	36		2879	37	
10	382	367	4	16	347	4	6
11	381	368	4	12	345	4	13
12	369	356	4	10	343	4	8
13	218	208	3	2	159	3	2
14	439	417	4	4	402	5	11
15	398	377	4	8	327	4	17
16	150	132	3	18	119	3	18
17	392	385	4	6	331	4	15
18	514	494	5	14	428	5	4
In	3243	3104	35		2801	36	
Total	6606	6336	71		5680	73	
Rating	71.1	69.9			72.3		
Slope	116	114			119		

GOLF COURSE DIRECTORY

RICH SPRING GOLF CLUB

18 Regulation Public

17467 Fairway Circle
Cold Spring, Minnesota 56320
612/685-8810 Clubhouse/Proshop

HOURS	7 am to Dusk
SEASON	April-November

RESERVATIONS	612/685-8810 3 days
	Walk-on: good/fair

GREEN FEES	M-F	S-S
Adult	$16/11	$18/12
Senior	$13/9*	$18/12
Junior	$16/11	$18/12
Twilight	NA	NA

*Before 10 am

PAYMENT	No credit cards accepted
	Non-local checks accepted

LEAGUES	Men: Th
	Women: T

MEMBERSHIPS	USGA, GCSAA, MGA

MANAGER	Dave Reichel
SUPERINTENDENT	Jim Johnson
PROFESSIONAL	Dave Reichel

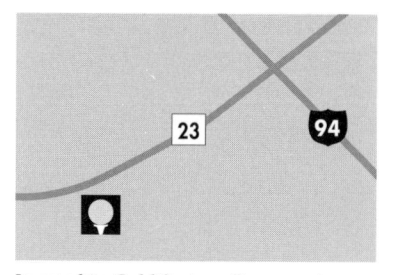

FEATURES	
Putting green	Y
Driving range	N
Practice area	Y
Golf carts	
Power (gas)	Y $19/11
Pull carts	Y $2
Club rental	Y $5
Club storage	Y
Caddies	N
Proshop	
Extended	Y
Refreshments	
Restaurant	Y
Lounge	N
Snacks	Y
Clubhouse	
Showers	N
Lockers	N
Lodging	N

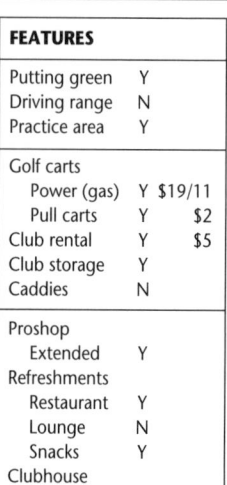

Located in Cold Spring. Course entrance is about ten miles southwest of I-94 on MN Highway 23.

	MEN				**WOMEN**		
	BACK	FRONT	PAR	HDCP	FRONT	PAR	HDCP
1	394	394	4	5	260	4	15
2	395	353	4	13	303	4	11
3	472	472	5	9	400	5	7
4	357	315	4	17	249	4	17
5	364	364	4	3	344	4	3
6	185	175	3	11	115	3	9
7	548	548	5	1	418	5	5
8	173	173	3	15	165	3	13
9	359	359	4	7	350	4	1
Out	3247	3153	36		2604	36	
10	330	330	4	16	320	4	10
11	186	176	3	14	166	3	14
12	400	369	4	10	289	4	18
13	345	337	4	8	327	4	6
14	544	534	5	2	449	5	2
15	150	143	3	18	125	3	16
16	537	511	5	6	430	5	4
17	400	387	4	4	307	4	8
18	403	403	4	12	330	4	12
In	3295	3190	36		2743	36	
Total	6606	6336	72		5347	72	
Rating	NA	69.7			70.0		
Slope	NA	119			110		

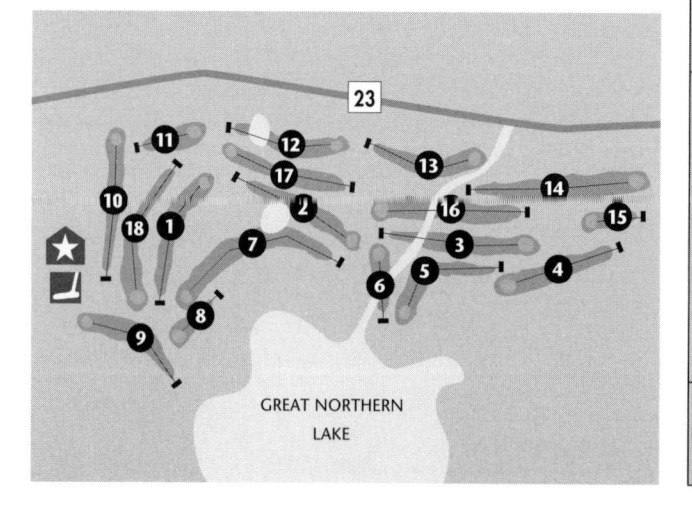

GREAT NORTHERN LAKE

RICH VALLEY GOLF CLUB

27 Regulation Public

3855 145th Street East
Rosemount, Minnesota 55068
612/437-4653 Clubhouse

RESERVATIONS	612/437-4653 1 week	
	Reservations required	
GREEN FEES	M-F	S-S
Adult	$14/9	$14/9
Senior	$10/7.50*	$14/9
Junior	$10/7.50*	$14/9
Twilight	NA	NA
	* Before 3 pm	
PAYMENT	No credit cards accepted	
	Non-local checks accepted	
LEAGUES	Men: Various	
	Women: Various	
MEMBERSHIPS	USGA, MGA	
OWNER	Ray & Rosie Rahn	
MANAGER	Rosie Rahn	
PROFESSIONAL	Sue Bremer, John Anderson	

HOURS	Dawn to Dusk
SEASON	April-November
FEATURES	
Putting green	Y
Driving range	Y $2-3.50
Practice area	N
Golf carts	
Power (gas)	Y $14/7
Pull carts	Y $1.25
Club rental	Y $3.50
Club storage	N
Caddies	N
Proshop	
Regular	Y
Refreshments	
Restaurant	N
Lounge	N
Snacks	Y
Clubhouse	
Showers	N
Lockers	N
Lodging	N

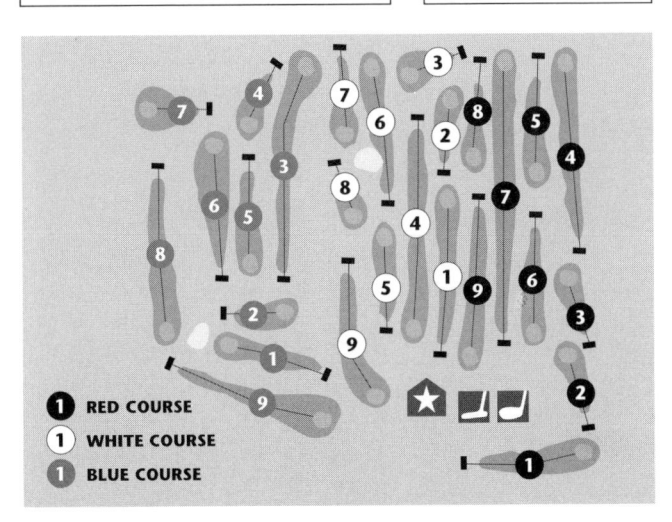

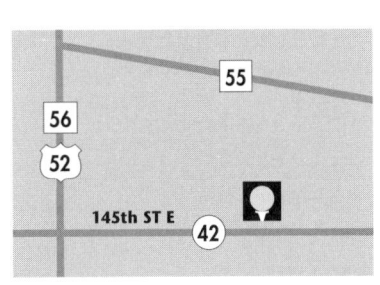

Located in Rosemount. Course is just 1/2 mile east of U.S. Hwy 52 on Cty Rd 42.

	MEN			WOMEN		
	FRONT	PAR	HDCP	FRONT	PAR	HDCP
1	348	4	5	335	4	5
2	184	3	7	172	3	7
3	137	3	8	125	3	8
4	373	4	4	364	4	4
5	234	3	3	226	4	3
6	258	4	9	229	4	9
7	540	5	1	434	5	1
8	223	3	6	160	3	6
9	451	5	2	366	5	2
RED	2748	34		2411	35	
1	414	4	1	403	5	1
2	201	3	6	191	3	6
3	124	3	9	116	3	9
4	507	5	2	383	5	2
5	170	3	7	159	3	7
6	358	4	4	348	4	4
7	135	3	8	123	3	8
8	269	4	5	193	4	5
9	363	4	3	353	4	3
WHITE	2541	33		2269	34	
1	350	4	3	317	4	3
2	100	3	9	85	3	9
3	464	5	2	346	5	2
4	137	3	7	124	3	7
5	278	4	5	252	4	5
6	327	4	6	259	4	6
7	109	3	8	95	3	8
8	438	5	1	370	5	1
9	335	4	4	280	4	4
BLUE	2538	35		2128	35	
N/E	5289	67		4680	69	
Rating	64.8			65.4		
Slope	93			96		
N/W	5079	68		4397	69	
Rating	62.4			64.2		
Slope	87			92		
E/W	5286	69		4539	70	
Rating	63.0			62.8		
Slope	94			95		

- 🔴 RED COURSE
- ⚪ WHITE COURSE
- 🔵 BLUE COURSE

GOLF COURSE DIRECTORY

RIDGEVIEW COUNTRY CLUB

18 Regulation Private

700 West Red Wing Street
Duluth, Minnesota 55803
218/728-5128 Clubhouse
218/728-3285 Proshop

HOURS	Dawn to Dusk
SEASON	April–November

| **RESERVATIONS** | 218/728-3285 2 days |
| | Members only |

GREEN FEES	M-F	S-S
Adult	$25	$25
Senior	$25	$25
Junior	$25	$25
Twilight	NA	NA
	Members and guests only	

| **PAYMENT** | No credit cards accepted |
| | Non-local checks accepted |

| **LEAGUES** | Men: Various |
| | Women: Various |

| **MEMBERSHIPS** | USGA, PGA, GCSAA, MGA |

| **MANAGER** | Tom Mellin |
| **PROFESSIONAL** | Jim Athey |

FEATURES		
Putting green	Y	
Driving range	Y	$3.50
Practice area	N	
Golf carts		
Power (gas)	Y	$19
Pull carts	Y	$3.50
Club rental	Y	$10
Club storage	N	
Caddies	N	
Proshop		
Extended	Y	
Refreshments		
Restaurant	Y	
Lounge	Y	
Snacks	Y	
Clubhouse		
Showers	Y	
Lockers	Y	
Lodging	N	

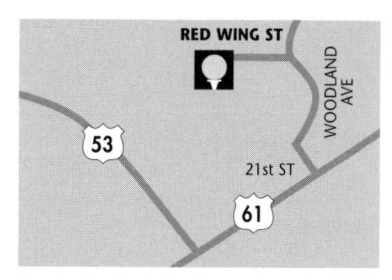

Located in Duluth. Course is west of U.S. Hwy 61 on 21st St, north at Woodland Avenue, then west on Red Wing Street.

		MEN			**WOMEN**		
	BACK	FRONT	PAR	HDCP	FRONT	PAR	HDCP
1	320	310	4	11	240	4	11
2	591	576	5	1	457	5	1
3	188	151	3	15	131	3	15
4	430	419	4	3	414	5	3
5	149	140	3	17	123	3	17
6	380	368	4	7	337	4	7
7	385	385	4	5	307	4	5
8	207	200	3	13	160	3	13
9	335	327	4	9	312	4	9
Out	2985	2876	34		2481	35	
10	206	195	3	16	142	3	14
11	366	356	4	8	310	4	16
12	180	170	3	18	130	3	12
13	506	476	5	6	413	5	6
14	485	480	5	4	415	5	4
15	342	305	4	12	286	4	18
16	557	542	5	2	451	5	2
17	165	140	3	14	109	3	10
18	405	393	4	10	370	4	8
In	3212	3057	36		2626	36	
Total	6197	5933	70		5107	71	
Rating	70.6	69.4			69.7		
Slope	128	126			123		

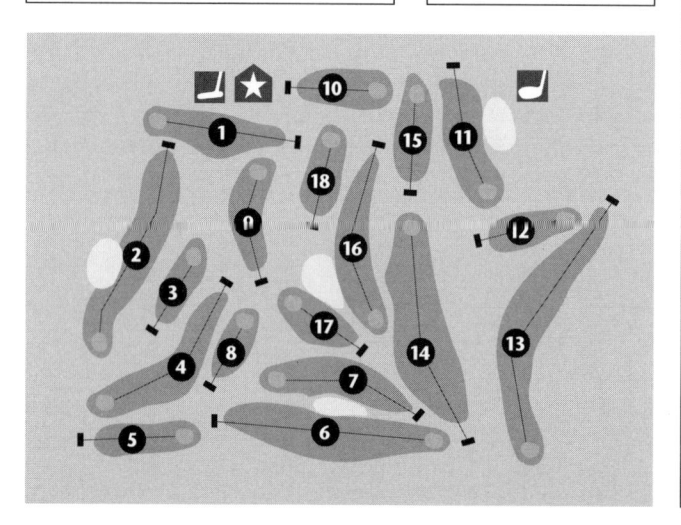

RIDGEWOOD COUNTRY CLUB

18 Regulation Public

Highway 7, P.O. Box 298
Longville, Minnesota 56655
218/363-2444 Clubhouse/Proshop

RESERVATIONS	218/363-2444 3 days	
	Walk-on: good/fair	
GREEN FEES	M-F	S-S
Adult	$13.50/7.50	$14/8
Senior	$13.50/7.50	$14/8
Junior	$10/5.50	$10/5.50
Twilight	NA	NA
PAYMENT	Credit: Visa® MC® AmEx®	
	Non-local checks accepted	
LEAGUES	Men: Various	
	Women: Various	
MEMBERSHIPS	USGA, MGA	
OWNER	Pat & Maralyn Tabaka	
SUPERINTENDENT	Bill Sexton	
PROFESSIONAL	Bernie Blackman	

HOURS	7 am to Dusk
SEASON	May to October

FEATURES		
Putting green	Y	
Driving range	Y	
Practice area	N	
Golf carts		
Power (gas)	Y	$15.50
Pull carts	Y	$2.50
Club rental	Y	
Club storage	N	
Caddies	N	
Proshop		
Extended	Y	
Refreshments		
Restaurant	Y	
Lounge	Y	
Snacks	Y	
Clubhouse		
Showers	N	
Lockers	Y	
Lodging	N	

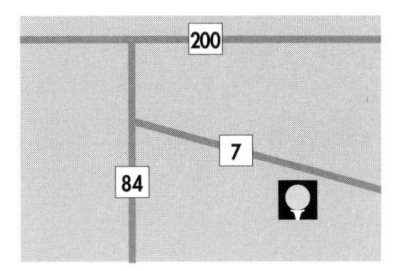

Located in Longville. Course is south of MN Highway 200 on MN Highway 84, then east on MN Highway 7.

	MEN				**WOMEN**		
	BACK	FRONT	PAR	HDCP	FRONT	PAR	HDCP
1	444	439	5	13	362	5	13
2	185	176	3	9	128	3	9
3	336	330	4	11	274	4	11
4	528	520	5	3	424	5	3
5	382	372	4	1	360	4	1
6	335	327	4	17	314	4	17
7	204	194	3	7	153	4	7
8	358	347	4	15	340	4	15
9	372	364	4	5	354	4	5
Out	3144	3069	36		2709	37	
10	201	188	3	16	178	3	16
11	445	435	4	2	376	4	2
12	544	524	5	8	454	5	8
13	411	391	4	14	370	4	14
14	443	423	4	6	413	5	6
15	286	276	4	10	266	4	10
16	414	399	4	4	337	4	4
17	117	117	3	18	106	3	18
18	477	457	5	12	457	5	12
In	3338	3210	36		2957	37	
Total	6482	6279	72		5666	74	
Rating	70.4	69.4			71.4		
Slope	117	115			116		

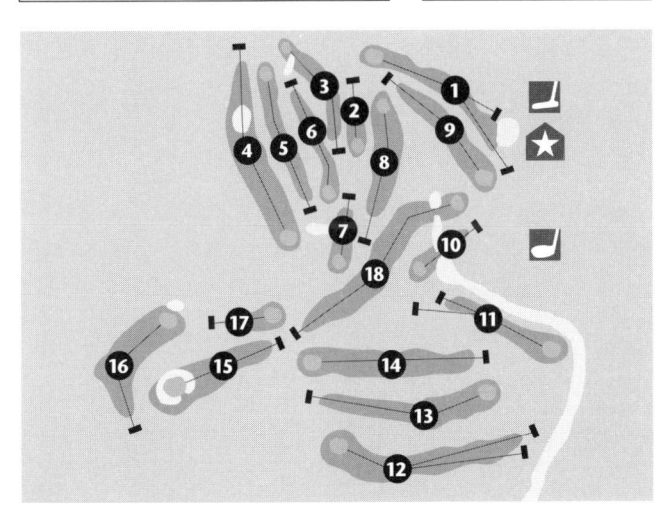

GOLF COURSE DIRECTORY

RIDGEWOOD COUNTRY CLUB

9 Executive Public

Highway 7, P.O. Box 298
Longville, Minnesota 56655
218/363-2444 Clubhouse/Proshop

HOURS	7 am to Dusk
SEASON	May to October

RESERVATIONS	No reservations accepted Walk-on: good/fair	
GREEN FEES	M-F	S-S
Adult	$4	$5
Senior	$4	$4
Junior	$3	$3
Twilight	NA	NA
PAYMENT	Credit: Visa® MC® AmEx® Non-local checks accepted	
LEAGUES	Men: Various Women: Various	
MEMBERSHIPS	USGA, MGA	
OWNER	Pat & Maralyn Tabaka	
SUPERINTENDENT	Bill Sexton	
PROFESSIONAL	Bernie Blackman	

FEATURES		
Putting green	Y	
Driving range	Y	
Practice area	N	
Golf carts		
Power	N	
Pull carts	Y	$2.50
Club rental	Y	$3.50
Club storage	N	
Caddies	N	
Proshop		
Extended	Y	
Refreshments		
Restaurant	Y	
Lounge	Y	
Snacks	Y	
Clubhouse		
Showers	N	
Lockers	Y	
Lodging	N	

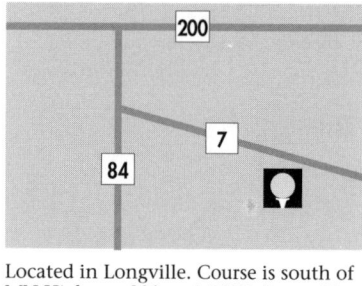

Located in Longville. Course is south of MN Highway 200 on MN Highway 84, then east on MN Highway 7.

	MEN			WOMEN		
	FRONT	PAR	HDCP	FRONT	PAR	HDCP
1	84	3	6	84	3	6
2	129	4	2	129	4	2
3	76	3	8	76	3	8
4	53	3	9	53	3	9
5	145	3	3	145	3	3
6	137	3	5	137	3	5
7	119	3	4	119	3	4
8	170	4	1	170	4	1
9	110	3	7	110	3	7
Out	1023	29		1023	29	
1	84	3	6	84	3	6
2	129	4	2	129	4	2
3	76	3	8	76	3	8
4	53	3	9	53	3	9
5	145	3	3	145	3	3
6	137	3	5	137	3	5
7	119	3	4	119	3	4
8	170	4	1	170	4	1
9	110	3	7	110	3	7
In	1023	29		1023	29	
Total	2046	58		2046	58	
Rating	NA			NA		
Slope	NA			NA		

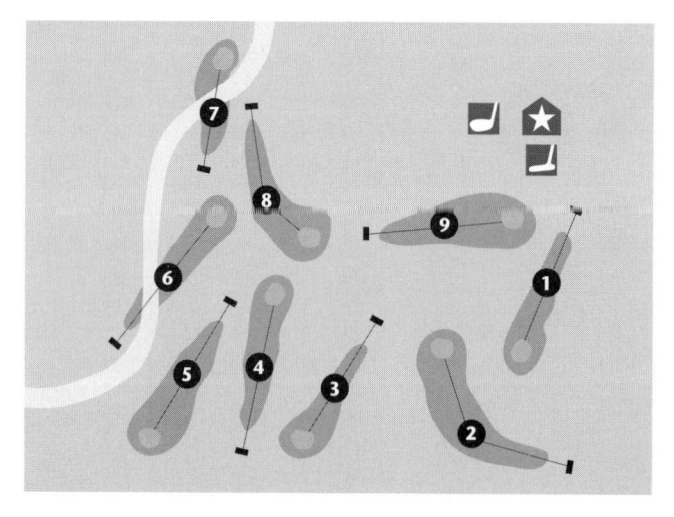

THE MINNESOTA ILLUSTRATED

RIVER OAKS MUNICIPAL GOLF COURSE

18 Regulation Public

11099 South Highway 61
Cottage Grove, Minnesota 55016
612/438-2121 Clubhouse/Proshop

RESERVATIONS	612/438-2121 3 days	
	Walk-on: fair/fair	
GREEN FEES	M-F	S-S
Adult	$16/12	$19/14
Senior	$13/10	$13/10
Junior	$13/10	$13/10
Twilight	$10	$10
PAYMENT	Credit: Visa® MasterCard®	
	Non-local checks accepted	
LEAGUES	Various	
MEMBERSHIPS	USGA, NGF, PGA, GCSAA, MGA	
OWNER	City of Cottage Grove	
MANAGER	Bruce Anderson	
SUPERINTENDENT	Tom Parent	
PROFESSIONAL	Bruce Anderson	

HOURS	6 am to Dusk	
SEASON	April-November	
FEATURES		
Putting green	Y	
Driving range	Y	$4.75
Practice area	N	
Golf carts		
Power (gas)	Y	$19/11
Pull carts	Y	$2
Club rental	Y	$7/5
Club storage	N	
Caddies	N	
Proshop		
Extended	Y	
Refreshments		
Restaurant	N	
Lounge	N	
Snacks	Y	
Clubhouse		
Showers	N	
Lockers	N	
Lodging	N	

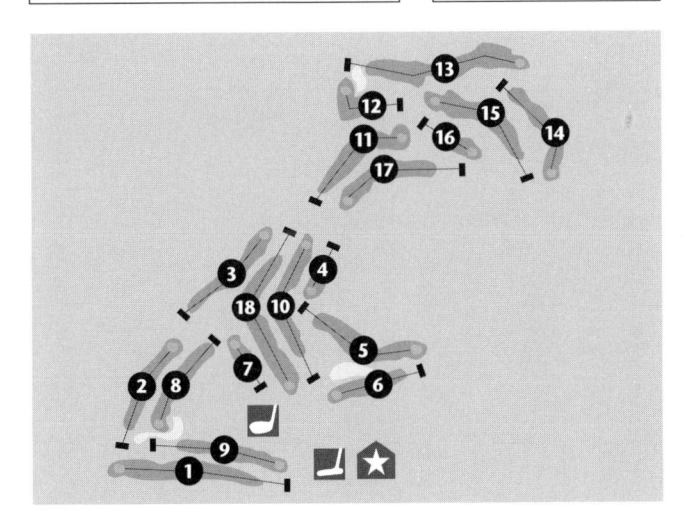

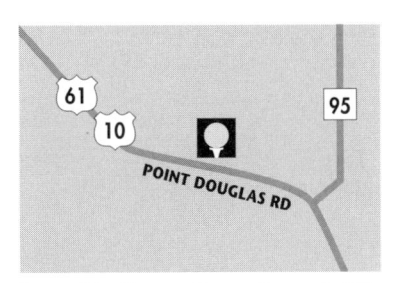

Located in Cottage Grove. Course is 1/2 mile north of MN Highway 95 on U.S. Highway 61/10.

	MEN				WOMEN		
	BACK	FRONT	PAR	HDCP	FRONT	PAR	HDCP
1	506	471	5	3	406	5	2
2	408	388	4	1	418	4	4
3	385	362	4	9	316	4	8
4	158	141	3	17	119	3	18
5	364	347	4	11	329	4	6
6	325	298	4	13	276	4	16
7	164	152	3	15	141	3	14
8	359	335	4	7	283	4	12
9	399	376	4	5	314	4	10
Out	3068	2870	35		2502	35	
10	408	384	4	6	346	4	5
11	388	367	4	16	339	4	7
12	193	169	3	8	129	3	3
13	521	490	5	4	432	5	13
14	334	319	4	18	250	4	11
15	405	377	4	14	340	4	17
16	207	180	3	12	143	4	9
17	413	381	4	10	321	4	1
18	496	481	5	2	422	5	15
In	3365	3148	36		2722	36	
Total	6433	6018	71		5224	71	
Rating	70.2	68.3			69.3		
Slope	121	117			117		

GOLF COURSE DIRECTORY

RIVER'S EDGE COUNTRY CLUB

9 Regulation Public

1455 County Road 27
Watertown, Minnesota 55388
612/955-2223 Clubhouse/Proshop
612/446-9185 Twin City Metro Area

HOURS	Dawn to Dusk
SEASON	April–November

RESERVATIONS	612/955-2223 1 week
	Walk-on: fair/fair

GREEN FEES	M-F	S-S
Adult	$13/8	$16/10
Senior	$13/8	$16/10
Junior	$13/8	$16/10
Twilight	NA	NA

PAYMENT	Credit: Visa® MasterCard®
	Non-local checks accepted

LEAGUES	Men: Various
	Women: Various

MEMBERSHIPS	MGA

OWNER	Tom Hollander

FEATURES

Putting green	Y	
Driving range	N	
Practice area	N	
Golf carts		
Power	Y	$10
Pull carts	Y	$2
Club rental	Y	$3
Club storage	N	
Caddies	N	
Proshop		
Extended	Y	
Refreshments		
Restaurant	Y	
Lounge	Y	
Snacks	Y	
Clubhouse		
Showers	N	
Lockers	N	
Lodging	N	

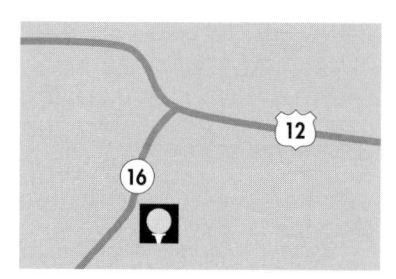

Located in Watertown. Course entrance is five miles south of U.S. Highway 12 on County Road 16.

	MEN				**WOMEN**		
	BACK	FRONT	PAR	HDCP	FRONT	PAR	HDCP
1	487	482	5	3	434	5	1
2	281	277	4	6	213	4	6
3	295	292	4	7	276	4	4
4	479	469	5	2	410	5	2
5	423	418	4	1	321	4	3
6	126	120	3	9	100	3	8
7	195	169	3	4	108	3	9
8	257	253	4	8	219	4	5
9	266	263	4	5	206	4	7
Out	2809	2743	36		2287	36	
1	487	482	5	3	434	5	1
2	281	277	4	6	213	4	6
3	295	292	4	7	276	4	4
4	479	469	5	2	410	5	2
5	423	418	4	1	321	4	3
6	126	120	3	9	100	3	8
7	195	169	3	4	108	3	9
8	257	253	4	8	219	4	5
9	266	263	4	5	206	4	7
In	2809	2743	36		2287	36	
Total	5618	5486	72		4574	72	
Rating	67.2	66.6			66.4		
Slope	111	110			112		

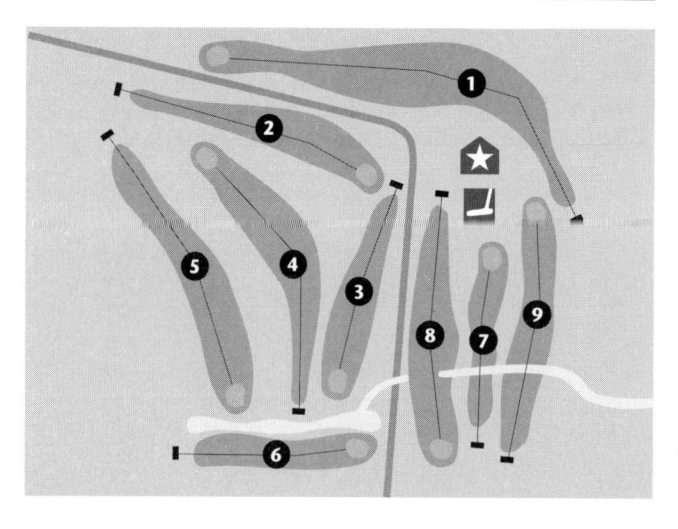

RIVERSIDE GOLF CLUB

9 Regulation Public

613 Golf Terrace, P.O. Box 387
Stephen, Minnesota 56757
218/478-2735 Clubhouse/Proshop

HOURS	Dawn to Dusk
SEASON	May to October

RESERVATIONS	218/478-2735	
	Walk-on: good/fair	

GREEN FEES	M-F	S-S
Adult	$10/6	$10/6
Senior	$10/6	$10/6
Junior	$10/6	$10/6
Twilight	$6	$6

PAYMENT	No credit cards accepted
	Non-local checks accepted

LEAGUES	Men: Various
	Women: Various

MEMBERSHIPS	MGA

MANAGER	Ralph Hvidsten

FEATURES		
Putting green	Y	
Driving range	N	
Practice area	N	
Golf carts		
Power	Y	$7
Pull carts	Y	$.50
Club rental	Y	$5
Club storage	Y	
Caddies	N	
Proshop		
Regular	Y	
Refreshments		
Restaurant	N	
Lounge	N	
Snacks	Y	
Clubhouse		
Showers	N	
Lockers	N	
Lodging	N	

Located in Stephen. Course entrance is about 1/4 mile west of U.S. Highway 75 on Main Street.

	MEN			WOMEN		
	FRONT	PAR	HDCP	FRONT	PAR	HDCP
1	385	4	1	385	4	1
2	380	4	2	380	4	2
3	280	4	7	215	4	7
4	480	5	3	410	5	3
5	280	4	6	280	4	6
6	160	3	8	160	3	8
7	130	3	9	90	3	9
8	320	4	4	270	4	4
9	300	4	5	300	4	5
Out	2695	35		2490	35	
1	385	4	1	385	4	1
2	380	4	2	380	4	2
3	280	4	7	215	4	7
4	480	5	3	410	5	3
5	280	4	6	280	4	6
6	160	3	8	160	3	8
7	130	3	9	90	3	9
8	320	4	4	270	4	4
9	300	4	5	300	4	5
In	2695	35		2490	35	
Total	5390	70		4980	70	
Rating	65.6			68.0		
Slope	103			110		

Course layout map not provided.

GOLF COURSE DIRECTORY

RIVERSIDE TOWN & COUNTRY CLUB

9 Regulation Semi-Private

P.O. Box 68
Blue Earth, Minnesota 56098
507/526-2764 Clubhouse
507/893-3677 Proshop

HOURS	7 am to Dusk
SEASON	April-November

FEATURES	
Putting green	Y
Driving range	Y
Practice area	Y
Golf carts	
Power (gas)	Y
Pull carts	Y
Club rental	N
Club storage	N
Caddies	N
Proshop	
Basic	Y
Refreshments	
Restaurant	N
Lounge	N
Snacks	Y
Clubhouse	
Showers	Y
Lockers	N
Lodging	N

RESERVATIONS	No reservations accepted
	Walk-on: good/fair

GREEN FEES	M-F	S-S
Adult	$20/12	$20/12
Senior	$20/12	$20/12
Junior	$20/12	$20/12
Twilight	NA	NA

PAYMENT	No credit cards accepted
	Non-local checks accepted

LEAGUES	None

MEMBERSHIPS	USGA, GCSAA, MGA

MANAGER	Claude Black
SUPERINTENDENT	Jim Brooks

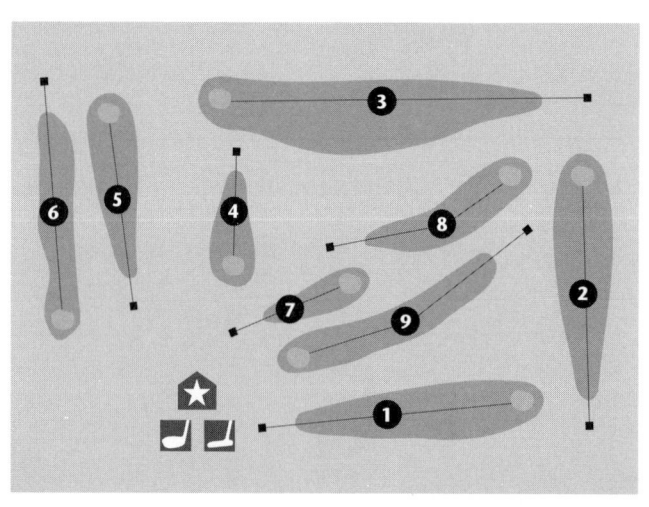

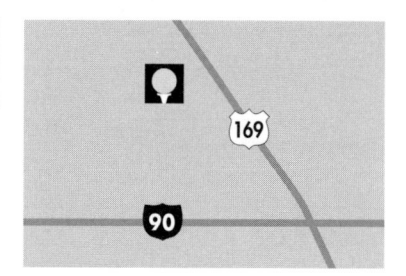

Located north of Blue Earth. Course is about four miles north of I-90 on U.S. Highway 169.

	MEN				WOMEN		
	BACK	FRONT	PAR	HDCP	FRONT	PAR	HDCP
1	412	400	4	1	384	5	1
2	337	327	4	4	307	4	4
3	499	486	5	5	466	5	5
4	220	154	3	9	132	3	9
5	357	335	4	7	315	4	7
6	339	332	4	2	322	4	2
7	179	161	3	8	143	3	8
8	400	362	4	3	333	4	3
9	466	456	5	6	452	5	6
Out	3209	3013	36		2854	37	
1	412	400	4	1	384	5	1
2	337	327	4	4	307	4	4
3	499	486	5	5	466	5	5
4	220	154	3	9	132	3	9
5	357	335	4	7	315	4	7
6	339	332	4	2	322	4	2
7	179	161	3	8	143	3	8
8	400	362	4	3	333	4	3
9	466	456	5	6	452	5	6
In	3209	3013	36		2854	37	
Total	6418	6026	72		5078	74	
Rating	70.0	69.8			73.4		
Slope	124	122			125		

THE MINNESOTA ILLUSTRATED

RIVERVIEW GOLF COURSE

9 Regulation Public

Box 32
New Richland, Minnesota 56072
507/465-3516 Clubhouse/Proshop

HOURS	Dawn to Dusk
SEASON	April to October

RESERVATIONS	507/465-3516	
	Walk-on: good/fair	

GREEN FEES	M-F	S-S
Adult	$12/8	$15/10
Senior	$12/8	$15/10
Junior	$12/8	$15/10
Twilight	NA	NA
	Rates for all day/9 holes	

PAYMENT	No credit cards accepted
	Non-local checks accepted

LEAGUES	Men: Various
	Women: Various

MEMBERSHIPS	MGA

PROFESSIONAL	Kari L. Phenix

FEATURES		
Putting green	Y	
Driving range	Y	$1
Practice area	Y	
Golf carts		
Power	Y	$14/10
Pull carts	Y	$1
Club rental	Y	$3
Club storage	N	
Caddies	N	
Proshop		
Extended	Y	
Refreshments		
Restaurant	Y	
Lounge	Y	
Snacks	Y	
Clubhouse		
Showers	N	
Lockers	N	
Lodging	N	

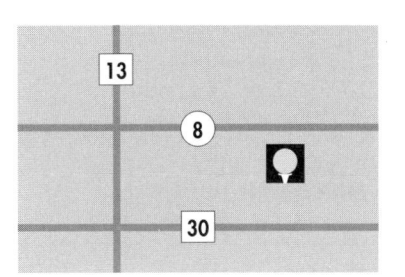

Located east of New Richland. Course entrance is about 1/2 mile east of MN Highway 13 on of County Road 8.

	MEN				**WOMEN**		
	BACK	FRONT	PAR	HDCP	FRONT	PAR	HDCP
1	344	334	4	7	314	4	7
2	410	400	4	3	346	4	3
3	360	344	4	15	330	4	15
4	354	348	4	11	323	4	11
5	164	152	3	17	144	3	17
6	512	508	5	5	446	5	5
7	193	181	3	9	160	3	9
8	370	321	4	13	306	4	13
9	507	487	5	1	430	5	1
Out	3214	3075	36		2799	36	
1	344	334	4	8	314	4	8
2	410	400	4	4	346	4	4
3	360	344	4	16	330	4	16
4	354	348	4	12	323	4	12
5	164	152	3	18	144	3	18
6	512	508	5	6	446	5	6
7	193	181	3	10	160	3	10
8	370	321	4	14	306	4	14
9	507	487	5	2	430	5	2
In	3214	3075	36		2799	36	
Total	6428	6150	72		5598	72	
Rating	70.8	69.6			72.2		
Slope	122	119			118		

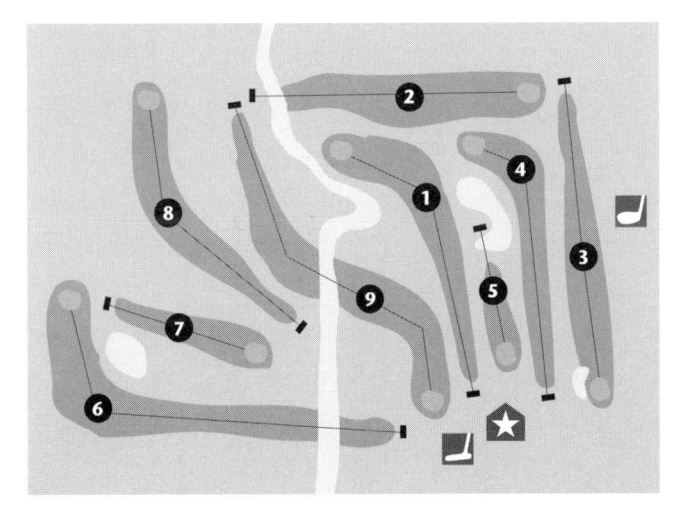

ROCHESTER GOLF & COUNTRY CLUB

18 Regulation Private

3100 Country Club Road
Rochester, Minnesota 55902
507/282-2708 Clubhouse
507/282-3170 Proshop

HOURS	8 am to Dusk
SEASON	April to October

FEATURES

Putting green	Y	
Driving range	Y	$2.75
Practice area	N	
Golf carts		
Power (gas)	Y	$27/16
Pull carts	Y	$3
Club rental	Y	$15
Club storage	Y	$60/yr
Caddies	Y	$15
Proshop		
Extended	Y	
Refreshments		
Restaurant	Y	
Lounge	Y	
Snacks	Y	
Clubhouse		
Showers	Y	
Lockers	Y	$55/yr
Lodging	N	

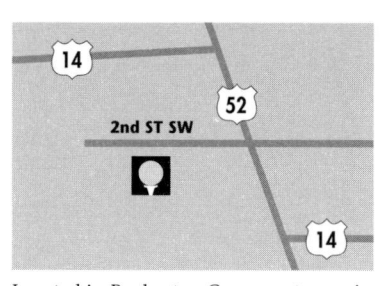

RESERVATIONS	507/282-3170	
	Members only	
GREEN FEES	M-F	S-S
Adult	$75	$75
Senior	$75	$75
Junior	$75	$75
Twilight	NA	NA
	Members and guests only	
PAYMENT	Fees billed to members	
LEAGUES	Men: Various	
	Women: Various	
MEMBERSHIPS	USGA, PGA, MGA	
PROFESSIONAL	David Richardson	

Located in Rochester. Course entrance is about three miles west of U.S. Highway 52 on 2nd Street SW.

	MEN				WOMEN		
	BACK	FRONT	PAR	HDCP	FRONT	PAR	HDCP
1	360	352	4	9	325	4	9
2	388	378	4	7	285	4	13
3	193	170	3	17	151	3	17
4	538	520	5	1	469	5	1
5	175	172	3	11	130	3	15
6	542	536	5	5	480	5	3
7	342	328	4	15	310	4	5
8	376	364	4	13	329	4	11
9	442	430	4	3	414	5	7
Out	3356	3250	36		2893	37	
10	339	318	4	16	224	4	16
11	121	113	3	18	106	3	18
12	455	445	5	4	422	5	2
13	345	335	4	12	326	4	4
14	161	151	3	14	139	3	14
15	416	405	4	2	317	4	8
16	382	373	4	10	300	4	6
17	400	391	4	6	288	4	12
18	393	385	4	8	366	5	10
In	3012	2916	35		2488	36	
Total	6368	6166	71		5381	73	
Rating	72.5	70.2			71.6		
Slope	132	130			131		

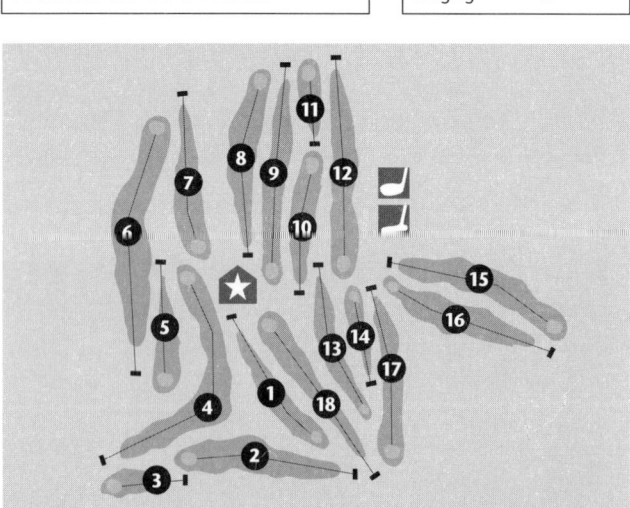

ROLLING GREEN COUNTRY CLUB

18 Regulation Private

400 Evergreen Road
Hamel, Minnesota 55340
612/478-6021 Clubhouse
612/478-6020 Proshop

RESERVATIONS	612/478-6021
	Members only

GREEN FEES	M-F	S-S
Adult	$42	$60
Senior	$42	$60
Junior	$21	$60
Twilight	NA	NA
	Members and guests only	

PAYMENT	Fees billed to members
LEAGUES	None
MEMBERSHIPS	USGA, NGF, PGA, GCSAA, CMAA, MGA
MANAGER	Ken Gullickson
SUPERINTENDENT	Pat Walton
PROFESSIONAL	Jim Terry

HOURS	8 am to 8 pm
SEASON	April-November

FEATURES

Putting green	Y
Driving range	Y
Practice area	Y
Golf carts	
Power (elec)	Y
Pull carts	Y
Club rental	Y
Club storage	Y
Caddies	Y
Proshop	
Extended	Y
Refreshments	
Restaurant	Y
Lounge	Y
Snacks	Y
Clubhouse	
Showers	Y
Lockers	Y
Lodging	N

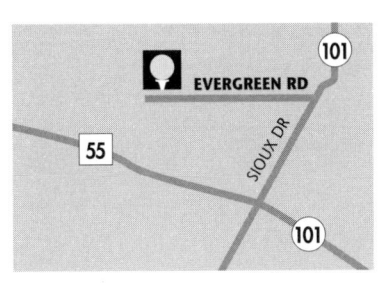

Located in Hamel. Course entrance is north of MN Highway 55 on County Road 101, then west on Evergreen Road.

	MEN				WOMEN		
	BACK	FRONT	PAR	HDCP	FRONT	PAR	HDCP
1	420	385	4	9	323	4	11
2	581	561	5	1	512	5	1
3	424	404	4	7	362	4	5
4	213	175	3	15	138	3	15
5	549	532	5	3	440	5	3
6	419	382	4	11	342	4	13
7	390	382	4	5	311	4	7
8	201	169	3	17	104	3	17
9	360	340	4	13	269	4	9
Out	3557	3330	36		2801	36	
10	412	380	4	10	314	4	12
11	506	488	5	16	451	5	4
12	369	359	4	8	302	4	14
13	248	218	3	6	146	3	16
14	537	525	5	2	491	5	2
15	378	356	4	14	346	4	6
16	400	375	4	12	340	4	8
17	170	160	3	18	100	3	18
18	453	413	4	4	369	4	10
In	3473	3274	36		2859	36	
Total	7030	6604	72		5660	72	
Rating	74.7	72.3			72.9		
Slope	134	129			124		

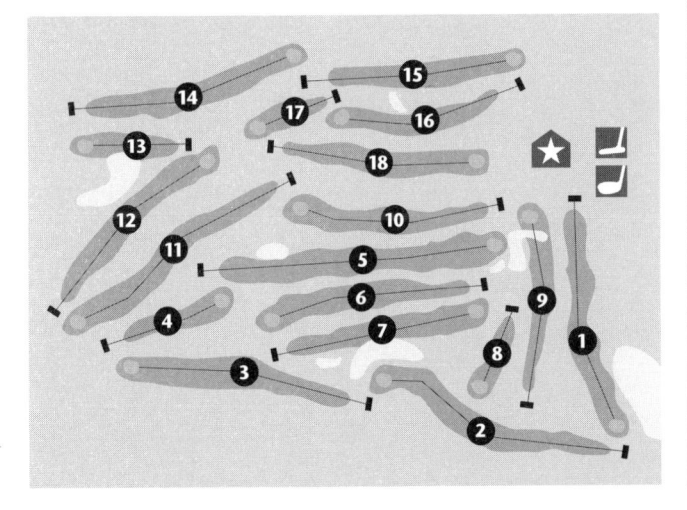

GOLF COURSE DIRECTORY

ROLLING GREEN FAIRWAYS

9 Par-3 Public

County Road 39
Fairmont, Minnesota 56031
507/235-9533 Clubhouse/Proshop

HOURS	8 am to Dusk
SEASON	April-November

| **RESERVATIONS** | No reservations accepted |
| | Walk-on: good/good |

GREEN FEES	M-F	S-S
Adult	$8/5.50	$8/5.50
Senior	$8/5.50	$8/5.50
Junior	$7/4.50	$7/4.50
Twilight	NA	NA

| **PAYMENT** | No credit cards accepted |
| | Non-local checks accepted |

| **LEAGUES** | Men: Various |
| | Women: Various |

| **MEMBERSHIPS** | NGF, MGA |

| **OWNER** | Fred Krahmer |
| **MANAGER** | Al Lidke |

FEATURES		
Putting green	Y	
Driving range	Y	$2.50
Practice area	N	
Golf carts		
Power	N	
Pull carts	Y	$1.35
Club rental	Y	$2.50
Club storage	Y	
Caddies	N	
Proshop		
Basic	Y	
Refreshments		
Restaurant	N	
Lounge	Y	
Snacks	Y	
Clubhouse		
Showers	Y	
Lockers	N	
Lodging	N	

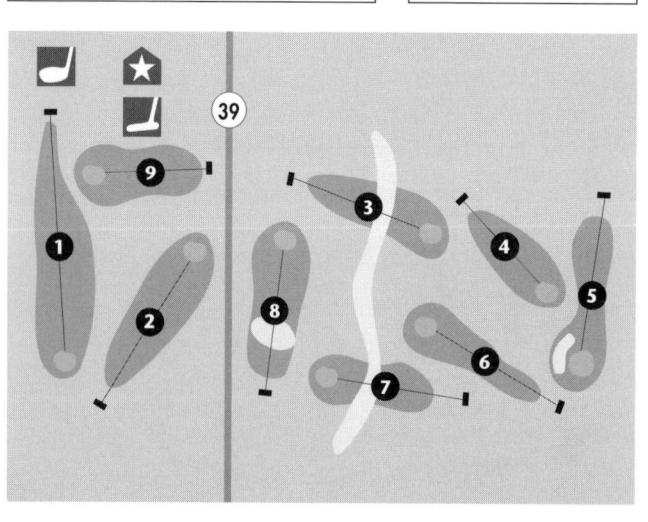

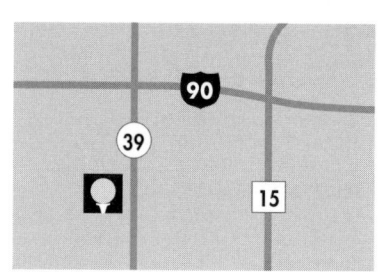

Located in Fairmont. Course entrance is about five miles south of I-90 on County Road 39.

	MEN			**WOMEN**		
	FRONT	PAR	HDCP	FRONT	PAR	HDCP
1	168	3	3	168	3	3
2	130	3	6	130	3	6
3	160	3	1	160	3	1
4	143	3	9	143	3	9
5	100	3	7	100	3	7
6	150	3	5	150	3	5
7	140	3	2	140	3	2
8	85	3	4	85	3	4
9	100	3	8	100	3	8
Out	1176	27		1176	27	
1	168	3	3	168	3	3
2	130	3	6	130	3	6
3	160	3	1	160	3	1
4	143	3	9	143	3	9
5	100	3	7	100	3	7
6	150	3	5	150	3	5
7	140	3	2	140	3	2
8	85	3	4	85	3	4
9	100	3	8	100	3	8
In	1176	27		1176	27	
Total	2352	54		2352	54	
Rating	50.1			51.8		
Slope	58			65		

ROLLING HILLS GOLF COURSE

9 Regulation Public

Route 2, P.O. Box 274
Pelican Rapids, Minnesota 56572
218/532-2214 Clubhouse/Proshop

HOURS	6 am to Dusk
SEASON	April to October

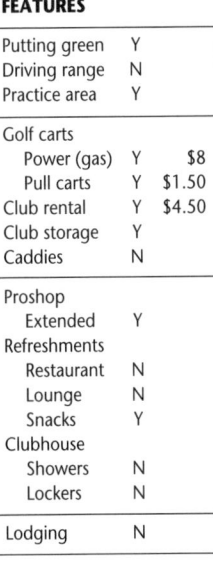

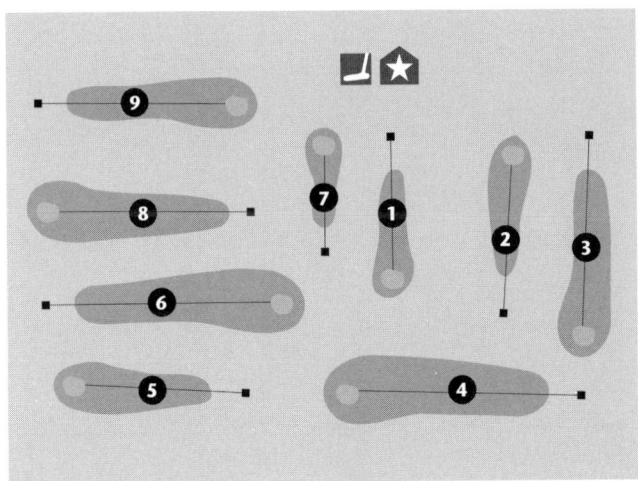

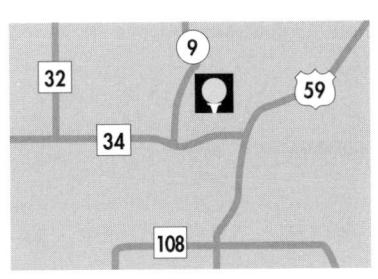

Located north of Pelican Rapids. Course entrance is north of MN Highway 34 on County Road 9.

RESERVATIONS	218/532-2214
	Walk-on: good/good

GREEN FEES	M-F	S-S
Adult	$12/8	$12/8
Senior	$12/8	$12/8
Junior	$12/8	$12/8
Twilight	NA	NA

PAYMENT	No credit cards accepted
	Non-local checks accepted

LEAGUES	None

MEMBERSHIPS	USGA, GCSAA, MGA

OWNER	Cyril A. Flem

FEATURES		
Putting green	Y	
Driving range	N	
Practice area	Y	
Golf carts		
Power (gas)	Y	$8
Pull carts	Y	$1.50
Club rental	Y	$4.50
Club storage	Y	
Caddies	N	
Proshop		
Extended	Y	
Refreshments		
Restaurant	N	
Lounge	N	
Snacks	Y	
Clubhouse		
Showers	N	
Lockers	N	
Lodging	N	

	MEN			**WOMEN**		
	FRONT	PAR	HDCP	FRONT	PAR	HDCP
1	285	4	8	285	4	8
2	300	4	5	300	4	5
3	365	4	2	365	4	2
4	440	5	9	440	5	9
5	195	3	1	195	3	1
6	390	4	3	390	4	3
7	120	3	7	120	3	7
8	305	4	4	305	4	4
9	325	4	6	325	4	6
Out	2725	35		2725	35	
1	285	4	8	285	4	8
2	300	4	5	300	4	5
3	365	4	2	365	4	2
4	440	5	9	440	5	9
5	195	3	1	195	3	1
6	390	4	3	390	4	3
7	120	3	7	120	3	7
8	305	4	4	305	4	4
9	325	4	6	325	4	6
In	2725	35		2725	35	
Total	5450	70		5450	70	
Rating	65.2			70.0		
Slope	98			108		

GOLF COURSE DIRECTORY

ROOT RIVER COUNTRY CLUB

9 Regulation Semi-Private

Route 1, P.O. Box 171A
Spring Valley, Minnesota 55975
507/346-2501 Clubhouse/Proshop

HOURS	8 am to Dusk
SEASON	April to October

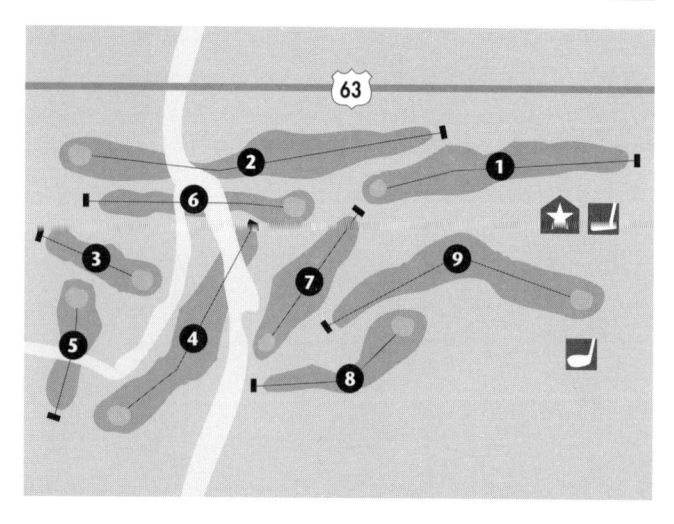

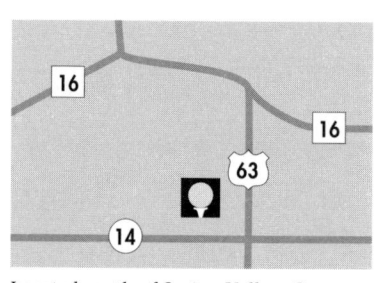

Located south of Spring Valley. Course entrance is five miles south of MN Highway 16 on U.S. Highway 63.

RESERVATIONS	507/346-2501	
	Walk-on: good/good	
GREEN FEES	M-F	S-S
Adult	$14/10	$15/11
Senior	$14/10	$15/11
Junior	$14/10	$15/11
Twilight	NA	NA
PAYMENT	No credit cards accepted	
	Non-local checks accepted	
LEAGUES	Men: Th	
	Women: T	
MEMBERSHIPS	USGA, GCSAA, MGA	
MANAGER	Shirley Berg	
SUPERINTENDENT	Rick Rannells	
PROFESSIONAL	Ted Hall	

FEATURES		
Putting green	Y	
Driving range	N	
Practice area	Y	
Golf carts		
Power (gas)	Y	$14/9
Pull carts	Y	$2
Club rental	Y	$5
Club storage	N	
Caddies	N	
Proshop		
Extended	Y	
Refreshments		
Restaurant	N	
Lounge	Y	
Snacks	Y	
Clubhouse		
Showers	Y	
Lockers	Y	
Lodging	N	

		MEN			WOMEN		
		FRONT	PAR	HDCP	FRONT	PAR	HDCP
1		370	4	4	361	4	3
2		510	5	1	453	5	1
3		185	3	6	170	3	6
4		348	4	2	326	4	4
5		180	3	8	163	3	8
6		305	4	5	258	4	5
7		297	4	9	287	4	9
8		275	4	7	262	4	7
9		489	5	3	477	5	2
Out		2959	36		2757	36	
1		370	4	4	361	4	3
2		510	5	1	453	5	1
3		185	3	6	170	3	6
4		348	4	2	326	4	4
5		180	3	8	163	3	8
6		305	4	5	258	4	5
7		297	4	9	287	4	9
8		275	4	7	262	4	7
9		489	5	3	477	5	2
In		2959	36		2757	36	
Total		5918	72		5514	72	
Rating		68.4			71.8		
Slope		116			121		

THE MINNESOTA ILLUSTRATED

ROSE LAKE GOLF CLUB

18 Regulation Semi-Private

Route 2, Box 264A
Fairmont, Minnesota 56031
507/235-5274 Clubhouse/Proshop

HOURS	Dawn to Dusk
SEASON	April-November

RESERVATIONS	507/235-5274	
	Walk-on: good/good	

GREEN FEES	M-F	S-S
Adult	$18/10	$18/10
Senior	$18/10	$18/10
Junior	$18/10	$18/10
Twilight	NA	NA

PAYMENT	No credit cards accepted
	Non-local checks accepted

LEAGUES	Various

MEMBERSHIPS	USGA, GCSAA, MGA

MANAGER	Linda Welchlin
SUPERINTENDENT	Scott Drever
PROFESSIONAL	Linda Welchlin

FEATURES		
Putting green	Y	
Driving range	Y	
Practice area	Y	
Golf carts		
Power (gas)	Y	$18
Pull carts	Y	
Club rental	Y	
Club storage	Y	$15
Caddies	N	
Proshop		
Extended	Y	
Refreshments		
Restaurant	Y	
Lounge	Y	
Snacks	Y	
Clubhouse		
Showers	Y	
Lockers	Y	$5-10
Lodging	N	

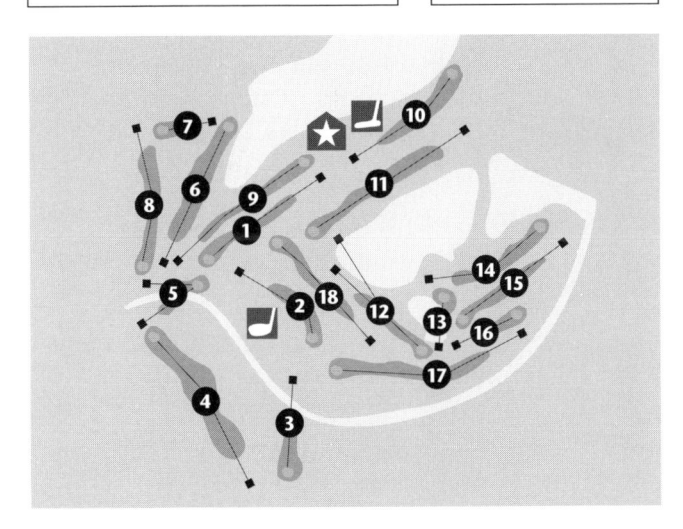

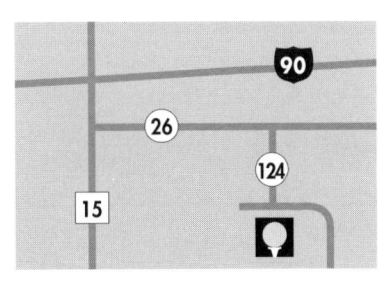

Located east of Fairmont. Course is three miles east of Hwy 15 on Cty Rd 26, then one mile south on Cty Rd 124.

	MEN				WOMEN		
	BACK	FRONT	PAR	HDCP	FRONT	PAR	HDCP
1	348	343	4	14	327	4	14
2	312	308	4	16	302	4	16
3	192	177	3	8	100	3	8
4	529	512	5	2	449	5	2
5	188	178	3	10	148	3	10
6	403	384	4	6	330	4	6
7	149	135	3	18	124	3	18
8	362	348	4	12	296	4	12
9	463	456	5	4	443	5	4
Out	2946	2841	35		2519	35	
10	375	373	4	9	352	4	9
11	461	469	5	1	426	5	1
12	401	356	4	7	313	4	7
13	160	156	3	13	106	3	13
14	415	404	4	5	350	4	5
15	341	322	4	17	275	4	17
16	183	183	3	11	151	3	11
17	540	531	5	3	426	5	3
18	374	366	4	15	358	4	15
In	3250	3160	36		2757	36	
Total	6196	6001	71		5276	71	
Rating	69.6	68.7			70.3		
Slope	121	119			120		

GOLF COURSE DIRECTORY

ROSEVILLE CEDARHOLM GOLF COURSE

9 Par-3 Public

2323 Hamline Avenue
Roseville, Minnesota 55113
612/633-5817 Clubhouse/Proshop

HOURS	6 am to Dusk
SEASON	April–November

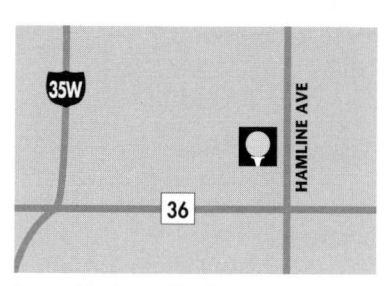

Located in Roseville. Course entrance is about 1/4 mile north MN Highway 36 on Hamline Avenue.

RESERVATIONS	612/633-5817 2 days
	Walk-on: good/fair

GREEN FEES	M-F	S-S
Adult	$6.50	$7
Senior	$6.50	$7
Junior	$6.50	$7
Twilight	NA	NA
	Sr/Jr rate $5 until 3:30 pm	

PAYMENT	No credit cards accepted
	Non-local checks accepted

LEAGUES	Men: Various
	Women: Various

MEMBERSHIPS	NGF, PGA, MGA

MANAGER	Sean McDonagh
PROFESSIONAL	Tom Jones

FEATURES		
Putting green	Y	
Driving range	N	
Practice area	N	
Golf carts		
Power	N	
Pull carts	Y	$1.50
Club rental	Y	$3.50
Club storage	N	
Caddies	N	
Proshop		
Regular	Y	
Refreshments		
Restaurant	Y	
Lounge	Y	
Snacks	Y	
Clubhouse		
Showers	Y	
Lockers	N	
Lodging	N	

	MEN			WOMEN		
	FRONT	PAR	HDCP	FRONT	PAR	HDCP
1	191	3	2	191	4	2
2	191	3	1	191	4	1
3	167	3	3	167	3	3
4	128	3	6	128	3	6
5	154	3	5	154	3	5
6	166	3	4	166	4	4
7	113	3	8	113	3	8
8	112	3	9	112	3	9
9	120	3	7	120	3	7
Out	1342	27		1342	30	
1	191	3	2	191	4	2
2	191	3	1	191	4	1
3	167	3	3	167	3	3
4	128	3	6	128	3	6
5	154	3	5	154	3	5
6	166	3	4	166	4	4
7	113	3	8	113	3	8
8	112	3	9	112	3	9
9	120	3	7	120	3	7
In	1342	27		1342	30	
Total	2684	54		2684	60	
Rating	51.6			53.8		
Slope	68			69		

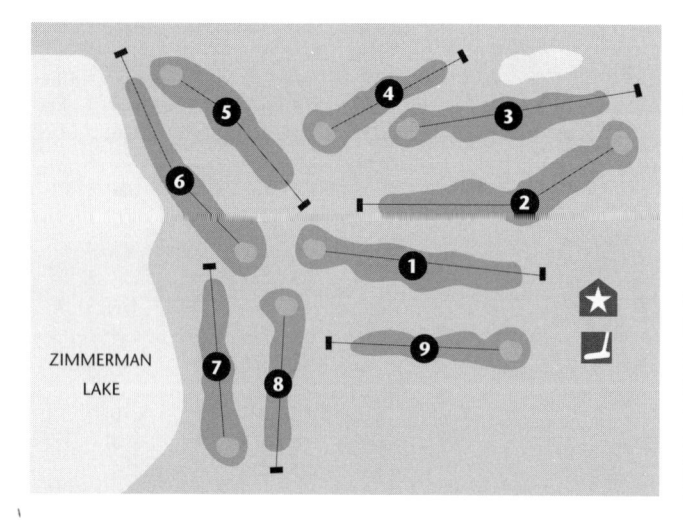

ZIMMERMAN LAKE

RUM RIVER HILLS GOLF CLUB

18 Regulation Public

16659 St. Francis Boulevard
Ramsey, Minnesota 55303
612/753-3339 Clubhouse/Proshop

HOURS	7 am to Dusk
SEASON	April-November

RESERVATIONS	612/753-3339	
	Walk-on: good/poor	

GREEN FEES	M-F	S-S
Adult	$18/11	$22/14
Senior	$11/5.50	$11/5.50
Junior	$11/5.50	$11/5.50
Twilight	$9	$9

PAYMENT	Credit: Visa® AmEx®
	Local checks only

LEAGUES	Men: T
	Women: W

MEMBERSHIPS	USGA, NGF, PGA, GCSAA, MGA

SUPERINTENDENT	Tom Stout
PROFESSIONAL	Jeff Tollette

FEATURES		
Putting green	Y	
Driving range	Y	$3
Practice area	N	
Golf carts		
Power (gas)	Y	$22
Pull carts	Y	$3
Club rental	Y	$6
Club storage	N	
Caddies	N	
Proshop		
Extended	Y	
Refreshments		
Restaurant	Y	
Lounge	Y	
Snacks	Y	
Clubhouse		
Showers	Y	
Lockers	N	
Lodging	N	

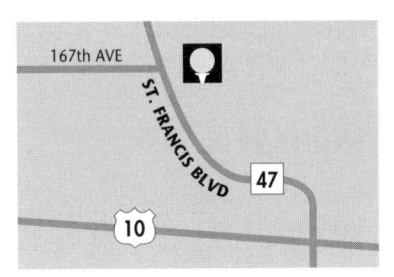

Located in Ramsey. Course entrance is five miles north of U.S. Highway 10 on Highway 47 (St. Francis Blvd).

	MEN				WOMEN		
	BACK	FRONT	PAR	HDCP	FRONT	PAR	HDCP
1	342	335	4	14	288	4	14
2	410	400	4	10	336	4	10
3	517	507	5	6	453	5	6
4	411	401	4	2	347	4	2
5	120	108	3	18	89	3	18
6	327	322	4	4	254	4	4
7	161	153	3	16	140	3	16
8	420	391	4	10	313	4	10
9	461	451	5	8	371	5	8
Out	3169	3068	36		2591	36	
10	459	409	4	1	343	4	1
11	525	510	5	11	436	5	11
12	358	348	4	5	272	4	5
13	160	142	3	17	100	3	17
14	416	403	4	7	362	4	7
15	205	190	3	13	151	3	13
16	385	358	4	9	310	4	9
17	303	293	4	3	202	4	3
18	358	348	4	15	328	4	15
In	3169	3001	35		2504	35	
Total	6338	6069	71		5095	71	
Rating	71.3	70.1			70.1		
Slope	122	119			119		

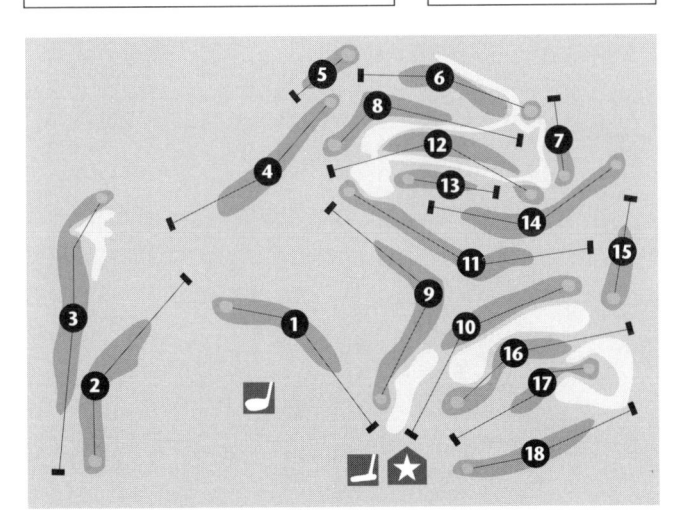

RUSH CREEK GOLF CLUB

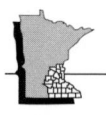

18 Regulation Public

7801 County Road 101
Maple Grove, Minnesota 55311
612/494-8844 Clubhouse/Proshop

HOURS	Dawn to Dusk
SEASON	April–November

RESERVATIONS	612/494-8844	
	Walk-on: fair/fair	
GREEN FEES	M-F	S-S
Adult	Call	Call
Senior	Call	Call
Junior	Call	Call
Twilight	NA	NA
PAYMENT	No credit cards accepted	
	Non-local checks accepted	
LEAGUES	Men: Various	
	Women: Various	
MEMBERSHIPS	USGA, PGA, GCSAA, MGA	
MANAGER	Ed & Lori Money	
SUPERINTENDENT	Tom Fuller	
PROFESSIONAL	Gerald McCullagh	

FEATURES	
Putting green	Y
Driving range	Y
Practice area	Y
Golf carts	
Power	Y
Pull carts	Y
Club rental	Y
Club storage	N
Caddies	N
Proshop	
Extended	Y
Refreshments	
Restaurant	Y
Lounge	Y
Snacks	Y
Clubhouse	
Showers	Y
Lockers	Y
Lodging	N

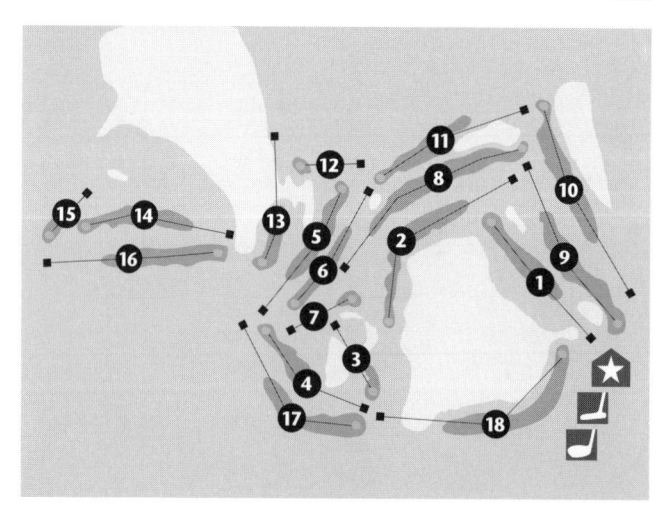

Located in Maple Grove. Course is west of I-494 on County Road 10/Bass Lake Road, then 1/4 mile north on Hwy 101.

	\multicolumn{4}{c	}{MEN}	\multicolumn{3}{c	}{WOMEN}
	BACK	FRONT	PAR	HDCP	FRONT	PAR	HDCP
1	393	361	4		315	4	
2	520	483	5		420	5	
3	173	160	3		139	3	
4	343	323	4		268	4	
5	373	350	4		318	4	
6	340	317	4		276	4	
7	202	187	3		163	3	
8	589	544	5		474	5	
9	450	414	4		358	4	
Out	3383	3139	36		2731	36	
10	529	495	5		408	5	
11	402	374	4		328	4	
12	183	169	3		132	3	
13	344	316	4		208	4	
14	369	297	4		269	4	
15	141	130	3		113	3	
16	453	405	4		315	4	
17	408	380	4		330	4	
18	557	516	5		450	5	
In	3386	3082	36		2625	36	
Total	6769	6221	72		5356	72	
Rating	NA	NA			NA		
Slope	NA	NA			NA		

RUTTGER'S BAY LAKE LODGE

THE LAKES/18 Regulation Public

Rural Route 2, P.O. Box 400
Deerwood, Minnesota 56444
218/678-2885 Resort
218/534-3432 Proshop

HOURS 7 am to Dusk

SEASON April to October

FEATURES

Putting green	Y
Driving range	Y
Practice area	Y
Golf carts	
Power (gas)	Y
Pull carts	Y
Club rental	Y
Club storage	Y
Caddies	N
Proshop	
Extended	Y
Refreshments	
Restaurant	Y
Lounge	Y
Snacks	Y
Clubhouse	
Showers	N
Lockers	N
Lodging	Y Call

RESERVATIONS 218/534-3432
Walk-on: good/fair

GREEN FEES
	S-Th	F-S
Adult	$34/20	$38/20
Senior	$34/20	$38/20
Junior	$34/20	$38/20
Twilight	$25/15 (4pm)	NA

PAYMENT Credit: Visa® MC® AmEx®
Non-local checks accepted

LEAGUES None

MEMBERSHIPS USGA, NGF, GCSAA, MGA

OWNER Jack Ruttger
MANAGER Perry Platisha
SUPERINTENDENT Patrick Kruper
PROFESSIONAL Brad Thompson

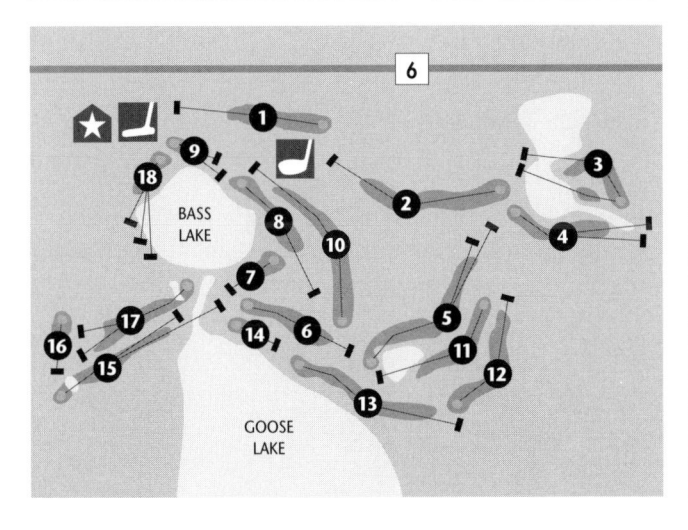

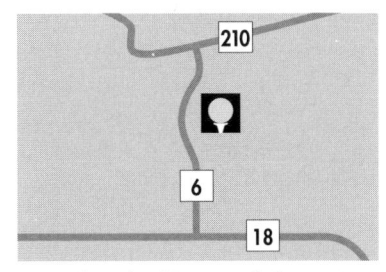

Located south of Deerwood. Course is about 5 miles south of MN Highway 210 on MN Highway 6.

	MEN				WOMEN		
	BACK	FRONT	PAR	HDCP	FRONT	PAR	HDCP
1	368	339	4	11	255	4	11
2	516	507	5	5	403	5	5
3	350	340	4	7	271	4	7
4	414	375	4	1	292	4	1
5	505	498	5	3	448	5	3
6	322	310	4	15	265	4	15
7	205	190	3	13	155	3	13
8	373	359	4	9	284	4	9
9	196	140	3	17	100	3	17
Out	3249	3058	36		2473	36	
10	574	550	5	2	489	5	2
11	410	390	4	6	311	4	6
12	343	331	4	14	255	4	14
13	507	494	5	12	408	5	12
14	136	129	3	16	104	3	16
15	500	480	5	10	390	5	10
16	148	135	3	18	122	3	18
17	386	374	4	8	335	4	8
18	232	213	3	4	165	3	4
In	3236	3096	36		2579	36	
Total	6485	6154	72		5052	72	
Rating	72.2	70.6			69.7		
Slope	131	128			124		

GOLF COURSE DIRECTORY

RUTTGER'S BAY LAKE LODGE

LODGE NINE/9 Executive Public

Rural Route 2, P.O. Box 400
Deerwood, Minnesota 56444
218/678-2885 Resort
218/534-3432 Proshop

HOURS	7 am to Dusk
SEASON	April to October

FEATURES

Putting green	Y
Driving range	Y
Practice area	Y
Golf carts	
Power (gas)	Y
Pull carts	Y
Club rental	Y
Club storage	Y
Caddies	N
Proshop	
Extended	Y
Refreshments	
Restaurant	Y
Lounge	Y
Snacks	Y
Clubhouse	
Showers	N
Lockers	N
Lodging	Y Call

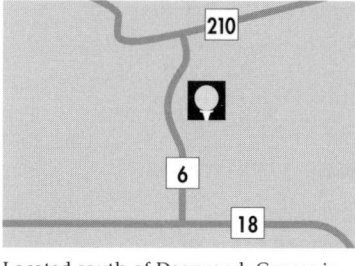

RESERVATIONS	218/534-3432
	Walk-on: good/fair

GREEN FEES	S-Th	F-S
Adult	Call	Call
Senior	Call	Call
Junior	Call	Call
Twilight	NA	NA

PAYMENT	Credit: Visa® MC® AmEx®
	Non-local checks accepted

LEAGUES	None

MEMBERSHIPS	USGA, NGF, GCSAA, MGA

OWNER	Jack Ruttger
MANAGER	Perry Platisha
SUPERINTENDENT	Patrick Kruper
PROFESSIONAL	Brad Thompson

Located south of Deerwood. Course is about 5 miles south of MN Highway 210 on MN Highway 6.

	MEN			WOMEN		
	FRONT	PAR	HDCP	FRONT	PAR	HDCP
1	317	4	3	307	4	3
2	250	4	7	233	4	7
3	135	3	9	120	3	9
4	264	4	6	244	4	6
5	310	4	1	301	4	1
6	172	3	8	155	3	8
7	300	4	2	300	4	2
8	268	4	5	248	4	5
9	269	4	4	269	4	4
Out	2285	34		2177	34	
1	317	4	3	307	4	3
2	250	4	7	233	4	7
3	135	3	9	120	3	9
4	264	4	6	244	4	6
5	310	4	1	301	4	1
6	172	3	8	155	3	8
7	300	4	2	300	4	2
8	268	4	5	248	4	5
9	269	4	4	269	4	4
Out	2285	34		2177	34	
Total	4570	68		4354	68	
Rating	60.6			60.4		
Slope	95			95		

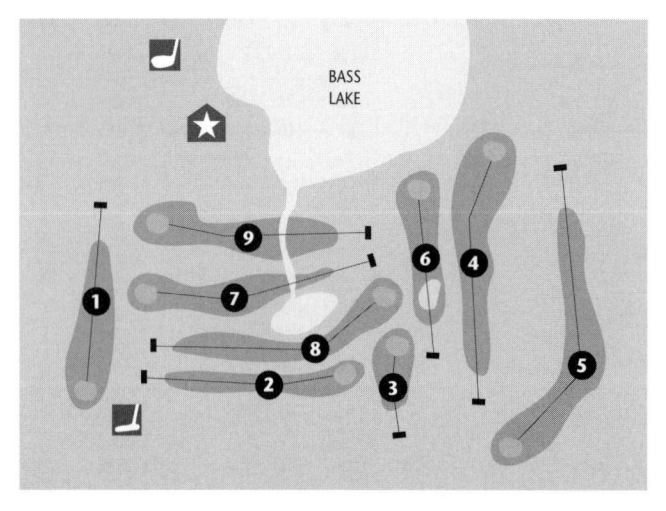

ST. CHARLES GOLF COURSE

18 Regulation Semi-Private

1920 Park Road
St. Charles, Minnesota 55972
507/932-5444 Clubhouse/Proshop

RESERVATIONS	507/932-5444 1 week
	Walk-on: good/fair

GREEN FEES	M-F	S-S
Adult	$17/10.50	$17/10.50
Senior	$17/10.50	$17/10.50
Junior	$17/10.50	$17/10.50
Twilight	NA	NA

PAYMENT	No credit cards accepted
	Non-local checks accepted

LEAGUES	Men: W
	Women: T

MEMBERSHIPS	USGA, NGF, PGA, MGA

OWNER	Wayne & Suzanne Idso
MANAGER	Michele Splittstoesser
PROFESSIONAL	Fran Rainey

HOURS	6 am to Dusk
SEASON	April–November

FEATURES		
Putting green	Y	
Driving range	Y	$3
Practice area	N	
Golf carts		
Power	Y	$17
Pull carts	Y	$1.75
Club rental	Y	$5
Club storage	N	
Caddies	N	
Proshop		
Extended	Y	
Refreshments		
Restaurant	Y	
Lounge	Y	
Snacks	Y	
Clubhouse		
Showers	N	
Lockers	N	
Lodging	N	

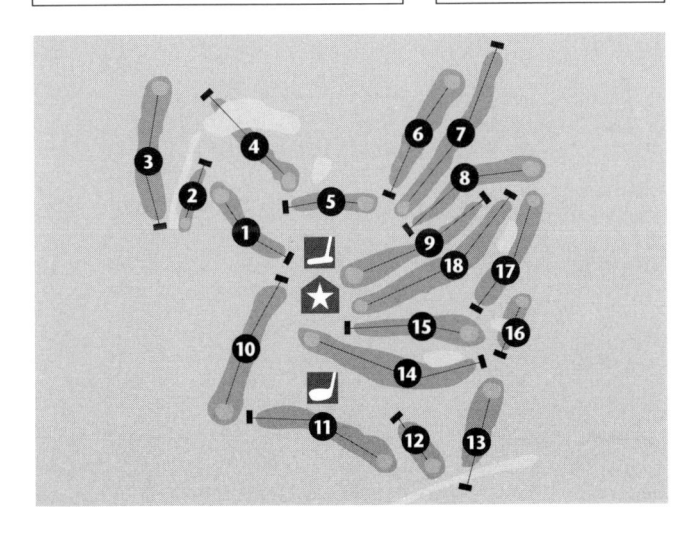

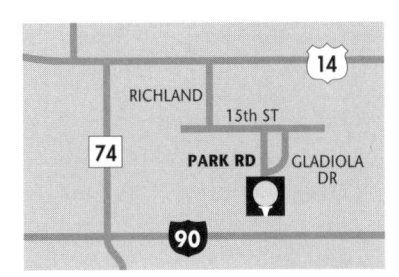

Located in St. Charles. Course is south of U.S. Highway 14 on Richland Ave, east on 15th St, then south on Gladiola Dr.

	MEN				WOMEN		
	BACK	FRONT	PAR	HDCP	FRONT	PAR	HDCP
1	292	274	4	17	256	4	17
2	174	168	3	15	162	3	15
3	377	367	4	9	357	4	9
4	343	337	4	11	331	4	11
5	213	203	3	13	193	3	13
6	384	368	4	7	352	4	7
7	416	400	4	3	384	4	3
8	388	382	4	5	376	4	5
9	501	483	5	1	465	5	1
Out	3008	2982	35		2876	35	
10	372	357	4	6	342	4	6
11	389	378	4	8	367	4	8
12	153	137	3	18	121	3	18
13	343	325	4	12	307	4	12
14	514	498	5	4	482	5	4
15	382	363	4	14	344	4	14
16	153	153	3	16	153	3	16
17	380	364	4	10	348	4	10
18	573	555	5	2	537	5	2
In	3259	3130	36		3001	36	
Total	6347	6112	71		5877	71	
Rating	69.7	69.0			71.6		
Slope	115	114			119		

GOLF COURSE DIRECTORY

ST. CLOUD COUNTRY CLUB　　　　　　　　　　18 Regulation Private

301 Montrose Road, Box 1064
St. Cloud, Minnesota 56302
612/253-1331 Clubhouse
612/253-1333 Proshop

HOURS	6:30 am - Dusk
SEASON	April to October

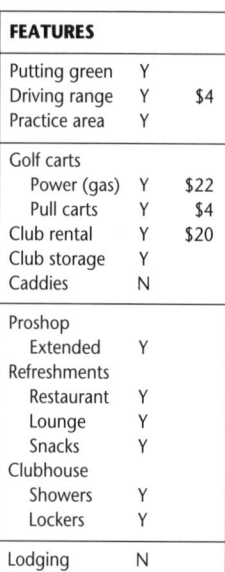

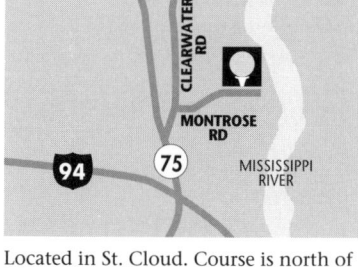

FEATURES

Putting green	Y	
Driving range	Y	$4
Practice area	Y	
Golf carts		
Power (gas)	Y	$22
Pull carts	Y	$4
Club rental	Y	$20
Club storage	Y	
Caddies	N	
Proshop		
Extended	Y	
Refreshments		
Restaurant	Y	
Lounge	Y	
Snacks	Y	
Clubhouse		
Showers	Y	
Lockers	Y	
Lodging	N	

Located in St. Cloud. Course is north of I-94 on Cty Road 75, east on Clearwater Road, then east on Montrose Road.

RESERVATIONS	612/253-1333 6 days	
	Members only	
GREEN FEES	M-F	S-S
Adult	$22/11	$28/14
Senior	$22/11	$28/14
Junior	$22/11	$28/14
Twilight	NA	NA
	Members and guest only	
PAYMENT	No credit cards accepted	
	Local checks only	
LEAGUES	Various	
MEMBERSHIPS	USGA, PGA, GCSAA,	
	CMAA, MGA	
PROFESSIONAL	Joe Malone, Tim LaVold	
SUPERINTENDENT	Rob Barr	

	MEN				**WOMEN**		
	BACK	FRONT	PAR	HDCP	FRONT	PAR	HDCP
1	440	433	4	5	426	5	7
2	369	364	4	13	261	4	13
3	184	174	3	15	165	3	15
4	440	444	5	1	322	4	5
5	422	410	4	3	332	4	9
6	130	123	3	17	115	3	17
7	428	417	4	11	330	4	11
8	358	348	4	7	290	4	3
9	529	522	5	9	433	5	1
Out	3300	3235	36		2674	36	
10	527	509	5	4	445	5	4
11	359	348	4	12	282	4	10
12	190	175	3	16	121	3	16
13	423	407	4	8	348	4	14
14	382	370	4	6	314	4	6
15	504	473	5	2	368	5	2
16	168	160	3	18	126	3	18
17	345	340	4	14	334	4	8
18	414	398	4	10	292	4	12
In	3312	3180	36		2630	36	
Total	6612	6415	72		5304	72	
Rating	72.1	71.2			72.7		
Slope	129	127			124		

SANBROOK GOLF COURSE

18 Regulation Public

2181 County Road 5
Isanti, Minnesota 55040
612/444-9904 Clubhouse/Proshop

HOURS	Dawn to Dusk
SEASON	April-November

RESERVATIONS	612/444-9904 2 days
	Walk-on: good/fair

GREEN FEES	M-F	S-S
Adult	$12/8	$14/9.50
Senior	$9.50/6.50	$14/9.50
Junior	$12/8	$14/9.50
Twilight	NA	NA

PAYMENT	Credit: Visa® MasterCard®
	Local checks only

LEAGUES	Various

MEMBERSHIPS	USGA, GCSAA, MGA

SUPERINTENDENT	Lyle Kleven

FEATURES		
Putting green	Y	
Driving range	Y	$2
Practice area	N	
Golf carts		
Power (gas)	Y	$18/9
Pull carts	Y	$2/1.50
Club rental	Y	$5
Club storage	N	
Caddies	N	
Proshop		
Regular	Y	
Refreshments		
Restaurant	N	
Lounge	N	
Snacks	Y	
Clubhouse		
Showers	N	
Lockers	N	
Lodging	N	

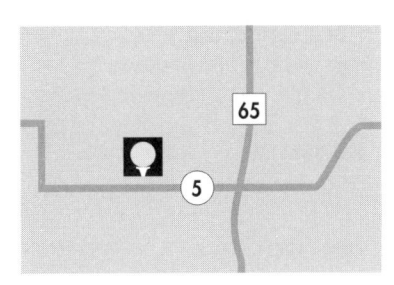

Located in Isanti. Course entrance is about one mile west of MN Highway 65 on County Road 5.

	MEN				**WOMEN**		
	BACK	FRONT	PAR	HDCP	FRONT	PAR	HDCP
1	444	407	4	15	288	4	1
2	617	591	5	11	426	5	3
3	138	123	3	17	103	3	5
4	542	531	5	7	424	5	11
5	288	273	4	5	258	4	9
6	185	175	3	9	165	3	17
7	389	374	4	3	283	4	7
8	326	316	4	13	306	4	15
9	368	356	4	1	301	4	13
Out	3297	3146	36		2554	36	
10	601	582	5	6	425	5	8
11	281	264	4	12	219	4	18
12	131	112	3	4	97	3	12
13	513	493	5	2	404	5	6
14	315	295	4	14	254	4	16
15	305	291	4	8	269	4	2
16	139	124	3	18	109	3	10
17	410	395	4	16	342	4	14
18	393	382	4	10	329	4	4
In	3088	2938	36		2448	36	
Total	6385	6084	72		5002	72	
Rating	NA	NA			NA		
Slope	NA	NA			NA		

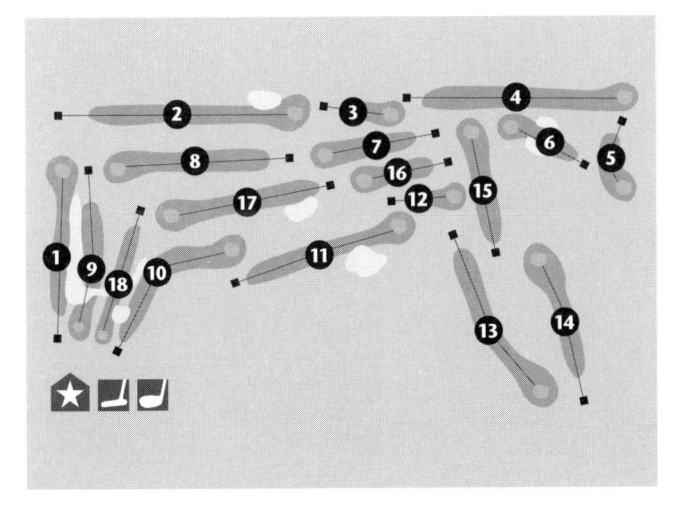

GOLF COURSE DIRECTORY

SANBROOK GOLF COURSE
9 Executive Public

2181 County Road 5
Isanti, Minnesota 55040
612/444-9904 Clubhouse/Proshop

RESERVATIONS	612/444-9904 2 days	
	Walk-on: good/fair	
GREEN FEES	M-F	S-S
Adult	$6	$7
Senior	$4.50	$7
Junior	$6	$7
Twilight	NA	NA
PAYMENT	Credit: Visa® MasterCard®	
	Local checks only	
LEAGUES	Various	
MEMBERSHIPS	USGA, GCSAA, MGA	
SUPERINTENDENT	Lyle Kleven	

HOURS	Dawn to Dusk	
SEASON	April-November	
FEATURES		
Putting green	Y	
Driving range	Y	$2
Practice area	N	
Golf carts		
Power (gas)	Y	$18/9
Pull carts	Y	$2/1.50
Club rental	Y	$5
Club storage	N	
Caddies	N	
Proshop		
Regular	Y	
Refreshments		
Restaurant	N	
Lounge	N	
Snacks	Y	
Clubhouse		
Showers	N	
Lockers	N	
Lodging	N	

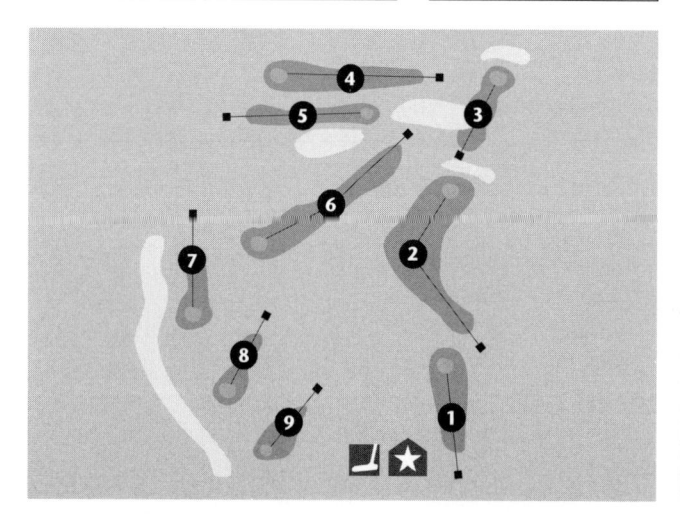

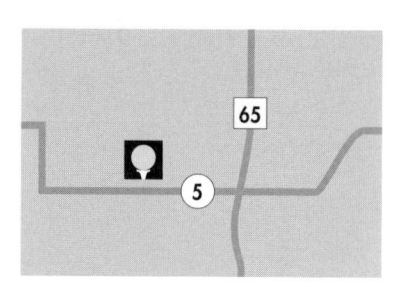

Located in Isanti. Course entrance is about one mile west of MN Highway 65 on County Road 5.

	MEN			**WOMEN**		
	FRONT	PAR	HDCP	FRONT	PAR	HDCP
1	197	3	4	188	3	8
2	373	4	1	357	4	1
3	189	3	2	179	3	2
4	159	3	5	152	3	6
5	131	3	7	131	3	3
6	271	4	8	248	4	7
7	169	3	3	156	3	4
8	156	3	6	146	3	5
9	129	3	9	121	3	9
Out	1774	29		1678	29	
1	197	3	4	188	3	8
2	373	4	1	357	4	1
3	189	3	2	179	3	2
4	159	3	5	152	3	6
5	131	3	7	131	3	3
6	271	4	8	248	4	7
7	169	3	3	156	3	4
8	156	3	6	146	3	5
9	129	3	9	121	3	9
Out	1774	29		1678	29	
Total	3548	58		3356	58	
Rating	56.2			58.4		
Slope	79			85		

SANDSTONE AREA COUNTRY CLUB

9 Executive Public

725 West 7th Street
Sandstone, Minnesota 55072
612/245-0471 Clubhouse/Proshop

HOURS	7 am to Dusk
SEASON	April-November

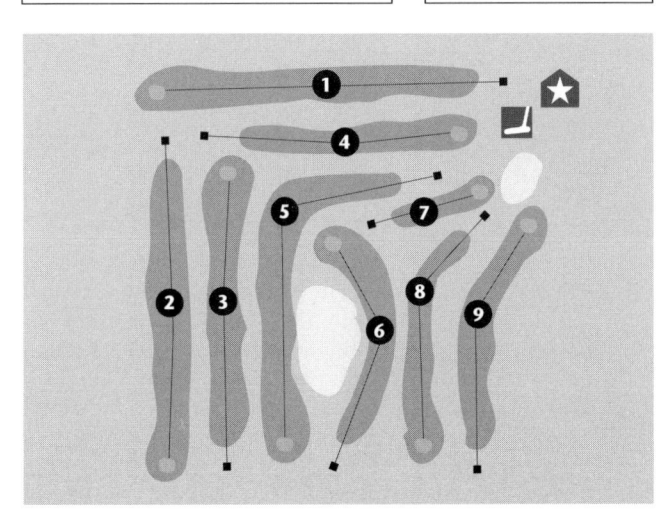

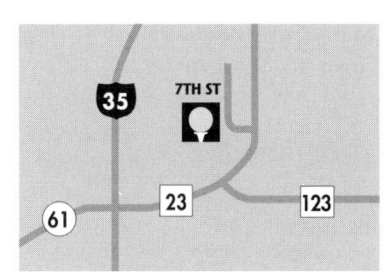

Located in Sanstone. Course entrance is about two miles east of I-35 on MN Highway 23, then west on 7th Street.

RESERVATIONS	612/245-0471
	Walk-on: good/fair

GREEN FEES	M-F	S-S
Adult	$10.50/7.50	$12.50/9.50
Senior	$10.50/7.50	$12.50/9.50
Junior	$10.50/7.50	$12.50/9.50
Twilight	NA	NA

PAYMENT	No credit cards accepted
	Non-local checks accepted

LEAGUES	Men: Th (4-7 pm)
	Women: T (4-7 pm)

MEMBERSHIPS	MGA

OWNER	City of Sandstone
MANAGER	Gary Bowen

FEATURES	
Putting green	Y
Driving range	N
Practice area	N
Golf carts	
Power (gas)	Y $12/6.5
Pull carts	Y $2
Club rental	Y $2.50
Club storage	N
Caddies	N
Proshop	
Basic	Y
Refreshments	
Restaurant	N
Lounge	N
Snacks	Y
Clubhouse	
Showers	Y
Lockers	N
Lodging	N

		MEN			WOMEN		
	BACK	FRONT	PAR	HDCP	FRONT	PAR	HDCP
1	377	292	4	3	266	4	3
2	331	331	4	5	269	4	5
3	263	263	4	8	238	4	8
4	306	306	4	7	277	4	7
5	422	422	4	1	395	5	1
6	187	187	3	2	170	3	2
7	133	133	3	9	110	3	9
8	285	285	4	4	276	4	4
9	277	277	4	6	259	4	6
Out	2581	2496	34		2260	35	
1	377	292	4	3	266	4	3
2	331	331	4	5	269	4	5
3	263	263	4	8	238	4	8
4	306	306	4	7	277	4	7
5	422	422	4	1	395	5	1
6	187	187	3	2	170	3	2
7	133	133	3	9	110	3	9
8	285	285	4	4	276	4	4
9	277	277	4	6	259	4	6
In	2581	2496	34		2260	35	
Total	5162	4992	68		4520	70	
Rating	64.6	63.8			65.4		
Slope	104	102			115		

GOLF COURSE DIRECTORY

SANDTRAP GOLF COURSE

9 Regulation Public

Route 3, P.O. Box 304
Cass Lake, Minnesota 56633
218/335-6531 Clubhouse/Proshop

HOURS	8 am to Dusk
SEASON	April to October

RESERVATIONS	218/335-6531	
	Walk-on: good/fair	
GREEN FEES	M-F	S-S
Adult	$14/9	$15/10
Senior	$14/9	$15/10
Junior	$14/9	$15/10
Twilight	$6 (5pm)*	NA
	*Tuesday & Fridays only	
	Reduced weekend pm rates	
PAYMENT	No credit cards accepted	
	Non-local checks accepted	
LEAGUES	Men: Th (pm)	
	Women: M (pm)	
	Doubles: W (pm)	
MEMBERSHIPS	MGA	
OWNER	Robert Reiblinger	
MANAGER	Gary & Bev Larson	

FEATURES		
Putting green	Y	
Driving range	N	
Practice area	N	
Golf carts		
Power	Y	$18/9
Pull carts	Y	$2/1.25
Club rental	Y	$3.50
Club storage	Y	$12.50
Caddies	N	
Proshop		
Basic	Y	
Refreshments		
Restaurant	Y	
Lounge	Y	
Snacks	Y	
Clubhouse		
Showers	N	
Lockers	N	
Lodging	N	

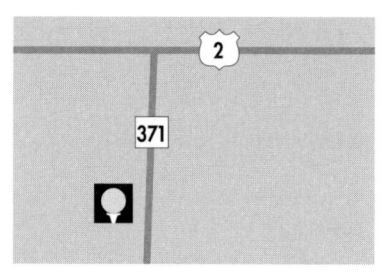

Located in Cass Lake. Course entrance is one mile south of U.S. Highway 2 on MN Highway 371.

	MEN			**WOMEN**		
	FRONT	PAR	HDCP	FRONT	PAR	HDCP
1	288	4		288	4	
2	170	3		170	3	
3	480	5		480	5	
4	474	5		474	5	
5	345	4		345	4	
6	144	3		144	3	
7	352	4		352	4	
8	348	4		348	4	
9	418	4		418	4	
Out	3019	36		3019	36	
1	288	4		288	4	
2	170	3		170	3	
3	480	5		480	5	
4	474	5		474	5	
5	345	4		345	4	
6	144	3		144	3	
7	352	4		352	4	
8	348	4		348	4	
9	418	4		418	4	
In	3019	36		3019	36	
Total	6038	72		6038	72	
Rating	68.4			72.6		
Slope	119			117		

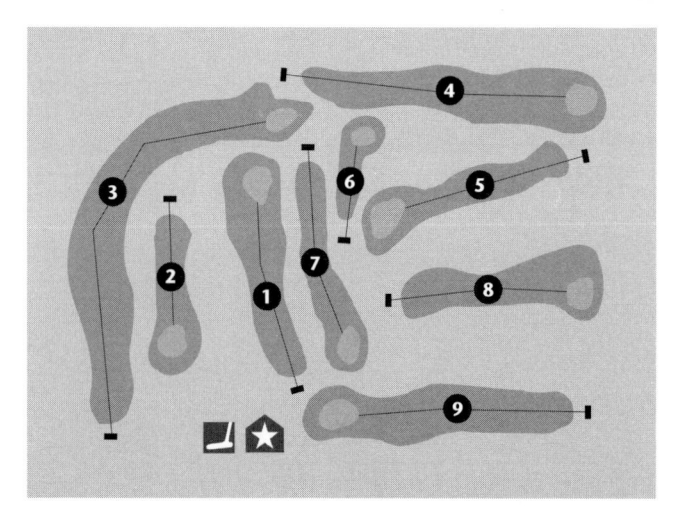

SARTELL GOLF CLUB

18 Regulation Public

P.O. Box 363
Sartell, Minnesota 56377
612/259-0551 Clubhouse/Proshop

RESERVATIONS	612/259-0551 2 days	
	Walk-on: good/fair	
GREEN FEES	M-F	S-S
Adult	$11/8	$13/10
Senior	$9/6	$11/8
Junior	$9/6	$11/8
Twilight	NA	NA
PAYMENT	No credit cards accepted	
	Non-local checks accepted	
LEAGUES	Men: Various	
	Women: Various	
MEMBERSHIPS	GCSAA, MGA	
OWNER	Jim Dahl	
MANAGER	Tom Wade	
PROFESSIONAL	Dick Culshaw	

HOURS	7 am to Dusk
SEASON	April-November

FEATURES		
Putting green	Y	
Driving range	Y	$2.50
Practice area	N	
Golf carts		
Power (gas)	Y	$15/8
Pull carts	Y	$5/2.50
Club rental	Y	$5
Club storage	N	
Caddies	N	
Proshop		
Basic	Y	
Refreshments		
Restaurant	N	
Lounge	Y	
Snacks	Y	
Clubhouse		
Showers	N	
Lockers	N	
Lodging	N	

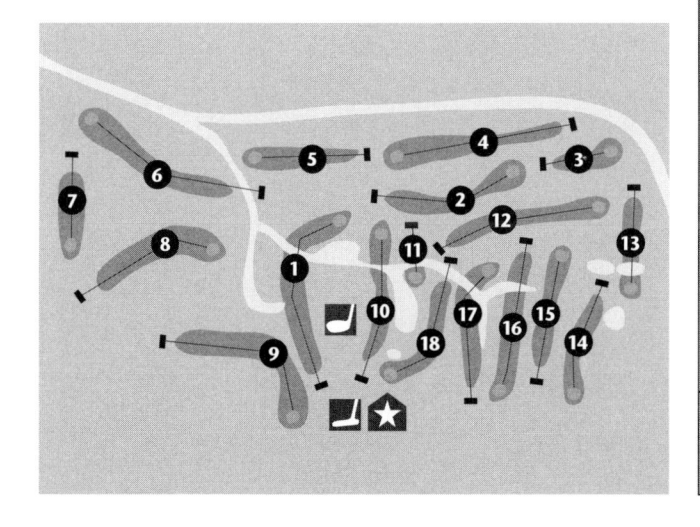

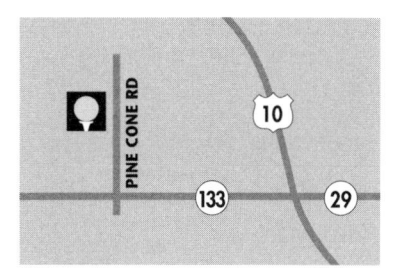

Located in Sartell. Course is west of U.S. Highway 10 on County Road 29/133, then two miles north on Pine Cone Rd.

	MEN			WOMEN		
	FRONT	PAR	HDCP	FRONT	PAR	HDCP
1	335	4	3	315	4	3
2	370	4	1	350	4	1
3	150	3	15	136	3	15
4	464	5	9	446	5	9
5	331	4	7	301	4	7
6	455	5	11	378	5	11
7	144	3	17	126	3	17
8	327	4	13	300	4	13
9	334	4	5	317	4	5
Out	2910	36		2669	36	
10	367	4	6	346	4	6
11	152	3	14	92	3	14
12	540	5	8	476	5	8
13	312	4	10	283	4	10
14	385	4	2	302	4	2
15	374	4	18	291	4	18
16	372	4	4	297	4	4
17	302	4	12	274	4	12
18	305	4	16	276	4	16
In	3109	36		2637	36	
Total	6009	72		5306	72	
Rating	68.3			69.9		
Slope	113			115		

GOLF COURSE DIRECTORY

SAUK CENTRE COUNTRY CLUB

9 Regulation Semi-Private

606 Lakeshore Drive, P.O. Box 173
Sauk Centre, Minnesota 56378
612/352-3860 Clubhouse/Proshop

HOURS	Dawn to Dusk
SEASON	April-November

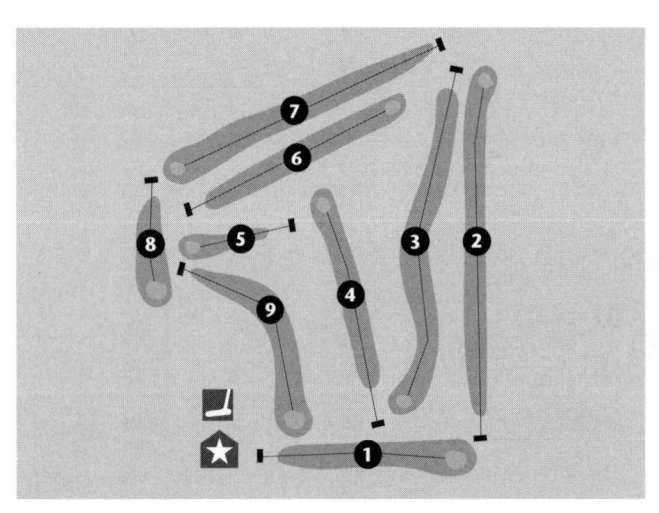

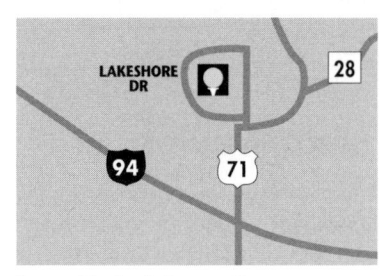

Located in Sauk Centre. Course entrance is north of U.S. Highway 71 on Main Street, then west on Lakeshore Drive.

RESERVATIONS	612/352-3860 2 days
	Walk-on: fair/fair

GREEN FEES	M-F	S-S
Adult	$12/8	$14/10
Senior	$12/8	$14/10
Junior	$12/8	$14/10
Twilight	NA	NA

PAYMENT	No credit cards accepted
	Non-local checks accepted

LEAGUES	Men: Various
	Women: Various

MEMBERSHIPS	USGA, MGA

MANAGER	Steve Schlotseldt

FEATURES	
Putting green	Y
Driving range	N
Practice area	Y
Golf carts	
Power (gas)	Y $16/9
Pull carts	Y $1.50
Club rental	Y $3
Club storage	Y
Caddies	N
Proshop	
Extended	Y
Refreshments	
Restaurant	N
Lounge	Y
Snacks	Y
Clubhouse	
Showers	N
Lockers	N
Lodging	N

	MEN			WOMEN		
	FRONT	PAR	HDCP	FRONT	PAR	HDCP
1	306	4	7	306	4	7
2	542	5	1	477	5	1
3	519	5	2	485	5	2
4	348	4	5	341	4	5
5	155	3	9	137	3	9
6	357	4	4	351	4	4
7	475	5	3	418	5	3
8	178	3	8	163	3	8
9	323	4	6	318	4	6
Out	3201	37		2996	37	
1	306	4	7	306	4	7
2	542	5	1	477	5	1
3	519	5	2	485	5	2
4	348	4	5	341	4	5
5	155	3	9	137	3	9
6	357	4	4	351	4	4
7	475	5	3	418	5	3
8	178	3	8	163	3	8
9	323	4	6	318	4	6
In	3201	37		2996	37	
Total	6402	74		5992	74	
Rating	70.4			74.6		
Slope	124			122		

SAVANNA GOLF & SUPPER CLUB

9 Regulation Semi-Private

HCR 4, P.O. Box 402
McGregor, Minnesota 55760
218/426-3117 Clubhouse/Proshop

HOURS	7 am to Dusk
SEASON	May-September

RESERVATIONS	218/426-3117
	Walk-on: fair/poor

GREEN FEES	M-F	S-S
Adult	$18/12	$21/15
Senior	$13/7.50	$21/15
Junior	$10/5	$21/15
Twilight	$7*	NA
	*Sunday-Thursday only	

PAYMENT	Credit: Visa® MC® AmEx® Discover®
	Non-local checks accepted

LEAGUES	Men: Th (2-5 pm)
	Women: T (8:30-10 am)

MEMBERSHIPS	NGF, MGA

MANAGER	McKinley Brown, Ron Blore
SUPERINTENDENT	Darrell Bruggman
PROFESSIONAL	Cathy Hughes

FEATURES		
Putting green	Y	
Driving range	Y	
Practice area	N	
Golf carts		
Power	Y	$14
Pull carts	Y	$2
Club rental	Y	$5
Club storage	Y	$35/yr
Caddies	N	
Proshop		
Extended	Y	
Refreshments		
Restaurant	Y	
Lounge	Y	
Snacks	Y	
Clubhouse		
Showers	Y	
Lockers	Y	
Lodging	N	

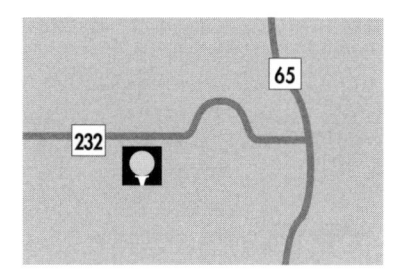

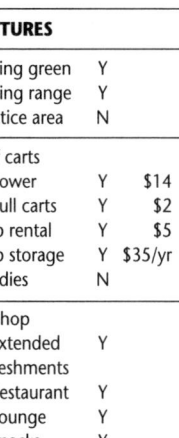

Located eight miles north of McGregor. Course entrance is 2 1/2 miles west of MN Highway 65 on MN Highway 232.

	MEN			**WOMEN**		
	FRONT	PAR	HDCP	FRONT	PAR	HDCP
1	387	4	4	303	4	4
2	393	4	1	309	4	1
3	547	5	2	480	5	2
4	193	3	7	121	3	7
5	287	4	9	227	4	9
6	557	5	3	459	5	3
7	203	3	5	150	3	5
8	330	4	8	262	4	8
9	357	4	6	312	4	6
Out	3254	36		2623	36	
1	387	4	4	303	4	4
2	393	4	1	309	4	1
3	547	5	2	480	5	2
4	193	3	7	121	3	7
5	287	4	9	227	4	9
6	557	5	3	459	5	3
7	203	3	5	150	3	5
8	330	4	8	262	4	8
9	357	4	6	312	4	6
In	3254	36		2623	36	
Total	6508	72		5246	72	
Rating	70.0			69.4		
Slope	113			111		

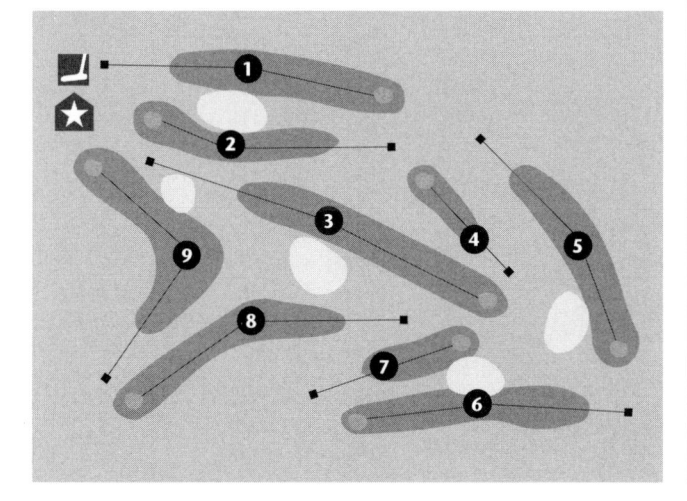

GOLF COURSE DIRECTORY

SAWMILL GOLF CLUB

18 Regulation Public

11177 McKusick Road
Stillwater, Minnesota 55082
612/439-7862 Clubhouse/Proshop

HOURS	7 am to Dusk
SEASON	April-November

RESERVATIONS	612/439-7862 3 days
	Walk-on: fair/poor

GREEN FEES	M-F	S-S
Adult	$18/12	$22/15
Senior	$16/9	$22/15
Junior	$16/9	$22/15
Twilight	NA	NA

PAYMENT	Credit: Visa® MasterCard®
	Non-local checks accepted

LEAGUES	Men: Various
	Women: Various

MEMBERSHIPS	USGA, PGA, MGA

MANAGER	John McCarthy
PROFESSIONAL	Scott Fenwick

FEATURES	
Putting green	Y
Driving range	Y
Practice area	N
Golf carts	
Power (gas)	Y $21/12
Pull carts	Y $3/2
Club rental	Y $6/4
Club storage	N
Caddies	N
Proshop	
Extended	Y
Refreshments	
Restaurant	Y
Lounge	Y
Snacks	Y
Clubhouse	
Showers	Y
Lockers	N
Lodging	N

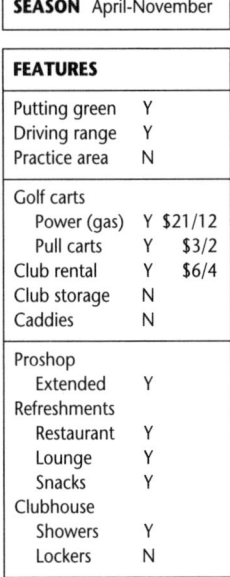

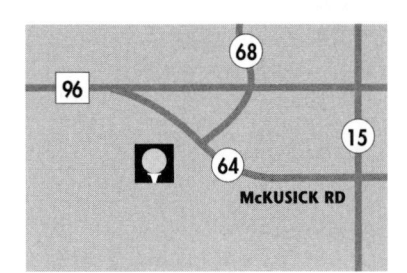

Located in Stillwater. Course entrance is south of MN Highway 96 on County Road 64/McKusick Road.

	MEN				**WOMEN**		
	BACK	FRONT	PAR	HDCP	FRONT	PAR	HDCP
1	485	468	5	11	408	5	13
2	318	306	4	9	300	4	7
3	172	152	3	15	145	3	15
4	430	425	4	5	420	5	3
5	164	154	3	17	107	3	17
6	390	350	4	7	283	4	1
7	580	576	5	1	412	5	5
8	166	154	3	13	124	3	11
9	415	325	4	3	278	4	9
Out	3120	2910	35		2477	36	
10	399	384	4	6	374	4	4
11	444	434	4	2	382	4	2
12	300	288	4	16	257	4	14
13	180	159	3	14	123	3	12
14	372	361	4	8	310	4	6
15	343	335	4	12	249	4	18
16	140	125	3	18	115	3	16
17	558	488	5	4	422	5	10
18	367	359	4	10	303	4	8
In	3103	2933	35		2535	35	
Total	6223	5843	70		5012	71	
Rating	70.2	68.1			69.5		
Slope	125	121			122		

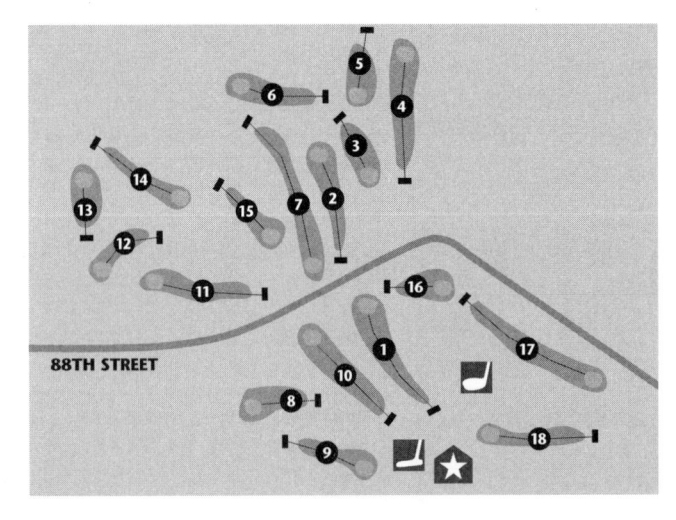

340

THE MINNESOTA ILLUSTRATED

SCOTTDALE GOLF CLUB

9 Regulation Public

19400 Natchez Avenue
Prior Lake, Minnesota 55372
612/435-7182 Clubhouse/Proshop

RESERVATIONS	612/435-7182	
	Walk-on: good/poor	
GREEN FEES	M-F	S-S
Adult	$22/12.50	$22/12.50
Senior	$19.50/11	$19.50/11
Junior	$19.50/11	$19.50/11
Twilight	$10.50	$10.50
	Special rates weekday am	
PAYMENT	No credit cards accepted	
	Non-local checks accepted	
LEAGUES	Men: T,W,Th (pm)	
	Women: M (pm), Th (am)	
MEMBERSHIPS	USGA, MGA	
MANAGER	Larry Enwall	
SUPERINTENDENT	Daniel Adelmann	

HOURS	6 am to Dusk
SEASON	April–November
FEATURES	
Putting green	Y
Driving range	Y $2.50
Practice area	N
Golf carts	
Power (gas)	Y $22
Pull carts	Y $2/1.50
Club rental	Y $6/4
Club storage	N
Caddies	N
Proshop	
Extended	Y
Refreshments	
Restaurant	Y
Lounge	Y
Snacks	Y
Clubhouse	
Showers	N
Lockers	N
Lodging	N

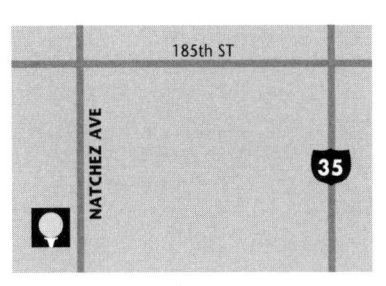

Located in Prior Lake. Course entrance is about two miles west of I-35 on 185th Street, then south on Natchez Avenue.

		MEN			**WOMEN**		
	BACK	FRONT	PAR	HDCP	FRONT	PAR	HDCP
1	377	362	4	5	244	4	8
2	210	204	3	4	198	3	2
3	504	395	4	3	390	5	9
4	149	145	3	7	142	3	5
5	301	290	4	8	283	4	7
6	473	467	5	9	331	4	3
7	417	395	4	1	274	4	4
8	539	535	5	2	415	5	1
9	360	354	4	6	260	4	6
Out	3330	3145	36		2537	36	
1	377	362	4	5	244	4	8
2	210	204	3	4	198	3	2
3	504	395	4	3	390	5	9
4	149	145	3	7	142	3	5
5	301	290	4	8	283	4	7
6	473	467	5	9	331	4	3
7	417	395	4	1	274	4	4
8	539	535	5	2	415	5	1
9	360	354	4	6	260	4	6
Out	3330	3145	36		2537	36	
Total	6660	6290	72		5074	72	
Rating	72.4	70.8			69.2		
Slope	123	119			121		

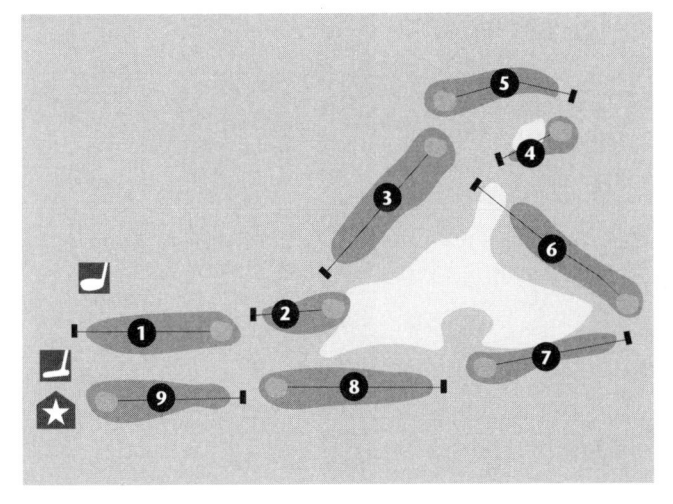

GOLF COURSE DIRECTORY

SHADOWBROOKE GOLF COURSE

9 Regulation Public

3192 State Highway 7
Lester Prairie, Minnesota 55354
612/395-4250 Clubhouse/Proshop

HOURS	Dawn to Dusk
SEASON	Mar–November

RESERVATIONS	612/395-4250	
	Walk-on: good/fair	
GREEN FEES	M-F	S-S
Adult	$16/10	$18/12
Senior	$10/7*	$18/12
Junior	$10/7	$18/12
Twilight	NA	NA
	* Before noon	
PAYMENT	No credit cards accepted	
	Non-local checks accepted	
LEAGUES	None	
MEMBERSHIPS	MGA	
OWNER	Elmer & Tom Schmiet	

FEATURES	
Putting green	Y
Driving range	Y
Practice area	Y
Golf carts	
Power (gas)	Y
Pull carts	Y
Club rental	Y
Club storage	N
Caddies	N
Proshop	
Extended	Y
Refreshments	
Restaurant	N
Lounge	Y
Snacks	Y
Clubhouse	
Showers	N
Lockers	N
Lodging	N

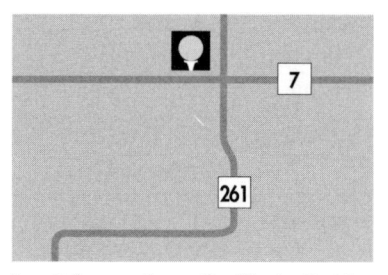

Located one mile north of Lester Prairie. Course entrance is just west of MN Highway 261 on MN Highway 7.

	MEN					**WOMEN**		
	BACK	FRONT	PAR	HDCP		FRONT	PAR	HDCP
1	570	545	5	2		430	5	2
2	170	160	3	9		115	3	9
3	395	370	4	3		315	4	3
4	355	340	4	7		290	4	7
5	560	535	5	1		450	5	1
6	185	170	3	6		130	3	6
7	520	500	5	5		400	5	5
8	390	375	4	4		305	4	4
9	175	160	3	8		120	3	8
Out	3320	3155	36			2555	36	
1	570	545	5	2		430	5	2
2	170	160	3	9		115	3	9
3	395	370	4	3		315	4	3
4	355	340	4	7		290	4	7
5	560	535	5	1		450	5	1
6	185	170	3	6		130	3	6
7	520	500	5	5		400	5	5
8	390	375	4	4		305	4	4
9	175	160	3	8		120	3	8
In	3320	3155	36			2555	36	
Total	6640	6310	72			5110	72	
Rating	71.0	69.6				68.2		
Slope	126	124				116		

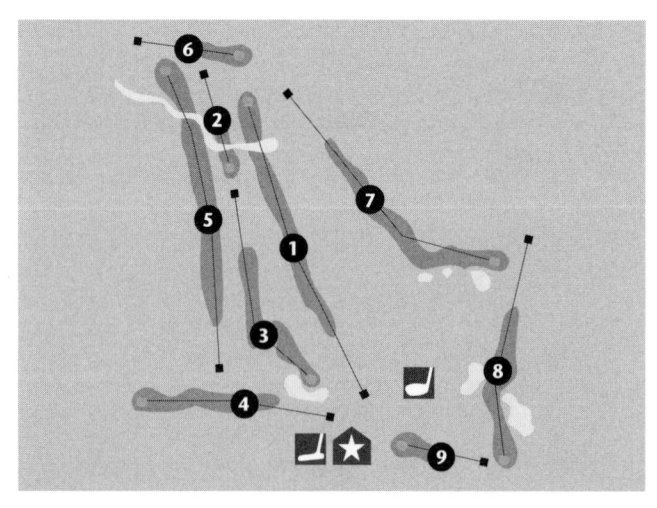

SHAMROCK GOLF CLUB

18 Regulation Public

19625 Larkin Road
Corcoran, Minnesota 55340
612/478-9977 Clubhouse

| RESERVATIONS | 612/478-9977 4 days |
| | Walk-on: good/fair |

GREEN FEES	M-F	S-S
Adult	$17/12	$19/13
Senior	$12/9	$19/13
Junior	$12/9	$19/13
Twilight	NA	NA

| PAYMENT | No credit cards accepted |
| | Non-local checks accepted |

| LEAGUES | Men: S,S (am), M (pm) |
| | Women: M,T (am) |

| MEMBERSHIPS | MGA |

| OWNER | Richard, Bill, George Deziel |
| MANAGER | Rick Deziel, Jr |

| HOURS | 5:30 am to Dusk |
| SEASON | April–November |

FEATURES	
Putting green	Y
Driving range	N
Practice area	Y
Golf carts	
Power (gas)	Y $20/11
Pull carts	Y $2
Club rental	Y $4.50
Club storage	N
Caddies	N
Proshop	
Extended	Y
Refreshments	
Restaurant	N
Lounge	N
Snacks	Y
Clubhouse	
Showers	Y
Lockers	Y
Lodging	N

Located in Corcoran. Course entrance is 5 miles west of I-494 on Bass Lake Road (County Road 10).

		MEN			WOMEN		
	BACK	FRONT	PAR	HDCP	FRONT	PAR	HDCP
1	542	533	5	5	510	5	1
2	414	404	4	1	394	5	5
3	377	357	4	9	337	4	17
4	159	149	3	17	140	3	11
5	360	350	4	13	305	4	13
6	466	451	5	15	436	5	3
7	380	358	4	11	351	4	9
8	224	215	3	3	211	4	15
9	386	376	4	7	366	4	7
Out	3308	3193	36		3050	38	
10	361	346	4	10	326	4	10
11	408	396	4	2	338	4	6
12	318	308	4	16	283	4	14
13	158	148	3	14	123	3	16
14	514	484	5	4	464	5	4
15	340	325	4	12	310	4	12
16	144	129	3	18	114	3	18
17	368	358	4	8	331	4	8
18	504	484	5	6	454	5	2
In	3115	2978	36		2743	36	
Total	6423	6171	72		5793	74	
Rating	68.4	67.3			70.9		
Slope	99	96			108		

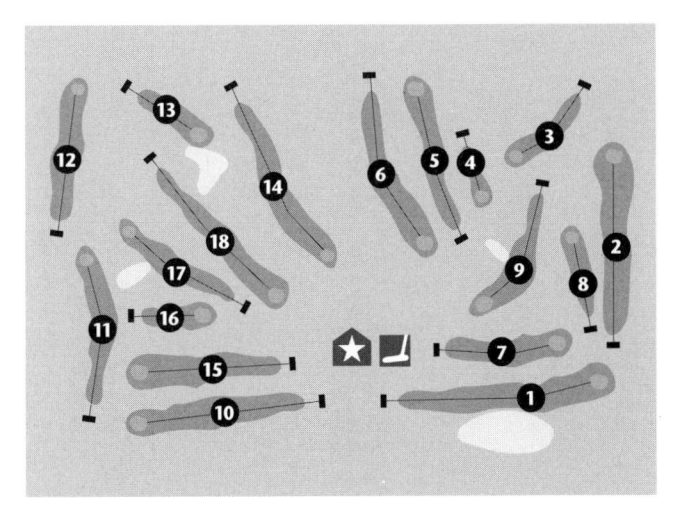

GOLF COURSE DIRECTORY

SHATTUCK–ST. MARY'S GOLF COURSE

9 Regulation Semi-Private

1000 Shumway Avenue
Faribault, Minnesota 55021
507/334-0230 Clubhouse/Proshop

HOURS	7 am to Dusk
SEASON	April to October

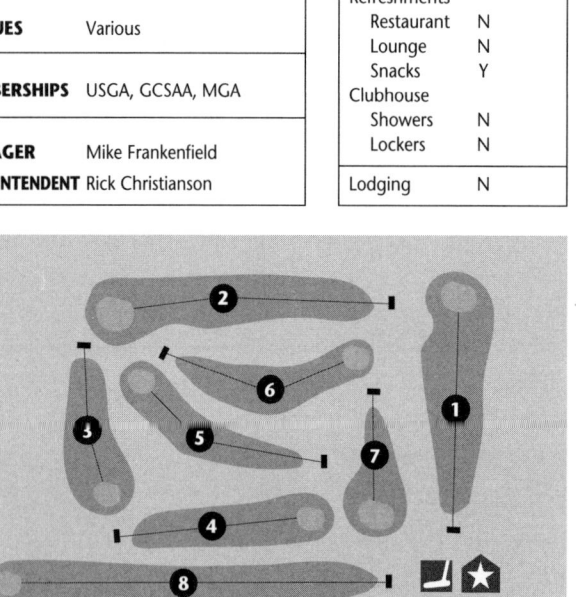

RESERVATIONS	507/334-0230
	Walk-on: good/fair

GREEN FEES	M-F	S-S
Adult	$12.50/8.50	$13.50/9.50
Senior	$12.50/8.50	$13.50/9.50
Junior	$8/4	$8/4
Twilight	NA	NA

PAYMENT	No credit cards accepted
	Non-local checks accepted

LEAGUES	Various

MEMBERSHIPS	USGA, GCSAA, MGA

MANAGER	Mike Frankenfield
SUPERINTENDENT	Rick Christianson

FEATURES	
Putting green	Y
Driving range	N
Practice area	N
Golf carts	
Power (gas)	Y $18/10
Pull carts	Y $1.50
Club rental	Y $4
Club storage	N
Caddies	N
Proshop	
Basic	Y
Refreshments	
Restaurant	N
Lounge	N
Snacks	Y
Clubhouse	
Showers	N
Lockers	N
Lodging	N

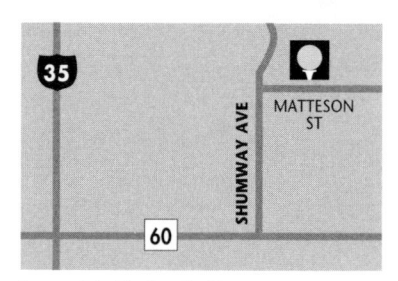

Located in Faribault. Course entrance is east of I-35 on MN Highway 60, then north on Shumway Avenue.

	MEN					**WOMEN**		
	BACK	FRONT	PAR	HDCP	FRONT	PAR	HDCP
1	292	292	4	15	292	4	15
2	355	355	4	3	355	4	3
3	225	195	3	5	195	3	5
4	304	304	4	11	304	4	11
5	297	297	4	7	297	4	7
6	295	295	4	9	295	4	9
7	127	127	3	13	127	3	13
8	458	458	5	17	458	5	17
9	426	377	4	1	377	4	1
Out	2779	2700	35		2700	35	
1	292	292	4	16	292	4	16
2	355	355	4	4	355	4	4
3	225	195	3	6	195	3	6
4	304	304	4	12	304	4	12
5	297	297	4	8	297	4	8
6	295	295	4	10	295	4	10
7	127	127	3	14	127	3	14
8	458	458	5	18	458	5	18
9	426	377	4	2	377	4	2
In	2779	2700	35		2700	35	
Total	5558	5400	70		5400	70	
Rating	66.4	65.6			70.4		
Slope	99	98			113		

SHORELAND COUNTRY CLUB

18 Regulation Private

Lake Emily Cty Rd 21, P.O. Box 516
St. Peter, Minnesota 56082
507/931-4400 Clubhouse
507/931-3470 Proshop

RESERVATIONS	507/931-3470 1 week	
	Members only	
GREEN FEES	M-F	S-S
Adult	$20/12	$20/12
Senior	$20/12	$20/12
Junior	$10/6.50	$10/6.50
Twilight	NA	NA
	Members and guests only	
PAYMENT	Credit: Visa® MasterCard®	
	Non-local checks accepted	
LEAGUES	Men: W (pm)	
MEMBERSHIPS	USGA, PGA, GCSAA, MGA	
PROFESSIONAL	Mike Luckraft	
SUPERINTENDENT	Greg Iden	

HOURS 7:30 am - Dusk
SEASON April-November

FEATURES

Putting green	Y
Driving range	N
Practice area	N
Golf carts	
Power (gas)	Y
Pull carts	N
Club rental	Y
Club storage	Y
Caddies	N
Proshop	
Extended	Y
Refreshments	
Restaurant	Y
Lounge	Y
Snacks	Y
Clubhouse	
Showers	Y
Lockers	Y
Lodging	N

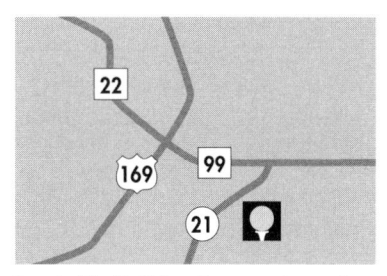

Located in St. Peter. Course entrance is about 1/2 mile south of MN Highway 99 on County Road 21.

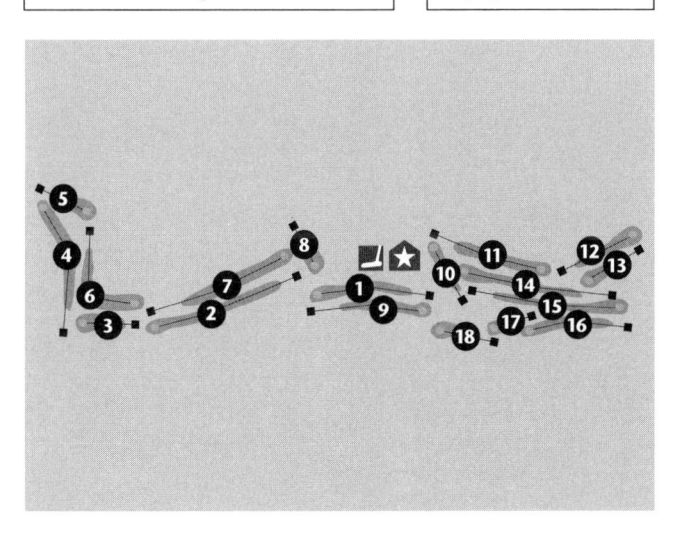

	MEN FRONT	PAR	HDCP	**WOMEN** FRONT	PAR	HDCP
1	355	4	12	335	4	12
2	492	5	4	452	5	4
3	210	3	14	200	4	12
4	412	4	6	372	4	6
5	141	3	16	131	3	16
6	367	4	8	317	4	8
7	481	5	2	444	5	2
8	133	3	18	123	3	18
9	340	4	10	305	4	10
Out	2931	35		2679	36	
10	215	3	11	202	4	11
11	355	4	5	321	4	5
12	270	4	7	240	4	7
13	177	3	13	120	3	13
14	507	5	3	489	5	3
15	528	5	1	488	5	1
16	315	4	9	305	4	9
17	110	3	17	100	3	17
18	167	3	15	122	3	15
In	2644	34		2387	35	
Total	5575	69		5066	71	
Rating	66.6			68.9		
Slope	112			117		

GOLF COURSE DIRECTORY

SILVER BAY COUNTRY CLUB

9 Regulation Semi-Private

P.O. Box 38
Silver Bay, Minnesota 55614
218/226-3111 Clubhouse/Proshop

HOURS	7 am to Dusk
SEASON	May to October

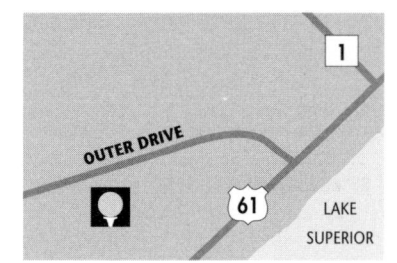

RESERVATIONS	218/226-3111 1 week	
	Walk-on: good/fair	
GREEN FEES	M-Th	F-S
Adult	$18/12	$18/12
Senior	$18/12	$18/12
Junior	$18/12	$18/12
Twilight	NA	NA
PAYMENT	No credit cards accepted	
	Non-local checks accepted	
LEAGUES	None	
MEMBERSHIPS	USGA, GCSAA, MGA	
OWNER	City of Silver Bay	
MANAGER	Norma O'Leary	
SUPERINTENDENT	Norma O'Leary	

FEATURES		
Putting green	Y	
Driving range	N	
Practice area	Y	
Golf carts		
Power (gas)	Y	$18/10
Pull carts	Y	$2
Club rental	Y	$4
Club storage	N	
Caddies	N	
Proshop		
Basic	Y	
Refreshments		
Restaurant	Y	
Lounge	Y	
Snacks	Y	
Clubhouse		
Showers	Y	
Lockers	Y	
Lodging	N	

Located in Silver Bay. Course entrance is about one mile west of U.S. Highway 61 on Outer Drive.

	MEN			WOMEN		
	FRONT	PAR	HDCP	FRONT	PAR	HDCP
1	378	4	5	295	4	13
2	176	3	15	149	3	11
3	373	4	11	293	4	15
4	432	5	17	358	5	9
5	425	4	1	360	5	5
6	484	5	9	401	5	3
7	347	4	7	334	4	1
8	158	3	13	107	3	17
9	400	4	3	385	5	7
Out	3173	36		2682	38	
1	378	4	6	295	4	14
2	176	3	16	149	3	12
3	373	4	12	293	4	16
4	432	5	18	358	5	10
5	425	4	2	360	5	6
6	484	5	10	401	5	4
7	347	4	8	334	4	2
8	158	3	14	107	3	18
9	400	4	4	385	5	8
In	3173	36		2682	38	
Total	6346	72		5364	76	
Rating	70.4			70.8		
Slope	121			123		

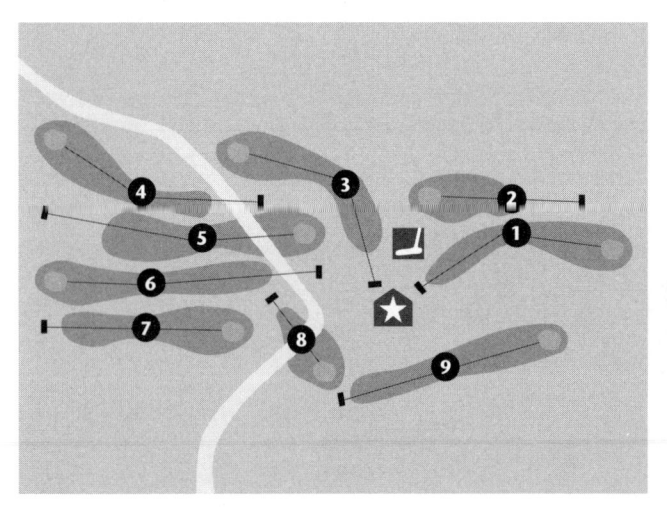

THE MINNESOTA ILLUSTRATED

SILVER BAY COUNTRY CLUB

9 Regulation Semi-Private

P.O. Box 38
Silver Bay, Minnesota 55614
218/226-3111 Clubhouse/Proshop

HOURS	7 am to Dusk
SEASON	May to October

RESERVATIONS	218/226-3111 1 week
	Walk-on: good/fair

GREEN FEES	M-Th	F-S
Adult	$18/12	$18/12
Senior	$18/12	$18/12
Junior	$18/12	$18/12
Twilight	NA	NA

PAYMENT	No credit cards accepted
	Non-local checks accepted

LEAGUES	None

MEMBERSHIPS	USGA, GCSAA, MGA

OWNER	City of Silver Bay
MANAGER	Norma O'Leary
SUPERINTENDENT	Norma O'Leary

FEATURES	
Putting green	Y
Driving range	N
Practice area	Y
Golf carts	
Power (gas)	Y $18/10
Pull carts	Y $2
Club rental	Y $4
Club storage	N
Caddies	N
Proshop	
Basic	Y
Refreshments	
Restaurant	Y
Lounge	Y
Snacks	Y
Clubhouse	
Showers	Y
Lockers	Y
Lodging	N

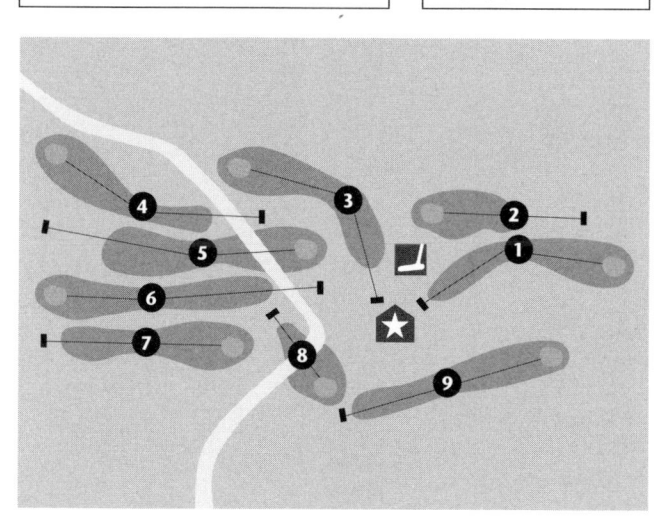

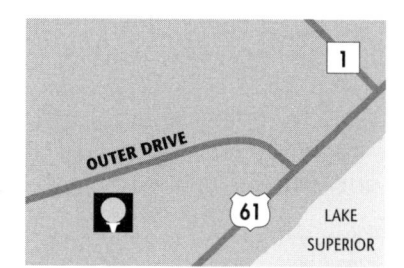

Located in Silver Bay. Course entrance is about one mile west of U.S. Highway 61 on Outer Drive.

	MEN			**WOMEN**		
	FRONT	PAR	HDCP	FRONT	PAR	HDCP
1	378	4	5	295	4	13
2	176	3	15	149	3	11
3	373	4	11	293	4	15
4	432	5	17	358	5	9
5	425	4	1	360	5	5
6	484	5	9	401	5	3
7	347	4	7	334	4	1
8	158	3	13	107	3	17
9	400	4	3	385	5	7
Out	3173	36		2682	38	
1	378	4	6	295	4	14
2	176	3	16	149	3	12
3	373	4	12	293	4	16
4	432	5	18	358	5	10
5	425	4	2	360	5	6
6	484	5	10	401	5	4
7	347	4	8	334	4	2
8	158	3	14	107	3	18
9	400	4	4	385	5	8
In	3173	36		2682	38	
Total	6346	72		5364	76	
Rating	70.4			70.8		
Slope	121			123		

GOLF COURSE DIRECTORY

SILVER SPRINGS GOLF COURSE

GOLD COURSE/18 Regulation Public

West County Road 39, P.O. Box 246
Monticello, Minnesota 55362
612/338-2207 Clubhouse
612/295-2951 Proshop

HOURS	Dawn to Dusk
SEASON	April-November

FEATURES	
Putting green	Y
Driving range	Y
Practice area	N
Golf carts	
Power (elec)	Y
Pull carts	Y
Club rental	Y
Club storage	N
Caddies	N
Proshop	
Extended	Y
Refreshments	
Restaurant	N
Lounge	Y
Snacks	Y
Clubhouse	
Showers	N
Lockers	N
Lodging	N

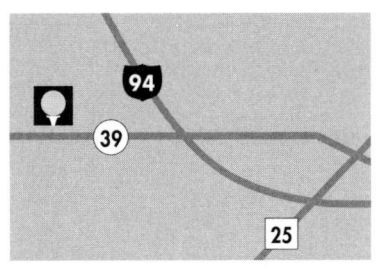

Located in Monticello. Course entrance is about 7 miles west of MN Highway 25 on County Road 39.

	RESERVATIONS	612/295-2951 1 week
		Walk-on: good/fair
GREEN FEES	M-F	S-S
Adult	Call	Call
Senior	Call	Call
Junior	Call	Call
Twilight	NA	NA
PAYMENT	Credit: Visa® MasterCard®	
	Non-local checks accepted	
LEAGUES	Men:	Various
	Women:	Various
MEMBERSHIPS	USGA, MGA	
OWNER	Peter & Pam Dane	
SUPERINTENDENT	Peter Dane	

	MEN					**WOMEN**		
	BACK	FRONT	PAR	HDCP	FRONT	PAR	HDCP
1	496	454	5	10	427	5	10
2	219	203	3	2	157	3	2
3	393	379	4	13	358	4	13
4	397	384	4	14	366	4	14
5	545	530	5	1	457	5	1
6	400	370	4	5	338	4	5
7	132	126	3	9	113	3	9
8	420	407	4	7	330	4	7
9	396	384	4	12	370	4	12
Out	3398	3237	36		2916	36	
10	355	335	4	17	320	4	17
11	162	152	3	8	138	3	8
12	338	331	4	6	322	4	6
13	568	560	5	3	520	5	3
14	375	365	4	15	353	4	15
15	195	183	3	16	170	3	16
16	404	375	4	11	360	4	11
17	380	355	4	18	330	4	18
18	555	545	5	4	530	5	4
In	3332	3201	36		3043	36	
Total	6730	6438	72		5959	72	
Rating	70.3	68.9			71.9		
Slope	108	105			111		

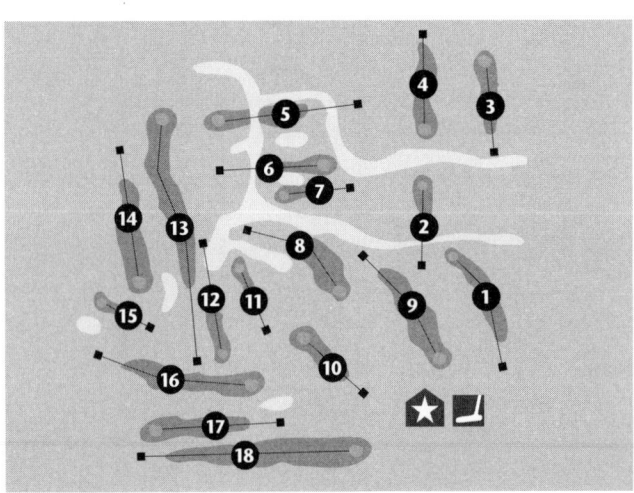

SILVER SPRINGS GOLF COURSE

SILVER COURSE/18 Regulation Public

West County Road 39, P.O. Box 246
Monticello, Minnesota 55362
612/338-2207 Clubhouse
612/295-2951 Proshop

RESERVATIONS	612/295-2951 1 week
	Walk-on: good/fair

GREEN FEES	M-F	S-S
Adult	Call	Call
Senior	Call	Call
Junior	Call	Call
Twilight	NA	NA

PAYMENT	Credit: Visa® MasterCard®
	Non-local checks accepted

LEAGUES	Men: Various
	Women: Various

MEMBERSHIPS	USGA, MGA

OWNER	Peter & Pam Dane
SUPERINTENDENT	Peter Dane

HOURS	Dawn to Dusk
SEASON	April-November

FEATURES	
Putting green	Y
Driving range	Y
Practice area	N
Golf carts	
Power (elec)	Y
Pull carts	Y
Club rental	Y
Club storage	N
Caddies	N
Proshop	
Extended	Y
Refreshments	
Restaurant	N
Lounge	Y
Snacks	Y
Clubhouse	
Showers	N
Lockers	N
Lodging	N

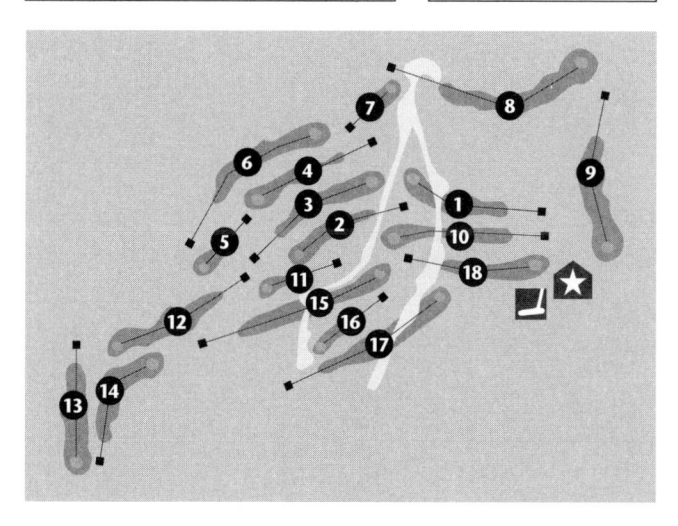

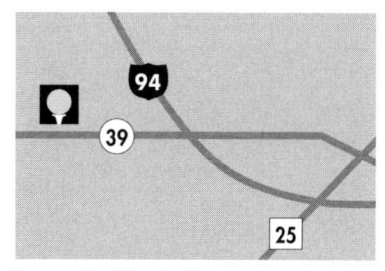

Located in Monticello. Course entrance is about 7 miles west of MN Highway 25 on County Road 39.

		MEN			WOMEN		
	BACK	FRONT	PAR	HDCP	FRONT	PAR	HDCP
1	442	410	4	1	393	4	1
2	420	400	4	3	385	4	3
3	414	396	4	5	378	4	5
4	386	368	4	13	350	4	13
5	183	169	3	17	155	3	17
6	485	471	5	15	440	5	15
7	184	162	3	7	140	3	7
8	505	505	5	9	435	5	9
9	424	408	4	11	392	4	11
Out	3443	3289	36		3068	36	
10	423	406	4	6	385	4	6
11	237	195	3	8	170	3	8
12	425	404	4	14	383	4	14
13	375	358	4	10	345	4	10
14	432	412	4	16	392	4	16
15	530	515	5	2	475	5	2
16	206	189	3	18	150	3	18
17	455	442	5	4	438	5	4
18	430	400	4	12	370	4	12
In	3513	3321	36		3108	36	
Total	6956	6610	72		6176	72	
Rating	71.3	69.8			73.2		
Slope	113	110			118		

GOLF COURSE DIRECTORY

SLAYTON COUNTRY CLUB

9 Regulation Public

Route 2, Highway 59
Slayton, Minnesota 56172
507/836-8154 Clubhouse/Proshop

HOURS 7 am to Dusk

SEASON April to October

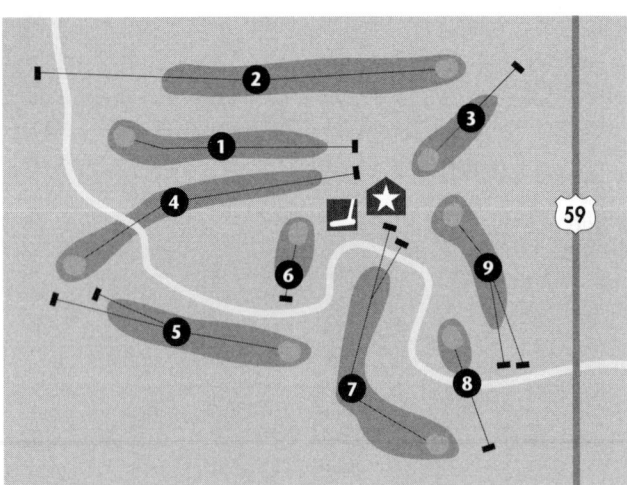

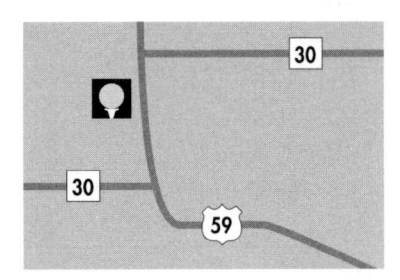

Located north of Slayton. Course is one mile north of Slayton on U.S. Highway 59 / MN Highway 30.

RESERVATIONS	507/836-8154	
	Walk-on: good/fair	
GREEN FEES	M-F	S-S
Adult	$12.50/8.50	$15/11
Senior	$12.50/8.50	$15/11
Junior	$12.50/8.50	$15/11
Twilight	NA	NA
PAYMENT	Credit: Visa® MasterCard®	
	Non-local checks accepted	
LEAGUES	Men: W (noon-dusk)	
	Women: T (noon-dusk)	
MEMBERSHIPS	GCSAA, MGA	
MANAGER	Ken Sagedahl	
SUPERINTENDENT	Sherwood Silvernale	

FEATURES		
Putting green	Y	
Driving range	N	
Practice area	Y	
Golf carts		
Power (gas)	Y	$15/10
Pull carts	Y	$1
Club rental	Y	$2
Club storage	N	
Caddies	N	
Proshop		
Extended	Y	
Refreshments		
Restaurant	N	
Lounge	Y	
Snacks	Y	
Clubhouse		
Showers	Y	
Lockers	Y	
Lodging	N	

	MEN			WOMEN		
	FRONT	PAR	HDCP	FRONT	PAR	HDCP
1	356	4	2	337	4	3
2	477	5	6	402	5	4
3	190	3	3	172	3	5
4	367	4	1	349	4	1
5	317	4	7	265	4	7
6	165	3	8	165	3	6
7	451	5	4	408	5	2
8	184	3	5	107	3	9
9	325	4	9	311	4	8
Out	2832	35		2516	35	
1	356	4	11	337	4	12
2	477	5	15	402	5	13
3	190	3	12	172	3	14
4	367	4	10	349	4	10
5	317	4	16	265	4	16
6	165	3	17	165	3	15
7	451	5	13	408	5	11
8	184	3	14	107	3	18
9	325	4	18	311	4	17
In	2832	35		2516	35	
Total	5664	70		5032	70	
Rating	68.8			70.0		
Slope	124			118		

THE MINNESOTA ILLUSTRATED

SLEEPY EYE GOLF CLUB

9 Regulation Semi-Private

Highway 14 West, P.O. Box 528
Sleepy Eye, Minnesota 56085
507/794-5249 Clubhouse/Proshop

HOURS	7 am to Dusk
SEASON	April-November

RESERVATIONS	507/794-9921 2 days
	Weekends only
	Walk-on: good/good

GREEN FEES	M-F	S-S
Adult	$14/7	$16/10
Senior	$14/7	$16/10
Junior	$14/7	$16/10
Twilight	NA	NA

| **PAYMENT** | No credit cards accepted |
| | Non-local checks accepted |

| **LEAGUES** | Men: Various |
| | Women: Various |

| **MEMBERSHIPS** | USGA, PGA, MGA |

| **MANAGER** | Duane Lee |
| **SUPERINTENDENT** | Arlyn Boddy |

FEATURES		
Putting green	Y	
Driving range	Y	$2-3
Practice area	N	
Golf carts		
Power	Y	$12
Pull carts	Y	$2/1
Club rental	Y	$3
Club storage	N	
Caddies	N	
Proshop		
Extended	Y	
Refreshments		
Restaurant	N	
Lounge	Y	
Snacks	Y	
Clubhouse		
Showers	Y	
Lockers	Y	
Lodging	N	

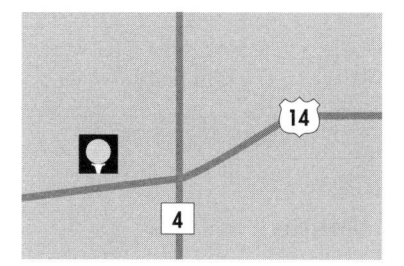

Located west of Sleepy Eye. Course is about 1/4 west MN Highway 4 on U.S. Highway 14.

	MEN			**WOMEN**		
	FRONT	PAR	HDCP	FRONT	PAR	HDCP
1	331	4		326	4	
2	250	4		244	4	
3	495	5		328	5	
4	135	3		129	3	
5	170	3		165	3	
6	313	4		309	4	
7	406	4		362	5	
8	507	5		402	5	
9	363	4		280	4	
Out	2970	36		2545	37	
1	331	4		326	4	
2	250	4		244	4	
3	495	5		328	5	
4	135	3		129	3	
5	170	3		165	3	
6	313	4		309	4	
7	406	4		362	5	
8	507	5		402	5	
9	363	4		280	4	
In	2970	36		2545	37	
Total	5940	72		5090	74	
Rating	68.0			68.8		
Slope	116			114		

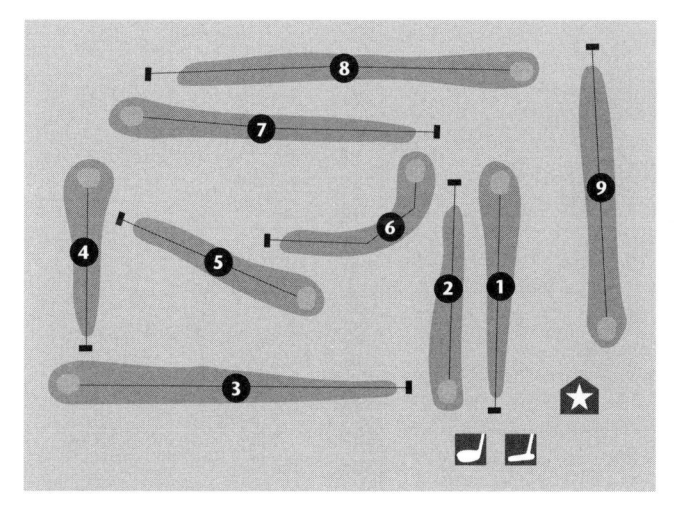

GOLF COURSE DIRECTORY

SOLDIERS MEMORIAL FIELD GOLF COURSE

18 Regulation Public

P.O. Box 1102
Rochester, Minnesota 55903
507/281-6176 Clubhouse/Proshop

RESERVATIONS	507/281-6176	
	Walk-on: good/fair	
GREEN FEES	M-F	S-S
Adult	$15/9	$15/9
Senior	$15/9	$15/9
Junior	$15/9	$15/9
Twilight	NA	NA
PAYMENT	No credit cards accepted	
	Non-local checks accepted	
LEAGUES	Men: Various	
	Women: Various	
MEMBERSHIPS	PGA, MGA	
PROFESSIONAL	Mark Olson	

HOURS	Dawn to Dusk
SEASON	April to October

FEATURES	
Putting green	Y
Driving range	N
Practice area	N
Golf carts	
Power	Y
Pull carts	Y
Club rental	Y
Club storage	N
Caddies	N
Proshop	
Extended	Y
Refreshments	
Restaurant	Y
Lounge	Y
Snacks	Y
Clubhouse	
Showers	N
Lockers	N
Lodging	N

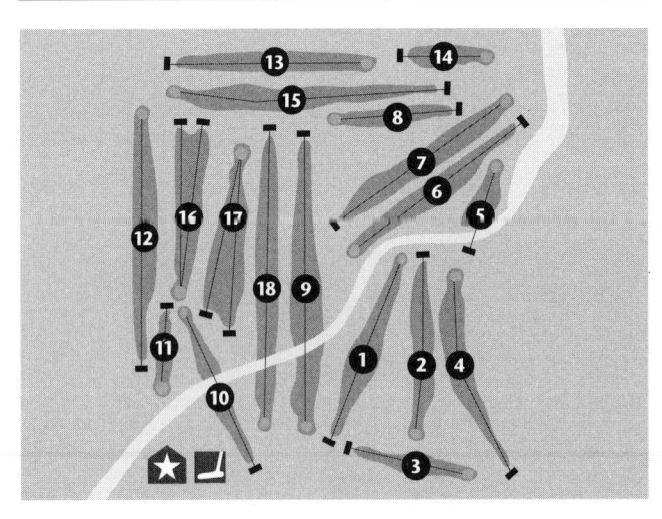

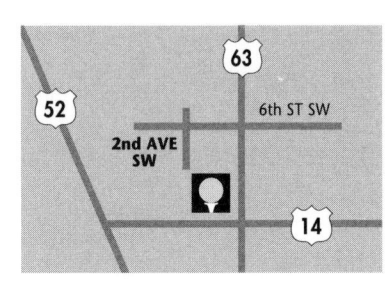

Located in Rochester. Course entrance is west of U.S. Highway 63 on 6th Street SW, then south on 2nd Avenue SW.

	MEN			WOMEN		
	FRONT	PAR	HDCP	FRONT	PAR	HDCP
1	324	4	12	312	4	12
2	308	4	15	296	4	14
3	187	3	14	165	3	15
4	365	4	8	352	4	6
5	165	3	16	150	3	16
6	365	4	6	338	4	10
7	367	4	4	358	4	4
8	212	3	10	182	3	8
9	476	5	2	442	5	2
Out	2769	34		2595	34	
10	277	4	11	221	4	11
11	150	3	17	122	3	17
12	434	4	1	427	5	5
13	355	4	7	342	4	7
14	147	3	18	140	3	18
15	477	5	5	471	5	3
16	287	4	13	275	4	9
17	320	4	9	288	4	13
18	490	5	3	456	5	1
In	2937	36		2742	37	
Total	5706	70		5337	71	
Rating	67.3			70.4		
Slope	118			120		

SOMERSET COUNTRY CLUB

18 Regulation Private

1416 Dodd Road
Mendota Heights, Minnesota 55118
612/457-1416 Clubhouse
612/457-1224 Proshop

RESERVATIONS	612/457-1224	
	Members only	
GREEN FEES	M-F	S-S
Adult	Call	Call
Senior	Call	Call
Junior	Call	Call
Twilight	NA	NA
	Members and guests only	
PAYMENT	No credit cards accepted	
	Non-local checks accepted	
LEAGUES	Men: Various	
	Women: Various	
MEMBERSHIPS	MGA	
PROFESSIONAL	Call	

HOURS	Dawn to Dusk
SEASON	April to October

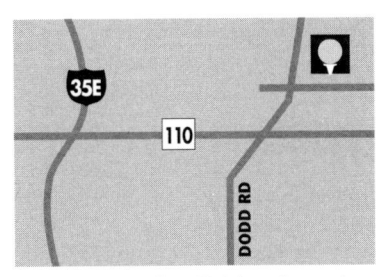

FEATURES

Putting green	Y
Driving range	Y
Practice area	Y
Golf carts	
Power (gas)	Y
Pull carts	Y
Club rental	Y
Club storage	Y
Caddies	Y
Proshop	
Extended	Y
Refreshments	
Restaurant	Y
Lounge	Y
Snacks	Y
Clubhouse	
Showers	Y
Lockers	Y
Lodging	N

Located in Mendota Heights. Course is about two miles north of MN Highway 110 on Dodd Road.

	\multicolumn{3}{c}{MEN}		\multicolumn{3}{c}{WOMEN}	
	BACK	FRONT	PAR	HDCP	FRONT	PAR	HDCP
1	354	351	4	15	308	4	11
2	500	486	5	1	453	8	1
3	424	400	4	7	351	4	5
4	185	177	3	13	156	3	17
5	418	378	4	5	318	4	9
6	429	400	4	3	344	4	7
7	366	354	4	11	326	4	13
8	157	153	3	17	132	3	15
9	539	511	5	9	465	5	3
Out	3372	3210	36		2853	36	
10	384	366	4	6	314	4	12
11	404	394	4	2	376	4	6
12	225	220	3	8	210	4	18
13	513	503	5	14	484	5	4
14	319	312	4	16	245	4	10
15	421	411	4	4	405	5	14
16	478	473	5	12	425	5	2
17	166	161	3	18	140	3	16
18	446	395	4	10	301	4	8
In	3381	3235	36		2900	38	
Total	6753	6445	72		5753	74	
Rating	73.5	72.3			74.8		
Slope	133	130			134		

Course layout map not provided.

GOLF COURSE DIRECTORY

SOUTHERN HILLS GOLF CLUB

18 Regulation Semi-Private

18950 Chippendale Avenue
Farmington, Minnesota 55024
612/463-4653 Clubhouse/Proshop

HOURS	6 am to Dusk
SEASON	April–November

RESERVATIONS	612/463-4653 1 week
	Walk-on: good/poor

GREEN FEES	M-F	S-S
Adult	$17/12	$23/15
Senior	$12.50/8.50	$23/15
Junior	$12.50/8.50	$23/15
Twilight	$8.50 (6pm)	$8.50 (6pm)

PAYMENT	Credit: Visa® MasterCard®
	Local checks only

LEAGUES	Men: Th (pm)
	Women: W (pm), Th (am)

MEMBERSHIPS	USGA, NGF, PGA, GCSAA, MGA

OWNER	NHD Golf Management
SUPERINTENDENT	Martin Terveer
PROFESSIONAL	Randy R. Inouye

FEATURES		
Putting green	Y	
Driving range	Y	$1.75-5
Practice area	Y	
Golf carts		
Power (gas)	Y	$20
Pull carts	Y	$2
Club rental	Y	$10
Club storage	N	
Caddies	N	
Proshop		
Extended	Y	
Refreshments		
Restaurant	N	
Lounge	N	
Snacks	Y	
Clubhouse		
Showers	N	
Lockers	N	
Lodging	N	

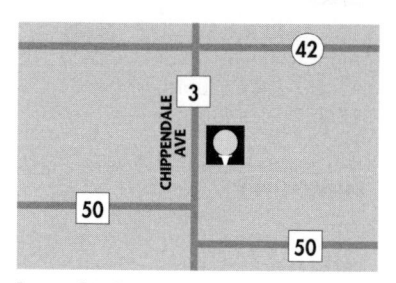

Located in Farmington. Course entrance is three miles south of County Road 42 on MN Highway 3 (Chippendale Ave).

	MEN				**WOMEN**		
	BACK	FRONT	PAR	HDCP	FRONT	PAR	HDCP
1	504	489	5	7	422	5	7
2	194	180	3	9	132	3	9
3	317	297	4	13	240	4	13
4	174	159	3	17	135	3	17
5	369	361	4	11	296	4	11
6	435	421	4	1	316	4	1
7	376	363	4	15	311	4	15
8	206	196	3	5	164	3	5
9	472	462	5	3	403	5	3
Out	3047	2928	35		2419	35	
10	417	411	4	2	341	4	2
11	163	155	3	18	121	3	18
12	547	534	5	6	446	5	6
13	351	339	4	12	258	4	12
14	407	383	4	8	312	4	8
15	147	128	3	16	119	3	16
16	366	358	4	14	277	4	14
17	355	347	4	10	264	4	10
18	514	490	5	4	413	5	4
In	3267	3145	36		2551	36	
Total	6314	6073	71		4970	71	
Rating	70.4	69.2			68.3		
Slope	123	121			116		

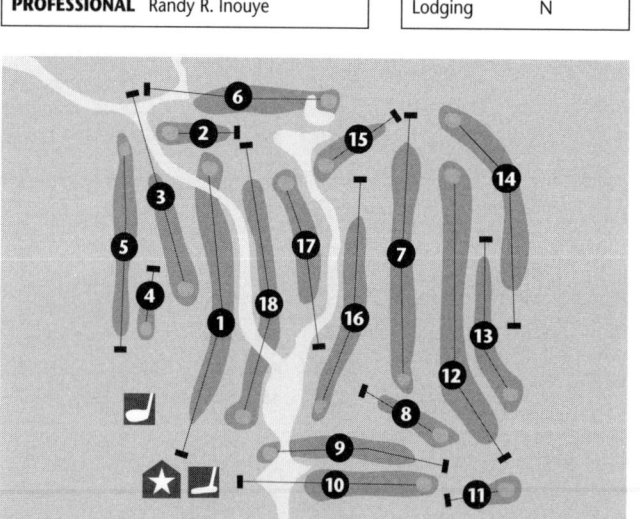

SOUTHVIEW COUNTRY CLUB

18 Regulation Private

239 East Mendota Road
West St. Paul, Minnesota 55118
612/451-6856 Clubhouse
612/451-1169 Proshop

HOURS	7 am to Dusk
SEASON	April to October

RESERVATIONS	612/451-1169 3 days
	Members only

GREEN FEES	M-F	S-S
Adult	$30	$30
Senior	$30	$30
Junior	$30	$30
Twilight	NA	NA
	Members and guests only	

PAYMENT	No credit cards accepted
	Non-local checks accepted

LEAGUES	None

MEMBERSHIPS	USGA, PGA, GCSAA, MGA

MANAGER	Mark McCahey
SUPERINTENDENT	Roger Kisch
PROFESSIONAL	Tom Dolby

FEATURES	
Putting green	Y
Driving range	Y
Practice area	Y
Golf carts	
Power (gas)	Y
Pull carts	Y
Club rental	Y
Club storage	Y
Caddies	Y
Proshop	
Extended	Y
Refreshments	
Restaurant	Y
Lounge	Y
Snacks	Y
Clubhouse	
Showers	Y
Lockers	Y
Lodging	N

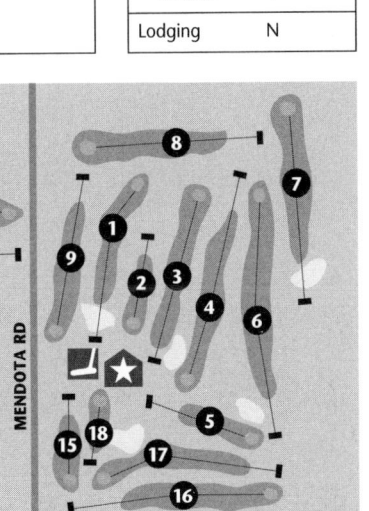

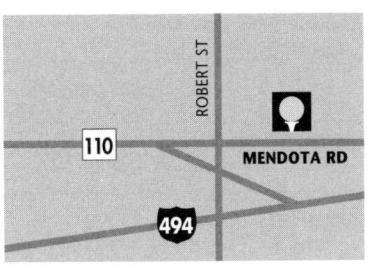

Located in West St. Paul. Course is one mile north of I-494 on Robert Street, then east on Mendota Road.

	MEN				**WOMEN**		
	BACK	FRONT	PAR	HDCP	FRONT	PAR	HDCP
1	361	353	4	3	294	4	11
2	185	166	3	15	166	3	17
3	385	374	4	7	346	4	9
4	490	468	5	17	450	5	3
5	220	220	3	1	211	4	15
6	487	476	5	11	469	5	1
7	396	388	4	5	373	4	5
8	371	362	4	9	350	4	7
9	340	331	4	13	315	4	13
Out	3235	3138	36		2974	37	
10	389	385	4	4	367	5	10
11	160	157	3	16	135	3	14
12	445	423	4	2	320	4	12
13	525	501	5	10	420	5	2
14	505	481	5	14	423	5	4
15	185	175	3	12	172	3	16
16	395	385	4	8	376	4	8
17	342	327	4	6	303	4	6
18	158	147	3	18	141	3	18
In	3104	2981	35		2657	36	
Total	6339	6119	71		5631	73	
Rating	71.4	70.5			73.5		
Slope	130	128			128		

GOLF COURSE DIRECTORY

SPRING BROOK GOLF COURSE

18 Regulation Semi-Private

Route 1, P.O. Box 46
Mora, Minnesota 55051
612/679-2317 Clubhouse/Proshop

RESERVATIONS	612/679-2317 2 days Walk-on: good/fair	
GREEN FEES	M-F	S-S
Adult	$18/12	$20/15
Senior	$18/12	$20/15
Junior	$18/12	$20/15
Twilight	$8 (6 pm)*	$12 (4 pm)
	* Mon and Wed only	
PAYMENT	Credit: Visa® MasterCard® Non-local checks accepted	
LEAGUES	Men: Th Women: T	
MEMBERSHIPS	USGA, PGA, GCSAA, MGA	
MANAGER	Alan Skramstad	
SUPERINTENDENT	Rob Heggernes	
PROFESSIONAL	Scott Heger	

HOURS 7 am to Dusk
SEASON April-November

FEATURES

Putting green	Y	
Driving range	Y	$3
Practice area	Y	
Golf carts		
Power	Y	$20
Pull carts	Y	$1.50
Club rental	Y	$9/6
Club storage	Y	
Caddies	N	
Proshop		
Extended	Y	
Refreshments		
Restaurant	Y	
Lounge	Y	
Snacks	Y	
Clubhouse		
Showers	Y	
Lockers	Y	
Lodging	N	

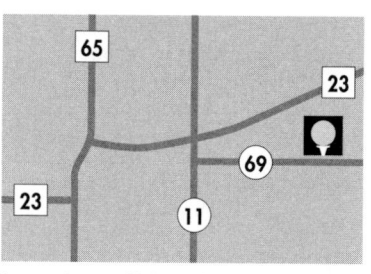

Located east of Mora. Course entrance is 1/4 mile south of MN Hwy 23 on Cty Rd 11, then 1/2 mile east on Cty Rd 69.

	MEN				WOMEN		
	BACK	FRONT	PAR	HDCP	FRONT	PAR	HDCP
1	364	336	4	11	275	4	11
2	137	124	3	17	105	3	17
3	313	301	4	13	265	4	13
4	355	325	4	9	264	4	9
5	561	514	5	3	438	5	3
6	389	380	4	7	313	4	7
7	191	175	3	15	127	3	15
8	512	481	5	5	415	5	5
9	427	408	4	1	361	4	1
Out	3249	3044	36		2563	36	
10	386	370	4	6	290	4	5
11	145	130	3	18	91	3	18
12	427	414	4	2	310	4	2
13	520	507	5	8	424	5	8
14	171	157	3	16	123	3	16
15	373	366	4	14	280	4	14
16	408	389	4	10	304	4	10
17	494	478	5	4	414	5	4
18	455	434	4	6	332	4	6
In	3379	3245	36		2568	36	
Total	6912	6522	72		5084	72	
Rating	73.4	71.8			71.3		
Slope	135	131			129		

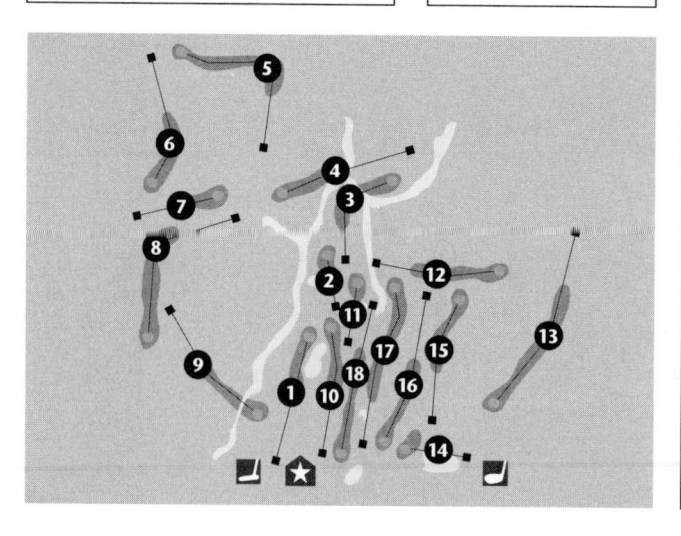

SPRINGFIELD COUNTRY CLUB

9 Regulation Semi-Private

South O'Connell Ave., P.O. Box 74
Springfield, Minnesota 56087
507/723-5888 Clubhouse/Proshop

HOURS	7 am to Dusk
SEASON	April-November

RESERVATIONS	507/723-5888
	Walk-on: good/good

GREEN FEES	M-F	S-S
Adult	$15/9	$20/12
Senior	$15/9	$20/12
Junior	$15/9	$20/12
Twilight	NA	NA

PAYMENT	No credit cards accepted
	Non-local checks accepted

LEAGUES	Men: Th
	Women: W
	Couples: M

MEMBERSHIPS	USGA, GCSAA, MGA

MANAGER	Craig Otto
SUPERINTENDENT	Craig Otto

FEATURES		
Putting green	Y	
Driving range	Y	$1.50
Practice area	N	
Golf carts		
Power	Y	$15/9
Pull carts	Y	
Club rental	Y	
Club storage	N	
Caddies	N	
Proshop		
Extended	Y	
Refreshments		
Restaurant	Y	
Lounge	N	
Snacks	Y	
Clubhouse		
Showers	Y	
Lockers	N	
Lodging	N	

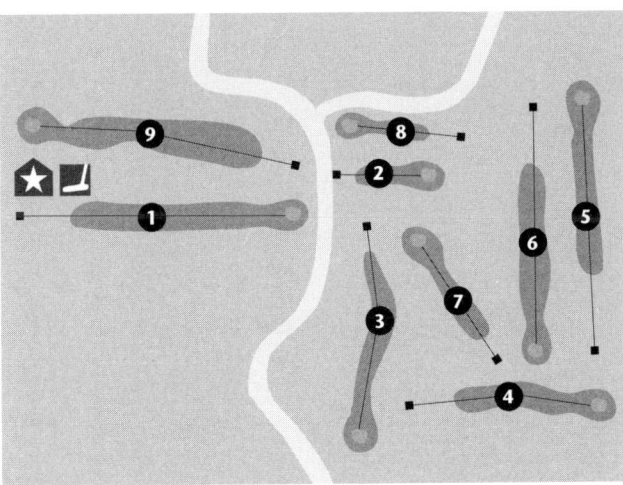

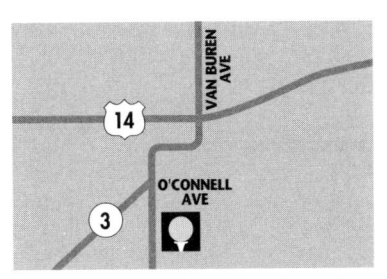

Located in Springfield. Course is south of Hwy 14 on Van Buren Ave, west on Central St, then south O'Connell Ave.

	MEN			**WOMEN**		
	FRONT	PAR	HDCP	FRONT	PAR	HDCP
1	504	5	4	429	5	4
2	143	3	8	137	3	8
3	366	4	2	336	4	2
4	329	4	6	249	4	6
5	380	4	3	310	4	3
6	368	4	5	301	4	5
7	296	4	7	281	4	7
8	135	3	9	117	3	9
9	552	5	1	416	5	1
Out	3073	36		2576	36	
1	504	5	4	429	5	4
2	143	3	8	137	3	8
3	366	4	2	336	4	2
4	329	4	6	249	4	6
5	380	4	3	310	4	3
6	368	4	5	301	4	5
7	296	4	7	281	4	7
8	135	3	9	117	3	9
9	552	5	1	416	5	1
In	3073	36		2576	36	
Total	6146	72		5152	72	
Rating	69.0			68.2		
Slope	122			118		

STILLWATER COUNTRY CLUB

18 Regulation Private

1421 North 4th Street
Stillwater, Minnesota 55082
612/439-7979 Clubhouse/Proshop

HOURS 6:30 am - Dusk
SEASON April-November

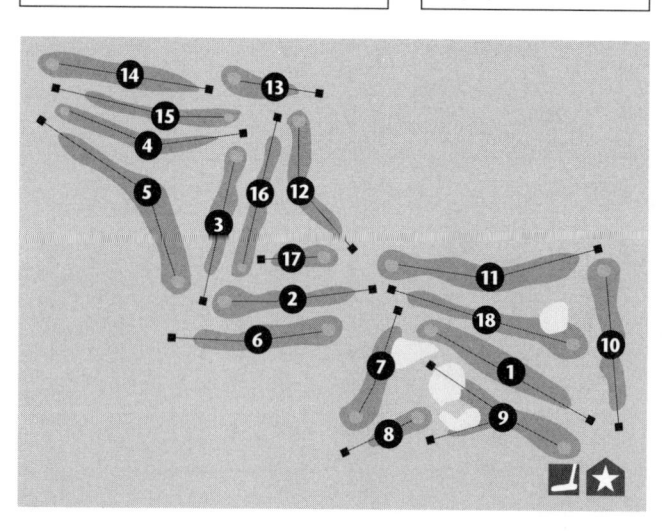

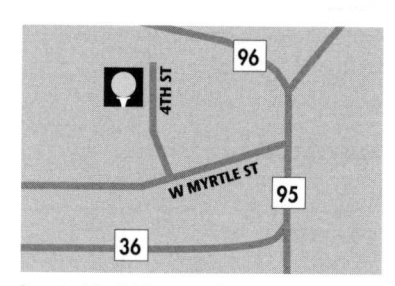

Located in Stillwater. Course entrance is 1/4 mile west on MN Highway 95 on Myrtle Street, then north on 4th Street.

RESERVATIONS	612/439-7979
	Members only

GREEN FEES	M-F	S-S
Adult	$28/15	$35
Senior	$28/15	$35
Junior	$28/15	$35
Twilight	NA	NA
	Members and guests only	

PAYMENT	No credit cards accepted
	Local checks only

LEAGUES	None

MEMBERSHIPS	USGA, PGA, GCSAA, CMAA, MGA

MANAGER	Jim Smith
SUPERINTENDENT	Marlin Murphy
PROFESSIONAL	Mike Tracy

FEATURES

Putting green	Y
Driving range	N
Practice area	Y
Golf carts	
Power (gas)	Y $18
Pull carts	Y
Club rental	N
Club storage	N
Caddies	N
Proshop	
Extended	Y
Refreshments	
Restaurant	Y
Lounge	Y
Snacks	Y
Clubhouse	
Showers	Y
Lockers	N
Lodging	N

	MEN				WOMEN		
	BACK	FRONT	PAR	HDCP	FRONT	PAR	HDCP
1	413	404	4	3	295	4	7
2	371	363	4	9	301	4	11
3	363	355	4	15	282	4	15
4	446	430	4	1	335	4	3
5	509	504	5	11	442	5	1
6	379	369	4	5	299	4	5
7	291	287	4	17	249	4	9
8	173	160	3	13	142	3	13
9	398	383	4	7	288	4	17
Out	3343	3255	36		2633	36	
10	373	363	4	6	356	4	6
11	493	485	5	8	335	4	8
12	360	345	4	10	317	4	12
13	175	175	3	18	125	3	18
14	440	415	4	4	296	4	10
15	435	418	4	2	410	5	4
16	368	348	4	12	304	4	14
17	161	148	3	16	143	3	16
18	524	499	5	14	415	5	2
In	3329	3196	36		2701	36	
Total	6672	6451	72		5334	72	
Rating	72.9	71.9			71.0		
Slope	130	128			127		

THE MINNESOTA ILLUSTRATED

STONEBROOKE GOLF CLUB

18 Regulation Public

2693 South County Road 79
Shakopee, Minnesota 55379
612/496-3171 Clubhouse/Proshop

HOURS 7 am to Dusk
SEASON April to October

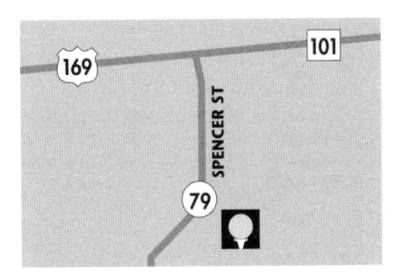

Located south of Shakopee. Course is three miles south of MN Highway 101 on Spencer Street (County Road 79).

RESERVATIONS	612/496-3171 3 days	
	Walk-on: fair/poor	
GREEN FEES	M-Th	F-S
Adult	$24/16	$30/16
Senior	$24/16	$30/16
Junior	$24/16	$30/16
Twilight	NA	NA
PAYMENT	Credit: Visa® MasterCard®	
	Local checks only	
LEAGUES	Men: Th (4-6 pm)	
	Women: T (5-6 pm)	
MEMBERSHIPS	USGA, NGF, PGA, GCSAA,	
	CMAA, MGA	
OWNER	Tom L. Haugen	
SUPERINTENDENT	Duane Slaughter	
PROFESSIONAL	Einar Odland	

FEATURES		
Putting green	Y	
Driving range	Y	$3.50-6
Practice area	Y	
Golf carts		
Power (gas)	Y	$22
Pull carts	Y	$3.50
Club rental	Y	$14
Club storage	Y	
Caddies	N	
Proshop		
Extended	Y	
Refreshments		
Restaurant	N	
Lounge	Y	
Snacks	Y	
Clubhouse		
Showers	Y	
Lockers	Y	
Lodging	N	

	MEN				WOMEN		
	BACK	FRONT	PAR	HDCP	FRONT	PAR	HDCP
1	545	512	5	4	440	5	4
2	168	155	3	16	129	3	16
3	367	344	4	14	310	4	14
4	172	153	3	12	136	3	12
5	550	519	5	2	377	5	2
6	415	373	4	8	325	4	8
7	148	125	3	18	110	3	18
8	406	355	4	10	195	4	10
9	411	379	4	6	346	4	6
Out	3181	2915	35		2368	35	
10	351	332	4	15	309	4	15
11	229	187	3	9	152	3	9
12	526	494	5	7	405	5	7
13	188	165	3	17	141	3	17
14	410	383	4	5	334	4	5
15	404	377	4	3	291	4	3
16	327	301	4	13	278	4	13
17	595	533	5	1	444	5	1
18	393	382	4	11	311	4	11
In	3423	3154	36		2665	36	
Total	6604	6069	71		5033	71	
Rating	72.0	69.4			68.9		
Slope	127	122			118		

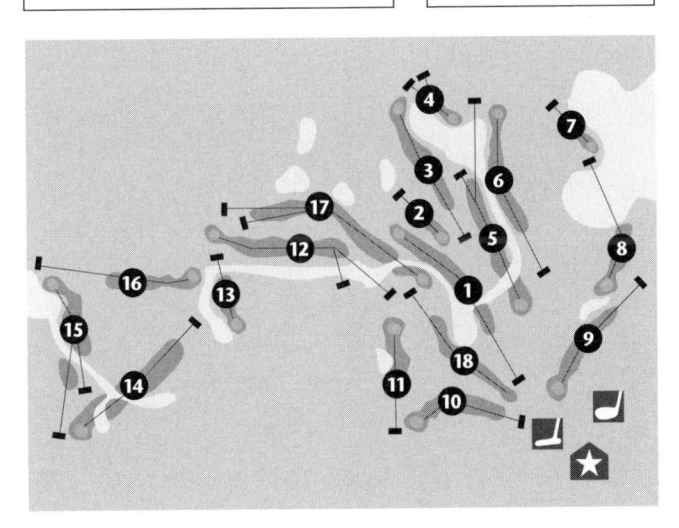

GOLF COURSE DIRECTORY

SUGARBROOKE GOLF COURSE

18 Regulation Public

Ruttger's Sugar Lake Lodge
1000 Otis Lane, P.O. Box 847
Cohasset, Minnesota 55721
218/327-1462 Clubhouse/Proshop

RESERVATIONS	218/327-1462 1 week	
	Walk-on: good/fair	
GREEN FEES	M-F	S-S
Adult	$26/16	$20/16
Senior	$26/16	$20/16
Junior	$26/16	$20/16
Twilight	$15	$15
PAYMENT	Credit: Visa® MC® Am\Ex®	
	Non-local checks accepted	
LEAGUES	None	
MEMBERSHIPS	USGA, PGA, GCSAA, MGA	
OWNER	Fred Bobich	
MANAGER	John Kellin	
SUPERINTENDENT	Steve Ross	
PROFESSIONAL	John Kellin	

HOURS Dawn to Dusk

SEASON April-November

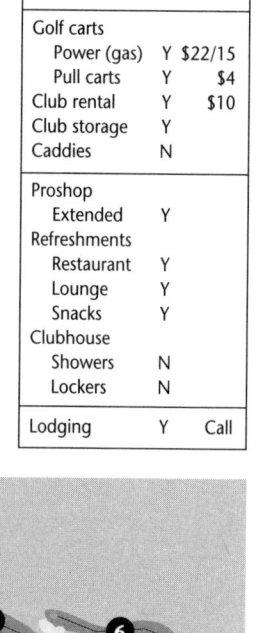

FEATURES		
Putting green	Y	
Driving range	Y	$3.50
Practice area	Y	
Golf carts		
Power (gas)	Y	$22/15
Pull carts	Y	$4
Club rental	Y	$10
Club storage	Y	
Caddies	N	
Proshop		
Extended	Y	
Refreshments		
Restaurant	Y	
Lounge	Y	
Snacks	Y	
Clubhouse		
Showers	N	
Lockers	N	
Lodging	Y	Call

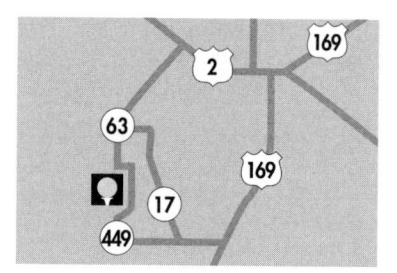

Located south of Cohasset. Course is west of U.S. Hwy 169 on Cty Rd 17, west on Cty Rd 449, then west on Otis Lane.

	MEN				**WOMEN**		
	BACK	FRONT	PAR	HDCP	FRONT	PAR	HDCP
1	404	389	4	9	316	4	5
2	571	549	5	1	473	5	1
3	414	397	4	5	301	4	9
4	353	326	4	13	270	4	15
5	225	211	3	7	163	3	13
6	470	467	5	15	389	5	7
7	424	405	4	3	338	4	3
8	357	342	4	11	276	4	11
9	163	150	3	17	103	3	17
Out	3381	3236	36		2629	36	
10	415	399	4	8	334	4	8
11	374	348	4	10	273	4	10
12	545	525	5	4	435	5	2
13	365	345	4	12	270	4	12
14	315	295	4	16	230	4	14
15	140	130	3	18	110	3	16
16	460	450	4	2	430	4	4
17	162	147	3	14	105	3	18
18	377	366	4	6	322	4	6
In	3153	3005	35		2509	35	
Total	6534	6241	71		5138	71	
Rating	71.5	69.9			68.8		
Slope	124	120			120		

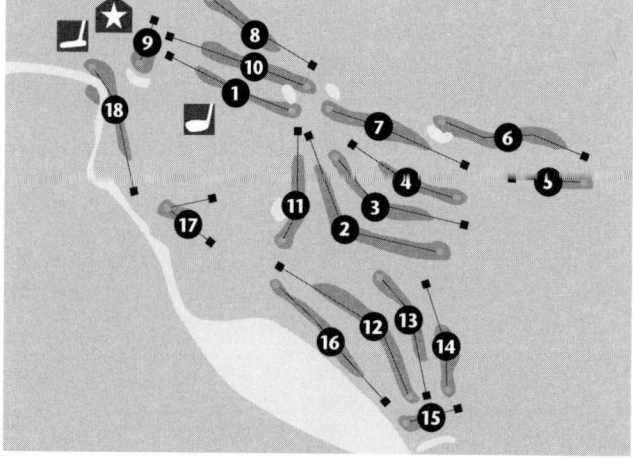

360

THE MINNESOTA ILLUSTRATED

SUNDANCE GOLF CLUB

18 Regulation Public

15240 North 113th Avenue
Maple Grove, Minnesota 55369
612/420-4800 Clubhouse
612/420-4700 Proshop

RESERVATIONS	612/420-4700 4 days
	Walk-on: fair/poor

GREEN FEES	M-F	S-S
Adult	$19/12	$22/13
Senior	$10/7	$22/13
Junior	$10/7	$22/13
Twilight	NA	NA

PAYMENT	Credit: Visa® MasterCard®
	Non-local checks accepted

LEAGUES	None

MEMBERSHIPS	USGA, PGA, GCSAA, MGA

OWNER	John Pierson, Bob Allen
SUPERINTENDENT	Rick Koring
PROFESSIONAL	David Leyse

HOURS 6 am to Dusk
SEASON April-November

FEATURES

Putting green	Y
Driving range	Y
Practice area	N
Golf carts	
Power (gas)	Y
Pull carts	Y
Club rental	Y
Club storage	N
Caddies	N
Proshop	
Extended	Y
Refreshments	
Restaurant	Y
Lounge	Y
Snacks	Y
Clubhouse	
Showers	Y
Lockers	Y
Lodging	N

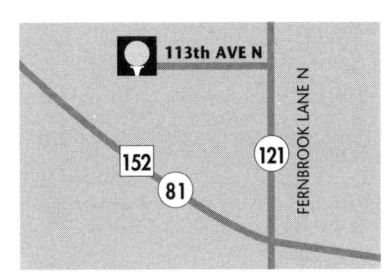

Located in Maple Grove. Course is north of County Road 81 on County Road 121, then 1/2 mile west on 113th Avenue.

	MEN				WOMEN		
	BACK	FRONT	PAR	HDCP	FRONT	PAR	HDCP
1	435	425	4	1	381	5	5
2	194	185	3	5	125	3	13
3	324	315	4	9	250	4	15
4	340	327	4	15	280	4	9
5	332	322	4	11	305	4	3
6	492	479	5	7	480	5	1
7	380	365	4	3	320	4	7
8	347	320	4	13	274	4	11
9	281	270	4	17	245	4	17
Out	3125	3008	36		2660	37	
10	330	322	4	14	250	4	14
11	155	145	3	16	114	3	18
12	395	389	4	4	365	4	4
13	401	395	4	8	325	4	8
14	568	561	5	10	501	5	10
15	425	379	4	2	338	4	6
16	359	328	4	12	320	4	12
17	134	120	3	18	100	3	16
18	554	543	5	6	535	5	2
In	3321	3182	36		2888	36	
Total	6446	6190	72		5548	73	
Rating	71.1	70.0			72.5		
Slope	129	127			129		

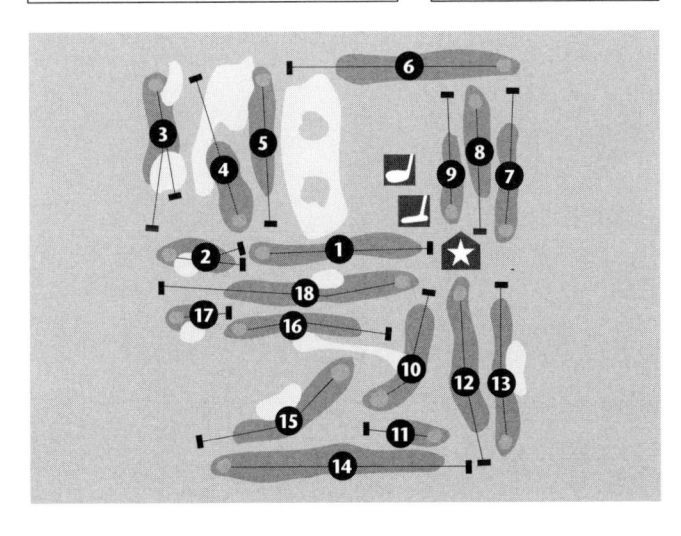

SUPERIOR NATIONAL AT LUTSEN

18 Regulation Public

P.O. Box 177
Lutsen, Minnesota 55612
218/663-7195 Clubhouse/Proshop

RESERVATIONS	218/663-7195
	Walk-on: good/poor

GREEN FEES	M-Th	F-S
Adult	$37/22	$37/22
Senior	$37/22	$37/22
Junior	$37/22	$37/22
Twilight	NA	NA
	Reduced fees M-Th (before June 13 or after October 1)	

PAYMENT	Credit: Visa® MasterCard®
	Non-local checks accepted

LEAGUES	Men: Th (pm)
	Women: Th (am)

MEMBERSHIPS	USGA, NGF, PGA, GCSAA, MGA

SUPERINTENDENT	Mike Davies
PROFESSIONAL	Gred Leland

HOURS	7 am to Dusk
SEASON	May-November

FEATURES		
Putting green	Y	
Driving range	Y	$2-3
Practice area	Y	
Golf carts		
Power (gas)	Y	$27/17
Pull carts	Y	$3/2
Club rental	Y	$6
Club storage	N	
Caddies	N	
Proshop		
Extended	Y	
Refreshments		
Restaurant	Y	
Lounge	N	
Snacks	Y	
Clubhouse		
Showers	N	
Lockers	N	
Lodging	N	

Located about 1/8 mile south of Lutsen. Course entrance is west of U.S. Highway 61 on Golf Course Road.

	MEN				**WOMEN**		
	BACK	FRONT	PAR	HDCP	FRONT	PAR	HDCP
1	401	371	4	5	332	4	5
2	142	130	3	17	119	3	17
3	347	329	4	11	315	4	11
4	361	332	4	1	277	4	1
5	495	478	5	7	411	5	7
6	174	160	3	15	136	3	15
7	351	331	4	13	233	4	13
8	496	480	5	3	425	5	3
9	321	290	4	9	252	4	9
Out	3088	2901	36		2500	36	
10	383	369	4	18	329	4	18
11	203	189	3	8	167	3	8
12	483	475	5	6	401	5	6
13	380	368	4	4	333	4	4
14	409	398	4	14	295	4	14
15	472	452	5	12	390	5	12
16	387	372	4	2	322	4	2
17	143	133	3	16	122	3	16
18	375	352	4	10	315	4	10
In	3235	3108	36		2674	36	
Total	6323	6009	72		5174	72	
Rating	71.5	70.0			70.6		
Slope	130	127			125		

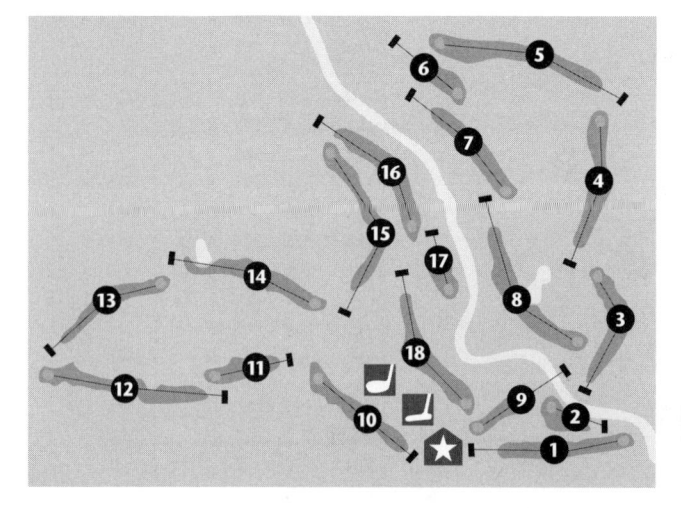

SUPERIOR NATIONAL AT LUTSEN

18 Regulation Public

P.O. Box 177
Lutsen, Minnesota 55612
218/663-7195 Clubhouse/Proshop

HOURS	7 am to Dusk
SEASON	May-November

RESERVATIONS	218/663-7195
	Walk-on: good/poor

GREEN FEES	M-Th	F-S
Adult	$37/22	$37/22
Senior	$37/22	$37/22
Junior	$37/22	$37/22
Twilight	NA	NA
	Reduced fees M-Th (before June 13 or after October 1)	

PAYMENT	Credit: Visa® MasterCard® Non-local checks accepted

LEAGUES	Men: Th (pm)
	Women: Th (am)

MEMBERSHIPS	USGA, NGF, PGA, GCSAA, MGA

SUPERINTENDENT Mike Davies
PROFESSIONAL Gred Leland

FEATURES		
Putting green	Y	
Driving range	Y	$2-3
Practice area	Y	
Golf carts		
Power (gas)	Y	$27/17
Pull carts	Y	$3/2
Club rental	Y	$6
Club storage	N	
Caddies	N	
Proshop		
Extended	Y	
Refreshments		
Restaurant	Y	
Lounge	N	
Snacks	Y	
Clubhouse		
Showers	N	
Lockers	N	
Lodging	N	

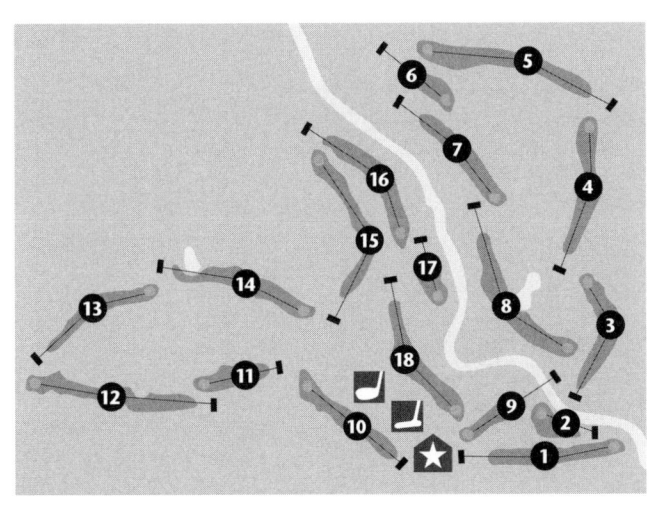

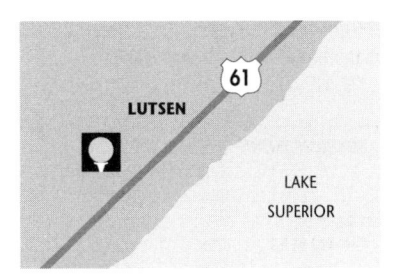

Located about 1/8 mile south of Lutsen. Course entrance is west of U.S. Highway 61 on Golf Course Road.

	MEN				**WOMEN**		
	BACK	FRONT	PAR	HDCP	FRONT	PAR	HDCP
1	401	371	4	5	332	4	5
2	142	130	3	17	119	3	17
3	347	329	4	11	315	4	11
4	361	332	4	1	277	4	1
5	495	478	5	7	411	5	7
6	174	160	3	15	136	3	15
7	351	331	4	13	233	4	13
8	496	480	5	3	425	5	3
9	321	290	4	9	252	4	9
Out	3088	2901	36		2500	36	
10	383	369	4	18	329	4	18
11	203	189	3	8	167	3	8
12	483	475	5	6	401	5	6
13	380	368	4	4	333	4	4
14	409	398	4	14	295	4	14
15	472	452	5	12	390	5	12
16	387	372	4	2	322	4	2
17	143	133	3	16	122	3	16
18	375	352	4	10	315	4	10
In	3235	3108	36		2674	36	
Total	6323	6009	72		5174	72	
Rating	71.5	70.0			70.6		
Slope	130	127			125		

GOLF COURSE DIRECTORY

TERRACE VIEW GOLF CLUB

9 Regulation/9 Par-3 Public

Highway 22 South, P.O. Box 3225
Mankato, Minnesota 56001
507/625-7665 Clubhouse/Proshop

HOURS	7 am to Dusk
SEASON	April-November

RESERVATIONS	507/625-7665 2 days	
	Regulation course only	
	Walk-on: good/fair	
GREEN FEES	M-F	S-S
Adult	$14/8.50	$16/9.50
Senior	$14/8.50	$16/9.50
Junior	$14/8.50	$16/9.50
Twilight	NA	$12 (4 pm)
	Prices for Regulation/Exec	
PAYMENT	Credit: Visa® MasterCard®	
	Non-local checks accepted	
LEAGUES	Men: W (pm)	
	Women: M (am)	
MEMBERSHIPS	USGA, PGA, GCSAA, MGA	
MANAGER	Jerry Carpenter	
SUPERINTENDENT	Dennis Owen	
PROFESSIONAL	Jerry Carpenter	

FEATURES		
Putting green	Y	
Driving range	Y	$2.50
Practice area	Y	
Golf carts		
Power (gas)	Y	$8
Pull carts	Y	$1.75
Club rental	Y	$4
Club storage	Y	$35/yr
Caddies	N	
Proshop		
Extended	Y	
Refreshments		
Restaurant	N	
Lounge	N	
Snacks	Y	
Clubhouse		
Showers	Y	
Lockers	Y	$35/yr
Lodging	N	

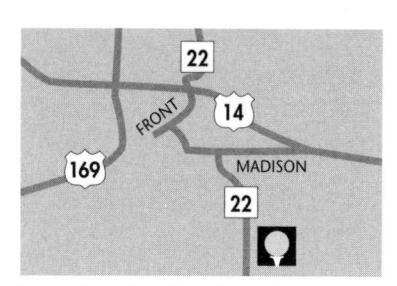

Located south of Mankato. Course is about 5 miles south of U.S. Highway 14 on MN Highway 22.

	MEN				**WOMEN**		
	BACK	FRONT	PAR	HDCP	FRONT	PAR	HDCP
1	333	313	4	13	246	4	13
2	511	476	5	9	402	5	9
3	353	330	4	15	264	4	15
4	380	355	4	7	282	4	7
5	137	129	3	17	109	3	17
6	535	509	5	3	405	5	3
7	439	409	4	1	318	4	1
8	197	177	3	11	131	3	11
9	419	395	4	5	307	4	5
REG	3304	3093	36		2464	36	
Rating	71.0	69.0			68.0		
Slope	118	114			110		
1	125	120	3	8	115	3	8
2	146	140	3	4	113	3	4
3	217	187	3	2	127	3	2
4	155	143	3	7	126	3	7
5	128	126	3	6	115	3	6
6	120	115	3	9	105	3	9
7	182	175	3	3	155	3	3
8	138	132	3	5	117	3	5
9	231	192	3	1	147	3	1
EXEC	1442	1330	27		1120	27	
Rating	52.9	52.0			51.8		
Slope	68	66			65		

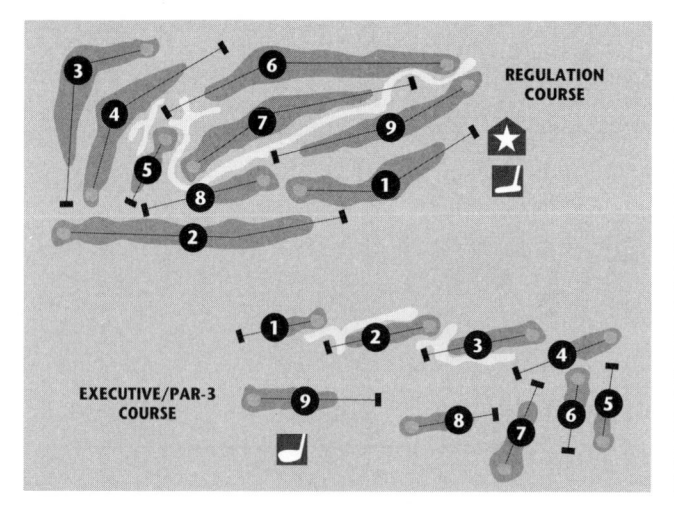

THIEF RIVER GOLF CLUB

18 Regulation Semi-Private

Highway 32 North
Thief River Falls, Minnesota 56701
218/681-2955 Clubhouse/Proshop

HOURS	7 am to Dusk
SEASON	April to October

RESERVATIONS	218/681-2955 4 days
	Walk-on: fair/fair

GREEN FEES	M-F	S-S
Adult	$21/11	$21/11
Senior	$21/11	$21/11
Junior	$21/11	$21/11
Twilight	NA	NA

PAYMENT	Credit: Visa® MasterCard®
	Non-local checks accepted

LEAGUES	Various

MEMBERSHIPS	USGA, NGF, PGA, GCSAA, MGA

MANAGER	Jim Lawrence
SUPERINTENDENT	Chuck Tuthil
PROFESSIONAL	Jim Lawrence

FEATURES	
Putting green	Y
Driving range	Y
Practice area	Y
Golf carts	
Power	Y
Pull carts	Y
Club rental	Y
Club storage	Y
Caddies	N
Proshop	
Extended	Y
Refreshments	
Restaurant	Y
Lounge	Y
Snacks	Y
Clubhouse	
Showers	Y
Lockers	Y
Lodging	N

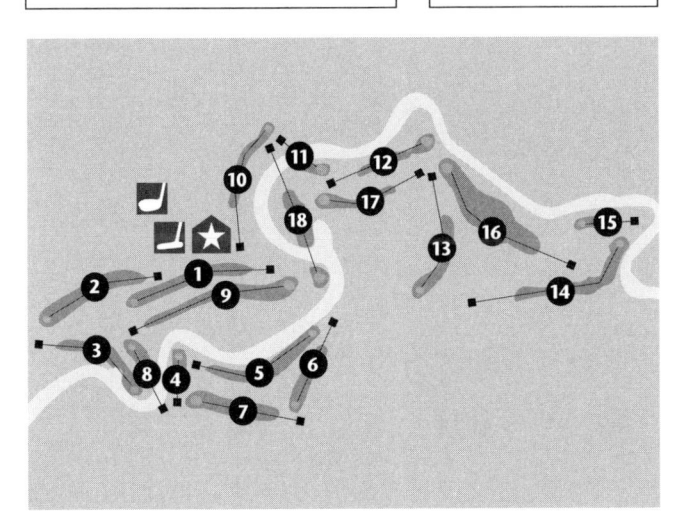

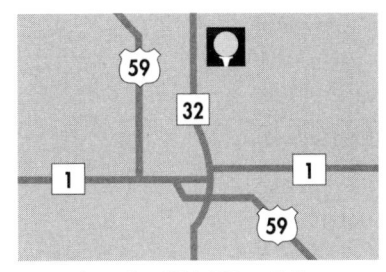

Located north of Thief River Falls. Course entrance is about 2 miles north of MN Highway 1 on MN Highway 32.

	MEN			WOMEN		
	FRONT	PAR	HDCP	FRONT	PAR	HDCP
1	397	4	4	397	5	12
2	368	4	15	368	4	6
3	356	4	11	356	4	3
4	146	3	13	107	3	17
5	414	5	17	414	5	7
6	254	4	18	254	4	14
7	367	4	10	309	4	10
8	206	3	6	206	4	15
9	519	5	12	444	5	8
Out	3027	36		2855	38	
10	332	4	8	313	4	4
11	143	3	14	81	3	18
12	344	4	3	317	4	2
13	365	4	9	321	4	9
14	570	5	2	548	6	5
15	128	3	16	118	3	16
16	532	5	7	457	5	1
17	322	4	5	274	4	13
18	351	4	1	305	5	11
In	3087	36		2734	38	
Total	6114	72		5589	76	
Rating	69.5			72.3		
Slope	118			123		

GOLF COURSE DIRECTORY

TIANNA COUNTRY CLUB

18 Regulation Semi-Private

P.O. Box 177
Walker, Minnesota 56484
218/547-1712 Clubhouse/Proshop

HOURS 6:30 am to Dusk
SEASON April-November

RESERVATIONS	218/547-1712	
	Walk-on: good/good	
GREEN FEES	M-F	S-S
Adult	$20/13	$20
Senior	$20/13	$20
Junior	$20/13	$20
Twilight	$13	$13
PAYMENT	Credit: Visa® MC® AmEx®	
	Non-local checks accepted	
LEAGUES	Men: M (am)	
	Women: T & Th (am)	
	Couples: Sun (4 pm)	
MEMBERSHIPS	USGA, NGF, GCSAA, MGA	
MANAGER	John & Thea Johnson	
SUPERINTENDENT	William Cox	

FEATURES		
Putting green	Y	
Driving range	Y	$2.50
Practice area	Y	
Golf carts		
Power (gas)	Y	$20/13
Pull carts	Y	$2
Club rental	Y	$4
Club storage	Y	
Caddies	N	
Proshop		
Extended	Y	
Refreshments		
Restaurant	Y	
Lounge	Y	
Snacks	Y	
Clubhouse		
Showers	Y	
Lockers	Y	
Lodging	N	

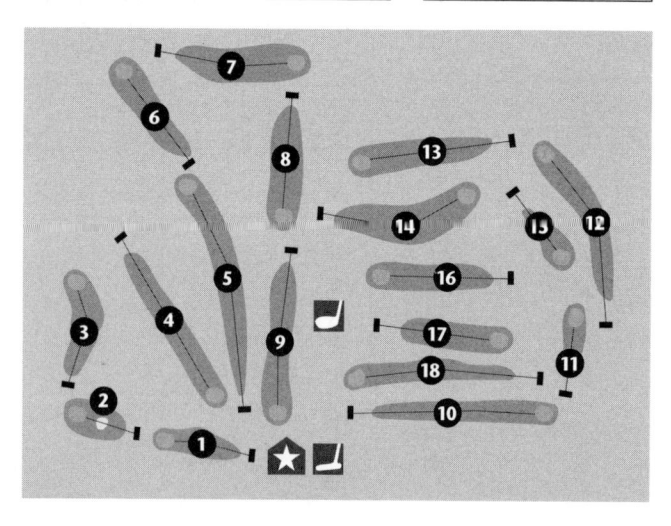

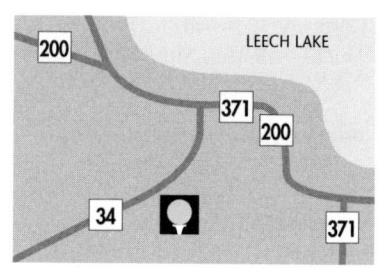

Located south of Walker. Course is 1 1/2 miles south of MN Highway 371/200 on MN Highway 34.

	MEN				WOMEN		
	BACK	FRONT	PAR	HDCP	FRONT	PAR	HDCP
1	306	296	4	16	286	4	13
2	177	170	3	18	153	3	17
3	271	268	4	14	254	4	15
4	435	429	4	2	413	5	3
5	540	531	5	6	514	5	1
6	270	264	4	12	226	4	9
7	330	316	4	8	300	4	7
8	277	270	4	10	240	4	11
9	422	410	4	4	395	5	5
Out	3028	2954	36		2781	38	
10	545	527	5	9	447	5	8
11	184	170	3	17	147	3	18
12	443	418	4	1	374	4	2
13	419	399	4	5	386	4	4
14	387	371	4	7	249	4	10
15	184	167	3	15	151	3	16
16	413	398	4	3	383	4	6
17	409	397	4	13	321	4	14
18	538	522	5	11	442	5	12
In	3522	3369	36		2900	36	
Total	6550	6323	72		5681	74	
Rating	72.0	71.0			73.5		
Slope	127	125			127		

THE MINNESOTA ILLUSTRATED

TIMBER CREEK GOLF COURSE

18 Regulation Public

9750 County Road 24
Watertown, Minnesota 55388
612/446-1415 Clubhouse/Proshop

HOURS	Dawn to Dusk
SEASON	April–November

RESERVATIONS	612/446-1415 4 days
	Walk-on: fair/fair

GREEN FEES	M-F	S-S
Adult	$14/10	$18/12
Senior	$14/10	$18/12
Junior	$14/10	$18/12
Twilight	NA	NA

PAYMENT	No credit cards accepted
	Non-local checks accepted

LEAGUES	Men: Various
	Women: Various

MEMBERSHIPS USGA, MGA

PROFESSIONAL Steve Haagenson

FEATURES		
Putting green	Y	
Driving range	Y	$4
Practice area	Y	
Golf carts		
Power (gas)	Y	$18/10
Pull carts	Y	$1.50
Club rental	Y	$5
Club storage	N	
Caddies	N	
Proshop		
Extended	Y	
Refreshments		
Restaurant	N	
Lounge	N	
Snacks	Y	
Clubhouse		
Showers	Y	
Lockers	Y	
Lodging	N	

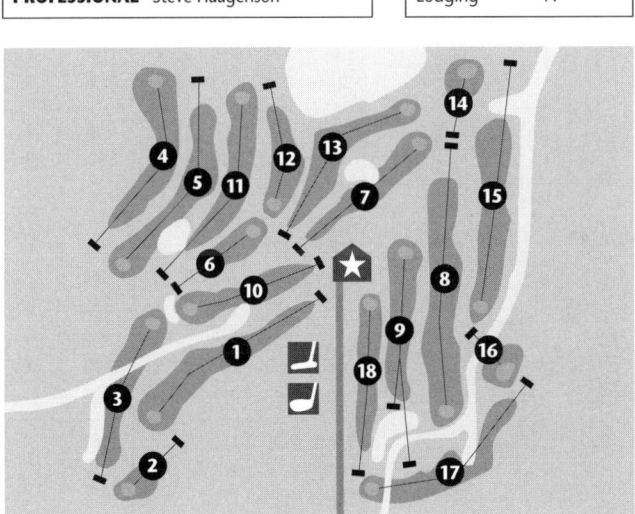

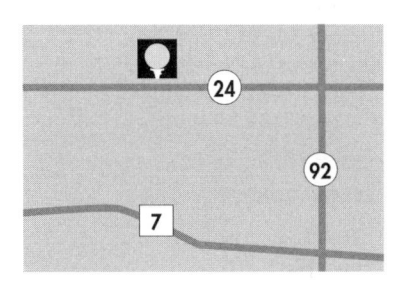

Located in Watertown. Course is 3 1/4 miles north of MN Hwy 7 on Cty Rd 92, then west 1 1/4 miles on Cty Rd 24.

		MEN			WOMEN		
	BACK	FRONT	PAR	HDCP	FRONT	PAR	HDCP
1	477	470	5	13	445	5	7
2	205	180	3	9	160	3	5
3	410	400	4	1	310	4	1
4	415	385	4	3	345	4	3
5	385	375	4	15	290	4	17
6	160	140	3	17	130	3	15
7	400	395	4	7	340	4	13
8	515	498	5	11	435	5	9
9	385	380	4	5	335	4	11
Out	3352	3223	36		2790	36	
10	376	360	4	10	346	4	8
11	354	350	4	4	295	4	10
12	344	334	4	14	300	4	16
13	465	455	5	8	415	5	12
14	200	165	3	16	140	3	14
15	540	480	5	12	430	5	6
16	160	140	3	18	120	3	18
17	406	365	4	2	310	4	2
18	410	400	4	6	310	4	4
In	3255	3049	36		2666	36	
Total	6607	6272	72		5456	72	
Rating	72.4	70.8			71.3		
Slope	132	129			125		

GOLF COURSE DIRECTORY

TIPSINAH MOUNDS COUNTRY CLUB

9 Regulation Public

County Road 24, P.O. Box 172
Elbow Lake, Minnesota 56531
218/685-4271 Clubhouse
800/660-8642 Proshop

HOURS	Dawn to Dusk
SEASON	April to October

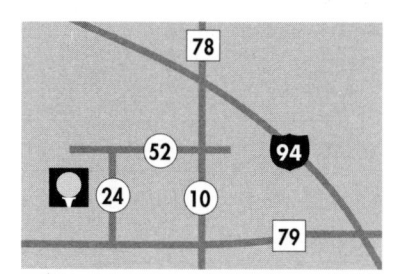

Located east of Elbow Lake. Course is 8 miles west of I-94 (Exit 82) on MN Hwy 79, then north on Golf Course Road.

RESERVATIONS	800/660-8642
	Walk-on: good/fair

GREEN FEES	M-F	S-S
Adult	$17/9.50	$17/10.50
Senior	$17/9.50	$17/10.50
Junior	$6/3*	$17/10.50
Twilight	$8 (5 pm)	$8 (5 pm)

* 10:30am-1:30 pm only
10-round cards available

PAYMENT	No credit cards accepted
	Non-local checks accepted
LEAGUES	Various
MEMBERSHIPS	USGA, NGF, PGA, GCSAA, MGA
MANAGER	Jan Ellingson

FEATURES		
Putting green	Y	
Driving range	Y	$2.25
Practice area	N	
Golf carts		
Power (gas)	Y	$16/11
Pull carts	Y	$1
Club rental	Y	$2.50
Club storage	Y	$15
Caddies	N	
Proshop		
Extended	Y	
Refreshments		
Restaurant	N	
Lounge	N	
Snacks	Y	
Clubhouse		
Showers	N	
Lockers	Y	
Lodging	N	

POMME DE TERRE LAKE

	MEN				WOMEN		
	BACK	FRONT	PAR	HDCP	FRONT	PAR	HDCP
1	390	380	4	8	325	4	8
2	355	340	4	9	275	4	9
3	190	185	3	7	135	3	7
4	525	510	5	5	410	5	5
5	420	400	4	1	320	4	1
6	405	385	4	2	305	4	2
7	195	190	3	3	135	3	3
8	510	495	5	6	385	5	6
9	175	170	3	4	140	3	4
Out	3165	3055	35		2430	35	
1	390	380	4	8	325	4	8
2	355	340	4	9	275	4	9
3	190	185	3	7	135	3	7
4	525	510	5	5	410	5	5
5	420	400	4	1	320	4	1
6	405	385	4	2	305	4	2
7	195	190	3	3	135	3	3
8	510	495	5	6	385	5	6
9	175	170	3	4	140	3	4
In	3165	3055	35		2430	35	
Total	6330	6110	70		4860	70	
Rating	69.8	68.8			67.2		
Slope	113	111			111		

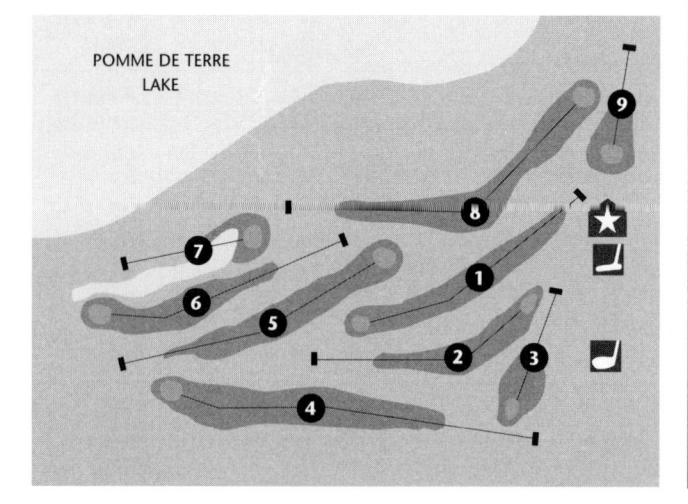

TOWN & COUNTRY CLUB

18 Regulation Private

2279 Marshall Avenue
St. Paul, Minnesota 55104
612/646-7121 Clubhouse
612/659-2549 Proshop

RESERVATIONS	No reservations accepted
	Members only

GREEN FEES	M-F	S-S
Adult	$40	$40
Senior	$40	$40
Junior	$40	$40
Twilight	NA	NA
	Members and guests only	

PAYMENT	Fees billed to members

LEAGUES	None

MEMBERSHIPS	USGA, NGF, PGA, GCSAA, CMAA, MGA

MANAGER	William Larson
PROFESSIONAL	Terry Hogan

HOURS 8 am to Dusk

SEASON April–November

FEATURES

Putting green	Y	
Driving range	Y	
Practice area	N	
Golf carts		
Power (gas)	Y	$26
Pull carts	N	
Club rental	N	
Club storage	Y	
Caddies	Y	
Proshop		
Extended	Y	
Refreshments		
Restaurant	Y	
Lounge	Y	
Snacks	Y	
Clubhouse		
Showers	N	
Lockers	N	
Lodging	N	

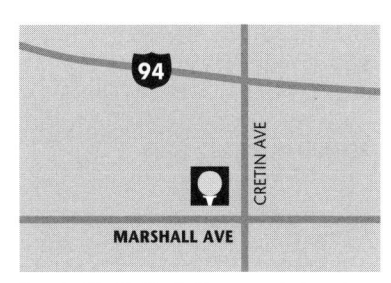

Located in St. Paul. Course entrance is about 1/2 mile south of I-94 on Cretin Avenue, then west on Marshall Avenue.

	MEN			WOMEN		
	FRONT	PAR	HDCP	FRONT	PAR	HDCP
1	314	4	13	299	4	8
2	105	3	17	91	3	18
3	144	3	9	132	3	16
4	479	5	15	404	5	10
5	319	4	11	315	4	4
6	458	4	1	392	5	12
7	347	4	7	340	4	6
8	364	4	5	361	4	2
9	410	4	3	406	5	14
Out	2940	35		2740	37	
10	372	4	2	360	4	1
11	165	3	8	129	3	15
12	526	5	6	450	5	9
13	263	4	18	256	4	11
14	229	3	4	222	4	17
15	493	5	14	486	5	5
16	510	5	10	501	5	3
17	481	5	16	458	5	7
18	132	3	12	119	3	13
In	3171	37		2981	38	
Total	6111	72		5721	75	
Rating	71.0			74.5		
Slope	130			137		

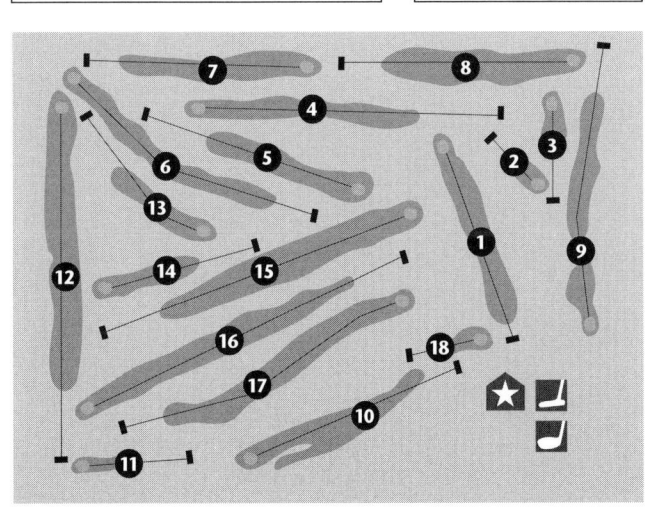

GOLF COURSE DIRECTORY

TOWN & COUNTRY GOLF CLUB

9 Regulation Semi-Private

Highway 59, P.O. Box 48
Fulda, Minnesota 56131
507/425-3328 Clubhouse/Proshop

HOURS	8 am to Dusk
SEASON	May to October

RESERVATIONS	507/425-3328
	Walk-on: good/fair

GREEN FEES	M-F	S-S
Adult	$13.75/9.25	$13.75/9.25
Senior	$13.75/9.25	$13.75/9.25
Junior	$13.75/9.25	$13.75/9.25
Twilight	NA	NA

PAYMENT	No credit cards accepted
	Non-local checks accepted

LEAGUES	Men: W
	Women: Th

MEMBERSHIPS	GCSAA, MGA

MANAGER	Jenny Aanenson
SUPERINTENDENT	Dale Burmeister

FEATURES		
Putting green	Y	
Driving range	Y	$3
Practice area	N	
Golf carts		
Power (gas)	Y	
Pull carts	Y	
Club rental	Y	
Club storage	N	
Caddies	N	
Proshop		
Extended	Y	
Refreshments		
Restaurant	N	
Lounge	N	
Snacks	Y	
Clubhouse		
Showers	N	
Lockers	N	
Lodging	N	

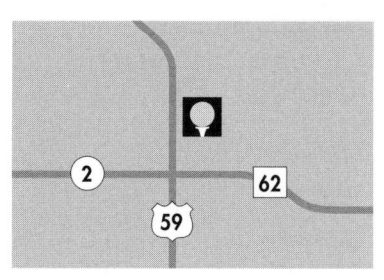

Located in Fulda. Course entrance is 1/2 mile north of MN Highway 62 on U.S. Highway 59.

	MEN				WOMEN		
	BACK	FRONT	PAR	HDCP	FRONT	PAR	HDCP
1	332	305	4	4	282	4	3
2	187	155	3	9	127	3	9
3	427	402	4	2	368	4	1
4	411	399	4	6	350	4	6
5	527	495	5	3	443	5	4
6	307	279	4	7	250	4	7
7	388	368	4	5	315	4	5
8	159	151	3	8	127	3	8
9	581	538	5	1	501	5	2
Out	3319	3092	36		2763	36	
1	332	305	4	4	282	4	3
2	187	155	3	9	127	3	9
3	427	402	4	2	368	4	1
4	411	399	4	6	350	4	6
5	527	495	5	3	443	5	4
6	307	279	4	7	250	4	7
7	388	368	4	5	315	4	5
8	159	151	3	8	127	3	8
9	581	538	5	1	501	5	2
In	3319	3092	36		2763	36	
Total	6638	6184	72		5526	72	
Rating	70.6	68.6			70.4		
Slope	110	106			112		

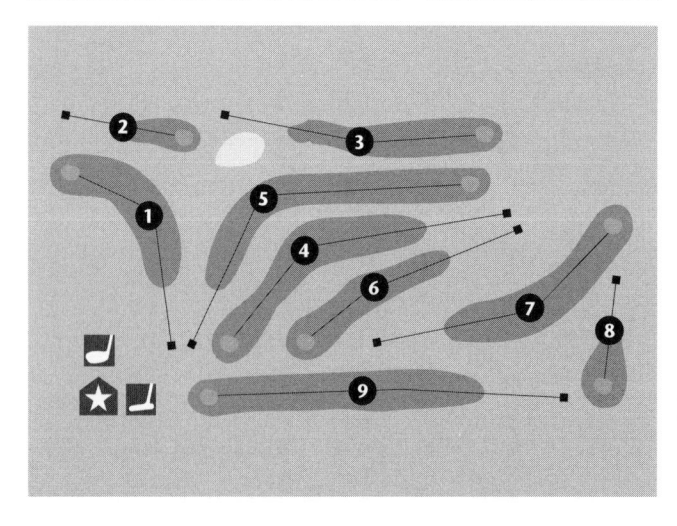

THE MINNESOTA ILLUSTRATED

TRACY COUNTRY CLUB

9 Regulation Semi-Private

Highway 14, P.O. Box 217
Tracy, Minnesota 56175
507/629-4666 Clubhouse/Proshop

HOURS	8 am to Dusk
SEASON	April to October

RESERVATIONS	507/629-4666	
	Walk-on: good/fair	
GREEN FEES	M-F	S-S
Adult	$16/9.60	$17/10.65
Senior	$16/9.60	$17/10.65
Junior	$16/9.60	$17/10.65
Twilight	NA	NA
PAYMENT	No credit cards accepted	
	Non-local checks accepted	
LEAGUES	Men: W	
	Women: T	
MEMBERSHIPS	MGA	
MANAGER	Ron Borchert	
SUPERINTENDENT	Wayne Jensen	

FEATURES		
Putting green	Y	
Driving range	Y	$1.50
Practice area	Y	
Golf carts		
Power (gas)	Y	$17
Pull carts	Y	$1
Club rental	Y	$2.50
Club storage	Y	$10
Caddies	N	
Proshop		
Basic	Y	
Refreshments		
Restaurant	N	
Lounge	N	
Snacks	Y	
Clubhouse		
Showers	Y	$.50
Lockers	N	
Lodging	N	

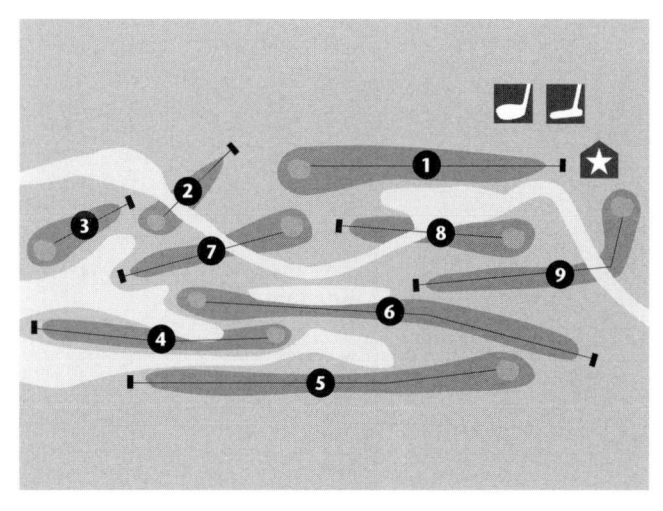

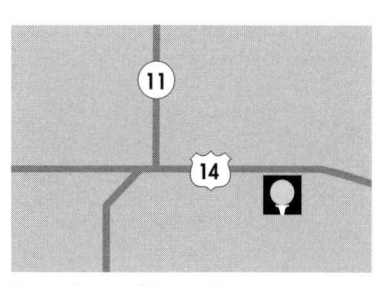

Located east of Tracy. Course entrance is about two miles east of County Road 11 on U.S. Highway 14.

	MEN				WOMEN		
	BACK	FRONT	PAR	HDCP	FRONT	PAR	HDCP
1	267	267	4	16	267	4	16
2	155	152	3	14	107	3	14
3	334	330	4	10	334	4	10
4	476	470	5	5	400	5	5
5	416	415	4	3	313	4	3
6	534	534	5	1	410	5	1
7	354	352	4	7	289	4	7
8	141	140	3	18	141	3	18
9	290	288	4	12	231	4	12
Out	2967	2948	36		2492	36	
1	267	267	4	17	267	4	17
2	155	152	3	15	107	3	15
3	334	330	4	11	334	4	11
4	476	470	5	6	400	5	6
5	416	415	4	4	313	4	4
6	534	534	5	2	410	5	2
7	354	352	4	8	289	4	8
8	141	140	3	9	141	3	9
9	290	288	4	13	231	4	13
In	2967	2948	36		2492	36	
Total	5934	5896	71		4984	72	
Rating	68.4	68.2			67.4		
Slope	121	121			116		

GOLF COURSE DIRECTORY

TWENTY NINE PINES GOLF COURSE

9 Executive Public

2871 Sundberg Road
Mahtowa, Minnesota 55707
218/389-3136 Clubhouse
800/397-4649 Proshop

HOURS	7 am to Dusk
SEASON	April to October

RESERVATIONS	800/397-4649
	Walk-on: good/good

GREEN FEES	M-F	S-S
Adult	$7.50	$8.50
Senior	$7*	$8.50
Junior	$7*	$8.50
Twilight	NA	NA
	* All day rate	

PAYMENT	No credit cards accepted
	Non-local checks accepted

LEAGUES	None

MEMBERSHIPS	USGA, MGA

OWNER	Virgil & Betty LaFond

FEATURES

Putting green	Y	
Driving range	N	
Practice area	Y	

Golf carts		
Power	Y	$9
Pull carts	Y	$1.50
Club rental	Y	$3.50
Club storage	N	
Caddies	N	

Proshop		
Regular	Y	
Refreshments		
Restaurant	Y	
Lounge	N	
Snacks	Y	
Clubhouse		
Showers	N	
Lockers	N	

Lodging	N

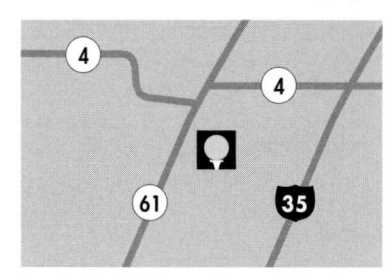

Located in Mahtowa. Course is 2 miles west of I-35 on Cty Rd 4, south on Cty Rd 61, then east on Sundberg Road.

	MEN			**WOMEN**		
	FRONT	PAR	HDCP	FRONT	PAR	HDCP
1	180	3		180	3	
2	230	4		230	4	
3	240	4		240	4	
4	215	4		215	4	
5	240	4		240	4	
6	120	3		120	3	
7	260	4		260	4	
8	220	4		220	4	
9	225	4		225	4	
Out	1930	34		1930	34	
1	180	3		180	3	
2	230	4		230	4	
3	240	4		240	4	
4	215	4		215	4	
5	240	4		240	4	
6	120	3		120	3	
7	260	4		260	4	
8	220	4		220	4	
9	225	4		225	4	
In	1930	34		1930	34	
Total	3860	68		3860	68	
Rating	NA			NA		
Slope	NA			NA		

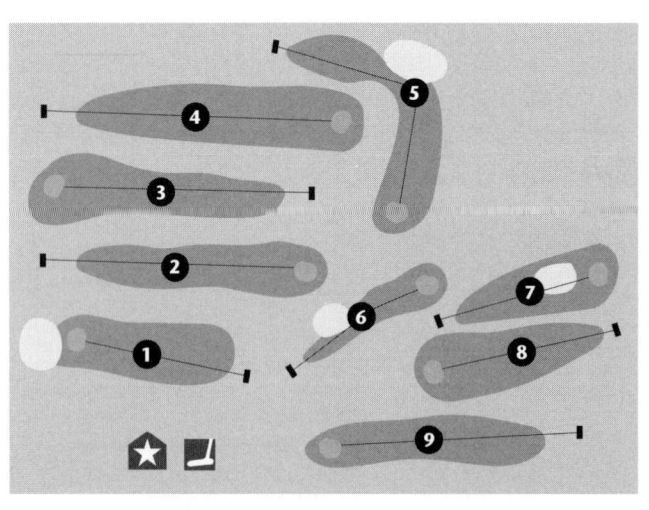

TWIN PINES GOLF COURSE

9 Regulation Public

P.O. Box 101
Bagley, Minnesota 56621
218/694-2454 Clubhouse/Proshop

RESERVATIONS	218/694-2454
	Walk-on: good/good

GREEN FEES	M-F	S-S
Adult	Call	Call
Senior	Call	Call
Junior	Call	Call
Twilight	NA	NA

PAYMENT	No credit cards accepted
	Non-local checks accepted

LEAGUES	Men: Various
	Women: Various

MEMBERSHIPS	MGA

PROFESSIONAL	Call

HOURS	Dawn to Dusk
SEASON	April to October

FEATURES	
Putting green	Y
Driving range	N
Practice area	N
Golf carts	
Power	Y
Pull carts	Y
Club rental	Y
Club storage	N
Caddies	N
Proshop	
Basic	Y
Refreshments	
Restaurant	N
Lounge	N
Snacks	Y
Clubhouse	
Showers	N
Lockers	N
Lodging	N

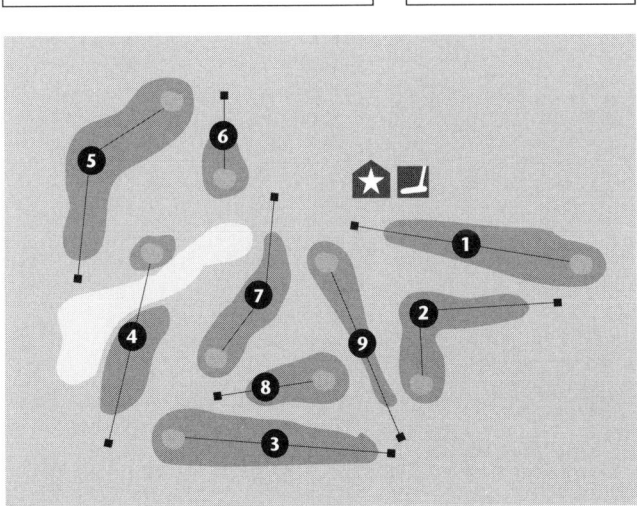

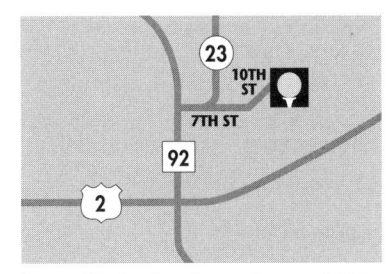

Located in Bagley. Course is east of MN Highway 92 on 7th Street/County Road 24, then northeast on 10th Street Road.

	MEN			WOMEN		
	FRONT	PAR	HDCP	FRONT	PAR	HDCP
1	389	4	3	389	5	3
2	337	4	7	332	4	7
3	485	5	5	430	5	5
4	380	4	2	293	5	2
5	460	5	6	336	5	6
6	175	3	8	169	3	8
7	417	4	1	319	4	1
8	312	4	9	304	4	9
9	207	3	4	207	3	4
Out	3162	36		2779	38	
1	389	4	3	389	5	3
2	337	4	7	332	4	7
3	485	5	5	430	5	5
4	380	4	2	293	5	2
5	460	5	6	336	5	6
6	175	3	8	169	3	8
7	417	4	1	319	4	1
8	197	3	9	197	3	9
9	340	4	4	335	4	4
In	3180	36		2800	38	
Total	6342	72		5579	76	
Rating	70.7			72.0		
Slope	121			117		

TWO HARBORS LAKEVIEW GOLF CLUB 9 Regulation Public

Highway 61 & 1st St., P.O. Box 355
Two Harbors, Minnesota 55616
218/834-2664 Clubhouse/Proshop

HOURS	6 am to Dusk
SEASON	May to October

RESERVATIONS	218/834-2664	
	Walk-on: good/fair	
GREEN FEES	M-F	S-S
Adult	$15/11	$15/11
Senior	$15/11	$15/11
Jr/Student	$11/8	$11/8
Twilight	NA	NA
PAYMENT	No credit cards accepted	
	Non-local checks accepted	
LEAGUES	Men: T,W (pm)	
	Women: Th	
MEMBERSHIPS	USGA, GCSAA, MGA	
MANAGER	Scott Larson	
SUPERINTENDENT	Scott Larson	

FEATURES	
Putting green	Y
Driving range	Y
Practice area	Y
Golf carts	
Power (gas)	Y
Pull carts	Y
Club rental	Y
Club storage	Y
Caddies	N
Proshop	
Extended	Y
Refreshments	
Restaurant	Y
Lounge	N
Snacks	Y
Clubhouse	
Showers	Y
Lockers	Y
Lodging	N

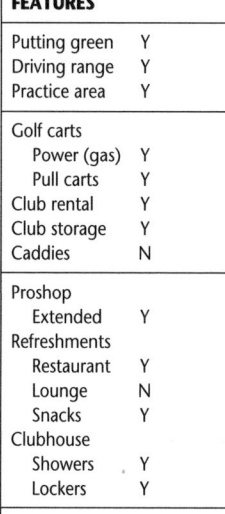

Located in Two Harbors. Course entrance is just east of 3rd Street (County Road 2) on U.S. Highway 61.

	MEN			WOMEN		
	FRONT	PAR	HDCP	FRONT	PAR	HDCP
1	335	4	17	335	4	5
2	470	5	11	470	5	1
3	170	3	6	135	3	17
4	520	5	7	420	5	13
5	330	4	15	330	4	7
6	365	4	1	365	5	15
7	185	3	5	185	3	11
8	365	4	13	365	4	3
9	375	4	3	375	5	9
Out	3115	36		2980	38	
1	300	4	14	300	4	8
2	453	5	16	453	5	2
3	200	3	4	135	3	16
4	485	5	8	420	5	12
5	330	4	12	330	4	10
6	365	4	6	365	5	14
7	120	3	18	120	3	18
8	325	4	10	325	4	6
9	430	4	2	430	5	4
In	3008	36		2873	38	
Total	6123	72		5853	76	
Rating	68.5			73.0		
Slope	116			120		

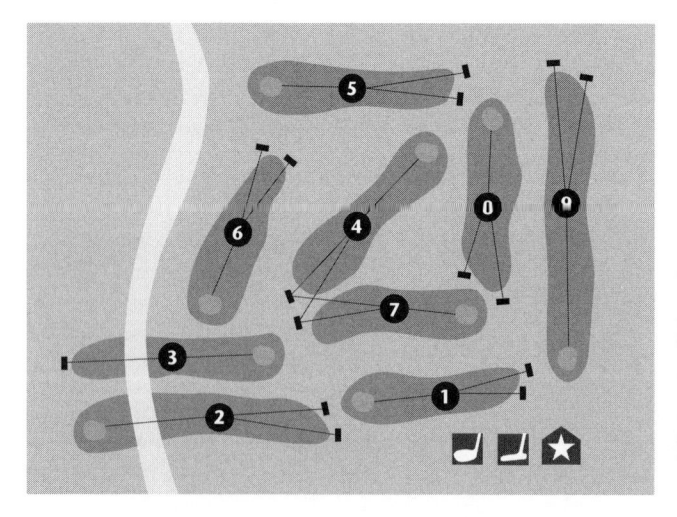

TWO RIVERS GOLF CLUB

9 Regulation Public

Highway 32 North
Hallock, Minnesota 56728
218/843-2155 Clubhouse/Proshop

RESERVATIONS	218/843-2155	
	Walk-on: good/fair	
GREEN FEES	M-F	S-S
Adult	$14/8	$15/9
Senior	$14/8	$15/9
Junior	$14/8	$15/9
Twilight	NA	NA
PAYMENT	No credit cards accepted	
	Non-local checks accepted	
LEAGUES	Men: W (pm)	
	Women: T (pm)	
MEMBERSHIPS	None	
PROFESSIONAL	None	

HOURS	8 am to Dusk
SEASON	May-September

FEATURES	
Putting green	Y
Driving range	N
Practice area	N
Golf carts	
Power	Y
Pull carts	Y
Club rental	Y
Club storage	N
Caddies	N
Proshop	
Basic	Y
Refreshments	
Restaurant	N
Lounge	N
Snacks	Y
Clubhouse	
Showers	N
Lockers	N
Lodging	N

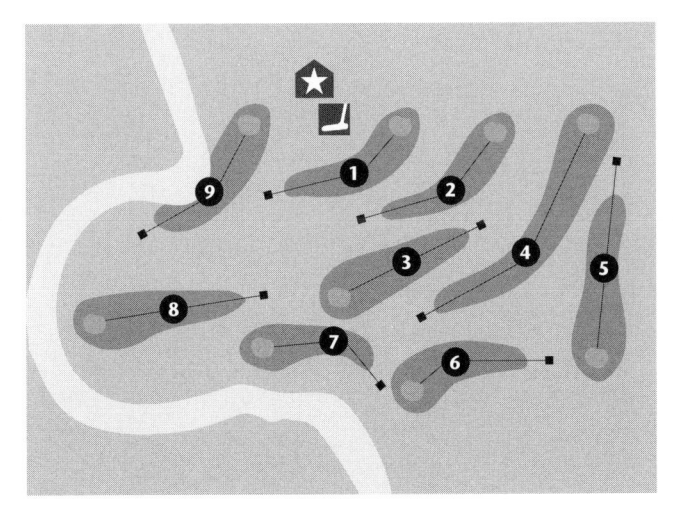

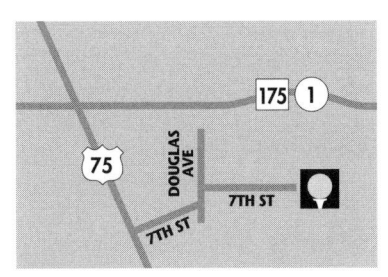

Located in Hallock. Course is east of U.S. Highway 75 on 7th Street, north on Douglas Avenue, then east on 7th Street.

	MEN			WOMEN		
	FRONT	PAR	HDCP	FRONT	PAR	HDCP
1	360	4	3	360	4	3
2	358	4	7	358	4	7
3	345	4	4	345	4	4
4	470	5	9	470	5	9
5	204	3	2	204	4	2
6	326	4	1	326	4	1
7	260	4	6	260	4	6
8	465	5	5	465	5	5
9	147	3	8	147	4	8
Out	2935	36		2935	38	
1	360	4	3	360	4	3
2	358	4	7	358	4	7
3	345	4	4	345	4	4
4	470	5	9	470	5	9
5	204	3	2	204	4	2
6	326	4	1	326	4	1
7	260	4	6	260	4	6
8	465	5	5	465	5	5
9	147	3	8	147	4	8
In	2935	36		2935	38	
Total	5870	72		5870	76	
Rating	64.4			68.6		
Slope	NA			NA		

GOLF COURSE DIRECTORY

TYLER COMMUNITY GOLF CLUB

9 Regulation Public

County Road 7, P.O. Box 447
Tyler, Minnesota 56178
507/247-3242 Clubhouse/Proshop

HOURS	8 am to Dawn
SEASON	April-November

RESERVATIONS	507/247-3242
	Walk-on: good/good

GREEN FEES	M-F	S-S
Adult	$12.25/9	$14.40/10.15
Senior	$12.25/9	$14.40/10.15
Junior	$12.25/9	$14.40/10.15
Twilight	$6.95	NA

PAYMENT	No credit cards accepted
	Non-local checks accepted

LEAGUES	None

MEMBERSHIPS	GCSAA, MGA

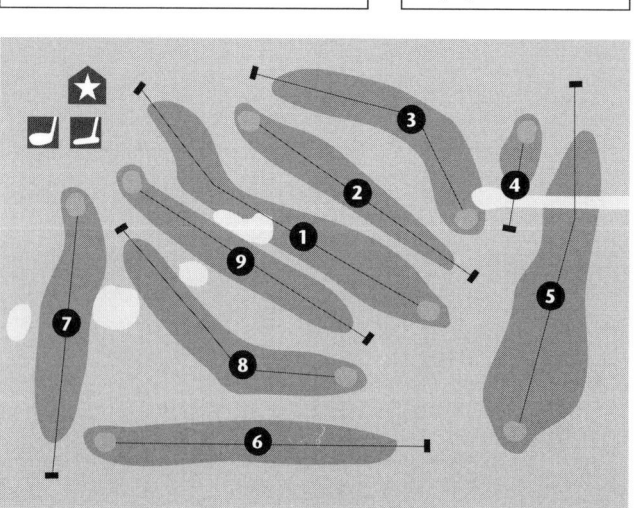

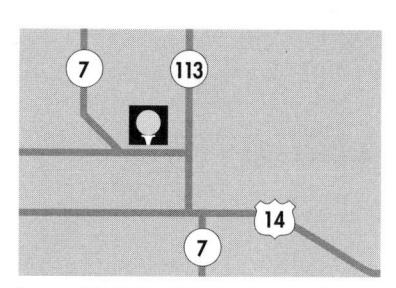

MANAGER	Joan Jagt

FEATURES	
Putting green	Y
Driving range	Y
Practice area	N
Golf carts	
Power (elec)	Y $12.75
Pull carts	Y $.50
Club rental	N
Club storage	N
Caddies	N
Proshop	
Regular	Y
Refreshments	
Restaurant	N
Lounge	Y
Snacks	Y
Clubhouse	
Showers	N
Lockers	N
Lodging	N

Located in Tyler. Course is one mile north of U.S. Highway 14 on County Road 113, then east on County Road 7.

		MEN			WOMEN		
	FRONT	PAR	HDCP	FRONT	PAR	HDCP
1	518	5	5	488	5	1
2	333	4	8	320	4	5
3	345	4	4	325	4	4
4	150	3	9	127	3	7
5	432	4	1	399	5	8
6	404	4	3	379	5	9
7	313	4	7	298	4	6
8	373	4	6	355	4	2
9	348	4	2	336	4	3
Out	3216	36		3027	38	
1	518	5	5	488	5	1
2	333	4	8	320	4	5
3	345	4	4	325	4	4
4	150	3	9	127	3	7
5	432	4	1	399	5	8
6	404	4	3	379	5	9
7	313	4	7	298	4	6
8	373	4	6	355	4	2
9	348	4	2	336	4	3
In	3216	36		3027	38	
Total	6432	72		6054	76	
Rating	71.2			74.6		
Slope	121			124		

U OF M LES BOLSTAD GOLF COURSE

18 Regulation Public

2275 West Larpenteur Avenue
St. Paul, Minnesota 55113
612/627-4000 Clubhouse/Proshop

HOURS	Dawn to Dusk
SEASON	April-November

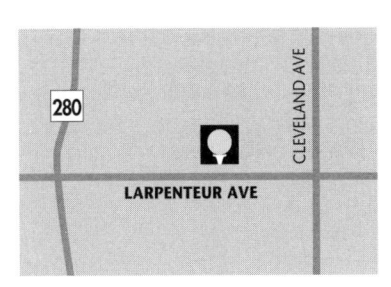

Located in St. Paul. Course entrance is about 5 blocks east of MN Highway 280 on Larpenteur Avenue.

RESERVATIONS	612/627-4000 1 week
	Walk-on: fair/fair

GREEN FEES	M-F	S-S
Adult	$17.75	$20.75
Senior	$17.75	$20.75
Junior	$17.75	$20.75
Twilight	$12.75	NA
	Student, staff and alumni discount rates available	

PAYMENT	Credit: Visa® MasterCard® Local checks only

LEAGUES	Other: M,W (pm)

MEMBERSHIPS	USGA, NGF, GCSAA, MGA

MANAGER	Chris Korbol, Deanne Miller
SUPERINTENDENT	Charlie Pooch, Jim Peloquin

FEATURES		
Putting green	Y	
Driving range	Y	$2-9
Practice area	Y	
Golf carts		
Power (gas)	Y	$20/11
Pull carts	Y	$2.50
Club rental	Y	$10
Club storage	N	
Caddies	N	
Proshop		
Extended	Y	
Refreshments		
Restaurant	N	
Lounge	N	
Snacks	Y	
Clubhouse		
Showers	Y	
Lockers	Y	
Lodging	N	

	MEN			**WOMEN**		
	FRONT	PAR	HDCP	FRONT	PAR	HDCP
1	393	4	4	375	4	7
2	163	3	10	130	3	13
3	400	4	6	382	5	9
4	355	4	2	340	4	1
5	150	3	16	135	3	17
6	306	4	18	294	4	11
7	464	5	12	450	5	3
8	185	3	8	178	3	15
9	472	5	14	444	5	5
Out	2888	35		2728	36	
10	339	4	11	281	4	12
11	347	4	13	268	4	16
12	415	4	1	411	5	4
13	525	5	9	430	5	2
14	280	4	17	268	4	14
15	390	4	5	383	4	10
16	388	4	3	384	5	6
17	145	3	15	137	3	18
18	406	4	7	394	5	8
In	3235	36		2956	39	
Total	6123	71		5684	75	
Rating	69.2			72.7		
Slope	117			127		

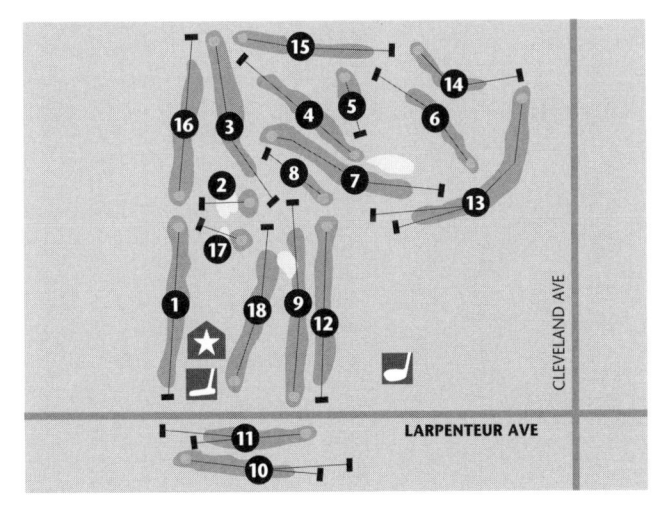

VALLEBROOK GOLF CLUB

9 Regulation Public

101 Vallebrook Road, P.O. Box 277
Lakefield, Minnesota 56150
507/662-5755 Clubhouse/Proshop

HOURS 8 am to Dusk

SEASON April-November

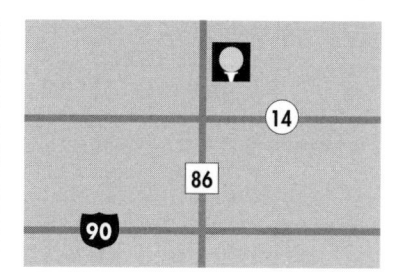

RESERVATIONS	507/662-5755 1 day
	Walk-on: good/fair

GREEN FEES	M-F	S-S
Adult	$14/9	$16/11
Senior	$6/6 (Th)	$16/11
Junior	$14/9	$16/11
Twilight	NA	NA

PAYMENT	No credit cards accepted
	Non-local checks accepted

LEAGUES	Men: W
	Women: T
	Couples: F

MEMBERSHIPS	USGA, GCSAA, MGA

OWNER	Doug Libra
MANAGER	Doug Libra
SUPERINTENDENT	Scott Sievert

FEATURES

Putting green	Y	
Driving range	Y	$3.25
Practice area	Y	
Golf carts		
Power (gas)	Y	$14/9
Pull carts	Y	$1.50
Club rental	Y	$3
Club storage	Y	$15/yr
Caddies	N	
Proshop		
Extended	Y	
Refreshments		
Restaurant	Y	
Lounge	Y	
Snacks	Y	
Clubhouse		
Showers	Y	
Lockers	Y	
Lodging	N	

Located in Lakefield. Course entrance is about three miles north of I-90 on MN Highway 86.

	MEN				WOMEN		
	BACK	FRONT	PAR	HDCP	FRONT	PAR	HDCP
1	134	128	3	8	94	3	8
2	309	298	4	9	207	4	9
3	155	112	3	7	99	3	7
4	187	181	3	6	137	3	6
5	364	354	4	5	272	4	5
6	185	182	3	3	145	3	3
7	507	498	5	2	406	5	2
8	411	405	4	1	296	4	1
9	476	471	5	4	416	5	4
Out	2718	2629	34		2072	34	
1	134	128	3	8	94	3	8
2	309	298	4	9	207	4	9
3	155	112	3	7	99	3	7
4	187	181	3	6	137	3	6
5	364	354	4	5	272	4	5
6	185	182	3	3	145	3	3
7	507	498	5	2	406	5	2
8	411	405	4	1	296	4	1
9	476	471	5	4	416	5	4
In	2718	2629	34		2072	34	
Total	5436	5258	68		4144	68	
Rating	64.8	64.6			62.6		
Slope	101	99			99		

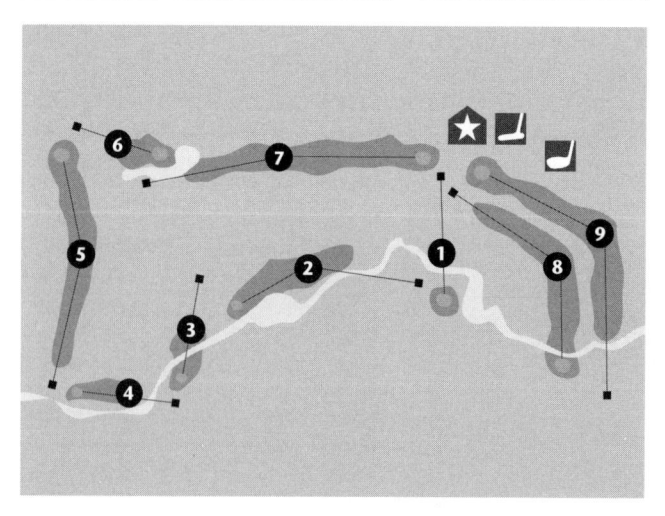

VALLEY COUNTRY CLUB

18 Regulation Semi-Private

1800 21st Street NW, P.O. Box 461
East Grand Forks, Minnesota 56721
218/773-1207 Clubhouse/Proshop

HOURS	6 am to Dusk
SEASON	April to October

RESERVATIONS	218/773-1207
	Walk-on: good/good

GREEN FEES	M-F	S-S
Adult	$12.50	$14
Senior	$12.50	$14
Junior	$6.25	$14
Twilight	$8.50	$8.50

PAYMENT	Credit: Visa® MasterCard®
	Non-local checks accepted

LEAGUES	Men: T (12 noon)
	Women: W (5:30 pm)

MEMBERSHIPS USGA, MGA

SUPERINTENDENT James Grassel
PROFESSIONAL Ken Hallgrimson

FEATURES		
Putting green	Y	
Driving range	N	
Practice area	Y	
Golf carts		
Power (gas)	Y	$16/9
Pull carts	Y	
Club rental	Y	$5/3
Club storage	N	
Caddies	N	
Proshop		
Extended	Y	
Refreshments		
Restaurant	N	
Lounge	N	
Snacks	Y	
Clubhouse		
Showers	Y	
Lockers	Y	
Lodging	N	

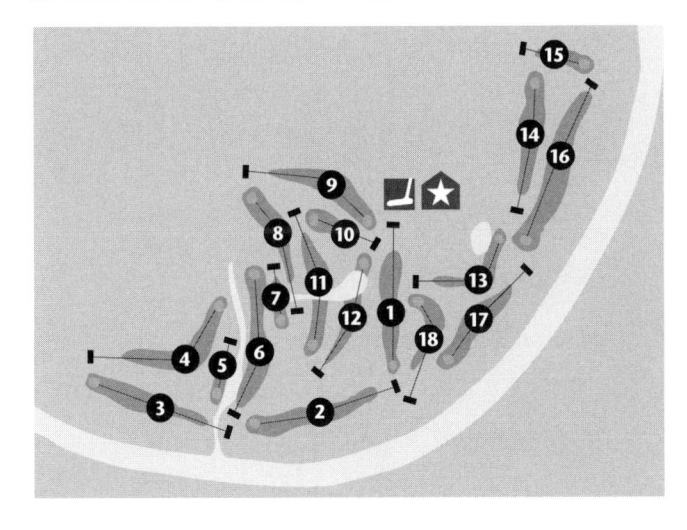

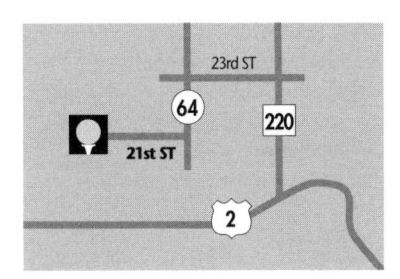

Located in East Grand Forks. Course is west of MN Hwy 220 on 23rd St, south on County Rd 64, then west on 21st St.

	MEN				**WOMEN**		
	BACK	FRONT	PAR	HDCP	FRONT	PAR	HDCP
1	355	341	4	4	325	4	4
2	524	509	5	10	457	5	10
3	346	334	4	17	248	4	17
4	383	378	4	1	300	4	1
5	150	145	3	13	134	3	13
6	481	468	5	8	374	5	8
7	118	102	3	14	88	3	14
8	400	382	4	7	358	4	7
9	345	338	4	16	330	4	16
Out	3102	2997	36		2614	36	
10	194	184	3	9	174	3	9
11	417	400	4	3	311	4	3
12	501	496	5	2	380	5	2
13	320	315	4	6	305	4	6
14	354	344	4	15	327	4	15
15	167	157	3	11	147	3	11
16	471	466	5	5	413	5	5
17	363	337	4	12	300	4	12
18	321	305	4	18	290	4	18
In	3108	3004	36		2647	36	
Total	6210	6001	72		5261	72	
Rating	69.6	68.6			70.5		
Slope	118	116			116		

GOLF COURSE DIRECTORY

VALLEY GOLF COURSE

9 Regulation Public

1900 East Becker Avenue
Willmar, Minnesota 56201
612/235-6790 Clubhouse/Proshop

HOURS 7 am to Dusk
SEASON April to October

RESERVATIONS	612/235-6790
	Walk-on: good/fair

GREEN FEES	M-F	S-S
Adult	$11/7	$12/8
Senior	$11/7	$12/8
Junior	$6/4.50	$9/6
Twilight	NA	NA

PAYMENT	No credit cards accepted
	Non-local checks accepted

LEAGUES	Various

MEMBERSHIPS	USGA, NGF, MGA

OWNER	Duane Westermann

FEATURES

Putting green	Y
Driving range	N
Practice area	Y
Golf carts	
Power	Y
Pull carts	Y
Club rental	Y
Club storage	Y
Caddies	N
Proshop	
Extended	Y
Refreshments	
Restaurant	N
Lounge	N
Snacks	Y
Clubhouse	
Showers	N
Lockers	N
Lodging	N

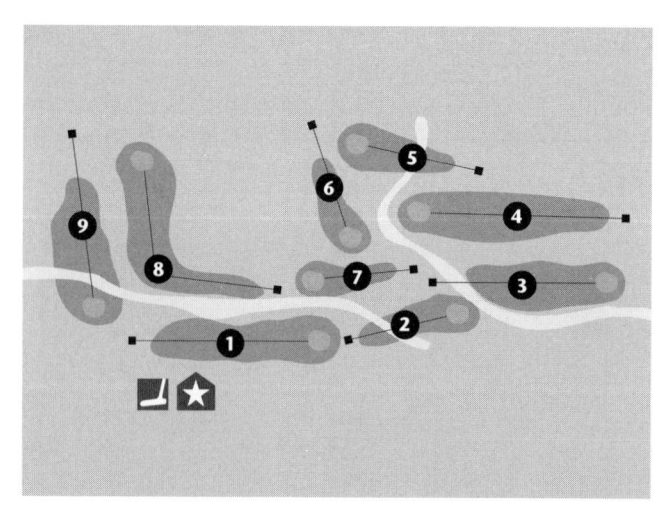

Located in Willmar. Course is south of U.S. Highway 12 on Lakeland Drive (Cty Road 124), the east on Becker Avenue.

	MEN			WOMEN		
	FRONT	PAR	HDCP	FRONT	PAR	HDCP
1	305	4	3	305	4	3
2	265	4	7	232	4	7
3	265	4	5	254	4	5
4	365	4	1	355	4	1
5	150	3	9	138	3	9
6	245	4	4	238	4	4
7	190	3	8	170	3	8
8	465	5	2	451	5	2
9	210	4	6	198	4	6
Out	2460	35		2341	35	
1	305	4	3	305	4	3
2	265	4	7	232	4	7
3	265	4	5	254	4	5
4	365	4	1	355	4	1
5	150	3	9	138	3	9
6	245	4	4	238	4	4
7	190	3	8	170	3	8
8	465	5	2	451	5	2
9	210	4	6	198	4	6
In	2460	35		2341	35	
Total	4920	70		4682	70	
Rating	63.6			67.2		
Slope	103			102		

VALLEY HIGH COUNTRY CLUB

18 Regulation Public

Route 2, P.O.Box 234
Houston, Minnesota 55943
507/894-4444 Clubhouse/Proshop

HOURS	7 am to Dusk
SEASON	April to October

RESERVATIONS	507/894-4444	
	Walk-on: good/poor	
GREEN FEES	M-F	S-S
Adult	$12/7	$13/8
Senior	$12/7	$13/8
Junior	$12/7	$13/8
Twilight	NA	NA
PAYMENT	No credit cards accepted	
	Non-local checks accepted	
LEAGUES	Men: Various	
	Women: Various	
MEMBERSHIPS	GCSAA, MGA	
OWNER	Mickey & Alta Meyer	

FEATURES	
Putting green	Y
Driving range	Y
Practice area	Y
Golf carts	
Power (elec)	Y
Pull carts	Y
Club rental	Y
Club storage	Y
Caddies	N
Proshop	
Regular	Y
Refreshments	
Restaurant	Y
Lounge	Y
Snacks	Y
Clubhouse	
Showers	Y
Lockers	Y
Lodging	N

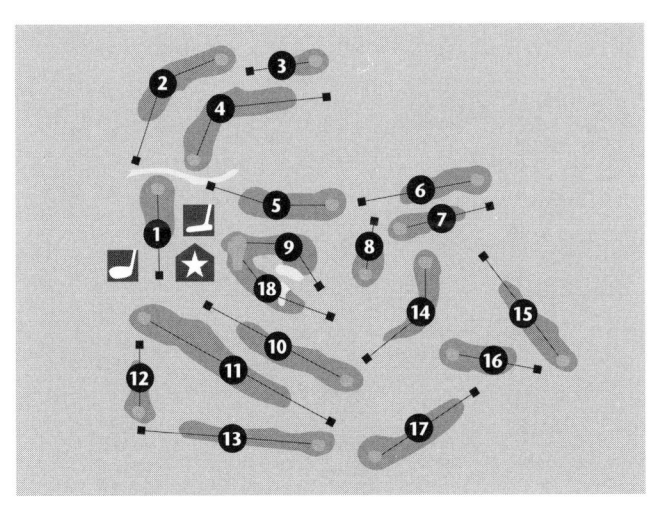

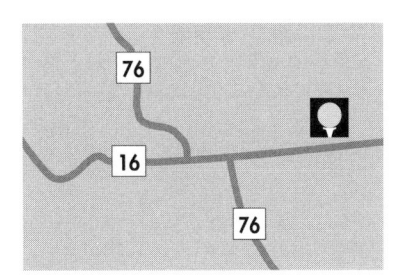

Located east of Houston. Course is about seven miles east of MN Highway 76 on MN Highway 16.

	\multicolumn{4}{c}{MEN}	\multicolumn{3}{c}{WOMEN}
	BACK	FRONT	PAR	HDCP	FRONT	PAR	HDCP
1	360	346	4	11	335	4	9
2	425	413	4	1	405	4	11
3	205	191	3	13	185	3	3
4	560	532	5	3	530	5	13
5	525	483	5	9	390	5	1
6	365	353	4	5	270	4	5
7	325	307	4	15	305	4	17
8	155	150	3	17	140	3	7
9	425	413	4	7	405	4	15
Out	3345	3188	36		2965	36	
10	404	397	4	12	371	4	6
11	525	515	5	14	461	5	14
12	137	116	3	18	98	3	18
13	478	406	5	8	355	4	8
14	263	201	4	4	182	3	12
15	272	257	4	2	243	4	2
16	111	104	3	16	98	3	16
17	328	316	4	10	265	4	4
18	367	357	4	6	346	4	10
In	2885	2669	36		2419	34	
Total	6230	5857	72		5384	70	
Rating	69.3	67.6			70.6		
Slope	113	109			116		

GOLF COURSE DIRECTORY

VALLEY VIEW GOLF CLUB — 18 Regulation Public

23795 Laredo Avenue
Belle Plaine, Minnesota 56011
612/873-4653 Clubhouse/Proshop

RESERVATIONS	612/873-4653 3 days Walk-on: fair/poor	
GREEN FEES	M-F	S-S
Adult	$18/12	$22/15
Senior	$18/12	$22/15
Junior	$18/12	$22/15
Twilight	NA	NA
PAYMENT	Credit: Visa® MasterCard® Non-local checks accepted	
LEAGUES	Men: Th Women: T	
MEMBERSHIPS	USGA, NGF, PGA, GCSAA, MGA	
OWNER	Dale Stier	
MANAGER	Brad Vold	
SUPERINTENDENT	Jim Hoffman	
PROFESSIONAL	Rob Lussenhop	

HOURS 6 am to Dusk
SEASON Mar-November

FEATURES

Putting green	Y	
Driving range	Y	
Practice area	Y	
Golf carts		
Power (gas)	Y	$22
Pull carts	Y	$3
Club rental	Y	
Club storage	N	
Caddies	N	
Proshop		
Extended	Y	
Refreshments		
Restaurant	N	
Lounge	N	
Snacks	Y	
Clubhouse		
Showers	N	
Lockers	N	
Lodging	N	

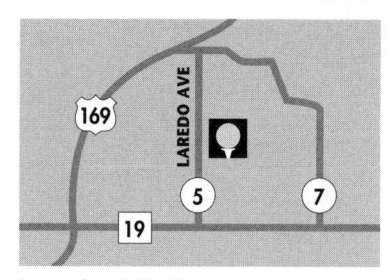

Located in Belle Plaine. Course entrance is east of U.S. Highway 169 on County Road 7, then south on County Road 5.

	MEN				WOMEN		
	BACK	FRONT	PAR	HDCP	FRONT	PAR	HDCP
1	458	450	4/5	5	351	5	5
2	244	190	3	7	160	3	13
3	545	520	5	1	438	5	1
4	276	258	4	15	225	4	9
5	139	132	3	17	117	3	17
6	374	361	4	11	254	4	15
7	389	376	4	9	294	4	7
8	345	328	4	13	317	4	3
9	235	208	3	3	161	3	11
Out	3005	2823	34/35		2317	35	
10	410	392	4	10	384	4	6
11	486	454	5	6	372	5	4
12	394	384	4	14	329	4	14
13	150	140	3	16	125	3	16
14	538	523	5	8	411	5	2
15	130	118	3	18	100	3	18
16	440	422	4	2	323	4	8
17	380	356	4	4	288	4	10
18	376	360	4	12	272	4	12
In	3304	3149	36		2604	36	
Total	6309	5974	70/71		4921	71	
Rating	70.1	68.7			68.5		
Slope	118	115			115		

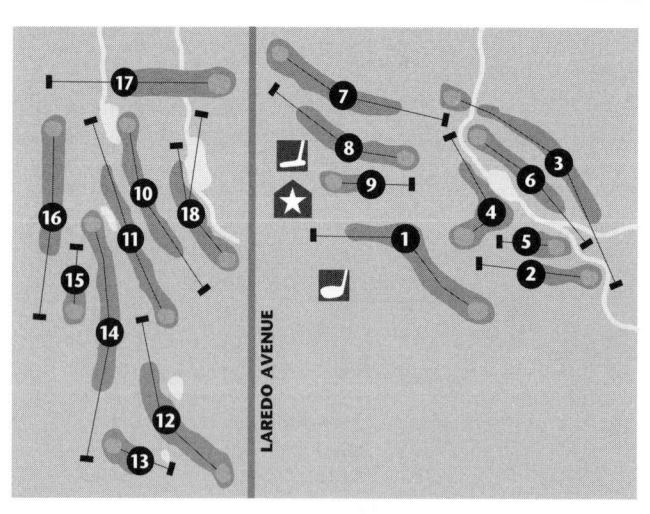

VALLEYWOOD GOLF COURSE

18 Regulation Public

4851 125th Street West
Apple Valley, Minnesota 55124
612/953-2323 Clubhouse/Proshop

HOURS	7 am to Dusk
SEASON	April-November

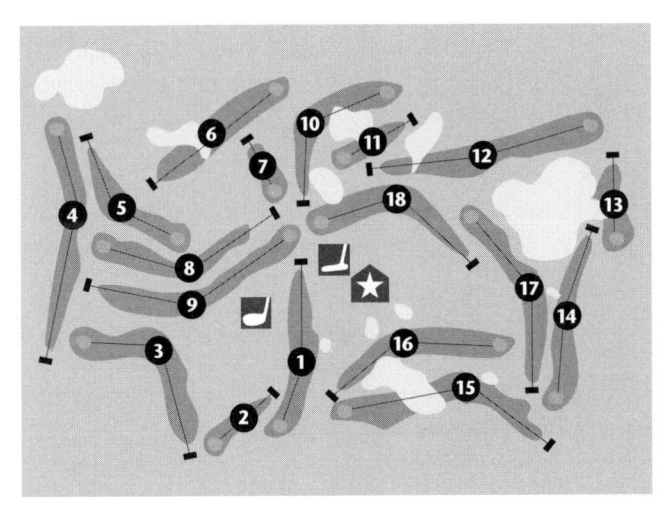

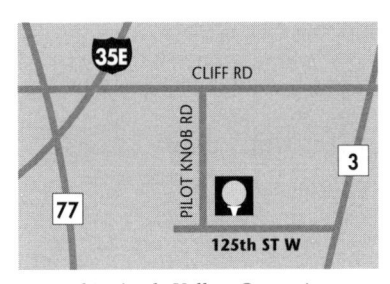

Located in Apple Valley. Course is east of I-35E on Cliff Road, south on Pilot Knob Road, then east on 125th Street.

RESERVATIONS	612/953-2323 5 days
	Walk-on: fair/poor

GREEN FEES	M-Th	F-S
Adult	$23/15	$23/15
Senior	$20/13	$23/15
Junior	$18/11	$18/11
Twilight	NA	NA

PAYMENT	Credit: Visa® MasterCard®
	Local checks only

LEAGUES	Men: W
	Women: T (am), Th (pm)

MEMBERSHIPS	USGA, PGA, GCSAA, MGA

OWNER	City of Apple Valley
MANAGER	Rick Dodge
SUPERINTENDENT	Scott Lockling
PROFESSIONAL	Rick Dodge, Jim Zinck

FEATURES

Putting green	Y
Driving range	Y
Practice area	N
Golf carts	
Power (gas)	Y $23/12
Pull carts	Y
Club rental	Y
Club storage	N
Caddies	N
Proshop	
Extended	Y
Refreshments	
Restaurant	Y
Lounge	Y
Snacks	Y
Clubhouse	
Showers	N
Lockers	N
Lodging	N

	MEN				WOMEN		
	BACK	FRONT	PAR	HDCP	FRONT	PAR	HDCP
1	334	320	4	8	318	4	4
2	157	148	3	16	126	3	7
3	393	385	4	6	225	4	18
4	475	463	5	12	458	5	9
5	325	308	4	14	275	4	13
6	333	323	4	10	280	4	6
7	167	161	3	18	130	3	15
8	447	431	4	4	308	4	17
9	464	454	4	2	420	5	12
Out	3095	2993	35		2540	36	
10	393	383	4	5	340	4	2
11	171	133	3	17	110	3	16
12	479	469	5	11	359	4	8
13	184	138	3	15	100	3	14
14	360	353	4	13	335	4	11
15	511	495	5	1	403	5	1
16	389	380	4	9	320	4	3
17	418	406	4	3	401	5	5
18	376	370	4	7	330	4	10
In	3281	3127	36		2739	36	
Total	6376	6120	71		5279	72	
Rating	70.6	69.5			70.3		
Slope	123	121			123		

GOLF COURSE DIRECTORY

VERMILION FAIRWAYS GOLF CLUB

9 Regulation Public

2407 Vermilion Drive
Cook, Minnesota 55723
218/666-2679 Clubhouse/Proshop

HOURS	Dawn to Dusk
SEASON	May-September

RESERVATIONS	No reservations accepted
	Walk-on: good/good

GREEN FEES	M-F	S-S
Adult	$15/10	$15/10
Senior	$9.50	$15/10
Junior	$7/4	$15/10
Twilight	$7 (5:30pm)	$7 (5:30pm)

PAYMENT	No credit cards accepted
	Non-local checks accepted

LEAGUES	Various

MEMBERSHIPS	GCSAA, MGA

MANAGER	Joan Norup
SUPERINTENDENT	Bill Peterson

FEATURES		
Putting green	Y	
Driving range	Y	$1.50
Practice area	Y	
Golf carts		
Power (gas)	Y	
Pull carts	Y	$2
Club rental	Y	$3.50
Club storage	N	
Caddies	N	
Proshop		
Regular	Y	
Refreshments		
Restaurant	Y	
Lounge	N	
Snacks	Y	
Clubhouse		
Showers	N	
Lockers	N	
Lodging	N	

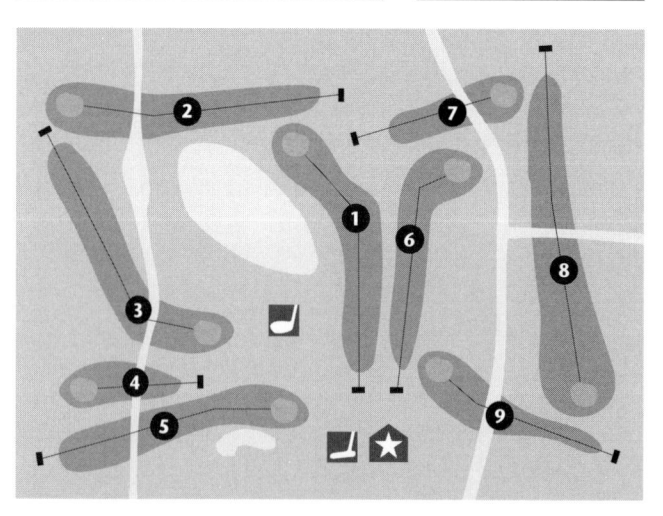

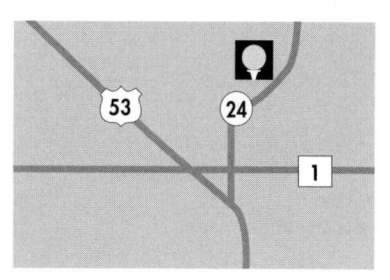

Located in Cook. Course entrance is four miles north of MN Highway 1 on County Road 24 (Vermilion Drive).

		MEN			WOMEN		
		FRONT	PAR	HDCP	FRONT	PAR	HDCP
1		367	4	5	345	5	5
2		385	4	3	385	5	3
3		388	4	4	342	5	4
4		195	3	8	155	3	8
5		480	5	2	420	5	2
6		380	4	6	357	4	6
7		185	3	9	145	3	9
8		525	5	1	485	5	1
9		340	4	7	340	4	7
Out		3245	36		2974	39	
1		367	4	5	345	5	5
2		385	4	3	385	5	3
3		388	4	4	342	5	4
4		195	3	8	155	3	8
5		480	5	2	420	5	2
6		380	4	6	357	4	6
7		185	3	9	145	3	9
8		525	5	1	485	5	1
9		340	4	7	340	4	7
In		3245	36		2974	39	
Total		6490	72		5948	78	
Rating		70.4			73.2		
Slope		122			126		

VERMILION RIVER GREENS

9 Regulation Public

5530 Crane Lake Road
Buyck, Minnesota 55771
218/993-2246 Clubhouse/Proshop

HOURS	8 am to Dusk
SEASON	May to October

RESERVATIONS	218/993-2246
	Walk-on: good/good

GREEN FEES	M-F	S-S
Adult	$10	$10
Senior	$10	$10
Junior	$5	$5
Twilight	NA	NA

PAYMENT	No credit cards accepted
	Non-local checks accepted

LEAGUES	Various

MEMBERSHIPS	NGF, GCSAA, MGA

OWNER	Kevin, Ban & Scott Hoffman

FEATURES		
Putting green	Y	
Driving range	N	
Practice area	Y	
Golf carts		
Power (gas)	Y	$10
Pull carts	Y	$1.50
Club rental	Y	$4.50
Club storage	Y	$15
Caddies	N	
Proshop		
Basic	Y	
Refreshments		
Restaurant	Y	
Lounge	Y	
Snacks	Y	
Clubhouse		
Showers	Y	
Lockers	Y	
Lodging	Y	Call

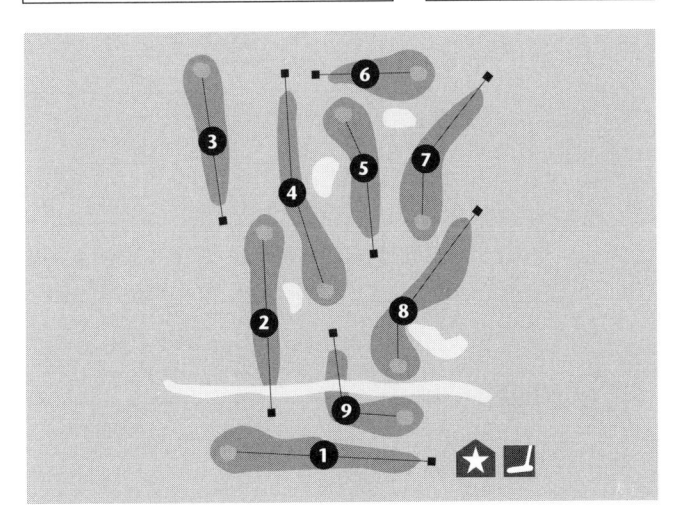

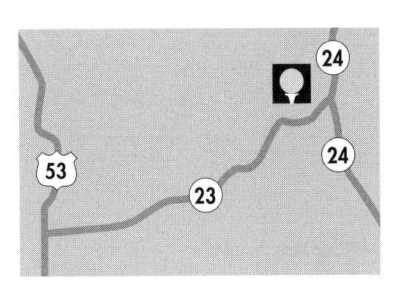

Located south of Buyck. Course entrance is east of U.S. Highway 53 on County Road 23, then north on Couty Road 24.

	MEN			WOMEN		
	FRONT	PAR	HDCP	FRONT	PAR	HDCP
1	180	3		163	3	
2	380	4		360	4	
3	320	4		310	4	
4	475	5		460	5	
5	350	4		335	4	
6	150	3		140	3	
7	295	4		285	4	
8	490	5		470	5	
9	300	4		280	4	
Out	2940	36		2803	36	
1	180	3		163	3	
2	380	4		360	4	
3	320	4		310	4	
4	475	5		460	5	
5	350	4		335	4	
6	150	3		140	3	
7	295	4		285	4	
8	490	5		470	5	
9	300	4		280	4	
In	2940	36		2803	36	
Total	5880	72		5606	72	
Rating	66.4			66.6		
Slope	101			105		

VIKING MEADOWS GOLF CLUB

18 Regulation Public

1788 Viking Boulevard, P.O. Box 41
East Bethel, Minnesota 55011
612/434-4205 Clubhouse/Proshop

HOURS	7 am to Dusk
SEASON	April-November

RESERVATIONS	612/434-4205	
	Walk-on: good/fair	
GREEN FEES	M-F	S-S
Adult	$15/10	$20/12
Senior	$12/8	$20/12
Junior	$12/8	$20/12
Twilight	NA	NA
PAYMENT	Credit: Visa® MasterCard®	
	Local checks only	
LEAGUES	Men: W (pm)	
	Women: T (pm)	
MEMBERSHIPS	NGF, PGA, GCSAA, MGA	
PROFESSIONAL	None	

FEATURES		
Putting green	Y	
Driving range	Y	$3
Practice area	N	
Golf carts		
Power	Y	$20
Pull carts	Y	$3
Club rental	Y	$6
Club storage	N	
Caddies	N	
Proshop		
Regular	Y	
Refreshments		
Restaurant	N	
Lounge	Y	
Snacks	Y	
Clubhouse		
Showers	N	
Lockers	N	
Lodging	N	

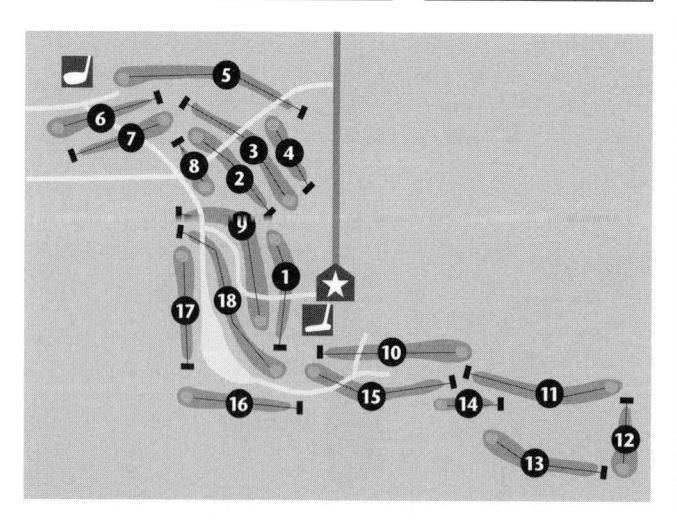

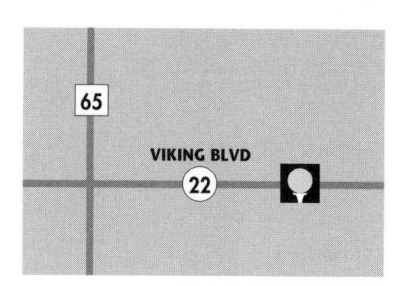

Located south of East Bethel. Course is 1 mile east of MN Highway 65 on Viking Boulevard (County Road 22).

	MEN				**WOMEN**		
	BACK	FRONT	PAR	HDCP	FRONT	PAR	HDCP
1	293	275	4	10	255	4	14
2	338	330	4	8	320	4	10
3	414	399	4	4	364	5	6
4	190	174	3	12	145	3	18
5	558	538	5	2	491	5	2
6	294	281	4	18	245	4	12
7	323	308	4	14	298	4	8
8	183	174	3	16	143	3	16
9	453	439	5	6	400	5	4
Out	3046	2915	36		2661	37	
10	430	415	4	5	350	4	7
11	465	453	4	7	394	5	3
12	230	220	3	3	170	3	15
13	364	352	4	13	300	4	9
14	140	128	3	17	118	3	17
15	500	490	5	1	455	5	1
16	317	307	4	11	267	4	13
17	334	322	4	15	296	4	11
18	484	474	5	9	385	5	5
In	3264	3161	36		2735	37	
Total	6310	6076	72		5396	74	
Rating	69.1	68.0			70.2		
Slope	113	111			114		

VILLAGE GREEN GOLF COURSE

18 Regulation Public

3420 Village Green Drive
Moorhead, Minnesota 56560
218/299-5366 Clubhouse/Proshop

HOURS	7 am to Dusk
SEASON	April to October

RESERVATIONS	218/299-5366 1 day
	Walk-on: fair/poor

GREEN FEES	M-F	S-S
Adult	$15/8	$17/10
Senior	$10/6*	$12/7 (4pm)
Junior	$10/6*	$12/7 (4pm)
Twilight	NA	NA
	* Before 1 pm	

PAYMENT	Credit: Visa® MasterCard®
	Non-local checks accepted

LEAGUES	Men: W (pm)
	Women: Th (am)
	Couples: M (pm)

MEMBERSHIPS	USGA, PGA, GCSAA, MGA

SUPERINTENDENT Rick Dauner, Mike Schroecher
PROFESSIONAL Russ Nelson, Matt Cook

FEATURES

Putting green	Y	
Driving range	Y	$3
Practice area	Y	

Golf carts		
Power (gas)	Y	$18/10
Pull carts	Y	$2
Club rental	Y	$5
Club storage	Y	$25/yr
Caddies	N	

Proshop	
Extended	Y
Refreshments	
Restaurant	N
Lounge	Y
Snacks	Y
Clubhouse	
Showers	Y
Lockers	Y

Lodging	N

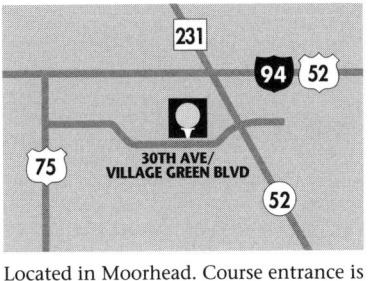

Located in Moorhead. Course entrance is south of I-94 (Exit 2) on County Road 52, then west on Village Green Blvd.

	MEN				WOMEN		
	BACK	FRONT	PAR	HDCP	FRONT	PAR	HDCP
1	489	483	5	17	443	5	17
2	400	387	4	11	305	4	11
3	400	385	4	7	320	4	7
4	404	392	4	13	327	4	13
5	178	166	3	9	121	3	9
6	448	433	4	1	359	4	1
7	520	505	5	3	457	5	3
8	193	180	3	5	165	3	5
9	378	367	4	15	308	4	15
Out	3410	3298	36		2805	36	
10	375	351	4	9	296	4	9
11	419	390	4	3	313	4	3
12	533	507	5	7	422	5	7
13	159	141	3	18	123	3	18
14	544	520	5	14	442	5	14
15	139	117	3	16	89	3	16
16	431	413	4	12	332	4	12
17	359	335	4	13	259	4	13
18	394	368	4	6	305	4	6
In	3353	3142	36		2581	36	
Total	6763	6440	72		5386	72	
Rating	72.0	70.5			70.5		
Slope	119	116			113		

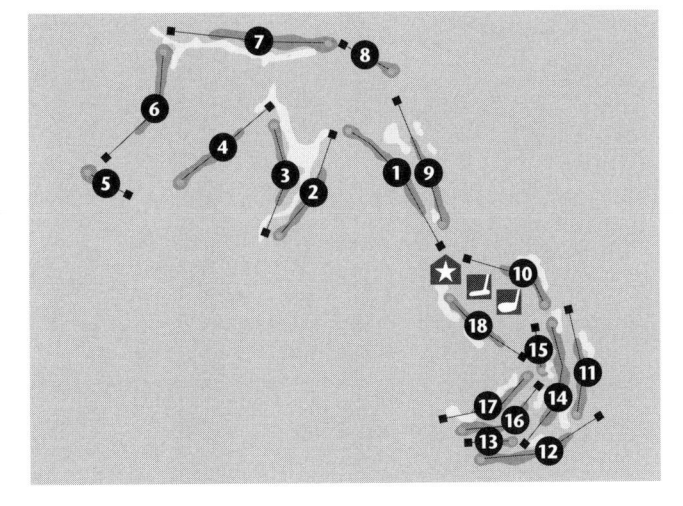

GOLF COURSE DIRECTORY

VIRGINIA MUNICIPAL GOLF COURSE

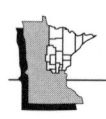

18 Regulation Public

9th Avenue North
Virginia, Minnesota 55792
218/741-4366 Clubhouse/Proshop

RESERVATIONS	218/741-4366
	Walk-on: good/good

GREEN FEES	M-F	S-S
Adult	$18/12	$18
Senior	$18/12	$18
Junior	$18/12	$18
Twilight	NA	NA
	Season tickets available	

PAYMENT	No credit cards accepted
	Non-local checks accepted

LEAGUES	Men: T,W (5:30 pm)
	Women: T (am), Th (pm)

MEMBERSHIPS	USGA, NGF, MGA

OWNER	City of Virginia
MANAGER	John Bachman
SUPERINTENDENT	Bill Kishel

HOURS 6:30 am to Dusk
SEASON April to October

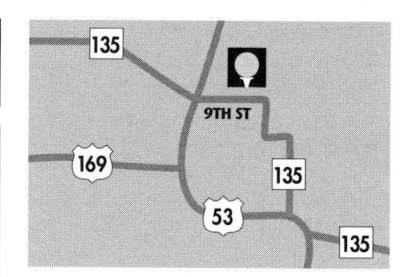

FEATURES

Putting green	Y
Driving range	N
Practice area	N
Golf carts	
Power (gas)	Y
Pull carts	Y
Club rental	Y
Club storage	N
Caddies	N
Proshop	
Extended	Y
Refreshments	
Restaurant	Y
Lounge	Y
Snacks	Y
Clubhouse	
Showers	Y
Lockers	Y
Lodging	N

Located in Virginia. Course entrance is about 1/2 mile east of U.S. Highway 53 on MN Highway 135/9th Avenue.

	MEN			WOMEN		
	FRONT	PAR	HDCP	FRONT	PAR	HDCP
1	483	5	17	483	5	17
2	437	4	1	372	5	1
3	392	4	4	302	5	4
4	338	4	7	218	4	7
5	135	3	8	118	3	8
6	493	5	18	480	5	18
7	292	4	16	242	4	16
8	367	4	13	367	4	13
9	160	3	9	150	3	9
Out	3097	36		2732	38	
10	381	4	10	381	4	10
11	421	4	2	356	4	2
12	335	4	12	215	4	12
13	388	4	3	320	5	3
14	313	4	15	284	4	15
15	225	3	5	180	3	5
16	381	4	11	348	4	11
17	182	3	6	137	3	6
18	478	5	14	443	5	14
In	3104	35		2664	36	
Total	6201	71		5396	74	
Rating	69.5			70.9		
Slope	118			120		

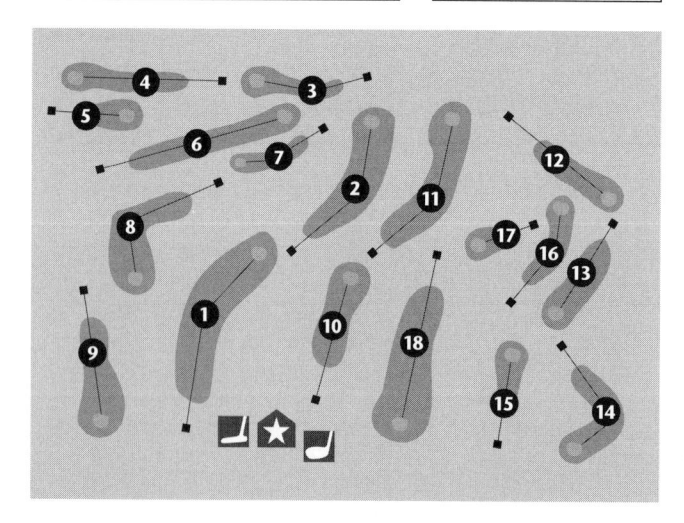

WADENA MUNICIPAL GOLF COURSE
9 Regulation Public

RR 2, P.O. Box 446
Wadena, Minnesota 56482
218/631-4010 Clubhouse/Proshop

RESERVATIONS	218/631-4010	
	Walk-on: good/good	
GREEN FEES	M-F	S-S
Adult	$16/10	$17/11
Senior	$16/10	$17/11
Junior	$16/10	$17/11
Twilight	NA	$6 (6 pm)
PAYMENT	No credit cards accepted	
	Non-local checks accepted	
LEAGUES	Men: W	
	Women: T (8-11 am)	
	T (4-6 pm)	
MEMBERSHIPS	GCSAA, MGA	
MANAGER	Bill Adams	
SUPERINTENDENT	Joe Peluso	

HOURS	7 am to Dusk	
SEASON	April to October	
FEATURES		
Putting green	Y	
Driving range	Y	$1-1.25
Practice area	Y	
Golf carts		
Power (gas)	Y	$17/9
Pull carts	Y	$2
Club rental	Y	$1
Club storage	Y	$7
Caddies	N	
Proshop		
Extended	Y	
Refreshments		
Restaurant	N	
Lounge	Y	
Snacks	Y	
Clubhouse		
Showers	Y	
Lockers	Y	
Lodging	N	

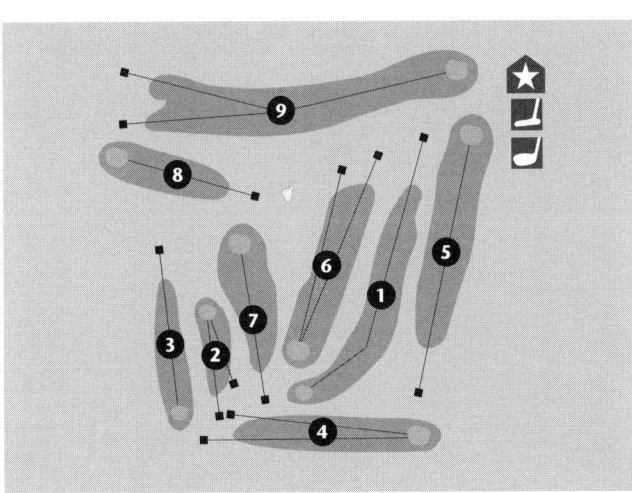

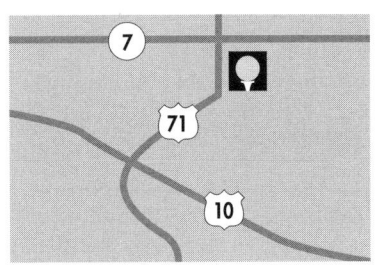

Located in Wadena. Course entrance is four miles north of U.S. Highway 10 on U.S. Highway 71.

	MEN				WOMEN		
	BACK	FRONT	PAR	HDCP	FRONT	PAR	HDCP
1	540	512	5	5	415	5	1
2	225	180	3	7	140	3	5
3	330	320	4	9	305	4	9
4	330	320	4	8	312	4	6
5	505	485	5	4	400	5	7
6	391	361	4	1	346	4	4
7	345	312	4	6	287	4	3
8	180	163	3	3	158	3	8
9	385	352	4	2	338	4	2
Out	3231	3005	36		2701	36	
1	540	512	5	5	415	5	1
2	225	180	3	7	140	3	5
3	330	320	4	9	305	4	9
4	330	320	4	8	312	4	6
5	505	485	5	4	400	5	7
6	391	361	4	1	346	4	4
7	345	312	4	6	287	4	3
8	180	163	3	3	158	3	8
9	385	352	4	2	338	4	2
In	3231	3005	36		2701	36	
Total	6462	6010	72		5402	72	
Rating	NA	68.0			70.6		
Slope	NA	115			116		

WAPICADA COUNTRY CLUB

18 Regulation Semi-Private

P.O. Box 73
St. Cloud, Minnesota 56302
612/251-7804 Clubhouse/Proshop

HOURS	6:30 am to Dusk
SEASON	April-November

RESERVATIONS	612/251-7804 2 day
	Walk-on: good/fair

GREEN FEES	M-F	S-S
Adult	$19	$22
Senior	$9	$22
Junior	$19	$22
Twilight	$12	$12

PAYMENT	Credit cards not accepted
	Non-local checks accepted

LEAGUES	Men: Various
	Women: Various

MEMBERSHIPS	USGA, PGA, GCSAA,
	CMAA, MGA

MANAGER	Jim Klaers
SUPERINTENDENT	Mike Kasner
PROFESSIONAL	Jim Klaers

FEATURES

Putting green	Y	
Driving range	Y	$3
Practice area	Y	
Golf carts		
Power (gas)	Y	$19
Pull carts	Y	$3
Club rental	N	
Club storage	Y	
Caddies	N	
Proshop		
Extended	Y	
Refreshments		
Restaurant	Y	
Lounge	Y	
Snacks	Y	
Clubhouse		
Showers	Y	
Lockers	Y	
Lodging	N	

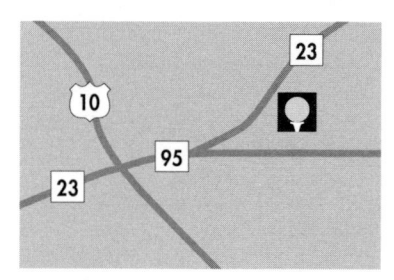

Located east of St. Cloud. Course is five miles east of U.S. Highway 10 on MN Highway 23.

	MEN			**WOMEN**		
	BACK	FRONT	PAR	HDCP	FRONT	PAR	HDCP
1	440	417	4	4	314	4	10
2	383	378	4	10	364	4	2
3	351	347	4	14	336	4	14
4	410	397	4	8	330	4	12
5	143	138	3	18	128	3	18
6	479	466	5	6	400	5	6
7	295	291	4	16	282	4	16
8	202	194	3	12	175	3	8
9	419	409	4	2	401	5	4
Out	3122	3037	35		2730	36	
10	521	454	5	9	439	5	9
11	198	178	3	15	152	3	13
12	379	371	4	7	350	4	7
13	312	290	4	13	258	4	15
14	516	502	5	5	455	5	5
15	458	438	4	1	360	4	1
16	172	158	3	17	141	3	17
17	385	350	4	11	289	4	11
18	513	503	5	3	425	5	3
In	3454	3244	37		2869	37	
Total	6576	6281	72		5599	73	
Rating	71.1	69.8			71.7		
Slope	121	118			122		

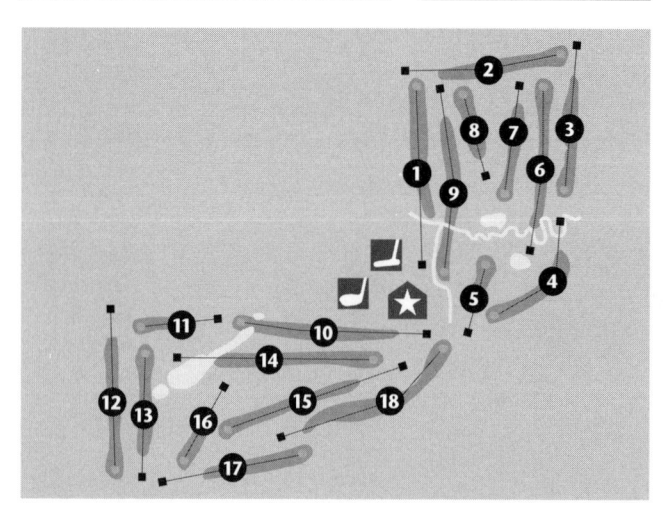

WARREN RIVERSIDE GOLF CLUB

9 Regulation Semi-Private

P.O. Box 128
Warren, Minnesota 56762
218/745-4028 Clubhouse/Proshop

HOURS	Dawn to Dusk
SEASON	April-November

RESERVATIONS	218/745-4028
	Walk-on: good/fair

GREEN FEES	M-F	S-S
Adult	$10/8	$12/10
Senior	$10/8	$12/10
Junior	$10/8	$12/10
Twilight	NA	NA

PAYMENT	Credit: Visa® MasterCard®
	Non-local checks accepted

LEAGUES	Men: W (3 pm)
	Women: T (3 pm)

MEMBERSHIPS	MGA

MANAGER	Steve Nelson
SUPERINTENDENT	Joe Yeado

FEATURES	
Putting green	Y
Driving range	Y
Practice area	Y
Golf carts	
Power (elec)	Y
Pull carts	Y
Club rental	Y
Club storage	N
Caddies	N
Proshop	
Extended	Y
Refreshments	
Restaurant	N
Lounge	N
Snacks	Y
Clubhouse	
Showers	N
Lockers	N
Lodging	N

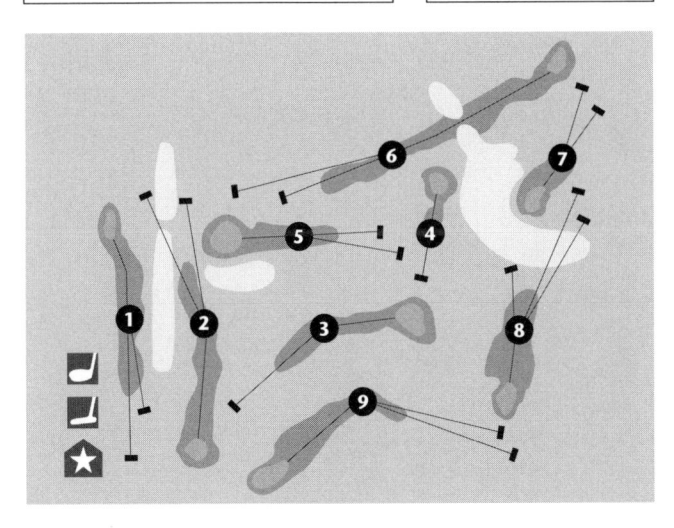

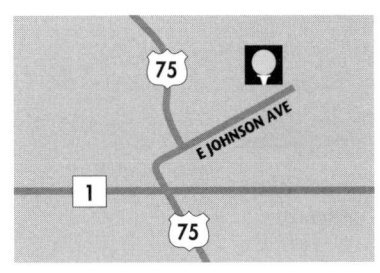

Located in northeast Warren. Course is about 1/2 mile east of U.S. Highway 75 on Johnson Avenue.

	MEN				WOMEN		
	BACK	FRONT	PAR	HDCP	FRONT	PAR	HDCP
1	395	385	4	3	365	5	3
2	387	372	4	4	355	4	4
3	370	330	4	6	310	4	6
4	167	150	3	5	125	3	5
5	280	245	4	9	215	4	9
6	480	460	5	8	392	5	8
7	190	155	3	2	135	3	2
8	371	335	4	1	252	4	1
9	470	460	5	7	380	5	7
Out	3110	2892	36		2529	37	
1	395	385	4	3	365	5	3
2	387	372	4	4	355	4	4
3	370	330	4	6	310	4	6
4	167	150	3	5	125	3	5
5	280	245	4	9	215	4	9
6	480	460	5	8	392	5	8
7	190	155	3	2	135	3	2
8	371	335	4	1	252	4	1
9	470	460	5	7	380	5	7
In	3110	2892	36		2529	37	
Total	6220	5784	72		5058	74	
Rating	NA	69.0			69.2		
Slope	NA	121			117		

GOLF COURSE DIRECTORY

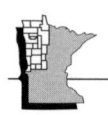

WARROAD ESTATES GOLF COURSE

18 Regulation Public

HC 2, P.O. Box 30
Warroad, Minnesota 56763
218/386-2025 Clubhouse/Proshop

RESERVATIONS	218/386-2025
	Walk-on: fair/poor

GREEN FEES	M-F	S-S
Adult	$13/10	$15/12
Senior	$10/8	$15/12
Junior	$6/3	$15/12
Twilight	$9	NA
	Discount packages available	

PAYMENT	Credit: Visa® MasterCard®
	Local checks only

LEAGUES	Men: W (5 pm)
	Women: M (6 pm)
	Senior: Th (1 pm)

MEMBERSHIPS	USGA, NGF, PGA, MGA

OWNER	Lee & Jan Leach
SUPERINTENDENT	Guy & Rick Leach
PROFESSIONAL	Lee Leach

HOURS	7 am to Dusk
SEASON	April to October

FEATURES	
Putting green	Y
Driving range	N
Practice area	N
Golf carts	
Power (elec)	Y $18/9
Pull carts	Y $2/1.25
Club rental	Y $8/5
Club storage	N
Caddies	N
Proshop	
Extended	Y
Refreshments	
Restaurant	Y
Lounge	Y
Snacks	Y
Clubhouse	
Showers	N
Lockers	N
Lodging	N

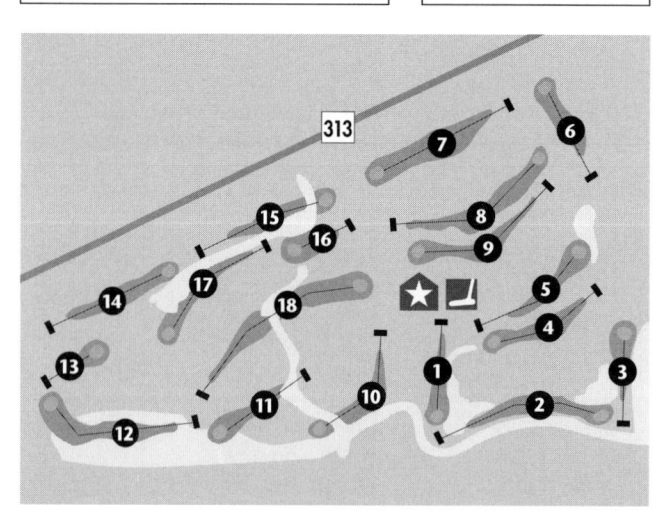

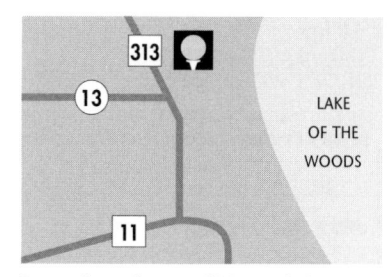

LAKE OF THE WOODS

Located northwest of Warroad. Course entrance is two miles north of MN Highway 11 on MN Highway 313.

	MEN				**WOMEN**		
	BACK	FRONT	PAR	HDCP	FRONT	PAR	HDCP
1	174	142	3	18	110	3	17
2	542	504	5	2	439	5	1
3	209	179	3	8	149	3	15
4	396	333	4	16	302	4	11
5	364	332	4	11	301	4	9
6	326	286	4	14	246	4	13
7	443	394	4	6	344	4	7
8	482	455	5	12	429	5	5
9	449	413	4	4	375	4	3
Out	3385	3038	36		2695	36	
10	420	363	4	5	331	4	8
11	355	304	4	17	245	4	12
12	545	499	5	3	406	5	6
13	219	193	3	10	167	3	16
14	402	369	4	13	337	4	10
15	458	433	4	1	407	5	4
16	198	170	3	15	143	3	18
17	410	354	4	9	271	4	14
18	550	482	5	7	453	5	2
In	3557	3167	36		2760	37	
Total	6942	6205	72		5455	73	
Rating	74.3	71.6			72.0		
Slope	128	123			121		

WASECA LAKESIDE CLUB

18 Regulation Semi-Private

P.O. Box 187
Waseca, Minnesota 56093
507/835-2574 Clubhouse/Proshop

HOURS	7 am to Dusk
SEASON	April to October

RESERVATIONS	507/835-2574 2 days
	Walk-on: good/fair

GREEN FEES	M-F	S-S
Adult	$20/13	$23/14
Senior	$20/13	$23/14
Junior	$20/13	$23/14
Twilight	NA	NA

PAYMENT	No credit cards accepted
	Non-local checks accepted

LEAGUES	Men: None
	Women: None

MEMBERSHIPS	USGA, PGA, GCSAA, MGA

MANAGER	Jeff Richards
SUPERINTENDENT	Rob Panuska
PROFESSIONAL	Jeff Richards

FEATURES	
Putting green	Y
Driving range	Y
Practice area	N
Golf carts	
Power (gas)	Y
Pull carts	Y
Club rental	Y
Club storage	Y
Caddies	N
Proshop	
Extended	Y
Refreshments	
Restaurant	N
Lounge	Y
Snacks	Y
Clubhouse	
Showers	Y
Lockers	Y
Lodging	N

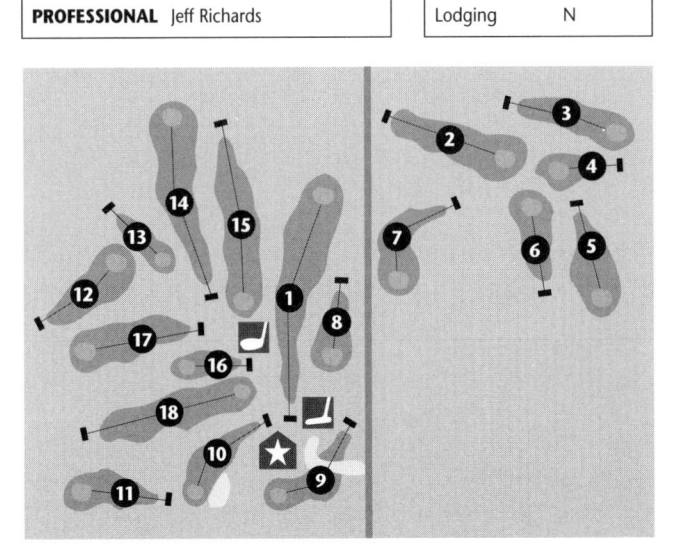

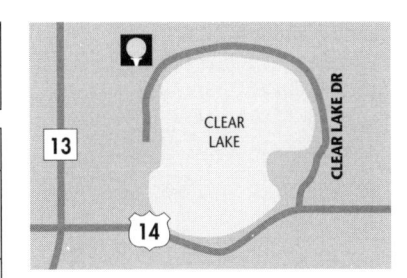

Located in Waseca. Course entrance is two miles north of U.S. Highway 14 on Clear Lake Drive.

		MEN			WOMEN		
	BACK	FRONT	PAR	HDCP	FRONT	PAR	HDCP
1	395	390	4	1	365	4	2
2	501	490	5	5	405	5	1
3	407	394	4	3	386	5	7
4	199	189	3	9	182	3	9
5	357	341	4	11	315	4	13
6	392	379	4	7	306	4	5
7	335	320	4	13	310	4	15
8	169	154	3	15	141	3	17
9	328	303	4	17	245	4	11
Out	3083	2960	35		2655	36	
10	181	168	3	10	156	3	6
11	275	269	4	14	260	4	8
12	298	294	4	16	261	4	16
13	199	189	3	8	178	3	14
14	479	471	5	12	404	5	4
15	470	458	5	6	370	5	12
16	125	115	3	18	107	3	18
17	411	403	4	2	394	5	10
18	504	495	5	4	488	5	2
In	2942	2862	36		2618	37	
Total	6025	5822	71		5273	73	
Rating	68.6	67.6			70.3		
Slope	116	115			115		

GOLF COURSE DIRECTORY

WATONWAN COUNTRY CLUB

9 Regulation Semi-Private

Rural Route 2, P.O. Box 147
St. James, Minnesota 56081
507/375-3849 Clubhouse
507/375-7213 Proshop

HOURS	8 am to Dusk
SEASON	April to October

FEATURES

Putting green	Y
Driving range	Y
Practice area	Y
Golf carts	
Power (gas)	Y
Pull carts	Y
Club rental	Y
Club storage	Y
Caddies	N
Proshop	
Extended	Y
Refreshments	
Restaurant	Y
Lounge	Y
Snacks	Y
Clubhouse	
Showers	Y
Lockers	Y
Lodging	N

RESERVATIONS	507/375-7213
	Walk-on: good/fair

GREEN FEES	M-F	S-S
Adult	$14/9	$15/10
Senior	$14/9	$15/10
Junior	$14/9	$15/10
Twilight	NA	NA

PAYMENT	No credit cards accepted
	Non-local checks accepted

LEAGUES	Men: Th
	Women: T

MEMBERSHIPS	USGA, PGA, GCSAA, CMAA, MGA

MANAGER	DeeAnn L. Nelson
SUPERINTENDENT	Karl Weiss
PROFESSIONAL	DeeAnn L. Nelson

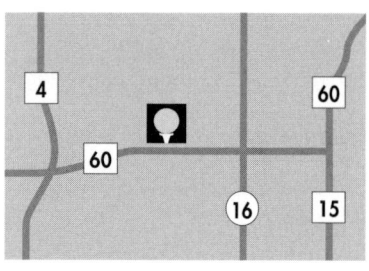

Located east of St. James. Course is about six miles east of MN Highway 4 on MN Highway 60.

	MEN				WOMEN		
	BACK	FRONT	PAR	HDCP	FRONT	PAR	HDCP
1	205	200	3	3	183	4	3
2	394	386	4	2	320	4	2
3	290	284	4	8	177	4	8
4	150	137	3	6	125	3	6
5	475	470	5	4	348	5	4
6	410	365	4	7	357	4	7
7	380	378	4	1	364	5	1
8	175	163	3	9	140	3	9
9	438	436	5	5	361	5	5
Out	2917	2819	35		2375	37	
1	205	200	3	3	183	4	3
2	394	386	4	2	320	4	2
3	290	284	4	8	177	4	8
4	150	137	3	6	125	3	6
5	475	470	5	4	348	5	4
6	410	365	4	7	357	4	7
7	380	378	4	1	364	5	1
8	175	163	3	9	140	3	9
9	438	436	5	5	361	5	5
In	2917	2819	35		2375	37	
Total	5834	5638	70		4750	74	
Rating	69.4	68.2			67.0		
Slope	120	118			105		

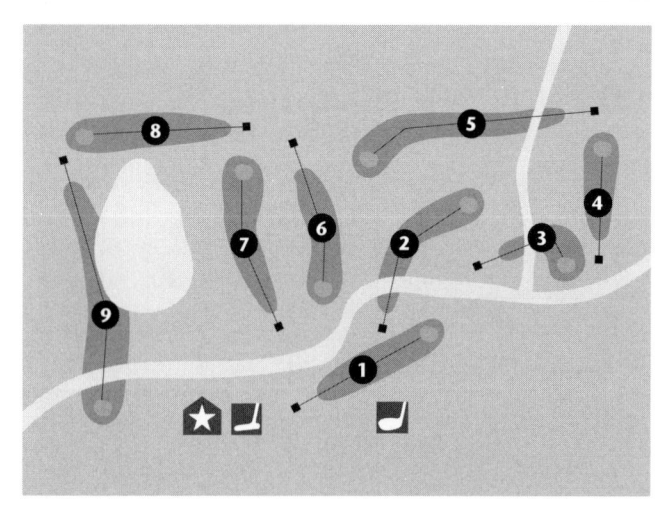

WAYZATA COUNTRY CLUB

18 Regulation Private

200 West Wayzata Blvd, P.O. Box 151
Wayzata, Minnesota 55391
612/473-8846 Clubhouse
612/475-9769 Proshop

HOURS	Dawn to Dusk
SEASON	April to October

FEATURES	
Putting green	Y
Driving range	Y
Practice area	Y
Golf carts	
Power	Y
Pull carts	Y
Club rental	Y
Club storage	Y
Caddies	Y
Proshop	
Extended	Y
Refreshments	
Restaurant	Y
Lounge	Y
Snacks	Y
Clubhouse	
Showers	Y
Lockers	Y
Lodging	N

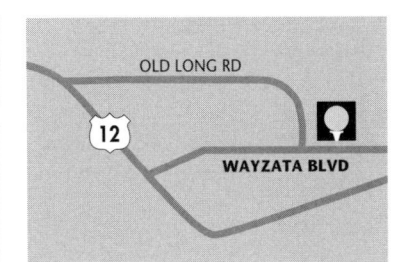

RESERVATIONS	612/475-9769	
	Members only	
GREEN FEES	M-F	S-S
Adult	Call	Call
Senior	Call	Call
Junior	Call	Call
Twilight	NA	NA
	Members and guests only	
PAYMENT	Fees billed to members	
LEAGUES	Men: Various	
	Women: Various	
MEMBERSHIPS	MGA	
SUPERINTENDENT	Robert Distel	
PROFESSIONAL	Gary Nutt	

Located in Wayzata. Course entrance is about 1/2 mile east of U.S. Highway 12 on Wayzata Blvd.

	MEN				WOMEN		
	BACK	FRONT	PAR	HDCP	FRONT	PAR	HDCP
1	425	400	4	9	361	4	5
2	496	483	5	11	448	5	1
3	383	374	4	7	312	4	11
4	212	172	3	15	156	3	15
5	441	425	4	1	331	4	7
6	520	499	5	13	462	5	3
7	395	385	4	5	315	4	9
8	151	134	3	17	122	3	17
9	444	432	4	3	409	5	13
Out	3467	3304	36		2916	37	
10	425	418	4	6	401	5	14
11	402	382	4	12	300	4	8
12	512	500	5	14	440	5	4
13	191	178	3	16	158	3	16
14	375	361	4	10	300	4	10
15	549	538	5	2	424	5	12
16	405	394	4	8	345	4	6
17	192	165	3	18	134	3	18
18	429	420	4	4	329	4	2
In	3480	3356	36		2831	37	
Total	6947	6660	72		5747	74	
Rating	74.8	73.4			74.8		
Slope	138	136			136		

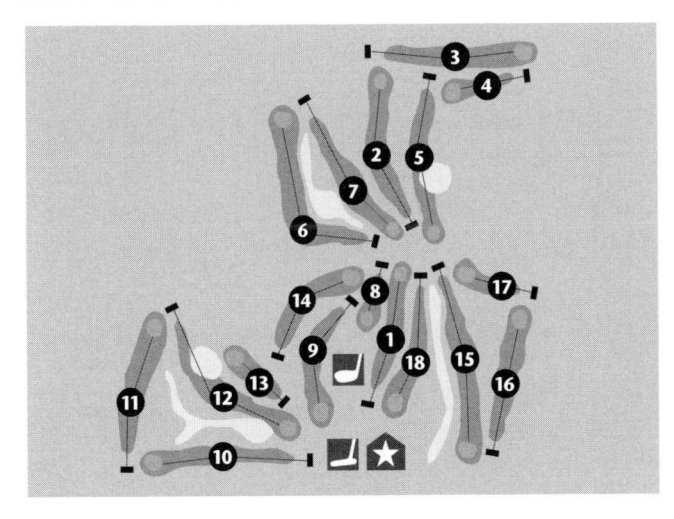

GOLF COURSE DIRECTORY

WELLS GOLF CLUB

9 Executive Public

Wells City Park, P.O. Box 236
Wells, Minnesota 56097
507/553-3313 Clubhouse/Proshop

HOURS 8 am to Dusk

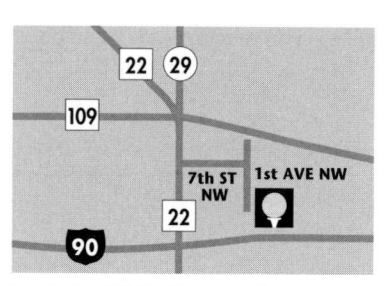

SEASON April to October

Located in Wells. Course entrance is east of MN Highway 22 on 7th Street, then south on 1st Avenue.

RESERVATIONS	No reservations accepted
	Walk-on: good/good

GREEN FEES	M-F	S-S
Adult	$5	$6
Senior	$5	$6
Junior	$2.50	$3
Twilight	NA	NA

PAYMENT	No credit cards accepted
	Non-local checks accepted

LEAGUES	Men: Various
	Women: Various

MEMBERSHIPS	MGA

OWNER	City of Wells
MANAGER	Gen Besser

FEATURES

Putting green	Y
Driving range	N
Practice area	Y

Golf carts	
Power	N
Pull carts	Y
Club rental	Y
Club storage	N
Caddies	N

Proshop	
Basic	Y
Refreshments	
Restaurant	N
Lounge	N
Snacks	Y
Clubhouse	
Showers	N
Lockers	N

Lodging	N

	MEN			WOMEN		
	FRONT	PAR	HDCP	FRONT	PAR	HDCP
1	153	3		153	3	
2	165	3		165	3	
3	195	3		195	3	
4	312	4		312	4	
5	285	4		285	4	
6	187	3		187	3	
7	224	3		224	4	
8	213	3		213	4	
9	320	4		320	4	
Out	2056	30		2056	32	
1	153	3		153	3	
2	165	3		165	3	
3	195	3		195	3	
4	312	4		312	4	
5	285	4		285	4	
6	187	3		187	3	
7	224	3		224	4	
8	213	3		213	4	
9	320	4		320	4	
In	2056	30		2056	32	
Total	4112	60		4112	64	
Rating	58.6			61.0		
Slope	85			90		

Course layout map not provided.

WENDIGO GOLF CLUB

18 Regulation Public

750 Golf Crest Drive
Grand Rapids, Minnesota 55744
218/327-2211 Clubhouse/Proshop

RESERVATIONS	218/327-2211 3 days	
	Walk-on: good/fair	
GREEN FEES	M-F	S-S
Adult	$20/14	$22/16
Senior	$20/14	$22/16
Junior	$20/14	$22/16
Twilight	NA	NA
PAYMENT	Credit: Visa® MasterCard®	
	Non-local checks accepted	
LEAGUES	Men: None	
	Women: None	
MEMBERSHIPS	USGA, PGA, GCSAA, MGA	
OWNER	Wendigo Corp.	
SUPERINTENDENT	Jim Haroldson	
PROFESSIONAL	Kent Baril	

HOURS	8 am to Dusk	
SEASON	April-November	
FEATURES		
Putting green	Y	
Driving range	Y	$2.50
Practice area	Y	
Golf carts		
Power (gas)	Y	$22/12
Pull carts	Y	
Club rental	Y	$10/5
Club storage	N	
Caddies	N	
Proshop		
Extended	Y	
Refreshments		
Restaurant	N	
Lounge	N	
Snacks	Y	
Clubhouse		
Showers	N	
Lockers	N	
Lodging	N	

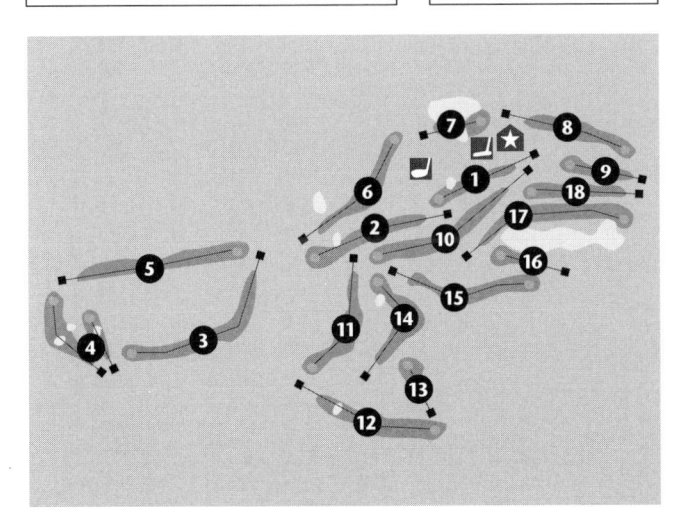

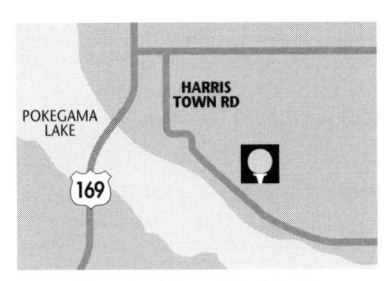

Located south of Grand Rapids. Course is 2 1/2 miles east of U.S. Highway 169 on Harris Town Road.

	MEN				WOMEN		
	BACK	FRONT	PAR	HDCP	FRONT	PAR	HDCP
1	306	294	4	17	231	4	15
2	409	394	4	3	295	4	3
3	545	530	5	7	436	5	1
4	324	311	4	11	235	4	7
5	572	542	5	1	428	5	5
6	433	418	4	9	323	4	9
7	211	187	3	5	127	3	11
8	376	356	4	13	301	4	13
9	202	193	3	15	150	3	17
Out	3378	3225	36		2526	36	
10	554	544	5	10	471	5	2
11	417	397	4	4	351	4	6
12	439	426	4	2	335	4	10
13	168	152	3	18	92	3	18
14	380	363	4	12	298	4	12
15	406	391	4	8	303	4	8
16	169	154	3	14	119	3	16
17	530	519	5	6	412	5	4
18	315	289	4	16	244	4	14
In	3378	3235	36		2625	36	
Total	6756	6460	72		5151	72	
Rating	72.0	70.7			70.0		
Slope	132	129			127		

GOLF COURSE DIRECTORY

WESTFIELD GOLF CLUB
9 Regulation Public

1460 West Fifth St.
Winona, Minnesota 55987
507/452-8700 Clubhouse
507/452-6901 Proshop

HOURS	6:30 am - Dusk
SEASON	April to October

FEATURES	
Putting green	Y
Driving range	Y
Practice area	Y
Golf carts	
Power	Y
Pull carts	Y
Club rental	Y
Club storage	Y
Caddies	N
Proshop	
Extended	Y
Refreshments	
Restaurant	Y
Lounge	Y
Snacks	Y
Clubhouse	
Showers	Y
Lockers	Y
Lodging	N

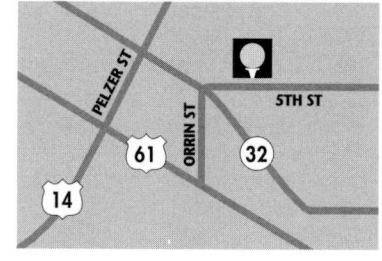

Located in Winona. Course is north of U.S. Highway 61 on Orrin Street, then east on 5th Street.

RESERVATIONS	507/452-6901 2 days
	Walk-on: poor/poor

GREEN FEES	M-F	S-S
Adult	$16/8	$16/8
Senior	$16/8	$16/8
Junior	$16/8	$16/8
Twilight	NA	NA

PAYMENT	No credit cards accepted
	Non-local checks accepted

LEAGUES	Men: Th
	Women: T (am), W (pm)

MEMBERSHIPS	USGA, MGA

PROFESSIONAL	Mike Brustkeur

	MEN				**WOMEN**		
	BACK	FRONT	PAR	HDCP	FRONT	PAR	HDCP
1	325	313	4	9	295	4	6
2	427	378	4	2	320	4	5
3	155	139	3	7	129	3	8
4	530	517	5	3	498	5	1
5	378	339	4	4	288	4	7
6	385	367	4	6	350	4	3
7	392	353	4	5	323	4	4
8	200	161	3	8	106	3	9
9	531	513	5	1	496	5	2
Out	3323	3080	36		2880	36	
1	325	313	4	9	295	4	6
2	427	378	4	2	320	4	5
3	155	139	3	7	129	3	8
4	530	517	5	3	498	5	1
5	378	339	4	4	288	4	7
6	385	367	4	6	350	4	3
7	392	353	4	5	323	4	4
8	200	161	3	8	106	3	9
9	531	513	5	1	496	5	2
In	3323	3080	36		2880	36	
Total	6646	6160	72		5760	72	
Rating	70.8	68.6			71.4		
Slope	121	116			121		

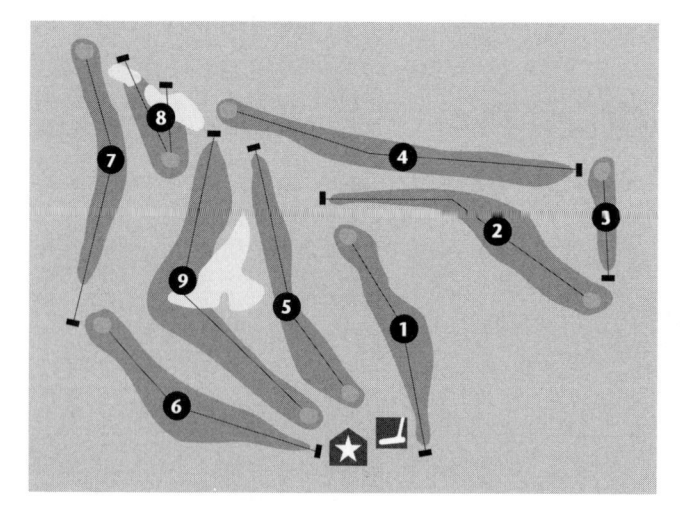

WHISPERING PINES GOLF COURSE

9 Regulation Public

County Road 6, P.O. Box 179
Annandale, Minnesota 55302
612/274-8721 Clubhouse/Proshop

HOURS 6:30 am to Dusk

SEASON March-November

RESERVATIONS	612/274-8721
	Walk-on: good/fair

GREEN FEES	M-F	S-S
Adult	$15/10	$18/12
Senior	$10/7	$18/12
Junior	$10/7	$18/12
Twilight	NA	NA

PAYMENT	No credit cards accepted
	Non-local checks accepted

LEAGUES	Men: Th (2-7 pm)
	Women: T (9-11 am)

MEMBERSHIPS	MGA

OWNER	Elmer & Dorothy Schmidt
MANAGER	Elmer & Dorothy Schmidt

FEATURES

Putting green	Y
Driving range	Y
Practice area	Y
Golf carts	
Power (gas)	Y
Pull carts	Y
Club rental	Y
Club storage	N
Caddies	N
Proshop	
Extended	Y
Refreshments	
Restaurant	N
Lounge	Y
Snacks	Y
Clubhouse	
Showers	N
Lockers	N
Lodging	N

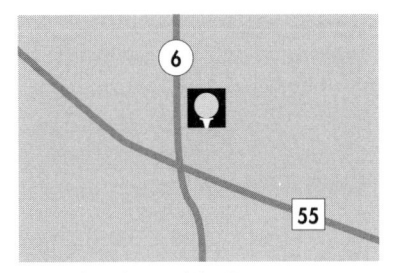

Located in Annandale. Course entrance is 1/4 mile north of MN Highway 55 on County Road 6.

		MEN			WOMEN	
	FRONT	PAR	HDCP	FRONT	PAR	HDCP
1	380	4	4	350	4	4
2	150	3	9	115	3	9
3	380	4	6	325	4	6
4	395	4	3	300	4	3
5	405	4	2	320	4	2
6	500	5	5	420	5	5
7	140	3	8	110	3	8
8	505	5	1	420	5	1
9	210	3	7	210	4	7
Out	3065	35		2570	36	
1	380	4	4	350	4	4
2	150	3	9	115	3	9
3	380	4	6	325	4	6
4	395	4	3	300	4	3
5	405	4	2	320	4	2
6	500	5	5	420	5	5
7	140	3	8	110	3	8
8	505	5	1	420	5	1
9	210	3	7	210	4	7
In	3065	35		2570	36	
Total	6130	70		5140	72	
Rating	69.4			70.0		
Slope	121			119		

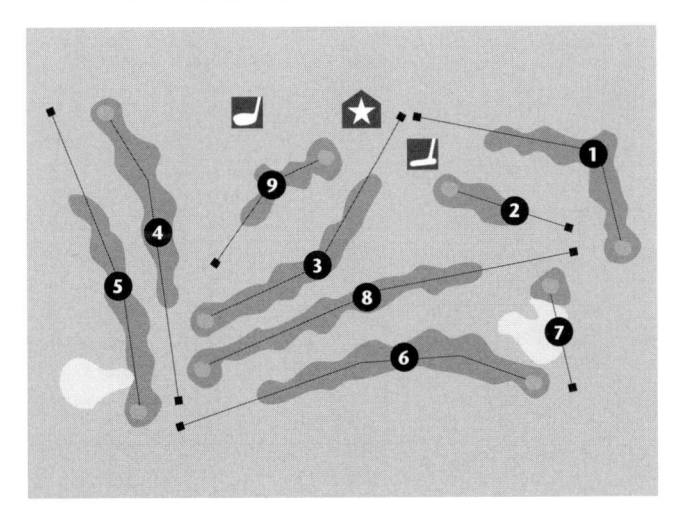

GOLF COURSE DIRECTORY

WHITE BEAR YACHT CLUB

18 Regulation Private

Highway 244, P.O. Box 10696
White Bear Lake, Minnesota 55110
612/429-4567 Clubhouse
612/429-5002 Proshop

HOURS	Dawn to Dusk
SEASON	April to October

FEATURES

Putting green	Y
Driving range	Y
Practice area	N
Golf carts	
Power	Y
Pull carts	N
Club rental	Y
Club storage	Y
Caddies	Y
Proshop	
Extended	Y
Refreshments	
Restaurant	Y
Lounge	Y
Snacks	Y
Clubhouse	
Showers	Y
Lockers	Y
Lodging	N

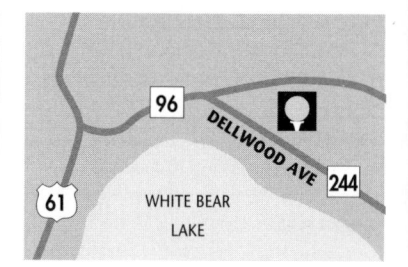

Located in White Bear Lake. Course is east of U.S. Hwy 61 on Hwy 96, then south on Dellwood Avenue/Hwy 244.

RESERVATIONS	612/429-5002	
	Members only	
GREEN FEES	M-F	S-S
Adult	Call	Call
Senior	Call	Call
Junior	Call	Call
Twilight	NA	NA
	Members and guests only	
PAYMENT	Fees billed to members	
LEAGUES	None	
MEMBERSHIPS	USGA, NGF, PGA, GCSAA, CMAA, MGA	
SUPERINTENDENT	John Steiner	
PROFESSIONAL	David Reitan	

	MEN				WOMEN		
	BACK	FRONT	PAR	HDCP	FRONT	PAR	HDCP
1	405	384	4	5	381	5	11
2	436	380	4	9	373	4	3
3	138	125	3	15	124	3	15
4	555	456	5	3	433	5	9
5	446	397	4	1	295	4	13
6	153	132	3	17	129	3	17
7	460	446	5	13	444	5	1
8	188	180	3	11	180	3	5
9	520	456	5	7	451	5	7
Out	3301	2956	36		2810	37	
10	337	300	4	14	287	4	12
11	179	145	3	18	145	3	16
12	387	350	4	12	350	4	4
13	525	471	5	4	471	5	2
14	332	314	4	10	314	4	8
15	427	377	4	2	377	5	14
16	482	456	5	6	442	5	6
17	209	136	3	8	134	3	18
18	349	318	4	16	318	4	10
In	3227	2867	36		2838	37	
Total	6528	5823	72		5648	74	
Rating	72.5	69.5			73.5		
Slope	133	127			130		

THE MINNESOTA ILLUSTRATED

WHITEFISH GOLF CLUB

18 Regulation Public

Route 1, Box 111B
Pequot Lakes, Minnesota 56472
218/543-4900 Clubhouse/Proshop

HOURS	6 am to Dusk
SEASON	April to October

RESERVATIONS	218/543-4900 3 days
	Walk-on: fair/poor

GREEN FEES	M-F	S-S
Adult	$26/17	$29/18
Senior	$26/17	$29/18
Junior	$26/17	$29/18
Twilight	$18/12	NA

PAYMENT	Credit: Visa® MasterCard®
	Non-local checks accepted

LEAGUES	Men:	Th (am)
	Women:	W (am)

MEMBERSHIPS	USGA, NGF, PGA, GCSAA, CMAA, MGA

OWNER	Ideal Development Corp.
MANAGER	Rick Ellested
PROFESSIONAL	Al Svejkovsky

FEATURES	
Putting green	Y
Driving range	N
Practice area	Y
Golf carts	
Power (gas)	Y
Pull carts	Y
Club rental	Y
Club storage	Y
Caddies	N
Proshop	
Extended	Y
Refreshments	
Restaurant	N
Lounge	Y
Snacks	Y
Clubhouse	
Showers	N
Lockers	N
Lodging	N

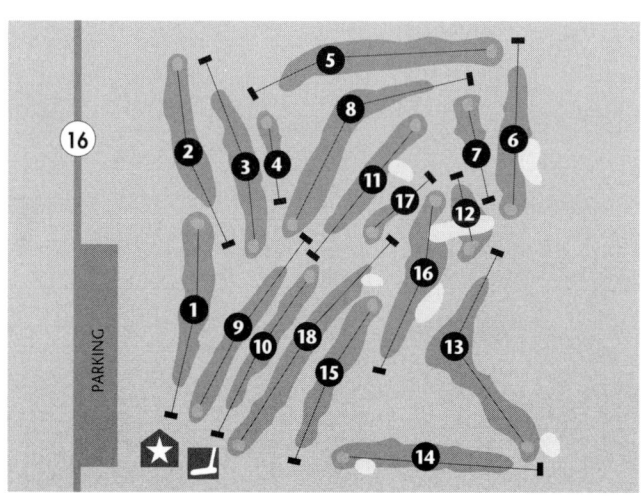

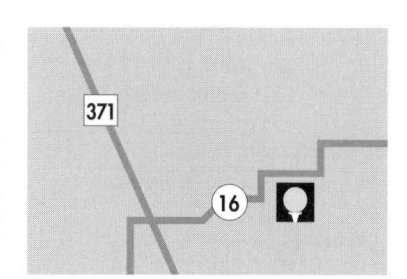

Located northeast of Pequot Lakes. Course entrance is five miles east of MN Highway 371 on County Road 16.

	MEN				**WOMEN**		
	BACK	FRONT	PAR	HDCP	FRONT	PAR	HDCP
1	377	360	4	9	332	4	7
2	389	379	4	7	336	4	13
3	365	357	4	15	304	4	15
4	156	142	3	17	125	3	17
5	509	501	5	1	486	5	1
6	326	319	4	13	294	4	11
7	184	177	3	11	162	3	9
8	482	471	5	5	456	5	3
9	377	361	4	3	342	4	5
Out	3165	3067	36		2837	36	
10	400	386	4	8	366	4	8
11	354	345	4	12	327	4	12
12	163	151	3	18	122	3	18
13	477	462	5	4	437	5	4
14	359	346	4	10	305	4	10
15	364	349	4	14	300	4	14
16	398	376	4	2	348	4	2
17	195	179	3	16	165	3	16
18	532	511	5	6	473	5	6
In	3242	3105	36		2843	36	
Total	6407	6172	72		5682	72	
Rating	70.4	69.3			72.6		
Slope	122	121			124		

GOLF COURSE DIRECTORY

WILDERNESS HILLS GOLF COURSE

18 Executive Public

591 Bley Road
Holyoke, Minnesota 55749
218/496-5751 Clubhouse/Proshop

HOURS	Dawn to Dusk
SEASON	April to October

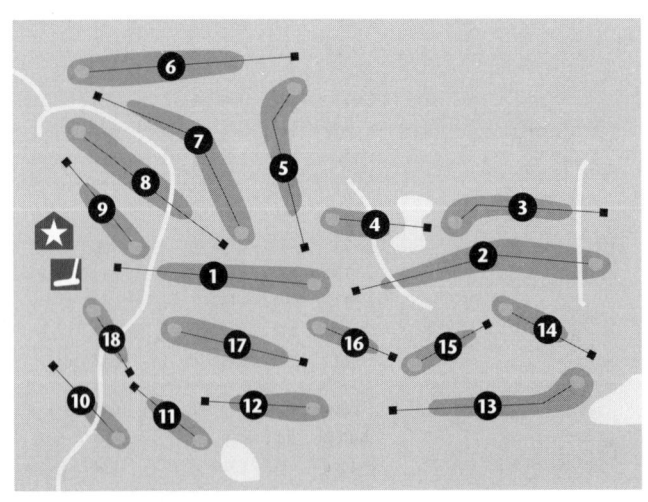

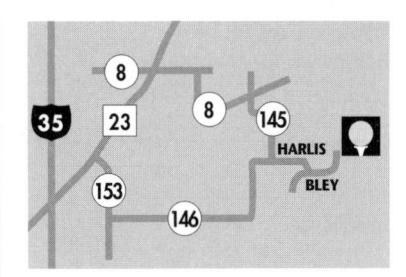

Located in Holyoke. Course is east of Hwy 23 on Cty Rd 8, south on Cty Rd 145, east on Harlis, then east on Bley Rd.

RESERVATIONS	218/496-5751	
	Walk-on: good/good	
GREEN FEES	M-F	S-S
Adult	Call	Call
Senior	Call	Call
Junior	Call	Call
Twilight	NA	NA
PAYMENT	No credit cards accepted	
	Non-local checks accepted	
LEAGUES	Men: Various	
	Women: Various	
MEMBERSHIPS	MGA	
OWNER	Tim Rogers	
MANAGER	Tim Rogers	

FEATURES	
Putting green	Y
Driving range	N
Practice area	N
Golf carts	
Power (gas)	Y
Pull carts	Y
Club rental	Y
Club storage	N
Caddies	N
Proshop	
Basic	Y
Refreshments	
Restaurant	N
Lounge	N
Snacks	Y
Clubhouse	
Showers	N
Lockers	N
Lodging	N

	MEN FRONT	PAR	HDCP	WOMEN FRONT	PAR	HDCP
1	380	4		368	4	
2	532	5		516	5	
3	327	4		315	4	
4	227	3		214	3	
5	478	5		452	5	
6	301	4		289	4	
7	485	5		467	5	
8	280	4		250	4	
9	160	3		146	3	
Out	3170	36		3017	38	
10	181	3		169	3	
11	138	3		128	3	
12	274	4		254	4	
13	265	3		223	3	
14	125	3		117	3	
15	164	3		152	3	
16	204	3		188	3	
17	308	4		278	4	
18	165	3		155	3	
In	1824	29		1664	29	
Total	4994	65		4681	67	
Rating	NA			NA		
Slope	NA			NA		

THE WILDS GOLF CLUB

18 Regulation Public

14819 Wilds Parkway
Prior Lake, Minnesota 55372
612/445-4455 Clubhouse/Proshop

RESERVATIONS	612/445-4455 5 days
	Walk-on: poor/poor
GREEN FEES	M-F	S-S
Adult	$95	$95
Senior	$95	$95
Junior	$95	$95
Twilight	$60	$60
	Fees include power carts
PAYMENT	Credit: Visa® MC® AmEx®
	Non-local checks accepted
LEAGUES	Men: None
	Women: None
MEMBERSHIPS	USGA, NGF, PGA, GCSAA, MGA
OWNER	Richard Burtness
INSTRUCTOR	Dan Simpson
PROFESSIONAL	Gaylen Allen

HOURS	6 am to Dusk
SEASON	April-November

FEATURES		
Putting green	Y	
Driving range	Y	$5.50-9
Practice area	Y	
Golf carts		
Power (elec)	Y	
Pull carts	N	
Club rental	Y	$25
Club storage	N	
Caddies	N	
Proshop		
Extended	Y	
Refreshments		
Restaurant	Y	
Lounge	Y	
Snacks	Y	
Clubhouse		
Showers	N	
Lockers	N	
Lodging	N	

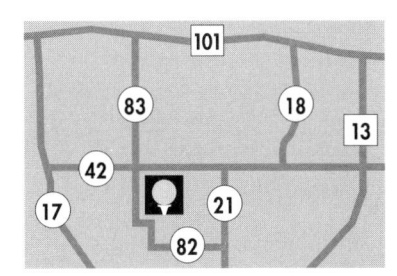

Located in Prior Lake. Course entrance is south of MN Highway 101 on Cty Rd 83, then east one mile on Wilds Parkway.

	MEN				**WOMEN**		
	BACK	FRONT	PAR	HDCP	FRONT	PAR	HDCP
1	406	360	4	15	317	4	15
2	517	471	5	9	401	5	9
3	170	148	3	17	96	3	17
4	340	286	4	13	237	4	13
5	478	400	4	7	370	4	7
6	460	398	4	1	363	4	1
7	174	159	3	5	148	3	5
8	540	518	5	11	372	5	11
9	378	345	4	3	247	4	3
Out	3463	3085	36		2551	36	
10	433	381	4	6	253	4	6
11	227	185	3	8	134	3	8
12	553	508	5	10	391	5	10
13	165	137	3	12	129	3	12
14	475	433	4	14	369	4	14
15	378	348	4	18	299	4	18
16	330	285	4	16	202	4	16
17	560	530	5	2	415	5	2
18	444	409	4	4	345	4	4
In	3565	3216	36		2537	36	
Total	7028	6301	72		5088	72	
Rating	74.7	69.0			70.2		
Slope	140	124			126		

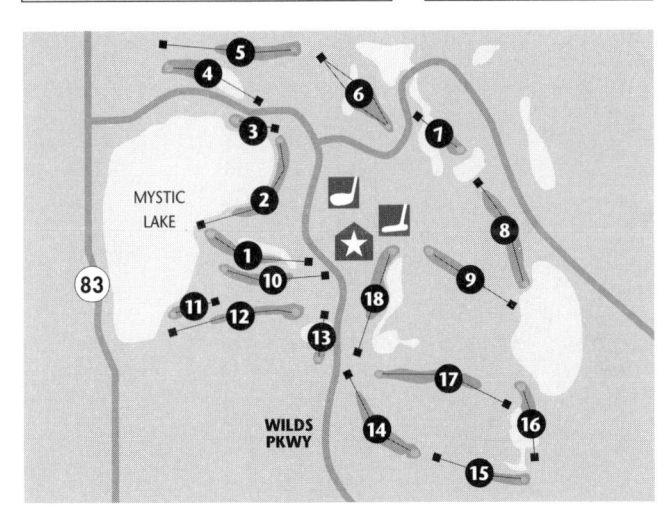

GOLF COURSE DIRECTORY

WILLINGER'S GOLF CLUB

18 Regulation Public

6900 Canby Trail
Northfield, Minnesota 55057
612/652-2500 Clubhouse/Proshop
612/440-7000 Twin City Metro Area

HOURS	Dawn to Dusk
SEASON	April-November

RESERVATIONS	612/440-7000	4 days
	Walk-on: fair/poor	

GREEN FEES	M-F	S-S
Adult	$23/17	$29
Senior	$20/17	$25
Junior	$18/17	$18
Twilight	$18	$22

PAYMENT	Credit: Visa® MasterCard®
	Non-local checks accepted

LEAGUES	Men: None
	Women: None

MEMBERSHIPS	USGA, PGA, GCSAA, MGA

SUPERINTENDENT Jim Kassera
PROFESSIONAL Howie Samb

FEATURES

Putting green	Y	
Driving range	Y	$1.50
Practice area	Y	
Golf carts		
Power (gas)	Y	$22
Pull carts	Y	$2.50
Club rental	Y	$9
Club storage	N	
Caddies	N	
Proshop		
Extended	Y	
Refreshments		
Restaurant	Y	
Lounge	Y	
Snacks	Y	
Clubhouse		
Showers	Y	
Lockers	Y	
Lodging	N	

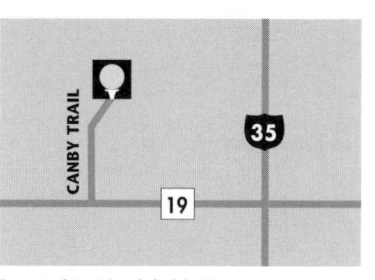

Located in Northfield. Course entrance is 1 1/2 miles west of I-35 on MN Highway 19, then north on Canby Trail.

	MEN				**WOMEN**		
	BACK	FRONT	PAR	HDCP	FRONT	PAR	HDCP
1	399	353	4	5	310	4	5
2	504	472	5	7	417	5	7
3	185	127	3	11	96	3	11
4	430	374	4	3	318	4	3
5	330	295	4	17	245	4	17
6	530	474	5	1	443	5	1
7	188	156	3	9	104	3	9
8	384	350	4	13	308	4	13
9	380	331	4	15	292	4	15
Out	3330	2932	36		2533	36	
10	370	331	4	12	282	4	12
11	390	334	4	10	294	4	10
12	445	405	4	2	365	4	2
13	362	325	4	14	288	4	14
14	183	155	3	16	123	3	16
15	503	440	5	8	409	5	8
16	419	365	4	6	339	4	6
17	143	101	3	18	93	3	18
18	566	471	5	4	440	5	4
In	3381	2927	36		2633	36	
Total	6711	5859	72		5166	72	
Rating	73.3	69.4			71.6		
Slope	140	132			130		

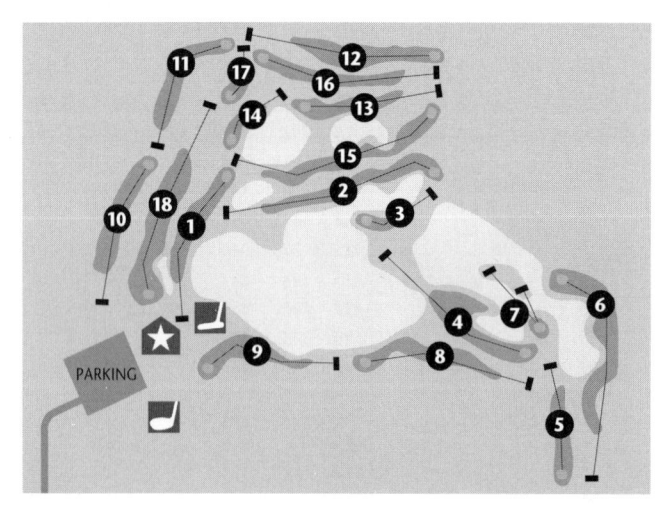

THE MINNESOTA ILLUSTRATED

WILLMAR GOLF CLUB

18 Regulation Semi-Private

1000 26th Avenue NE, P.O. Box 751
Willmar, Minnesota 56201
612/235-1166 Clubhouse/Proshop

HOURS	7 am to Dusk
SEASON	April-November

RESERVATIONS	612/235-1166 1 day
	Walk-on: good/fair

GREEN FEES	M-F	S-S
Adult	$22/13	$22/13
Senior	$22/13	$22/13
Junior	$22/13	$22/13
Twilight	NA	NA

PAYMENT	Credit: Visa® MasterCard®
	Non-local checks accepted

LEAGUES	Men:	T (1 pm-dusk)
		Th (1-6 pm)
	Women:	W (7 am-noon)
		W (4-6 pm)

MEMBERSHIPS	USGA, NGF, PGA, GCSAA, MGA

SUPERINTENDENT	Jim Wodash
PROFESSIONAL	Jeff Wahl

FEATURES		
Putting green	Y	
Driving range	Y	$3
Practice area	Y	
Golf carts		
Power (gas)	Y	$20
Pull carts	Y	$4
Club rental	Y	$9
Club storage	Y	
Caddies	N	
Proshop		
Extended	Y	
Refreshments		
Restaurant	Y	
Lounge	Y	
Snacks	Y	
Clubhouse		
Showers	Y	
Lockers	Y	
Lodging	N	

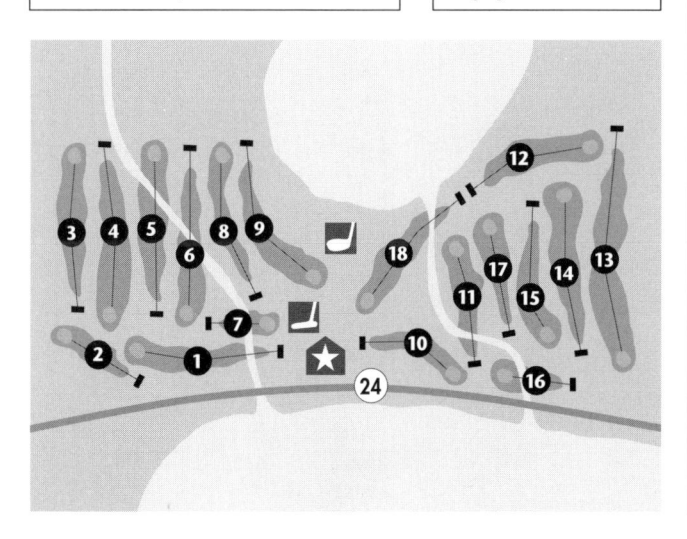

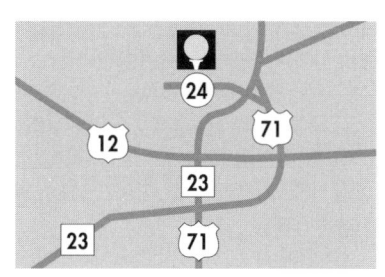

Located north of Willmar. Course is west of U.S. Highway 71 on 26th Avenue NW (County Road 24).

	MEN				**WOMEN**		
	BACK	FRONT	PAR	HDCP	FRONT	PAR	HDCP
1	497	482	5	11	402	5	15
2	168	153	3	17	141	3	13
3	413	403	4	3	335	4	5
4	480	471	5	15	411	5	9
5	418	405	4	1	336	4	1
6	182	156	3	9	123	3	17
7	389	374	4	5	329	4	3
8	364	352	4	7	311	4	7
9	346	331	4	13	305	4	11
Out	3257	3127	36		2693	36	
10	322	310	4	6	300	4	6
11	258	258	4	12	254	4	2
12	332	318	4	14	258	4	10
13	518	510	5	10	432	5	4
14	408	398	4	2	387	5	8
15	394	382	4	4	280	4	14
16	183	163	3	8	125	3	12
17	300	284	4	18	272	4	15
18	345	335	4	16	270	4	18
In	3060	2958	36		2578	37	
Total	6317	6085	72		5271	73	
Rating	70.8	69.7			70.9		
Slope	129	127			127		

GOLF COURSE DIRECTORY

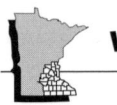

WILLOW CREEK GOLF COURSE

18 Regulation Semi-Private

1700 48th Street SW, P.O. Box 68
Rochester, Minnesota 55903
507/285-0305 Clubhouse/Proshop

HOURS	6 am to Dusk
SEASON	Mar-November

RESERVATIONS	507/285-0305 1 week	
	Walk-on: good/fair	
GREEN FEES	M-F	S-S
Adult	$15/10	$15/10
Senior	$15/10	$15/10
Junior	$15/10	$15/10
Twilight	NA	NA
PAYMENT	Credit: Visa® MasterCard®	
	Non-local checks accepted	
LEAGUES	Men: T (pm)	
	Women: T (am), W (pm)	
MEMBERSHIPS	USGA, NGF, PGA, GCSAA, MGA	
OWNER	Wendell Pittenger	
MANAGER	Scott Rindahl	
SUPERINTENDENT	David Erickson	
PROFESSIONAL	Scott Rindahl	

FEATURES		
Putting green	Y	
Driving range	Y	$3-4
Practice area	Y	
Golf carts		
Power	Y	$17
Pull carts	Y	$3
Club rental	Y	$8
Club storage	N	
Caddies	N	
Proshop		
Extended	Y	
Refreshments		
Restaurant	Y	
Lounge	Y	
Snacks	Y	
Clubhouse		
Showers	Y	
Lockers	Y	
Lodging	N	

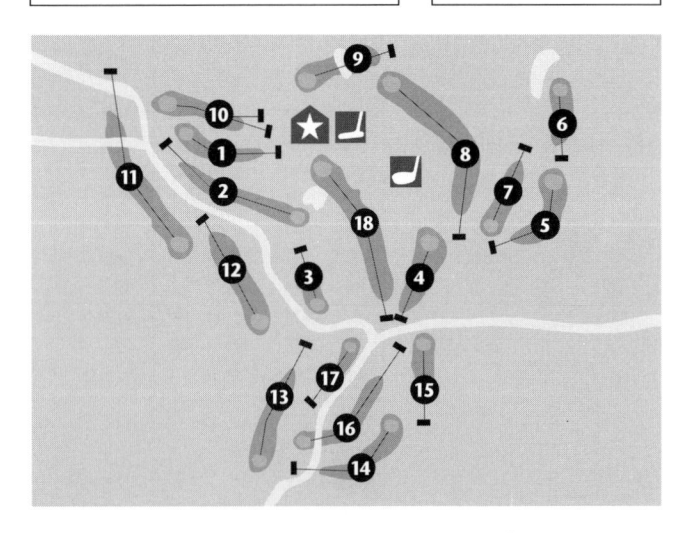

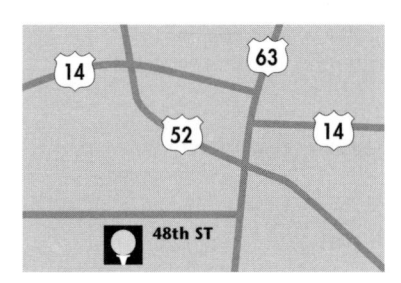

Located in southwest Rochester. Course is about one mile west of U.S. Highway 63 on 48th Street.

	MEN				**WOMEN**		
	BACK	FRONT	PAR	HDCP	FRONT	PAR	HDCP
1	325	321	4	13	307	4	13
2	493	459	5	3	419	5	3
3	195	163	3	9	153	3	9
4	372	359	4	11	348	4	11
5	383	333	4	7	303	4	7
6	165	151	3	17	134	3	17
7	338	307	4	5	290	4	5
8	521	515	5	1	501	5	1
9	171	164	3	15	151	3	15
Out	2973	2772	35		2606	35	
10	435	412	4	4	394	4	4
11	481	471	5	2	454	5	2
12	364	348	4	8	331	4	8
13	341	322	4	14	302	4	14
14	391	380	4	12	350	4	12
15	175	165	3	18	120	3	18
16	341	306	4	10	258	4	10
17	171	157	3	16	130	3	16
18	381	369	4	6	348	4	6
In	3080	2930	35		2687	35	
Total	6053	5702	70		5293	70	
Rating	69.1	67.5			70.1		
Slope	117	114			121		

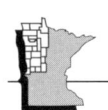

WILLOW CREEK MUNICIPAL GOLF COURSE

9 Regulation Public

Route 1, P.O. Box 550
Barnesville Minnesota 56514
218/493-4486 Clubhouse/Proshop

HOURS	8 am to Dusk
SEASON	April to October

RESERVATIONS	218/493-4486	
	Walk-on: good/good	
GREEN FEES	M-F	S-S
Adult	$11/7.50	$12/8.50
Senior	$11/7.50	$12/8.50
Junior	$9.50/6	$12/8.50
Twilight	NA	NA
PAYMENT	No credit cards accepted	
	Local checks only	
LEAGUES	Men: W (pm)	
	Women: Th (am)	
MEMBERSHIPS	MGA	
PROFESSIONAL	None	

FEATURES		
Putting green	Y	
Driving range	N	
Practice area	N	
Golf carts		
Power (elec)	Y	
Pull carts	Y	
Club rental	Y	
Club storage	N	
Caddies	N	
Proshop		
Basic	Y	
Refreshments		
Restaurant	N	
Lounge	N	
Snacks	Y	
Clubhouse		
Showers	N	
Lockers	N	
Lodging	N	

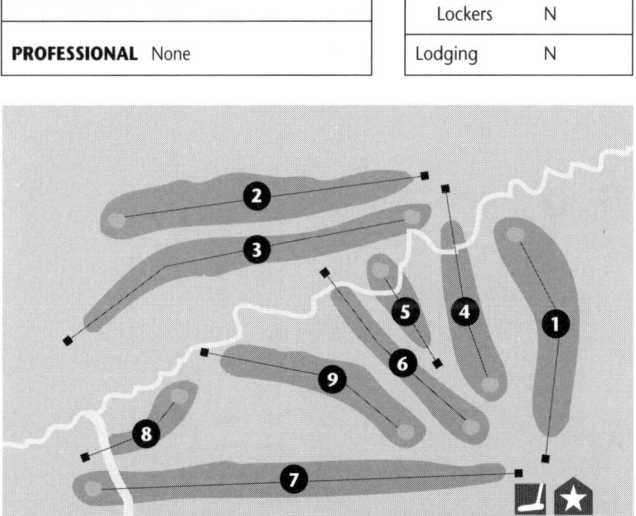

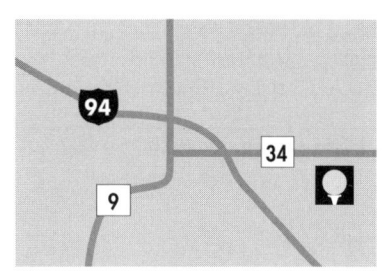

Located 2 1/4 miles east of Barnesville. Course entrance is about 1 1/2 miles east of I-94 on MN Highway 34.

	MEN				WOMEN		
	BACK	FRONT	PAR	HDCP	FRONT	PAR	HDCP
1	340	333	4	5	326	4	5
2	369	364	4	2	316	4	2
3	440	431	5	1	334	5	1
4	288	279	4	6	264	4	6
5	117	117	3	8	117	3	8
6	291	287	4	4	264	4	4
7	528	520	5	3	417	5	3
8	175	175	3	9	127	3	9
9	283	277	4	7	241	4	7
Out	2831	2783	36		2407	36	
1	340	333	4	5	326	4	5
2	369	364	4	2	316	4	2
3	440	431	5	1	334	5	1
4	288	279	4	6	264	4	6
5	117	117	3	8	117	3	8
6	291	287	4	4	264	4	4
7	528	520	5	3	417	5	3
8	175	175	3	9	127	3	9
9	283	277	4	7	241	4	7
In	2831	2783	36		2407	36	
Total	5662	5566	72		4814	72	
Rating	64.8	64.4			65.4		
Slope	100	99			104		

GOLF COURSE DIRECTORY

WIN-E-MAC GOLF CLUB

9 Regulation Public

Rural Route 2, P.O. Box 147B
Erskine, Minnesota 56535
218/687-4653 Clubhouse/Proshop

HOURS	7 am to Dusk
SEASON	May–November

| **RESERVATIONS** | 218/687-4653 2 days |
| | Walk-on: good/fair |

GREEN FEES	M-F	S-S
Adult	$7.50/7.50	$9.50/7.50
Senior	$7.50/7.50	$9.50/7.50
Junior	$4.50/4.50	$9.50/7.50
Twilight	NA	NA

| **PAYMENT** | No credit cards accepted |
| | Non-local checks accepted |

| **LEAGUES** | Men: Various |
| | Women: Various |

| **MEMBERSHIPS** | MGA |

| **MANAGER** | Randy Johnson |

FEATURES		
Putting green	Y	
Driving range	Y	$2
Practice area	N	
Golf carts		
Power (gas)	Y	$8.50
Pull carts	Y	$2
Club rental	Y	$3.50
Club storage	N	
Caddies	N	
Proshop		
Regular	Y	
Refreshments		
Restaurant	N	
Lounge	N	
Snacks	Y	
Clubhouse		
Showers	N	
Lockers	N	
Lodging	N	

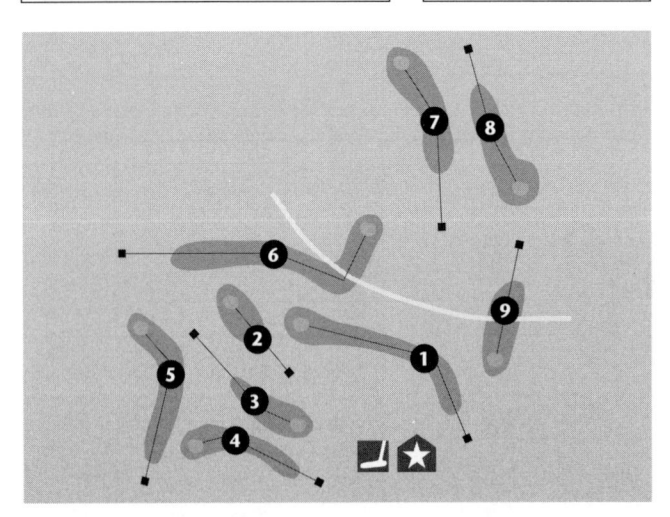

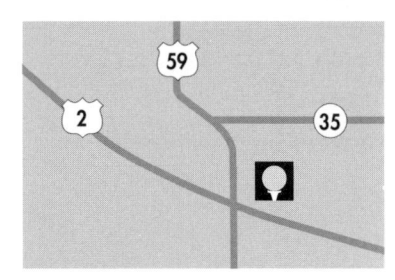

Located one mile east of Erskine. Course entrance is north of U.S. Highway 2 on U.S. Highway 59.

	MEN			**WOMEN**		
	FRONT	PAR	HDCP	FRONT	PAR	HDCP
1	400	4	1	387	5	1
2	145	3	6	120	3	6
3	255	4	9	255	4	9
4	260	4	8	250	4	8
5	315	4	5	305	4	5
6	430	5	3	420	5	3
7	335	4	2	305	4	2
8	325	4	4	310	4	4
9	155	3	7	155	3	7
Out	2620	35		2507	36	
1	400	4	1	387	5	1
2	145	3	6	120	3	6
3	255	4	9	255	4	9
4	260	4	8	250	4	8
5	315	4	5	305	4	5
6	430	5	3	420	5	3
7	335	4	2	305	4	2
8	325	4	4	310	4	4
9	155	3	7	155	3	7
In	2620	35		2507	36	
Total	5240	70		5014	72	
Rating	65.4			68.8		
Slope	105			116		

WINDOM COUNTRY CLUB

9 Regulation Semi-Private

River Road, P.O. Box 74
Windom, Minnesota 56101
507/831-3489 Clubhouse/Proshop

HOURS	8 am to Dusk
SEASON	April-November

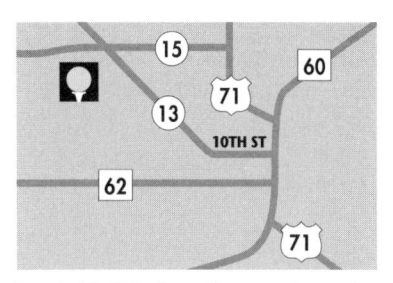

Located in Windom. Course entrance is west of of U.S. Highway 71 on County Road 15.

RESERVATIONS	507/831-3489 1 day
	Walk-on: fair/poor

GREEN FEES	M-F	S-S
Adult	$12/8	$15/10
Senior	$12/8	$15/10
Junior	$12/8	$15/10
Twilight	NA	NA

PAYMENT	No credit cards accepted
	Non-local checks accepted

LEAGUES	Men: Th
	Women: T
	Couples: W

MEMBERSHIPS	USGA, GCSAA, MGA

MANAGER	Ron Crawley
SUPERINTENDENT	Ron Crawley

FEATURES	
Putting green	Y
Driving range	N
Practice area	Y

Golf carts		
Power (gas)	Y	$8
Pull carts	Y	$1
Club rental	Y	$2.50
Club storage	Y	
Caddies	N	

Proshop	
Extended	Y
Refreshments	
Restaurant	N
Lounge	Y
Snacks	Y
Clubhouse	
Showers	Y
Lockers	N

Lodging	N

		MEN			WOMEN	
	FRONT	PAR	HDCP	FRONT	PAR	HDCP
1	300	4	8	294	4	7
2	304	4	6	293	4	6
3	473	5	7	453	5	3
4	164	3	4	158	3	4
5	527	5	3	415	5	5
6	400	4	1	357	4	2
7	156	3	5	111	3	8
8	362	4	2	273	4	1
9	248	4	9	243	4	9
Out	2939	36		2597	36	
1	300	4	8	294	4	7
2	304	4	6	293	4	6
3	473	5	7	453	5	3
4	164	3	4	158	3	4
5	527	5	3	415	5	5
6	400	4	1	357	4	2
7	156	3	5	111	3	8
8	362	4	2	273	4	1
9	248	4	9	243	4	9
Out	2939	36		2597	36	
Total	5878	72		5194	72	
Rating	67.6			68.8		
Slope	113			113		

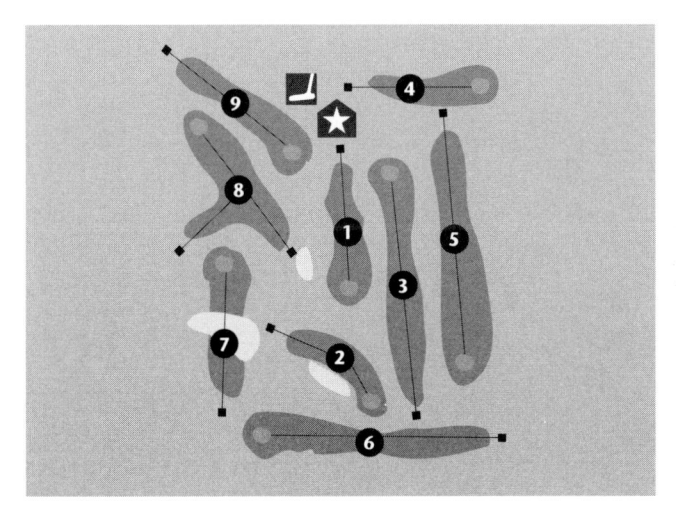

GOLF COURSE DIRECTORY

WINONA COUNTRY CLUB

18 Regulation Private

Pleasant Valley Road
Winona, Minnesota 55987
507/454-3767 Clubhouse
507/452-3535 Proshop

HOURS 7 am to Dusk

SEASON April–November

FEATURES
Putting green	Y
Driving range	Y
Practice area	Y
Golf carts	
Power (gas)	Y
Pull carts	Y
Club rental	Y
Club storage	Y
Caddies	N
Proshop	
Extended	Y
Refreshments	
Restaurant	Y
Lounge	Y
Snacks	Y
Clubhouse	
Showers	Y
Lockers	Y
Lodging	N

RESERVATIONS	612/472-4909	
	Members only	
GREEN FEES	M-F	S-S
Adult	$35	$35
Senior	$35	$35
Junior	$35	$35
Twilight	NA	NA
	Members and guests only	
PAYMENT	No credit cards accepted	
	Non-local checks accepted	
LEAGUES	Men: Various	
	Women: Various	
MEMBERSHIPS	USGA, PGA, GCSAA, MGA	
PROFESSIONAL	Bradley D. Thompson	

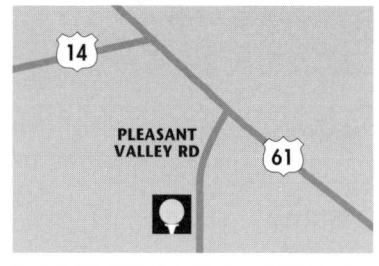

Located in Winona. Course entrance is one mile southwest of U.S. Highway 61 on Pleasant Valley Road.

	MEN				WOMEN		
	BACK	FRONT	PAR	HDCP	FRONT	PAR	HDCP
1	377	372	4	11	360	4	7
2	195	160	3	17	136	3	17
3	552	547	5	3	475	5	1
4	412	404	4	1	331	4	9
5	518	515	5	13	423	5	3
6	201	191	3	15	130	3	15
7	406	394	4	9	325	4	11
8	379	367	4	7	294	4	13
9	423	413	4	5	402	5	5
Out	3463	3363	36		2876	37	
10	153	141	3	18	100	3	18
11	565	557	5	2	482	5	2
12	448	423	4	4	411	5	4
13	350	344	4	12	332	4	10
14	353	334	4	10	308	4	8
15	204	190	3	14	165	3	16
16	414	356	4	8	299	4	12
17	413	409	4	6	409	5	6
18	350	325	4	16	265	4	14
In	3303	3079	35		2771	37	
Total	6766	6442	71		5647	74	
Rating	73.2	71.9			72.8		
Slope	136	134			130		

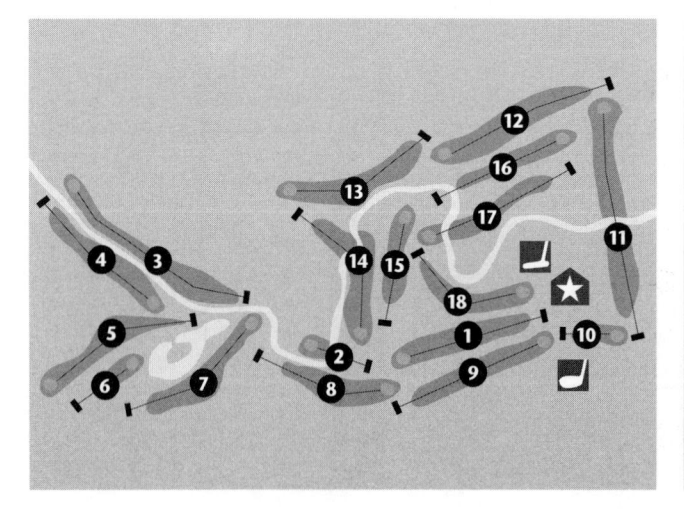

WINTHROP GOLF CLUB

9 Regulation Semi-Private

P.O. Box 544
Winthrop, Minnesota 55396
507/647-5828 Clubhouse/Proshop

HOURS	6 am to Dusk
SEASON	April to October

RESERVATIONS	507/647-5828 3 days
	Walk-on: fair/poor

GREEN FEES	M-F	S-S
Adult	$15/10	$18/12
Senior	$15/10	$18/12
Junior	$15/10	$18/12
Twilight	NA	NA

PAYMENT	No credit cards accepted
	Non-local checks accepted

LEAGUES	Men: Various
	Women: Various

MEMBERSHIPS	GCSAA, MGA

MANAGER	Kermit Moen
SUPERINTENDENT	George Weier

FEATURES		
Putting green	Y	
Driving range	N	
Practice area	Y	
Golf carts		
Power (gas)	Y	$10
Pull carts	Y	$1
Club rental	Y	$4
Club storage	Y	
Caddies	N	
Proshop		
Extended	Y	
Refreshments		
Restaurant	N	
Lounge	Y	
Snacks	Y	
Clubhouse		
Showers	Y	
Lockers	Y	
Lodging	N	

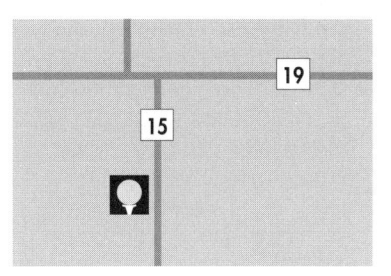

Located south of Winthrop. Course is two miles south of MN Highway 19 on MN Highway 15.

	MEN			**WOMEN**		
	FRONT	PAR	HDCP	FRONT	PAR	HDCP
1	350	4	7	350	5	7
2	462	5	5	366	5	5
3	344	4	11	294	4	11
4	451	5	9	374	5	9
5	218	3	1	177	3	1
6	394	4	3	394	5	3
7	125	3	13	85	3	13
8	297	4	17	230	4	17
9	271	4	15	271	4	15
Out	2912	36		2541	38	
1	350	4	8	350	5	8
2	462	5	6	366	5	6
3	344	4	12	294	4	12
4	451	5	10	374	5	10
5	218	3	2	177	3	2
6	394	4	4	394	5	4
7	125	3	14	85	3	14
8	297	4	18	230	4	18
9	271	4	16	271	4	16
In	2912	36		2541	38	
Total	5824	72		5082	76	
Rating	68.0			68.8		
Slope	114			112		

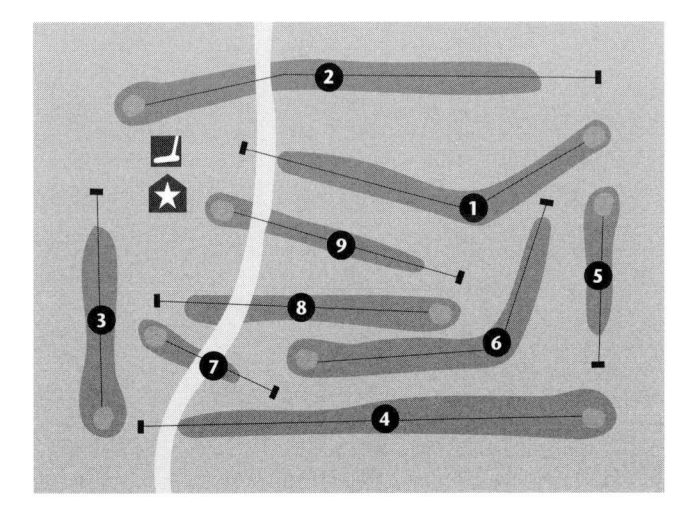

GOLF COURSE DIRECTORY

THEODORE WIRTH GOLF COURSE

18 Regulation/9 Par-3 Public

1300 Theodore Wirth Parkway
Minneapolis, Minnesota 55422
612/522-4584 Clubhouse/Proshop

HOURS	Dawn to Dusk
SEASON	April–November

RESERVATIONS	612/522-4584 4 days
	$2 fee for weekends
	Walk-on: good/good

GREEN FEES	M-F	S-S
Adult	$18/13	$18/13
Senior	$18/13	$18/13
Junior	$18/13	$18/13
Twilight	NA	NA

| PAYMENT | No credit cards accepted |
| | Local checks only |

| LEAGUES | Men: Various |
| | Women: Various |

| MEMBERSHIPS | USGA, NGF, GCSAA, MGA |

| MANAGER | Scott Nelson |

FEATURES	
Putting green	Y
Driving range	N
Practice area	Y
Golf carts	
Power (gas)	Y $18/10
Pull carts	Y
Club rental	Y
Club storage	N
Caddies	N
Proshop	
Basic	Y
Refreshments	
Restaurant	Y
Lounge	N
Snacks	Y
Clubhouse	
Showers	Y
Lockers	Y
Lodging	N

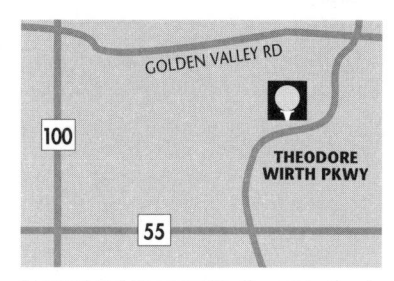

Located in Minneapolis. Course is about 1/2 mile north of MN Highway 55 on Theodore Wirth Parkway.

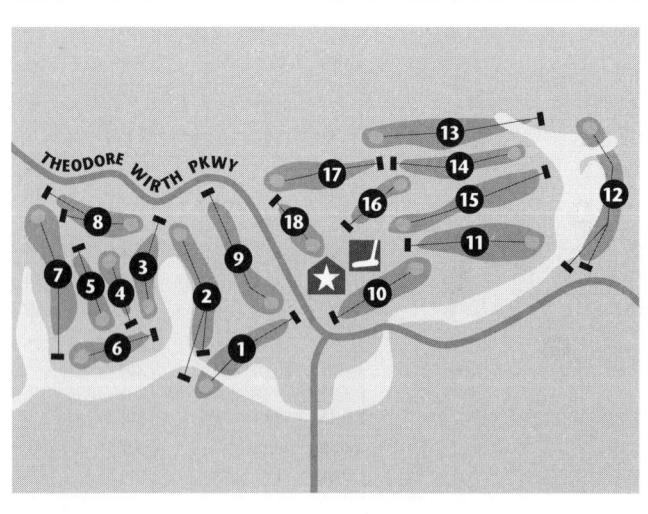

		MEN				WOMEN		
	BACK	FRONT	PAR	HDCP		FRONT	PAR	HDCP
1	375	365	4	7		349	4	3
2	477	471	5	1		341	4	1
3	320	311	4	9		274	4	11
4	208	202	3	13		196	3	9
5	338	332	4	17		285	4	17
6	233	222	3	11		215	4	15
7	457	410	4	3		392	5	7
8	334	325	4	15		248	4	13
9	392	377	4	5		372	4	5
Out	3134	3015	35			2672	36	
10	380	370	4	8		363	4	8
11	358	346	4	14		335	4	12
12	518	471	5	2		461	5	2
13	422	410	4	6		342	4	4
14	372	367	4	12		358	4	14
15	491	485	5	4		436	5	6
16	180	175	3	16		156	3	16
17	407	402	4	10		391	4	10
18	146	143	3	18		125	3	18
In	3274	3169	36			2967	36	
Total	6408	6184	71			5639	72	
Rating	72.7	71.2				72.5		
Slope	132	129				124		

WOODBURY GOLF & FITNESS

9 Par-3 Public

3351 Woodlane Drive
Woodbury, Minnesota 55125
612/735-4401 Clubhouse/Proshop

HOURS	6 am to Dusk
SEASON	April-November

| **RESERVATIONS** | No reservations accepted |
| | Walk-on: good/fair |

GREEN FEES	M-F	S-S
Adult	$7	$7.50
Senior	$5*	$7.50
Junior	$5.50*	$7.50
Twilight	NA	NA

*Before 2 pm

| **PAYMENT** | Credit: Visa® MasterCard® |
| | Non-local checks accepted |

LEAGUES	Women: M (5:30 pm)
	Adult: W (5:30 pm),
	T (9 am)

| **MEMBERSHIPS** | PGA |

| **MANAGER** | Michele Dahlberg, Pat Murphy |
| **SUPERINTENDENT** | Dave McCarty |

FEATURES	
Putting green	N
Driving range	N
Practice area	Y
Golf carts	
Power	N
Pull carts	Y $1.35
Club rental	Y $3.25
Club storage	N
Caddies	N
Proshop	
Basic	Y
Refreshments	
Restaurant	N
Lounge	N
Snacks	Y
Clubhouse	
Showers	N
Lockers	N
Lodging	N

Located in Woodbury. Course is east of I-494 on Valley Creek Road, then south 2 1/2 miles on Woodlane Drive.

	MEN			**WOMEN**		
	FRONT	PAR	HDCP	FRONT	PAR	HDCP
1	174	3	5	174	4	5
2	130	3	7	130	3	7
3	195	3	1	195	4	1
4	128	3	9	128	3	9
5	96	3	8	96	3	8
6	162	3	3	128	3	3
7	172	3	4	172	4	4
8	148	3	2	132	3	2
9	110	3	6	110	3	6
Out	1315	27		1265	30	
1	174	3	5	174	4	5
2	130	3	7	130	3	7
3	195	3	1	195	4	1
4	128	3	9	128	3	9
5	96	3	8	96	3	8
6	162	3	3	128	3	3
7	172	3	4	172	4	4
8	148	3	2	132	3	2
9	110	3	6	110	3	6
In	1315	27		1265	30	
Total	2630	54		2530	60	
Rating	NA			NA		
Slope	NA			NA		

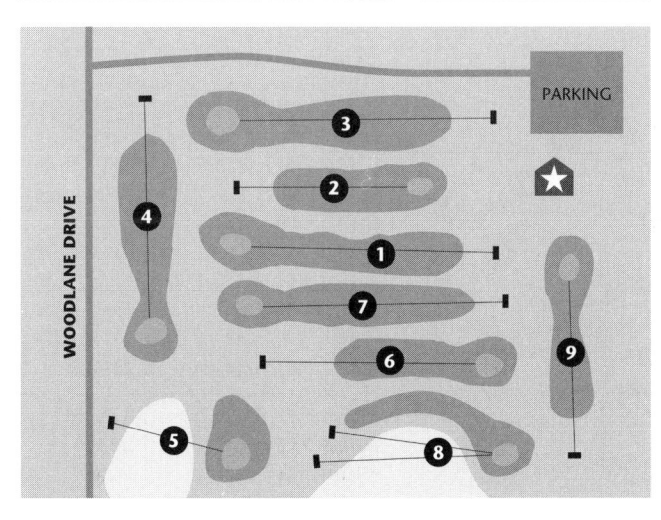

GOLF COURSE DIRECTORY

WOODHILL COUNTRY CLUB
18 Regulation Private

200 Woodhill Road
Wayzata, Minnesota 55391
612/473-7333 Clubhouse
612/473-5024 Proshop

RESERVATIONS	612/473-5024	
	Members only	
GREEN FEES	M-F	S-S
Adult	$35/19	$45/25
Senior	$35/19	$45/25
Junior	$7/7	$20/20
Twilight	NA	NA
	Members and guests only	
PAYMENT	Fees billed to members	
LEAGUES	None	
MEMBERSHIPS	USGA, PGA, GCSAA, MGA	
MANAGER	Rick Fredrickson	
PROFESSIONAL	Phil Reith	

HOURS Dawn to Dusk
SEASON April to October

FEATURES

Putting green	Y
Driving range	Y
Practice area	N
Golf carts	
Power (elec)	Y $24/19
Pull carts	Y
Club rental	Y
Club storage	Y
Caddies	Y
Proshop	
Extended	Y
Refreshments	
Restaurant	Y
Lounge	Y
Snacks	Y
Clubhouse	
Showers	Y
Lockers	Y
Lodging	N

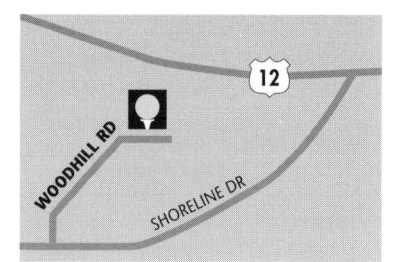

Located in Wayzata. Course entrance is south of U.S. Highway 12 on Shoreline Drive, then north on Woodhill Road.

	MEN				**WOMEN**		
	BACK	FRONT	PAR	HDCP	FRONT	PAR	HDCP
1	415	401	4	5	378	5	15
2	137	131	3	17	123	3	17
3	487	478	5	11	466	5	1
4	421	401	4	3	358	4	5
5	385	378	4	7	361	4	3
6	424	422	4	1	392	5	7
7	341	334	4	13	329	4	11
8	221	214	3	9	180	3	13
9	342	338	4	15	332	4	9
Out	3173	3097	35		2919	37	
10	383	378	4	6	362	4	6
11	426	410	4	2	395	5	10
12	561	531	5	10	401	5	8
13	210	203	3	8	196	4	16
14	509	496	5	12	446	5	2
15	411	406	4	4	374	4	4
16	163	155	3	18	133	3	18
17	386	339	4	14	317	4	12
18	355	348	4	16	324	4	14
In	3404	3266	36		2958	38	
Total	6577	6363	71		5877	75	
Rating	73.0	71.9			75.8		
Slope	134	132			134		

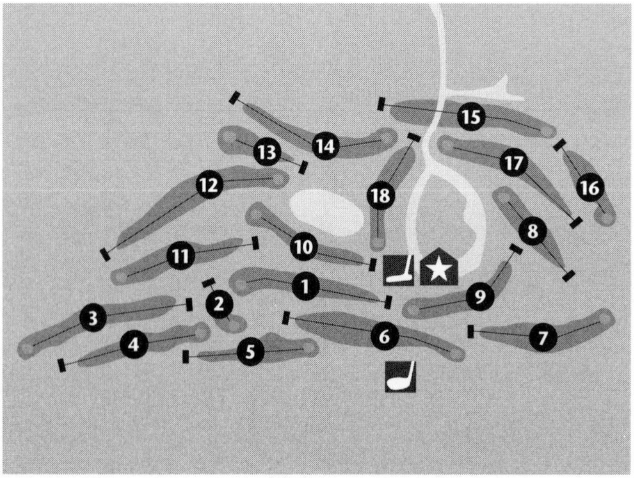

414

THE MINNESOTA ILLUSTRATED

WOODLAND CREEK GOLF CLUB

9 Regulation Public

3200 South Coon Creek Drive
Andover, Minnesota 55304
612/323-0517 Clubhouse/Proshop

HOURS	Dawn to Dusk
SEASON	Mar-November

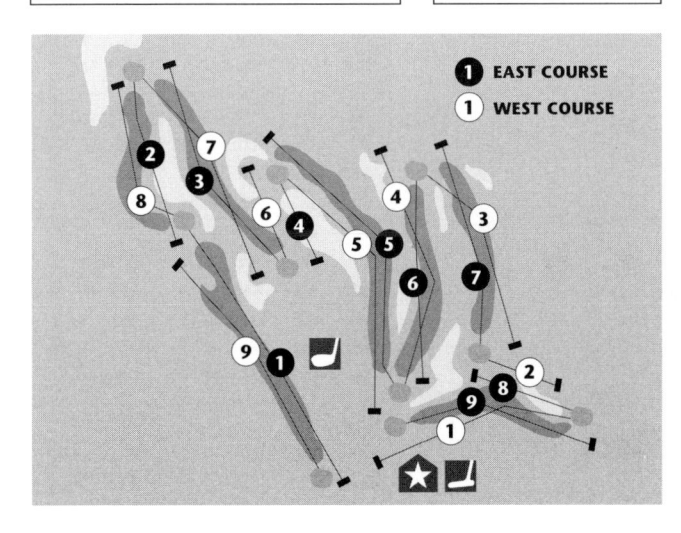

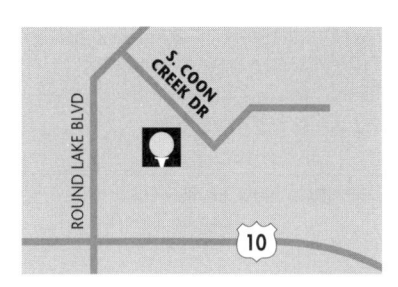

Located in Andover. Course is one mile north of U.S. Hwy 10 on Round Lake Blvd, then south on Coon Creek Drive.

RESERVATIONS	612/323-0517	
	Walk-on: good/fair	
GREEN FEES	M-F	S-S
Adult	$14/8	$16/9
Senior	$11/6	$11/6
Junior	$11/6	$11/6
Twilight	NA	NA
PAYMENT	No credit cards accepted	
	Non-local checks accepted	
LEAGUES	Men: M	
	Women: Th	
	Couples: F	
MEMBERSHIPS	USGA, NGA	
SUPERINTENDENT	Kim Sandvig	
PROFESSIONAL	Gordy Skaar	

FEATURES	
Putting green	Y
Driving range	Y $2.50-4
Practice area	N
Golf carts	
Power (gas)	Y
Pull carts	Y
Club rental	Y
Club storage	N
Caddies	N
Proshop	
Extended	Y
Refreshments	
Restaurant	N
Lounge	N
Snacks	Y
Clubhouse	
Showers	N
Lockers	N
Lodging	N

	MEN			**WOMEN**		
	FRONT	PAR	HDCP	FRONT	PAR	HDCP
1	471	5	3	388	5	2
2	300	4	8	285	4	6
3	415	4	2	323	4	3
4	156	3	9	91	3	9
5	465	5	1	401	5	1
6	337	4	6	253	4	4
7	362	4	4	299	4	7
8	187	3	7	182	3	8
9	353	4	5	287	4	5
EAST	3046	36		2509	36	
1	359	4	6	281	4	5
2	145	3	9	138	3	8
3	330	4	5	240	4	6
4	390	4	2	305	4	2
5	476	5	1	401	5	1
6	171	3	8	122	3	9
7	469	5	4	396	5	4
8	304	4	7	248	4	7
9	409	4	3	402	4	3
WEST	3053	36		2533	36	
Total	6099	72		5042	72	
Rating	69.2			69.0		
Slope	112			114		

❶ EAST COURSE
❶ WEST COURSE

GOLF COURSE DIRECTORY

WORTHINGTON COUNTRY CLUB

18 Regulation Semi-Private

1414 Liberty Drive, P.O. Box 306
Worthington, Minnesota 56187
507/376-5142 Clubhouse
507/376-4281 Proshop

RESERVATIONS	507/376-4281 1 day	
	Walk-on: good/fair	
GREEN FEES	M-F	S-S
Adult	$17/10	$20/12
Senior	$17/10	$20/12
Junior	$17/10	$20/12
Twilight	NA	NA
PAYMENT	No credit cards accepted	
	Non-local checks accepted	
LEAGUES	Men: Th	
	Women: T	
MEMBERSHIPS	USGA, PGA, GCSAA, MGA	
MANAGER	Larry & Cheryl Bjore	
SUPERINTENDENT	Tom Meier	
PROFESSIONAL	Larry Bjore, Kevin Reese	

HOURS	8 am to Dusk	
SEASON	April to October	
FEATURES		
Putting green	Y	
Driving range	Y	$2.50
Practice area	N	
Golf carts		
Power (gas)	Y	$15
Pull carts	Y	$1.50
Club rental	Y	$5
Club storage	N	
Caddies	N	
Proshop		
Extended	Y	
Refreshments		
Restaurant	Y	
Lounge	Y	
Snacks	Y	
Clubhouse		
Showers	Y	
Lockers	N	
Lodging	N	

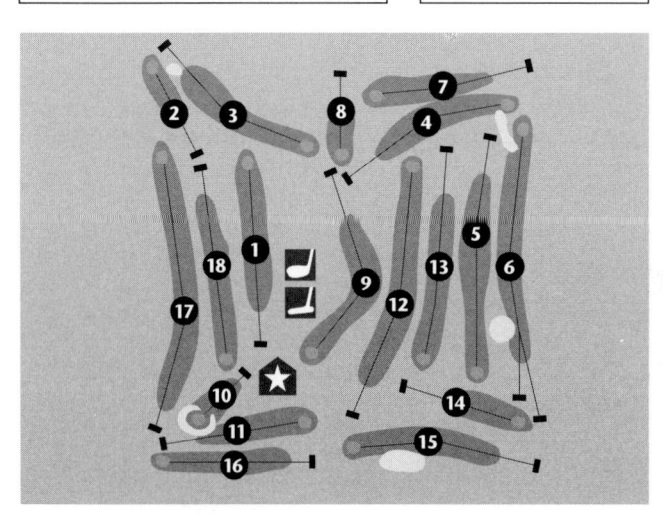

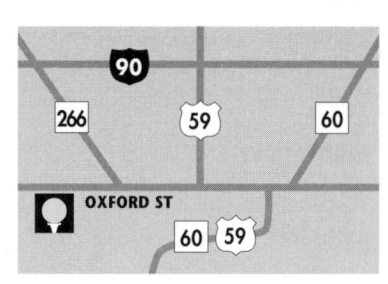

Located in Worthington. Course is south of I-90 on MN Highway 266, then 1/2 mile west on Oxford Street.

	MEN				**WOMEN**		
	BACK	FRONT	PAR	HDCP	FRONT	PAR	HDCP
1	349	344	4	9	337	4	9
2	173	155	3	17	146	3	15
3	390	364	4	1	336	4	3
4	328	320	4	13	240	4	13
5	435	411	4	3	403	5	5
6	510	461	5	7	338	4	7
7	374	342	4	11	315	4	11
8	166	158	3	15	133	3	17
9	402	391	4	5	361	4	1
Out	3127	2946	35		2609	35	
10	115	110	3	18	103	3	18
11	305	300	4	16	289	4	14
12	499	490	5	12	376	4	2
13	382	365	4	10	341	4	4
14	229	186	3	8	211	4	16
15	379	385	4	4	324	4	8
16	312	306	4	14	295	4	12
17	523	515	5	6	461	5	6
18	390	385	4	2	308	4	10
In	3134	3042	36		2708	36	
Total	6261	5988	71		5317	71	
Rating	70.5	69.2			70.5		
Slope	125	123			122		

416

THE MINNESOTA ILLUSTRATED

ZUMBRO VALLEY GOLF CLUB

9 Regulation Semi-Private

P.O. Box 76
Kasson, Minnesota 55944
507/635-2821 Clubhouse/Proshop

RESERVATIONS	507/635-2821 1 day	
	Walk-on: good/fair	

GREEN FEES	M-F	S-S
Adult	$16/9	$16/9
Senior	$16/9	$16/9
Junior	$16/9	$16/9
Twilight	NA	NA

PAYMENT	No credit cards accepted
	Non-local checks accepted

LEAGUES	Men: Th (pm)
	Women: T (am)
	Junior: M (am)

MEMBERSHIPS	USGA, MGA

PROFESSIONAL	Call

HOURS	7 am to Dusk
SEASON	April-November

FEATURES	
Putting green	Y
Driving range	Y
Practice area	Y
Golf carts	
Power (gas)	Y
Pull carts	Y
Club rental	Y
Club storage	N
Caddies	N
Proshop	
Regular	Y
Refreshments	
Restaurant	Y
Lounge	Y
Snacks	Y
Clubhouse	
Showers	N
Lockers	N
Lodging	N

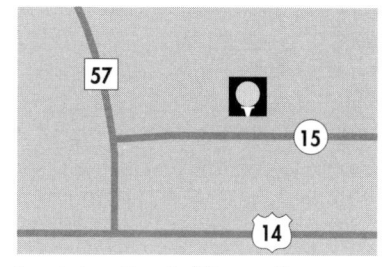

Located northeast of Kasson. Course entrance is east of MN Highway 57 on County Road 15.

	MEN			WOMEN		
	FRONT	PAR	HDCP	FRONT	PAR	HDCP
1	237	4	5	237	4	5
2	254	4	7	254	4	7
3	283	4	4	233	4	4
4	348	4	1	348	5	1
5	165	3	9	135	3	9
6	451	5	2	321	5	2
7	309	4	6	309	4	6
8	276	4	8	276	4	8
9	269	4	3	189	4	3
Out	2592	36		2302	37	
1	237	4	5	237	4	5
2	254	4	7	254	4	7
3	283	4	4	233	4	4
4	348	4	1	348	5	1
5	165	3	9	135	3	9
6	451	5	2	321	5	2
7	309	4	6	309	4	6
8	276	4	8	276	4	8
9	269	4	3	189	4	3
In	2592	36		2302	37	
Total	5184	72		4604	74	
Rating	65.8			68.8		
Slope	117			116		

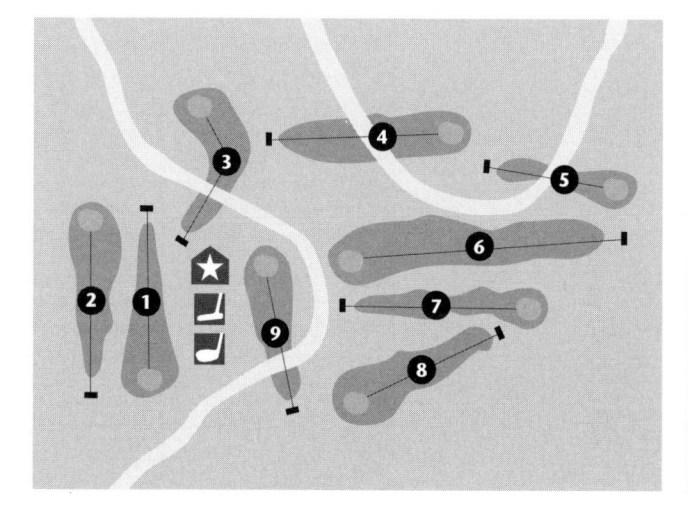

ZUMBROTA GOLF CLUB

9 Regulation Semi-Private

P.O. Box 208
Zumbrota, Minnesota 55992
507/732-5817 Clubhouse/Proshop

HOURS	Dawn to Dusk
SEASON	April to October

RESERVATIONS	507/732-5817
	Walk-on: call

GREEN FEES	M-F	S-S
Adult	$15/10	$15/10
Senior	$15/10	$15/10
Junior	$15/10	$15/10
Twilight	$NA	$NA

PAYMENT	No credit cards accepted
	Non-local checks accepted

LEAGUES	Men: Various
	Women: Various

MEMBERSHIPS	MGA

PROFESSIONAL	Call

FEATURES		
Putting green	Y	
Driving range	N	
Practice area	Y	
Golf carts		
Power	Y	$12/7
Pull carts	Y	$1
Club rental	Y	$3
Club storage	N	
Caddies	N	
Proshop		
Regular	Y	
Refreshments		
Restaurant	N	
Lounge	N	
Snacks	Y	
Clubhouse		
Showers	N	
Lockers	N	
Lodging	N	

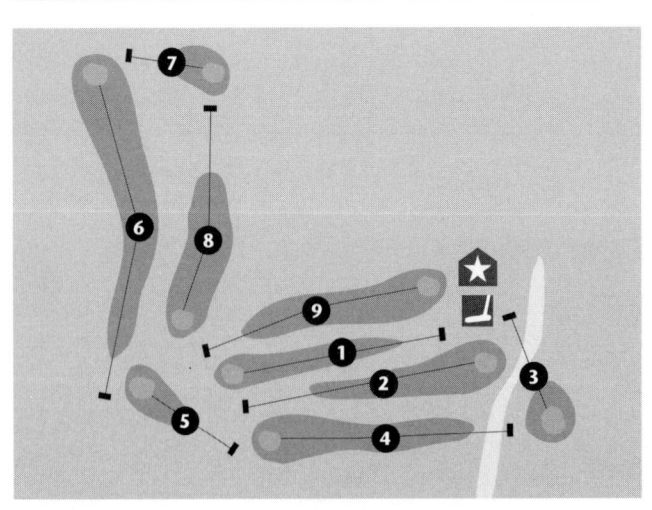

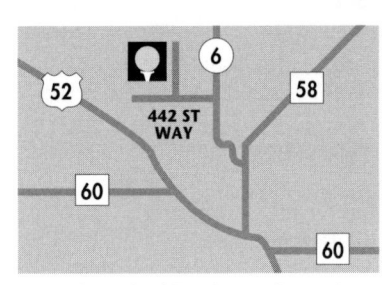

Located north of Zumbrota. Course is west of MN Hwy 58 on County Road 6, then west on 442 Street Way.

	MEN				**WOMEN**		
	BACK	FRONT	PAR	HDCP	FRONT	PAR	HDCP
1	341	331	4	15	315	4	9
2	409	362	4	9	340	4	7
3	163	152	3	11	140	3	15
4	363	357	4	3	343	4	5
5	190	173	3	7	150	3	11
6	501	479	5	5	446	5	1
7	147	132	3	13	121	3	17
8	332	321	4	17	285	4	13
9	360	341	4	1	315	4	3
Out	2806	2648	34		2455	34	
1	341	331	4	15	315	4	9
2	409	362	4	9	340	4	7
3	163	152	3	11	140	3	15
4	363	357	4	3	343	4	5
5	190	173	3	7	150	3	11
6	501	479	5	5	446	5	1
7	147	132	3	13	121	3	17
8	332	321	4	17	285	4	13
9	360	341	4	1	315	4	3
In	2806	2648	34		2455	34	
Total	5612	5296	68		4910	68	
Rating	67.2	65.8			68.8		
Slope	120	117			116		

INDEXES

COURSE INDEX

CITY INDEX

COURSE INDEX

A
Afton Alps Golf Course 1
Albany Golf Club 2
Albert Lea Golf Club.....................3
Albion Ridges Golf Course 4
Alexandria Golf Club 5
All Seasons Golf Course.................6
Angushire Golf Courses.................7
Apple Valley Golf Course 8
Appleton Golf Club.......................9
Applewood Hills Golf Course......10
Arrowwood Golf Club................11
Austin Country Club...................12

B
Babbitt Golf Course.....................13
Baker National Golf Course ...14-15
Balmoral Golf Course 16
Bearpath Golf Club 17
Bellwood Oaks Golf Course.........18
Bemidji Town & Country
 Club...19
Benson Golf Club........................20
Bent Creek Golf Club 21
Bentwood Climax Municipal
 Golf Club................................22
Big Lake Golf Club 23
Birch Bay Golf Course 24
Birchwood Golf Course 25
Birnamwood Public Golf
 Course 26
Blackduck Golf Club 27
Blooming Prairie Country Club ..28
Blueberry Pines Golf Club 29
Bluff Creek Golf Course 30
Brackett's Crossing Country
 Club...31
Braemar Golf Club 32-33
Brainerd Golf Club (Now Pine
 Meadows at Brainerd) 289
Breezy Point Resort 34-35
Bridges of Mounds View, The 36
Brightwood Hills Golf Course 37
Brockway Golf Club 38
Brookland Executive Nine Golf
 Course 39
Brooklyn Park Golf Course.........40

Brooktree Municipal Golf
 Course 41
Brookview Golf Course 42
Buffalo Heights Golf Course 43
Buffalo Run Golf Club................44
Bunker Hills Golf Course 45-46
Burl Oaks Golf Club 47

C
Canby Golf Club 48
Cannon Golf Club.......................49
Carriage Hills Country Club........50
Cass Lake Golf Course (Now
 Sandtrap Golf Course)..........336
Castle Highlands Golf Course 51
Castlewood Golf Course..............52
Cedar Hills Golf Course..............53
Cedar River Country Club..........54
Cedar Valley Golf Course 55
Cedarholm Golf Course,
 Roseville 326
Centerbrook Golf Course 56
Chaska Par 30 Golf Course.........57
Chippendale Golf Club (Now
 Southern Hills Golf Club) 354
Chippewa National Golf Club 58
Chisago Lakes Golf Course.........59
Chomonix Golf Course...............60
Chosen Valley Golf Club 61
Cimarron Golf Course.................62
Clark's Grove Golf Course..........63
Clearwater Estates (Now Eagle
 Trace Golfers Club) 90
Cleary Lake Golf Course.............64
Cloquet Country Club 65
Coffee Mill Golf & Country
 Club...66
Cokato Town & Country Club....67
Columbia Golf Course 68
Como Park Golf Course 69
Cottonwood Country Club.........70
Country View Golf 71
Countryside Golf Club 72
Creeks Bend Golf Course............73
Crestwood Hills Golf Course......74
Crosslake Golf Course 75
Crystal Lake Golf Course............76

Cuyuna Country Club.................77

D
Dahlgreen Golf Club 78
Dawson Golf Club.......................79
Daytona Country Club................80
Deer Run Golf Club....................81
Dellwood Hills Golf Club...........82
Detroit County Club 83-84
Dodge Country Club 85
Double Eagle Golf Club..............86
Driftwood Resort &
 Golf Course 87
Dwan Golf Club 88

E
Eagle Ridge Golf Course 89
Eagle Trace Golfers Club 90
Eastwood Golf Club 91
Edge Of The Wilderness Golf
 Course 92
Edgewater Golf Club (Now
 Albert Lea Golf Club) 3
Edina Country Club 93
Edinburgh USA...........................94
Elk River Country Club 95
Elm Creek Golf Links 96
Elmdale Hills Golf Course 97
Ely Golf Course...........................98
Emily Greens Golf Course 99
Enger Park Golf Course 100
Eshquaguma Club 101
Eveleth Municipal Golf
 Course 102

F
Fair Hills Golf Course 103-104
Falcon Ridge Golf Course...105-106
Falls Country Club 107
Faribault Golf & Country
 Club.......................................108
Farmers Golf & Health Club 109
Ferndale Country Club..............110
Fiddlestix Golf Course...............111

COURSE INDEX

Fifty Lakes Golf Center
  (Howard's Barn)....................161
Forest Hills Golf Club................112
Fort Ridgely State Park Golf
  Course 113
Fort Snelling Public Golf
  Course 114
Fosston Golf Club.....................115
Fountain Valley Golf Club........116
Fox Hollow Golf Club 117
Fox Lake Golf Club...................118
Francis A. Gross Golf Course.....139
Frazee Golf Course....................119
French Lake Open Golf
  Course 120
Fritz's Resort & Golf Course 121

G

Garrison Creek Golf Course 122
Gem Lake Hills Golf Course......123
Glencoe Country Club 124
Golden Valley Country Club 125
Goodrich Golf Club...................126
Graceville Golf Club..................127
Grand National Golf Club.........128
Grand View Lodge..............129-130
Grandview Golf Club 131
Grandy Nine Golf Course 132
Granite Falls Golf Club..............133
Green Lea Golf Course 134
Green Valley Golf Course.........135
Greenhaven Golf Course...........136
Greenwood Golf Course............137
Greenwood Golf Links 138
Gross Golf Course, Francis A.....139
Gunflint Hills Golf Club 140

H

Hampton Hills Golf Course 141
Harmony Golf Club 142
Hastings Country Club..............143
Havanna Hills Golf Course 144
Hawley Golf & Country
  Club..145
Hayden Hills Executive Golf
  Course 146

Hazeltine National Golf
  Club..147
Headwaters Country Club.........148
Heart of the Valley Golf
  Club..149
Hiawatha Golf Course 150
Hibbing Municipal Golf
  Course 151
Hidden Creek Golf Club...........152
Hidden Greens Golf Course 153
Hidden Haven Country Club....154
Highland Park Golf Course 155
Highland Park Nine Hole
  Golf Course 156
Hillcrest Country Club..............157
Holiday Park Golf Course..........158
Hollydale Golf Club 159
Howard Lake Greens 160
Howard's Barn/Fifty Lakes
  Golf Center............................161
Hoyt Lakes Country Club..........162
Hyland Greens Golf Course 163

I

Indian Hills Golf Club...............164
Interlachen Country Club.........165
Interlaken Golf Club 166
Inver Wood Golf Course....167-168
Irish Hills Golf Course...............169
Ironman Golf Course 170
Island Falls Country Club 171
Island View Golf Club 172
Izatys Golf & Yacht Club...........173

J

Jackson Golf Club......................174

K

Kate Haven Golf Course............175
Keller Golf Course 176
Kenyon Country Club...............177
Kimball Golf Club 178

L

Lafayette Club 179
Lake City Country Club 180
Lake Hendricks Country
  Club..181
Lake Miltona Golf Club.............182
Lake Place, Links at 183
Lakeview Golf Club, Two
  Harbors..................................374
Lakeview Golf Course................184
Lakeway Golf Course.................185
Lanesboro Golf Club 186
Les Bolstad-University of
  Minnesota Golf Course 377
Le Sueur Country Club..............187
Lester Park Golf Course 188
Lewiston Country Club.............189
Links at Northfork, The.............253
Litchfield Golf Club 190
Little Crow Country Club 191
Little Falls Country Club...........192
Lone Pine Country Club 193
Long Prairie Country Club........194
Loon Lake Golf Club.................195
Lost Spur Country Club 196
Lutsen, Superior National at 362
Luverne Country Club 197

M

Ma-Cal-Grove Country Club.....198
Madden's on Gull Lake 199-201
Madelia Golf Course..................202
Madison Country Club 203
Mahnomen Country Club 204
Majestic Oaks Golf Club 205-207
Manitou Ridge Golf Course.......208
Maple Hills Golf Center 209
Maple Hills Golf Club 210
Maple Valley Golf & Country
  Club..211
Marshall Golf Club....................212
Mayflower Country Club 213
Meadow Greens Golf Course 214
Meadowbrook Country Club 215
Meadowbrook Golf Club...........216
Meadowlark Country Club........217
Meadows Golf Course 218

COURSE INDEX

Meadowwoods Golf Course 219
Mendakota Country Club 220
Mendota Heights Par-3..............221
Mesaba Country Club 222
Midland Hills Country Club 223
Milaca Golf Club 224
Mille Lacs Lake Golf Resort 225
Minakwa Golf & Racquetball
   Club..226
Minikahda Club 227
Minneapolis Golf Club..............228
Minneopa Golf Club 229
Minnesota Valley Country
   Club..230
Minnetonka Country Club 231
Minnewaska Golf Club..............232
Minniowa Golf Club 233
Mississippi Dunes Golf Links 234
Mississippi National Golf
   Links.......................................235
Montevideo Country Club........236
Montgomery Golf Club.............237
Monticello Country Club..........238
Moorhead Country Club...........239
Moose Lake Golf Club 240
Mora Country Club (Now Spring
   Brooke Golf Course) 175
Mount Frontenac Golf
   Course 241
Mountain Lake Golf Club 242

N
New Hope Village Golf
   Course 243
New Prague Golf Club..............244
New Ulm Country Club 245
Nordic Trails Golf Course..........246
Normandale Executive Golf
   Course 247
North Branch Golf Course 248
North Links Golf Course 249
North Oaks Golf Club 250
Northern Hills Golf Club 251
Northfield Golf Club 252
Northfork, The Links at............253
Northland Country Club 254

O
Oak Glen Country Club.....255-256
Oak Harbor Golf Club 257
Oak Hill Golf Club 258
Oak Knolls Golf Club 259
Oak Ridge Country Club 260
Oak Summit Golf Course 261
Oak View Golf Club 262
Oak View Golf Course...............263
Oakcrest Golf Course.................264
Oakdale Country Club 265
Oaks Golf Club 266
Oakwood Golf Course 267
Olivia Golf Club 268
Olympic Hills Golf Club 269
Oneka Ridge Golf Course 270
Orchard Gardens Golf Course...271
Orono Golf Course 272
Ortonville Golf Club 273
Osakis Country Club 274
Owatonna Country Club 275

P
Parkview Golf Club 276
Pebble Creek Country Club.......277
Pebble Lake Golf Club...............278
Perham Lakeside Country
   Club..279
Pezhekee Golf Course................280
Phalen Park Golf Course 281
Pheasant Run Golf Club............282
Pierz Golf Course.......................283
Pike Lake Country Club 284
Pine Beach East-West, Madden's
   on Gull Lake..................199-201
Pine City Country Club 285
Pine Creek Golf Course 286
Pine Hill Golf Club 287
Pine Island Golf Course.............288
Pine Meadows at Brainerd........289
Pine Ridge Golf Club 290
Pine River Country Club 291
Pinewood Golf Course 292
Piney Ridge Lodge, Irish Hills ...169
Piper Hills Golf Club 293
Pipestone Country Club............294
Pokegama Golf Course..............295

Pomme de Terre Golf Club 296
Ponderosa Golf Club 297
Prairie View Municipal Golf
   Course 298
Preston Golf & Country Club ...299
Prestwick Golf Club...................300
Princeton Golf Club 301
Purple Hawk Country Club......302

Q
Quadna Hills Golf Course 303

R
Ramsey Golf Club......................304
Red Oak Golf Course 305
Red Rock Golf Course................306
Red Wing Country Club 307
Redwood Falls Golf Club..........308
Rich Acres Golf Course..............309
Rich Spring Golf Club 310
Rich Valley Golf Club................311
Ridgeview Country Club 312
Ridgewood Country Club ..313-314
River Oaks Municipal Golf
   Course 315
River's Edge Country Club 316
Riverside Golf Club 317
Riverside Town & Country
   Club..318
Riverview Golf Course...............319
Rochester Golf & Country
   Club..320
Rolling Green Country Club.....321
Rolling Green Fairways 322
Rolling Hills Golf Course 323
Root River Country Club..........324
Rose Lake Golf Club 325
Roseville Cedarholm Golf
   Course 326
Rum River Golf Club (Now
   Princeton Golf Club)............301
Rum River Hills Golf Club.......327
Rush Creek Golf Club...............328
Ruttger's Bay Lake Lodge ...329-330
Ruttger's Sugar Lake Lodge
   (Sugarbrooke Golf Course)...360

GOLF COURSE DIRECTORY   421

COURSE INDEX

S
St. Charles Golf Course 331
St. Cloud Country Club 332
Sanbrook Golf Course 333-334
Sandstone Area Country Club...335
Sandtrap Golf Course 336
Sartell Golf Club 337
Sauk Centre Country Club 338
Savanna Golf & Supper Club 339
Sawmill Golf Club 340
Scottdale Golf Club 341
Shadowbrooke Golf Course.......342
Shamrock Golf Club 344
Shattuck–St. Mary's Golf
    Course 345
Shoreland Country Club 346
Silver Bay Country Club............347
Silver Springs Golf Course..348-349
Slayton Country Club 350
Sleepy Eye Golf Club 351
Soldiers Memorial Field Golf
    Course 352
Somerset Country Club.............353
Southern Hills Golf Club...........354
Southview Country Club 355
Spring Brook Golf Course..........356
Springfield Country Club..........357
Stillwater Country Club 358
Stonebrooke Golf Club..............359
Sugarbrooke Golf Course..........360
Sundance Golf Club 361
Superior National at Lutsen 362

T
Tartan Park Golf Club 363
Terrace View Golf Club 364
Theodore Wirth Golf Club........412
Thief River Golf Club 365
Tianna Country Club 366
Timber Creek Golf Course.........367
Tipsinah Mounds Country
    Club 368
Town & Country Club 369
Town & Country Golf Club 370
Tracy Country Club...................371
Twenty Nine Pines Golf
    Course 372

Twin Pines Golf Course.............373
Two Harbors Lakeview Golf
    Club......................................374
Two Rivers Golf Club 375
Tyler Community Golf Club.....376

U
University of Minnesota Golf
    Course, Les Bolstad 377

V
Vallebrook Golf Club 378
Valley Country Club 379
Valley Golf Course 380
Valley High Country Club 381
Valley View Golf Course............382
Valleywood Golf Course 383
Vermilion Fairways Golf Club...384
Vermilion River Greens.............385
Viking Meadows Golf Club 386
Village Green Golf Course.........387
Virginia Municipal Golf
    Course 388

W
Wadena Municipal Golf
    Course 389
Wapicada Country Club 390
Warren Riverside Golf Club 391
Warroad Estates Golf Course.....392
Waseca Lakeside Club 393
Watonwan Country Club 394
Wayzata Country Club..............395
Wedgewood Golf Club (Now
    Prestwick Golf Club) 300
Wells Golf Club.........................396
Wendigo Golf Club 397
Westfield Golf Club...................398
Whispering Pines Golf Club......399
White Bear Yacht Club..............400
Whitefish Golf Club..................401
Wilderness Hills Golf Course 402
Wilds Golf Club, The 403
Willinger's Golf Club 404
Willmar Golf Club.....................405

Willow Creek Golf Course 406
Willow Creek Municipal Golf
    Course 407
Win-E-Mac Golf Club................408
Windom Country Club.............409
Winona Country Club 410
Winthrop Golf Club..................411
Wirth Golf Course, Theodore ...412
Woodbury Golf & Fitness.........413
Woodhill Country Club 414
Woodland Creek Golf Course ...415
Worthington Country Club......416

Z
Zumbro Valley Golf Club..........417
Zumbrota Golf Club 418

422

THE MINNESOTA ILLUSTRATED

CITY INDEX

A
ADA
    Heart Of The Valley Golf Club....................149
ADAMS
    Cedar River Country Club 54
ALBANY
    Albany Golf Club 2
ALBERT LEA
    Albert Lea Golf Club 3
    Green Lea Golf Course 134
ALEXANDRIA
    Alexandria Golf Club 5
    Arrowwood Golf Club 11
    Crestwood Hills Golf Course 74
    Nordic Trails Golf Course 246
ANDOVER
    Woodland Creek Golf Course 415
ANNANDALE
    Albion Ridges Golf Course 4
    Whispering Pines Golf Club 399
ANOKA
    Greenhaven Golf Course 136
APPLE VALLEY
    Apple Valley Golf Course 8
    Valleywood Golf Course 383
APPLETON
    Appleton Golf Club 9
ATWATER
    Island Falls Country Club 171
AUSTIN
    Austin Country Club 12
    Meadow Greens Golf Course 214
    Ramsey Golf Club 304

B
BABBITT
    Babbitt Golf Course 13
BAGLEY
    Twin Pines Golf Course 373
BARNESVILLE
    Willow Creek Municipal Golf Course........407
BATTLE LAKE
    Balmoral Golf Course 16
BAUDETTE
    Oak Harbor Golf Club 257
BELLE PLAINE
    Valley View Golf Club...............................382

BECKER
    Pebble Creek Country Club 277
BEMIDJI
    Bemidji Town & Country Club...................19
    Castle Highlands Golf Course 51
    Greenwood Golf Course............................137
BENSON
    Benson Golf Club 20
BIG FORK
    Edge Of The Wilderness Golf Course...........92
BLACKDUCK
    Blackduck Golf Club 27
BLOOMING PRAIRIE
    Blooming Prairie Country Club 28
BLOOMINGTON
    Dwan Golf Club 88
    Hyland Greens Golf Course 163
    Minnesota Valley Country Club................230
BLUE EARTH
    Riverside Town & Country Club...............318
BRAINERD
    Birch Bay Golf Course 24
    Madden's on Gull Lake 199-201
    Pine Meadows in Brainerd 289
BREEZY POINT
    Breezy Point Resort 34-35
BROOKLYN CENTER
    Centerbrook Golf Course 56
BROOKLYN PARK
    Brookland Executive Nine Golf Course 39
    Brooklyn Park Golf Course 40
    Edinburgh USA..94
BUFFALO
    Buffalo Heights Golf Course 43
    Buffalo Run Golf Course 44
BUFFALO LAKE
    Oakdale Country Club 265
BURNSVILLE
    Birnamwood Public Golf Course 26
    Orchard Gardens Golf Course...................271
BUYCK
    Vermilion River Greens.............................385

C
CALEDONIA
    Ma-Cal-Grove Country Club.....................198

CITY INDEX

CAMBRIDGE
 Purple Hawk Country Club..........................302
CANBY
 Canby Golf Club 48
CANNON FALLS
 Cannon Golf Club 49
CARLTON
 Pine Hill Golf Club.......................................287
CASS LAKE
 Sandtrap Golf Course 336
CEDAR
 Hidden Haven Country Club......................154
CHASKA
 Bluff Creek Golf Course 30
 Chaska Par 30 Golf Course 57
 Dahlgreen Golf Club 78
 Hazeltine National Golf Club 147
CHATFIELD
 Chosen Valley Golf Club 61
CIRCLE PINES
 Kate Haven Golf Course..............................175
CLARKS GROVE
 Clark's Grove Golf Course 63
CLEARWATER
 Eagle Trace Golfers Club 90
CLIMAX
 Bentwood Climax Municipal Golf Club.......22
CLOQUET
 Big Lake Golf Club 23
 Cloquet Country Club 65
 Pine Hill Golf Club.......................................287
COKATO
 Cokato Town & Country Club 67
COLCRAINE
 Eagle Ridge Golf Course 89
COHASSET
 Sugarbrooke Golf Course 360
COLD SPRING
 Rich Spring Golf Club 310
COOK
 Vermilion Fairways Golf Club 384
COON RAPIDS
 Bunker Hills Golf Course 45-46
CORCORAN
 Pheasant Run Golf Club..............................282
 Shamrock Golf Club....................................344

COTTAGE GROVE
 All Seasons Golf Course 6
 Mississippi Dunes Golf Links 234
 River Oaks Municipal Golf Course............315
COTTONWOOD
 Cottonwood Country Club...........................70
CROOKSTON
 Minakwa Golf & Racquetball Club 226
CROSSLAKE
 Crosslake Golf Course 75

D
DALTON
 Lakeway Golf Course 185
DAWSON
 Dawson Golf Club...79
DAYTON
 Daytona Country Club 80
 Hayden Hills Executive Golf Course..........146
DEERWOOD
 Cuyuna Country Club 77
 Ruttger's Bay Lake Lodge 329-330
DELLWOOD
 Dellwood Hills Golf Club.............................82
DETROIT LAKES
 Detroit Country Club..............................83-84
 Fair Hills Golf Course..........................103-104
 Ironman Golf Course 170
DODGE CENTER
 Dodge Country Club....................................85
DULUTH
 Enger Park Golf Course 100
 Grandview Golf Club..................................131
 Lester Park Golf Course.............................188
 Northland Country Club 254
 Pike Lake Country Club.............................284
 Ridgeview Country Club..............................31

E
EAGAN
 Carriage Hills Country Club 50
 Lost Spur Country Club 196
 Parkview Golf Club 276
EAGLE BEND
 Double Eagle Golf Club................................86

424   **THE MINNESOTA ILLUSTRATED**

CITY INDEX

EAST BETHEL
　　Viking Meadows Golf Club 386
EAST GRAND FORKS
　　Valley Country Club 379
EDEN PRAIRIE
　　Bearpath Golf Club 17
　　Bent Creek Golf Club 21
　　Cedar Hills Golf Course 53
　　Olympic Hills Golf Club 269
EDINA
　　Braemar Golf Club 32-33
　　Edina Country Club 93
　　Interlachen Country Club........................165
　　Normandale Executive Golf Course..........247
ELBOW LAKE
　　Tipsinah Mounds Country Club...............368
ELK RIVER
　　Elk River Country Club 95
　　Pinewood Golf Course 292
ELMORE
　　Minniowa Golf Club 233
ELY
　　Ely Golf Course 98
EMILY
　　Emily Greens Golf Course........................99
ERSKINE
　　Win-E-Mac Golf Club.............................408
EVELETH
　　Eveleth Municipal Golf Course.................102
EXCELSIOR
　　Minnetonka Country Club 231

F
FAIRFAX
　　Fort Ridgely State Park Golf Course 113
　　Mayflower Country Club 213
FAIRMONT
　　Interlaken Golf Club 166
　　Rolling Green Fairways 322
　　Rose Lake Golf Club 325
FARIBAULT
　　Faribault Golf & Country Club 108
　　Shattuck–St. Mary's Golf Course 345
FARMINGTON
　　Fountain Valley Golf Club 116
　　Southern Hills Golf Club 354

FERGUS FALLS
　　Pebble Lake Golf Club..............................278
FIFTY LAKES
　　Howard's Barn/Fifty Lakes Golf Center 161
FOREST LAKE
　　Castlewood Golf Course 52
　　Forest Hills Golf CLub............................112
FOSSTON
　　Fosston Golf Club 115
FRAZEE
　　Frazee Golf Course 119
　　Maple Hills Golf Club 210
FREEBORN
　　Oak View Golf Club 262
FRONTENAC
　　Mount Frontenac Golf Course 241
FULDA
　　Town & Country Golf Club 370

G
GARRISON
　　Garrison Creek Golf Course 122
　　Mille Lacs Lake Golf Resort 225
GLENCOE
　　Glencoe Country Club.............................124
GLENWOOD
　　Minnewaska Golf Club 232
　　Pezhekee Golf Course..............................280
GLYNDON
　　Ponderosa Golf Club 297
GOLDEN VALLEY
　　Brookview Golf Course 42
　　Golden Valley Country Club 125
GRACEVILLE
　　Graceville Golf CLub...............................127
GRAND MARAIS
　　Gunflint Hills Golf Club 140
GRAND RAPIDS
　　Pokegama Golf Course............................295
　　Wendigo Golf Club 397
GRANITE FALLS
　　Granite Falls Golf Club 133
GREENBUSH
　　Oak View Golf Course.............................263

CITY INDEX

H
HALLOCK
 Two Rivers Golf Club 375
HAM LAKE
 Majestic Oaks Golf Club 205-207
HAMEL
 Rolling Green Country Club..................321
HARMONY
 Harmony Golf Club 142
HASTINGS
 Afton Alps Golf Course 1
 Bellwood Oaks Golf Course 18
 Hastings Country Club 143
 Hidden Greens Golf Course 153
HAWLEY
 Hawley Golf & Country Club 145
HAYFIELD
 Oaks Golf Club..266
HAYWARD
 Holiday Park Golf Course............................158
HENDRICKS
 Lake Hendricks Country Club....................181
HENNING
 Oakwood Golf Course 267
HIBBING
 Hibbing Municipal Golf Course.................151
 Mesaba Country Club 222
HILL CITY
 Quadna Hills Golf Course 303
HINCKLEY
 Grand National Golf Club 128
HOFFMAN
 Red Rock Golf Course 306
HOLYOKE
 Wilderness Hills Golf Course 402
HOPKINS
 Meadowbrook Golf Club............................216
 Oak Ridge Country Club............................260
HOUSTON
 Valley High Country Club 381
HOWARD LAKE
 Howard Lake Greens 160
HOYT LAKES
 Hoyt Lakes Country Club 162

I
INTERNATIONAL FALLS
 Falls Country Club 107
INVER GROVE HEIGHTS
 Inver Wood Golf Course.....................167-168
ISANTI
 Sanbrook Golf Course 333-334
ISLE
 Fiddlestix Golf Course.................................111

J
JACKSON
 Jackson Golf Club 174
 Loon Lake Golf Club 195

K
KASSON
 Zumbro Valley Golf Club...........................417
KENYON
 Kenyon Country Club.................................177
KIMBALL
 Kimball Golf Club 178

L
LA CRESCENT
 Pine Creek Golf Course 286
LAKE CITY
 Lake City Country Club 180
LAKE PARK
 Green Valley Golf Course 135
LAKE ELMO
 Tarten Park Golf Club 363
LAKEFIELD
 Vallebrook Golf Club 378
LAKEVILLE
 Brackett's Crossing Country Club................31
 Crystal Lake Golf Course.............................76
LANESBORO
 Lanesboro Golf Club 186
LE SUEUR
 Le Sueur Country Club 187
LEECH LAKE
 Chippewa National Golf Club 58
LESTER PRAIRIE
 Shadowbrooke Golf Course 342

CITY INDEX

LEWISTON
    Lewiston Country Club 189
LINDSTROM
    Chisago Lakes Golf Course 59
LINO LAKES
    Chomonix Golf Course 60
    Cimarron Golf Course 62
LITCHFIELD
    Litchfield Golf Club 190
LITTLE FALLS
    Little Falls Country Club 192
LONG PRAIRIE
    Long Prairie Country Club 194
LONGVILLE
    Ridgewood Country Club 313-314
LUTSEN
    Superior National at Lutsen 362
LUVERNE
    Luverne Country Club 197

M
MABEL
    Meadowbrook Country Club 215
MADELIA
    Madelia Golf Course 202
MADISON
    Madison Country Club 203
MAHNOMEN
    Mahnomen Country Club 204
MAHTOWA
    Twenty Nine Pines Golf Course 372
MANKATO
    Minneopa Golf Club 229
    Terrace View Golf Club 364
MAPLE GROVE
    Rush Creek Golf Club 328
    Sundance Golf Club 361
MAPLEWOOD
    Country View Golf 71
    Goodrich Golf Club 126
MARSHALL
    Marshall Golf Club 212
MCGREGOR
    Savana Golf & Supper Club 339
MEDINA
    Baker National Golf Course 14-15

MELROSE
    Meadowlark Country Club 217
MENAHGA
    Blueberry Pines Golf Club 29
MENDOTA HEIGHTS
    Mendakota Country Club 220
    Mendota Heights Par-3 221
    Somerset Country Club 353
MIESVILLE
    Elmdale Hills Golf Course 97
MILACA
    Milaca Golf Club 224
MILTONA
    Lake Miltona Golf Club 182
MINNEAPOLIS
    Columbia Golf Course 68
    Francis A. Gross Golf Course 139
    Hiawatha Golf Course 150
    Minikahda Club 227
    Minneapolis Golf Club 228
    Theodore Wirth Golf Course 412
MINNEOTA
    Countryside Golf Club 72
MINNETONKA
    Meadowwoods Golf Course 219
    Minnetonka Country Club 231
MINNETONKA BEACH
    Lafayette Club 179
MONTEVIDEO
    Montevideo Country Club 236
MONTGOMERY
    Montgomery Golf Club 237
MONTICELLO
    Monticello Contry Club 238
    Silver Springs Golf Course 348-349
MOORHEAD
    Meadows Golf Course 218
    Moorhead Country Club 239
    Village Green Golf Course 387
MOOSE LAKE
    Moose Lake Golf Club 240
MORA
    Spring Brook Golf Course 356
MORRIS
    Pomme de Terre Golf Club 296
MOTLEY
    Pine Ridge Golf Club 290

CITY INDEX

MOUND
- Burl Oaks Golf Club 47
- Lakeview Golf Course 184
- Red Oak Golf Course 305

MOUNDS VIEW
- Bridges of Mounds View, The 36

MOUNTAIN LAKE
- Mountain Lake Golf Club 242

N

NEW BRIGHTON
- Brightwood Hills Golf Course 37

NEW HOPE
- New Hope Village Golf Course 243

NEW PRAGUE
- Creeks Bend Golf Course 73
- New Prauge Golf Club 244

NEW RICHLAND
- Riverview Golf Course 319

NEW ULM
- New Ulm Country Club 245

NISSWA
- Birch Bay Golf Course 24
- Fritz's Resort & Golf Course 121
- Grand View Lodge Pines 129-130

NORTH BRANCH
- North Branch Golf Course 248

NORTH MANKATO
- North Links Golf Course 249

NORTH OAKS
- North Oaks Golf Club 250

NORTHFIELD
- Northfield Golf Club 252
- Willinger's Golf Club 404

O

OAKDALE
- Lake Place, Links at 183

OLIVIA
- Olivia Golf Club 268

ONAMIA
- Izatys Golf & Yacht Club 173

ORONO
- Orono Golf Course 272

ORTONVILLE
- Ortonville Golf Club 273

OSAKIS
- Osakis Country Club 274

OSSEO
- French Lake Open Golf Course 120

OWATONNA
- Brooktree Municipal Golf Course 41
- Havana Hills Golf Course 144
- Hidden Creek Golf Club 152
- Owatonna Country Club 275

P

PARK RAPIDS
- Headwaters Country Club 148

PELICAN RAPIDS
- Birchwood Golf Course 25
- Rolling Hills Golf Course 323

PEQUOT LAKES
- Breezy Point Resort 34-35
- Whitefish Golf Club 401

PERHAM
- Perham Lakeside Country Club 279

PIEZ
- Pierz Golf Course 283

PINE CITY
- Pine City Country Club 285

PINE ISLAND
- Pine Island Golf Course 288

PINE RIVER
- Driftwood Resort & Golf Course 87
- Irish Hills Golf Course 169
- Pine River Country Club 291

PIPESTONE
- Pipestone Country Club 294

PLAINVIEW
- Piper Hills Golf Course 293

PLYMOUTH
- Elm Creek Golf Links 96
- Hampton Hills Golf Club 141
- Hollydale Golf Club 159

PRESTON
- Preston Golf & Country Club 299

PRINCETON
- Princeton Golf Club 301

PRIOR LAKE
- Cleary Lake Golf Course 64
- Scottdale Golf Club 341
- Wilds Golf Club, The 403

CITY INDEX

R
RAMSEY
    Northfork, The Links at 253
    Rum River Hills Golf Club 327
RED LAKE FALLS
    Oak Knolls Golf Club 259
RED WING
    Mississippi National Golf Links 235
    Red Wing Country Club 307
REDWOOD FALLS
    Redwood Falls Golf Club........................... 308
RICE
    Oak Hill Golf Club 258
RICHFIELD
    Rich Acres Golf Course.............................. 309
ROCHESTER
    Eastwood Golf Club 91
    Maple Valley Golf & Country Club 211
    Northern Hills Golf Club 251
    Oak Summit Golf Course 261
    Rochester Golf & Country Club................ 320
    Soldiers Memorial Field Golf Course 352
    Willow Creek Golf Course 406
ROGERS
    Fox Hollow Golf Club 117
ROSEAU
    Oakcrest Golf Course 264
ROSEMOUNT
    Brockway Golf Club 38
    Rich Valley Golf Club 311
ROSEVILLE
    Roseville Cedarholm Golf Course 326
    Midland Hills Country Club 223
RUSHFORD
    Ferndale Country Club 110

S
ST. ANTHONY
    Francis A. Gross Golf Course.................... 139
ST. CHARLES
    St. Charles Colf Course 331
ST. CLOUD
    Angushire Golf Courses 7
    St. Cloud Country Club 332
    Wapicada Country Club 390
ST. JAMES
    Watonwan Country Club 394

ST. PAUL
    Como Park Golf Course 69
    Fort Snelling Public Golf Course.............. 114
    Highland Park Golf Course 155
    Highland Park Nine Hole Golf Course...... 156
    Hillcrest Country Club 157
    Keller Golf Course 176
    Maple Hills Golf Center 209
    Phalen Park Golf Course 281
    Town & Country Club 369
    U of M/Les Bolstad Golf Course............... 377
ST. PETER
    Shoreland Country Club 346
SANBORN
    Farmers Golf & Health Club 109
SANDSTONE
    Sandstone Area Country Club 335
SARTELL
    Sartell Golf Club....................................... 337
SAUK CENTRE
    Sauk Centre Country Club 338
SHERBURN
    Fox Lake Golf Club 118
SHOKOPEE
    Lone Pine Country Club 193
    Stonebrooke Golf Club............................. 359
SILVER BAY
    Silver Bay Country Club........................... 347
SLAYTON
    Slayton Country Club 350
SLEEPY EYE
    Sleepy Eye Golf Club 351
SPICER
    Little Crow Country Club 191
SPRING VALLEY
    Root River Country Club 324
SPRINGFIELD
    Springfield Country Club.......................... 357
STACY
    Falcon Ridge Golf Course................... 105-106
STANCHFIELD
    Grandy Nine Golf Course 132
STEPHEN
    Riverside Golf Club 317

CITY INDEX

STILLWATER
- Applewood Hills Golf Course.......................10
- Indian Hills Golf Club..................................164
- Oak Glen Country Club......................255-256
- Sawmill Golf Club..340
- Stillwater Country Club 358

T
THIEF RIVER FALLS
- Thief River Golf Club 365

TRACY
- Tracy Country Club 371

TWO HARBORS
- Two Harbors Lakeview Golf Club 374

TYLER
- Tyler Community Golf Club........................376

V
VICTORIA
- Deer Run Golf Club......................................81

VIRGINIA
- Eshquaguma Club 101
- Virginia Municipal Golf Course.................388

W
WABASHA
- Coffee Mills Golf & Country Club...............66

WACONIA
- Island View Golf Club................................172

WADENA
- Wadena Municipal Golf Course 389

WALKER
- Tianna Country Club..................................366

WARREN
- Warren Riverside Golf Club.......................391

WARROAD
- Warroad Estates Golf Course 392

WASECA
- Waseca Lakeside Club 393

WATERTOWN
- River's Edge Country Club 316
- Timber Creek Golf Course 367

WAYZATA
- Wayzata Country Club 395
- Woodhill Country Club..............................414

WELLS
- Wells Golf Club..396

WEST ST. PAUL
- Southview Country Club 355

WHITE BEAR LAKE
- Gem Lake Hills Golf Course......................123
- Manitou Ridge Golf Course 208
- Oneka Ridge Golf Course..........................270
- White Bear Yacht Club...............................400

WILLMAR
- Valley Golf Course.....................................380
- Willmar Golf Club 405

WINDOM
- Windom Country Club..............................409

WINONA
- Cedar Valley Golf Course............................55
- Westfield Golf Club...................................398
- Winona Country Club 410

WINTHROP
- Winthrop Golf Club...................................411

WOODBURY
- Prestwick Golf Club...................................300
- Woodbury Golf & Fitness 413

WORTHINGTON
- Prairie View Municipal Golf Course 298
- Worthington Country Club.......................416

WYOMING
- Greenwood Golf Links 138

Z
ZUMBROTA
- Zumbrota Golf Club..................................418

Order direct from the publisher!

Use this handy order form.
Available in book and software formats.

Order your copies of the Minesota and Wisconsin Illustrated Golf Course Directories!

	Qty x	Price*	= Total
❏ Book ($24.95)	_____	$ 24.95	$ _____
❏ Software ($39.95)			
❏ Windows™	_____	$ 39.95	$ _____
❏ Macintosh©	_____	$ 39.95	$ _____
	Shipping at $4/title		$ _____
*Tax Included		Grand Total	$ _____

NAME (PLEASE PRINT) _____

ADDRESS _____

CITY _____ STATE _____ ZIP _____

PHONE (DAY) _____ (EVENING) _____

Send to: **Evergreen Publications**
         3824 Willow Way, Eagan, MN 55122

Order direct from the publisher!

Use this handy order form.
Available in book and software formats.

Order your copies of the Minesota and Wisconsin Illustrated Golf Course Directories!

	Qty x	Price*	= Total
❏ Book ($24.95)	___	$ 24.95	$ ___
❏ Software ($39.95)			
❏ Windows™	___	$ 39.95	$ ___
❏ Macintosh©	___	$ 39.95	$ ___
	Shipping at $4/title		$ ___
*Tax Included	Grand Total		$ ___

NAME (PLEASE PRINT) _____

ADDRESS _____

CITY _____ STATE _____ ZIP _____

PHONE (DAY) _____ (EVENING) _____

Send to: **Evergreen Publications**
3824 Willow Way, Eagan, MN 55122

Order direct from the publisher!

MINNESOTA
ILLUSTRATED
GOLF COURSE DIRECTORY

WISCONSIN
ILLUSTRATED
GOLF COURSE DIRECTORY

Use this handy order form.
Available in book and software formats.

Order your copies of the Minesota and Wisconsin Illustrated Golf Course Directories!

	Qty x	Price*	= Total
❏ Book ($24.95)	_____	$ 24.95	$ _____
❏ Software ($39.95)			
❏ Windows™	_____	$ 39.95	$ _____
❏ Macintosh©	_____	$ 39.95	$ _____
	Shipping at $4/title		$ _____
*Tax Included	Grand Total		$ _____

NAME (PLEASE PRINT) _____

ADDRESS _____

CITY _____ STATE _____ ZIP _____

PHONE (DAY) _____ (EVENING) _____

Send to: **Evergreen Publications**
    3824 Willow Way, Eagan, MN 55122

Order direct from the publisher!

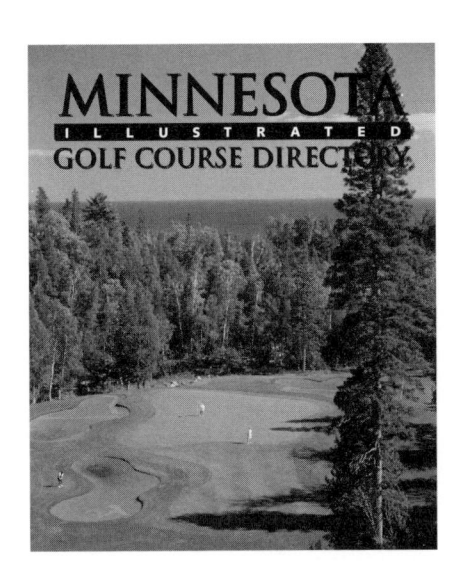

Use this handy order form.
Available in book and software formats.

Order your copies of the Minesota and Wisconsin Illustrated Golf Course Directories!

	Qty x	Price*	= Total
❏ Book ($24.95)	_____	$ 24.95	$ _____
❏ Software ($39.95)			
❏ Windows™	_____	$ 39.95	$ _____
❏ Macintosh©	_____	$ 39.95	$ _____
	Shipping at $4/title		$ _____
*Tax Included	Grand Total		$ _____

NAME (PLEASE PRINT)

ADDRESS

CITY   STATE   ZIP

PHONE (DAY)   (EVENING)

Send to: **Evergreen Publications**
3824 Willow Way, Eagan, MN 55122